Unheard
Voices

Unheard Voices

The Rise of Steelband and Calypso in the Caribbean and North America

A. Myrna Nurse

iUniverse, Inc.
New York Lincoln Shanghai

Unheard Voices
The Rise of Steelband and Calypso in the Caribbean and North America

Copyright © 2007 by A. Myrna Nurse, PhD

All rights reserved. No part of this book may be used or reproduced by any means, graphic, electronic, or mechanical, including photocopying, recording, taping or by any information storage retrieval system without the written permission of the publisher except in the case of brief quotations embodied in critical articles and reviews.

iUniverse books may be ordered through booksellers or by contacting:

iUniverse
2021 Pine Lake Road, Suite 100
Lincoln, NE 68512
www.iuniverse.com
1-800-Authors (1-800-288-4677)

ISBN-13: 978-0-595-40153-6 (pbk)
ISBN-13: 978-0-595-84533-0 (ebk)
ISBN-10: 0-595-40153-8 (pbk)
ISBN-10: 0-595-84533-9 (ebk)

Printed in the United States of America

And then I saw or rather heard it: the pebbles of the pan, the plangent syllables of blue, the on-rolling syncopation, the rhythmic tidalectics; and it was the islands' own sound, not taken or borrowed from no where else or if borrowed borrowed so creatively it becomes our own: & the irksome wonder/*why so long?* why did it take so long, take me so long to come to this so natural so obvious so beautiful so easily our own:

> Kamau Brathwaite's *Barabajan Poems* ("History" IV.5.10–14)
> (Used by permission)

Contents

Introduction xi

CHAPTER 1 Tell the Truth about Pan: A Vignette by Ray Anthony Holman 1

CHAPTER 2 A Gem of Pan and a Father of Panmen: Neville Jules's Story 11

CHAPTER 3 The First Family Band: A Vignette by Hugh Borde 50

CHAPTER 4 Ingenuity in Steelband's Social and Political Organization: Albert Jones's Story 57

CHAPTER 5 Pan's Arrival in the United States: Rudolph V. King's Story 96

CHAPTER 6 You Only Die Once: A Vignette by Desmond Bravo 112

CHAPTER 7 Law Enforcement on Carnival Day: Randolph Babb's Story 122

CHAPTER 8 Toward a New and Different Triangular Trade: Calypsonian Shirlane Hendrickson Thomas's Story 135

CHAPTER 9 The Inversed Triangular Trade: A Vignette by Vincent Hernandez 151

CHAPTER 10 We're Not Materially Rich: A Vignette by Jeff Narell 161

Chapter 11	From the Decks of the U. S. Navy: A Vignette by Franz Grissom............................	168
Chapter 12	The Introduction of Modern Music Technology: A Vignette by James Leyden.................	180
Chapter 13	Bridging Cultural Divides: Clifford Alexis's Story.....................................	186
Chapter 14	Launching an Academic Program: G. Allan O'Connor's Story...........................	218
Chapter 15	A Thriving Family Business: Philbert Solomon's Story.....................................	231
Chapter 16	Breaking Class and Genre Barriers: Othello Molineaux's Story.............................	254
Chapter 17	New Wine in New Wineskins: The Last Social Experiment: Leroy Alí Williams's Story.........	270
Chapter 18	Trying to Make a Dollar: A Vignette by Trevor Stubbs.....................................	285
Chapter 19	When Behaviors Eclipse Talent: Ruth and Terrance Cameron's Story....................	291
Chapter 20	The Classical and Academic Business of Pan: Dawn K. Batson's Story.....................	306
Chapter 21	We Can Move Forward as a Literate People: Lennard V. Moses's Story....................	315
Chapter 22	From the Rawness to the Beauty of Steel: A Brief Biography of Elliott Mannette..............	335

Glossary.. 419
Conclusion... 423
Notes... 427
Other Interviewees....................................... 455

Acknowledgments

Special thanks to Professor Susan Wells, Associate Professor Keith Gumery, and Professor Emeritus Dennis Lebofsky of my alma mater for making a place for me in the first-year writing program upon my return from South Carolina. Your kindness has sustained me in ways you do not know.

The following very kind people encouraged me directly and indirectly to persevere toward the completion of this project. First, special thanks extend to Professor Cornel West, whom I first met in spring 2001 while he was visiting Presbyterian College (Clinton, South Carolina). At the time, I was there in a tenure-track position, which I relinquished for personal reasons. After discussing my project with him, he pointed out that the work, though unfunded, was much too important to be left languishing. I remain grateful that he took time to advise a junior faculty member to stay the course. Nonetheless, languish the work did for a few years after I completed all the interviews and needed to distance myself from each man's and woman's voice toward making the work a whole one.

Selwyn Cudjoe, Professor of Africana Studies of Wellesley College, continues to champion my professional pursuits. Many thanks for your support.

In summer 2005, I received an unexpected e-mail from Professor Kamau Brathwaite whom I'd met in 1992 and discussed with him my interest in his poetry. A chapter of my dissertation (1999, unpublished) is based on his poetry and essays. His e-mail of interest in my work and encouragement not to give up on this project were just what I needed toward its completion. My warmest thanks and undying gratitude to this other giant in our discipline and world community who took time to befriend and encourage me.

Deirdre David, Professor Emerita and former dissertation director, has remained my advisor for the past few years, for which I'm eternally grateful. I am very grateful that you also are a friend.

I cannot say thanks enough to my second sister, Rhoda Greenidge (University of the West Indies, St. Augustine's alumna and resides in Missouri City, Texas), who read a large portion of the manuscript and made excellent suggestions toward revisions.

Deepest appreciation to Carolyn Gregg for an outstanding job on editing portions of the final draft of the manuscript.

My late mother, Editha Virginia Kirton (née Raeburn, of Glencoe and Petit Valley; d. September 3, 2003), never did waver in her love and support of my scholarly endeavors. Hence, this work is dedicated in loving memory of a mother and teacher of her family and school communities of Four Roads Government School, Eastern Girls' Government School, and Point Cumana Government School. I also dedicate this work to my late father, Clyde Luther Kirton (d. August 27, 2006) who brought and kept the joy of music in my life.

Throughout my research, my immediate family members have helped me stay the course toward the project's completion. Alex, my son (Chinese martial arts instructor), cheered me on when he sensed that I was discouraged and lacked the will to persevere. My daughter, Miranda (John Hopkins University and the University of Miami School of Law alumna), read large portions of the manuscript and with an editor's eye suggested many revisions. My husband, Keith (financier, photographer, musician, reader/editor, critic, and best friend), has guided me in too many ways to enumerate here. Thank you, loved ones, for being so wonderfully supportive.

I feel especially honored that LeRoy Clarke, a great Trinbagonian poet/prophet/artist, granted me a two-hour interview at his home on October 30 and gave his blessings on this project. The fact that this work is self-published attests that it is a labor of love for my fellow Trinbagonians and for Steelband. Since I'm a naturalized U.S. citizen, I've sought to honor my fellow U.S. citizens in this endeavor as well. My hope is that I've served you all well.

Introduction

The Discommodious Bodies of Pan's Violent Birthing

Undoubtedly, the end of the twentieth century brought much international attention to the Steelband movement, which originated during the 1930s among the Fanonesque wretched of the earth in Trinidad and Tobago (T&T). This compilation of narratives is based on interviews with some Caribbean and America pan-people in Steelband who live in the United States and Canada. The Caribbean portraitures describe the perpetual struggle against poverty as a catalyst for violence, intertwined with the innate will to creativity and voicing that could not be silenced. The U.S. ones similarly intimate the grit and determination involved in furthering "the pebbles of the pan." The narratives in sum intensify the poignancy of the question implicit of this work: what is there about steelband music, this *thing* (as the men refer to their art form) of great love, that promises social equilibrium toward validating the sensibilities and sentience of all people? The answer to the question resides in the primary purpose of this work, which is to show how the movement began in the Caribbean, was transplanted to and grew in North America, and today can break the boundaries of class, race, gender, academic, and other barriers.

I approached the interviewees with the objective of learning firsthand about this thing that Trinidadians and Tobagonians (also called Trinbagonians) were at one time misled to despise, simply because it originated among the despised underclass. Since mine was a quest for knowledge, I did not wish to impose questions of epistemic or academic discourse and trusted that the interviewees' knowledge was sufficient to provide fodder for further dialogue. Surely, what they had to say would emerge within the historical and social contexts of their own Caribbean colonial and American metropolitan experiences. Invariably, their stories inform on these, as well as the confluence of the musical inventions of the African diaspora that produced Calypso and Soca, Steelband, Jazz, and Reggae, as well as T&T Indian music.[1] Additionally, Trinidad has produced a hybrid music style, Chutney-soca, which is a synthesis of Indian tassa drumming and calypso rhythms.

Contemporaneously, in T&T this first generation of panmen's voices emerged with those who were calling for West Indian Federation,[2] since both activities occurred during the decades of the 1930s to 1960s. Consequently, the invention of Steelband informs that the downtrodden and underclass were not complacent, quiet, or stoic in their suffering. Rather, they were actively pursuing paths toward ending their social and economic oppression. For these reasons, the narrative format befits presenting how their story is Pan's, Pan having been created in Limbo, according to Lloyd Best. Quite eloquently, Best argues that Limbo is not a place of despair or uncertainty but of creativity and innovation, a locus for voice to express itself through various art forms, of which Pan is the last and follows Mas,[3] Carnival, and Calypso.[4]

To be in Pan was, and still is, these panmen's innate will to voice, as Elliott "Ellie" Mannette (Morgantown, West Virginia) who is generally recognized as one of the fathers of the movement, describes his compelling desire to build a family of pans. Yet, such voicing is not just Mannette's passion but that of all the pan-people, first and second generation, whose perspectives are presented here. They delineate how Pan is a consuming desire, affecting every fiber of their being. In some cases, their involvement has taken an exacting toll on social and marital relationships. Hence, Mannette's brief narrative images primarily his early days in Steelband and the stark violence that shaped the movement, his innovations, his early travels and immigration to the United States in 1967, the price he paid in his private life, and some of his work and accomplishments in the United States as an artist-in-residence at West Virginia University (WVU).

At times apologetic for his actions that contributed to the violence, Mannette hopes his story would allow for an understanding of being born and bred in a sociopolitical environment whose colonial leaders could not care less for those deemed beneath them. Such indifference to fellow humans, stemming from a failure to recognize and respect people's humanity, was insidious and another cause of the violence. For Mannette, when pan-building and -tuning came along, the arduous work brought a channel for redirecting his anger, rage, and impetus to lash out at society. Rather than vent on a fellow oppressed, as a pan-builder-tuner he could pour that energy onto a discarded oil drum, wrestle with and temper cold, rigid steel into a thing of beauty that produced marvelous sound and music and feel immensely thrilled and satisfied. Few people understood that for him and other panmen their work offered such joy, along with the opportunity to contribute to society with dignity and honor what they could, which are innate human desires. One such person who understood this drive in Mannette was Maria "Vera" Pereira (Riverdale, Georgia) whose vignette is appended to his story to accentuate how complex being in Steelband has been for Mannette, as well as other T&T panmen.

The work begins with a vignette by Ray Anthony Holman (Seattle, Washington), a dear friend of Mannette. Recognizing the focus on Mannette at the time of our conversation, Holman kept his insights trained on Mannette's accomplishments but with one mandate, that I pursue the truth of the movement. He insisted that I interview Neville Jules (Brooklyn, New York), another father of the movement, toward truth's pursuit, because though he loves Ellie dearly, he cannot ignore that Steelband is larger than any one man and its story must be the truth. T&T, North America, and the world deserve nothing less. Yet, the effort to answer the call for truth is not without impediment because one person's truth is often another's moral relativism. For example, Jules and Albert Jones (Brooklyn, New York), former elected president and vice president of the National Association of Trinidad and Tobago Steelbandsmen (NATTS) during the '50s and '60s, describe some underlying tensions between east and west. They refer to the men from Laventille as *the east* and those from Woodbrook as *the west*. Because *the east* and *the west* did not readily collaborate primarily due to class differences, the facts regarding who did what when are contestable.

Truth withstanding, Jules and Jones portray how the men within their respective vicinities borrowed and shared their innovations, but all the new ideas generated among *the east*. Hence, their narratives are invaluable toward counterposing Mannette's truth-telling about his claim to what he invented, and that of anyone who, in lacking intimate details of what was evolving among *the east*, has misrepresented the movement's overall activities. Jules provides an invaluable perspective on the early days of Pan before it began to move westward, the creation of the Trinidad All Stars Percussion Orchestra (TASPO),[5] which is not to be confused with T&T's TASPO (Trinidad All Steel Percussion Orchestra) of 1950, his own innovations, and the Bomb's origination.[6] The Bomb is an off-stage competition on Carnival Monday morning that helped to transform positively the movement. From an organizational perspective, Jones's narrative shows how the men resisted colonial attempts to stifle their creativity.

Both reiterate Holman's call for an authentic historical narrative of the movement, a demand that became somewhat of a voluntary refrain among the other interviewees. Hence, regarding truth-telling, as I met with or conversed via telephone with all these first-generation panmen, I became aware that I was embarking on this work at a critical time in the movement. With a rising international interest in Steelband, its birthing people wanted that the truth be told, one that emphasized that Steelband was larger than anyone's individual life or contributions, and that any work that spoke of Pan must reflect this, for one may speak with authority but necessarily with authenticity. Thus, their call for historical truth becomes ancillary to the work's major argument.

One truth that remains constant and ineffaceable is the violence that shaped the movement during the '40s and '50s, which sometimes threatened its life. The rivalry that fueled band clashes on Carnival days and during Carnival's off-season almost always resulted in fatal injuries and imprisonment. The vignettes of Randolph "Rannie" Babb (Brooklyn, New York), former member of Chicago Hill Sixty and head of T&T's Criminal Investigation Department, Narcotics Division, and of the late Desmond Bravo (Philadelphia, Pennsylvania), former leading iron-man of Casablanca Steel Orchestra, provide further insight into how violence affected the movement. Babb offers from a police inspector's perspective how the police on street duty on Carnival days sometimes directed or misdirected the bands and inadvertently contributed to the violence.

Bravo states that he, though not an instigator of the violence, loved it: "It was when I left the Rising Sun band and joined Casablanca and met all those other young fellas involved in this rioting affair that I truly began to love this [being in Steelband]. I'm not going to pretend with you. I loved the rioting." Bravo, who later joined the West Indian Regiment during World War II and was deployed to Egypt for two tours of duty and in the United States became a member of the Willow Grove Police Department of Pennsylvania, wants it to be known that Steelband accommodated all aspects of human nature, including men with a penchant for violence. Thus, the narratives in sum speak of men who were creative, destructive, disciplined by enforcers (described in Jules's and Jones's narratives), intractable, and violent.

All the emphasis on violence reminds us that the men warred against the violence of poverty linked to oppression, the violence of a colonial machine that attempted to grind to dust all resistance to oppression, and the violence of competition both for social and economic gratification. This poverty and its ensuing violence in resistance to the poverty have relayed to the present and are portrayed in some T&T poetry and novels: Henry Beissel's 1966 poem "Pans at Carnival"; John Agard's 1982 poem "Pan Recipe";[7] Marion Patrick Jones's 1973 novel *Pan Beat*; and Earl Lovelace's 1979 novel *The Dragon Can't Dance*. In Calypso, David Rudder's calypso, "Dedication (A Praise Song)" (*No Restriction: The Concert*, 1996) celebrates how "ten thousand flowers bloom" from "a muddy pond." The classic calypso, "Voices from de Ghetto" by Singing Sandra, Calypso Monarch of 1999, reminds us that some people of the Pan world in T&T are still ghettoized as discommodious bodies whose escape from the ghettos' hellish poverty is in Steelband's music.[8]

To counter all forms of violence, the first-generation panmen organized and challenged the social status quo as the movement journeyed toward social acceptance. That journey was precarious and contentious, and the men today hold strong opinions and counter-opinions about the roles of Dr. Eric Williams, the government, and societal leaders—such as Beryl Mc Burnie, Lennox Pierre, Albert Gomes, and others—in assisting them. While Jones and Jules hold firmly to the position that Dr. Williams could have done more, others such as Philbert "Phil" Solomon of Pittsburgh, Pennsylvania (born in Guyana and lived in Trinidad for approximately ten years) and Babb counterpose that he was a godsend. Solomon argues that Dr. Williams did for Pan the inverse of Forbes Burnham, who literally destroyed the movement in Guyana by retracting all funding for steelbandsmen. Burnham's actions set back Pan in Guyana for decades, Solomon maintains. Concomitantly, Babb thinks Dr. Williams did all he could for the time in which he lived, for instance, by helping to promote Steelband as a positive cultural image. Granted the validity of both sides of this debate, nonetheless, Jones acknowledges that Dr. Williams's best contribution was through the Development and Environmental Works Division (DEWD). Referred to as the project, the men were employed during the Carnival off-season and aware that DEWD by implication was never intended to elevate their social or economic status. The project was merely to provide a means of occupation to mitigate the violence. To improve their status, the men had to rely on their own initiatives.

Jones's narrative describes one such initiative. He details that based on his efforts through NATTS that Steelband redefined its participation in the 1960 Music Festival and began to revolutionize its image. The first generation of panmen—musically illiterate but possessing a keen ear for music and a remarkable memory—themselves were already proving their ability to perform competitively the most intricate of European classical music with dexterity and aplomb at the Bomb competition. Jones delineates how he argued with the 1960 Music Festival committee for the right of the men to continue to demonstrate this ability and the pan's versatility by performing genres of their choice and being judged on their own merit. The standard that he helped establish at the 1960 Music Festival has evolved into today's World Steelband Music Festival (WSMF).

In regard to giving people due credit for their work in the movement, Pan has since corrected its oversight of Jones and Pan Trinbago, T&T's professional Steelband organization, awarded him due recognition for his labors at the 2005 WSMF held at Madison Square Garden on Father's Day. Pan Trinbago also recognized Clifford "Cliff" Alexis of Northern Illinois University (NIU) and residing in DeKalb, Illinois, for his work in Pan in the United States and the Caribbean. That the movement took so long to honor these men probably has more to do with the fact that they have resided for years in the United States where the movement is increasing in momentum. Yet, this momentum must not obscure the fact that T&T has generally taken its time in recognizing the men, and a part of that has much to do with classism linked to color stratification, compounded by social tensions. For instance, the *east-west* strains were exacerbated when the movement began to receive governmental recognition and funding toward writing and publishing, and such opportunities went to the middle-class west whose narrators slanted the truth, most likely unintentionally. Hence, many questionable facts about the movement have stood uncontested until now, and the men's call for truth-telling cannot be glossed over as we begin to right some wrongs of the legacy of British colonialism, one being class division.

Intertwined Roots and Their Colored Branches

Classism linked to color stratification most definitely shaped the movement, evident in the narratives of Holman, Dawn Batson (Miami, Florida), Othello Molineaux (Miami, Florida), and Shirlane Hendrickson Thomas (Orlando, Florida), the niece of the late Andrew "Pan" de la Bastide, another father of the movement. All their stories include poignant reminders that T&T still has much work to do regarding class injustices. In the case of Andrew "Pan," it is somewhat unconscionable that he died with his whereabouts being relatively unknown throughout the Pan world. Some of the interviewees had no idea where he resided until after he died and his obituary was published in the T&T's newspapers.[9] Should such anonymity surround someone who invented a section of the steel orchestra? Should panmen be victimized, so to speak, simply because of the indifference the world reserves for those considered "nobodies"? Thomas's story is included in this collection because she is the closest relative of Andrew "Pan" to whom I could get, and of equal importance is the voice she brings to Calypso.

Thomas iconicizes some bridges that connect us to the plight of panmen from Calvary Hill, East Dry River—another area "Behind the Bridge"—Belmont, and places where the lower and poor classes, usually the black-skinned, resided and were socially ostracized. Also, her story reverberates with the class injustice so many suffered then and now, of color stratification, and more positively the inter-relationships within the movement and society itself. Her voice echoes the general criticism that the men so eloquently articulate, that they lived in a society whose general perception was that nothing good or of social value could come from among the wretched, interchangeably "niggers" and "coolies." On the contrary, she reminds us that Trinbagonian calypsonians began making their mark on U.S. and world music as early as the 1930s.[10] For this reason, her call is valid for an interpolation of Calypso into school curricula and appends to the men's calls for Pan's inclusion in curricula, also. We recognize, of course, that such inclusion is a drastic step toward a comprehensive analysis of, toward validating, all Trinbagonians of all class levels and all their contributions, whether African, Indian, Chinese, or White, which is a focus of Jones's narrative.

He has long argued that the roots of Pan are found in Dahomean Rada, which is not to obscure the fact that the Shango and Orisha traditions also shaped Pan's origin and evolution. Jones's argument first published in a 1998 *Sunday Express* article by Kim Johnson[11] is that efforts to ascertain the truth of Pan's origin must confront the historical reality that *the west* did not accommodate or tolerate drumming. Drummers resided in the hills of Laventille, in Belmont, and in other areas where West African religions thrived in marginality. Deductively, the western men could not have invented the pan because they were not among the Dahomean, Shango, and Orisha drummers, the men of Pan's embryonic stage.

On the other hand, *the west* was cultivating a thriving middle class, some who embraced Pan's culture and were instrumental in promoting effectively the instrument. Most notable were White panmen Curtis Pierre and Junior Pouchet. For this, they must also receive due credit as the interviewees bestow upon them. Jones also wants remembered other non-Africans who caught Pan's vision early, promoted the instrument, and quietly revolutionized human relationships. Among the Indians are Jit Samaroo, the most famous; Dudley Rouff, the captain of Tokyo from the '40s to the '60s; Lennox "Bobby" Mohammed of Guinness Cavaliers, the band's historic and legendary arranger. Among the Chinese, Hugh Loy and Kim Loy Wong are well-known. Chan LeePow (Hockessin, Delaware) continues to be a vital force in Pan in the Philadelphia, Pennsylvania region. The total recognition of racial and ethnic diversity in Pan is integral toward bringing to cessation the deeply entrenched class prejudice that is even more divisive than racial differences, another arresting societal issue toward which this work merely intimates.

Yet, Pan in the African diaspora has been advanced by many pan-lovers who immigrated to the United States, Canada, and elsewhere. In the United States, its technology was advanced by Americans the late Franz Grissom (Boulder City, Nevada) and James Leyden (Banks, Oregon), and its program first introduced into schools by the late Murray Narell and into colleges and universities by G. Allan O'Connor (DeKalb, Illinois). Pan's migration to the United States may have begun as early as the 1940s. The late Rudolph "Rudy" V. King (Brooklyn, New York) shares that when he arrived in 1949 from Trinidad and began pan-tuning, some Trinidadian immigrants who arrived before he did assisted him. He speculates that though they may have brought Pan with them, they were not actively promoting the instrument. His work involved pioneering activities, such as registering the instrument with the Music Union, meeting Louis Farrakhan during his days as Mighty Charmer in the 1950s, and marketing a specific island/tourist/calypso image that engendered the politics of Pan's economy in the United States.

Overall, King calls attention to the fact that the men whose livelihood depended on gigs had to meet the demands of the gig's contract, for steel bands were hired with expectations that harked back to what some interviewees refer to as a "Yellow Bird" calypso image. While this projected image may not have been the men's preference, the band's attire had to match a prescribed one that included bright, floral shirts, white pants, and straw hats, when the hats were specifically requested. The narrative of Ruth and Terrance Cameron[12] (Philadelphia, Pennsylvania) presents how the men in their band, Steel Kings, sometimes challenged this prescription and confounded things further with their obnoxious behavior. Such, they argue, hindered Pan's growth during the 1970s and '80s. They and other interviewees are concerned that Pan's prevailing calypso-tourism image may be hindering more than propelling Steelband into mainstream U.S. culture.

Conversely, one GE television "ecoimagination" commercial aired during 2004 redefined somewhat the calypso stereotype by using steelband music in association with a future that is charting a new course in energy consumption.[13] Still, the implicit call is for an examination of the stereotype that keeps Pan relegated to summer activities rather than seeing the steel orchestra as the orchestra of the twenty-first century, which Solomon argues. He is of the opinion that we are witnessing the slow death of the symphony orchestra as an art form, to be replaced by the steel orchestra. Maybe Solomon's opinion cannot be lightly dismissed. After all, the 2005 WSMF at Madison Square Garden performed to a sold-out audience of over five thousand, while one of the most e-mailed articles from the June 25, 2005 *New York Times* lamented the crisis in symphony orchestras.[14]

With one hand stretching backward to an ineffaceable past and the other stretching forward into a future that calls for much, pan-people's faith in humanity is undiminished. With confidence they hold to a vision that includes

- a Steelband future realized in more cultural inclusion recognized in the establishment of a Pan theater and museum both in Trinidad and the United States;

- more business enterprises and endeavors to revolutionize the Caribbean region economically, which will not only redefine globalization but signal international consumerism that does not necessarily begin with the United States;

- more literacy within the movement and invariably more academic awareness of the movement that already is erasing some academic boundaries.

These inclusions, and in particular the emphasis on literacy, will speak volumes for a world commitment to economic and educational growth. In Steelband, stringent boundaries between the arts and humanities, science, and engineering are already being blurred, the narrators maintain. An organic collusion of the disciplines is already constructing new curricula for students at all levels.

In music, Solomon points out that his middle and high school Pan students are as familiar with Mighty Sparrow as they are with Beethoven. No other instrument is bridging European classical music to Calypso and Soca, to the enjoyment of players and listeners. No other instrument promises to rescue those White dinosaurs in music from extinction than the pan's pebbles. What a rich, promising future for all cultures! Should such a future be wholly embraced, we may break once and for all the cycle of poverty and violence of which Singing Sandra bewails is endemic of all developing countries, not just T&T, the U.S. urban ghettos, and the non-integrating gaps throughout the world. Should such a future be wholly embraced, every nation can become a land of opportunity for its people, and people would not have to look to the United States or other metropolises for a good quality of life. This is not to say that Caribbean pan-people are ungrateful for how they have prospered in the United States. Rather, to reiterate Alexis and Jones, nothing is wrong with a prophet receiving honor in his own country, for the men wanting to be recognized as well as make a decent living in their birth-land.

This evolution toward a complete revolution in national economies entails ceasing to exoticize the Caribbean as the United States' and Europe's tourism playground, the image under which Pan was initially marketed. Dennis Le Gendre's *Steelband in Perspective* (1973), printed with government support, describes how the government inadvertently promoted the image of Steelband primarily in association with tourism. Invariably, with the Caribbean marketing itself as the winter getaway, the site of multi-colors—people, florae, and fauna—to fascinate and invigorate northerners, island music became an attractive advertising device for airlines and cruises. In terms of how this image was further promoted, Grissom, former Chief Musician of the U.S. Navy Steel Band (disestablished in 1999), shares how the Navy Steel Band during the early '60s used the steelband music of each Carnival season for its performances and unconsciously allowed Carnival to shape a festive portrayal of Steelband in the United States and on international travels.

However, these marketing devices are not solely responsible for promoting this image. The fact is that the United States today holds to a fixed idea of backyard/underdeveloped/third-world Caribbean and South American neighbors,[15] suitable for U.S. consumerism but not for competing on the global market. Once Steelband became somewhat established in the United States, the image then evolved around a folk one, which the Camerons and Jeff Narell (San Francisco, California) interrogate. They, along with Grissom, are concerned that the image of Steelpan conjoined to a tourist one keeps its music marginalized as folk music in the United States. The concerns revolving around marginality point to how Steelband and its image implicitly remain bound to a multicultural-racist one, which is not so far removed from classism, an issue that both Narell and Grissom address.

The Pebbles' Global Presence

Pan as international presence brings some controversial questions that cannot be easily dismissed or ignored. The narrators are concerned that T&T is not sufficiently pursuing research and development (R&D) to compete with the United States, Europe, and Asia. They see that Japan and Sweden are poised to dominate the future of pan-building, and T&T will have to purchase pans from them. Others think that T&T is not sufficiently developing music literacy among pannists for T&T bands to compete internationally. Alexis thinks that a T&T conservatory of music is long overdue. He also would like to see an indoor venue that accommodates visiting bands at the WSMF when held in T&T, for it is inexcusable for visitors to be distracted by raindrops falling on their pans during performances. He, Solomon, and Leroy Alí Williams (formerly of Santa Clara, California, and now residing in Charlotte, North Carolina) would like the instruments to be standardized for increased productivity, marketability, and economy.

Linked to these concerns is the question of what to call the instrument. How do we sensibly engage the question of one's consciousness of consciousness (Paulo Freire[16]); the right to Creole, the nation language of the Caribbean collective, according to Kamau Brathwaite;[17] and, the right to one's linguistic expressions, according to Edouard Glissant,[18] which allow the naming of one's own thing, an issue the panmen raise? Their questions regarding what to call the instrument, whether steelpan or steel drum, point to their right to name the instrument that they invented and not have that name or the right to naming effaced or diminished by any gesture, neo-colonial or otherwise. Yet, the multifaceted nature of the debate on this matter relates to the complexity of naming one's invention and the power of the voice rooted in the African drum.[19] King is adamant in his position that the name steelpan is ambiguous in its association with the cooking pan and bedpan and hence prefers steel drum. Molineaux is of the opinion that the movement is making an historical down-turn, one being propelled by those who want the instrument to be named "steelpan" over "steel drum" and ignore that the international community for the most part already identifies the instrument as a steel drum. Mannette agrees with the instrument being called steel drum; hence, his company established in 2000 is Mannette Steel Drums Ltd. Admittedly, Mannette's, King's, and Molineaux's perspectives run counter to how everyone else refers to the instrument as pan or steelpan, including Solomon whose company is named Solomon Steelpan Company, previously mentioned. One recognizes that all the stances are critical and useful to a balanced perspective on and within the movement, and the right to naming and voice.

At some time in the near future, the question on what the international community would call the instrument should be settled, probably here in the United States. Should the WSMF continue to be held here, as proposed, I cannot perceive that Pan Trinbago would concede to the title being revised to read "World Steeldrum Band Music Festival" to satisfy what can be regarded as provincial or neo-colonial penchants. Without apology, I weigh in favor of Simeon L. Sandiford's cogent argument based on his critical analysis of the instrument's name. He argues that since the instrument is neither a member of the idiophone nor membranophone family of percussion instruments, the instrument is a steelpan.[20] Furthermore, the name pan resonates of the history of nineteenth-century colonial oppression that banned the use of drums, and the men's circumvention of the ban to voice their musicality. Thus, the narratives raise these and many other provocative issues for debate and dialogue across the academic boundaries of science and technology, the humanities, postcolonialism, and intimate the need for forums and/or symposiums on Steelband.

Much work has been and is being done in Steelband, work that remains marginalized for the most part because, indeed, Pan needs to be taken more seriously, as many interviewees aver. We must continue to document rigorously all its history and developments before all the repositors of Pan's history are no longer with us—King died on March 18, 2004; Bravo died on August 10, 2004; and Grissom died on July 26, 2005. It takes a compilation of all their stories to complete Pan's history. While this compilation brings to light how sponsorship originated—see the vignette of Hugh Borde (Ypsilanti, Michigan), it leaves unanswered some questions, such as: in which year did steel bands first participate in the Music Festival? Jules's story implies it was 1952. The men admittedly cannot specifically recall some exact dates because, as they say repeatedly, they did not know they were making history, so they paid little attention to dates. Consequently, the facts of one story contradict those of another. Also, I have not exhausted all the pan-people living in the United States and have not dented Canada, where Tommy Crichlow resides and is the arranger of Toronto's Pan Masters Steel Orchestra. I'm sure his perspective is invaluable. The stories of American Andy Narell, the Trinbagonian founders of Brooklyn's CASYM Steel Orchestra, Trinidadian Ken "Professor" Philmore, the founders of Panyard, Inc., and many others most likely would have enriched this work. In truth, I desired to be all-inclusive; in reality, I just could not be due to limited time, resources, and format of this work.

Meanwhile, all the concerns about who first did what in the movement are valid, and an accurate as possible documentation is the responsibility of diligent researchers. Such work does not necessarily fly in the face of the knowledge that the identity of many men who contributed to Pan's innovations will probably never come to light. For instance, Robert "Robbie" Greenidge (California) who plays with Jimmy Buffett thinks that Trickster god will keep obscured from us the first man to invent the first pan as a musical instrument.[21] Even so, the concern underpins the demand for authenticity that withstands historical interrogation without belying the efficacy of these men's experiences. Truly, their experiences have been multi-variegated and dichotomous. They were poor and middle class, oppressed and privileged, uneducated by occidental standards and educated, and prone to violence and to peace. Today, as successful business-people, educators, musicians, community leaders, and other positions of leadership, they continue to share in common: the will to voice that refuses to be silenced, and the desire for the world to know of their relevance and contributions to a dynamic musical art form and its emerging literary discourse.

At some point, after sufficient rigorous research, the time will come for a catalog of who's who in the Steelband movement, a catalogue that recognizes all who made major contributions to Pan, internationally, and interpolates postcolonial discourse. To that end, this work is then a mere ripple in Pan's ocean, one that is possible only because each interviewee shared his/her story gratis. They have shared of themselves so selflessly during the days of Steelband's inception and growth, and today their generosity, graciousness, and kindness continue as a monolith of the Pan spirit. For these reasons, I share their confidence in Pan's promising future.

In closing, these narratives, whether presented objectively or subjectively, derive from conversations that were held formally from 2000 to 2003. All the interviewees were mailed a transcribed copy of our conversation/s for revision suggestions. Some made considerable revisions via phone conversations toward a comprehensive narrative. All but one insisted that the work met marketing standards and their story adhered to the rules of Standard English. In so doing, I took some liberties, retained some T&T Creole, and consequently accept full responsibility for the work's final outcome, one being retaining when they addressed me directly in the second person. It begins with Holman's vignette and its injunction to pursue the truth of the movement. It continues with Jules's story, Jules being an authority who fearlessly challenges Mannette's truth-telling. Some of the vignettes and stories leading to Mannette's, the last one, speak of Mannette's contributions. However, the dominant focus is on what each narrator has contributed to Trinidad and Tobago's and the United States' respective cultures and how they have triumphed over much adversity.

Not previously mentioned, the Bravo and King stories describe the origin of Brooklyn's Labor Day Parade, invaluable information to the movement, since the Labor Day Parade is acclaimed as the largest cultural event of the United States and generates much revenue for New York City.[22] The work portrays a movement that is microcosmic of human dynamic activities, of people engaged in immigration, cultural collusion and confluence, science and technology, education and literacy, and the promise of equilibrium realized in the appreciation of the tapestry of all human creativity and genius. Finally, the work brings to light most notably the following pioneering information about Steelband that is not commonly known:

1. the first band to be sponsored in 1945;

2. a rare Casablanca steelband recording made in 1947;

3. Pan's migration to the United States in 1949;

4. an international Steelband festival in 1953;

5. the U.S. Navy Steel Band, which began in Puerto Rico in 1956 and its appearance at the Brussels Expo in 1958;

6. the presence of an impressive steel band in Grenada in 1957;

7. Hill Sixty South American tour in 1958 to 1960, with visits to Brazil, Argentina, Chile, Peru, Ecuador, Colombia, Panama, Guatemala, Honduras, Costa Rica, El Salvador, Mexico and California;

8. Guyana's activities inclusive of its national steel band's performance of T&T's national anthem at its Independence in 1962;

9. Pan being introduced to Nigeria in 1972;

10. the first steelpan company being built in 1990 in Pittsburgh, Pennsylvania.

1
Tell the Truth about Pan: A Vignette by Ray Anthony Holman[1]

Ray Anthony Holman *is considered a legend in Pan, nationally and internationally. A Visiting Artiste at the University of Washington, Seattle (1998–2001), his indefatigable spirit and energy continues to radiate positively to those with whom he associates. Some of his original compositions include "Secrets of the Pan" and "Pan on the Run" (1973) and "Heroes of the Nation" (2001). Our conversation was held at the 2001 Meet Me in Morgantown Workshop and followed up by phone.*

Meeting Ellie

I met Ellie in 1957 when I was living on Roberts Street. Invaders yard was on Tragarete Road, between Lewis Street and Rosalino Street. Little Carib Theatre was on White Street. So, I lived say maybe 160 yards from Invaders panyard. According to Ellie, I looked like about eight years old when I started hanging around the panyard, but I was a little older. Roy Rollock, Beryl McBurnie's nephew, introduced us. He and I were friends. He lived even closer to the panyard, in a house next to the Carib [Little Carib Theatre]. Ellie was making instruments for Beryl McBurnie. She had the foresight to have a steel band accompany her dance troupe and to encourage the development of the instrument. Rollock's father was also a musician and band leader. He invited Roy and me to try out the pan, to go around with him for a couple of days by Invaders and see how we liked it. I went to the yard and touched the pan. We had heard the name Ellie Mannette, but I had never seen him or known exactly who he was. We stood outside the yard and he saw us and called us in. That was my first meeting.

After that first meeting, I became a member of Invaders then later switched over to Starlift but maintained contact with Invaders. I still used to go back and play with them if they needed players. If I had to do a Jazz concert on TV, he always lent me a pan to use for that TV appearance. So, I always maintained that contact until he left Trinidad in 1967. After he left, I lost all contact with him. Even though I visited New York infrequently, I never saw him. I always inquired about him but was always told he was somewhere or the other.

Then, in 1989 when the Invaders organized a reunion, I thought it would be such a joyous occasion that I made an effort to contact him and see if he would be willing to return to Trinidad for that. I sent a message to him and then got a phone call from him. That was sort of amazing. I got a call from Kaethe George who then put him on. I told him that Birdie was organizing the reunion and encouraged him to come. He said he would think about it, and we talked some more about *ole* times. So, that was the first time since 1967 I was in contact with him.

I remember the last time I saw Ellie in Trinidad was just before he left for the States. I was standing at the corner of Tragarete Road and Rosalino Street, which was right by Invaders yard. He was riding his bicycle coming home from work and I called out to him, "Hi, Skip! How ya doin'? Wha' goin' on?" He said, "I'm going to New York and you will never see me again." I asked, "How's that?" He replied, "I'm outta here." I will never forget those words. And, he kept his word because from 1967 to 2000, it took thirty-three years for him to break his promise. I don't think it is really a promise that should have been made. You can't say you will never do something. You never know what will happen in life. I was happy that he broke it. So, I reestablished contact with him first in 1989 and then later again in 1996 when he invited me to come here [to the workshop].

To do that, I had to give up a contract I had to do summer seminars every year in Japan. But I gave that up. It was so good to be reunited with him! I considered that if he asked me to come here for a week then it must be an important thing. I was happy to know that he really needed me. I was even thinking about how much longer he was going to live. Kaethe said something about having heard so much about me from Ellie and that she was looking forward to meeting me. I think in response I said something like, "All right, you'll meet me in Morgantown," which is how the title for the workshop "Meet Me in Morgantown" was coined.

Beginning Problems between the East and the West

You must understand, Ellie was a legend even before coming to the United States. From what I know, and I do not know everything, when I met him, he was considered brilliant. His reputation was enormous. Without question, he was considered the premium tuner of pans in Trinidad. Coming from Woodbrook, Invaders always attracted the middle class around Carnival time. The who's who in association with Carnival aligned themselves with Invaders. Plus, he was associated with Little Carib. In my mind, I have Invaders and Little Carib linked as two cultural marks, icons, institutions of those days. To me, the two are inseparable. Both came from Woodbrook. Both were excellent showcases for culture, and Invaders was inextricably linked with Ellie's name. The few Woodbrook people, the patrons of the arts, were among the minority who really lent their support and did not wholly look down on the steel band. They really supported the art: Bruce Procope was one, a senior counsel/lawyer. Some important people like him were patrons. Ellie was in that milieu.

At the same time, remember, the People's National Movement (PNM) had not too long come into power with Independence in 1962. Black people for the first time in T&T's history were beginning to feel that they now had something. You must remember, too, that PNM was the party of the people and the movement was doing everything to secure votes for the next election. They were looking to do this among the Laventille people, the people who lived right there on the outskirts of Port of Spain (PoS). And, it's true, too, that the east PoS region—John John, Laventille, Behind the Bridge, those areas—was a major center for the development of the pan. Some people in government then decided to make a concerted effort and moved to give attention to the men of this area; hence, the name "Spree" Simon gained prominence and was exaggerated, and the name Ellie Mannette lost significance and was downplayed.

This is my recollection of what was going on at the time and the context, I think, for the bad feelings that were stirred up among the panmen. I, myself, felt this. From my perspective, Ellie felt some of this and took it very badly. He was not being given the recognition he deserved, of which I'm in total agreement. Following this rise of Spree Simon, Pan Am North Stars led by Anthony Williams became the leading band.

Invaders was the most popular band around 1956 to '57, which was when I came on the scene. They'd won some competitions and made some popular records. Theirs was a unique sound, different from the Pan Am North Stars' sound, led by Anthony Williams. And, this was obvious at the first Panorama held in 1963 when North Stars won that first Panorama. I believe that Invaders was doing well at music festivals. Anthony Williams's sound was a different sound from Ellie's. His was a sound that captivated people. It was a combination of the sound of the instrument and the arrangement of the classical pieces. You could tell they practiced, were very dedicated to the instrument.

When I left Invaders, a lot of the younger players followed me. This was a hard blow to Invaders and Ellie, to lose all their young players, and it took the band a long time to recover from the loss of almost all of the youth. With the emergence of Pan Am and Tony Williams—remember he was also the arranger—one band was descending and another was ascending. Also, with Bertie Marshall bringing out the double tenor, we had another innovation on the scene, a different pan. We had all these factors: Tony Williams with a different sound, his spider-web pan, and the brilliant band he had; then Bertie Marshall; then Wallace Austin. All these guys had a different sound, a different tone coming from their bands. Invaders would always be known for its sweetness, but these guys with their instruments were more powerful. Their vibrations were not as warm, but they were more exciting in sound. We were attracted to some of the new sounds coming from the other bands, which were beginning to grow in prominence. It was then a combination of all these things happening in the Steelband movement and in Trinidad itself.

Trinidad was an uninviting place for panmen, so Ellie experienced a lot of hurt there. He probably saw things slipping away from him a bit, also. Additionally, some pressure in his personal life, which still remains undisclosed, may have been relevant. Who knows?

Let me say here that what we're talking about is the truth, and I'm trying to be as truthful as possible. He came under pressure in his personal life and the Steelband movement, which he put above everything else. I do know he never missed a day's work. Every day, you could see him riding his bicycle to and from work. But I think he saw that he wasn't getting anywhere with the development of the pan. From what I could see, tuning was something he did after he came home from work. It was a side-line for him, even though in '56 to '57 everybody wanted a pan from Ellie Mannette. But he was never a full-time tuner. He wasn't doing it day in and day out. He couldn't.

People didn't make money from tuning pan. Seven dollars. Eight, nine, or ten dollars, which back then may have been a lot of money, if people could afford to pay it. You couldn't make a living doing that in those days, not like today when pan-tuning is all you do and could make a living like he is now. So, his pans were in high demand but he couldn't deliver as rapidly as they demanded, which forced people to learn to do it themselves.

You know how they say necessity is the mother of invention. By necessity, pan-tuners came into existence. People were forced to learn. So, everyone didn't have to get a pan from Ellie Mannette any more. Little by little, he stopped getting this recognition, too. He was suddenly a prophet without honor in his own country. So, he began to get sour about that. A little resentment came about. And, he loved tuning the instrument. Something he'd put his heart and soul into. All of a sudden, other pan-tuners were getting more recognition than he was. That also hurt. So, I understood his promise not to return to Trinidad, even though it saddened me to hear him say that. That is what I know.

One Cause of the East-West Rivalry

The rivalry goes back in history to that whole feeling of massa day done. In regard to panmen like Ellie and other light-skinned men in the movement, it was not only his complexion but his accent that caused Ellie to come across as more educated, more charismatic, well spoken, and privileged. Politicians, while they were trying to promote other people, the black-skinned—Rupert Nathaniel of the Symphonettes; Rudolph Charles; and a set of men who just loved pan, men like Corbeau Jack—in Ellie's case he was just trying to help everyone he could who loved pan. He went up the Hill to Desperadoes and helped those men himself. Then, Invaders became a meeting point for all people, panmen as well as the patrons of the arts, and he didn't think twice about helping people. But the politicians didn't see it that way. They only saw that it was time for change and tried to downplay Woodbrook and Invaders by playing the color card, playing one tuner off the other.

I think he felt that he was being disposed of. It all just finally got to him and he decided to leave, never to return. I was really sorry, even though I understood what drove him away and I wasn't even in the band at the time. But I admired him then. I always did, always will. I think it was better for him that he left when he did. Things happened the way they did. He had these connections with the [U.S.] Navy band and then Murray Narell, and he made good on those connections.

I can offer only my perspective regarding the role color played in the movement. What I myself experienced and hence know. So, know that this is not a question about perception or misperception. People stereotyped the panman as uneducated and rough. They felt you had to fit that stereotype and dealt with you in that way. If you came with a different image, you became a threat, so they had to downplay that. I was myself called a high-colored Trinidadian, so I experienced that. Again, I am not talking about misperceptions and connotations and a deluded imagination. I experienced what Ellie went through. It was the absurdity of class and color differences, of thinking of some people as the elite.

I was a QRC [Queen's Royal College] boy and my principal didn't want me playing pan.[2] I was caught in the middle. To be associating with the hooligans who played pan when I was a college boy and too good to be playing pan. I myself wasn't being given what I was due. On both sides I was being pressured. The politicians and some panmen were rejecting me for not being one of them, and the educated were pressuring me to not play pan because I was a college boy. They felt I was too good to be playing pan. I got it from both sides. They couldn't understand that we all shared this common love, and it didn't matter if you were light-or dark-skinned, cultured or uneducated. I went on to UWI, graduated from there, lectured there, and so on. This image of a panman was incongruent to the stereotype. It was what I experienced. The effort, on one hand, was to keep the pan down, while there were some of us who loved the instrument and couldn't deny this love. To do so would have been dishonest to one's true self. How could you expect us to deny this love? No. We couldn't.

In terms of Ellie: today, I see him as the leader of pan-tuning and developing the large steel orchestra capable to performing symphonies. His vision as a teacher is very powerful. His desire to transfer these voices into sound, as a master teacher, complements his ability to explain his vision to others so that they can grasp his teaching. These are the markings of a master teacher. He can explain cause and effect and show how things relate. Some people who call themselves teachers cannot do that. Anyone listening to Ellie explain Pan [the instruments and the movement's history] can grasp easily what he is talking about. His mind is so clear and methodical, it is very impressive. His legacy is master tuner/master teacher, and it will ensure the continuance and survival of the instrument.

But, this survival is not stunted at his visionary level. This survival is already to surpass what he envisioned. And, he does not feel threatened by his students excelling him. He delights in that. That, again, is the mark of an excellent teacher. Not only his students but all humanity can learn from him. We have never been contented with remaining at one level of doing things. Human activities have always been evidenced by growth and improvement. That is what we're all about. People who see that and promote it are the ones who go down as great in history. Small minded people don't want growth, improvement, or change. Not Ellie. Eventually, the people of Trinidad will come to see and recognize this about Ellie and appreciate him. Time will exonerate him not as a traitor of the culture. Not a traitor at all.

This is why you have to talk to other people to get right whether he is a traitor to Trinidad culture. You should contact Darway of St. James for accurate dates. You should also check with Neville Jules about the claim that another man was the first to use the oil drum, and someone else was the first to use rubber on the sticks. I love Ellie dearly and would do anything for him. Anyone knows that. But the story of Pan is bigger than Ellie, so you have to get to the truth. All I'm saying is that if you're writing a story about the truth of the movement, you have to talk to other people. Maybe, you'll also learn that Ellie was not the first to tune the double second. I myself can recall that at the Roxy Theatre either in '56 or '58 for the first Music Festival, I saw the first double second there being played by a man from San Fernando, one of the Bonaparte brothers. However, the double second as we know it now was made by Ellie.

You don't have any other choice. It's a responsibility, a mandate. You want to write and publish something that in the long run will make everyone in the movement feel good that you got to the truth. I don't know how you'll get to all these people. Some of them are already dead. But you have to do your best.

People also want to know my full story, I know. Well, that's another story for another book....

2001 Meet Me in Morgantown Workshop Summary

Holman and Robbie Greenidge who shared the spotlight at the 2001 MMIM offered attendees firsthand accounts on T&T's hybrid culture during a morning session. Holman shared how he played J'ouvert (explaining how the names for Carnival events reflect the strong French economic and cultural influences) then returned home to come back out around one o'clock on Monday afternoon to play "sailor mas" and Indian. The Mas band used baby powder quite liberally and the coined phrase defining sailor mas: "If yuh *fraid* ah powder / Doh play a sailor."

Holman further recalled how Sparrow's "The Outcast" (1963) points to the stigma associated with panmen, one they all struggled to rise above, so that that first Panorama of 1963 with twenty bands entering the competition indeed marked a turning point in Steelband. He and Greenidge emphasized how sponsorship, though affording primarily pans and basic steel bands' needs, did help improve behavior. However, they pointed out that companies were not generally supportive of panmen or the Carnival season, which began immediately following Christmas. As Carnival approached and men devoted more time to the panyard and Mas camps, they lost their jobs, as codified in the late calypsonian Lord Kitchener's (né Aldwyn Roberts) "No Work for Carnival."

Both men noted that Panorama also caused a shift from the Bomb competition to the Panorama stage competition, whose results in those early days reflected more so the crowd's response and biases than the judges' objective evaluation. They further pointed out that as pans graduated to stands and wheels, fights occurred among men who wanted to pull the pans of excellent players in various bands, seeking to identify with these talented panmen who were taking Steelband to soaring heights. These pan-pushers invariably caused more trouble than their labor merited and contributed to the stigma. Nevertheless, any disruptions had to cease completely once the band entered the "barber green," a paved stretch that led to the entrance of the stage.

They informed that in the early days of Panorama, bands learned up to eleven songs for the road, which has been drastically reduced to one for the road, two to three for Dimanche Gras, and big Sunday which rolled into Monday. Those days of playing multi songs on the road led to piracy of songs by tourists or visitors. Eventually, the organization had to come quickly into step with copyrighting laws to protect material from theft. A type of protectiveness that is atypical of panmen's generous attitude had to come into existence.

The men further shared how the Red Cross Kiddies Carnival, now a big event, intrudes upon Panorama time, and that other Steelband competitions for schools and small bands point to how the art form has proliferated. Despite its pervasiveness, Carnival is not without controversy, which is not insurmountable if the steelband association and the Carnival Development Committee maintain open and honest dialogue.

Holman concluded the session with sharing that one of his ambitions is one day to present his full perspective on Pan and Steelband before the movement's history becomes too jaded by many misrepresentations.

Author's note: I also very briefly interviewed Greenidge; however, it was not transcribed because it was much too short and lacking of substance of his own vast contributions to Pan in T&T and the United States. He spared me what time he could before departing to perform with Jimmy Buffet on NBC's *Today*, an annual appearance for many years and counting. I am, however, in much gratitude for his knowledge and insight of the movement. We all eagerly anticipate his full story, too.

Holman's calypso in tribute to calypsonians, "Heroes of the Nation," was performed at the finale concert of the workshop. Its lyrics are presented here by permission.

Verse 1
While in their earthly state
They made the country great
Icons of our culture
Treasures that is what they are
Beings of a wonderland,
Touched by the master's hand
Their deeds were so great,
Therefore I now beg you please
Come and let us sing in tribute to these

Chorus
Heroes of the nation
Poet, calypsonian
Talkin' 'bout the great Denis Williams
Talkin' 'bout the Maestro Kitchener
And Ras Shorty, musically
What a loss for this blessed country
We cannot replace their artistry
They gone, gone, gone
But the music will live on
They were ambassadors
We cannot forget because

Music for the nation
Was their ultimate passion
Loved by the populace
No one can take their place
Many going to come and many will leave and go
They deserve honor all because they were.

Verse 2
Let every steelband man
And every calypsonian
Stand in recognition
Of these great artisans
They deserve more than this
And shall surely be missed
Their contribution being as worthy as it has
Come and let us remember all them as

Verse 3
Genius has come and gone
Leaving us all to mourn
Soca music no more
Will be as it was before
Gone are the heart and soul
To leave a gaping hole
Get behind your pan if you are a pan-player
Jam something sweet to serenade our.

2
A Gem of Pan and a Father of Panmen: Neville Jules's Story[1]

Neville Jules's *following list of accomplishments is in association with his leadership of Trinidad All Stars Philharmonic Orchestra (also abbreviated TASPO), formed in 1946 with Prince Batson, the captain.* Jules *cites the band's name as having been suggested by Kenny, a tailor and artist who designed Mas costumes. The band's achievements include:* **1952**, *third place winner, Steelband Music Festival held at the Globe Theatre;* **1953**, *participated in International Steelband Festival in British Guiana (BG);* **1954**, *second place winner, Steelband Music Festival held at the Roxy Theatre;* **1957**, *BG tour;* **1958**, *the famous Bomb "Minuet in G" was a big hit on the road for Carnival;* **1968**, *Steelband Festival champion, first time competition after a fourteen-year absence;* **1969**, *first place, Bomb competition, played "Ballet Egyptian";* **1970**, *first place, Bomb competition; Madison Square Garden performance;* **1971**, *first place, both uptown and downtown Bomb competitions.*

Pan Innovations and Some Controversies

I was born May 21, 1927, in East Dry River, PoS. I first heard and saw Steelband in Hell Yard in 1939 when I followed the sound of the music to where I saw players such as Tackler, Brassy, and Elmo "Bully" Alleyne. That motivated me to play and eventually to start tuning pan with Rudolph "Fisheye" Ollivierre around 1943.

The first pan I made was a ping-pong. It had three notes that played only rhythm, no melody. Later, I also made the tenor kettle. I saw Zigilee's[2] and copied it after he refused to let me play his. I continued to make pans and was the first to bring out the caustic soda drum—the first single bass pan—and later two caustic soda drums that set the groundwork for the multi-bass section we have today. I also made the *grundig* to play the rhythm with chords. That was a background pan, now called the cello.

I also was the first to make the single guitar pan, which I originally called the quatro pan. I was inspired to make that pan around Christmas-time when a parang band was practicing in a house on Duke Street, between Charlotte and Henry Streets. I stopped and listened to them and paid attention to the guy strumming on the quarto. I decided to make a pan to imitate that sound and call it the quatro pan. The guys in the band talked quite a bit about it and the talk spread. When we came on the road, a lot of people from different bands—Spree, Philmore "Boots" Davidson, and other people—came to hear it. A few days later, Boots made an identical one and called it the guitar pan and the name stuck in association with him. While he may get the credit for it, he copied it from me. That could have been around '48 or '49. In those days, time didn't really matter to us. We were just doing all these things. I was concentrating on building a family of pans, even though then I wasn't even consciously doing that. What I mean is that I didn't start out saying to myself I was building a family of pans. I was just imitating sounds I heard, such as the tune boom.

I was the first to create the tune boom, a pan that's no longer around. Paul Robeson inspired me to made the tune boom, the bass sound. It was a drum made from the Bermudez biscuit tin, and the first steel bands we had used this drum and the bass drum, which was played similarly to the way the drum-set is played. The tune boom was also inspired from another instrument. I saw a guy playing a box bass—that's a box with a hole in it, similarly to the guitar or bass—and at the hole were three springs cut at different length. Some guys were playing the guitar and singing, and he was imitating a bass by plucking at the strings. It was not musical but had the heavy sound of a bass. I wanted to imitate that sound and made the tune boom. You can say that the tune boom was the real predecessor of the bass.

To return to the caustic soda drum: when I tuned the tune boom, it was to accompany the ping-pong that played the melody. One of the first melodies played on the ping-pong was "Mary Had a Little Lamb" because the notes were easy to pick on a four-note pan. Imagine a guitar playing bass chords, and you wanted not just chords but the real song. I wanted something to do that and tried the caustic soda drum. There were some advantages and disadvantages to the caustic soda drum. It was a very light pan and longer than the ping-pong, much like the drums we have now but light enough for a guy to carry all day. But because the caustic drum material was so light and thin, it could only endure the two or three days of playing for Carnival. It cracked and broke too easily while playing. This is why the men looked for something more durable and adopted the 55-gallon oil drum. When the guys first started to use the 55-gallon drum, they would cut it very short then weld on the skirt of these lighter caustic drums to make them longer. But carrying those pans caused the guys to develop blisters, which is why someone eventually came up with the idea to add wheels to the drums for Carnival. So, the evolution was from the caustic to the oil drum to drum on wheels. It was a transition from one thing to the next based on convenience. In my case, it was based on instruments I wanted to imitate.

TASPO [mentioned in the Introduction] helped to establish the transition. The men were using the oil drums for the tenor, second, and guitar second pans, and whatnot. To establish the time all this was happening, we could go to the controversy around Ellie Mannette. We used to use small pans for ping-pong pans that may have been eighteen to twenty inches in diameter and could hold twelve, maybe even fourteen, notes. There was a competition in Tunapuna at the Palladium Theatre, or it may have been the Monarch, on Eastern Main Road. I don't remember the exact year. I entered the competition, as well as Ellie, as a ping-pong soloist with the small pan.

We were all backstage and when our name was called we went up on stage to play and sat with our pan positioned between our legs. When this guy named Snatcher was called—his real name is Cyril Guy[3]—he came out with this huge pan, a 55-gallon drum, and couldn't sit the way we sat. He had to position the pan between his knees to play. The whole theater laughed at the guy, because they saw this pan was so huge and it became a big joke to them. They couldn't see what he probably saw. Ellie came first at that competition and I came second. Within a few months, two to three, Ellie, I, and everyone else began using the big pan, the 55-gallon drum. The next competition we entered in Mucurapo Stadium, Ellie had a big pan and I had a big pan, which we entered as soloists. Snatcher, who first came out with the big pan, won that Mucurapo competition and got a bicycle. I came second and Ellie came third. Now, he's telling everybody he was the first to come out with the big pan.

But, Ellie cannot really get anyone to back his claim. Too many people are still alive today who saw Snatcher—people say he's still alive and living in Tunapuna—when he came out with the big pan, and they can vouch for what I'm saying. Too many people who were at that Tunapuna competition can well remember who were there, who won, and what type of pan the competitors played. I know this because when I spoke with some of them, they verified what I'm saying about who played on a big pan and who played on a small pan. Ellie and I played on a small pan and Snatcher played a big pan. When men like Ellie rise to a top position, they have to be careful with what they say. They must remember that other people can still remember the way things really were. I, on the other hand, don't have to brag about what I did and didn't do because I have nothing to prove to anyone but myself. So, when I say I created this or that, I speak the truth and also have people who can back me up.

I also made a pan I called the trombone pan—a single pan—and like the *grundig* it didn't play the way I wanted it to play and so I discarded it, as I did the *grundig*. I think that's the complete list of the pans I experimented with—the trombone, the tune boom, the *grundig*, the caustic soda, and the guitar or the quatro.

When Pan Trinbago was on Edward Street, the organization wanted to get to the bottom of how and when Pan started and invited quite a few old panmen. This was on an Ash Wednesday. They invited people from the radio and TV stations. Everybody in his little group was being questioned. After all the questions were finished, everyone came together as a large group and they began taping as questions were being asked of each panman for verification. The question regarding Spree first came up: who was the first man to play a song on a pan? They asked me that question. I answered, "Look, everybody thinks that Spree was the first person to play a song on a pan, but that is not so." I then explained what I did and what I knew. Other people backed me up. Andrew de la Bastide (they called him Andrew "Pan") who went abroad with TASPO started talking.[4] Still backing up what I said, our stories varied a little. He said that where I was—because I had left Charlotte Street and went up the Hill at some friends—is where he saw the pan and played it. He claims that I threatened him for playing the pan. Then he said he went and made one. My story was that I went up the

Hill playing the pan, he heard it, and then I made one for him. He went on to say that he made a pan for himself and later on he made one for Spree. Spree was later then trying to claim something that he knew nothing about, but instead should have gone back and looked at what he really did and did not do.

Then, the talk came up about the big pan, which was introduced before Ellie says it was. But as I said before, anyone can go to Trinidad now and find people who will tell the truth about the big pan. In fact, men in Invaders also know the truth but out of loyalty to Ellie wouldn't come right out and say the truth. Pan Trinbago used to have all this on file, but a big fire destroyed all their records of everything—the history of Pan, everything. Questions regarding the big pan went so far that during the discussion someone else said it wasn't Snatcher but Andrew Beddoe. Beddoe was a drummer,[5] a very good folk drummer who used to beat pan, too. Somebody suggested that he made and tuned the pan and gave it to Snatcher. A guy who was in the audience said, "I know the man," and called the man's name, the band he was in, and the song Snatcher played in the competition. All this was documented.

There's just too much controversy around who did what first. For example, some people say that Fisheye made the first tune boom, but that's not true. If you asked Fisheye, he would tell you that I, in fact, made the tune boom. Believe it or not, he was once captain of Second Fiddle, my first band, not because of what he could do in Pan but because the band was in his yard on Charlotte Street. Because of the wrong things he did to me and to the other members, we had a split and from that split came All Stars. Though he wouldn't say so, he couldn't tune or do anything, but he somehow ended up in Invaders. A short time after he was there, apparently *Look* magazine—Invaders was a popular band—went to the band to do a story on it. Whose face was on the cover? Fisheye's, with his two big eyes and wearing an officer's cap. Not Ellie Mannette's or any other Invaders man's. The Invaders story was inside with pictures of Ellie and others. That magazine was on display in the Pan Trinbago office before the fire.

Sorry to say: but Ellie doesn't know all the facts because some things he just doesn't know about. For instance, we went down one Christmastime with the tune boom to Invaders yard and played. When we were leaving, they all stood up and watched us as we were walking back up Tragarete Road. That may have been the first time some people saw the tune boom, connected it to Fisheye, and came to conclude that Fisheye made it. But, Fisheye didn't make anything. Many things being attributed to Fisheye are false. He was just there at the time the thing was happening. But as a panman who played a song you would listen to and like, or to tune a pan and whatnot, he was not into any of that. In certain instances, I gave him some opportunities, such as when I showed him what to play, and because he was a very showy fella, he got credit. Sometimes, he got credit that he didn't deserve.

One night, we were on the street—at the time we were still using the small pan. To draw attention, he made a coil with a kerchief and with his eyes opened wide he placed the coil and the pan on a little boy's head and played it, with everybody watching him. All for show. Also, when he walked into the yard, he did so with such bravado that everybody would say, "Look at Fisheye!" He did a lot of things to draw attention to himself. Imagine, he had just arrived at Invaders yard and *Look* magazine put on its cover his photograph, not Ellie's or any other Invaders boys like "Birdie" or Francis. That must tell you something.

In regard to the controversy around who did what first: I attended the last WSMF in 2000. I traveled home with my son, who lives in another state, not here in Brooklyn. He invited me and paid for my fare because I wasn't enthusiastic about going. While there, I didn't plan to attend any Pan event, not the Festival or Panorama; however, someone insisted that I attend the Festival and even got me a ticket to make sure. At the Festival, Patrick Arnold greeted me, "Neville, you're here? If I knew you were here I would have taken you to Ellie." He left and went and found Ellie and brought him over to me. Ellie and I talked for a while and he brought me up to date on all he was doing at the university, blah, blah. Then, he was called because Invaders was about to play.

Either the next day or two days later, he was interviewed on TV. To my great surprise, he claimed to do a lot of things, which he didn't do. For example, he claimed he was the first person to put rubber on sticks, which is a lie. I did it before him, and it wasn't my idea. The idea was my friend's, Prince Batson, the first captain of All Stars. He said, "Neville, why yuh doh wrap rubber on the sticks?" because we were playing with raw tips and after a while the ends frazzled. And I did, which was in the '40s. Now on that show, Ellie claimed that he used to use a pallet stick then a coconut branch, and all that sort of thing. I found that claim real curious, not the truth.

He also claimed the fifty-five-gallon drum. Well, that claim made me call *The Guardian* right away. I said, "This is Neville Jules speaking. Ellie Mannette is right now telling a pack of lies on TV. He is claiming he is the first person to make the fifty-five-gallon drum. That's a lie. Nobody has to tell me. Both of us were at that competition with our small pan when a fella came to the competition with a big pan and played." It so happened that I had to leave Trinidad the next day but was there long enough to raise questions regarding Ellie's claims. I figure, if it was anyone else who had called the paper, the newspeople might not have reacted the way they did. I said to them, "Not so," and they published it.

After being home in Brooklyn a few days, someone said to me of having read on the Internet where Ellie said I should put my money where my mouth is. I should put up or shut up. But, I'm willing to do that any time. It was not an accident that I was in Trinidad at the same time as Ellie. I was supposed to be there, because the guy was telling so many lies. Another example is when he said that to go some place to play he'd put his pan in a crocus bag to take it to where he was going. He turned to the fella who was interviewing him and said, "And you can call that the first pan case." That may be so: but who's to believe it when it now looks like he's just trying to grab everything for himself?

Here's another story. Prince Batson, Fisheye, another guy named Markoff who's passed away now, and I—the four of us—used to go all the way to Woodbrook to get drums. Now, where we used to go for the caustic soda drums was a place I knew for having a lot of drums. Because, after we made the first bass, Ellie came to me and I told him where to go. The pans that we used to go there for were used for the same ping-pong and tenor kettle pans, but they were just so big. Getting back to the story: around two o'clock in the morning we would go down to the river, because this place was at the mouth of the river near the sea. We would see if the tide was in and the water was backing up, and then some of us would walk through the water to get to the factory. When we got there, we would jump up onto the river wall, jump over the fence, and steal the drums. The rest of the guys would remain on the other side of the fence and we would pass the drums to them. When we were finished, we would walk up the river and when we reached Besson Street Police Station we would walk by there easy, easy, so the police wouldn't see or hear us. Then, we would continue up the river into Hell Yard and leave the pans there. The next day, we would start tuning the pans. This was around '44, '45, even before the end of the war. This is what we used to do and I've told this story to many people in Tunapuna at the Palladium Theatre—or it may have been the Monarch—on Eastern Main Road.

Listen to what Ellie Mannette told the same guy that morning on TV, to my surprise. He jumped on his bicycle, rode it to Carenage, Chaguaramas. Once there, he swam out into the sea, waited there in the water until the soldier was gone, climbed over the fence, stole a 55-gallon drum, threw it into the sea, and swam back to shore with it. Now, who could believe that? How high was this fence? How strong was he? Where was the fence in relation to the sea? Didn't the sound of the drum splashing into the water alert the guard? If you went on to the U.S. base with soldiers guarding it constantly, how you could steal a drum and get away with it? He had to swim from Carenage to that part of the base to get the drum. How long and far was the swim? That story raises more questions than gives a clear picture of that whole scenario. People have to question the veracity of the story. This sounds to me like he merely wants to have one better than my story. So, people need to question the crocus-bag-as-a-pan-case story and all Ellie's claims in order to give credit where credit is due. I know an Invaders man who told me that the first double second pan he saw was in Southern Symphony from La Brea. That's the band with the Bonaparte brothers. He said, "Neville, look, I only want the truth, you know. I want to know the truth." And, this fella is a staunch Invaders man. He's not in Invaders now, but he was. He said, "I saw that pan there. How come Ellie claim to make that?" I said to him, "Boy, Ellie didn't make that."

You see, I was interviewed on the radio program, *Pan for the People*,[6] this year by Cyril Diaz—the former captain of Starlift. I'd promised to be in Trinidad last year and didn't go but went this year. During the interview, again the story of the second pan came up. A caller to the program insisted that Ellie Mannette tuned the second pan for Bonaparte. I told him, "Do you know what you are saying?" I was challenging him because I used to spend weeks in La Brea in Bonaparte's panyard and also because I had friends from La Brea. I said, "I know that both Bonaparte brothers used to tune their own pan, and they even used to tune pan for other bands. So, why would they come to Ellie to tune their pan? Who told you that?" He answered his father. I said that he had better get his information right, because those guys used to do their own tuning.

Something is going on with the people west of Green Corner. They want everybody to believe that everything happened down there [*the west*]. Some will die supporting what they believe, which is most everything came from Woodbrook, whether that is the fact or not. Here's an example. Another guy who wasn't originally around when the whole thing was happening was the first to criticize me for not knowing what I'm saying. This guy, who obviously wasn't around when Ellie's barracuda was stolen, said the tree from which it was hung was at the corner of Charlotte and Duke Streets. He was quoting from some newspaper article whose writer not only didn't have the facts right but didn't know the lay of the land. Anyone who knew the area then will tell you that no tree was at the Charlotte and Duke, which streets have had houses for as long as I could remember. It certainly didn't have a tree there when Ellie's pan was taken and hung in John John, which is not Charlotte and Duke. Another article called me Neville "Fisheye" Jules. So you must know that some writers don't take time to check the facts and get their information right. Even [Felix] Blake[7] and others didn't take the time to get the facts right, so I don't give that much credit to his book.

Returning to the radio program: another fella called and challenged me about the fifty-five-gallon drum, saying it was a fory-five-gallon drum pan. I said, "You can say what you want. But were you there? 'Cause I know different." I insisted, "I am telling you that it was a fifty-five-gallon drum pan. I was there." I was also there in 1950 when no band had the fifty-five-gallon drum yet.

There's also Norman Darway who quotes from the newspapers and gets the facts wrong. Yet, Darway and those Western guys want to claim everything for *the west*. They ought to at least get the facts right first.

What I don't like about this whole thing is: Ellie Mannette and his followers—his die-hard people—are apparently trying to rob Trinidad and the world of the true history of Pan. That I don't like. As a fellow Trinidadian, I don't like that at all. Give Jack his jacket! When people come to me, I say to them that Ellie Mannette is the guy who sank the pan, put the grooves in the pan to separate the notes, and at one time he was the best tuner in Trinidad. I give him that credit. Back then, a lot of people wanted to be like him when it came to tuning because of how sweet Invaders pans were. That is also to his credit. But he shouldn't try to take away from what the other guys have done. Don't do that, man!

I also question his claim that he invented seven out of the ten sections of the steel band. The sections include: tenor, double tenor, double seconds, single guitar, double guitar, triple guitar, quadruple guitar, cello, tenor bass, and bass. Tony Williams gets credit for the spider-web tenor/the circle of fifths; Bertie Marshall gets credit for the double tenor; and people give me credit for the bass, guitar, and the *grundig*, which we don't use. Now, remember people—Ray Holman is one—say that a man in the south came out with the double second before Ellie did. That leaves five not seven remaining sections for him to take credit for. People who listen to him think he's the bible on Pan and they must believe what he says. But, I'd like people to consider the other side of the story and take all this information into account in order to give Jack his jacket and Jim his *gym-boots*. I think Ellie could give Jack at least his shirt, and then there won't be any controversy.

I want to return to some of the chronology regarding the inventions: remember, Prince Batson, the first captain of All Stars, suggested that I wrap the sticks with rubber. He was captain and I was lance corporal, the rank I wanted to hold in the band because I wanted to be just one level above the regular guys. Later, I became captain. I adopted the title of lance corporal from the police organization that had one, two, and three stripes for lance corporal, corporal, sergeant, and so on. To maintain discipline in the band, we followed the suggestion of the leader. So, when Prince Batson said for me to wrap the sticks, I did. This happened after V-J Day because before V-J Day nobody was really playing a song on a pan but playing rhythm. The rubber-tipped stick was to enhance song-playing, which came into full swing after the end of the war. All Stars was the first band to play a song on a pan. All before that, people were only playing rhythm. If Ellie or anyone challenges that, their credibility is at stake.

Here's another fact. I was the first person to make the double second, but I didn't follow through with it. It wasn't to be a double second but ended up like that. The two-pan thing. I made it and tuned it, and hung it on one leg. Nowadays, we use three legs. My double pan had a single metal pole with a round base and a cross-piece welded to the pole. I bore one hole for the pan on one side of the rim and another hole on the other side of the rim. I used a bolt with a nut and tightened it. The side of the pan with the nut and bolt changed and went out of tune, while the notes away from the nut and bolt were fine. Because I became busy with other responsibilities, I put it aside with the intention of returning to it later. This happened around '50 or '51. Before long I heard, "Boy, somebody come out with the double second." I kept quiet. I don't know when Ellie says he came out with the double second, but I question any of his inventions that were supposed to have happened before V-J Day.[8]

When New York planned to honor some of the old panmen up here in the States, the organizers planned to bring Invaders from Trinidad. We were at the Trinidad ambassador's office for a meeting that was to be aired over the radio. I was invited to give a talk. After I finished, the man who arranged for Invaders to come to the States approached me and said, "Listen, man, Invaders is coming up from Trinidad, you know. Do you want a ticket to come to the show?" I said, "Yes. I heard that Ellie Mannette has said for me to put up or shut up, so I would like to talk to him." He confirmed that Ellie was coming to the show. I said, "I'll be there to meet and confront him."

The night of the show, I was there sitting in the audience and waiting. Suddenly, someone announced, "Mr. Ellie Mannette would not be here tonight because he is scared of flying, and there's too much snow where he is, and blah, blah, blah." Scared of flying? Since when? Did he come from Trinidad by boat? Or, did he know we were waiting to confront him with the truth and backed down? I wonder.

I am still waiting to have a talk with him, since that time in Trinidad. Before he went on that interview, we spoke very nicely and he shared with me all that he was doing. I remember that people were asking him all about the pan and who the first person was, and he claimed that we can't give credit to one person only because pan was not invented. Right? Well, there's nothing wrong with that claim. But when he begins claiming things that he didn't do, who wouldn't be angry?

Yes, the history of Pan is embroiled in controversy, with Ellie Mannette dead smack in the middle of things because he has created the controversy. The rubber-tipped stick, the crocus bag-pan case, the seven of ten sections he invented, when songs were being played on pan, and on the list goes.

Until now, I've questioned the authenticity of the history of Pan, including Blake's, as I said before. You can't have an accurate history until you get to talk with all the main players of that history. You, Doc, will have to talk to men in Trinidad, men whom no one is talking to, before you can write a true history of Pan. People have a lot of work to do to get this right. And, the more people you talk to and include, the fuller the story gets.

A part of that history includes the transition to the stands. The stand for the tenor pan was metal because you needed a solid base. I recall that some were made of wood, too, but the first stand was metal. I know I used metal with the first double second I made and set aside. It should be easy to figure out who made the first stand, but it wasn't me. You see, once bands began to travel, whether it was by boat or plane, the men had to put the pans in something. But someone had to have done it, and I don't know who that person is. Unlike other fellas, I can talk of what I know and of my contributions, and I wouldn't try to overstep that, because you can never tell what is really going on in another's backyard. So like La Brea, I can talk about that because I used to visit there constantly, spend weeks there. I can tell you about Hill Sixty, which no longer exists. That's the area I took the pan to Andrew "Pan," which is where he used to be. I can talk about Casablanca.

There's a guy—he's dead now—Sonny Jones. He had made a seven-note pan, which I had liked how it sounded. Many times when I wanted to play in a competition, I used to borrow that pan. He's a guy from the very early days of Hell Yard, when I was a little boy hanging around the bigger guys. I remember he went to Lacou Harpe and he might have been around a couple of steel bands. I think Kim Johnson interviewed him, and he told Kim that he was in about twenty-five different steel bands—bands from the country [rural area], from all over. He also mentioned he was in All Stars, which was a lie. Something had to be wrong with me if I didn't know that: you understand? So, I *know* that a lot of these guys lie.

It seems like almost everyone I meet who talks about Pan and about the Garrot tells me how he was in the Garrot as a little boy. How could all these people be up in the Garrot? The last person who came to me with the Garrot talk was Abu Bakr. He came into the panyard and wanted me to talk to the captain to get some pans for him. The Garrot was a club on Charlotte Street and used to be around where Najib Elias Hardware Store was. You would go upstairs to the first floor, through the gambling room where there was the stairway to the Garrot or attic on the top floor. I even have a picture that someone gave me of Winston Gordon who used to be in the band and now arranges for a band in Tobago. It was a picture of him and me playing iron in the Garrot. When he saw it, he was so happy and said it was for the archives. What's nice about when people talk about the Garrot in those days is they always have something good to say about it. No bad memories.

After the split with Second Fiddle, a member of Cross of Lorraine suggested that we get some good guys to join us and call the band Trinidad All Stars. In the history of All Stars, the band was in one fight with one steel band, Casablanca. It really involved two or three guys from All Stars who were doing all the fighting with Casablanca. The other guys didn't really get into that. This also happened during the late '40s or early '50s.

Understand that in those days things were happening, but we weren't paying attention at the time because the idea that Pan would reach where it is now never crossed our mind. Remember that in those days it was a disgrace to be a panman. If we went from one place to the next, we would have a pan-stick in our pockets. We didn't have an office file in our hands. I remember there were times on the road mothers would come and just snatch their children by the scruff of their neck and pull them out the bands. Anyone who was playing or jumping in the band between the pans, they would just pull them out. They didn't want their children around pan. With that sort of attitude, we weren't paying attention to a lot of things that are now considered significant.

From Hell Yard to All Stars

In addition to what I remember as my innovations is the first ping-pong pan I made to play a song on. There was a rumor that somebody was playing a song on a pan, a story I'll give in a little while. But first, I want to give some history on Hell Yard, which I only mentioned before, as well as some stories of my boyhood.

My good friend Elmo, called Bully, had told me about Bighead Hamil who was in Hell Yard at the time—this was before the fellas from Hell Yard had abandoned their yard. During the war, when the bands used to be on the street for

Carnival or whatever festivity, the authorities stopped the bands from parading. Since the police stopped the fellas from Hell Yard and they couldn't play their pan, they went about their business and hardly returned to use the yard. Hell Yard had a sailor band named Bad Behaviour, and Hamil was one of the youngest guys in that band. That band was captained by a guy named Sagiator. The name of their steel band was Second Fiddle, so Hell Yard was the home of Bad Behaviour and Second Fiddle, and we called them all the fellas from Hell Yard.

After the older guys—the fellas from Hell Yard—left, we the younger guys made Hell Yard our home with Hamil who was their youngest guy becoming our oldest guy in the yard. Fisheye and I were much younger than he was. He was about nineteen and I was about fifteen, if so old. All of us hung out in Hell Yard, with Bully who was with the older guys staying around, but he didn't do any pan-playing. I remember him saying the first person he heard playing a song on a pan was Bighead Hamil. At the time, I was around Hamil helping tune pan—the ping-pong and the bass kettle and whatnot—I didn't hear him play any songs on a pan.

Hell Yard was located where All Stars' yard is right now, at the corner of George and Duke Streets. Years ago when I was a little boy in the '30s and lived in Laventille, the Dry River overflowed. There may be some people still alive in Trinidad who could give you a first-hand account of that flood. Anyhow, after the river overflowed, the people who lived in the houses there abandoned them. At the back of those houses on Duke Street, there was the hollow area with weeds growing where the Bad Behaviour boys played cricket. That hollow area was called Hell Yard. Right now the land is leveled, and that is where today's All Stars yard is.

The people who lived in that East Dry vicinity knew the area from Charlotte Street to Duke Street like the back of their hands. If I were at the Salvation Army on Charlotte Street and I wanted to go to the corner of Nelson and Duke Streets, I didn't have to come all the way down to Charlotte Street then on to Duke Street. I could cut across anyone of those backyards. Here's a good story related to that.

At Christmas, in those days we used to play on the road. Steal chances to go and play on the Hill or in town. We played on the Hill on any given night once we were in the mood. And, we were always in the mood. Once we were on the Hill, we would meet Despers—at the time they used to call themselves Laventille Band, not Desperadoes—Casablanca, Hill Sixty, which is no longer in existence, Tokyo: all these bands would be playing on the Hill. Of course, there weren't any radios and stereos like now. So, you could have stood on Prince Street or Duke

Street or Charlotte Street and heard the echo of the steelband at night. The police followed that echo up the Hill in their Black Maria, that big van, to raid the bands. The men would drop their pans and run. But that Christmas, a particular friend of mine said, "Let's go on the road, man. If police come, me ent runnin' at all." I said, "All right." We made a search for the police then went up on the Hill playing. When we were ready to come back down and go to town, we were on Piccadilly Street—right where All Stars yard is now—near Duke going toward Park Street. We were beating pan while going down the Hill into town.

A police guy who was a member of Casablanca Steel Band and used to serve warrants was there. He came into the band and said nothing. As a matter of fact, he was even directing the band and the traffic, so we figured everything was easy and we continued beating pan onto Park Street then onto Charlotte Street. Just before we got to Duke Street, we looked back and saw the Black Maria coming. We said we weren't running at all. As the van reached us, tens of policemen jumped out to arrest us and everybody scattered. One man had a bass around his neck. I had one around my neck, too. A policeman stopped me, a sergeant, keeping his hand on the pan. "You're under arrest." I said, "Just give me a chance to take off the bass from around my neck." I lifted the string from around my neck and was off. The policeman couldn't run after me because he was old. He said to a younger policeman, "Get him!" I swung up Duke Street and into one of those yards, and once I was in that yard I was like mandrake. The policeman didn't know where I was gone. He couldn't find me in that yard once I was over that fence. And it was so good, I remember that while I was running everyone was clapping. It was so nice. I was gone.

We knew that area very, very well. We only walked in the street when we felt like walking. From Charlotte Street to Duke Street, almost all the yards on that stretch we knew. The police raided us because they didn't want us playing pan. It was rumored at one time they were going to come into the yard and take away our drums. But (it was) not only the police who didn't want us playing pan.

Here's another story. Right now where All Stars is, there was a vacant lot. When you entered the yard there was a house to the right, and the people who used to live there their name was—. They hated Steelband and steelbandsmen. At the back of Hell Yard was a breadfruit tree that provided shade from the sun. Their kitchen was not attached to the house at the back of their yard. A window was at the back of the kitchen. Hell Yard was down in a hollow and their house and kitchen were at the top. I would be down in the yard pounding and tuning my pan. Their kitchen was above me, and they would open their window and dump their garbage onto me. I had to move out of the way of the garbage coming down on my back.

On the Duke Street side of that same house, there was a lamp-post. At night, we'd sit around the lamp-post talking. Something was sold at Bonanza Drugstore at the corner of Frederick and Queen Streets named calypso. It was used for killing *bachacs*.[9] It was sold by the pint, twelve cents a pint, in liquid. That thing smelt like ten rotten eggs. Whenever we were talking outside by the lamp-post, they opened their window quietly and dropped two drops. That's all they needed to drop, and no one could stay in that area. You had to hold your nose and move, because that thing was really stink. Like a stink bomb. Today, they're gone and All Stars is still there in that very spot.

Regarding the first ping-pong I made to play a tune, I remember it was Empire Day, May 24, on a Thursday morning. The rain had fallen and I went to the Royal Theatre at nine thirty. I had a pan in the yard at Fisheye's that I had made four notes on. This could have been between May and July when I made the pan, because I also remember that it was after the victory over Europe when the authorities allowed people back on the streets in 1945. We returned to the streets and paraded for about three days. The police didn't stop anybody. The band played the rhythm while the people sang to the tune of "Mary Anne": "*Five years, eight months we ent play no mas / Whole day, whole night we go play de—.*" All right. Fill in the blank. For three days, they couldn't stop us. Somewhere between V-E Day [May 7, 1945] and V-J Day [August 6, 1945] I made the four-note pan for the Royal Theatre event. The first two songs I played on it were: "You Want to Come Kill Me" by Lion and "Do-Re-Mi."

For V-J Day, we came on the road playing the songs because on V-E Day no one was playing songs. It was just the usual rhythm they were playing on the ping-pong pan. When we came out on V-J Day and was the only steel band playing a song, this guy by the name of Eric Stowe, a member from the old Hell Yard band, came in front of the band as the conductor. Every corner we came to, he stopped the band, then Fisheye would start the band with his rendition of "Do-Re-Mi." The other bands weren't playing any music, you know. It was only a clackety-clack that kept rhythm as they moved down the road. So, it was a big thing to be playing a tune and the talk spread, "Boy, you hear what that fella was playing?!" We were still carrying the Second Fiddle name from Hell Yard. We played those two songs for the victory over Japan, and by the first Carnival in 1946 everyone else was playing a song, including Spree Simon. He was originally there and knew nothing about those first two songs.

Now, I'm not claiming I was the first person to play a song on pan but that I preceded Spree, and not only me but Fisheye, too. When I made my [four-note] ping-pong pan, I gave it to Fisheye to play because I used to play the tenor kettle. I liked to play the tenor kettle. So, Fisheye played the songs on the pan I made, and I accompanied him.

The name of my band was Second Fiddle, the name originally taken from the guys from Hell Yard. After that, we were called Cross of Lorraine, a French name. Those were the two names before All Stars. So, we boys, as members of the first two little bands we had between the time Bad Behaviour left and V-J Day, were calling ourselves Second Fiddle. Then, we changed the name to Cross of Lorraine. After the split with Fisheye and we left his yard, we became Trinidad All Stars. Fisheye, because he had no band, went and joined Invaders.

Discipline and the Bomb

My vision during those days of bad Steelband riots was to develop a strong sense of discipline and respect. One of the first things we would tell the members, especially the new members, was, "We doh want you arguing with nobody from another band. Yuh not supposed to go by another band and even listen to what they playing." We also had certain rules laid down about being on time for rehearsals, and stuff like that, and we let the members know that they would be fined if they broke the rules. We also had someone stationed by the door. If a rehearsal was at a certain time, everyone had to be there at that time. We tried to maintain that.

As a matter of fact, when guys came to join as first-year members, we told them that around Carnival time not to look for any money when they played. They were not going to be given any money. If the person performed well, we could decide to give him something. But they all knew up front not to expect any money. Then, too, the entire band was playing pretty well and people liked to hear the band and what we were doing. With our reputation, these guys wanted to be in the band, which made it easier for them to do what we in authority said, if they wanted to remain.

I made a guy responsible for imposing fines, and I gave him the authority to fine whoever broke the rules, whoever he wanted to fine. He used to fine more than I did. Sometimes, someone gets a post and he wants to see everything go well, and he wants everything done in a particular order. That was him. Up to this day, whenever we meet as a group, the guys always heckle him about that. They tell him he was a bad man. Stuff like that. But it worked. It kept us out of a lot of trouble with the other bands.

Not only that, we always tried to do something different. We were the first to go and play for the police every Tuesday night at their headquarters. Other bands followed suit. We always wanted, even with the rivalry with Invaders—in the early days the Invaders was the best playing band in Trinidad and won most of the competitions—to outdo them, but in a friendly sort of way. I remember for a competition in 1948 in the Savannah—I think it was for Carnival—when a lot of the bands decided not to compete, Invaders made it known that they would compete. We asked not to be judged, even though we played. So we all played but not to be judged, and they still said Invaders won the competition. They were very popular, and whenever they left Woodbrook and came into town for Carnival, the entire town returned to Woodbrook with them. So I said, "This thing's got to stop." I began looking for them anywhere they were so the people could judge between them and us. I decided to surprise them by playing something they didn't hear or the public didn't hear, and that's the way the Bomb started.

I started doing it secretly and people used to wonder how they used to come around the band and hear us practice this or that calypso but never hear us practice that song. What happened was: we would rehearse with everyone there, and then I'd say to the members, "All right, time for lunch. We're finished"—the cue for them and the public to leave. The band had to go and eat and return because they knew we were going until late that night into the morning. They all knew that they had to learn whatever classical piece we were doing, sometimes with their fingers. We practiced upstairs in the Garrot and became known as the Garrot Boys. Downstairs, the people were gambling. Someone who might be a member of the band would be downstairs with the gamblers to listen to whether he could hear the pan. If he could, he would shout out, "Too loud!" I'd say, "All right, no sticks. Fingers." Not until Carnival Monday morning when we assembled to play, then everyone in the band really knew what the song really sounded like. The men knew what they were playing without knowing how the whole band sounded. It worked because our supporters and other people in a fête on Sunday night would be anticipating when All Stars would drop this bomb on Charlotte Street. They would leave the dance before it was finished and assemble outside the Garrot until we came down. Even the members didn't know the name of the classical piece. They knew only numbers, our code. When I said number one or number two, they knew what to play. No names. Not until Carnival Monday morning.

This gave us the edge over everybody, not only Invaders. We had an edge over Ebonites and all the bands from the west: North Stars, Crossfire, you name them. They had to come across Charlotte Street and stop, whether we were there or not, and play their classical piece. I remember a Carnival Monday morning we were coming up Henry Street and about five or six bands were coming down Charlotte Street: Invaders, Crossfire, and some others. When we swung onto Prince Street going toward Charlotte Street toward the Market, so many bands were coming down Charlotte Street that we had to wait till all these bands passed. All the bands from the west plus other bands. I think that was the very first year we had women police and there was one standing at the corner. So, we stood there playin' and jammin' while the bands passed by. Crossfire came by while we were on Prince Street but we didn't give them a second thought. We stayed there for so long at the corners of Charlotte and Prince Streets that Crossfire had time to go up Henry Street into Duke Street.

Finally, when the time came for us to go through, the crowd was thick, and I decided to follow the policewoman's direction to go straight ahead on Prince Street. Because of the thickness of the crowd, we had to raise our pans over our heads and walk through the throngs of people. Some of them there didn't like All Stars, and when they saw us walking with our pans over our heads they said, "Dem other bands beat better than All Stars, so All Stars put dey pans up in the air and surrender." Anyhow, after getting through, we played an old piece, not our special piece, and when we reached the corner of Nelson and Prince Streets, Crossfire was there again playing their best piece. They played that one piece all the time, like they had no other tune to play, with the crowd bawling, "Crossfire today beat All Stars!" The rest of that year, everybody who didn't like All Stars spread around that rumor. I said, "Okay, next year we'll see what will happen." This was in 1957, I think. I went and we started to practice "Minuet in G," very easy, the usual way for the next year.

All that year, I forgot Invaders, whoever. When the time came in 1958, I was looking for one band—Crossfire. We were coming up Henry Street by the telephone company—we had scouts on the road, you know, looking to find out where what band was. That year, we were looking for Crossfire. The scouts reported that Crossfire was coming down Frederick Street. We went and waited for them at the corner of Duke and Frederick Streets while we were jammin' "Minuet in G." After that, there was no more talk of Crossfire. No more. That talk was finished.

Then, sometime in 1959 there was talk about Invaders' "Liebesträume" on a recording. True, Invaders played "Liebesträume" the same year we played "Liebesträume," but the two cannot be compared. What people heard on that record was Corbeau Jack soloing with the Invaders band accompanying him. If anyone can get a record of our "Liebesträume," he will hear our entire band playing, not one person soloing. I remember Ellie's older brother had just come out of prison—it was the first Carnival after he came out of prison—and we were coming from Independence Square and going up Henry Street. He came into our band and said, "Playing 'Liebesträume'?" as if to say that we were sounding better than Invaders. At one time, the radio station played both recordings and had people compare them. How could you compare one person soloing with an entire band's playing? Also, remember that recordings then weren't like now. There was no set of recording tapes available. Mainly, the radio stations and people in that business had them.

I used to do everything in my band. I was pan-builder,-tuner, and arranger. Now, this was the tradition of the steel band in the past, as far as I know it. The guy who could do the most in the band, when the time came for naming a captain most likely would be nominated. So, it was me, Sonny Roach, Ellie Mannette, Boots Davidson, the guy from Pan Am North Stars, and so on. Eventually, all this began to be too much for one person—building, tuning, arranging, and captaining. So, I had somebody helping me with the tuning and gradually stopped tuning. In addition to doing all that, I was also financier, because when we hadn't a sponsor, I would spend my own money on the band.

On Sponsorship and Other Financial Matters

Some people think the first sponsor we had was Hilton Hotel, but that wasn't really so. Some members of the band used to go up there and play, especially when tourist boats came in. To keep the job for them, we began merely calling ourselves Hilton All Stars. The men kept that job for quite some time, but then I realized that was hampering the band. If a company was looking for a band to sponsor, it wouldn't consider All Stars. And as I said, I was the one spending money to buy the instruments and have them tuned. After the band played for Carnival and for dances after Carnival, all the money we made was counted and I would be reimbursed any money I used.

The Green Giant Company then came along and considered sponsoring us. The guys who played in Hilton who were calling themselves Hilton All Stars wanted to use some of the pans I had made. I told them no, that since they were working throughout the year they could tune their own pans. To audition for Green Giant, so to speak, I then took some of the pans, used the Panorama uniform we had, and with some extra men went to play for the Green Giant people who came to the Hilton to hear us. It so happened that the manager of the Hilton heard the band and didn't know it was All Stars. He asked the guy who was in charge of the band, what band that was, and then learned it was All Stars. The manager responded that he was seeing different people in a different uniform, and the pans were painted a different color. So, the Hilton guys blamed me and said I, as the captain, didn't want them to use the other pans, blah, blah. The manager said to guys, "Okay, you have a band then get your own pans." Hilton All Stars then went to the newspapers and accused me of stealing all the money. They used this line as an excuse to leave, when I wasn't even involved with the band's money. At the time, I was in the city and was merely asked to hold the money for them, which I did. But to say I stole it: they merely used that story to break away and form their own band and call their new, little band, Boston Something or the other, I can't remember. But it didn't last long.

Anyhow, we did not get the sponsorship from Green Giant but from Catelli, mainly because of Peter Pitts. From the early days when he was a young man during the late '40s, he used to be in our band with us on the streets and wherever. He, Mr. Hales, and their friends were from Catelli and all came out with our band. I remember once when we were going up for Panorama for the final night, a call came for me from Peter Pitts while we were in the Savannah. He asked whether I would consider being sponsored by Catelli. I said yes. He said, "What about if you go on stage right now and introduce your band as Catelli All Stars?" I said, "Sure." So, our first real official sponsor was Catelli. This was in '68, I think.

Peter Pitts was a very interesting person. I think his father, or someone with close connections, at one time was the editor of the *Trinidad Guardian*. He's a White Trinidadian, and was very much into Calypso. He sang calypsos in shows, not the tents. He lives in Maraval still and was a staunch member of our band and we became good friends. He's the kind of person on a J'ouvert morning would come by All Stars yard, wherever we were, sit down on the sidewalk, and if one of the guys was eating a roti or something, he would say, "Give me a piece," take it, have a bite, then hand it back. Nice, nice guy. Regular like that. About four or five White guys were like that. Patrick [Stanisclaus] Castagna, the Guyanese who lived in Trinidad and composed our national anthem, also became a friend of our band. So, all these men were in our band and got drums for us, and stuff like that.

Most of the time, I wasn't employed. I began working seriously from around 1952 for the port as a longshoreman. Before that, I did little jobs here and there because I was more into Pan. I used to tell Fisheye or a couple of other guys around, "Let's go down to Woodbrook or some place and steal some pans." When the people put their garbage outside, we would go and inspect them. Those that looked good, we emptied the garbage on the ground and took the pans. My work with the port was more like the side job, and Pan was the main job because I stopped working a week before Christmas and didn't return until about two weeks after Carnival.

Meanwhile, though Pan was my life I didn't become too involved with TASPO. My band wasn't a part of it because All Stars was not a member of the steelband association. After hearing all the negative things about Pan, as a steelbandsman, of course I was a little suspicious of certain middle class people like Lennox Pierre who were suddenly interested in Pan. I decided then to stay back and look and see what was going on first. I was wary of the whole thing. That's the only reason I didn't get involved with the association.

Even though we weren't a part of TASPO when it was going to England, we helped them raise money for the trip. We played at different venues, and so on, to make money for them. But also around that time they wanted six people to go and play somewhere in Washington, D.C. My name was among the first they called. Hugh Borde from Crossfire, some other people, and I were going to be a part of that, but it eventually fell through. So, at the same time they were making arrangements for TASPO to go to England, they were talking about a six-man pan-side ["pan-side" refers to a regular steel band] to go to Washington, D.C.

A Panoramic View of the Movement, Carnival, and Calypso

Let me now to give a decade-by-decade sketch of my life, of the main events, and on how I came to depart for the States. The late '30s, based on general knowledge, is marked by the appearance of Alexander Ragtime Band, a band from the west. At that time, I lived in Laventille, East Dry River, so wouldn't know much about what was happening in the city. I was about ten to eleven during that time. I remember we had to leave the Hill and follow the tamboo-bamboo band when it went into town on Carnival. Now, people say that Pan started in the west, and I don't dispute that based on Bully and Hamil's knowledge of when they first heard Alexander Ragtime Band in 1939 and Hell Yard's pan-band which started after 1939.[10] I do know that the tamboo-bamboo bands started in the east, where the men had better access to bamboo.

Then, the family moved from the Hill around 1939 to live on Mango Rose, which was near Duke and Piccadilly Streets. As a little boy in the yard there, around either Christmas or Carnival, all around all you could hear was pan. I heard this pan playing, so I left Mango Rose and walked toward it. To give you an idea of where Mango Rose was: if you left Duke Street and walked toward the bridge, when you reached the bridge, Duke Street continued to the left, Piccadilly Street to the right, and Mango Rose was at that fork. In that yard, there were barrack houses where a lot of people lived. That was Mango Rose. I followed the sound of the pan and came to Piccadilly Street, crossed the road, and followed the sound to Hell Yard. I leaned over the wall and watched them while they were playing. Bully was one of the guys there. He was also from the Hill, another little fella like me. That was my first encounter with Steelband. I knew about the bamboo but not about Steelband until that moment, around late '39 or early '40.

As time went by, I used to go into the river to play with Fisheye. There was an old motorbike with a clamp. We used to push it up the Hill then ride it down. This was during the war and brings us to the '40s, the early part of which the government had banned parading in the streets. What I remember is: the ban didn't start exactly at the same time as the war. I recall that one year as a little fella I wanted to play Mas with Hell Yard's Bad Behaviour, and I didn't play and regretted it. I said the next time I had to play, which I did after I paid my sixteen-cent fee to play with the band. In those days, Carnival was not like now. Back then, the masqueraders used to have disguises. The marching sailor bands were also marching. I want to believe—I could be wrong—that the phrase 'Road March'[11] that defines Calypso for Carnival originated around that time, because there were many different types of sailors: the proper, marching sailors; the fancy sailors; and, the Bad Behaviour sailors who arrived clean but left dirty, because when they yelled, "Roll, Bad Behaviour, roll!" they had to roll on the ground and that white suit got dirty. If you didn't roll, they threw you onto the ground and rolled you in canal water. Serious. Do you know the bags used for selling coals? They would get that black coals bag and wet it and beat you with it. They would go to the slaughter house and get the cow bladder and beat you with that.

Then, there were sailor bands that would only march. On Carnival Tuesday morning, the admiral came in the open-back car with the plunge. But before coming, the band used to go and march in their competition, where they didn't jump up and down. They marched with a drill instructor. You joined that band and went on a road march. LEFT TWO-LEFT RIGHT! They barked out their orders. When you heard them say they were going on a road march tonight, you knew they meant business. So, I could be wrong but I believe that's where the term and tradition for Calypso road march came from.

For the first year or two of the war, the people were allowed to play. Then, when the authorities proclaimed the following year, "No Mas, no parade," bands still came out. As a matter of fact, I, as a little fella, was with one of the booms. I remember the police raided the bands, and I dropped my drum and ran. A lot of people got arrested and locked up, and from that time it stopped. They used to have the air-raid warden going around at night—when there were the air-raid practices—with the search light, and if you lit a candle or anything, you heard somebody bawling, "Out that light!" They were very strict.

But these guys who used to be with the pan, they just kept everything quiet and still used to take chances going up on the Hill. Because, this pan was like a disease [an addiction] for a lot of people. It only took one man to say, "Lewwe go up the Hill," and everybody said, "Yes." And because we were by the river we had no problem. What we could do, those guys in town couldn't do, because we had the Hill: you understand? We would jump into the river with the pan, sneak up easy over Calvary Hill, Piccadilly Street, and we were gone up on the Hill. While we were up there, it was like Carnival: Casablanca, Desperadoes, Hill Sixty were all up there. Then the police would come up there with the Black Maria to raid us. That was the type of activity during the war with the steel band.

The first time the steel bands came out was on V-E Day, along with other music bands. We came out again for V-J Day. About the innovations, let's see: in '45 to '46 there was the ping-pong and song on the pan, the tune boom, and the guitar pan. The caustic, *grundig*, and trombone came in the '50s. Other people were doing things, also, like Bertie Marshall who came out with the double tenor. He also introduced harmonics to the notes to make them sound much better. People much later came out with the bore pans—I was already in America when they came out with the bore pan—and all different types of things. People just kept on moving with this, all the time.

In the '50s, like I said, we were in the Garrot and as the pan and the movement started to grow, we could no longer accommodate the one-, two-, or three-bass section. We started with one, then someone from St. James put two wheels on the bass with a handle at the back for one person to push the pan while the player played. Then came the two-bass followed by three. Once we got up to three then four basses, the Garrot couldn't hold them. We had to leave the Garrot and went next door by an Indian place opposite to where we were, and from there we went to Henry Street where there was a vacant lot. It was right near to Duke Street. By that time, we'd grown to four and five basses. So, the family of Steelpan was growing and everything was improving, and after we got our sponsor we had to go to festivals, and stuff like that. In 1952 and '54, I went to the first two festivals then quit. I said no more festivals for me because I didn't like what was going on.

The first festival we played and they gave us eighty-seven points for either the tune of choice or whatever it was. In those days, they were using the indelible lead—what you wrote with those lead could not be erased. They gave us eighty-seven, then tried to turn that seven into a three. That placed us third. The second year we went back. Judging from what Northcote[12] said in '52 about what the steel band should and should not do, we followed those instructions. There were six bands and we played number five. Southern All Stars played number six. When band number six went up to play, we were at the back of the stage. That competition was being held at Roxy Theatre. When we heard what was going on with them, we said that couldn't win. Dr. Wiseman was the adjudicator that year, '54. The year before it was Dr. Northcote who said what we shouldn't do, and we followed his instructions. While listening to band six, we knew they couldn't beat us.

After they were finished playing, the time came for them to announce the scores. Band number one was called and they announced what they did and what they shouldn't have done, and so on. When he announced our band, number five, he gave us a lot of credit, because a lot of what we did none of the other bands did; in fact, no other band ever did that. Other bands never had a conductor or used the bongos. When we arrived on stage, we first set up then waited for the conductor. When he arrived, we stood up and bowed. We started all that. All Stars was, and is, the trendsetter. When the adjudicator began his comments, he announced, "Band number five, here came Sir Thomas Beecham," referring to our conductor, because when Beecham arrived on stage, he knocked on a pan, everyone stood up and bowed. He continued talking about all the good things the band did. When he called out the points the band made, they were the highest points for the night and the crowd cheered. So, we were sure that band number six, after we'd heard them play, couldn't score higher than us, even though in that band a guy did something similar to what Corbeau Jack did. He alone played, and the band accompanied him. He soloed a lot, and Northcote had said that we shouldn't be doing that. We were sure that band couldn't win.

Then the adjudicator said, "Wait, more runs are to come after lunch," using that cricket term. When I heard that, I knew we had lost. Later after lunch, when he commented on their performance, he talked about how amazed he was that the members' hands moved so quickly and gave them first place. We came second. I said, "No more Festival for me." We didn't return until 1968.

Dr. Northcote and Dr. Wiseman were British. There's a book published on all this: their comments, points, and so on. As a matter of fact, there's talk still going around about me at the first Festival we had when I performed as a soloist. All the top soloists at that time were there. During the test piece when I started to play, the audience thought I didn't know what I was doing, because everyone else went up and began playing the test piece right away. They had no introduction, nothing at all. When I went up, I had an introduction that I played, and you could hear all their murmuring. Then suddenly they heard the test piece starting to be played. They started to talk even louder, and that threw me off. Now, a lot of betting had passed: Jules will beat this one, that one cannot beat that one, and whatnot. In the middle of the tune, I stopped playing and stood up and walked off the stage. Northcote, Pat Castagna, and all the other judges left and came back-stage to encourage me to return to the stage and complete my performance. I refused. They continued for about five minutes or so, insisting for me to return and play. Eventually, I said okay. Then, Northcote went on stage to talk to the audience about how they must behave. He told them that when artists were performing, there must be total silence. He continued that when Jules returned to play, all who had placed bets had to take off their money. I returned and played and came second. I couldn't come first. Dudley Smith won that solo competition. That was in '52. A lot of guys still remember that: "Ah, you walked off the stage. You remember that?" So that's what happened in the early '50s.

During the late '50s, we started with classical music. After we had the encounter with Crossfire, we played "Minuet in G" in 1958. The next year we played "Liebesträume," then Museta's Waltz" in '61, and in '62 or '63 "The Marriage of Figarro," the most difficult song to learn. Quite a few classical pieces in all. We used to give the pieces numbers, not names. Not until Carnival day the men knew the names of the pieces they practiced.

All this time, I was trying to keep my head above the water, and I really wasn't into the pan as I was before. But things were moving along in the Pan world. I know that Bertie Marshall said to me that he wanted to be as good as or even a better tuner than Ellie Mannette. In '64 or '65, he called and showed me the double tenor where he put in the harmonics, and so on. Now, if we wanted to be really controversial, to emphasize that always there's someone with knowledge of something else that was happening, once a former Dixieland man, a White Trinidadian, gave me a picture from a newspaper article of another Dixieland man, a White Trini, with a double tenor. This photo predates Bertie Marshall. You can tell by the clothing of the people in the photo that the pan was in the man's lap—two pans bolted together. So, someone connected with Dixieland is not getting his due credit. The point I want to emphasize here is even though at that time things weren't moving as fast as when Pan first started, I think the men were still looking at how they were doing things and finding ways to improve. Because in Trinidad in those days, you could count the number of good tuners on one hand: Ellie Mannette, Bertie Marshall, and Tony Williams. There were others but they weren't as good as these three.

Then Panorama started, I think in 1963. At first, All Stars band didn't go. It's the members who pressured me to go eventually. All I can remember is the year we went, the calypso we played was "Patsy" by Sparrow. After that, we've attended all the Panoramas.

Personally, as I said, I was trying to stay afloat. I began working steadily around 1952 at the Port. Things were so rough in the Steelband world that sometimes after we played on the road for Carnival and we packed away the pans, we would hardly get to play anywhere, except for a christening or wedding. We got to play at a lot of dances around Carnival time, but things kind of slowed down afterward. The panman in the early days hoped to get work, to go out and play abroad, because Pan wasn't as popular as now. Everybody is now playing pan. But then, that was just a dream, and the work wasn't really coming in. We had to look for other means for making a dollar. As I got older, I wasn't as enthusiastic about the Pan world.

My attention wasn't into Pan as it was before, because at the time I started to have kids and needed money, and it was rough.

I remember that I made a record and wanted to christen my first daughter. I went to Christopher who had a record store on Nelson Street and he told me he didn't have any money. I made enough noise in the place to embarrass him. To avoid the embarrassment, he made out a check and gave me. Things were slow at the time and I was more interested in working, because even with the job I was doing, not every week I got to work because it depended on when the ships came into the Port with the cargo. It was really hard in those days. That was on the personal side.

I think Eric Williams could have done a little more for panmen. I remember he offered some assistance to Desperadoes, because at one time they could have gotten visas to go abroad, and so on. Then, too, instead of just focusing on the steel band he focused on things on a wider scale. There was this ten-day work program for the guys to earn some money, and a lot of the men who were tradesmen—masons, carpenters, shoemakers—left their trade to do this work. They could put in just two hours of work for the day and have the rest of it to themselves. I'm sure some of them got into that program, whatever it was. I know of one man in the Pan world who ended up being a foreman in one of these jobs. At that time, I was already working at the Port.

I guess in the government's way, it tried to help the men. In the early days, men like Albert Gomes tried to get things together. I didn't attend many meetings with them when they were trying to get things together. Then, Lennox

Pierre came along and helped form the steelband association. You have to remember that Pan then wasn't what it is now. It was more remote and we did what we could. As Pan began to move forward, to gain ground and become popular, the government and private businesses didn't do what they could. By not doing what could have been done, the way was left open for people from abroad to do what Trinidad should have been doing. There's a Pan factory in Ohio and you can get anything you want in Pan from there. These people first employed panmen from Trinidad to make the pans. They carefully observed what they were doing and once they learned to make pan for themselves, they no longer had need for the Trinidadian panmen. Now, they're doing their own building and tuning, and everything you need in Pan you can get from them. Also, we have this latest controversy regarding the hydroforming process.

I think in Trinidad Pan is only a name. It's on the BWIA plane and is the national instrument, but it's still only a name because Trinidad is not treating it as a national instrument. What I also don't like—and I spoke to Patrick Arnold about this—is how panmen are treated differently from calypsonians. I'm not complaining about what calypsonians are receiving. They deserve every dollar and prize they earn. The comparison between the people in the two art forms is this. Calypsonians sing every night around Carnival time in the tents and are paid, then some of them are picked to sing in the different categories. The winner—Sugar Aloes or whoever—gets one hundred thousand dollars and a car. On the other hand, panmen must practice almost every night during the Carnival season into all hours of the morning, which costs them a whole lot of money. Then they have to go to the preliminaries, north finals, semi-finals, and finals. And *if* they win, that band might get one hundred thousand dollars. What will that do for a whole panyard? They have one hundred men, plus those who push pan, plus those who do so many other things to keep the yard going. In *Kaiso* [another name for Calypso], one man gets the same amount *plus* a car. Plus, he still earns what he does for singing in the tent. That sort of imbalance I don't like at all.

This year (2002), All Stars won Panorama, and they got the one hundred thousand dollars and a van. But, I think they can increase the prize money. All Stars is in the big band category, and big bands go on stage with one hundred men. The pannists are not the only ones to be paid. The tuner, arranger, painters who paint the pan, those who push the pans, those who clean the yard all have to be paid from that one hundred thousand dollars. So, you're looking at the players as well as the non-players who help grease the wheels of the panyard who all need to be paid. How much money is each getting?

I've seen a man soloing at Music Festival and the rest of the band accompanying him and winning. I've lived through two to three weeks of not going to work on the docks to get pans ready for the next Festival, a time that was hard on the family. Because I was so unlucky, that was the time a lot of ships were in port and I could have made a lot of money like the other guys who worked there. I made nothing because I'd given up that time to prepare for the Festival. And after we played and I was confident that we had won the competition fair and square, we were placed second. I was totally discouraged from competing again in the Festival. I stopped, as I said before. Panmen had to put up with too much and get too little in return.

As I told someone else, maybe I myself am to be blamed. I was one of the people who started this thing from early, the kind of competitive spirit that I had to go looking for Invaders, which led to the clashes on the road. All of this trickled down to today's panmen. So now, all they're studying is how to win. Here in New York, almost anywhere now, all the players want to do is go up on that stage and play for Panorama and to win. If a new band is created and members begin joining and you tell them the band is not going to Panorama, suddenly the panyard is empty. They're going to bands that are going to Panorama. But the cost to the people who are bringing out bands is too much. Some bands for Panorama must send for Clive Bradley and other arrangers or a tuner from Trinidad. The band who wants these people from Trinidad must lay out the money for airfare, living accommodations, arranging, tuning and blending—blending is the term for tuning pans that are already made so that they blend with newly-made pans, and retuning all pans just prior to competition. Money is also laid out to buy these new pans, stands for the pans, and whatever else the band needs. Some bands have to pay several thousands of dollars to rent a place to have rehearsals because they don't have a yard.

In addition to renting yard space, they have to rent lights, portable toilets, and tarpaulin or build tents to cover the pans. You getting an idea of how much money these bands have to lay out? If that band wins Panorama, the money it gets cannot compensate for those expenses or break even. Why are they doing it? I think it's because we established this competitive spirit that trickled down to today, so that everybody only wants to compete regardless of the cost. All they want to know is that they beat all bands and hold that winner's title. But they don't see how much someone is making money off them and exploiting them. Trinidadians typically associate Pan with J'ouvert, the Bomb competition, wanting to be the best band on the road, and winning Panorama. Pan-people focus on winning these titles. Once they win, this is all they can boast about. They seem to have a tunnel vision that does not extend beyond the competitive spirit of winning these titles.

When I came here in '71, I stayed out of Pan. It wasn't until '96 I returned to Pan, and a lot of things happened between those years. I occasionally returned to Trinidad for short stays.

On Immigrating to the United States

I immigrated for the same reasons a lot of people immigrate—for a better opportunity to make a living for myself. I was working at the Port, and we were given the option to retire voluntarily with a pension. I decided that after all the years in Steelband I really couldn't live off it. The engagements were so few, and there were so many problems with the steel band with getting the men to rehearse and other different types of problems, I said, "You know what? I think I'm going to America." A lot of people weren't pleased with the decision, but I'm not sorry at all. So, I left in 1971, returned in '73 when the band won its first Panorama, and then occasionally to listen to the band, give any solicited advice on what they were doing for Panorama and things like that. Then toward the end of '95 into '96, a group wanted me to bring out a band from All Stars, Old Boys from All Stars. They invited me to be the manager, offering that I didn't have to do anything else. I had reminded them that I was out of Pan for too long. They insisted that they wanted me.

I attended the first meeting one Sunday morning, and a guy handed me a tape of a calypso and asked me to listen to it. He wanted to play that calypso on the road and wanted me to arrange it for them. I did that, then another, then they wanted a Bomb tune, and that's how I got back in, slowly.

In the in-between years, I started to return to Pan. I had a band that came out one Labor Day. A guy who'd had a lot of problems with teaching them the tune ended up high himself and couldn't play a note on Labor Day. Then after Labor Day and the time came to rehearse and learn other songs, no one came to rehearsals. So, I said to myself that since 1943 I was in Pan and went through all sorts of things. Once, I was so sick a woman was telling people I had tuberculosis. That happened, I think, from wearing wrong clothes. Some of us wanted to be different and decided to dress in corduroy pants and sweaters. Imagine that! In that hot weather! With sweating under such heavy clothing and heating the pan over a big, open fire, the change in body temperature from getting wet in the rain or simply from removing the heavy clothes caused my chest to open, and all that. It was a bad cold and the sickness crept down even to my knees, so I walked with my shoulders drawn and back bent. This is why a woman said I had tuberculosis and belonged in the PH [Poor Hopes] ward. It was just a bad cold though. I also had too many problems in Pan. So, I said to myself that enough was enough. That's it. I'm not going to be in America and start over again and be aggravated by guys who sometimes wanted to come to rehearsals, and whatnot. I don't need that. But before that, after I arrived and I was looking for work, I was applying for night jobs only, so that I would have time during the day to go around looking for pan to tune. Whatever. Then after that started, I said that's it.

What really happened is: we had this band up here, and I did "Somewhere over the Rainbow." Now, a guy from All Stars in Trinidad came up while we were doing the song and he liked it, but he didn't say anything to me. After Labor Day, he came and said to me, "Cap, do you mind if I take this song down to Trinidad to score?" I said, "That's all right." So, he learned all the different parts and took the song down to Trinidad. Every competition they entered with that tune, even the Bomb, they won. They sent and informed me that they'd won, and so on. So, the second year I did a medley and the guy did the same thing. He took it down to Trinidad and they won again. Now, four different competitions are on the road and a band must enter all four to qualify. With the points the band earns—for Panorama, an old-time calypso, the Bomb, and one other category—the Bomb tune that I arranged and they used put them over the edge. They won over one hundred thousand dollars. So, they kept asking me to arrange the Bomb tune for them. That's what I now do—their Bomb tune. Right now, I'm considering stopping that.

Also, I was teaching some kids at one time, who were beginner players. But then the guy who ran the school and I had a falling out, so that came to a halt.

I never went back to tuning. As a matter of fact, the level where these guys have taken tuning to, it will take me a long time to catch up if I started back tuning. So, at my age I can't even think about that.

Vision for Pan

I'd like to see some changes in Pan. Let the panman think more about himself first. Here in America, panmen are sacrificing too much just to win Panorama. When they win, they're not getting their money immediately. They sometimes have to wait an entire year to get the prize money. Yet, the next year they go through the same thing. The men not only aren't being business-like enough, they're not valuing their talent and what they really have to contribute. They fail to see that they're being exploited. What I'm trying to say is today's panmen have to stop letting somebody invest money in having them come to play in full houses without in turn compensating them for what they are worth. They shouldn't accept waiting a whole year before getting their prize money either. They have to think more of themselves and what they are worth. You see, all they're thinking about is to compete, like two boxers who want to beat up each other and the promoters are getting the larger percentage of the money. This is what is going on right here in Brooklyn. I don't know if the same thing is happening in London, where they also have Panorama, but I think so, because the attitude is the same: to win.

I've lived in this country from 1971 and have gone to three maybe four Panoramas at the most, because I've retired. I told myself that this one I went to last year (2001) might be the last one. I was on the road on the Parkway years ago on Labor Day and they invited me to become a judge, but I declined. It's time for something different to happen.

Panmen should have an association that plans all events, and when it is time for Panorama the association deals with the promoters and specifies what the bands need, the conditions under which the bands will play, and the association presents whatever is necessary. Then, if the promoters want to negotiate, they can do so with the association. Come to some sort of agreement that clearly stipulates what is to be expected and by when, and all that. The United States Steel Band Association (USSBA) isn't doing that, as far as I know. But neither they nor the players are the ones footing the bill. The owner of the band is. The players are in the band to play and some of them are students. Some players even bring their own pan to the band and pack up and leave when it's all over. They're not interested in how the owner gets money to pay the pan tuner and arranger. The only thing they see themselves giving up is time. But time is money, in this place. The panmen need to hold themselves and everybody else to higher standards.

It's the old panman, the pan-lover, who is still sacrificing. In most cases, the owner is an older panman from years ago in Trinidad with Pan in his blood. He was in a band in Trinidad, and he came here with the desire to recreate what he had in Trinidad. So, he creates a band and calls it by the same name as the band he was in in Trinidad, but then proceeds to treat the whole business like it was a hobby. I tell fellas that the only way a guy should put out money like that for a steel band is if it's merely a hobby. That's how you look at things if you're putting out that amount of money and getting little to nothing in return. It takes thousands of dollars to run the panyard here in Brooklyn, as I mentioned before. That's how things used to be in Trinidad. One person puts out and gets back little or nothing. But even in Trinidad today, it's better than it is here. The majority of bands in Trinidad have a sponsor. These Brooklyn bands have no sponsor. Here, the owner is the captain *and* the sponsor. If he has a couple of friends from the same band and the same district, those friends would help.

All Stars has a sponsor. Sometimes when All Stars goes to their sponsor and asks for something, they don't get it. Yet, some bands have no sponsors at all. And, a lot of these bands after Labor Day don't function. They stack the pans in a basement until the next year comes around and the time to begin rehearsing for Labor Day.

Many things must change in Pan. It's true we've seen a lot of change. Take, for example, the rhythm section now called the engine room, which is a term that came about after I left Trinidad, so it is not that old. If it was around before I left in '71, it wasn't called by that name. We had the rhythm section—the iron section, which is what we called it—that included any instrument that didn't play melody. To understand how that came about, we have to go back to the days of tamboo-bamboo.

In the front of the bamboo band were men who had their bottle and spoon. They half-filled the bottle with water and with the spoon created a sound while the music was sung by voices. Bully told me once that a guy from Hell Yard named Looly got a piece of iron to use to imitate the bottle and spoon. This became similar to the cymbals of a drum set, which sounded louder and eventually replaced the bottle and spoon because the bottle sometimes broke. According to Bully, Looly was the first to do that. Now, after that we had the bass kettle or the doo-doop, the boom, the caustic soda drum that created a heavier sound than the doo-doop so we used to call it the Paul Robeson, the kettle and other similar instruments used to keep rhythm. Once the pan with notes came to bring songs into the band—later the tune boom followed by the drum set—we began to do away with those earlier instruments. Remember, I mentioned that All Stars was the first to introduce the congas to the band. The congas also replaced an earlier instrument. The rhythm section then also evolved along with the pans. This is why, despite the controversy around who did what first, no one person can claim being the inventor of the steel band or even the pan itself. A lot of people put their two bits into it, with people borrowing ideas from each other.

When it came to the quality of the music, it was the same. Ellie had a good quality, and everybody was happy with that. Then along came Bertie Marshall who tried something else by adding something, which sounded better than Ellie's, and on and on. But the way pan sounds today makes the way it sounded long time [in the past] *jokey*. That's the real truth. The people who have been in

Pan for a long time sometimes are amazed at these changes. Where Pan is going will follow along a similar evolutionary pattern.

You say that people question whether the time will come for Pan to take its place along side other instruments in the symphony orchestra. Maybe. Until the whole family of Steelband instruments is standardized there will be a problem in seeing the pan as having arrived. In a lot of bands the way the pans are tuned—the formation of the notes—may be alike, like the tenor pans where you have fourths and fifths. A lot of bands have these tenor pans. In that way, you can say the tenor pan is almost standardized. But some bands still have tenor pans that are not fourths and fifths, namely the older bands like All Stars. In All Stars, we have both pans because people bring their own pans to play, and in addition the band has some fourths and fifths for those who are accustomed to those pans. The formation of the pans I had from the early days is what they still have. Desperadoes and Amoco Renegades have their own style too from the old days. These variations are just with the tenor pan. For the basses, there are about three to four different styles, because even as a musical instrument a bass is a bass, not so in the steelpan. You can have a six-bass and go into say "Band A" and play the bass, but if you go into "Band B" you can't play that bass. This is not only because the notes might be different but the pans even though with identical notes can be set up differently, too. That's the problem.

We need to have the instruments made in a way that anyone from anywhere in the world can play. Pan hasn't reached yet the same level the instruments of a symphony orchestra have reached. In the symphony, their different instruments—wind, string, and so on—are tuned to the same pitch. I don't know that we're doing that yet, either. So, we have to get to that level.

I'm not calling for a standardization of the size of the notes. Not really. If the tuner is dealing with a machine or a factory that is mass producing pan who knows the metal of the steel, its mixture, and its width, and all that, then he can talk about precise size. But right now, tuners are getting pans from wherever they can. A lot of different factories are making pans and using different mixtures to make the metal, so that each pan is not the same. Many times when I used to tune pan, I would get a pan and sink it and whatnot with no big problem. I would get another one and it's too much problem to work with. I would tune one pan to sound one way and another pan for the same section—tenor or second—the same way, but the two pans would sound different. The composition of the steel for each pan is so different that you cannot get the same sound. So, that has to become standardized, the composition of the steel to be used for all the pans. Once we have that, then we could use the same measurement for all the notes. While I haven't studied metal and don't know much about it, that much I understand based on my tuning days.

With a pan, I used to draw out the note and groove it based on what I thought it would be. For instance, I estimated Middle C to be one size on one pan but a slightly bigger or smaller size on another pan. Then, after I decided to put Middle C in one spot I realized that I could put a lower note there to sound better, and that's all because of the metal. Then, I had to figure the age of the pan and what it was used for before I got it. Back then, we weren't dealing with drums that were made strictly for Pan, as you know. We weren't so lucky, and if we did that was a rare occasion. Sometimes, we had to get pans from Jamaica and other places, wherever we could get them from. This is not talking about the early days when we used to steal whatever we could lay our hands on. This is later, and we still had no reliable source. So, when the drums came in from wherever, we had to examine them and if they looked good we bought them. Then after we had them, we had to decide which one would make a good bass or tenor or guitar, and whatnot.

From these beginnings, you say that now some are talking about size and standardization, and so on. Whenever those who're pushing for this determine standardization, they must first establish the source of the material being used and have some control over that. That's where they must start, as they probably know. They must know what it takes to produce the tonal quality of the standardized G, A, or F. From my experience with pan-building and -tuning, the steel composition of the various pans caused the C on one pan to sound different from the C on another pan.

Then, when you come to talking about the pan in the symphony along side the violin and other strings, you have to remember that the manufacturers of strings have specially treated wood and specially made strings to make that finished product. The same must be happening for Pan, and they have to get it just right, too. I see that years in coming, which might be sooner than later because pan is well known and well loved by people throughout the world. When Pan is standardized, people from anywhere in the world can walk into any band and play the instrument of that section they know.

At the same Pan Trinbago meeting I mentioned earlier, when we talked about Spree and Ellie, I had told them about standardizing the pan. This meeting was about six to seven years ago when I brought up that topic. I pointed out to them that bands are having a lot of problems with the transportation of pans. I used for an example the fifty-pan band. If the pans were standardized, the only problem would be that each band may want to arrange the pans a little differently for

Music Festival or Panorama competitions, or whatever the occasion. Everybody would practice at home and travel only with their sticks. There could be some extra pans in case one falls or gets damaged for whatever reason. Once players arrive there for the competition, all would be judged on the same pans. Then, because it's much less time to set up and pull down the pans on stage, the competitions would go more quickly and efficiently.

The members of one band entering the stage while the other band is leaving will all be so much easier. The venue for the competition will already be fixed, so people can travel from all over to world to take part in these competitions with more ease. This idea came up because the year before a band from San Fernando was supposed to play first. It couldn't; their truck broke down and they arrived late. Right now, there's a fifteen-minute gap between the bands. That time can be less, with still enough time for band members to rearrange pans or replace damaged ones and so on. And that's it. Competitions can start on time and finish on time, with the program going more smoothly. For festivals, this will cut down on the transportation expenses for bands, too. A lot of bands lately are calling on the government of Trinidad to help them transport pan. You would see right now the fire trucks pulling something with pans, and all that. Establishing a place with standardized pans for competitions wouldn't hamper business either. Bands would still need to purchase pans for their panyards and for gigs on the road. It's now that these competitions are getting bigger and now international, the country has to move in this direction. Pan Trinbago should own its own set of instruments, already.

This idea, as well as the call for standardization, is a long way off, to me, but they must still think about it, and when the time comes, more than think. They have to make the effort, if they want to see the pan on par with all other instruments that have long been standardized. Anywhere you go, a piano is a piano; a guitar is a guitar; a saxophone is a saxophone, and so on. They may be made by different people, but all these people are working along the same principles.

Conclusion: Some Demands Remain

To wrap this up: from a youth I always had an interest in some sort of rhythm thing. I remember as a little boy when my mother left the house to go sell her things, I used to beat the hell out of a chair. Then came my interest in the tamboo-bamboo. Rhythm is something that is in me.

My personal life is not a big secret. I'm divorced from my wife of sixteen years. Everybody who knows me knows that. It's no secret. She lives here in America, too. I have seven children, and believe it or not, none of them is in Pan. None. I want to believe if things back then were like now, they would have been in Pan. Back then, with the stigma pan carried and they were so small—four, five, six—you couldn't get them into Pan. As a matter of fact, I remember a Carnival I took two of them and had them in the sailor band. We had one of the largest sailor bands Trinidad ever saw. They were to the front of the band and when I passed by they said, "Daddy, the people only *bouncin'* me." I had to leave and take them back home. For all the years I was in Pan, they were never around the band. I bought an organ for my daughter and she did quite well on it. But Pan? Nothing.

I didn't willfully keep them out. It was like this. In the heat of the time of Pan and with where I was living in Barataria, the band was in town. I could make only so much time in the day if I was learning classical pieces while they were in school. Then the time they came home was the time I was ready to leave, and they had their homework, and so on. The situation just wasn't good for them to get into Pan and I didn't force it.

Musically, I played music by ear. I learned all those classical pieces from the records and wrote them out in my way. I then took this to the men who led the various sections and showed them what to play. The section leaders then taught their individual sections then the entire band came together and played.

I enjoyed all my efforts, and today I have a few awards for my contributions to Pan. I received awards from many organizations: The Hummingbird Bronze from the government of T&T; a few from Pan Trinbago; from some here in America. For my birthday this past twenty-first of May—I'm now seventy-five—All Stars had three days of celebration with five bands in its panyard playing. They also hosted a candlelight dinner and invited the mayor, two or three ministers, Patrick Arnold and other Pan Trinbago officials, and the owner of Exodus who presented me an award. They all came together and gave me a very good occasion. I appreciate all that. Here in the United States, the Trinidad Folk Art Institute gave me two awards. For the last one—I think it was in 2000 or 2001—they invited quite a few people in Pan: Clive Bradley, Ray Holman, Austin Wallace, Herbert Johnson who I think has died, Junior Pouchet, and others. We all got awards from the city of New York as well as the Institute. I still have awards in Trinidad they have given me in my absence, which someone may bring for me when he travels.

All in all, I'm happy with my contributions and involvement. What I like about it is: we now have a group of people who were followers of All Stars, including some players. When we get together in a party, we love to talk about the old days. All good memories, none negative. We laugh and have a good time recollecting those memories. The best part though is where All Stars is going.

The property next to the yard was for sale, and the band had spoken to the bank and had made a bid and a small down payment on the property. A guy who loves the band and is a fan of All Stars asked me what was happening with the band. I said things were all right and explained about the intention to buy the property next to the yard. Since he seemed interested, I went on to explain that the band approached their sponsor but didn't get any money from them. He invited me to a birthday party he was having for his wife in a few days. I went. A few of his friends were there and during the party he called us all together into a separate room and invited me to share with them the situation the band was facing. I did. When I was finished, one guy asked the price of the property and I told them—$125,000. He wanted to know whether that was U.S. or T&T currency. I replied T&T. Next thing, the men all began naming how much each could give and didn't stop there. I contacted some former members of the band in California and other states and Canada. Today, that group of men is a part of the organization, the Trinidad All Stars Old Boys and Girls Association, the American chapter. They organize boat rides and other fund-raisers and every penny goes down to Trinidad—three, four thousand U.S. dollars stretch a long way in Trinidad with the exchange rate. The property was bought and is now being developed. This guy right here, Lennox Nelson, is one of the live-wires of that project. So, we are another first.

The American chapter donates money to meet whatever need the band has: pans, whatever. One member came to me and said, "I'm thinking about sending down a chromed nine-bass." Imagine that, a chromed nine-bass. So, I sent and asked the captain how much that would cost. When we heard the price, he decided that the band could be better served with three bass sections for the same amount of money. That's the kind of generous people we have. They continue to love the band and what it is doing, and anywhere the band turns they continue to support it especially through the purchase of that piece of property. This group continues to raise money to invest in the property.

We have some long-range plans. First, we want to establish something so that the band can become self-sustaining and not dependent solely on the sponsor. We are looking to make some sort of investment that will turn over money. This will allow the band to support its unemployed members in some sort of employment capacity. We give them some work to do and pay them. We can give something back to the community. That's where we are right now. Trendsetting, again. All Stars is continuing to focus on going in the right direction. We had some negative ones in the band who didn't approve of what the band did by buying the property. Now, they realize that the move was a very good one.

The American chapter is open to anyone, including those who have no prior membership or association with All Stars. We have people with no prior involvement who have joined and receive the monthly newsletter. They are supposed to pay a small monthly fee, and if you're a member you receive an All Stars pin. We have T-shirts and other tops. When the guys are going certain places like a funeral or other formal event, they wear their pin. Then, when you enter the yard wearing a pin, the people immediately know who you are.

Our vision is to be in the position to eventually reach down and help the next generation. We want to leave more than a pan legacy. On that same property, we plan to build a building and do a lot of different things. All that needs money. One guy called me to show me a picture of a place in England called The Yard, a place where Shakespeare and others used to perform in the past centuries. The building is shaped in a semi-circle and three stories high. This guy went to Trinidad and took pictures of buildings from Nelson Street to Charlotte Street. He had a vision of preserving the area as an historic Pan site, an imitation of the Shakespeare Yard. But I don't know how realistic that idea is when he discussed it with me. He also asked me all sorts of questions regarding our plans, and I referred him to the captain of All Stars who happened to be here in the States at the time. They met and talked, and what plans they've come up with I don't know.

We have a building fund set aside for only property development. We also have a separate fund for pans and other purchases, and so on. We have a very good support system and network going, all moving in the right direction. So, I'm happy about all that. We have something rooted in Pan in Trinidad and are beginning to show the steelbandsman how to just stop competing against each other in Panorama and toward leaving a more tangible legacy with a business purpose. That thing is putting money into one or two people's pocket and not really benefitting the movement. We have moved away from that. So, while we may have started that competitive spirit, we've moved on and paving the way to something better for the millennium. I have no regrets.

At my age, I may not have remembered all the dates accurately, and sometimes people tell me of things I did which I have no recollection of. Sometimes they tease me saying that I was too strict and bad. But it was necessary in those days and to what I wanted to accomplish. Once, there were three guys who didn't know the Bomb tune. I dismissed the whole band and kept just the three of them there. I told them they weren't leaving until they learned the tune. The first guy learned it and I allowed him to leave, then the second guy, the same. The last guy said, "Capt, I *kyar* stay. Ah gotta go." I said, "There's the door. If yuh go, doh come back!" He left and never came back.

Another guy was the secretary of the band and used to gamble a lot. Remember the Garrot was over a club. Carnival time, people coming to play gave him money for music, and as fast as he got the money he gambled it. When they told me about it I said, "All right." Afterward, when the time came to give everyone their money, I asked him how much he was supposed to get. I fined him that exact amount. He didn't get a penny. I told him he got all his money already. He didn't argue with me.

I also had a friend with whom I was really close and everybody knew it. In those days, we didn't drink. Somebody left a bottle of rum in the Garrot, and I said nobody was to touch that bottle of rum. But because we were close, he decided to get a glass and have a drink. I said, "Nobody is to drink." He left and got a glass. When he came back, I told him I was going to fine him if he ignored my directive. He said, "So what? Yuh fine me, yuh fine me." He had a first drink then went on to have a second one. I said again, "If you pick up that bottle, I'm going to fine you." He went ahead and poured a second drink. When he made to have a third one I said, "I'm going to fine you everything you're going to get for Carnival." He didn't believe me, you know, and had his third drink. Carnival day came and his envelope was blank. Empty. If I didn't do that, I would have lost all respect. Everybody was watching because they knew we were friends and they wanted to see if I would show favoritism. Not me. With me you do something against the rules and you pay. So, those are examples of how strict I was and why they now say I was bad....

3

The First Family Band: A Vignette by Hugh Borde[1]

Hugh Borde's *vignette uncovers the very first steel band in Trinidad to gain sponsorship and the role of Esso Trinidad Tripoli in touring with Liberace in the 1960s.*[2]

I first started to be involved with Pan, as some people call it, when I was six years old in 1939 and remained involved ever since. In those days, pans were not the 55-gallon drum. They were Klim pans on which we played "Mary Had a Little Lamb" and other simple, little melodies, as far as I can remember. Back then, there were five notes that could carry, "All day all night, Miss Mary Anne" and "Mary Had a Little Lamb." Those were the two songs played on Pan.

I first heard the bigger pans made by Sonny Roach of Bournes Road in St. James. I remember going up the Bournes Road river where he used to tune his pans and seeing him pounding and pounding into the bigger type of pan. In those days, my mother was the first to bring a piano into her home in St. James, and Sonny Roach used to come down to our house so that I could give him just the notes he was looking for, which were, "Do, Re, Mi, Fa, So"—those five notes. He would keep pounding on those drums on the side of the house, and sometimes my mother would get fed up, I remember distinctly, and would come with a bucket of water and wet him down. I could never forget those days. So, Sonny Roach was the first person I ever heard with the steel drum. He got up to seven notes. Then my elder brother, Carlton Borde, took one of my father's Vaseline drums and tuned it. My father owned one of the first businesses in St. James, which was People's Pharmacy. He was a druggist and chemist. Carlton put nine notes on the pan, which was more than the scale of seven notes. There was a point in time when Carl went to even fourteen notes.

We started our little children's band in the back of my father's premises on 56 Western Main Road, St. James. That was a family band that included: Carl, myself, my younger brother, all the next-door neighbors like the Murrays—Hamil Murray, Hutchinson, Errol Murray, Kenneth Questel, John Cole—we called him Daddy Cole in those days, Sterling Betancourt, Roy St. Rose and his brother Kelvin, "Ming" McKenzie, Arnim Worrel, Irwin Clement, and Dennis and Mervyn Thomas. These were the people we started out with in the family band. The band was called Hell's Kitchen. We were the first sponsored steel band *ever*, sponsored by Robinson Crusoe Rum Company in 1945. For V-J Day, we played on the street on a truck, the whole band. I remember we played for the entire day for five dollars, which we divided among the band. In those days, that was plenty money. I stuck with the steel band since, and it started to develop. Then, the 55-gallon drum came in afterward. Ellie Mannette and Sonny Roach were the men responsible. Ellie had his Oval Boys band going during that time, too.

The only two bands in St. James at the time were Tripoli and Harlem Nightingales, which was later called St. James Sufferers. They called it St. James Sufferers after the Mas they played in those days, and that name remained with them. From there, other bands began breaking out. I wasn't a member of Tripoli then because we had our family band.

Our family band formed around 1940 to '41. This happened long before WW II and V-J Day, and all those happenings. This is what I've been trying to get straight with people who may say that Pan started during WW II in 1945. Pan was there before 1945, you see.

Other people who came up from the country [rural area] continued to make pan, and from there it continued to grow. But as far as who was the first to make those big drums, it was somewhere between Sonny Roach, Ellie Mannette, and Neville Jules. Those were the three people I knew around that time.

History has it that Spree Simon started Pan, which I don't see how that could be possible. It is said that he started Pan when he began to come down to St. James where I was living. We used to take Spree up to Bournes Road where Sonny Roach was making these drums. There are people who can testify to that. He has family still in John John: Neville "Bakernose" McCloud who's still alive. He can testify to this.

At a symposium a couple of years ago, I heard Oscar Pile say the first song he ever heard played on a pan was Spree Simon's "I Am a Warrior." This couldn't be possible. This is probably the first that *he* heard. He was talking about in the 1940s. For you to play "I Am a Warrior" on a pan, you must have at least one scale to do it. This is where the technicality comes in and what I was trying to show Oscar Pile at the symposium, that it couldn't be that way. Pans were made before he heard "I Am a Warrior." When Spree played that song, I was about fourteen years old, which is to say that Pan started *before* "I Am a Warrior." But it was after this that Pan started to develop, along with the image of panmen as hooligans and vagabonds, and so on.

My father and mother were staunch Catholics and, as they used to say, had nothing against the pan. What they were against (in those days) were the people who used to play the pan. The poor, the underprivileged, and so on. William Henry Carter, my uncle, my mother's brother who was the first Black college master in Trinidad and taught at St. Mary's College, thought it was a disgrace for us to be playing pan. So much so that he kept away from visiting our home because we the children, his sister's children, were playing steel drum. It was after the pan began to receive recognition in the '50s and to keep music festivals—this was after the music association joined with the steelband association to organize Steelband music festivals—then my uncle began to show interest. When there were shows at Queen's Hall, he started visiting us at home, asking for complimentary tickets, and so on. That's how it started with us. We remained a steel band until Hell's Kitchen was no more.

After that, I went and joined a band in Bellevue called Five Graves to Cairo. In those days, the bands took their names mostly from movies, war pictures. Now, history has it that Cairo started in Bellevue but it actually started in St. James. The leader was Hugo Besson, who is still alive. He started the band with Mac Kingsale. I remember that clearly because I was one of the people he started with at his aunt's home in St. James. From there, after his aunt died he left his aunt's and went to live in Bellevue and the band went up there to Bellevue with Besson. It was a little strenuous to go up Long Circular Road to continue with the band, but I did stay with them until they played in the first Steelband competition. After that, my brother and I left Cairo and I joined Sufferers for a little while then went and joined Tripoli. I took over leadership from the original leader, Joseph "Joe" Crick[3] who left Trinidad in 1951 and now lives in Philadelphia, Pennsylvania. I've been leading Tripoli from then till today. I'm the oldest leading Steelband leader ever, which people don't realize. No one who has led a band for so long is still alive, with the same band. Other people have led bands that have changed their names and the band went through different names, and so on. Since I began leading Tripoli from '51, I've continued to lead through 2002.

I've had my band here in the United States since 1967, when we toured the United States and Canada and we performed for the T&T Pavilion at the Expo

'67 in Montreal. That is how Liberace met us and immediately booked us. We opened with him at the Shrine Auditorium in Los Angeles. To get from Montreal to Toronto to Los Angeles, we purchased a bus and drove in the United States for the first time, driving 3,500 miles. We didn't know anything about highways or maps or anything. We just drove. Eventually, we did arrive at Los Angeles on time to be ready for our first show with Liberace. That's where we started, with Liberace giving us our start. We toured with Liberace for two years. We were the only act who toured with him for two years. Most of his acts he booked for six month or one year; that's it. But the steel band went over so well that we got a standing ovation after every performance. The people asked Liberace to bring back the band the following year, which he did. We toured forty-six states with him.

Liberace placed us on *The Ed Sullivan Show, The Mike Douglas Show, The Tonight Show* with Johnny Carson, *The Merv Griffin Show, The David Frost Show*—we did every major TV show in the country with Liberace. That's when the steel band really began to get popular because after that we played at Carnegie Hall, at Radio City Music Hall, and at the Waldorf Astoria. All these facts today's youth in Trinidad don't know. They have no idea. These are the things that Pan Trinbago ought to make known to the modern panmen, the young kids. What and where and with whom the steel band really started to become popular. This knowledge is lacking.

If you go into Pan Trinbago's office now, you will see all sorts of things they can't even identify. They called me when I was there recently to ask me about the pictures of some bands they have hanging on their walls—who was who, what was this person's name in this and that band. So many things in the movement are lost, which is a pity. We fought so many battles to bring Steelband to where it is today. I've done my best even since I've been here. Every year, I return home for Carnival. I've been an adjudicator for Panorama since 1975, and I still try to help every year I go home. I contribute what ideas I can, to which they say, "Yes, yes." But once I leave and gone, they return to what they're doing, which is keeping things at a standstill.

Up to this present day, I believe the only progress the steel band has made is in the tuning of the drums, and even that is not by very much. You can't compare hardly anyone today with one of the greatest pan-tuners of T&T, Alan Gervais from Egypt Village, Point Fortin. He was around when the National Steel Band [of T&T] was formed in 1963, when the idea originated with Eric Williams and George Goddard and I was secretary. Later, when Williams became prime minister, he said we should have a national steel band where we would bring together all the leading Steelband players in Trinidad and Tobago, and that was how the National Steel Band came to prevent riots. Up to today, no credit is given to the National Steel Band and Dr. Williams for his foresight in bringing us together, when all the members started to reunite and the fighting began to decrease. The National Steel Band brought a fella from Tokyo, from Tripoli, from Invaders, from Desperadoes, from San Juan All Stars, from Free French in San Fernando, from Fontclaire in San Fernando, from Tobago—fellas from all these bands became a family and began looking out for one another.

To answer the question: who was responsible for this? You have to give Dr. Eric Williams credit. It was his idea for the steelband association with Mr. George Goddard, president and Albert Jones, vice president. This was the idea of Williams and the Steelband movement, to form a national steel band to prevent riots. So, this is how the rioting part was prevented. And, people don't give him credit. As a matter of fact, people today, the modern panmen, don't even know there was a national steel band back then. Conrad Hunte,[4] who was vice captain of the West Indies Cricket Team, was the one who first brought the National Steel Band to the United States in 1964. He brought us to Michigan, to Mackinac Island, for the Moral Rearmament Conference. Peter Howard was the leader of the conference, and Conrad Hunte was one of the directors. They organized and brought in people from England, Scotland, Germany, France, China, Japan, from all over the world. We were all assembled there. As a matter of fact, that's where we met Sidney Poitier and his two daughters, and we showed them a little of the steel band. They invited Sidney Poitier to come to the islands, too. He was a guest at the conference. The prime minister of India was also at the conference. Many prominent people were there. The National Steel Band toured with the conference through twenty-two of the states. Then, we returned to Trinidad at the end of '64 after the conference was finished. From then on, a lot of little different things started to develop with the Steelband movement.

Since then, I still don't see much progress, because all the people seem to be interested in one thing—Panorama. After Panorama, there's no life for the steel band in Trinidad. If you look at what is happening now, everything appears at a standstill once Carnival is over. Even the panmen are fed up with those who lose. The only ones satisfied are those who win. From the second place winners to everyone on down, they're dissatisfied. Today, it's like another stigma has remained with the steel band that cannot be erased for one reason or another. Everyone seems dissatisfied. I don't know if the birth of Panorama has brought this new type of stigma associated with losing.

The reason that I even bring this up is: this year I had accompany me one of the directors of National Public Radio, Davia Nelson. She went to Trinidad for the first time to see the steel bands and have her own image of Carnival days, a time when we should be parading the streets and for the tourists to hear our culture. Instead, all we were hearing were the DJs with their set of noise overpowering the steel bands. When the DJs passed, the bands could not play. This should not be taking place, not in these modern times. This is one of the things we should get rid of completely. Leave steel band for the masqueraders and the steelbandsmen at Carnival time. The DJs are the people killing Carnival. For bands to get back together, for pans and for people to start back playing Mas and the steelpan like it was when we left it in '68, we also got to bring down the size of the band.

One, all these suspended bass drums in the air, there's no room for that. People don't have the time or energy to be pushing these many drums along the streets. It's not like it was before when there were the tenors and double tenors, double seconds, guitars, the cellos, and the bass. That was it, with everything on the ground. It was a pleasure for people while they were jumping up to reach over holding the pans on the side and pushing them while they still jumping up. In those days, people could have played Mas while in the steel band. Right now, how many bands do you see on Carnival day? I could count them: All Stars, with a little sailor band; Desperadoes, even though they are now on top of a truck; Starlift; and Exodus. Look at that; I could count them on one hand. In our day, all the steel bands participated on Carnival day. Now, it's a big, big difference. That's just a little of how things have changed but not so much for Pan. I can go on for a long time on some of the other things I've observed, but we don't have enough time for that.

Before concluding, I want to share a little more details on the first steel band to be sponsored, ever, which I mentioned before, Hell's Kitchen. It was in 1945, as early as that, and this information is not found in any book people have written about the history of Steelband because they did not include people like me in their narrative. Here's how that came about. One day the Robinson Crusoe Rum delivery people saw us, little children, while we were performing in the backyard. They were making their deliveries to a rum shop. Hell's Kitchen backyard was across from the DeSouza Rum Shop, White Eagle Rum Shop. They heard this music and came across and Mr. Whitehead approached us and asked, "How would you all kids like to play on a truck for us?" That's how that got started. They came up with the idea to put us on this truck with our steel drums with a big banner across that read: Robinson Crusoe Rum Hell's Kitchen. They used us to promote their product. The idea caught on afterwards, when a lot of sponsors realized that they could use other bands to promote their product. Not steel bands, at first, that came later. But they sponsored music bands to play during masquerade time.

Some people give Williams credit for that. He can get credit for some things but not that. There was no Williams at this time. He came around in '56 and I'm talking about '45. Ask me anything about the history of Pan and most likely I can give you an answer. I'm not senile and still have my senses and my memory is still very good. There's also the story about what the Tripoli Steel Band continues to do in the United States, which is not very well known. I'm still doing lectures at colleges and universities for the instrument to get the recognition it deserves in this country. All that is information for your next book....

4

Ingenuity in Steelband's Social and Political Organization: Albert Jones's Story[1]

Albert Jones *is considered a foremost authority on Steelband, having been involved in the movement since 1945 as a member of Belmont's Rising Sun Steel Band. He has held distinguished offices in the movement's organization: vice president of the National Association of Trinidad and Tobago Steelbandsmen (NATTS), (1963–64); member of the first National Steel Band of Trinidad and Tobago (1963); assistant secretary-treasurer of NATTS (1957–58); elected president of NATTS (1959–60).* Jones *also was president-general of the Postmen's Union of Trinidad and Tobago (1966–67) and president of the Postmen's Union (1968). Since living in Brooklyn, New York, he has lectured on many occasions on Steelband throughout the New York metropolitan area.*

Some Early Cultural Roots

I left Trinidad in 1969 without an academic degree, having worked there as a civil servant—a postman—for eighteen years beginning in 1950. I first became involved in Steelband five years earlier, in 1945.

I was born on June 28, 1929, in Laventille, on the border between Quarry Street and Laventille Road, after the family moved from Toco into town [PoS]. There, we lived on Duke Street, right next to the yard opposite George Street where All Stars practiced, which wasn't called All Stars in those days. The yard's name was Hell Yard and the home of Bad Behaviour, a tamboo-bamboo and biscuit-drum band. No pan yet, even though those times were shaping it and influencing me and everybody else. It was bottle and spoon with everybody singing as the band moved down the street. The *chantwell* in the front of the band went

Call: Bo-lay, bo-lay, bo-lay!
Response: Achee, bo-lay!
Call: We ent workin', no-way!
Response: Achee, bo-lay!
Call: Ai-yai-yai-yai!
Response: Achee, bo-lay!

A real nice call-response melody that was accompanied by bottles, spoons, and bamboos. What they called the jammin'. It was no real fast thing. Everybody moved in an easy rhythm and was dressed up in their old clothes. That's what I got involved with when I played Mas with Hell Yard around 1935. But my involvement was short-lived for a couple of reasons, one of them being playing Mas.

I got to play because of my sister who was half Negro, half Chinese and taunted when she walked down the road with the jeer, "Nigger Chinee." Even though I was little, I had enough sense to see that my mother favored her and wanted the best for her because she was nice-looking, while I was this little Black boy who made do with what was left over. My mother raised us in a single-parent home and got advice from her brother, my uncle, for big decisions. Playing Mas was a big thing because it was costly. That year, my mother was letting my sister play as a fairy in Kiddies Carnival,[2] and because I wanted to play I asked my mother, "What about me? I want to go, too." Even though she couldn't afford it, I was persistent and even got my friend named Stowe to have his uncle talk to my mother. Whatever payment arrangements were made with my mother, my uncle, and my friend's uncle, I got to play a sailor-boy and carried a petit-quart bottle and a tin of powder.

When the morning of the Masquerade came, I remember a guy nicknamed Wahjank put me on his shoulder because I was too small to walk. My great-aunt filled my bottle with green tea, which I had in my back pocket. I really don't know how rum got into my bottle, or if it was accidentally switched somehow. Anyhow, I ended up with a bottle with rum, which I drank. I remember going down Charlotte Street, swinging on to Duke Street, back up Piccadilly Street to come across to go to the Savannah, and that was the last thing I remembered. I awoke Ash Wednesday morning at a relative's home. That was the last time I played Mas.

The other reason I wasn't involved with Bad Behaviour for long was: Hell Yard was also the home of stick-fighters who didn't allow us little ones to be around them. They were real bad with their sticks, which they sometimes burst each other's heads with. We weren't allowed to witness that. The most I—all we little fellas—used to do was go and peep to see them stick-fighting.

Sometime after playing Mas, the family moved to Behind the Bridge on Clifton Street. There, my mother came into some money—I think through some sweepstakes—and used it to purchase a share in a shop that Edwin Ash owned on Laventille Hill. Laventille, in those days, was just tracks, no roads, and we didn't have water. I had it tough, coming from PoS and going to live there.

Things eventually went wrong between Ash and my mother. When she heard about a land deal in Belmont, she had enough money saved to buy the land and build a house there. We moved from Laventille even before the house was finished being built.

Early Days in Rising Sun and a Catalogue of Innovators and Their Inventions

I started working at Davidson and Todd as a cash-boy during the Christmas season. I was fifteen going on sixteen when I started to work and fortunate to earn the favor of Miss Todd, who got me a position at the library, a new place opened for White people and aristocrats from St. Ann's and other rich neighborhoods. I worked there, at the store and the library, for three to five years then got laid off on V-E Day. Leaving the store and heading home, I saw a whole set of bands on the street. I went up Henry Street, and right at the corner of Henry Street this band was coming from Queen Street heading up to Rosary Church. I decided to jump in the band, called Valley Band, because I saw some players I knew in the band and felt right at home. I jumped until we reached Belmont. While jumping, I noticed that the band was made up of three different sections. One section was from Warnerland by Cadiz Road near the Savannah, one from up St. François Valley Road, and one from Belmont Valley Road.

You could say that my full involvement with Pan began on V-E Day with jumping in Valley Band. It continued about three to four days later when I met up with Dudley Smith who eventually became captain of Rising Sun. I was walking down Belmont Valley Road when he called out to me, "Town-man!" because I was from PoS. I stopped and waited to see what he wanted. He said, "I see yuh jumpin' up. You like de jump?" I said, "Yes." With that, we started talking, and that talk became an invitation, of sorts, to join them. Because I wasn't working and wasn't really looking for work because I had a little money saved, every day when I passed by the yard I stopped and we chatted.

They used to beat pan in a place opposite to the Chinese Savannah. The Chinese Savannah was that little spot men used to play cricket and football. The place where they used to beat pan has houses now, but back then they called it the Shango Yard, even though it was really a Dahomey sect, Rada.[3] Everything sounded alike because when you heard a drum you believed it was Shango. But this was a special sect. Only women danced while the men beat the drums. They were young guys from the same family who started beating pan.

In those days, the pan-band was really a one-note thing, doo-doop, a boom, and iron. Later on, between the two victories, V-E Day and V-J Day, the bands started changing their names. The three Belmont sections mentioned before became Belmont United. Carl "Carli" Byer from St. François Valley Road was this band's captain. But Carli had an attitude. If you were beating pan in the Warnerland section and came over and made a mistake in his section, he would hit you on your hand. So, the main guys in the area, those from Warnerland and Belmont Valley Road, joined and became Rising Sun and left out the guys from St. François Valley Road who called themselves Corsican Brothers. Carli became their captain. He's living now somewhere in Harlem, Manhattan. Eventually, the Rising Sun band split, with Warnerland separating from Valley Road. Jack named the Warnerland band Step Yard and the Valley Road band kept the name Rising Sun with Dudley Smith becoming its captain.

All this time, I wasn't a member yet because my mother insisted that I learn a trade and sent me to learn industrial engineering. So, I only used to pass by and stop in now and then to talk. It was at the time of the split Dudley invited me to join them on their rounds at night, and I became fully involved after that.

The men used to beat pan while going down the road and would go over the Hill because the police used to harass them. The police couldn't follow them over the Hill because they used to drive this big police van called the Black Maria, which couldn't climb hill; it could only drive on the street. About twelve or thirteen policemen would be in the van and they'd jump out and stop the band, beat the guys and take away their pans. This was why the boys went over the Hill, to avoid the police who couldn't follow them over the Hill. The police became so dangerous you couldn't take your pan anywhere. They had more pans in the police station than on the road. If you went to the Belmont police station, all you would see was pan lined up in the back of the building.

You see, most of the guys were poor and couldn't afford to buy pan. But they had access to the Bermudez Biscuit Factory right by Dry River and they used to go there and get their pans. Then, they also got their pans from the Industrial Centre's lard factory. That's the difference between the guys down in the west and those in the east, and why we must say the claim the western guys are trying to make that they started these things in the west is false because they couldn't. At the time, they didn't have ready access to tins and pans.

Anyway, that night when Dudley invited me to come along, we went up Valley Road and came down St. François Valley Road. Whilst coming down the Hill the guys from the other pan-side,[4] the Corsican Brothers, joined with the Rising Sun band and we became as one. After that night, the two bands began interchanging. There was no war between them or anything. If they didn't like one captain they left and went over to the other band.

Once when we returned to the yard after the jump, the guys wanted to practice. But the people in the tent said they were having their religious service in the Rada-Shango tent, and the band moved down Valley Road to a yard owned by a lady named Miss Girlie whose last name was Toussaint. She died last year.

Between V-E Day and V-J Day when the bands began going into town, they started to change their names, taking names from the movies, and so on. Our band became Rising Sun. Ellie Mannette's band, Oval Boys whose captain was Stanley Hunt at the time, became Invaders. Destination Tokyo was also from a movie. There was also Gay Desperadoes. All Stars didn't come in yet. All Stars used to be Cross of Lorraine, a name, I think, from the French. Then there was Casablanca. Red Army (that *saga* boy band from Sackville Street, Green Corner) came out later. Those were the main bands that started fragmenting and from the fragments came more bands.

Rising Sun started going into town and returning with Dudley who was inspired to look for better sounding pan to improve Rising Sun's quality. We started checking around and I came to find out that "Zigilee," whose real name was Carlton Barrow, had a pan with three notes. They say he used a stone to make his pan with three notes, and was the first one to make a three-note pan and called it "Chufac." His band's name was Waterloo and was in the same vicinity with Renegades, the area that goes up the Hill by Bart Street and Piccadilly Street, around by Duke Street. Zigilee controlled the band. Whenever he stopped playing, the whole band stopped. He was beating, counter-beating, while doing his own thing and everything else. Zigilee had this pan long before Spree Simon who came after the three-note pan was invented.

In fact, the next person to make an invention was Neville Jules. Jules and Zigilee lived close to each other. Zigilee lived up on the Hill, and Jules lived close to Dry River by All Stars. Jules was the one who added the fourth note. Then he started tuning pan with a broomstick. He was getting a lighter sound and was more interested in being artistic. He made four notes right in that Dry River. His band, as I said before, was Cross of Lorraine. The first people in charge of that band at the time were the Ollivierres brothers; one was called Fisheye. Jules wasn't the captain then. Somewhere along the line, he and Fisheye must have had a falling-out. But Jules and Zigilee were interchanging ideas.

Spree Simon came into the picture later and started playing the four-note pan and was very versatile. But another person who came even before Spree was a guy by the name of Andrew "Pan" de la Bastide. He was from Clifton Hill, between Desperadoes and Tokyo yards. His band was named Hill Sixty. Andrew was the first one to make the seven-note pan and improve on Pan. He got in touch with Jules and they used to visit one another. I think Jules took his pan up to Andrew and showed him his four notes, and then Andrew tuned *seven* notes. Then Spree made his seven-note pan and played "Mary Had a Little Lamb" and the songs the Baptists used to sing called Sankee Soca. He and the others playing those songs didn't play whole melodies but got as close as possible to what the people used to sing. When they were missing notes on the pan, they filled in those missing notes by singing them. And, we used to enjoy it because the whole thing, the playing mixed with the voices, had a steady rhythm.

Spree was also the one who in 1946, I think, played for Governor Sir B. Clifford at this big event in Marine Square, which was how Spree got his recognition. All the talk of the town was how Spree played for the governor. He played on the lead pan of the Tokyo band, "Juju Warrior." People came to recognize it as the first full tune that was played on pan. He later played "I'm a Warrior," a Baptist Sankee. Beside that, the next song he played for the governor was "God Save the King." So, he became recognized at the time for these things as very versatile, as I said before. Very, very good. After this, the bands really started getting into music.

The point I'm making here is that Spree came along and made a seven-note pan, too, and after he played for the governor the seven-note began to spread with everybody putting more notes on a pan. Everybody was openly experimenting because nothing was hidden. The Behind the Bridge guys were exchanging their ideas because they had to meet each other. For instance, if my band was leaving on Christmas morning from Belmont and your band was coming over the Hill around midday from Laventille Road—and that was a long stretch between Belmont and Picton Hill, St. François Valley Road, Belle Eau Road—when the bands met up they partied and exchanged ideas. Down in town or in the west, they didn't have that privilege or opportunity. Bands would also go up in the Hill to play and practice. It was this type of thing happening.

All this time, Ellie wasn't there to make a name for himself playing pan. Ellie came in later with his change, the concave with pushed up notes.

The next innovation was Jules's creation of the *grundig*, the big drum. He then added the tune boom, which he also created from a biscuit tin. He did this by cutting the top of the ordinary oil drum and putting the biscuit drum (this biscuit drum was made of tin and steel) inside it, which was lighter. He made that into the tune boom, which created a loud sound. Since it was lighter, they could carry that.

After Ellie became captain, following Stanley Hunt, the Invaders started getting involved through his innovations. He and his brother, Birdie, started tuning. At the same time, the men were beginning to use bigger drums on which they could put more notes. But no one was using the chromatic scale at this time. Ellie was also the first to start using the chromatic scale, and I think that was because of the influence of Lennox Pierre who with his violin showed Ellie how to build pans using the chromatic scale. Pierre was a devout musician, a lawyer living in Woodbrook, and an influential person. He was a part of the Youth Centre, and would take his violin there to play and give them ideas on how to improve the pan. That is how Invaders began to use a style different from the rest. While people were tuning and putting their notes anywhere, Ellie began to develop a pattern, an active principle for tuning. He took it to a further stage, which was happening around the time TASPO was formed, when I was just beginning to really get involved with the Steelband movement.

Others were also improving, too. Competition was the whole idea among all of them. Ellie stood out because he remained with building and tuning pan, and he also had more ideas about metal since he was a machinist. But he came in a long time after others had got this thing started.

If we're talking about the first men with the idea to put notes on pan, we have to go back to these men of the past. It's good to talk about Ellie and Bertie and so on, but we must not forget that they came later in the evolution of things. This is why I insist that we must remember the men who established the foundation for what Pan is now and what it will be in the future. And, it looks like Trinidad will really lose out on its development, because first, the outside world is more advanced in science and technology than Trinidad, and also the old stigma of panmen still remains in Trinidad. These men were of the underworld. The underclass. The downtrodden. These were the men who did it, whose names we may never know.

All this is to say that the innovative ideas were coming mostly from the Hill. These men had more access to pans than the guys from the west so they were able to experiment more, and they were exchanging their ideas more freely. Here's one example. In those days, the ping-pong used to be in the front of the band. Now, remember that the ping-pong was held in one hand and with the other hand you played it. So, you had to be a very strong guy to play ping-pong. The guy who made the change to strapping it around the neck [called pan-around-the neck][5] was Zigilee, the same year Tokyo played "Juju Warriors," with Spree playing the lead for the governor.

My wife, Cynthia, has some history of the movement, too. A St. James band named Nob Hill used to practice in her father's backyard and she snuck on to the pans to beat them after the men were gone. Her brother, Ralph "Pablo" Springer,[6] was a member of the band, which was how the band got permission to use the yard. She was very young then and as you know in those days women couldn't get involved in Pan. This same band broke up and one faction formed into North Stars, captained by Anthony Williams, and later sponsored by Pan Am. Williams introduced the spider-web lead pan and is responsible for improving Pan, just as much as Ellie and Jules.

Williams was also known for his versatility. He has won both Panorama and Music Festival. He has always arranged, tuned, and played, unlike Mannette who mostly tunes and does not arrange, I think. Williams, similarly to Jules, has not received his due recognition because he does not talk much. These quiet men often retreat in the face of publicity but are quite multi-talented. Without any formal classical knowledge, Williams arranged excellent classical pieces for his band. North Stars of today sounds no better than the North Stars under Williams's captaincy. The band back then was very advanced and were it not for Williams's illness, the band would be even further along. Williams's illness is from what we all suffer—being ignored or rejected by the very country and people we sought to establish the culture of Steelband among.

I am very familiar with the level of recognition the men received away from home compared with the snobbery they received at home, and how such treatment hurts. That lack of respect is very painful, enough to drive anyone to any type of breakdown. The captain of Rising Sun, Dudley Smith, went with Katzenjammers and played in Fire Down Below Steel Band. He never returned to Rising Sun because after that event he and the band went away to the Bahamas. He never returned to Trinidad. Both his mother and father died and he never returned for their funerals. A lot of talented guys left in the early days, and we see the high acclaim they receive away from home. Mannette is one. The kind of respect they get away from home, it grieves them not to get it at home. I could only hope that one day Trinidad will really give the men the respect that they receive from outside.

It also saddens me to see that a lot of people who never really made any significant contribution to Pan are getting the recognition in the Pan world. They could just beat a good pan, and that's it. They came along and found things the way they were, jumped on the boat, and now are getting everything.

Social and Political Organizations

As stated before, I got involved in Pan in 1945 with Rising Sun then started playing pan. In 1946, the movement began to indicate its first signs of organization with a guy by the name of Rannee Phillips. He was like an impresario. He owned clubs, about three or four in PoS. He would have dancers and so on at these clubs. This was during the time we called the Yankee days. In 1947 he opened a club on Belmont Valley Road and called it the Rose Bowl. The club was next to the Shango Yard—where the guys used to hang out—and opposite the Chinese Savannah. The majority of people who used to patronize the Rose Bowl were Americans and the girls who entertained them. The cars would pull up and they'd get out, that sort of business.

Anyway, Phillips organized the first steelband competition, which was held at the Mucurapo Stadium. Know that Sonny Roach won the ping-pong soloist category at one of these early competitions. Eventually, Phillips got a break, got contracts and could afford to send bands abroad. In 1946, he sent the first steel band to travel, Red Army, to BG, as it was called in those days. The next band went to St. Vincent for a trade fair, Rising Sun, the band I was in. We traveled in '47 at Christmastime. With more contracts, he was also responsible for sending bands to America, too. Much later, the Chicago band with de la Bastide traveled in '64.

They'd changed their name from Hill Sixty when de la Bastide became their leader. De la Bastide remained in the States then and never returned to Trinidad. I'm not sure where in the States he's living.

After Rising Sun returned from St. Vincent—we spent two weeks there, I started to attend school to train in industrial engineering. My mother insisted that I do something other than Pan. But before completing school, I saw this position advertised for the Post Office job, went and sat the exam, passed it, and got in. That was in 1950, and I was beating pan less and less while being in school. Actually, I became an administrator of the band and started bringing in Mas/Carnival into the band, and organizing the band itself without beating pan.

During those years, in 1947 the Trinidad and Tobago Steelband Association (TTSA) started in Piccadilly Street by St. Paul Street. When TTSA started, the idea was twofold: to quell the rioting and to manage unbalanced contracting, because people were hiring only some bands to play here and there, which was causing a lot of conflict. We wanted to channel contracts in a proper manner and at the same time address the rioting, which also started with people in the movement that the Americans called *saga* boys and *saga* girls. But the rioting was also going on because of envy, whose pan was better than whose and that sort of thing. The advice to start the association came from Canon Farquhar, Andrew Carr, and other big people who saw something in Pan and wanted to channel it in a different direction. The suggestion was for each band to send someone to the association's meeting who represented the band's pan-side.

The men held the first meeting Behind the Bridge at a center on St. Paul Street. I did not attend that first meeting because I was not an active member of the pan-side. Our two representatives from Rising Sun were Carlton Bedhi and Dudley Smith. Carlton Bedhi was elected as treasurer, Sydney Gollop as president, and Sonny Harewood as secretary.[7] Then, Sydney Gollop became president and Nathaniel Crichlow from City Syncopaters became vice president. He was a senator at one time and in charge of the trade union affair.

After Crichlow's time a few years later, Rising Sun sent me to represent the men. While Crichlow was there, things went downhill because he was involved with the trade union. That's when George Goddard representing Invaders came in. He was the one who called us back together, advised us to have a new meeting and get rid of the existing executive body. To start from scratch with a whole new association. Goddard was elected president. I think someone else returned and had a problem with the structure. At a later time, Goddard decided that the whole association needed to be reformulated. That's when I became active in it.

Much later, in 1956, we marched as a trade union, with All Stars representing the association. We marched to begin to receive recognition. Sometime around 1956 to '57, the name was changed to the National Association of Trinidad and Tobago Steelbandsmen (NATTS). To keep NATTS going, we got Lyle Lashley, a real estate businessman from Frederick Street, to lend us his office space. We used to keep general meetings at Progressive High School because we had no other place. All our equipment was in a briefcase. All this time, we were getting fed up because the guys didn't want to stop the rioting. We really had problems among the steel bands.

I remember when I had to stop Renegades and Sun Valley (from Nelson Street) from fighting. The police came and got me from my job. They had the two leaders locked up in the Besson Street Police Station. I went up and found Goldteeth and a member from Desperadoes named Pa. I knew Goldteeth as Stephen and when I went in I said to him, "Stephen, what happenin' here?" He said, "I doh know. Dey bring me here an' tell me I causin' riot." I turned to Pa and asked him what he was doing there. He said, "I from the Hill so dey bring me here." Now, even though Pa was from Desperadoes and that fight was between Renegades and Sun Valley, the police decided they could bring in Desperadoes.

Something had happened between Renegades and Sun Valley, and the Sun Valley boys couldn't go to Royal Theatre or play in the Savannah. Meanwhile, the Renegades guys couldn't hang out at a favorite rum shop on Nelson Street. I suggested to the police for us to go to the boys' hang-out at Calvary School. I met a fella there named Luta Blaize (or Luther Blade, I'm not too sure of the spelling) that I knew from five years before and asked him what was going on, how it was that some fellas couldn't come down to Nelson Street. He said he wasn't involved in that. So, I asked if the guys came down for a drink if they'd be left alone, so that there'd be no more fighting and the boys getting locked up. He said that was okay. I asked for fifteen minutes to negotiate with Goldteeth, because even though he wasn't involved in that particular fight, he was the head. I had only five dollars in my pocket and knew that could buy a bottle of wine.

I walked down Nelson Street, and at the corner of Nelson and Prince Streets I decided to hang out there with the Sun Valley boys. While there, I asked Pa how he got involved. His response made me realize that it was all about pride. So, I negotiated for the fellas to come down and drink, for them to play in the Savannah, and for them to get into Royal Theatre. Three days later, Goldteeth found me to say that three of his boys were locked up. They were fighting over a different matter. It was always one thing or another.

Goddard was fed up and wanted to go into religion, so he joined the Jehovah's Witnesses and resigned. I was the organizing secretary and the vice president, Dave Harding, was a custom officer. Prior to Harding, Lennard Morris was vice president. Morris really didn't want any leadership role and only wanted to be on the executive committee. So, there was a meeting. At the time, Goddard and I were really running things by moving around, visiting places to organize bands, and getting them to join the organization. At that meeting, an election was called and I was nominated as president. I accepted on condition that I was going to change the entire original structure. They agreed to allow me to do what I wanted to do. This was happening in 1959, and I don't think we had a music festival the year before because of polio or something.

I called a meeting early in '59 at Progressive High School because the 1960 Music Festival was coming up, and its music association had begun advertising for the different groups to compete. In order to compete we needed funds. So, I decided that the music association's call was a good opportunity for steel bands to get back involved, as well as change the old structure that included positions for a president, a secretary-treasurer, and an assistant secretary-treasurer.

The guy holding the position of secretary-treasurer was sort of inactive. His name was Egbert Allen. He eventually became the mayor of Arima but at the time was pay-master with Harriman and Company. So, more often than not he would just drop in. At other times, we had to wait while trying to get in touch with him to get letters written. However, he managed the money well, was good for that post as treasurer. But when you're ready to move, you want somebody who is active, who can get things done right away. So, I decided that I would change the structure and the men agreed. We elected as secretary a teacher named Selwyn Heyward who taught at Eastern Boys School—very intelligent fella. Franky Maillard became assistant secretary and Allen remained treasurer. From that time, we could move forward more quickly. With the reorganized executive committee, I could concentrate on the music festival toward organizing the preliminaries' rounds. Meanwhile, the branches in town, down south, and in Tobago had nothing actively working, so I had to revamp that structural part of the association.

I visited San Fernando and reorganized that branch. The organizing committee—all members of the steelband association—comprised of Mr. Alfred Cooper (organizing secretary), Franky Maillard (assistant secretary), Ossie George from San Fernando, and Lennard Morris (vice president of the steelband association and a member of Merrymakers Steel Band). The father of Bobby Mohammed, Guinness Cavaliers' captain, was a representative of Gondoliers, I think. I called the meeting at Palms Club in San Fernando. Ossie George helped organize it with me and got the group to attend the meeting that Sunday. Lo and behold, also present at the meeting as an observer was a woman named Muriel Donawa who eventually became a member of PNM and later a minister in the government. Ossie George was elected secretary, Steve Regis as president, and Muriel Donawa as the public relations officer. Few people know that. That branch then was able to start organizing its preliminary round.

Then, I went to Tobago and organized the branches there, too. Incidentally, the Tobago bands were on strike because they were more lucrative than the Trinidad bands, since Tobago was a more tourist island. The bands used to play in all the clubs, so they had a strike on the clubs. They'd sent an SOS to NATTS to come and straighten things out. Little bands had begun to form to take the jobs of the bigger bands who started to panic and call us. Mr. Lashley and I went to Tobago. Mr. Lashley played a very significant role by being there for us when nobody really was. He has never got the credit and thanks he deserved, and I want him to get his due credit. When we had nothing, he loaned us his office space and became our public relations officer. With his assistance, we were able to draw up some papers and become a legal organization. Before that, Flavius Nurse, who was working with the PNM office as secretary-treasurer, allowed us to use his office. He got a contract for Boystown at that time. But Goddard hadn't liked that operation and got the association away from being so closely linked to the government. This is how Mr. Lashley came in and remained with us when no one else wanted to.

Before he and I left for Tobago, we found out that the person in charge of Crown Point Hotel was Fletcher Johnson, the owner of J.T. Johnson in Trinidad. We realized we had a good basis to work from. Lashley, an excellent businessman, knew Fletcher and began conversations with him. By the time we got to Tobago and met with the manager of the hotel, a price for the bands had been decided upon. The men were asking for a much higher price than the hotel was willing to pay. So, we came to a compromise.

The secretary of the Tobago bands, who is now a professor right here in Brooklyn at Medgar Evers, was John Gibbs. I think his field is chemistry. He was representing a band in Tobago. The present president of Pan Trinbago, Patrick Arnold, is from Our Boys. He was also there. But at the time, Gibbs represented the Tobago bands, was studying in Trinidad, and also was getting ready to travel abroad. When we arrived in Tobago, we got the bands together so they, too, could begin getting ready for their preliminary. By this time, we'd decided for sure we would hold the preliminaries, because everything was beginning to come together. Back home in Trinidad, I'd gathered all the heads of the bands to lay out the plans for our preliminary.

All this time, know that Invaders didn't want to join the association at all. Goddard was a member of Invaders, but he and Ellie Mannette never pulled, never got along. Ellie had an attitude, you must understand. He didn't do much talking but wanted his way. Had to have his way. Because of that, he and Goddard couldn't pull. He gave the impression that he could get along without the association because he was from Woodbrook, getting all the lucrative jobs, and was in with Beryl McBurnie, so he didn't care about any association. All Stars also wasn't much interested in the association, for their own reasons, too.

I had to use strategy to get Invaders to join, whose opportunity came due to something that was taking place at that very time. A guy named Colin Agostini, I think was his name, was an impresario. Now, Brute Force from Antigua was coming to Trinidad around September or November of '59 to make a steelband recording—something I learned later on. In fact, the first steelband music we heard over the radio was theirs, not a Trinidad band.[8] Imagine that! When I found out they were coming to Trinidad, and at the time still didn't know why they were really coming, I pointed out to the men that we had a steelband association and an outside band shouldn't just be coming to Trinidad to play without the association being notified. They were coming to play at the Yacht Club, at Normandie, and other places we also had bands playing. So, I went seeking some advice.

I remember well the Saturday of the show to be held in San Fernando. Brute Force, Invaders, Dixieland, and a special band from San Fernando were advertised, for what was supposed to be a show featuring only the élite, the best of Trinidad meeting the best of Antigua. But I felt this was wrong because the association wasn't involved. That morning, I went to visit Bruce Procope, one of our pro bono advisors who liked all these cultural things and was working with Beryl McBurnie. Andrew Carr was another advisor. I went to Procope because he was a lawyer. Selwyn Heyward, the secretary, went with me. (Selwyn, though from Nelson Street, was educated and sharp—a teacher.) I said to Procope that the organizers wanted to cause riot by leaving out bands that were members of the association, but Procope said he couldn't do anything about it. They were bands coming in to play and he couldn't stop them. So we left, and while going downstairs Selwyn said, "Listen, we have to try something, you know. We can't just let them come here and do this without us doing something." While we were walking up Queen Street trying to figure out what to do, a mind told me to try some technique business [street-smartness]. I wondered how to formulate that, and the chance came when we reached Frederick Street on the Bata Shoes Store side.

Some Casablanca boys were *liming* there with "Barong" Areata and others; and on the opposite side by Y. de Lima, Curtis Pierre and a side [group] of White boys were *liming*, too. I went first to Curtis Pierre, 'cause he was with Dixieland and connected to Invaders and some other band that Curtis and his boys used to play in. I said to him, "Curtis, you're a member of the steelband association. How come you didn't tell us anything? According to the rules you're supposed to inform us when you're playing, and they're advertising this thing that we know nothing about. What going on?" He said, "I thought you knew. You all don't know anything?" I said, "We only now know and, in fact, we're calling off the show." He watched me and said, "Anything you say is fine." I said, "I'm coming back just now," and went over to "Barong" on the next side of the street and said to him, "Barong, I want you to help me out with something." He asked, "With what?" I said, "Listen, we want to stop a show in San Fernando, but I will need your support." He replied, "Wha'ever yuh say." He had about six guys there hanging out with him. I gave each one a band—one was from Tokyo, another from Desperadoes, and so on—and said, "I'm going back to Bruce Procope to talk. Remember which band each of you from." I knew that Procope knew Barong Areata because Barong was what they called an enforcer. Everybody knew him. I invited them to follow me across the street to Curtis and said to him, "Curtis, I want you to go with us. I'm going back to Mr. Procope." He said, "Okay," and he and two other guys followed us.

Whilst going down St. Vincent Street, I met Comandos, a guy from St. James, who I knew for a long time. He was wearing a white shirt, but it was brown in color from the cement work. I invited him to come with us, too, saying to him all he had to do was *grind*. "Just look vex, don't do any talking. Let me do the talking. You're from San Fernando and you came up just to tell me that the boys from San Fernando out to *mash up* the show."

We went down Queen Street, back to the office, and asked to speak to Mr. Procope. When he came he said, "You were just here. What is the problem?" I said, "This is important." I looked at Comandos then said to Procope again, "This is important. I went back to the office and found these members waiting for me because they have plans to go down to San Fernando to *mash up* the show." Pointing at Comandos I said, "This guy here he, too, just came from San Fernando." He said, "All right. All you come in and sit down. What's the matter?" I, playing vex too, said, "They want to stop the show. These guys come to Trinidad and they playing all over the place, nobody telling them anything, and then you're billing Mr. Curtis Pierre as the best band in Trinidad, the band from south as the best band from south, and Invaders as the best, too. Something wrong." He said, "Listen, man, you say they out to *mash up* the show, but we don't want us to go back to twenty years. We're trying to move ahead." I said, "Well, tell us what to do." He said, "I'll tell you what. I know the person who brought Brute Force." You hear that? All the time he couldn't do anything. "The guy's name is Mr. Goldfish of Cook's Caribbean. He brought them down to make a record with the best bands in Trinidad." I said, "Well, you will have to talk to Mr. Goldfish." He said, "All right, let me talk to him."

He called Mr. Goldfish and they set a meeting for the Monday. On the phone, he told Mr. Goldfish not to allow Brute Force to go on at all because there was a protest now, a call for the show to stop. Agostini came in now. He said that the show was based around Brute Force because all the recordings on the radio were from Antigua.[9] He agreed that it looked like the show was about to be called off.

I then contacted the newspapers for them to print that news. In the evening, I decided to go visit Invaders. I was out to close down the show and I had put that out to the newspapers, "Steelband Association Stops Show in San Fernando," because all the time Ellie used to say, "All yuh ent have no power. All yuh playing the fool." I got a copy of the evening news and went straight down to Invaders yard with this information.

I used to get around by bicycle or just walked from one panyard to another to visit bands. Once, I walked to San Juan and back. This time, I used my bicycle and when I got there I said to him that I came to find out what was going on with Invaders and to let him know that I stopped the show. He said, "What show?" I said, "Read the papers." He watched me. I said, "Listen nah, man, you have to support the association. Goddard is no longer in the association. We're starting something new and want to move ahead. As a main band in this thing, you know you're supposed to—." He cut me off saying, "It's not me, you know. What dem fellas say to do, that is what I do. So is whatever they say." I said, "All right." An arranger named Zypherine was there. Remember, Ellie was just the tuner. I talked to him and said, "Listen," and laid out a plan. He said, "Leave everything to me. I'll talk to them."

You see, talk was getting around that the association was beginning to prepare to enter Music Festival and Zypherine wanted to play in the Festival. We wanted participation in the Festival to feature bands that went through all the rounds: preliminary, quarter-finals, semi-finals, and finals. I was looking for the association to organize all the rounds. Ellie was the man who would stand up and say he didn't want anything to do with the association and would have his own way. This guy knew this and said for me to leave it up to him. He said that regardless of what the guys said he would be there and Ellie would go along with them. He went on to say that he planned to take part in the Festival and that I will hear from him. I left the newspaper with them to remind them of what the association could do.

Eventually, he came back to us and said Invaders was willing to join. I began operating with more leverage from then on. I then went to All Stars, but Jules was adamant. He said the band wasn't practicing, and that was that.[10] So, for that Festival I don't think All Stars participated. North Stars was somewhat defunct at the time and they didn't participate either.

When I began to organize for the preliminary in early '59, I recognized that the association needed money. We had nothing, nothing at all when I checked the records. I called on Mr. Allen, the treasurer, and couldn't get him. He was always busy with one organization or another, involved with four or five of them at the same time—Boys Scouts, PNM, and who knows what. I was ready to move on and he had no time. Next, I asked the secretary to contact him about the bank book. When I got the bank book, I saw that we had $150. The problem was then how to start with that amount.

My first challenge was to get Roxy Theatre. I went to Miss Teelucksingh, I think was her name. She said, "No, no, boy. I don't want no steel band in my theater." I wanted to rent, even though we had no money, and she was already saying no. I said, "Listen, I'm actually doing you a favor." She said, "Oh, yes? How?" I said, "Because we have Queen's Hall. But you were with us from the early days when things were hard and I didn't want to leave you out. This is why I've come to you first to give you an opportunity to make good on this." She said, "Well, those boys like to *mash up* the place." I reassured her that wouldn't happen and we would guarantee that the boys would behave. We would be in charge because we wanted to give her the chance to make some money off us. With that persuasion, she finally agreed.

I gave her seventy-five dollars as an advance deposit to hold the date and time. All this time, no band had started to get ready yet. I was just moving things along steadily. I next went to Y. de Lima and asked them to sell some tickets. Jack de Lima agreed. The next day, I went to Radio Trinidad and asked Frank Prado, a Guyanese announcer, if he would be the MC [master of ceremonies]. He agreed. With this, I started to get free advertisement over the radio, which was good because I couldn't pay if I had to. I needed the remaining seventy-five dollars for another job.

I went to a friend named Pollonaise, who went to school with me and owned a printery on Henry Street. He decided to accept the seventy-five dollars to print the program and tickets. I went back and got a floor plan from Miss Teelucksingh and he used that for printing the tickets. Next, I sectioned off PoS, because that was where the money was—Invaders, Tripoli, the bands of the west—and started advertisements in that area. I had six or seven bands in this western division. Then, Hugh Borde's sister agreed to sell the tickets for us. Hugh Borde was in charge of Tripoli and also a member of my executive committee.

The day came for the preliminary and we held them. Invaders wasn't as prepared but they always had good tunes. I think Dixieland won the Festival and Invaders came second, so Invaders did well, along with the six bands, and we made some money, I think over one thousand dollars—a good profit. The first thing I did was to purchase a copying machine. We were still using Lashley's office, so I started to give him sixteen dollars a week for using his office, typewriter, and secretary. That money was more for her because she was doing all that work for us; it wasn't really for the rental space. I also wanted to move from Lashley's office, even though the secretary was a big help to us, because I felt we needed our own place. Then, I bought a typewriter for the Association. I had a lot of things to do because the other preliminaries—in the south and Tobago—were coming up and I had to pay for more printing and tickets. That profit-money stretched far.

The next preliminary was in south, in San Fernando. By this time, I had a growing legacy, which started out with one hundred fifty dollars. Goddard had set up a steelband association dance at Seamen and Waterfront. He'd paid down money on the place and on an advance on the band. I had to carry out that obligation to Norman Texwilliams. We decided to use two bands for that dance: Silver Stars and Norman Texwilliams's band. The dance was not successful because, in those days, I didn't know much about that type of business. I merely wanted to carry through on a prior commitment. I think that was the first NATTS dance we had. Then, south wanted a dance because they heard we'd had one up north. So, we planned a second dance for South. At that dance, I don't think we used a music band, a DJ—we didn't call them DJ at the time. Merrymakers and two southern bands organized it. It wasn't successful but we didn't lose any money. Whatever money came in went to the southern branch to help its organization. That's how we started moving.

In those days, I had a vision for Pan. I wanted Pan to move forward from the environment it was in toward being viewed differently, a raised status for Pan's social acceptance. Pan had started getting the White boys from college involved who formed Dixieland and Silver Stars steel bands. I also believe that by taking part in the Festival the standard of the music improved because after the Festival the men continued to practice and play the classics. Plus, the pans themselves began to improve. I could see how my vision could be realized. The association also started to get some prominence, too.

After the Festival, I changed our stationery. For the Festival, I got the *Guardian* to print a formal letterhead with our coat-of-arms on it. Using this stationery, we invited all the ambassadors and councilors to the Festival. Afterward, I received some dinner invitations and other invitations to various functions at the American, British, and Canadian embassies. These foreigners began giving us acceptance at a level we didn't get even among our own.

I was president for one year and did so much that I began to get bad feedbacks. Goddard wanted to return. He was finished with the church. I started hearing this and that about money, and whatnot. So, I decided that since I was working with the post office that my time was consumed with that. The guys there wanted me to assist them. They felt I was wasting my time with Pan boys when they were the ones appreciative of my assistance. So, they elected me president of the Post Office Workers Union. With that, I left NATTS.

After my leaving, I think Junior Pouchet became president for about five to six months. Ellie was supposed to be elected but he was absent from that meeting, and to be elected you had to be present. However, Pouchet didn't last long because he was more committed to his steel band. For the remainder of that year, a caretaker committee held the organization together. In 1962, Cecil Hunte was elected and it was during his term the organization became NATTS Trade Union, complete with a constitution. Then came Independence.

Independence time was a good one. Crossfire won the Festival that year. The guy who wrote the test piece, "Steelband Started Here"—or something like that—was Cecil Hunte. For Independence, Crossfire played at the Rock Gardens. A band from BG was there as a guest artist. I think Bookers sent them.

The following year Goddard returned to office. He called me to say they wanted to form a national steel band. I returned and was elected as a second vice president, and Goddard put me in charge of the National Steel Band when it was formed. But before they traveled, I left. The secretary, Kathleen Gill, and I weren't pulling. She and Goddard were friendly and she was acting at a higher level than she was supposed to. For instance, we once went to Radio Trinidad to play and I asked her to help me organize getting the pans out of the building. She refused. If I got them upstairs, then I could get them back downstairs. I pointed out to her that I was working. All I wanted her to do was make sure things were going smoothly, and this she refused. So, I decided that under those circumstances I couldn't be bothered. I had my own job to see about and eased myself out of NATTS at this time.

While I was involved with Pan, I had a good time and have very good memories. Other memories revolve around the idea that Eric Williams did a lot for Pan.

Eric Williams, Development and Environmental Works Division (DEWD), and the Music Association

Eric Williams started getting involved with Steelband by having several meetings with the men. But apparently, NATTS hadn't a real plan and he wanted to hear much more than the men were putting forward at the time. So, he backed out and we decided to form the National Steel Band. All Eric Williams and the government gave us was money to pay for the pans, and Williams personally gave us a drum set. I was a member of the National Steel Band, too, but only beating congas. I'd stopped beating pan years ago. The proposal we put forward to him, we had thought, was for them to accept the steel band as the national instrument of the country, and the National Steel Band would play alongside the police band. The members of the national band would be paid something, trained to read music, become a part of the official music program, and represent Trinidad, along with the police band. But they never gave us that support, recognition, or status. Williams just backed out completely and the association was left on its own. The band went so far as to get help from the Moral Rearmament who sponsored them on that tour to the United States. But by that time, I'd left NATTS, as said before. And, that was the end of that regarding Williams, the government, and the association.

Here's another reason I say that Williams really didn't do anything to enhance Pan. True, he gave the panmen a little job here and there because they were rioting. But after those jobs: nothing. I mean nothing, despite all the appeals to him. So, I don't know where people get the impression that he made the *bad-johns* into ambassadors of T&T. What did he do, for example, about those days of rioting between Desperadoes and Marabonters, those big riots, when we didn't have the DEWD project, yet? They were threatening to use dynamites and so on to blow up each other. Serious. I was the organizing secretary at the time and Goddard was the president in 1955 to '56.

A member of the PNM hierarchy, Dr. J. D. Elder, who was also researching to write about the culture of the country, attended one of our association meetings to ask us to do something, anything to stop these guys. There were other riotings all over the place, but the biggest ones were between Desperadoes and Marabonters. Elder discussed this with Goddard, who was, at the time, friendly with a girl from John John, whose brother was the vice captain of the band. But Goddard said that was a matter for the police and the church and he wasn't getting involved in that. When I asked him privately why he took that position, he said that he was going up to John John to talk with the boys, and he and the girl were getting along well. But if things went wrong, he couldn't count on any policeman for protection so he was making sure he stayed on the boys' good side. He suggested that I, instead, say something to them. You see, I was a postman and knew the area and all the guys in the area. So, I agreed to go.

The Sunday morning, I went up and asked to meet with one of the main guys named Danna to see if, as both the government and the police in fact wanted, we could hold this meeting toward the bands making peace. They said they didn't know where Danna was and if I wanted I could go and see if I could find him at the La Basse, down over the line. I went and found a fella called Buh-here, who told me that Danna wasn't there but might be up in Laventille. I wasn't going all the way back there and asked him and Kid Coolie, a Marabonters *bad-john*, to give Danna the message that a meeting was being held the next Sunday. The meeting was scheduled to be at the same place Uriah Tubal "Buzz" Butler held his meetings on St. Joseph Road, his former office turned into a club, which I'd got permission to use. Two police superintendents—one of them was Inspector Barnes—Lennox Pierre, Lyle Ashley, and three men from the Ministry of Culture were supposed to attend.

The meeting was held on a Sunday, but I couldn't attend. A follow-up meeting was set to be held in Laventille. I wasn't involved in organizing that meeting but went to it. At that meeting, we realized that the cause of all the trouble among the men was no work, and they wanted to work. They were unemployed and most likely if they had something to occupy them they wouldn't be fighting. That was how the DEWD project came into being. They decided to have these guys clean the canals and do other road-work. George Yeates was in the Laventille truck business. He had attended college but didn't finish any degree. They decided to utilize him as leader, as a top man in the project, which extended to John John, then Belmont, then all over T&T. That's how things started to quiet down among the boys.

With that going, the panmen started to support Williams and the PNM. But apart from giving the men those little jobs around the place through the project, he didn't do anything big. People must understand that. True, the majority of men in the project were steelbandsmen, but when the time came to promote the thing as the culture of the country, he wasn't really doing that. It was really we steelbandsmen who ourselves organized and got things turned around by doing for ourselves, which many people are unaware of. We had to fight the government. At one time, we had to fight with them real hard to get a little bit of money, because we didn't have any money and couldn't do much of anything. We went through a whole lot, had to do a lot of fighting. One example of how we had to fend for ourselves relates not to the government but the Music Association, when May Johnstone was in charge. I was president at the time.

The music professors, the adjudicators, said that the steel bands were not to play classical pieces because the instrument was not suitable. They said Steelband was not suited for that sort of music and the men had to play other types of music. They held a meeting on Sackville Street to present this to me. Those present were: Vernon Evans; another man named Alladin, who represented the Ministry of Culture; Mr. Johnston, the president of the Music Association; and representing NATTS were Egbert Allen, Mr. Lashley, Mr. Harding, two other guys, and me.

I arrived a little late because, as a postman, I had to complete my rounds; and, I apologized for my late arrival. They apprised me on what had taken place before I arrived. The Music Association had brought to the meeting music sheets for what they considered appropriate for the steel bands to play for the Music Festival—island music, some sort of mambo-tango nonsense.[11] At the time, NATTS was not in charge of the steel band category/class of Music Festival. From their discussion, I gathered their main concern was finals. I was surprised that the men from NATTS agreed to that: but not me. I informed them not to limit me. I knew if I'd allowed them to do that, the steelbandsmen would have found themselves in a tizzy. I also saw that they were setting us back by years, despite how much we'd advanced. I just couldn't agree to that.

I pointed out to them that we were not competing against conventional instruments and we had to be judged based on our performance among ourselves. They could use their ten-point system of evaluation, if they so chose, but appropriate it to how we performed among ourselves. I pointed out that we were not in the same category as the guitars or clarinet. Therefore, they couldn't compare us with those instruments. They could only do so based on how one band did in comparison with or contrast to another band. They eventually agreed. You see, I just couldn't sit there and go along with them telling us that we couldn't play this or that and had to play that mambo-tango stupidness. Because they were the Music Association of T&T, holding the competitions at Queen's Hall, that didn't mean they had to hold us back. So, from my negotiations I was able to get us into that festival at Queen's Hall on our terms for the first time, in 1960.

I gathered also that they wanted us there only for the finals, and I refused to agree to that, too. I argued that all the years we were generating money for the festival, with the steel band performances being the biggest part of it and bringing in the most money, I thought it was time for them to begin to see that Steelband was our culture and for us to hold the full rounds of competition there. We compromised based on some behind-the-scenes negotiations with Mr. Codallo, the manager of Queen's Hall. They finally agreed that the quarter-finals through finals would be held at Queen's Hall. They said they were concerned that the men would *mash up* the place, and so on. So, I stopped them from limiting us to playing mambos and tangos and keeping us out of Queen's Hall until the finals. I called the shots regarding what the men would play, and I helped establish the basis for judging us.

All this time, we didn't even used to call Panorama by that name. We called it Friday Night Bacchanal. Then, around '63 the name changed to Panorama with Goddard.[12]

These are some of the reasons I'm reluctant to say the government really assisted NATTS during the Williams's era. The one who really assisted NATTS was Albert Gomes. Unlike the other so-called White people, he used to live on Belmont Valley Road, two houses from the Rada drummers, right there with the steel bands as they were starting up. He was also a member of the Federated Trade Union and a member of the city council. When he became minister, he moved to St. Clair. He was the one who used to stop the police from harassing us, because he knew that these fellas were really only beating pan and not really looking for trouble. He, Canon Farquhar, and others like them who were more culture-minded are the ones who really did something for Steelband. The majority of Trinidadians only used to complain about the set of noise we were making and the amount of violence we were causing and having. It was a crime to be a steelbandsman. Things are at such a higher level now. It's good to see how far Pan has come.

So as for the riotings, Albert Gomes did more than Williams ever did to quell the riotings by having the police go easy on the men, then went one step further to help organize the Six-to-Nine Parade for us. He called us to a meeting and outlined what we could and couldn't do to avoid getting arrested and locked up.

Before that parade, we couldn't go out on the streets without the police harassing us. I reiterate that with Williams's amount of power, Steelband would be much more advanced today if he'd done more. The government as a body didn't do what it could. They gave only a lot of mouth service then.[13] They're still doing that today.

Some of their attitude and behavior changed when the college boys started to get involved. That's when people on the whole started easing up a bit on us, with the arrival of bands like Dixieland, Silver Stars, one or two from San Fernando like Gondoliers. Curtis Pierre was largely responsible for that movement to bring in college boys. At the time, he was in college when he formed a little band named Stromboli. Dixieland and Silver Stars grew out of Stromboli. Curtis Pierre deserves a lot of credit for helping to change the image of panmen because at the time people like him weren't beating pan. Once he started to bring in college boys, panmen began to receive some acceptance and toleration. He and Junior Pouchet take that credit. These two, I see, were responsible for bringing the total acceptance of Pan in Trinidad society.

If anyone wants to hail the cause for Pan's social acceptance, I'll say it was because of a combination of things. One, the men began to play classical music. Two, pan was beginning to sound better and the whole thing was becoming more enjoyable. True, in the early days it was a lot of noise—the foundation period. But with the improved tonality, quality of music, the presence of the college boys, panmen's overall changing image, things began to change. And, three, the men organized themselves, using all the help they could get from various sources.

All in all, even though when I first got involved I was beating pan, when I saw the need to organize I did my part. I put myself into that little niche because I really wasn't that versatile on pan, that dexterous, and knew that I couldn't move around with the bands because I was with the post office. But I looked for all ways to promote Steelband as our culture. One of those ways was working with the children through City Kids.

City Kids

One other group I helped formed at the same time I became president of NATTS was City Kids.[14] I came to organize City Kids while I was organizing Mas and different events, having stopped beating pan. I'd brought out "Back to Africa" with George Bailey and the year before that, La Toco. It was after La Toco that Bailey came up to Belmont and asked us to join up with him to bring out the biggest section. After we agreed, he never even mentioned Dudley Smith. He registered "Back to Africa" under his name, but Rising Sun brought him out. In those days, bands didn't get any money for playing Mas but Bailey must have got something for winning. Anyway, after that we had a meeting to decide what to do the following year, but I didn't like how business was conducted at that meeting and washed my hands off Rising Sun. Then, I heard about this group of kids beating old pans, coal-pot, and whatnot, and was asked to help them by getting them organized. At the time, they were young boys still in school. Roderick Toussaint was their leader/captain. After I helped organized them, his older brother Horace became the manager. They came out of that same Toussaint yard that Rising Sun used to beat pan in and, in fact, used the old pans Rising Sun abandoned after Rising Sun became defunct. I got more pans from Casablanca, Invaders, Sunland, and Desperadoes—all different styles of pan—and asked Scorpion, a tuner from Arima, to bring them into tune for the band. Later, I got Corbeau Jack to tune for us.

After they were organized and called City Kids, I helped to get them gigs through the Tourist Board playing on the wharf for the tourists. I used to get them out of school, with permission, of course, to go and play. The money they got from doing that was whatever the tourists gave them. The larger, organized bands couldn't afford to play under those circumstances, which is how I got City Kids to do that. Soon afterward, we began getting jobs at the Normandie and other tourist places.

Robbie Greenidge was a City Kid and grew up in that versatile environment of playing different pans. We used to put him on a soap box to stand on to reach the pan. After organizing City Kids, I helped organize the National Steel Band. When the National Steel Band asked for a representative from City Kids, we sent Robbie. Rudolph Charles took Robbie under his wings. Charles was beating cellos in the National Steel Band. Eventually, Robbie went over to Desperadoes because his uncle Carl was tuning pan for Desperadoes. But he developed his versatility in City Kids because he learned to play all the different pans. A lot of the little fellas started out with City Kids and once they knew how to beat, they left and joined the bigger bands.

But we have a problem, our people, with organizing and supporting each other. We can't seem to sustain anything with that love and understanding for the betterment of each other. People are still looking out too much for themselves only. The attitude is: what I can get out of it for myself is the only thing that matters. It's what's happening right here in Brooklyn.

I happen to know that Neville Jules is still trying to help out the best he can, but others are only trying to take advantage. He's still the kind of person who'll give more than he'll get. Always did a lot. Always tried to give a true picture of the way things were and not give any false impressions of himself because he always had a bigger picture in mind for Pan. That included helping others. Then, when with his help people got so big that they forgot who helped to get them where they are, they overlooked him. Some of these boys here in the States behave so badly, I really don't know what to say. But not Jules. His story gives a good picture of how Pan evolved.

To get a clear understanding of how Pan is to evolve, we have to look at the way the piano people looked at piano. Everyone contributed toward improving the piano, brought it to the best level it could be, and then it gained wide acceptance. That's what we have to do. Get away from this individual wanting to do his thing and that one trying to do his thing, then talking only about how his pan is better than the other one's pan. That's not helpful.

Furthermore, we also have to see how to use the pan for more than just the Carnival season.

On Calypso: Its Link to Pan and Pan's Spiritual Roots

Remember, the roots of Carnival are in the people mimicking their betters, and vice versa. In fact, I call Trinidadians mimic men. We're like monkeys in some ways. We like to take on everybody else's thing and leave our own behind. Look at the Reggae. Once, I went down for Carnival and all I was hearing was Reggae. At *Carnival*! No calypso! And, Calypso is one of the highest musical cultures in the world.

Our calypsonians are poets, some of the best in the world. Some Trinidadians continue to marvel at Shakespeare and forget about our own Chalkdust. Our calypsonians have punned everything, from a fly to a politician, in a way that you can dance to the calypso. Our calypsos are also topical and sensible. We don't know the culture we have but are quick to latch on to what everybody else is doing. Take Reggae, for example, which itself is a copy thing, too. They take everybody's music and put a beat to it. For that matter, they can take a calypso and put a beat to it, too. It's an art form, yes, but it's still a beat.[15]

The difference with the calypso as its own unique art form is that it takes what is happening in nature and society and makes it into a topic, sometimes so simple that a child can understand. It can also be really sophisticated, so that you have to try to get to the subtle meanings. It's that double entendre that makes Calypso so great, a high form of art. But because it comes from home, some Trinidadians don't even recognize it as such. It will take somebody from the outside, like with the pan, taking it from them and making it their own before they realize what they *used* to have. *Used to have,* because today you're not hearing any good calypsos. They're singing a lot of foolishness: "Wave yuh hand an' jump up, jump up!" Where have all the good calypsonians gone? They used to sing about a foolish policeman or woman, or about the obeah man, or about a big man with a small woman, or about a bird or horse or snake. Songs you could listen to and understand what was going on and laugh. But they've lost that. The young ones coming up are not thinking about any of this. They just pick up a few words, put a little melody to the words, and they're looking to make a million dollars.

David Rudder is the only one we have who sings like the old calypsonians. And, even he, too, is trying to formulate something else in Calypso. He's trying to take it to another level by making the calypso into a song. So, even though he has the Calypso bent, he's losing the Calypso flavor of the old days. Even so, he's the only one who is keeping somewhat true to the genre. He's still singing about a topic and explaining it, and you can even dance to it. That's the beauty of Calypso and David Rudder is the only young, bright light in Calypso, which some people say is the music of Pan.

The beauty of Pan is that it can play all music. However, it's best suited for Calypso. You see, it originated from calypso music, with the people who were developing an instrument to go with the calypso tradition. So, Pan evolved in the Calypso tradition. You can feel most comfortable playing calypso on pan. A guy in England will play his type of music on pan and feel comfortable doing that, and the same for a guy from France or Germany, or wherever. But Trinidadians feel most comfortable playing calypso, I think.

A culture is something, eh. Our culture is Calypso and Steelpan. The piano was made for the European classics, and that is their culture. Drums and jumping and dancing go together, as you can see among some Africans and Native Americans. That is how culture evolves, with one activity complementing another. For us, it's Steelpan and Calypso. That's our culture.

If anyone knows the history and background of Pan and Calypso, he will know that they originated simultaneously out of colonial efforts to suppress African culture. Most of us are descendants of African people. Now, if you study the places where Pan first came from, you'll find it came from those places where there was Shango, an African presence. Every band from the old days that you can identify, if you search where it originated, you'll find it was next to or near a Shango yard. Every single band was either in front or behind or next to or near a Shango yard. The majority of those early beaters of pan come from Shango. Tokyo, Desperadoes, Rising Sun, Casablanca, Checnick—they were all close to a Shango yard.

We called everything Shango because that is how we came to know these people and their practices. I was under that impression, too. But in reality, there were different sects with different affinities of African religion that came to Trinidad and settled in various places, and we came to call them all Shango. For instance, in Belmont Valley Road where they beat drums, too, we called it Shango but it was not. It was Rada from the Dahomey tribe. Their playing sounded alike, their original beating. But if you studied it carefully, you could hear the subtle differences and would recognize one as Shango and one as Rada.

About Rada, which I think was from the West African Dahomey tribe, the people brought with them their customs and settled in an area where they preserved this. It's like how the Caribbean people tend to congregate in certain spots in Brooklyn, depending on which island they came from. The Bajans live on upper Nostrand Avenue, the Bajans being among some of the earliest arrivals from Barbados. They established their enclaves and hold on to them. It's a similar process that happened in Trinidad.

With the steel band, it started with the drumming in the Shango tent then went to the bamboo because the colonials passed the law prohibiting them from beating drums after the camboulay riots.[16] They passed those laws with the intention of curbing the riots. But the people still wanted to enjoy their festivities during camboulay time, so they went to using bamboo to make their sound. Once they had their rhythm, they were happy to make their festivities. From the bamboo, they added the dustbin, then the tin can, and so on, until somebody eventually came out with the oil pan, and so on. You know about that from talking with the other men. But it really started with the idea of drumming and the Shango tent. I remember that Carnival of 1946 or '47 during a festivity for Discovery Day when someone got killed. They blamed the bands for that and said no more pans for Discovery Day. So, everybody went out with Shango drums because pan was banned. Different bands came out with their drums. Do you see the relationship between Shango, African religion, and what eventually came to be the steel band?

The African is a tympani person. He's always beating something, and that is what he's evolved from. Now, to accompany the beating, he had to sing, and back then the only thing he could sing about was what the master was doing, what the neighbor was doing, and what the authorities were doing. That is how the calypso came about. It poked fun at any and everybody. The master didn't know one word of what the calypsonian was saying, when all the time he was talking back to the master, and the master dancing along too. He didn't have a clue that he was dancing along and having a good time to something that was making fun of him.

Remember, too, that the English never really colonized Trinidad, meaning, lived on the island as the French did. The French lived there as a part of the society, which is why we have a strong French Creole presence—French names for places, and so on. They didn't really fraternize with the people, but they were more connected than the English. The English merely sent their representatives to manage and control their interests, to set up their law and order. So, you find the French started Carnival and later we copied it. When the French started Carnival, their celebration lasted from Christmas through the Lenten season. They didn't have Mas but (had) the balls and dances, which began at Christmas and culminated on the two big days of going from house to house in their fancy costumes. Eventually, when the lower class French started to imitate the upper class, they couldn't get involved in the house visits. So, they took to the road and began parading, and when the slaves were freed, this is what they began mocking, all of them, when playing Mas or masqueraders. They played dukes and duchesses, lords and ladies, and the other aristocrats. Eventually, they brought in their drums, which were later banned, then they switched to bamboo, and all that, which I already said. So, it was giving vent to their repression that shaped the way Carnival and Steelband have evolved in Trinidad. From Mas and drum to bamboo to tin can to pan.

This is something that was happening at the time. No one person was doing this. One thing we can say is that the first band that came out with pans included a guy by the name of Humbugger of Alexander Ragtime Band, and he made a name for himself. I remember seeing that band on Henry Street in the late '30s to early '40s before the war. Humbugger was wearing a pair of thermal underwear and a top hat. The pans had music sheets stuck on them, but the men weren't reading the music. They were just beating and Hamburger was waving his stick. The movie had just come down to Trinidad and they named the band after the movie. They were from Newtown, Woodbrook.

Also, they didn't really have notes on those pans. Notes on pan started with "Waterloo," Zigilee, and True Facts, which everybody knows about. Later, Jules improved on their three notes to make it four, and so they continued. They were interchanging ideas and sharing what they were doing. This was happening Behind the Bridge, the place where creativity was shaping this thing. Andrew, then Spree, added to it. Those two were very dexterous players. In those days, they played with one hand, not two hands as today, and if you could move that one hand well while strong enough to carry the pan, you made a name for yourself.

On Sponsorship

Sponsorship was a gradual process. I recall that the bands in the south, because of their environment, picked up sponsorship before those in the north. Guys who were working with Texaco and the other oil companies that had money got their companies to pick up sponsoring. The companies picked up on the idea when they recognized the bands offered free advertising. As you know, most of the guys in steel bands were the underprivileged. They had no money to buy pans, and it began to be expensive to maintain a band. In the earlier days when pans were carried around the neck, they weren't as expensive as when stands were introduced. Then tuners began to demand more money and pans became more expensive. Once Panorama began, only sponsored bands were winning because they had what was necessary to win. Unsponsored bands participated for the experience and lacked the finesse of the sponsored bands. But to answer the question on how sponsorship all began, I don't really know.

I remember that Coco-Cola sponsored Silver Stars and because of some problem Silver Stars lost their sponsorship. We were also able to get sponsorship for Desperadoes. Despers had just begun to stop rioting, and we promised them if they continued to stay away from the violence, we would help them pick up a sponsor. So, when the time came for a [cricket] test match at the Oval and they requested the association to send a band, we told them we were sending Desperadoes. They threatened to cancel the match, and we insisted that their only request was to send them a band and we were sending our best band. They'd given us their promise that they would behave, and everyone knew they would perform well. That was all we could guarantee: their good word and best performance. Since Coco-Cola had just dropped Silver Stars and was looking to pick up a new band, someone probably recommended Desperadoes as the best band for Coco-Cola to sponsor and to go to the match. We also thought that once Coco-Cola picked them up they could discipline them as they saw fit, and whatnot. This is how sponsorship eventually became the norm.

Often, it happened through guys working for a company who approached those companies and sold themselves to the company. It wasn't companies who went looking for bands to sponsor but guys taking that initiative and using their inside contact to help pull it off. The role the association played was to ask for help through approaching people who worked for these companies. But it didn't come about through some organized method. We needed the financial help and once we recognized the potential in sponsorship, we went about getting help in the manner I just described. No government official was behind that either. So, if anyone gives Williams credit for that, that's wrong. He's received *too* much credit. A lot of people really don't know how things really happened within the movement. True, he did a lot for education in the country, but as for the culture of the country, he didn't do that much. People like Beryl McBurnie of Little Carib Theatre and the Julia Edwards Dance Company, they're the ones who did a lot.

The Enforcers

The Steelband movement grew through various ways and methods. One aspect that people are unaware of is the role the enforcers played. Society called them *bad-johns*. Without the enforcers, half of the steel bands would not have existed.

Now, there was always a miserable member of a band, someone who wanted to do things his own way. Came to practice when he wanted to, or when he came to practice then didn't want to practice. That's when the enforcer stepped in and announced that anybody who didn't feel like practicing could leave. And, because he was a *bad-john*, you dared not wrangle with him. A lot of times it was the enforcer who got practice going because no one dared stand up to him. Then, if the band was practicing every night and you decided you were coming only one or two nights, one night he'd show up at your door wanting to know what happened, if you'd stopped liking the band or what. You'd better have a good reason for missing practice. So, they were called enforcers to stop everyone from taking his own little liberty. Some men felt the band couldn't do without them, that they were big and important. The enforcers reminded them of their real place and commitment. They also protected the panyard, the territory. The captain couldn't do that. He had to concentrate on getting the men to memorize the tune and play it well. The enforcers or *bad-johns* also protected the bands on Carnival days. No one from another band could come into your band to make trouble just like that.

However, these enforcers were good and bad, because a lot of the riots occurred because of these same *bad-johns*. They did things in the name of the band, and the whole band got into trouble. People on the outside had the impression that the entire band supported what these bad-johns-enforcers did. So, while they maintained discipline within the band and provided good protection, they themselves got into trouble and gave the band a bad name.

Some enforcers were pan-players, but the majority of them did nothing else but act the enforcer role. They gambled; they rioted. But when the time came for the band, they didn't make any joke. You didn't play with them at all.

Every band had its enforcers. They *had* to have them. Goldteeth was with Renegades. He never played pan, though once he was captain. Then there were Ossie and Batman from Casablanca; in fact, Casablanca had plenty of them. Donald Stedman was one from Desperadoes. He used to beat a pan when he went looking for those men who used to come to practice when they felt like it. When they heard that pan coming, they slipped out their backdoor to get to the yard before Donald could find them to remind them that the band was learning a new tune and *everyone* had to be at practice. Belmont had Albert Thompson and Carli Byer from St. François Valley Road. Byer was a real enforcer. This is the same Carli Byer I mentioned before, the one who broke up the band that used to be Belmont United. In those days, one guy was the ping-pong man and all the rest were strumming. If Carli Byer heard you were off beat, he would hit you on your hand, *bah-daow*! The fellas got tired of that kind of enforcement and broke off and formed a band without his presence. Then, there was Eddie Boom from Sunland, a band he helped form. He never beat a pan but showed up for every Carnival, having been in charge of everything. He told every man what to play and really enforced order in the band.

There was Mastifé from Tunapuna. He lived five to six years in town then lived in Tunapuna. He had a girl living in John John near the Tokyo band. He made Tokyo get into trouble sometimes. One Christmas day, they were beating pan and decided to go down to the south east. In those days, not many people had cars. This guy came by in a car with a canvas top and wanted to drive through the band. Mastifé, who was half-drunk, jumped onto the car to stop him from crashing through the band. Well, the man drove off and returned with police who arrested and locked up some people.

About Mastifé, he wasn't an enforcer of this particular band, but he was what they called a devil, a *saga* boy from Red Army. He could stick-fight and *wine* a lot. He had what they called a *jook-waist*. He was one of the men who took up *jook-waist* and when he was at a dance, a whole crowd would gather around with him in the center *jooking* his waist like crazy. Mastifé was popular around Red Army's time, during the Yankee days. As a *saga* boy, he looked like a Spaniard—curly haired, good-looking, and very strong. When Mastifé arrived in town, that was it! They even had a calypso on him. Even though he was from Tunapuna, he was accepted in all the panyards because he was an overall badman who operated at a different level from the *bad-johns*.

Another bit of information that is not well-known today is that a member of our band, Rising Sun, was the ex-commissioner of police—Randolph Burroughs. In those days, there was no commissioner of police; in fact, he wasn't even a policeman yet. When I heard he'd joined the police force, I learned he'd joined as a driver. His rise was meteoric! But I knew him as a member of Rising Sun when he was a doo-doop, rhythm player. With him was a guy named Leo "Bams" Bailey who used to work on the railway as a coker. He worked nights and every morning he and Burroughs came into the yard. Every panyard long time [in the past] had a breadfruit tree. Under the tree you boiled your breadfruit and saltfish—they call it codfish here—while burning your pan. They came every morning for their breadfruit and saltfish for breakfast. Though Burroughs used to live in Tunapuna, he came to Belmont for his "Rising Sun" breakfast. At one time after the war [WW II], every band had a tattoo. I never took one because I wasn't really a true member. Rising Sun's tattoo was the sun, and both Burroughs and Bailey had one.

During his time, I think the riots had already begun to diminish, so I can't say he did much in that regard. When he came into his position, cricket was the emphasis and the Black Power Movement was starting up. He became famous by tracking down the guerillas living in the hills. In his law enforcement days, there were individual bad men to deal with, not the collective riotings of the early days of Pan.

Racial and Ethnic Diversity

A lot of other individuals also made a lot of contributions to the movement, and we don't talk much about them—Indians, Chinese, and Whites.

Jit Samaroo is well-known.[17] His story is waiting to be told.

Then, there was Dudley Rouff, an Indian who was Tokyo captain from the '40s till the '60s, when he left and came here to the States. He was a conscientious steelbandsman, even though he didn't beat pan. A very quiet man. Once, they lost a competition and his father threw out all the pans—he used to keep all the pans in his father's yard. The father couldn't tolerate that the band lost and threw out all the pans. Also, in every band there was an Indian.

Indian Patrick Thomas, a former member of the Savoys, helped to build the stands. Ralph "Pablo" Springer, a member of North Stars and Cynthia's brother, was the first one to come up with the idea for wheels for the bass. He was a turner and Patrick was a fitter. Ralph suggested it to Anthony Williams who agreed and Patrick helped him. Patrick has a Christian name, which one day caused him to have to prove to the police he was really Patrick Thomas. Many Indians, like

Patrick, have Christian names and so when their names are mentioned in Pan you don't think they're Indian. It's only now the Indians are bringing their chutney flavor into the culture. Before time, Pan was a Trinidadian thing. "All ah we is one" marked everybody's attitude. Back then, the people were together as one. So, in every Belmont area there were Tambi, Sampath, and "Guppee"—Indian things.

Let's not forget Bobby Mohammed from San Fernando who used to arrange for Renegades but was from Cavaliers. Cavaliers has won some Panoramas.

Among the Chinese—no pure Chinese—were Hugh Loy and Kim Loy Wong. People referred to as "Jap" [Japanese] were really Chinese. Once they were a little mixed, we called them Jap, but they were really Chinese.

Then, we had plenty *douglas*, too, those mixed with Indian and African, like me. My mother was a dougla and father an African. Anthony Williams was a *dougla*, too. Trinidad has a whole lot of mixtures. Ellie Mannette would be considered mixed, too.

Among the Whites were Curtis Pierre, who I already mentioned, and Junior Pouchet. Those are just some of the names. There were many more Whites than the few names I mentioned.

Everybody made some contribution in his own time and in his own way.

Exile and a View on Pan's Growth

I came to the United States for economical and personal reasons. The circumstances that led to my emigration, however, had to do with being president of the Postmen's Union, an interesting set of circumstances that are unrelated to Steelband. Suffice it to say that as the president of the Post Office Workers' Union (POWU), I stuck my neck out doing what I could to help improve conditions for postal workers. For that, I drew much unwanted attention to myself that caused me to go to court to defend my innocence, then had to take drastic measures to keep myself safe, so when the opportunity came for me to emigrate, I took it.

Once I was in the United States, I continued to serve the community here. But adjusting to life in the States at that time wasn't easy. The year I arrived, 1969, wasn't the best time to come. The situation was somewhat perilous for Caribbean people. They used to call us from the Caribbean "monkey chasers." They'd say to us, "You come here from climbing your coconut trees. Go back to climbing your coconut trees." Any time we opened our mouths to speak and they heard our accent, they'd mutter the climbing-coconut-trees nonsense, which was the image created by the movies and the White people who organized that industry. So, African Americans couldn't see that we came with a drive, much less understand that drive, which was our desire to get somewhere.

In spite of everything, life has been good to me, on the whole. It would have been good to have received some recognition from Pan Trinbago in Trinidad, as well as from the Brooklyn Panorama organization because I assisted them. Before I left Trinidad, Arnim Smith was the only one who showed me any respect and appreciation for all I did—bicycling all over the place, walking sometimes.

Three years ago, I was down there and ran into Sterling Betancourt, who was recently knighted by the Queen. I was visiting the new Pan Trinbago office. The old one was burnt down and all the records destroyed. When I got there, the present president who I knew from long time [the past] since the '50s could only tell me he had no extra tickets for Panorama to spare. I had to tell him I didn't come for free tickets or to beg for favors. I came only to visit, since I was here for a short stay and wanted to say hello. All he could then find to say was how he was busy, and so on. I turned and walked out the office. So, I've got little to nothing at all from Pan Trinbago.[18] How quickly they forget what some of us did and now treat us with little to no respect. How hard can it be to be respectful? Brooklyn Panorama, at one time, never offered me a free ticket to Panorama. I've always bought my tickets for myself and Cynthia. I have since gotten a pioneer pass.

I've remained involved in many ways. In 1974, we started an organization called the National Association of Steelband, Carnival, and Festival, with myself as president, Kim Loy as vice president, and Ingrid Armstrong as secretary. So much has happened since then. Take, for instance, the current Panorama split, which I agree with,[19] because the Brooklyn Panorama organizers are full of self-seekers.

To go all the way back to '74, I know Clyde Henry very well, 'cause I helped him start his business. When they had bands on the Parkway [meaning, Eastern Parkway] for the first time, I brought out a steel band. That first time the bands came up the Parkway from Washington Avenue. The following year, Vincent Hernandez and I joined up. At first, we used to go to Pennsylvania to practice with John Gibbs. He was working as a chemist advisor with the Alcon Company, and he asked for the band to come. He had ideas, so I decided to go because I helped organize the band. Every Saturday we went down to Philadelphia, Pennsylvania, but were just playing and nothing else was happening, so I stopped. But Vincent remained with the side, while Gibbs tried to get a sponsor in Philadelphia. He had big plans, but I couldn't see with his plans and felt he was wasting time. Besides, I had a family to take care of and could be using every Saturday to make money right here. So, I stopped pursuing Pan business. Eventually, Gibbs himself returned to Brooklyn and got a position at Medgar Evers.

Later, they asked me to help the people who organized the Brooklyn Museum event, WIADCA, when they were beginning to organize. I did but noticed that they weren't dealing with the players and masqueraders. They were looking out only for themselves. I found that was wrong so I backed out. I decided to just bring out a band and get a steel band to play. I had a little band on Nostrand Avenue, and Vincent had a band that used to practice on Vernon Avenue. We decided to join together. He and I brought out that band, the first one, on the Parkway. That was either in '73 or '74.

In those days, we didn't have much mobility and we were promised a float from WIADCA. On that day, I personally saw about the Mas with plans to bring out a sailor band called "Under Sea Kingdom." When I went that morning, I learned that they weren't getting the amount of floats they were expecting. I realized that we had no wheels, and with our steel band on Vernon Avenue I had to figure out what to do.

While I was on Eastern Parkway, a Spanish guy in a truck pulling a float came by. I called out, "What's happening?!" He called back, "(Si!" I called out again, "What's happening?!" He said, "(Si, si, si!" and started to drive off. I said, "Follow me." I stole a float. I really did! I don't know who they brought that float for because they told me I couldn't get one. He followed me down Washington Avenue and straight to Vernon. There, we loaded the pans up and that's how we got our float. He was talking Spanish and I couldn't understand what he was saying, he couldn't understand me, so I made the most of that opportunity. Anyway, that was the last of my dealing with Pan. I decided to concentrate on my family and myself.

Pan today is not like yesterday. I had to spend a lot of my time trying to make peace among the men, and had to do that with my own money sometimes. Today, they have nothing like that to worry about and whatever money they make they're keeping for themselves. And, I don't enjoy the Parkway like I used to. I prefer J'ouvert. Before, you could look forward to meeting up on the Parkway with those you hadn't seen for a long time. Now, the crowd is so big that it doesn't have the same feeling to it. It's people from every where and you don't know who is who. J'ouvert has that old feeling because the crowd is more a Trini one and strictly steelband music. The Jamaicans were sort of vexed because of that, but they couldn't do anything about it. J'ouvert is Trinidadian Carnival culture and we want only pan. We have fifteen or sixteen bands lined up waiting to go up the Parkway, and all of them playing Mas, too. Big mas band with elaborate costumes. No DJ and Reggae music. They have the rest of the day for their music.

I've done my part and my satisfaction is that the Creator gave me the influence, the love, and the wherewithal to get things done. So far, I've come out of the whole thing unscathed. There's nothing wrong with me. I still have my good health and my mind's working pretty good. I am thankful to the Creator for all that. God has blessed me with my little piece of property and a nice, beautiful wife. My children are grown and healthy. I'm happy. I can still travel. Two weeks ago, I visited a friend in Miami. I'm planning to attend this year's Music Festival in Trinidad. I'm taking my wife and we're going and will enjoy ourselves.

Meanwhile, the Caribbean still continues to treat the pan with little respect. T&T government should have a special place for Pan at UWI, a special course just for Steelpan, its history, the inventors and innovators, everything. This is something that should have been done years ago. Take this new government who with UNC organized the national band. It's through the Indians that came about. It has taken so many years for them to accomplish just that, and the band is still not enjoying the status it's supposed to enjoy. If this is your national instrument and your national band is performing somewhere, they should have them set up like the police band. They should be practicing every day, reporting on time, and playing at the important events, just like the police band. The National Steel Band still doesn't have the same status as the police band. We need our own venue for performance. We need a place where people can go to learn music and enhance their music literacy.

Pan has a right to be more advanced than it is. It's only now that they see it's getting out of hand with the foreigners and outsiders looking to take over, they're trying to put forward some effort. But the government lacked the foresight to push pan the way Manley pushed Reggae, which, by the way, got started in Jamaica by a Trinidadian. Before Reggae, the Jamaicans were into Ska and this Trinidadian who was there working at one of their radio stations started playing this music, later called Reggae, on his guitar. Then it caught on and really took off with Bob Marley, and our Trinidadian boy's name is forgotten. I hope someone remembers it and will share. The Jamaicans know how to push what got started in their land. Not us. Our government still treats our culture with scant courtesy while mourning that we still don't have a place to teach Pan. The U.K. and the United States established pans in schools before we did in Trinidad. We had a right to have done this many years ago. We'd put forth a proposal to get a place in Cocorite called Copacabana as our center. We never got it. After my time, somebody gave them some land down in Chaguaramas and they're still trying to get it.[20] So, they're just mouth service.[21] They'll only try to do something when they see progress in places like Japan, which will lead the world in Pan R&D.

Why? Japan is more industrious in science and technology, and they're doing all kinds of research. Everybody knows the kind of people the Japanese are. Whatever you do, they can do a little bigger and better. Right now, they may be behind, but they're making slow and steady progress. Very soon now, Trinidad will be at crossroads because the oil drums they're accustomed to getting are outdated. The big companies, I understand, are using a type of plastic now. So, you have to have a special alloy and other special compositions for the pan. They're not using oil drums anymore, because steel is becoming hard to get. There's a firm here in the United States that is experimenting with sinking the pan and selling them to Trinidad so that when it gets there all Trinidad has to do is tune it. That company will make money. Add to that the possibility of closing markets for importing steel or pans or drums and Trinidad is in trouble. All their boasting about having invented this pan thing will mean nothing if plastic replaces steel. Places like Japan are experimenting, as I just said. I spoke with a guy who was there recently, and he said they're trying to get the right type of alloy that will last regardless of how much you beat it. A machine presses it to form the note and sound. If they perfect that process, they will have a light, household instrument that will be smaller. The need for tuners will decrease. That is the scary part of this R&D, to me.

As far as I can see, Trinidad will have to get away from the idea of this large band with so many people beating pan. They have to reduce to a smaller size band and even consider electrifying it. I think that will give more mobility. Pan as a novelty is wearing off. When it was a novelty, a large band with all those sets of drums to move around the place was good. But those days are gone. If they really want to make money, they have to consider all these things. We'll end up with players who stay with it just for the love of it but still can't make a living off this thing. I can already see that pan will become a household item, if these people are successful with their experiments. Families will be purchasing an entire set for their children to play, and that will come after Pan evolves further in the future. Why? Because children can't play a saxophone and some of those other instruments as easily as they can play pan.

America, as far as I know, is not doing anything major in R&D, not like Japan and Sweden who are way ahead of America. I think it's because a Black man invented it and then again it is an import. It wasn't invented here.

I really thought Black Americans would have responded to this better. I thought they would have picked up on this novelty and moved with it. They're so musically inclined, which is why I don't understand their aversion to Pan. Probably because they didn't create it, this is why they just keep away. The Whites, on the other hand, jumped on this thing. They were drawn to it a long time ago. So, we have problems on many levels.

I can only say that if the Japanese or Chinese really get the chance to take this thing over, look out. The Japanese are not making any big fanfare about what they're doing now. They're going about it the business-conscious way—keeping quiet about their thing until they're ready to release it on the larger market. That is what has me scared. We'll be buying our pans from (the Japanese). I can see that.

5
Pan's Arrival in the United States: Rudolph V. King's Story[1]

Some distinctions of the late Rudolph "Rudy" V. King *include: honorary member of the Music Union Local 802,* **2003**; *featured in article in* **2003** *New York Times;*[2] *Pan Ivory Steelband, Appreciation Award, November* **2002**; *West Indian American Development Carnival Association Inc., Appreciation Award,* **August 15, 2002**; *Cheryl Byron & Something Positive Inc., Youth Solo Pan Music Festival* **1999**, *Outstanding Pioneer Award* **1999**; *J'ouvert City International Inc., Certificate of Appreciation,* **September 5, 1995**; *Caribbean Research Center, Medgar Evers College, Appreciation Award,* **April 13, 1994**.

Pan's Many Influences

I was Rudolph Carter back in Trinidad. I used to go to school by that name and most of my friends knew me by that name. So if you say Rudy King, they wouldn't know who you're talking about. I came to this country under my mother's name, which was when I changed my name from Carter to King.

I first got into Pan in 1939 as a kid and was about nine or ten years old when I began experimenting with making my own pan. I can't remember the specific year. All I can remember is a song that came out at that time that went, "This is the story of a starry night, / Happiness, glory of a new delight...." That song was popular at the time and that's how I remember when I got started in Pan in Trinidad, by the songs that were popular at the time. But it's so long ago that I can't even remember the title of that song, too.

I remember as a kid seeing the bamboo band, which faded out because the war started. I believe the steel band started with the surrender of Germany. When news came of the surrender, everybody went wild and picked up anything and played. Everybody in Trinidad was beating a garbage can. Even American soldiers were beating garbage cans, too, and I believe they took part in the creation of Pan. I saw everyone celebrating with my own eyes, rejoicing over the surrender. So, I believe the whole transition from the bamboo band to the steel band came with the rejoicing over the surrender of Germany and the end of the war. Other people I've talked to said they also believe this was how the steel band started.

The rhythm of Pan came with the Africans, which they played on the bamboo and then on the garbage pan, biscuit tins, whatever they could find. But I don't understand why people want to go back to Africa to say the roots of Pan are found there. Some people claim that the first steel band came out of a bamboo band from Gonzalez and that has a ring of truth to it. The next bamboo band came out of Lacou Harpe. This was before Casablanca and Invaders and Desperados. It was everybody coming up with ideas—how to sink the drum, how to groove with the nail, and so on.

First, the pan had two notes. Then it went to three, four, five then seven notes. No one man did that. Everybody put in their little piece. I have talked with Neville Jules, a man I admired a lot when I was small, and he agrees that no one person started it. What I could recollect from that time is that no one man claimed to be the one who invented the steel band. How Winston "Spree" Simon fit into it, I'm not too sure, but I know he didn't invent Pan. I mean, he is dead and can't defend himself. But to be truthful, he and I were kids at the same time, of the same age. So, how could he invent pan if he was a boy when I was a boy? It was the older guys who did it.[3]

Carlton "Zigilee" Barrow has to get a lot of credit for Pan. He's the first man that I know of and was the best kettle drum player around. He died at about eighty-something years old. He was the most famous guy in Trinidad at the time I was going to school, although he was playing only two notes. If he was doing that at the time, where was Spree? Who can say who invented Pan? No one man can say that he invented Pan when it started with two notes. You can't play music with two notes. But you could play rhythm. Right? Later, guys like Spree came along and made improvements. So, he couldn't have picked up a drum and said, "I will sink this drum and make a pan." As they went along, they improved till they got a better sound. At one time, they didn't even burn the drum.

I can recall that when I started tuning I was attending Calvary Hill School, before I even attended Rosary RC School. As soon as school let out, I'd run down the hill and go by Hell Yard by the Piccadilly Street bridge and lean over the bridge and listen to what new song Hell Yard had. As soon as I heard what they were doing, I'd run back up the hill and do the same thing. So, we were all were copying from each other.

I grew up in the Quarry Street area. My band was called East Side Kids, a name Sonny Jones gave us from a Hollywood movie that had just come out. All of us were from Lacou Harpe: Kelvin Hart, "Pie," "Acco," Kim Loy Wong, and "Yankee Boy" were some of the kids in the band. Little kids who're all still alive today. We were the smallest of kids, little boys, who got started around the same time I started experimenting with pan-tuning and so our band wasn't recognized. Renegades was also started by boys and at first wasn't recognized. Renegades was in our area, too.

The first person I saw and admired playing pan was Zigilee, as I said before. But Zigilee, even though he was playing only two notes, he was the one who made Neville Jules get into Pan. I was listening to him [Zigilee] and seeing how famous he got, and this was before Spree. This is why I'm puzzled when I hear people say Spree Simon invented pan and spread other distorted versions of the history of Pan. Even some published works don't include the facts that I know myself, facts that date before 1949 when I left for the States. I can't say much about Pan in Trinidad after I left, but I know about Pan before that.

For instance, I took part in stealing drums, tin cans, washtubs, whatever we could find. If I passed and saw a wash tub, I reported it back to the guys. We'd wait until it was dark, and whether the owners had dogs or not, we were getting that pan. We used to jump over the coconut grove and steal drums. Now, there's this story I read in a book that the Americans came to Trinidad, and the base had all these empty drums, and the fellas didn't have any money to buy these drums, so they took these drums and began using them. I wished I knew where you could have got those drums at that time. The only band that used to get drums from the base was Invaders because they had connections. But we had to go and "thief" drums, as we used to say in Trinidad.

We used to go to the biscuit factory, because we used to play drums with our hands at that time, and biscuit tins were good for that. Those were the boom drums. So, we used to go down to the factory and help ourselves to what was on the sidewalk, tins full of biscuits. We took those drums, biscuits in them and all. We used to sell half of the biscuits, swear to God. After the biscuits tin ran out, we went after the Vaseline drums from a drugstore on Oxford Street. We used to take those drums, too, Vaseline in them or not. One time, we stole from Chacon Street a drum full of kerosene. The drum was heavy, quarter full of kerosene. About eight of us were taking turns carrying this drum when a police stopped us and asked where we got the drum from. We told him a man down the street gave it to us. He wanted to know who was the man and wanted us to take him to the man. Now, we were little boys and he couldn't run with us. We dropped the drum and went running down by the Dry River. And, that was it. Once we hit the Dry River, we knew the river and he couldn't catch us. An hour or two later, we returned for the drum. We did these things because we couldn't buy drums in those days, so we begged for and more often stole drums.

After all that trouble, when those big fellas saw us little guys with drums, they took them away. Once, we went down to the La Basse to get a drum we saw down there, near the Tokyo panyard. The Tokyo fellas saw us with the drums and called out, "Hey, where all yuh going with dat? Leave dat drum right dere!" We had to leave it. They were Tokyo fellas, and you didn't mess with them. They used to look wild. All that is a part of the history of Steelband.

This history of Pan is unbelievable, especially the amount of fighting. There used to be too much fighting, which I believe came from the guys called vagabonds, fellas called *bad-johns* who don't give a damn about anything, including Steelband. Those were the people who used to play pan, because it was easy to play the pan at that time. It was the one-stick pan, the ping-pong, which you used to hold in one hand and play with the other. Then came pan-around-the-neck, which you could play with two sticks. With two sticks, it got harder for them vagabonds, them dummies, to play the pan because they didn't know or care a thing about music. But even then they continued to influence Steelband and cause fighting.

For instance, while one fella would take a drink of rum and let the music, a kind of spiritual music, get into his soul, another fella under the influence of the rum would start a fight or a wild jump-up to the steel band music. But, on the whole, the steelband music had a calming effect on the men. So, I witnessed how the music and the rum made people wild but also calmed people down. And, when those fellas got wild, if you were in that band you'd better watch out, because it was bottle pelting and dodging fellas with cutlass. I even wrote a song about that once, and I think it was Nap Hepburn who sang it, "No More Fighting."

For a while, that sort of violence hindered the movement, I think. Some bands were trying to get famous by becoming the worst band in Trinidad. Everybody was afraid of Tokyo the most. They were from Behind the Bridge on St. Joseph Road, going toward the country [rural area]. I was most afraid of that band. We used to call it the "baddest" band around. The fellas in the band worked at the slaughter house and would cut you up in a minute. Those guys were *very* bad. Then, there was the Bar 20 band, which was respected, too, because a lot of criminals were in that band. There were also Casablanca, Rising Sun, Invaders, the top bands that were respected because those men were so bad. But, by far, the worst band of all at that time was Tokyo.

Bar 20 guys used to come to my band, East Side Kids, and take our pans. After they took my pan and gone, all I could do was sit down and cry. I couldn't fight or talk back to those bigger men. You know who you talking to? They were *bad-johns*: Audrey, Bitterman, and another *bad-john* who was Battasbee, his nickname. He wasn't a pan-player but nobody was messing with him or any of those *bad-johns*. You couldn't tell those guys a thing. They were killers, if you know what I'm talking about. Is a helluva story, this Pan story. I wished I'd paid more attention to what was going on back then. But we didn't know we were making history. All we knew was we wanted to play pan.

I used to cut those guys' hair, too: Zigilee, Battasbee, Bitterman, and Ossie from Casablanca. One day, I was pitching marble in the yard and Ossie came in for a haircut. He said, "Hey, I want ah hair cut." I said, "After this game." He said, "De game finish now. Go and get yuh tools." I had to go and get my tools, right away. When he sat down for the haircut he said, "Lemme tell yuh somet'ing, little one. If you cut me, I cut you back." I used to shave with a razor blade because I didn't have a razor to give them their mark. Then he continued, "And I want a long sheik" [side-burns], and the guy hair was growing only to the bottom of his ear lobe. Another guy who was there said, "Why yuh getting de little boy frighten, man? You can't have no long sheik. You ent have no hair there."

One time, the Invaders fellas did me something when I went to buy a netball. The guys from Bar 20 went and told everyone that the guys from Invaders hit me in the Savannah. When I got back they said, "Hey, come here. We hear they beat you up in the Savannah." I said, "Nah." They said, "We going with you tomorrow." I said, "No, no. Nobody ent beat me up." One guy spoke up, "Yes, I was there." You know, all those guys used to carry cutlass in their waists. So, the next day they came with me. We saw all the Invaders guys sitting around a house. When the Bar 20 guys showed up, I saw all of them scatter before I went and hide. Those guys pulled out their cutlass and I saw all the Invaders fellas run for so. I saw Ellie running like hell that day. I never told Ellie about that day, because I didn't know him in Trinidad. He was with the Invaders from Woodbrook and I was from up my side; and Ellie's older than me. I was a kid to them.

Steelband in the United States in the 1950s

Look at what we have today. We have people from different universities interested in this instrument, so we already know where this thing is going. All I can say is the steel drum is an itinerant instrument, and the movement is growing and hasn't arrived yet. How it will get to wherever it can get depends on you and me. People with vision can take steel drum to any height. I had my own vision when I came to the United States in 1949.

I didn't actually bring a drum. I had to find what I could to use. I didn't know of anywhere in Brooklyn to find drums and talked to a friend named Bertie Griffith. I shared with him my desire to make pan and so I needed drums. He knew of a guy who might be able to help, a caretaker of a place with abandoned drums. He promised to talk to him and did. A few days later, we got a car and went and picked up those drums.

Then, the problem was where I was going to make these drums. I was staying on Livonia Avenue with an aunt and decided to use the backyard. Those houses had a lot of windows. While I was sinking the drums, I made quite a lot of noise and somebody threw something out the window on me. I didn't know if it was water or pee; I'm (still) not too sure. I got a little sprinkle of it and decided to stop and go to the park at the corner of 123rd Street, Morningside Park. Bertie took me there. I was fixing a fire to burn the drum and so concerned with that that I didn't notice a police standing behind me. He asked what I was doing. I said I was making a pan. He said, "A pan?" I said, "Yes, a steel drum that you play music on." He said, "Well, it's against the law to burn a fire in the park." I said, "I didn't know it was the law to do this, because in my country we used to burn this thing in the park." He said, "But this is not your country." I said, "All right." Then, he asked me where I was from and I told him Trinidad. He wanted to know how long I had been here and I told him a few months. He said it looked like I didn't know better and gave me a break. That was the end of that but not my desire to make pan. I returned to my aunt's backyard and took whatever abuse necessary to make my pans.

Later, Clyde Holdip, from Casablanca, and I decided to make a band. We started this little band of about five to six guys: Clyde, Carl Williams, Bertie Griffith, Wallace "Shakespeare" Reid, and me. Those guys were here before me. They probably came here in '47 or '48. At the time they left, steelpan hadn't improved that much in Trinidad. So, when I came I showed them what we were doing, and it's on these latest pans we started to practice. We began by playing in little parties for free. Then after one party, I decided we needed money for transportation and charged twenty dollars for the whole band. That was nice, because it meant that we had started doing something. Then at the next party, I charged fifty dollars because it was in the Bronx and we needed two cars. After that, I got a gig for a boat ride. By this time, the band got bigger, about seven or eight guys playing. I got one hundred dollars for that gig. That was big! At that time, a train ride cost five cents; newspaper cost two cents. So, in those days, one hundred dollars was good!

After the boat ride, we got to play in a dance. At the dance, a delegate from the Musician Union came and stopped the band from playing. He asked if I had a contract to play there and I said no. He said I couldn't play without a contract and I told him I didn't know that. He gave me a break and warned me to never let him see us playing any where without a contract. After that gig, I went to join the Union. There, I was told that I couldn't join because the Union didn't know anything about this instrument. However, I was taken to meet the president of the Union because everyone was excited and saying, "Come and see this thing this guy has. A garbage can that he plays music on." The president finally approved and I joined the Union as a percussionist in 1950, the year I'm recorded as having joined, which is now on their computer so anyone can check that fact. Then, the other guys had to join the union, too. We were put on an installment plan to pay our membership dues, which we paid with the money we earned on gigs.

The band also played at the Apollo Theater on amateur night and came in second with another group. To my knowledge, years later a second band from Barbados also played at the Apollo. I don't know of any other band that played there.

Some time later, I got a call to go to a job by myself, to tour with a woman named Massie Patterson on a Calypso Carousel that first went north then south. We stopped in Texas, Ohio, all those different places. When I returned, I got another job without the band with Sam Manning in Chicago at the Blue Angel. I was there for a two-week option, and at the end of the two weeks Manning took me on for another eight weeks.

While there, this guy by the name of Mighty Charmer[4] came. We had a rehearsal during which time I was practicing. He also came out and practiced his solo. This guy used to get about three encores a night, and once in a while I got two because the people were so impressed with this steel drum. Then this guy's contract was up and he had to move on to some place else. But he decided that he was finished with this show business. He wasn't going to mess with it any more and was going to join the Muslims and invited me to come with him. I said all right but didn't go. I used to have a photo of him and me but lost it. I lost many photos of those early days in the States. After I closed there, after having done twelve weeks at the Blue Angel, I returned to New York. Years later, I recognized that the same Mighty Charmer was none other than Louis Farrakhan. I saw him one day on TV and recognized him. He was very good—could sing calypso and play a ukulele and the violin. Now, I sometimes wonder if I'd followed Farrakhan that maybe I would have been second to him.

I returned to the Blue Angel about three more times. I went with a group led by Sam Manning who'd formed a group of dancers. I learned a lot from him because he knew how to put shows together. Once, we played at the Edgewater Beach Hotel, a large hotel. At the time, everything was in black and white—the toilet doors were painted black for Black people and white for Whites. Then, you couldn't eat because they weren't serving you, with the signs marked, "No Niggers Allowed." All these things, it was a helluva experience, you know. Still, when we played at places, the people used to appreciate the group. But that's all you did. You played and then got out of there. After that stint, when I returned home I formed a band named Tropican (officially named Tropicana), which used to be called at first "the Trinidad band that grew."

When the Labor Day parade began in Harlem, we joined it.[5] Much later came the Panorama competition, and I won the first two Panoramas. This was during the '60s. During the '70s, I started going to Myrtle Beach, South Carolina, at the Hilton Hotel. I played down there for about ten years every summer. Then, I went to Hilton Head. I kept on going and then returned to Brooklyn and concentrated on making drums. I eventually decided to get out of the band because it got too expensive—to go on the road, to build the racks for the pans—it was emptying my pockets. I decided to join a small group.

The Tropican band changed its name to Moods after I left, a band that still exists. Regardless of the name change, call it Tropican or Moods, this is the oldest steel band in this country. Moods didn't compete in the last two Panoramas, but the band still exists.

My involvement in Pan continued with Despers USA. All this time, I continued to and still make and tune pans.

Naming One's Invention: It's More than an Image

I really don't like the idea of referring to the instrument as a pan and prefer to call it a drum, steel drum. You have a frying pan and a bed pan, and these are pans. But this is an instrument. We have the second pan: but what is a second pan? What is a double second pan? What do these names mean? The men figured that this pan followed that pan, and so they call them a first pan and second pan. They don't have a third pan or fourth pan, but they have a four-pan section.

If you go in a strange place and say, "I'm a pan-player but I forget my pan home," and somebody responds, "I got a pan," and goes and brings a frying pan and says, "You're a pan-player, then play this," then what? I believe it was a pan in the early days when if you were a pan-player you were a nobody. After people started to appreciate the music as coming from *the* pan, then they changed the name. But it is still an instrument that was outlawed as a pan. The people who used to go by the name pan-players in those days had to go through a lot, so I really don't like to hear people call it a pan. I wish that somebody would put a name to it and give it some respect, any other name but pan.

All other instruments have a name: saxophone, xylophone, and all the other instruments. Those made from wood are not called a wood flute. This is why I say that this instrument doesn't have a name because nobody changed it from pan. And, that name might remain forever. Regardless of what we decide to call this instrument, which is headed for mass production because it's being played all over the world in Africa, Sweden, and Germany, this instrument is getting more attention than any other.

We get call backs to play a second and third time. If people didn't like us, they wouldn't have us. And, I don't have a problem with playing according to the terms of my contract. If it is a concert or dance, we prepare accordingly.

Some groups are versatile. In our band, we include singing. Some pan-players do only calypso, and when they do, they sing somebody else's song. But you have to do your own thing. Make your own music. Make your own song, so you can show how this instrument can play any type of music.

I agree with the argument that people can take steel drum to any height. But what pan-players must understand is they have to be prepared for the future. It looks like Trinidad pan-players are only interested in what Trinidad did in the past, what happened in Trinidad. If you're living in the States, we have to get into how things are done here. In this regard, it looks like the older heads are pushing the movement more than the young people, because we are trying to have a direction of our own and not follow others. If you keep following, then the same thing will be repeated all the time. So, you have to change your direction and go your way, and this is what I want to do. I want to show people that we can do our own thing and make our own music, instead of listening to a record of some song somebody else composed, taking take that song and putting it on a tape, a CD, and saying, "This is my record." That's not original. People want to see this thing go places? Get original. Get as creative as the man who brought this thing into existence. The young people only copying what we older ones did. Where's their originality?

I mean, the older heads tried to lift pan a little higher, while if you tell the younger players come and let us back up some singers, they tell you they're pan-players. But if you're a musician, you have to show yourself as a musician. Don't criticize by saying, "We ain't doing this. We don't want to do this because that's not what they're doing in Trinidad." A lot of these guys all they're doing is patterning themselves after Trinidad. Not me. I want to do my own thing, so when the public hears me, they will hear something different. I'm not saying don't play a Shadow song from Trinidad, a Sparrow song. But understand that Sparrow and Shadow are doing their own thing.

And, by the way, it's time for Sparrow to hire a steel band to back him up. I've never seen Sparrow perform with a steel band. He could make things better for the steel drum player. He's leaving Trinidad and hiring musicians. Hire a steel band. Surely, he can do that. It's our own people who are keeping back the thing, too. All this goes to the debate regarding where the movement is going.

I went to a show in the Trinidad Consul and this question was asked, where Pan was headed. I find it doesn't make sense for them to try to see where Pan is going, when we all know that these White folks from Sweden are playing pan as good as those guys in Trinidad. How did Pan get to Sweden? This means somebody had to take it there, and we're not talking about just going around the corner. These places—Sweden, Germany, Africa—are not just around the corner from Trinidad.

Then, there's the question regarding the image of pan. Based on my experience, I believe that the people who hire the band helped to set the image. For instance, I went to Canada with a guy who'd called me one night and asked me to go with him that very night. I didn't know the fella and he was giving me my first and last notice to go with him. He came at twelve o'clock to get me for the trip. I'd never heard the guy sing, see him do a thing. On the way, I asked him what songs we'll be doing. He said mostly Harry Belafonte songs. I said all right because I was familiar with those songs. When we got there, he told me we were doing first "Scarlet Ribbon." But "Scarlet Ribbon" is not a calypso, yet I had to work with him. He also sang "Day-O." The songs he selected were one thing. The way he sang them was another, which was not calypso-style. The guy was very good with a very nice voice, but he was too dead and the colors he was dressed in were drab. The manager of the club said, "You're all closing tonight." The guy replied, "We just opened." The manager said, "You're closing tonight." I was so embarrassed, eh. I told the manager, "Listen, I came up here for two weeks and I haven't made one night yet and you're closing us out of the show." He said, "You all are not doing calypso and you all don't look like calypso people." I was dressed festive. But the guy was dressed in black with a black scarf, black shoes, black tie, and black shirt. So, the manager didn't think we looked like Calypso. I asked him to give us until the next night. He agreed to give us the following night to see what we could do. I took the guy downtown shopping right there in Canada. We bought him a flowered shirt and a straw hat, and that night when we appeared, the manager was excited. He said, "Now you'll look like Calypso." He then allowed us to finish the two weeks.

To emphasize my point: let's go back to the Blue Angel gigs. One night, a Russian whose name was Fadouly (I'm not sure how it's spelled) was there. Also there were Menovitch and Boris. Fadouly told me a new show was coming and he offered to keep me with it. He mentioned that it was the Mighty Panther, who I had heard of. The night the Mighty Panther appeared to do the show, he came out dressed in a flannel suit and bow-tie. The manager blew up. "Man, you're a calypso singer dressed like that?! You come here to do opera in this place? No. You have to look like a calypso-man now." Depending on what kind of show it is, if you're playing the steel drum and dressed in bow-tie and so on, you're out of character if the people want to see you in a floral shirt, bright colors. That was what they hired you for because that was their expectation. The Mexicans and Spanish people perform in the bright bolero shirts, and whatnot, according to that traditional performance. So, when people expected to see you in bright, colorful clothes, that's what you gave. That was one image.

Now, if you go to Carnegie Hall and the occasion calls for more formal attire, you'd be out of character if you showed up in bright, flowered shirts. Obviously. I don't have a problem with dressing formally and playing pan. I have pictures of myself in all sorts of outfits. I was in a tuxedo because the occasion called for us to wear tuxedos. I have other pictures of us dressed according to the various characters we were required to play. The point I'm making is to give the people what they want in order to get that job, to get the band to go places, to get those call-backs. If you didn't dress how they wanted, you were not going to get called back. You didn't fit that description of what they expected. I know some people from Trinidad who wouldn't do Harry Belafonte songs. If I went along with that I wouldn't have got work. It was a business. True, some images fit some stereotypes. But when you're looking for work, for money, damn the stereotype! We did what we must.

These issues used to bother me. I still don't like to see a band looking like the members are out of place. I remember once at the Renaissance this guy, a very good pan player, all day he was walking around in suit and tie. The night the band was to play he came in wearing a flowered shirt to play with the band, while the rest of the band was wearing suit. They told him, "We gave you a tie to wear with your white shirt. Why you didn't wear it?" He said, "All day I walking around wearing that, I didn't feel like wearing tie tonight." But he was looking different, like he didn't belong to the band.

Another time was when we were at Myrtle Beach. Every time we appeared, the people applauded. Sometimes we wore white pants, other times black shirt, sometimes flowered shirt. It all depended on the day. But every day we wore a different outfit, which was nice, because we were always clean-looking and fitting the character. I know of some guys when you tell them we're going on a gig, they come with sneakers or any old thing. I can't go for that.

On the Issue of Music Literacy

Music literacy is still to come. You see, a lot of the guys are getting into reading the music. This means it is better for the band, in that it can save a lot of time which is a good thing. A good example is this. The bands for Panorama start practicing say two or three months ahead of time. But what they practice tonight they forget tomorrow night because they have the music stored in their head and not on paper. With reading the music, it wouldn't take two to three months to get ready for Panorama. All they have to do is have some dress rehearsals closer to Panorama. With the sheet music, people could practice on their own and then come together for a mere three to four days. We know that some musicians go into the studio today, see that sheet music for the first time, and play what's on that sheet. But because the fellas have to memorize the music, it takes them much longer to get it. In the future, people will take only two or three days to learn a Panorama song. So, learning to read the music will save time, and reading music is the right way. I know some people say they could listen to any song and play it, so they don't need any music. But the literacy is still important.

That's the opportunity the young people have today. The older people are going out of the business and they don't need music sheets. Some of them can retain things really well. But those of the younger generation who don't care about learning to read music will find themselves at a disadvantage. It's up to the individual, too. My suggestion is for today's young people to learn to read music. Ignorance will say don't learn to read music. We have a lot of that talk among the older heads, and we can't change them. Some of them if you say you want to take them on a gig and ask them if they know "Yellow Bird," they will say they don't play that. But if they want to go out and make money, they will have to learn to play "Yellow Bird." If they stay home, how are they going to make money? And, if they could read music, it would take them a matter of a few days to learn it. So, if you could read the music, you could learn to play any song, go out and play it, collect your money, and go back home. Right? This goes to the argument of giving people what they want, whether it is "Yellow Bird" or "Mary Anne" or another very old song. And, don't make them have to ask you two or three times, which is not good for business. Don't make them wait too long either, which also is not good for business. My advice is: give people what they want and get it done in as little time as necessary. That's what we should be looking at in the future of Steeldrum. We're competing with the world.

I remember working for this guy Art Delougoff (I don't know how that named is spelled either—all these names) who used to run the Village Gate. Every weekend, we used to do Carnegie Hall, the small hall, and share the door. Whatever we made at the door, we split it, after expenses. I got some new guys from Trinidad in the band and these guys changed the whole band. They wanted to practice only Shadow's songs. The night we were playing the agent came by wanting to know what was wrong with the band. I said, "Nothing," and wanted to know if the band sounded better. He said no, it sounded worse. I told him I had better players now. He said the band didn't sound the way it used to because he was not hearing the songs we were supposed to play. The guys didn't want to play "Mary Anne" and "Yellow Bird." They wanted to play like in Trinidad. But the agent who hired me didn't want to hear that music. They wanted to hear what they knew. So, what could I do?

To further make this point, take these popular bands here in the States. When you go to hear them play, what are they playing? Look at James Brown, for example. He's playing all the songs he did from way back. If he doesn't play certain songs that people come to hear, that they familiar with, that they could follow and sing along, he would lose his popularity. And, that's not just James Brown; that's the musical field I'm talking about. You have to remember that the American crowd is different from the Trinidadian crowd. Trinidad people will say, "Why he playing dem same ole songs?" Here, it's different and if you want your band working, you have to give the people what they want, what they like. Mikey [Enoch][6] got three hundred dollars one day from one man who wanted him to play "Jamaica Farewell" and two other songs the man wanted to hear. If Mikey said he wasn't playing them, he'd have lost three hundred dollars right there. People are willing to pay to hear what they like. This thing is a business, too. If they want to hear Jazz, Indian music, Chinese music, any type of music on this instrument, pan-players must be able to play, and play well, not just shadow good players in the band who know what they're doing. Some players can play Jazz beautifully on the pan, which is great. Some people limit themselves to only Calypso, which could hurt them. If you only want to limit yourself to playing certain things, then you're not versatile.

I agree that if you asked say James Brown, for example, to sing a calypso, he may not sing it like a calypsonian from Trinidad. He will put it in his own way and do it, as a musician. My point is the musician will get the job done. The versatile musician will get any job done.

See Victor Brady. He's a guy who doesn't like White people but will play White people music. When you hear him play, you want to know how he doesn't like White people but is only their music he's playing. He can't play calypso, you know. But if you hear him play classical music, you'll be amazed. I say, be versatile and don't limit yourself. Know your instrument and know how to play it well.

A Pan-Steeldrum Lover and Proud

My life has been Steeldrum, the thing I love. These days, I love making mementoes of Pan. About seven to eight years ago, I made the clock-drum for a friend. It stopped working and he brought it back for me to fix. It simply needed replacement batteries. But I wanted to change the whole outlook before returning it to him and never did. I have it here for about two years now. What I'm planning to do is something else. I'm planning to make another one with the map of Trinidad, a map-drum. I make miniature drum-trophies for Panorama. A lot of people order them. They take a lot of time to make, more time to make than the regular size drums because of their small notes. I began making these about ten years ago. They play, too.

I consider myself as a pan-lover. As far as I can remember, this occupies my time without any pressure. We live in a world with so much stress and we have to have something to fall back on. A lot of people my age don't want to have anything to do with Pan. These are people who used to play pan and stopped. As far as being relaxed in my mind, I can sit here with this drum and mess with it, and forget all about what else is going on around me. I forget that I don't have money; I forget that I don't have a wife; but I got this. Something to lean on. A lot of people go crazy because they have nothing to lean on. They worry and lose their mind. They get nervous and die from heart failure. This takes away all that for me.

I have a friend named Alston Jack (also an arranger and song writer) who teaches women over forty years old. They have a band. Some of them as old as sixty and seventy years and playing pan. They've been on TV. I believe that he is helping these women. Before that, they thought they were old and life was over for them. Now, he says they're full of life. So, this instrument is playing a good part in many people's lives. It gives people something to look forward to. Some people don't have that, or else the only thing they look forward to is going to church. But church is only Sundays, man. What are they doing during the week? You have to have something to share in this life. When you get to my age, you need more than all the bad news you hear on radio and TV that could make you feel like life is over. This thing gives you a spark, an energy.

Steelband has taken me many places and allowed me to do a lot of things. In addition to being recognized as a percussionist, I'm a limbo dancer, fire-eater, bottle dancer, and mini-pan maker. While a workman is worthy of his hire, I never became wealthy in this business. I never tried to get rich in this thing. My satisfaction came, still comes, from doing something I love. I'm satisfied to have seen Steelband improve, gone from tin cans to chromed pans that cost an arm and a leg, a pound and a crown, as they used to say back home. Some prices are too steep, like Ellie Mannette's. Those high prices in the long run are only hurting the business. But it's good to see how pans are chromed now. I always liked to have my pans look nice. I take my miniature pans to New Jersey to be chromed. Chroming is an expensive process. But I always took pride in how my pans looked, always wanted them to be clean and attractive. I've always felt I could do something more to make it look like an instrument, instead of just using paint. I don't claim that I was the first one to chrome my pans because I don't know if anyone was doing that before me when I started in the '60s.

This brings me to the controversy about who did what first. This thing didn't even used to be a matter, but now it is. So, I want to state clearly that I don't know if I was the first one to start a steel band in the United States, because I don't know if someone else had a band during the early '50s when I first started my band. Like in Trinidad, people everywhere were doing things that other people didn't know anything about. What I know is when I started my first band, and that was in 1950. I have lots of memories of my life in Steelband, lots of good memories.

In Memoriam

Rudolph "Rudy" V. King died March 18, 2004. He was born September 1, 1930. His memorial service on March 22, 2004, held at the Woodward-Thompson Chapels in Brooklyn, New York, brought hundreds of people who came to honor a man who leaves behind a rich legacy in Steelband. He leaves to cherish his life and work: his mother, Carol King-Walling; sister, Elva Lewis; daughters, Estrellita and Shelly; son, Rudolph; four grandsons; and a host of nieces, nephews, relatives, and friends.

6

You Only Die Once: A Vignette by Desmond Bravo[1]

The late Desmond Bravo *was a former soldier of the West Indian Regiment who served in El Alemain, Egypt, during World War II. An ex-police officer of Willow Grove, Pennsylvania,* Bravo *was a former member of Casablanca and was an iron-man of Pan Stars (now Pantastic), Philadelphia, Pennsylvania.*

I was born in Sangre Grande, Trinidad, on May 22, 1922, and from there moved to Belmont when I was eight. I grew up in Belmont. I also lived in Toco. I joined a steel band at age twelve. The first steel band I knew was Rising Sun in Belmont. Nap Hepburn, the calypsonian from Belmont, was involved in it. He was one of the headmen. Jack, Otto Reds, and Dudley Smith (one of the leading kettle men at the time) also were some of the early men. Some other men were Patrick "Mickey Roonie" Moore, Albert Thompson, and Felix Pan.

I joined the army in '41, served overseas with the West Indian Regiment, and returned home in '45.

I didn't get back into Steelband until '47 when I joined Casablanca Steel Band (referred to as 'Blanca). They originated in Gonzales, moved to Argyle Street, then to Observatory Street. The band had one of the leading tenor men at the time named "Patsy" Haynes. The arranger was Arthur Decoteau, and another tenor man was Leon Bentick. The leader of 'Blanca was Oscar Pile (who has died), and then there was "Barong" and "Zoro"—the more or less founders of Casablanca. I remained with 'Blanca until I married and later came to the United States in 1958. As one of the leading bands in Trinidad, anywhere you went people knew Casablanca. One year, we played "The Bells of St. Mary" and won Panorama, with Patsy Haynes leading the tenors.

I think that same year Invaders played "In a Monastery Garden." Pan Am North Stars later came back and took the cake when they played "Poets and Peasants." Winnifred Atwell was the band's conductor. We have to give that lady credit; she was very good. Anthony [Williams] was the best arranger and tuner. I have as a souvenir here one of his original pans, which I'll never part with. He and Elliott Mannette were the best tuners those days. Tony lived in St. James. He's very sick now; everybody knows that. He's one the government could have done a whole lot more for. He was a very, very quiet man, he and Bertie Marshall. Quiet men who did a lot but never did any thing to draw attention to themselves. Bertie knows pan and is very, very good.

Another very, very good player is Boogsie Sharp. About ten years ago when I visited [Trinidad], I saw him. I used to put him on a soap-box in Benary Street to beat pan. Now, he is a big man with beard and all. He said to me, "Ah bigger than you now, you know." None of them pass me straight and still like to heckle me, always have something nice to say to me. All of them were little boys to me. I admire them when I go down to Trinidad. The same Nap Hepburn, the calypsonian, I met him in Duke Street; he was with Terror. They said, "You ent getting bigger, you ent getting smaller." I said, "I going remain the same and you *kyar* do me nutten, you know." Nap said, "Since you come from America, give me a beer, nah." I said, "Give you a what?" I have a nice time whenever I visit.

When I first came here, I joined with Pops McCarthy. He had a band in New York, called Harlem All Stars. At that time, calypsonian Melody's "Mama, Look a Boo-Boo" calypso was reigning in Brooklyn. They were selling T-shirts celebrating Calypso, and that sort of thing.

When Sparrow performed a night in Carnegie Hall, there were about sixty people, and we made a big show about it. I even remember the tune that I got down on my knees and played on three tenor pans. Conrad Mojé was the captain of the band and arranged "Love Me Tender" calypso-style. I remained with them and was one of the first guys to play pan at Carnegie Hall with Pops McCarthy, Rudy King (now of Despers USA), Mojé, Hughey, and some other guys I can't remember now. Sparrow was performing. At that performance, we danced a limbo. I was the guy to dance a limbo with Sparrow on the stage. This was in 1958.

One event happened at the Apollo Theater when we played there. I had to slap a boy who came talking fresh to me because I had just come from the islands. I didn't care who he was. You don't talk to me like that, so I slapped him, Frankie Lyman. I swear; they would have deported me for that. He and I became somewhat friendly after that.

Rudy King also got into a little trouble, though not at the same time. He was accused of something he didn't do, and eventually whatever charges they brought against him were dropped. We used to call him Goatee Face. He and I were good friends, too, and I had just gone back to Trinidad for a short visit when the news came. I was shocked and refused to believe any thing they said about him. Not him. So, I was glad when the thing was resolved and his name cleared. It cost him a lot, a lot. When I came back and we saw each other, we were glad that it was with good news.

I returned to Trinidad in '60 and rejoined the Regiment who'd called me back. The Black Power movement came up while I was there, and that affected all of us. I think we have to thank Dr. Williams. A little before the nonsense started, he got the different merchants to represent a band and promoted sponsorship: Old Oak, Neal & Massy, Trinco, and so on. Band sponsorship was also being managed by the association, and if any band interfered with another band the association threw the trouble-making band out of the association. Getting thrown out meant that band lost face and was misrepresenting the company that sponsored it. So, when the Black Power movement came along, I think panmen behaved themselves because they didn't want to lose sponsorship. Too much was at stake: purchasing pans, uniforms, traveling, and so on.

I think the association helped to reduce the violence among the bands, too; Carib Tokyo, Desperadoes, and all the bands started behaving. Things in Steelband started to get much better and go better for the men. I think Dr. Williams helped play a part in that and we have to give him his due praise. He liked Tokyo, so that everybody in Laventille voted for PNM.

I remained in Trinidad for ten years and while there was in Casablanca with my cousins and nephews. One-Man, his nickname, was running the band at the time with Chandler. Patsy Haynes came back, too, and we all were there. Once the Black Power uprising died down, I came back to the States.

I didn't get back into Steelband again until '73 here in Philadelphia. I met one or two of the guys—Rick who had a little band asked me to join them. I stuck around but kept an eye on Harlem All Stars, which to me was more committed to what they were doing. Harlem All Stars got started the Labor Day parade, which is now this big event in Brooklyn.

That event started in Harlem with just that one band involved, along with the New York Fire Department (NYFD). I think it used to be called the NYFD parade. This was in '61 or '62. The event moved to Brooklyn because the NYFD would allow only one steel band to participate. The relocation occurred maybe in '66 or '67. All the old boys were still involved. Then Pops McCarthy got killed one Saturday night in a dance in Harlem and I decided to stay away from Harlem and Brooklyn, to stick to Philadelphia. I usually go back every Labor Day and meet the old guys.

The men living in Philadelphia decided about ten years ago to start a band named Philly Ville. It got started with Ossie, Wayne Mattack, "Friction," and Daniel. I joined later and we went pretty good. We traveled to New York and made our history on Labor Day, with everybody hearing us for the first time. People wanted to know what band we were. We were swinging. But then, like the usual story in Steelband, things began to go astray. This one went this way and that one went that way. Then, Ken started his own band. Philly Ville remained and I stuck with them for a while. Rick had his own band. So, in this area we had two bands.

In the '80s, "Dinks" and Ken said, "Look, it's time for us to get together and form a band to represent Philadelphia." I thought it was a good idea and we decided to join up with Philly Ville. Things went well for a while and then there was a falling out and a split of the band. Same *ole* story.

Some time after that, one night Pompey Bishop, who used to lead Tokyo at one time, Brian, and others of us formed Pan Stars. The first place we played was in Camden and from then it was no turning back. We're about ten in size. One girl, a former Invaders player named Tricia, is with us. Then, we have Tony who used to play for Jamboree; he's our leading tenor-man. Brian is from Tokyo; he was their treasurer and used to play the treble pan and still plays it with us. One of the double-second players, Dinks, used to play with Ebonites from Morvant. Another is from Solo Harmonites. I am the only one from Casablanca Steel Band. I was a noted Casablanca man from the rebel days.

"Pompey" is still with us. He had decided to go back to the time when they used to play pan around the neck and brought out here the first Pan-Around-the-Neck steel band. The band is unique. I don't play pan anymore and play the congas. I used to play the tenor pan and still have my tenor pan from home with the T&T flag embossed on the front. I play tunes for the old folks living in this building. At Christmas-time, they have me play downstairs in the community room. Sometimes one person will join in with a chac-chac and another with something else. It's all fun, really good fun, and something for me to amuse myself in these later years of my life.

The Rebel Days

I never made or tune pan. The most I ever did was a little pounding and marking. They told me what to do: how to mark and burn the pan. But I couldn't take that noise, sitting down there whole day and night with that hammer. I really couldn't take that kind of noise. That was for Rudolph Charles and all those guys who went up Gonzales Hill to do that. Later, I didn't have the patience to learn tunes and decided that I was good with iron, so I became the leading iron-man of the rhythm section. That's what I'm doing in our band right now, too. I hit, *one-two-three*, and the music starts. Practice and performance don't get started without me.

I always loved Pan since growing up in Belmont. My cousin, Felix, was a second-pan man. My parents didn't encourage me in Pan and wanted me to leave it alone. I used to run away during evening time and go and listen to the band. During the day, as soon as my mother left the house I was in the panyard. But it was when I left the Rising Sun band and joined Casablanca and met all those other young fellas involved in this rioting affair that I truly began to love this [being in Steelband]. I'm not going to pretend with you. I loved the rioting.

Tokyo and Casablanca were always at war. Invaders and 'Blanca were always at war, too. The only steel band during that time that kept out of it was the Free French, the only band with four bugles. You could hear and know from a distance when they were coming up the road. We used to say, "Here come the Free French men." They had the girls wearing jerseys and the boys in their berets. That was a unique band; it was sweet enough. The other rioting bands were Desperadoes and later on T&TEC Power Stars from St. James. Pan Am North Stars with Winnifred Atwell—ivory and steel—was a very good band. Then, there was Five Graves to Cairo. But Red Army was the band where I got into trouble.

One day, I met up with them. They held me and started to beat me when I pulled out a blade and cut from left to right. I didn't make prison but cost the family a lot of money. My big brother put a licking on me for that. He's the only one I took licks from. I got a name from that running with Red Army. Afterward, everybody called me Little One. I was always sharp, clean as a whistle, well dressed and looking my best. My appearance also caused trouble with All Stars. We used to go and hang around them and all the girls used to admire me, always clean and tidy. "All yuh look at Little One: looking so good." When the girls left All Stars and came over to Casablanca, their boyfriends didn't like that. They started pelting bottle, and whatnot, at us. And me? I wasn't running any where.

Once, three guys cornered me on Goat Street. I decided that before they half-killed me I would take them out first. I cut each of them. That was when my reputation started to grow. Another time when there was a Coney Island near the Savannah by the Princes building, they cornered me there again and I had to protect myself. The boys didn't know what was going on then. It seemed like it was a long time before Ossie Campbell, the strongman of Casablanca, Zoro, and those fellas came up the road and saved me that night from those guys.

'Blanca [Casablanca] was a band that people used to love. When we came down the road the tune we used to play was, "Tell them we ent *fraid* / Tell them we ent *fraid* / Because we young, we strong, and we brave." People used to leave and come running. It was fame for us.

Crossfire was another trouble band from St. James. We had a little riot with them once, too, for the same nonsense over girls. Eventually, I became friends with the Crossfire boys. I married a girl from St. James and when the kids were born I moved to St. James. Then, everybody in 'James got to know me. By that time, things were beginning to quiet down, too, and I joined with Crossfire. One night, Crossfire was coming up the street, with my wife and cousins in the band. I had got the wire that any band coming from the west was going to get a beating from Tokyo. It was around nine o'clock that Tuesday night and we were coming up to Las' Lap when we saw people coming running saying, "Fight! Fight! They beating all St. James people." I saw 'Blanca coming up Charlotte Street and took over saying, "Nobody coming in this band."

That night, everybody was bareback. We had the children in the front, ladies in the back, and men in front and behind. Protectors in front of the band, protectors at the back of the band, and the band going up the road. I had put a lot of people from St. James into our band, down to my cousin-in-law and all. The captain of Tripoli, the real captain back then, the founder of Tripoli—his name is Joe Crick and he's living right across the street from here—I hid in our band. Tokyo men might have killed him that night. They all had to take off their shirt or jersey with their Tripoli name on it. They couldn't show they were in Tripoli at all. We went straight up Charlotte Street, pass the hospital, made a left onto Queen Street and headed back to St. James. Our side didn't go to St. James. After sending Tripoli on to St. James, the rest of us went around and back up Park Street. That side met up with Renegades, which was from Belmont.

What was happening that night had started with two fellas, one of them from Sun Valley, another trouble band. The thing started that Carnival Monday when they came to town and caused a lot of problems with some kind of robbery. I can't remember the names of the six Blackhead brothers from the other band—two have died—who were plenty bigger than me. I was never scared of them or cared for them either. I lived with the attitude: only once man had to die. This was why they were intimidated, sort of scared of me. I wasn't afraid to die. I use to tell them up front, "If you ent *fraid* to die, I ent *fraid* either." I thank God I never got cut. I got stabbed in my back but never cut. Fellas didn't use to take any chances with me.

There was a guy called Carli Byer who threatened my family. He lived in Brathwaite Street and was with Invaders. I got up one morning about five o'clock, wrapped a nice little cutlass, and went and sat on his step and waited for him. He lived on a big barrack yard. He came out and went to the pipe in the yard, scrubbing his mouth [brushing his teeth]. When he looked around, he saw me. I hadn't even touched him, didn't even tell him a word, and the boy started to bawl, "Oh gawd! Murder!" I coolly got up and walked through the yard, and still didn't touch him. Afterward, people couldn't stop laughing and saying, "Desmond, yuh good yuh know. What yuh went in de yard for?" And I saying, "I went for a drink ah water." They saying, "Buh you ent living there."

What was so funny was Carli used to stammer. He would go, "Wh-wh-you-you go-go," and stuff. And people would go, "What you mean, 'Wh-wh-you-you go-go?'" Then, he would want to knock them down. He couldn't take that fatigue [teasing] at all. So, when Carli saw me and started to bawl, his mother and everybody come running outside to see what going on. I was walking out the gate with him saying, "L-l-look, he-he go-go-goin'." And, I didn't run. I just walked out the gate, real cool. Afterward, he and I became friends. Whenever 'Blanca passed by, he would ask, "Yu-yu-yuh all right?" I would say, "I good."

Goldteeth was another *bad-john* from Casablanca. He came to America and got killed. Got stabbed. They lied and said that was not the cause of his death, but I know he got stabbed.

Gangs came out of steel bands. Like Marabonters. They were from Grenada. Those men came over on schooners and mostly worked on the wharves. Some of these men joined Tokyo. I think, in fact, half of Tokyo people were Grenadians.

They were very hardworking and weren't afraid of anybody. This was another cause of the riots. Fellas from St. James and Belmont couldn't let them Grenadians make them look bad.

One big incident that made the papers was concerning Elliot. I don't recall the year it happened though. They used to call Elliott Barracuda back then, not his pan but him. I know because one of Ellie's sister and my brother were together. He and I never had anything [any trouble], though we were from rival steel bands, except for once. His brother, Birdie, they also used to call him Pablo, was the cutter-man for Invaders. He made prison—a big incident that made the papers—and came out and we became very good friends. He and my son were very good friends, too. Eventually, all of us became very good friends. This is some real history of this thing, straight from the horse's mouth.

A lot of families made some painful sacrifices for Steelband. Some of these sacrifices out of respect I remain discreet about. But this much I can say. I know what I'm saying and not saying. Ellie is from Toco. I'm from Toco. I am one of the guys who painted the lighthouse in Toco. I was in my teens then. So, I knew about the Mannettes, the Stuarts, and all those families from Toco. Nuff [enough] said.

All of us started with nothing. Alexander Ragtime Band, starting off in Woodbrook, had just one pan, a Bermudez biscuit drum, iron, and other things. That was the same way for Casablanca and all bands at that time. Winston Spree from Tokyo, the first man to beat "Mary Had a Little Lamb" on a pan, started off with nothing. The leading kettle-drum man from Rising Sun, Dudley Smith—I think he went to Miami and formed a little side there—started off the same way. Bagga Hillary—he's living now in St. Thomas and wants me to come down there—is another one. But I like it here.

I still do push-ups to keep myself in shape. I like being a good example to the young people now, and they like having me around them. Some of the women still want to dance with me, too. I'm having a good time at this time of my life, especially with Pan Stars. We have a lot of gigs coming up. Our band is not like other bands. We have all pans. That is what people like about us. All the players are very good, including Tricia, the only woman to play with us. Her grandfather was one of the leading Tripoli tenor-men, Manuel Camps. He is still a very, very good player. I'm enjoying life, still, and live good with people. Those rebel days are long behind me. I'm living now to laugh and love people. What else is there to life?

Author's note: I later met with the members of Pan Stars (now Pantastic) at their rehearsal site at Cobbs Creek Parkway, Philadelphia. The following is a summary of my animated discussion with these second-generation panmen: Rondell "Pompey" Bishop, Neil "Fat-man" Dodds, Lee-jah, Clarence "Dinks" Mundy, Brian Raymond, Red Man, Terro, and Wendell. Also present were Rena, secretary, and visitors Diane, Bravo's granddaughter and great-granddaughter Destiny.

One point of discussion was the men's perspective on the persistent stereotypes that dog people who come from the John John area, despite the fact that John John people have made excellent contributions to society in various leadership positions. They complained that society generally has been reluctant to give John John people the credit due to them, sometimes going so far as punishing those who tried to help them; consequently, some people have lost their jobs.

In concurrence, I shared with them that Chan LeePow, with whom I had spoken the week before, said he was reprimanded for helping with a bank loan Winston Bruce, a.k.a. Dr. Rat (later known as Docile Rat), a former Renegades *badjohn*. The bank manager was upset with LeePow for granting Bruce the loan, which he claimed was reserved for more deserving clients. The event occurred in the '70s. They knew Dr. Rat, who died earlier this year in 2003, but not LeePow.

We also discussed the history of Steelband, which served to reinforce the necessity for an accurate chronology of Steelband's evolution. Even they, born in the cradle of the movement, held to conflicting and wrong versions of Pan's origination by maintaining that Invaders and Tokyo are the two oldest steel bands in the world. When I pointed that Mannette himself narrates he was inspired to begin Oval Boys, Invaders' precursor, by Alexander Ragtime Band, they conceded that we have to get to the bottom of the truth, one that emphasizes that the bands adopted their new names from Hollywood movies, which was one of the causes of Steelband violence.

In concurrence with the objective to pursue the truth, Dinks, an older band member, claimed he learned from his uncles in Pan that the violence perpetuated in these movies was a major contributing factor to the men's behavior. He pointed out that prior to the movies the men had a great degree of respect and acceptance of each other. However, they turned to the increased level violence to copy the western cowboys and other gangs portrayed in the movies, having adopted the names for their steel bands accordingly. Except for bands such as All Stars and others who adopted names that identified with a different perspective, the majority of band-members mindlessly followed the nonsense portrayed in these movies.

Dinks eloquently recalled for his younger fellow musicians those days when, "Come Ash Wednesday, you couldn't even hum a calypso. From then until Christmas, you couldn't enjoy your calypso. That was the typical colonial thing. We had to fight to change all that." He continued, "What at first we didn't realize was this was our culture. Eventually, we did and decided to put a stop to the nonsense, all the violence we picked up from the Hollywood movies. We had to get back to respecting what was ours. With the slow progress, we also had to fight real hard to get the church to accept Pan as not the devil's instrument." Dinks continued that he was referring to the historical devaluation of all things African, and the fact that Indian drumming was never outlawed hence never historically disrespected.

Addressing me directly, he continued, "You probably know about when they outlawed the drum in Trinidad. Again, it was the colonials who did that. So, it was one battle after the next we had to fight and win. We met with negativity up, down, left, right, and sideways. We have a very colorful history, and look how now this thing gone world-wide...."

In Memoriam

Desmond Bravo died on August 10, 2004. One of his sons, Michael, reports that a one-week wake was held in his honor, which concluded with a steel band playing at Soca Village, Philadelphia. Almost four hundred people packed the funeral-home to pay tribute to a man most dearly loved. A part of his obituary included the following from a poem written by one of his grandsons, Jeremiah: "The life is done / but the legend lives on / ... Pick up your drum sticks in hand / Play from the heavens / Send your music down for us / For you are the steelpan man." Upon conclusion, another steel band played again in his honor.

All of Bravo's seven children survive him: sons Terry, Danny Gabriel, Michael, Dennis, and Walter; and daughters Rosanna and Laura. He is further fondly remembered by all his children-in-law, grand and great-grandchildren, nieces and nephews, relatives, and friends.

7

Law Enforcement on Carnival Day: Randolph Babb's Story[1]

Randolph "Rannie" Babb *is one of the founding panmen of Hill Sixty, for which Andrew "Pan" de la Bastide tuned; former police superintendent and one of the first police officer to head of Trinidad and Tobago's Narcotics Division of the Criminal Investigation Department (CID).*

Babb *is currently co-chairman of the Steelband Committee for the West Indian American Day Carnival Association (WIADCA), 1998 to present.*

Early Beginnings of Hill Sixty

I was born in East Dry River or Behind the Bridge, that place recognized as home of the underprivileged and oppressed. In truth, a bridge crossed the river from PoS to the other side. That other side was called Behind the Bridge. I was born on Clifton Hill in 1928, the second son of Prince Edward Babb, a soldier, a tradesman, and a community worker.

Long time [in the past], a little boy growing up in an area like that was under the strict supervision of his parents. Some parents kept their children so strict that these children couldn't even come out on the street to play. They could only look out the window at the other children playing. Other people who lived in the neighborhood also kept a strict eye on us children, and we respected them so much we could not afford to do anything wrong for them to see. They would have berated us for it. Unlike now. Kids today would stand there and curse out grown-ups for trying to correct them. We couldn't do that. We would get licks both places, from the grown-ups and then our parents. That's where I was born and grew up, with people who had two things in common: they tried to live a decent life and bring up their children in the proper way; and they tried to keep out of trouble. But, as usual, and you know how people are; some people moved into the area and people looked up to them as martyrs and clung to them. As a result of that kind of favoring, some people were spoiled and some were saved. Like Mr. Jones here, we were lucky. He and I are among those who were saved. I was older than he was, but we both went to school around the same time. The children of the strict parents tended to go to the same school.

I attended Piccadilly School. The other boys' schools were Nelson Street, Market School, Richmond Street, and Tranquility: that's as far as we could have gone if we didn't win a scholarship or our parents couldn't afford to send us to college.

While growing up, I started to play sports and get involved in other activities. There were some big men who lived on St. Paul Street, Rodney Street, and Clifton Street. Right where those three streets met, those men used to play tamboo-bamboo, lard pan, and kettle pan. As little boys, we would stop and watch these men, listen to their certain rhythm. The way they played encouraged anybody to stop and look and listen to these men playing these things. So, while going to school, these men's activities attracted us.

These men were also producing Mas.

More and more, I couldn't help myself from wanting to copy what these men were doing. It wasn't before long that I started playing the kettle. The big fellas then got interested and began calling me to play with them. They probably favored me, too, because I had a god-brother who ran the band. He was nicknamed Topi, a brown-skinned guy. You know how we used to look up to those guys with color. So, Topi being there with them could have helped.

Some time shortly after I started playing the kettle, I began hearing about Spree Simon and his side who was from John John, which they later called Tokyo. They started something for the young fellas and I felt I should be with them. I went across to their side [of the Hill], but their behavior was not in accordance with my upbringing. So, I left them and returned to my side and was there when we decided to form a band on the Hill. All this time, I didn't know that a similar thing was happening in other areas of the country.

Living in our area was Andrew de la Bastide. His mother used to live on Reservoir Hill. His sister became Calypso Princess and wife of Lord Blakie, and his brother became calypsonian All Rounder. A musical family, strong in the culture. One day, we were where Reservoir and Clifton Hills meet, he suggested that we form a band. We were small and didn't quite know what that meant. But Pachai [or Patcheye], his real name was Fitzroy Henry Pachot,[2] said to us, "You know what? I will get the instruments." You know the biscuit drum that biscuits were sold in? A round drum with a hole? He meant that. Another guy nicknamed Mummee said, "I will produce the tune boom." That was the same as the doo-

doop. To me, he was the first person to produce this pan. I'm not saying he was the first but that to me he was the first. There were also paint pans, about four to five inches in diameter.

One day, while the fellas were sitting rhyming and trying to sing calypso, Andrew brought this pan and started hitting it on different sides. When we were finished, he left it there and went home. Another evening, he came with this pan. It wasn't cut. He had a piece of stick, no rubber, and said, "All yuh hear dis." Every side he hit was a different note. But we couldn't have made out whatnot was what.

Around this time, we began to hear about Neville Jules also experimenting doing the same thing. Jules must have heard about Andrew, too. Jules used to live across on Laventille Hill. We didn't pay Jules any attention though.

One day, Andrew came across to our hill and said, "All yuh listen to dis," and he played three distinct notes on his pan. He left and returned later, and this time he said, "Ah got somethin', yuh know. Listen." This time he played five notes. Distinct as ever. Well, this news spread so far that people started coming to the Hill to see what was going on. It then looked like people left and went to experiment.

All this time, I didn't know too much about Ellie Mannette.

The next step in the process was the cutting of the paint tin and pushing the inside upward. In that way, the boys could hold it in one hand and beat it with the other with a stick. Shortly after, the Ray brothers came on the scene. After them came Theo Pachot, Pachai's brother. The seven of us formed this band, for which Andrew made about three pans for us. Later, Pachai became the manager and architect of all plans; Andrew was the musician, technician, master, and teacher; and I maintained the discipline. But when we first started, it was with *jooking* at these pans, with Andrew directing us on what to do, which is how he became our musical director. He used to go home and experiment on the pan and come back the next day and tell us what to do. One day, he said, "All yuh know something? I put another note on this pan and I got a part of the 'Bugle Call,'" and he played it for us. Another fella named Jones was a very good bugler and living not too far from where we were heard us and came over. He said, "Y'all don't know the other part of the Call?" We said, "No." He was instrumental in teaching us the other part of the Call. All this could have been happening in the early '40s, before the war. I will tell you about another development.

We started to play these pans and people got interested, but others complained that it was too much noise. John Slater was living in the area, too, a very good panman. One day, he came over and joined us. We used to practice in

Pachai's yard. Ellie Mannette, Jules, Spree and all these fellas heard what was happening and came to see what was going on. So, for them to say Spree invented pan, that couldn't be true. Andrew helped Spree build and tune his pan.

Before V-E Day, we used to celebrate Discovery Day. Prior to Discovery Day, every area that had a steel band organized used to print T-shirts in bright colors to outdo each other and parade with whatever instruments they had, which, of course, was just in the embryonic stage of the instrument. By this time, some bands already had five or six notes on their pans. Some bands were playing "Mary Had a Little Lamb." Our band was also learning to play this tune, too. We had buglers in our band who helped us with rhythm. 'Cause, we didn't have the cello pan, the guitar pan, the five-bass, and all that sort of thing yet. Our bass was the biscuit drum, and Pachai was one of the best player of this drum.

You could say that's how we started to develop the area with pan. From then on, we started going to the lard factory near to Gaiety Theatre in St. Joseph Road for pans. Gaiety Theatre was a prominent theater in Behind the Bridge.

Around that same time, Ellie Mannette, a smart man, sank the pan and increased the number of notes to seven. Following that, Andrew one day was at home playing "When Your Body Lie Down in the Grave" and didn't know his mother was listening attentively. When he was finished, she called him and said, "Son, I was against the pan. But having heard you play this, you now have my permission to play pan all the time." He came back to us with that news, and that was when we truly began to practice diligently.

Desperadoes wasn't the powerful band at the time. They used to come across to listen to us. They weren't in that community spirit yet. Jules's band of little fellas used to be called Bad Behaviour, at the time. [See Jules's story for the correct name of his band.] He was a young fella then and had to beckon [answer] to the big fellas. So, the bands we had were from Charlotte Street, John John, Clifton Hill, and Woodbrook.

What we started to do was: in the night we formed bands that beat pan and went over the Hill. We went over the Hill to get away from the police who used to run us down and take away our pans. This really caused the people in the community to suffer because we used to empty their garbage cans and use them to make new instruments. We became like a thorn in the side to some. We were doing all this in preparation for Discovery Day when we brought out our bands. Our first breakthrough was on V-E Day.

When we heard the war was finished, it was Mas. Different bands that had advanced in their trek of pan came out. Bands from the west, east, south—Arima and other places weren't involved in Pan yet—hit the streets. The bands came from PoS and San Fernando. San Fernando had their own thing going, too, because since they were close to the oil fields they made their pans from the empty oil drums. We weren't getting pans from that source yet. So, Mas on the days celebrating the end of the war included a masquerade of bands and the street bands with the best ones beating pans.

Bands had begun giving themselves names from various movies, and we called ourselves Hill Sixty without even knowing what that name meant. We didn't realize that our name was after a graveyard in England. Not until much later. But we didn't bother with that and kept the name. I was a leading tenor panman, and we had the Ray brothers who I mentioned before. We also had a tuner who with Andrew used to tune our pans.

Pan progressed from seven to nine notes. Our band began playing at various competitions and sometimes clashed with other bands at these competitions. Some of these competitions would have five bands. We learned "God Bless America" for when we competed. We drilled that tune into our heads. But all this time, we didn't take these competitions too seriously. We were happier just knowing we could play our instruments. We loved the art form.

V-J Day is when all hell broke loose. Bands playing tunes came out around that time. Full tunes. Bands came from Belmont—"Patsy" Haynes's Casablanca, Betancourt's band—all these fellas and their bands came out and played full tunes.

Meanwhile, these bands started to treat us like outcasts because they felt that with us coming from Behind the Bridge we didn't have much. But we had very sweet pan from Behind the Bridge.

Now, St. Paul Street used to bring out a mas band called "Hit the Deck," a sailor band. That Mas band wanted Hill Sixty to play for them on the road. After we decided to become a part of the Mas band, we changed the name of our band to Chicago. I suggested the name, which was a ship (I think a battleship), and we became known as Chicago Hill Sixty.

Alternate Perspective on the Cause of the Violence

A lot of other things started to happen, too. Infringements of band upon band led to fights among the men with people getting seriously hurt, and so on. We, the younger ones, who weren't violent or being violent decided we didn't want any part in that violence. Of course, some bands kept entirely to themselves, but then there were those warrior ones: Tokyo, Casablanca, Despers, and some bands from the west that had some bad fellas. But these bad fellas were not the ones playing pan. They were followers and the ones making trouble, while we panmen were playing really nice music.

When the fighting started escalating, my uncle, who is now deceased, said to me, "Fella, I am seeing that you are heading for problems. It's either you look for a good job—you just come out of school—or you leave your father's place." Leave my father's place? I looked at him. I had a great respect for him so I didn't say anything back to him. One day, he came by for us to talk. He asked, "You want to join the police service?" He asked me this when we young Trinidadians and Tobagonians didn't want to have anything to do with the police service because the nucleus of the police service was foreigners: Bajans, Antiguans, and all these people. That was work for small-island people.

I think around the same time Mr. Jones and his consorts had formed an association that the idea of TASPO grew out of, the search for the best panmen to go away [travel abroad]. We were always practicing, and when people came up the Hill and heard us, they used to ask who I was and I got to know they had their eye on me. But I remembered my uncle's words that this pan thing was leading me into trouble. I decided then instead to join the police service, because when TASPO was finished I wouldn't be getting anything more from that. I also wanted to be able to get something from being in the police service. Now, I wonder what the end results of my getting involved in TASPO would have been.

I had my own instrument and by that time I was living at Alexander Place. Next to me was another stalwart called Winthrop who didn't know anything about pan at that time but used to listen to me playing my pan in my gallery. When I was about to join the police service, he asked me, "Can you give me your pan?" I said, "All right." I felt that joining the service meant my pan career was finished. I gave him that pan and from there he went on to become a top musician. I can't think of his first name, but he went on to become well-known. This was a pan made by Andrew who made pans for our band.

I want to jump over a few years into the future. As anyone knows, after you've been in something for a while when you leave it you miss it, for a time. We had a man in our company [circle of friends] named Le Gendre who was working at the government printery. Now, tourism was one of the focal, money-making industries in Trinidad. The tourist industry wanted to promote the steel band as the first innovation of its kind in the world in order to bring people to the island to see this attraction. The industry then began to promote the sponsoring of bands. Some time later, they decided to write this book to this end. This book I'm talking about was eventually published in 1973, *Steelband in Perspective*. This was before Goddard. I assisted Goddard with his book, which fails to include many facts about the movement. He makes only a passing reference to Mr. Jones here, and much of what has been written about the movement has not included the truth. Mr. Jones and I are not upset that we have been slighted. We're more upset that the truth has been [obfuscated]. We experienced these stages of growth in the movement that people have so far [glossed over], and we stand unequivocally by what we say.

Going back, as a result of the decision to use Steelband to boost the tourism industry, we had to do something if anything was to come of Steelband. We realized that the fighting amongst ourselves must stop, come to an end. As a police then, I knew what was going on on both sides and worked with Mr. Barnes, a top police officer, to help bands stop rioting. Barnes was the one who helped stopped the warfare between Tokyo and Despers. According to Mr. Jones, he was one of the guys who came to the association to ask to help stop the riot between Laventille, Desperadoes, and Tokyo. I was one of the guys who was nominated to work with a contingent of policemen under Mr. Barnes to see how we could quell the violence and bring love among the panmen. Of course, that wasn't any fly-by-night attempt. Eventually, we got the violence to cease to a point, and during the time of peace Mr. Barnes died. We took it over from there and then began a new upsurge of violence. San Juan All Stars, some very tough fellas, started rioting in PoS: this was a very bad section of Tokyo. They came into town and made a lot of trouble.

We had a program and a project that before every Carnival we would go into the yards with the bad fellas and search the place for weapons. That incentive, the knowledge that the police was on to them, eventually helped to curb the violence. There still used to be some fracas, though. The last big riot I can remember took place one Carnival at the Queen's Park Savannah because of false rumor. That was in '69. Black Power came in around that time and was taking effect on how the men were behaving, too. As I was saying, a false rumor caused that riot. Word got around that a man was trampled on the tarmac leading up to the stage. A police officer on horseback was supposed to have done that. They went on to say that the man got beaten up, and so on. But none of it was true. The insurgent crowd turned and bore down on the officer who discharged a round into the air. That caused the whole thing. A lot of people got injured. I was working on Charlotte and Duke Streets when the crowd started bearing down on that area.

My partner, Vernon Headley who's deceased now, wanted to run. I said to him, "Where you're running going? You don't even know what is happening." So, we stood there and watched the crowd capsize all the vending carts of the roadside vendors who set up their business for Carnival. Then, we got word that the crowd was dispersed. We inquired about what really happened and learned the truth. A lot of people were placed under arrest for starting the riot and for rioting, for disturbing the peace. But they didn't receive any heavy penalty. Some were charged and some sent to prison and then released. But after that, there wasn't anymore rioting.

Certain people began to get more involved. Pan Trinbago came out of the steelband association that Mr. Jones and others had kept going. The point I want to make here is that a lot of people were instrumental in quelling, and eventually, stopping the violence. Some people opened avenues for panmen who could then begin to display their talent. These opportunities helped the men turn their attention more to Pan and where it could go.

The men generally needed some guidelines, and once they got them through the association then things began to improve. Those who didn't ended up in prison, which meant the end of their career. Finished. The men didn't want that. So, one of the things that happened to stop the violence was the association. Mr. Jones will tell you that when he took over the association in '59, the panmen expected to be in control of things.

I was in and out of Steelband while working with the police and seeing how things changed. I became a police officer in 1953 to '54. I was one of the officers responsible for routing all the bands. As a matter of fact, if we knew Tokyo was coming down one street and that Despers was coming down a road where they were bound to meet up and clash, we would re-route Despers to another street and let Tokyo through so they would not collide. So, no one could say the police was responsible. Why would we do that? That would mean more work for us. The police would have accidentally routed one band onto the same street as another, but when that happened it was due to human error.

Some people think that the presence of the police was the cause of the violence. That is troubling to me. It's true that early on the police used to seize the pans. But when the men organized, that is what they wanted stopped. They didn't want every time they made a pan the police would come along and take it away. Eventually, the seizing of pans stopped.

There also used to be meetings at the police headquarters. All the steel bands used to be invited, especially the bands from around PoS. Band representatives used to go to headquarters and tell the police what they wanted, and so on. The representatives had to sign up names stating who was in charge of the bands, and whatnot. According to Mr. Jones, in 1960, the association printed flags, white cotton flags with a logo with a pan inscribed onto it. The same logo was on their letterhead. To avoid clashing, each band that was a member of the association was given a flag. So when one band passed another band and saw the flag, the men knew that band was a member of the association. Member bands then knew to keep the peace on Carnival days.

You see, a lot of people believe that everything bad was because of Steelband. But a majority of times when things happened they were caused by the followers, as I mentioned before. In fact, I won an award from the Council of Arts (run by Les Slater), about three to four years ago. I was invited to present a talk on Steelband and *Bad-johnism* and honored for being a part of the police team that worked with panmen to improve things for them. This was one venture that Dr. Williams pushed because he was trying to make things better for panmen. Anyhow, this talk was to clear up misconceptions that panmen were *bad-johns* who caused the violence, which is not true. The followers caused the violence. They weren't beating any pan. They lived in your area, jumped up in your band, and made trouble. They had a grievance with someone else in another area, because most of those fellas were *bad-johns* who weren't studying pan but were gambling, then coming on Carnival day to jump in a band, looking to get back at and do something to someone. Most of the times, that's how the trouble went down. So, it wasn't really panmen themselves but the bands' followers who used to get involved in trouble or make the trouble.

The then Prime Minister Dr. Eric Williams who had visited different areas and introduced certain things for the steel band, like schools, helped make progress. That was a result of the association's doing. When he came into power and these things were going on, his presence in different areas helped to make a difference. Like the 1973 Chaguaramas Convention Centre event where he introduced the courses for panmen, who hailed the event as the Emancipation of the Panman. Like his visits to various bands such as Blue Diamonds and Trinidad Tripoli. However, Jones and I disagree on Dr. Williams's contributions. He remembers that it was Inspector Barnes who came to that meeting with Tokyo, Marabonters, and Desperadoes to help make peace.

To get back to the early days of Pan, Le Gendre in his book points out that Hill Sixty was one of the pioneers of the Steelband movement in the early 1930s, not the late 1930s as some people say. And, I can tell you that this is true. Andrew who played "When Your Body Lie Down in the Grave" was one of the first panmen to play a complete melody on pan, called at that time the ping-pong. [*Note*: de la Bastide played this melody during the early '40s, prior to the war, as this narrator previously mentioned.] This is something the pundits on Pan don't know and so don't talk about. But I was there and could tell you what Le Gendre says about Pan is true. Andrew was one of the old pioneers. I'm preserving Le Gendre's *Steelband in Perspective* as a part of the true record of the Steelband movement.

Another of Andrew's first is that he was the first person to teach a woman pan. Norma Callender was the first female to learn to play the ping-pong. She mastered it under Andrew, not Ellie, who probably didn't even know she learned to play pan. So, Le Gendre is right about that, too. She's living right here in Brooklyn, New York. Had a stroke recently and is recovering from it, so she has hibernated herself from people.

All that time, the Clifton Hill residents were astonished at the sounds coming from the pan, and the word spread that Andrew's ping-pong was talking.

It's so much that has happened in Steelband. Let me draw your attention to another fact. Ten members of Hill Sixty traveled in 1958 to California, a trip organized by Ranny Phillips who also organized the first competition in the stadium. At the end of the trip, Pachai was the only one who returned to Trinidad. All the rest remained in California, including Andrew. He died there last year but was buried in Trinidad, which is good.

Respect People and Get the Story Right

Before retiring from the police force, I went away on a scholarship to England. I stayed at a guy nicknamed Baby Jones. He used to be a member of Hill Sixty and retired to England. He became one of the top pan-tuners in England. While I was there, after he left for work I would play one of his pans and it came back to me. They built a pan with about fifty-something notes—they soldered the drum to make it into a pan—and I realized that I still had the thing in me for Pan. After that, I think, is when someone made the pan in the circle of fourths and fifths and standardized the tenor pan.

A friend of mine who had a band, his name is St. Louis, every time I visited Trinidad I would visit him to hear the band. One day, he asked me, "You want to try your hand?" I said, "Boy, I stop beating pan so long, I don't know." He said, "Try your hand." The first thing I looked for on the pan was the scale: Do, Re, Mi, Fa, So, La, Ti, Do. Once you find the scale on a pan, you're on your way. If you can't find the scale on that pan, you can't beat a tune. He gave a pan to me and that's the pan I brought to New York. I practiced a lot to return to my level of perfection and when I returned to Trinidad I found that I was missing something. I went to the factory and bought another pan and kept it in Trinidad. In that way, I was playing on two different types of pan. From that, I started using written music to enhance the playing, and that's where I am now.

One of the reasons I won't return to a band is because of the discipline. I do not want anyone to disrespect me because I'm not going to disrespect anyone. Nobody. I go around to the different bands and see how these kids behave. I can't take that. I will give them some ideas if they want me to. Just the other day, I played somewhere and afterward the fellas came up to me quarreling with me to come back and play with the band. No. Not me. It's not like long time [in the past]. When a captain of a band said, "You can't do that," you bowed your head. You would not cuss the captain. You couldn't do that. He would drop you from the side [pan-side] immediately. You were out. When as a member of Hill Sixty, I was responsible for the discipline in the band, for the road-side part of the band, and the men didn't talk back to me. That's what I'm used to. It was that same sense of discipline I took with me into the police force.

As a police officer, I was the first man in charge of narcotics at the CID Headquarters and narcotics experts. That time the drugs were marijuana, the barbiturates and amphetamines. Today, coke and heroin are destroying the youth. I was in the force for twenty-eight years. While I was in the service, I got my first scholarship to the States to see how the anti-drugs innovation programs were running. I also went to Canada and England to see their programs, too. They were always surprised to see how much we in the Caribbean knew about drugs. That was around '64 to '65.

After that, I received a scholarship to John Jay College to do criminology then return home. Instead, I started attending a law program at a law school in England but stopped because my wife died, and when I returned I had some conflicts with Immigration. With the conflicts and the death of my wife, I lost interest. Up to recently, I received a letter requesting my interest in completing the program. After all this time.

I came to the States in '85, shortly after my wife's death, and settled here.

Mr. Jones and I go back a long way. Usually, when people come to me for information on Steelband I'm skeptical. Too many people have come looking for information and after giving them what I knew they turned around and said something else. A lot of things already published about Steelpan and steelbandsmen have not been nice to read. You understand? As I said before, a lot of trouble in steel bands was caused not by panmen but by the bands' followers. Then, the panmen got blamed for it. Only one steel band I know of had *bad-johns* beating pan: Red Army. Eventually, they faded so that even that image was gone. So, the real panmen were not *saga* boys or *bad-johns* or anything else they say about panmen. The followers were responsible for much of the trouble that reflected on panmen. Mastifé was a Red Army man, and even he wasn't beating pan. All the other *bad-johns* were in Red Army, and I don't think they were beating pan either. So, when I read all those things about panmen it does hurt me. People should make sure and get the story right.

When Jones explained what you were doing, I then decided to give it one more try. I hope this time somebody gets it right. If I can be of any further assistance, feel free to call me. This art, we are quickly losing it. Some of us are not paying enough attention to the greatest musical invention of the twentieth century. It came from us, and now we're losing it.

One of the things I've been trying to do for the longest while is to form a pioneer steel orchestra. Bring together all the pioneers, but that is so hard to come about because a lot of these men have lost all interest. Of course, when you are a musician you don't really lose interest in music. I saw a show here the other night that had some of the old stalwarts playing pan. If all we old fellas could come together and form a symphony orchestra, that would be a good thing. A pioneer band would show people where we came from and where we are today. This is a part of the history. This is what we still can contribute to the community.

It's a shame that some of us have to worry only about the money aspect of this thing because today you can't get by without money. But we started off doing this thing for the sheer love of it, the art of it. You heard about the university courses that they've now started for young tuners? That idea began with Williams. He used to work with Rudolph Charles a lot then. Mr. Jones will tell you that Trinidad still doesn't have a place, if, say a professor from England visits Trinidad to learn about Pan he can go to a museum. I think that's what Pan Trinbago is now working on to put together. They have a lot of researchers working hard to pull all this together. They're making some progress

I hope that now we are beginning to get the whole story of Pan. But there's more, too, in regard to Steelband and Calypso and the presence of women in the movement. You really need to talk to some women. Find out about the days when calypsonians sang in Bamboo tents, later called Calypso Tent; about Calypso Princess, Andrew Pan's sister and his brother All Rounder who were singing in the '60s into the '70s. Princess and Lord Blakie were not the first husband-and-wife calypso team. There were Lord and Lady Iere from San Fernando. They were the first husband-wife team I know of. But talk to some women....

Author's note: Our conversation concluded with Babb's view on what was occurring in regard to Brooklyn Panorama 2003. The event was scheduled to take place at the parking lot of the Brooklyn Museum, with the prior split being mended. Babb reported that the two groups—United States Steel Band Association (USSBA) and WIADCA—have put aside their differences and come to a compromise in the interest of introducing and promoting Steelband programs in schools. The leaders were working with District 17, where many students who are already members of steel bands attend schools, and with the New York City's Board of Education toward realizing this goal.

The organization also planned to award Michael "Mikey" Enoch posthumously for his contributions to Steelband. Enoch, a former tuner for Despers USA, died in September 2002.

8

Toward a New and Different Triangular Trade: Calypsonian Shirlane Hendrickson Thomas's Story[1]

Shirlane Hendrickson Thomas *reigned as Calypso Queen for four consecutive years, 1998 to 2001. The niece of Andrew "Pan" de la Bastide, she is proud to have represented her country and culture on her international travels as Calypso Queen. Thomas, owner of her own record label Alco Productions, has put that work and her singing career on hold while she pursues her doctorate.*

An Inheritor of the Colonial Legacy

I was born October 29, 1961, in Troumacaque, Laventille. I attended Calvary RC School, which was burnt down. From there, I went to Mucurapo Junior Secondary and was there one week when the authorities presented me with the option of choosing a five-year school. I chose South East PoS because it was close to town where the family lived. I didn't know that I was a scholarship winner, not until years later while attending UWI, St. Augustine, and Dr. Bernard explained to me what had happened then. My name was deleted and another child from a choice school, according to Cro-Cro, was given my position. I never forgot that after investigating I learned that I got 233 out of 236 in Common Entrance [Examination]. Of course, deleting my name had to do with racial and class prejudices against me for coming from Behind the Bridge.

I didn't attend St. Joseph's Convent until years later, after leaving South East. One of Makandal Dagga's sister, Mrs. Cynthia Niles, walked with me. She told Mummy, "You stay home. I'll walk with her." We went to the Ministry of Education. The then officer, Mr. Donovan Palmer, gave her a slip of paper and told her, "Good luck." We went to St. Joseph's Convent and Sister Paul, who at the time was the principal, told me, "Well, you finally reach here." I should have gone there from the beginning. Even then I didn't know the full story, only that I qualified for St. Joseph's. Every time I tell people of this experience, they can't believe it.

After learning of this injustice, I decided that nothing was stopping me. I started my first degree at UWI, completed my degree in Business Management at Buffalo State University, and went on to complete my master's, also in Business. I'm now pursuing the doctorate, which may take some time because I'm juggling many things right now.

Launching a Calypsonian Career

My career as a calypsonian actually began when I was a background vocalist to my father's and sister's performances, whether in a calypso tent or at private or charity shows. I was also the dancer-actress on stage, which all began when I was an early teenager. I had never sung solo until 1985 when my name accidentally appeared in the evening news of the *Sun* newspaper as one of the performers for Queens in Concert. Of course, I was not a queen. I was not even a frontline performer. Yet, there was this long story about me doing my first degree at UWI, St. Augustine, and I'm like, "What is this?! Wow!" I knew my sister regularly performed at queen competitions and she was the one to look for. The promoter of the show—Makandal Dagga, the political leader of the National Joint Action Committee (NJAC)—looked at the article and said, "You know what? If this is what it is, you'll have to get up on stage and do something." He and his wife—the female leader of women's arm of the committee—used to host a series of programs. These programs were held during the early years of the Black tradition in art where my father, Black Stalin, Valentino, and all those calypsonians, performed. They had this concert throughout the year, and my name appeared on the list of performers.

I couldn't even think of a calypso to sing, not even one of my sister's or Dad's, so I decided to do my own thing on stage. I rehearsed one of Miriam Makeba's African songs and another named Crying's Easy by a Trinidadian entertainer. That night, that was it. After the performance, the gentleman told me, "Well, you know you will be on the cast from now on." The next article was billed, "A Star is Born." I still can't believe how I was propelled into the limelight after being only a back-up singer.

It also happened that at a concert in San Fernando where Super Blue—at the time he was Blue Boy—was supposed to close and was late, I believe, or just didn't show up. They asked me to close. I did, and that was the clincher.

When I immigrated to America in 1990, things turned around for me. Realizing that I was on my own, I decided to really give my singing a chance. At first, I lived in Bronx at one of my dad's close friends, then moved to Brooklyn and stayed with Glenda Cadogan, a female reporter and agent for CASYM Steel Orchestra. She and I became close friends over the years. I met her years ago in Point Fortin at one of those same said concerts. She says that she recognized back then that I was meant to sing.

In 1990, after I moved to Brooklyn, I joined a band called Impact 40, which was at the Golden Pavilion at that time. Gene and Gold were the promoters-owners of the club. There, I met a couple of the guys who all later went on to do various things. Impact 40 performed there for a time until it dispersed and we went separate ways. That was when I went solo and started performing all over Brooklyn and Bronx, along side [Mighty] Sparrow, [Calypso] Rose, and others of their status. In either 1992 or '93, Rose took me on tour with a couple of other performers to Atlanta, Georgia, and the Carolinas. We traveled in an RV and had a helluva time.

At one of the clubs, for the first time we came to understand the difference between north and south. It was close to two in the morning and one of the guys was drinking a beer. He put it down, turned his back, and when he looked again the beer was gone. There was a strict rule about alcohol-drinking after hours. We all were amused. It was comical to us the way that bottle disappeared. In Brooklyn, we could carry on into the wee morning. That's a glimpse of some of the experiences I've had.

I started my own label, Alco Productions. Before Alco Productions, in 1991 I met with a guy called Fitzroy Mackintosh, now passed on, who decided to produce me that year. I did that first recording called "Big Wood," a double entendre based on the different kinds of wood you find in Trinidad: teak, mahogany, and so on. He took it off the shelf immediately because people started to bootleg the record. The following year, I had a song which won me an award from *Everybody's Magazine*, owned by Herman Hall, for best upcoming female entertainer. The song was "Nanny Wanted." I based it on a classified ad I saw in a Long Island newspaper placed by a Jewish guy who was looking for a nanny, specifically from the West Indian community. I created another double entendre out of that and it rocked the whole of the Labor Day parkway that year. There was I on top a truck, dressed like a nanny in apron and everything, *wining* in a frenzy, and having the whole crowd in an uproar. We sold records from off the truck, which was something that year. I continued performing every Carnival, Labor Day, and at every other event I could across the globe, meanwhile pursuing my studies in Business Management and starting my own business.

I met my husband Frank Thomas in 1992. At that time, he had a travel agency, Alco Travels. We teamed and became Alco Productions as the second part of the travel agency. I had my label for the first time, which was one of my mission statements as a cultural performer. It is difficult to survive as a female entertainer in the world of Calypsodom, as we call it. So, to have my own production label is a triumph.

To continue the chronology, around 1993 to '94 I met George Kirton, Anslem Serrette—two arrangers—and began working with them. A spin-off from my business is to offer opportunities toward educating the younger people on the ins and outs of the business. I learned a lot from the prior years, 1990 and '91, about writing a song from scratch, taking it to the pressing plant with Mr. Mackintosh, going through each stage until the record was produced. That included lifting the boxes along with the guys, going into the record stores to distribute them, doing every little stage of the process. I have that experience to share with younger ones about what to do when they are coming out. I can teach them that one of the very first things they must have is a press kit that includes a biography, photos, and a video tape.

When I began interacting with other entertainers, one of the things I remembered when I studied Economics and Art for A-levels at St. Joseph's Convent and learning about all the-gies—sociology, anthropology, and psychology—was how to interact with others. When you're in the classroom, you don't understand much because your mind is elsewhere. You want to do other stuff. Eventually, you begin to understand how all these things fit into your daily schedule. As you go along in this business, you have to have a lot of discipline, self-control, and at the same time be able to stand up for your rights, especially as a woman. It's not at all easy.

Sometimes, too, as an entertainer you want to be a diva, but you have to know how to be a diva. Instead of turning people off, you have to know how to have that pleasing personality. I've seen and been in experiences with some of the top-named entertainers who because of their popularity they would demand certain things and behave quite obnoxiously. This turned people away from them rather than endear people to them. I've learned to invite people to come and sit with me. I've also learned that you never know who is at the other end, who's sitting in that audience. So, I learned to be willing to greet people and smile, *all the time*. It helps and you never know when in an unguarded moment you create the wrong first impression, which can cost you a lot in the long run. It also helps at the same time to be humble. So, it's one thing to perform along with the top entertainers and hold your own on stage and another to rise to each occasion.

Having role models like my sister and father and all I call the aunties and uncles helped me, too. Uncle Stalin, Aunty Rose (Calypso Rose), and Aunty Sandy (Singing Sandra) were excellent role models. Rose would tell you that in the early days her father was a spiritual Baptist, strong in that faith. So, to even mention the word calypso was like a stink in the house. One wouldn't believe her experiences about when she came out singing calypso along side guys like Sparrow, and the kind of challenges she had to put up with. She and they all paved the way for us and we're so fortunate to have them.

Now that I'm a songwriter, I appreciate them even more, understanding what writing and performing were like in those times. Today, it's still so difficult for a woman to get a calypso to sing. Some demands are still being made, even though not as much as back then. So, we encourage the ladies to sit down and write right. My first calypso in 1985 was called "Victimisation." Either my dad or sister sang it years ago. That was the first time I sat down and wrote a full-length calypso with four verses, and I've continued writing from then on. I've written all my calypsos and normally wrote my sister's calypsos. The two years, she won prior to my winning in 1998, she sang the winning calypsos I wrote for her in 1996 and 1997.

When it comes to performing, it's amazing how much we can learn from all of these veteran entertainers. Some of them to this day, though they may be getting on in age, still have the vocal techniques that some of us younger ones really need to grasp. Some still have the ability to perform well, too. They might be singing things that the crowd may not want to hear, but they have that stage personality that is critical to success. So, it's that whole-rounded image we need to have or develop or encompass to make us as versatile as these veteran stage-performers. Some people can really portray the one part they are strongest in. But when you see someone who is versatile, you know that is what counts. I try to tell people how much versatility is important.

I also like to emphasize the importance of knowing the history of our music and its culture. As a calypsonian, we have so much history outside our Caribbean islands that the average Trinidadian doesn't know. While studying and researching, I learned about all this history we have in New York City,[2] about guys like Tiger, or Tigre, and Roaring Lion who when they came here landed on Ellis

Island to get into New York, and how long it took them to get a visa. Some of it is written and some is oral. Some texts are by Dr. Hollis Liverpool (Mighty Chalkdust) and Donald Hill. When you listen to the recording by Decca Records, you hear how these calypsonians included the real calypso and callaloo in their song, which Hill writes about. People wouldn't think that Calypso is all that big until they begin to learn about the impact that these guys had in those days. We really haven't done enough in documenting our history and getting it into the schools. When I go out and am asked to lecture or give a talk, even a simple thing like talking to the children, I usually go right to the educational part of it.

The other thing is: how does one go about writing a calypso? It's just like writing a poem. It must have a story line, a theme that is developed, and so on. You write and revise it. You begin, and then by the middle you wonder how good it is, or you lose interest in it because you realize it's a bunch of nonsense that even you yourself wouldn't want to hear. Then, you go and listen to the guys from yesteryear and what they did to get you focused again. Daddy always used to talk about [Lord] Kitchener. In 1967, when my dad started singing Calypso, that's where he went, to Kitchener, né Aldwyn Roberts. He opened on Friday, January 6, 1967, the night he started singing. He would tell you that over the years Kitchener always talked about rhyme, rhyme, rhyme, and to stick to the theme of the song. Pretender used to get upset any time you did not rhyme and would not listen to you. It's that kind of thing: it must rhyme; make sense; tell a story that can hold your interest; and the melodic structure must make sense. These things I go back to to help me write the good calypso.

So, when George and I sat down together, that's what we worked on. We always tried to teach each other things as we went along. He and Anslem were more used to the new Soca style and I'm from the old school, especially under guys like those in the police band. I remember going with Dad to the police band room and meeting Anthony Prospect, who is now passed on. I worked with Ronnie Mackintosh's father, another top arranger, who like Prospect never made jokes. They were like, "Hey! What sort of crap is this? We need to have something that makes sense here." So, when I worked with George and some other guys, we sang slowly the melodic structure and the melody line then went on to the rest. Once we had that structure, what I call the belly, then we added the hands, and whatever else. Without that basic structure, we didn't even know where we're going. The new style is, of course, now all this computerized stuff, where guys are sampling music from every Tom, Dick, and Harry. An experienced calypsonian would say, "That has no melodic structure." When there's a melodic structure, the song has a full body. These are all the little learning experiences that young, upcoming entertainers in the art form need to take note of. I always tried to do something with a lyrical message that had more of the traditional calypso-style in it. I followed what I learned from those old guys, even though I brought some variation to it here and there.

Because life is a cycle, one's music will go right back to the original. [Thomas is alluding to Ernest D. Brown's "Carnival, Calypso, and the Steelband in Trinidad," published in *The Black Perspective in Music.* Brown argues that calypsonians began competing during the days of slavery, and the first calypso king was crowned by the famous slaveholder Pierre Berogorrat who gave the title to a man named Gros Jean, *Maît Caiso*, or Master of *Caiso*, who lived near Diego Martin. Calypso is sometimes called *Kaiso*.[3]] In as much as technology has advanced and you find people going toward that stuff, they're still already starting to go back to the old techniques. What you find is the younger guys are now sourcing music from the older ones. They're actually taking the old songs and doing them over. Look at the teamwork with Rose and Double Dee this year. For two years he'd been hunting her down, he said, to work with her on "Fire, Fire." He rapped part of it and she sang part, and together they created a blast. Allison Hinds teamed up with Sparrow last year and they did a calypso. It's that kind of thing happening.

I always say if we have an avenue where we can cherish the veterans who are still with us and market their kind of music and stick to the original but nice it up, we would do the art form a great service. I know that every generation brings to the art form a new style of music, but if we can incorporate the tradition with the new style then we have a blast.

After four years of winning four titles consecutively, I decided that was it. I had made a pledge and lived up to it. I had told myself that I would win this thing for four years.

An International Performer in West Africa

I was the first Caribbean entertainer, and female at that, to participate in Emancipation in Ghana, the first African country to host Emancipation. Prior to that in 1997, the then-president, J. J. Rowlings had gone to Jamaica and witnessed Emancipation there. Subsequently, on his visit to Trinidad of the same year, he saw the same Emancipation and was impressed. He took back the concept. Remember, in Trinidad and the other islands we were used to Emancipation celebrations, since God knows when. In Ghana, I was privileged to perform there and attend all the youth rallies, youth seminars, and sit down and talk about our historical perspective as a Caribbean person. I was able to share our experiences with slavery and all of that. But, mind you, the young people in West Africa at the time weren't interested in slavery and what it involved. They were more interested in America and being fully Americanized. I think in '98 Clinton had visited and they were still reeling from the impact of that visit. It seemed that he left a lasting image in West Africa.

Everybody was like, if you wore a Tommy Hilfiger T-shirt you were a big deal. I remember that a young African guy wanted my husband's hat, and I wanted to exchange whatever for what African things I could have. But when he grabbed for this hat, I was amazed and said to myself, "Eh, eh! We Caribbeans need to get inside ah here!"

I returned later that year for their Carnival then again in '99. In all, I made three visits and also performed in Senegal, which is predominantly French. I passed French in high school but am not fluent, no Frenchie. But for one performance I got up on stage and greeted them with the three words known best, "Je t'aime beaucoup." The crowd went hysterical, and I made the front page of their newspaper all written in French.

There're so many things I can say about visiting and performing in Africa. I was offered citizenship of Ghana but couldn't accept it because I already have dual citizenship, U.S./T&T. They wanted to offer me so many things that I felt like a home-girl. There's one remarkable story that I must share.

The first time that I went in '98, my husband hooked up an interview for me with one of the local newspapers. I remember it was a Tuesday morning and I had told the guy to come to the hotel around ten o'clock. After breakfast, I went downstairs but was wearing jeans and a top. There, I saw all these camera crews entering the lobby and thought they were there to interview a celebrity staying here. I investigated and found out that Rita Marley was also staying at the hotel. In 1991, during my days as a freelance journalist for *Everybody's Magazine*, I interviewed her for the celebration of the tenth anniversary of Bob's death. The interview was at the Mayflower Hotel in Manhattan and included two of their children, Stephen and Cedella. I later interviewed Ziggy over the telephone. That was a real plus for me as a young freelance journalist. I told myself that she wouldn't remember me from back then. Seeing all the camera crews gathering around the pool, I pulled on Frank's sleeve and told him they were there to interview Rita.

Then, I saw her at the far end having breakfast and ran to greet her and introduce myself again. She remembered me after I told her who I was and we hugged. Then, she asked me what I was doing there and I explained that I had come to perform for Emancipation, which she didn't know about. She went to Ghana every year to celebrate her birthday on July 25 and to relax and exhale. After asking her whether she was giving an interview, she immediately realized that they'd come to interview me and said so.

I couldn't believe it. Three TV stations were there to interview me. *Me!* TV3, the main station, and another station were there. She then pretended to be one of my agents for one of the shows and said to them, "You would have to go through me to get to her." Then, she looked at me and nodded. It was hilarious! Later, the interviews portrayed me as a real home-girl, like I belonged there. Really beautiful!

That Tuesday night, the Deputy Minister of Tourism at the time, Mr. Amofa, invited us to the airport for the return of two slaves' remains. I didn't know it was a part of the Emancipation program. The remains of one who had been made a queen mother had been kept by a lady in Jamaica, and the other's remains were from North Carolina, I believe. Their remains were being returned for reburial, and the ceremony was aired on TV. We attended the ceremony, which was very touching. One should see their rituals for a wake. It was like what we call a J'ouvert carnival. They burst carbide; people danced some dances that required tremendous physical strength; and all the drumming. We also visited the slaves' dungeons and actually walked the slave path into the dungeons and attempted to relive the whole experience. I feel quite fortunate to have been invited to share that experience and give praises to the ancestors.

A tourist guide in Ghana took us to a place called the Canopy Trail. We didn't know where the hell we were going. Picture something like the Trinidad Zoo. He dropped us off at this place and said, "You can take it from here. Have fun." We said, "Okay," and proceeded to follow the path. But before leaving us, he took us along this uphill path and all the time we heard voices screaming and laughing but didn't see anybody. Then, we came to signs that read: "Do not make noise. You will awake the monkeys." Next, he stopped by some trees, one called mortar and the other called pestle, which may have a connection to what we in Trinidad called mortar and pestle. He cut the bark of another tree, and that scent from that bark was sweeter than any perfume I'd ever smelt. I said to Frank, "If America got a hold of this one, then that would be the end of this natural resource."

When we got to a higher point Frank said, "I'm not going on that." We were about to cross a roped bridge that was so high when we looked down we saw only forest. They said seven Canadians and two Ghanaians built this roped bridge that connected the branch of one tree to another, and built it from the barks of some very tall trees—so tall their tops disappeared into the clouds. Once you got on to the bridge, you either turned back right away or after a certain point you kept on going. Now, these tree trunks are so large, they cut away some points into a platform that then reconnected the rope. We had this other guard about half my size who was just skipping along this roped bridge, making the whole thing look like nothing. When you looked at the thing, you realized it was only a rope you were holding on to. Your feet were shaking because this bridge was not firm or steady but constantly swaying. But I made it over, of course. I looked back at Frank who shook his head and said, "I'm not crossing that thing." Another older man said, "My heart can't take that." I was brave enough for both of them and went running behind the guard, following him the same way he ran, refusing to look left or right because that was too scary. The whole thing is truly remarkable. That men actually built that!

At the University of Lagos in Nigeria, I found that there are more similarities than differences in our music. Working with some of the African performers from across there was illuminating. I tried to understand how they *wine* and they tried to understand how we *wine*. I couldn't understand how those women could *wine* like that, go right down almost to the ground.

In Senegal, I found the Senegalese were more sophisticated than the Ghanaians in the way they behaved at concerts. They're very, *very* calm and somewhat non-expressive. I was told that I was the only one in a long time who was able to move them. You know me. I come with my Trini self and at that first show I performed, there were some gentlemen who were sitting quite sedately so they could understand. Across the street, I saw this guy who was well dressed. They were all well dressed in their African fineries. During one of my songs, I went and took his hat off and played with his bald head. They came to Frank and me the next day and told us, "If you can move the audience the way you did, then you could perform three times tonight." When I realized what he was saying, I said, "Oh! Is that what you want me to do? Get the crowd up and jumping?" That is all part of our culture, what we entertainers can really do. I understood that the Ghanaians would jump and wave while the Senegalese would sit and look at you and clap their hands politely. If you tried to get them to jump up and clap their hands, they would be like, "Hell, no!"

A couple of years later when I returned, I was honored to perform on Dodi Fayad's father's ship. That stage was gold plated. I can't imagine being honored to perform anywhere grander than that. I loved every moment of it.

So, all these have been parts of my experiences, as well as trying to gather knowledge about the diverse cultures where I've sung and performed. Funny enough, I've always found a bit of similarity. Wherever I've gone, I've found something that caused me to take a second look because it was something being done similarly to the way we do things back home and called by a different name or referred to in a different manner. From this, I know we're all one God's children. That's just how it is.

An International Performer: Pan in Sweden

I got an e-mail from a band in Sweden inviting me. Frank was on the computer and saw the e-mail. The leader of the band, Lars Hanssen of Soca Rebels—he's married to an Indian from San Juan, Trinidad, who's living there with him—has an all-White band called Soca Rebels. I remember that theirs was the first band in Europe to redo Crazy's 1992 "Nanny Wine." Just last month, Crazy performed with them in Sweden, which got a lot of coverage in the *Trinidad Guardian*.

In Sweden, I enjoyed all the highlights. There, it was something to see those White folks' dedication and commitment. I'd seen it in London and elsewhere, but it was amazing to see how the Swedes played pans in such a synchronized way. They had lights attached to the pans that swayed in synchrony. That band had one Black guy, according to Frank. He played the chac-chac and when we asked him where he was from he said, "Trinidad." Imagine that! A Trinidadian playing only the chac-chac, not even pan. When I told George and others about that, they couldn't believe what they were hearing.

I took Anslem with me to Sweden, and before even arriving I had hooked up with the promoter to find out where I'd been performing. When we got there, I had no idea where the place was, of course. It was amazing to perform with them without any prior rehearsal. How that came about was like this. I had just returned from Africa and had a two-day lay-over in New York before continuing to Sweden through London. I got there the same day and was to perform that same night. All I did was send them a CD, and during the sound check I was amazed. They played that music exactly as George and the guys had arranged it. I couldn't believe it.

The organizer had told me they would also have dancers and all that, too. I'd wondered, "Dancers?" They had their Mas band from Stockholm who plays Mas every year with Barbarosa in Trinidad come out on stage in their costumes. For the entire performance, they *wined* down the place and the crowd bawled the whole night, "Soca! We want Soca!" You should have seen their itsy-bitsy pieces of clothing, worse than what the girls in Trinidad wear. I was like, "Well! Hello!"

I performed in five places that year: Stockholm, Göteborg, Norrköping, and two others. It was amazing to have these kinds of experiences along side the African ones. I traveled all in the interest of promoting the Calypso Queen title.

The whole experience, of visiting various parts of West Africa and Europe, is something I'll always cherish. Some queens, because of their unfortunate circumstances, after winning they can't do much with their crown. Thank God for me being able to travel to various places and talk about these travels.

On Andrew "Pan" de la Bastide

I have always looked up to my Uncle Andrew Pan who passed on last year. I have not forgotten him. As a matter of fact, the 1999 Calypso Queen crown that I won was a Steelband calypso, which was won for Steelpan. My husband used to play for Syncopaters and still fiddles on the pan. I sometimes took the pan sticks and did my little thing then called my uncle. He was able to tell me over the phone which wrong note I was playing. I went, "Uncle, you didn't have to go and embarrass me," and he was, "Yeah, you need to get to middle C," then proceeded to tell me the whole history of middle C on the pan. Afterward, I got to thinking that one of my missions—but God took him before I could complete it with him—was to get all the older pan-guys who were still alive to do a forum.

We also want to cherish those who are still with us, even though they're still not being given their full dues. Some of the young people might have heard just a name or two, because of the lack of interest shown to them and also because these same young people feel these older pan-guys are simply dying. They don't see them as anything else. But we should be putting these older guys into the schools to lecture, telling people about how this thing got started because they have so much to offer. Do we really know and understand what it is to tune a pan? To me, that's a whole history in itself.

I didn't grow up close to him but I know he could have told you how a pan-player was viewed and treated derogatorily. The stigma that society had placed on them during the '40s and '50s and subsequent decades is unconscionable. During the early decades, you couldn't tell people you were a pan-player.

He himself used to run away from home. It was when his name was called on the radio as a member of TASPO, his same mother who used to lambaste him and *cut his tail* for running away to play pan, couldn't stop bragging to everyone that her son was chosen: "My son is going on tour! You hear my son's name called on the radio? That was him." I have a record of him back in those days with Ellie when the group went on tour. I look at the photo and can't believe he was my uncle.

He used to tell me his tales. He liked talking to me because he said I was going places. So when I returned from a trip, I called him to tell him where I'd been, whether it was to Africa or Europe. He always said, "You remind me of me so much." Then, he would give me stories of all the places he'd been, and I'd be loving them but could only say, "Wow!"

During his last days, he was there still loving up his pan and having groups over. I think these are the guys we should really try to cherish. We need to document all their experiences.

A Promising Future Born from a Rich and Diverse Past

On my Mum's side of the family is the Indian fraternity. This led me to enter the Chutney-soca competition. I went in the full regalia: the nose stuff, hair, and everything. This is my Hindu side. My uncles were staunch Hindus from the country [rural area] and used to tell us some of the Hindi words. So, it's amazing to have to do the two things.

We're really cosmopolitan, we Trinis, and I teach about that whenever I lecture, especially under Liberal Arts. Some people tend to leave this out, but it's good to know all the roots of your family history, and I see family and cultural history in who I am and the people I meet. Well, at least I want to know if there's some family history in those I meet. We have to go back to the past, to the tradition, sometimes, before we can understand where and how we're going forward. All this new-wave music is a spin-off from something old. In Calypso, whatever new they're trying to do is coming from the veterans. Life being a cycle takes us right back to the past, as I said before.

Young entertainers are actually taking some of the old-style calypso and putting it into the new-wave thing. Some of them so bold-faced they're calling it theirs without giving the true credit to the source. They don't see this as a form of plagiarism. That's another word they might take and make into a calypso: plagiarism.

The thing is: we need to have a cultural dome, a building of about six or seven floors. We need one on Trinidad and one in New York City. You know that New York is the next thing outside Trinidad Carnival. I wrote about this in one of the calypsos for Lady Wonder who won her title with it.[4] It was all about this cultural dome, because when you arrive in Trinidad and land in Piarco [International Airport], especially if you visit at Carnival time, you need to know, to have ready access to what is going on in the culture. You shouldn't have to be asking around. You can go straight to the dome and find one floor that deals with Calypso, one that deals with Soca, another with Pan, another with another art form, and so on.

All the history should be laid out before your eyes. Then, if you wanted additional information on any social event, any party, that would be available there, too. We still don't have a home for our music history.

We don't have a Pan theater, of all things, which St. Thomas has. Years ago, I remember going there to do back-up for Dad and the others. We went into one of the Pan theaters, and there was a Trini guy playing the pans. All the shelves were laden with different pans in the different stages of the development. We need this in Trinidad. We lost some of our history in '73 with the OPEC oil boom, one may remember. We've been exporting pans a lot since then. Instead, we have people coming in from Japan and elsewhere and entering our WSMF and almost beating us. If we're not careful we can lose all this. The competitions and our history. We have to hold on to our history and have it down-pat. For too long, we've had people from the outside coming and telling us what we need to do, and we're still not doing it. We need to go way back into our history, prior to those days of Quevedo.[5]

My husband's father was Lord Iere. The Lady Iere of that time is not the same one you hear of today. I'm going back to the late '50s into the early '60s. She died in the '70s. I remember Dad talking about them, about Lord Iere's special vocal tone and Tigre, whom we know as Tiger but Dad called him, "Tigre." I remember actually speaking with him once. He took his time and articulated his words. Then, there was Lady Trinidad who I think won one of the very early Calypso Queen contests. I think she died a couple of years ago and was honored by NJAC. Over the years, NJAC has been honoring a lot of the queens.

The first year I won, they honored Calypso Rose. So, it was an honor to win at the same time she was being honored. To sing and perform and have her in the audience! And, of course, Denyse Plummer and the impact she made on stage is well-known. The ladies have been there battling over the years, both young and old. Singing Francine has a soprano voice that is unsurpassed. I dare not pass her anywhere without saying hello. She would demand to know what the hell was wrong with me. She's another one whom I call "Aunty."

I honor all calypsonians. For women, our history begins in the '50s. But the real breakthrough came with Calypso Rose and her name marks the turning point. She sang in Sparrow's tent until 1979, which was the year my sister started singing. Abby Blackman came out that year, too, and won the queen title. Prior to her, we have Lady Trinidad and Lady Iere. Calypso Princess came later in the '60s going into the '70s. Her history is linked with Lord Blakie, whom I call Uncle Blakie, and they have some history together. You know, today he's still performing with that powerful tenor voice. Still singing with his stick, too. Continuing with the men, I remember Stalin and Valentino, who along with Blakie are called the blood brothers. Valentino is still very cool. Keeps you waiting till he makes that next sentence that brings thunderous applause. In the early days, my Dad toured with people like Barron and he remembers those songs they sang in Guyana like, "He Lick She."

Only calypsonians know what it's like to sing in a tent, *every night*. They call it stamina. You go every night and perform wherever the tent went, right through Carnival Tuesday. Come Ash Wednesday and it's all over, and you begin to miss it.

On Borrowing and the Need for Documentation

We know how much others have "borrowed" from our tradition. Belafonte in the United States made Melody's "Mama, Look a Boo-Boo" big. The Andrews sisters redid "Rum and Coco-Cola," which another Trini wrote.[6] We know that "Hot, Hot, Hot" is originally Arrow's, but Poindexter[7] redid it and it became this world-wide phenomenon. It's unfortunate that others made these songs popular, which I'm sure they didn't do intentionally. Nonetheless, the original people haven't got the fame or fortune from their creativity.

All this is to say that if our stuff is not properly documented and marketed in the right way, others will get credit for what we did, and it will be like we weren't even the ones who made the original contribution. We have to know the value of copyrighting and patenting what we do. People feel that it's okay just to sample other people's music and put it in their songs, as though this is an okay thing to do. But this is not an okay thing to do.

If you look at some of Western music closely, you will find a lot of that Caribbean musical structure in it. Belafonte's band is made up of musicians from all over the world. I remember him saying in an interview, that once a musician is good he will use him, regardless of where he comes from, Africa or wherever. That goes to the diversity in music.

People have still not grasped the potential of calypso music. When Colin Powell came to Trinidad, he said that during the Gulf War/Desert Storm the only songs he knew to sing were Sparrow's calypsos. He played Sparrow's songs in those army camps and was happy to say that he knew Sparrow's songs from back then and to now. Imagine, Powell having a Sparrow collection!

Also, I remember once—going back to Africa—this guy was selling land in the mountains. I think it's opposite to this place where Rita has her castle, so to speak. The guy took out this stack of records and among them I saw one of my sister and me when we backed up Lord Nelson and Lala. This guy had a whole series of calypso albums. I was so surprised! In Jamaica, I visited a guy who had a room that was like a record store, which was full of traditional calypsos, his love. I was surprised there, too. A lot of Calypso die-hards are out there in the world.

Even so, we still need a big market for the music, which I believe will happen when Calypso gets into the schools. Songs with good lyrics, I mean. Even though we have the spin-offs of the Calypso—Soca and Chutney-soca, the basic calypso has still remained within its traditional form. People will still love it the same way. The younger people, because of their taste in the different musical genres, believe only when it has crossed over it's marketable. But how come Bob Marley's Reggae isn't crossing over? Any part of the world you go, it's Bob Marley's Reggae.

Interestingly, a Jamaican and one other person said so to me that a Trini invented Reggae. Today's average Jamaican may not want to admit it, and is only if you want war you say so. But that's the truth, and some Jamaicans won't hesitate to say so. These are people who have kept Jamaican music history intact. They can tell what was before Ska, when Ska came, and then finally Reggae. But, you see, it's all part of the Caribbean influence. In Jamaica, they have a soca version of music, too. They don't use as many instruments as we do in Trinidad. We use five and six horns, guitar, bass, keyboard, and all that. They just use a guitar, a bass, and a keyboard. So their sound is much different from ours. Right now, people are hardly even using the instruments. They get a sound off the computer and go with that.

Trinis have been making their mark all over the place and some places have documented this. We haven't done so because our music has been stigmatized in our own country and confined as a seasonal thing. Who could forget that it was only around Carnival time you could hear this kind of music, and come Ash Wednesday it's like it didn't exist? Today, we don't really have Lent in Trinidad in the way that used to keep silent the music. People just continue singing and playing whatever music they like. But still we have to be begging the radio stations to play our music. They don't mind playing Reggae and all other kinds of music. It's sad like that. What we will do? We can't give up. And, the more unity we have in the art form the more we will bind together and more forward better.

When all is said and done, we have something of quality to take to the schools and make a difference. If we're not in the schools we're not anywhere.

9
The Inversed Triangular Trade: A Vignette by Vincent Hernandez[1]

Vincent Hernandez's *awards include: Dem Stars Steel Orchestra, Recognition in the Art Form,* ***2001****; Renegades Steel Orchestra, Honors in Appreciation for His Years of Work,* ***2000****; Member, National Steel Band of Trinidad and Tobago.*

With all due respect and with his permission, I acknowledge that Mr. Hernandez *granted me the interview only one month following his release from hospitalization for the treatment of prostate cancer. Our short time together reinforced my awareness that the men who were involved in the early days of the movement were indeed warriors, possessing indomitable spirits of love and compassion, generosity and kindness. They are all advanced in years, and their remaining days with us are so short. As with all the men and women with whom I spoke, I felt so honored to be in the presence of another Steelpan hero.*

The narrative highlights briefly Hernandez's *role in pioneering Steelband in Nigeria in the 1970s and his view on machine versus man in pan-tuning.*

Days of Hunger

I was born in 1929 in Success Village, Laventille in PoS, Trinidad. I went to Western Boys RC School on Richmond Street. For a while, I lived in Arima, approximately sixteen miles from PoS. At that time, we used to have fêtes in the street during Christmas-time with bands playing, but what we had before the war you couldn't really call a steel band. It was people using sticks and pans and so on to keep rhythm. I was about seventeen years old at that time and my nickname was Yittie. Everyone in Arima knew me as Yittie, the panman, because I was the first to start Steelband in Arima. I was around sixteen when I started my first steel band, and we called it The Vigilantes because everything then was bad. The band had about six to seven people, and every one of them was bad except me. Those boys were young, too, and liked to fight and break up dances, but I was the music man.

In 1945, when I first started tuning pan, I had no method. I started when we had two or three notes on the pan and used pan more for timing, rhythm. Whatever spot on the pan I placed the note and tuned it and it sounded right, I left the note there. Then, we advanced to six to seven notes on the pan. We used to call those pans ping-pong and had two of them to play a song. I would play on one ping-pong and another player would answer on his ping-pong. When I started making pan, I was trying to make better what had already come into existence.

I taught myself to tune and to play by copying from Neville Jules. I knew him but only from a distance and he didn't know me. To teach myself to play, I used to run away from Arima to his group, which was a big size. Whatever his group was playing, I would race back to Arima and try to do. I, being the big boss in my band, used to puzzle my boys who wondered where I got that from. This is probably the first time Jules will know that I used to *fudge* [cheat or steal] all the time from him. Later, we all went to bands in town that we could hear and listen to then ran back to the country [rural area] and practiced what we fudged. That was how my band was the best one in Arima, and I was the best tuner.

Soon after I developed my skills, another band called Atomic formed in Arima, on Cocorite Road. It's now called Melodians and is still there on the same street. I tuned their pans and almost all the pans in Arima. All those guys still know me, and when I return for Carnival we meet and talk about those old days. I go back for almost every Carnival.

While still living in Arima, and before moving to Belmont, I started San Juan All Stars. Once I moved to Belmont, I started tuning pans for a small band located on Sandhurst Street, which called itself Satisfiers. The calypsonian Nap Hepburn lived on Sandhurst, too. This band was a good one and had no part in the rioting and fighting, even though sometimes some other guys would come and *mash up* our front-line pans. Our band was made up of decent men who wouldn't fight back. We didn't even go looking for those men responsible for *mashing up* our pans. We just let it go. Because we weren't into fighting or rioting, we didn't make it into the news and such. Our focus was to come out every Carnival and play Mas.

I tuned pans under a breadfruit tree in the band captain's yard, Derrick Greenidge. No relationship to Carl or Robert Greenidge. Those were days when you often didn't have anything to eat or drink and some people weren't kind. Mrs. Greenidge, every morning when she left for work, locked up her kitchen door so I couldn't get to eat anything, and she knew I was hungry. When a breadfruit fell, I would roast one on the wood I was burning the pan on and eat it just like that, without any salt or seasoning or anything. Doing Steelband was really hard, especially for those in the country [rural area]. People in town had things a little easier. Sometimes, I tuned pan for a flask of rum, even though I wasn't any real drinker. But that was how people paid me because they didn't have any money. So *I* didn't have any money. The most pay I got was a dollar or two, and that was all I did for a living. In those days, you ain't getting anything from nobody! It was while tuning and playing for Satisfiers that Greenidge recommended me to the National Steel Band. I was the best player from the band.

I have a photograph of the twenty-two of us on my mantel. I have another photo of when we went to Jamaica in '65 for almost three months. That was a part of the National Steel Band, too, but included just fourteen of us. On our way to Jamaica, we stopped at the various islands along the way. I was the only tuner in that group and made pans for people in all the islands where we stopped. At that time, we could make pan in one day, not like today. Once the boat docked in the harbor, I would find a drum, make a pan from it and sell it. I was trying to make an extra dollar or two. When we got to Jamaica, I had to make pans for three schools. That earned me enough money to return to Trinidad by plane. The rest of the guys remained in Jamaica for a couple more months.

Later, after being home for a while, I became involved with Renegades. Now, I always visit them when I go home. They're still by Charlotte Street where it goes up to Oxford Street. I stay in that area, too. Renegades was one of the most popular bands of the day.

Reflecting on how hard things were for panmen back then, Eric Williams and the government could have done so much more. Williams helped with promoting the idea of sponsorship of bands but that was all. What we really needed was money just to live, and as a band we eventually needed uniforms, a place for the band to practice, and we always needed food. Imagine this. A roti was fifteen cents in those days. The National Steel Band began with forty-four members, a member from each leading steel band, and traveled with twenty-two. In those days, some of us didn't have that fifteen cents to buy a roti before going to practice. We had to beg somebody for money to spare. That's how hard things were for us.

A Pan Entrepreneur and Pioneer

After I returned to Trinidad, I continued making drums for Murray Narell. I first started making drums for him in '62. When I first started off, he didn't know me personally and I didn't know him. I used to send the drums up here to New York and he'd send down his checks. We did this for three to four years. Since he was dealing with schools, he must have been using the drums in the schools. What I know is: he had a family band because I have another photo on my mantel of his band with Andy Narell and his brother Jeff. Their band was named Steel Bandits and sponsored by one of those Hudson River boats, the Graceline.

I came to the United States when Mrs. Narell invited me to New York in '66. We didn't know each other either. It was a Sunday when I arrived at JFK International Airport. She came right up to me and asked me if I was Vincent Hernandez. I said, "Yes," and she took me home to their house.

I knew the Narells before Ellie did. In fact, I was the one who recommended Ellie to them. At the time, Patrick Arnold and I were tuning pan in Flushing, New York, for Murray Narell. One day, I was tuning a drum and Mr. Narell asked me who I thought as the best pan-tuner in Trinidad. I answered, "Of course, Mr. Ellie Mannette." He didn't even know of Ellie Mannette. He'd heard of Corbeau Jack and asked, "What about Corbeau Jack?" I said, "No, Ellie Mannette is the best." This was in late 1966. Then, I suggested that we go to Trinidad at that time because the Music Festival was happening right then at Queen's Hall, and I was sure he would be able to meet Ellie Mannette there. He agreed that was a good idea and I went back to tuning the drum. Two hours later, he returned and said, "We're going to Trinidad." When we got there, I introduced him to Ellie at Queen's Hall, and from then they began discussing their business. The following year, Ellie came to New York.

But sorry to say, he's such a funny guy he wouldn't mention to anyone the fact that I introduced him to Narell, really. Before we left in '66, he and Narell must have finalized things because Ellie came to me, in a sort of showing off way, and said, "I going to New York next year." He didn't know I was already here or that I was the one who first mentioned him to Narell. I said, "Okay, see you up there." He acted in this surprise manner, "You see me up there?!" His attitude was that I couldn't possibly be in New York. I simply said, "Yes, that's right." After he came, we all met up and tuned drums together for Murray Narell.

When I first came to the United States, I stayed with the Narells for one night. I came on a Sunday, and on Monday morning he gave me, I think, his son's car to drive to New Jersey. I had arrived the day before and didn't know how to drive in this place. He wrote the directions on a sheet of paper for me to get to where I was going. At this time, I still only knew to drive on the left side and managed to get to New Jersey somehow or the other, with him following behind me. When we got there, he found a room for me to stay, and I stayed in Jersey for a while making drums for him.

That first place he found was with some White people and I stayed there only for two days. The owner destroyed his own flowers then complained that I was destroying his place and couldn't stay there any longer because they couldn't have a Black man living there. They threatened to burn down the house if I remained living there. Narell helped find me another place. There, during the night all I could hear was the sound as if someone was falling down. This was a place they sold drugs. I got fed up with that and decided to move to Brooklyn. By that time the following year in '67, my wife had come and was living with a friend in Brooklyn. We saw each other when I came from Jersey to visit. I moved to Brooklyn and we lived on Lewis Avenue.

A little later after more men arrived, Clifford Alexis and I formed a band that was quite good. We played in all the basement parties. Rudy King was a member as well as our driver. The name of that band was Troubadours, and we had nine members total and made a lot of money. Eventually, we played in Carnegie Hall and all those big places.

A changing moment in my life came a few years later. Now, I came here legally and had all my papers. So, when someone asked for one of us to go to Lagos, Nigeria, to build and tune pans for Mobil Oil Company, I got the job. I don't know if Ellie had his legal papers, but I know he didn't particularly want to go. I was glad to go because I was willing to go anywhere related to Steelband. The first time I went to Nigeria was in '72 when I started up a band named Mobil Oil Steel Band. I went back eight times. Since Mobil Oil Company invited me, I could build, tune, and arrange only for the company. The band had about twenty-five members, all working for the company. It could have been a much bigger band but they restricted it to only company workers. The fella in charge was named Tom Iyamu. Another member of the band, I think his name is spelled Akwé, always comes to New York and comes to see me.

Apparently, the company heard about Pan here in New York. So when they wanted to get a band started in Nigeria, they came to us. In traveling to Nigeria, I had the chance also to visit Morocco, Germany, London, and other places, and make some pans for people there. This is how my name is known throughout the world, not just throughout the Caribbean.

Pan Now and in the Future

I'm still tuning pans, which is all I do for a living, and have a full set of drums, a complete band, in my basement. I still make drums for Carroll Sound on 41st Street in New York City, for Drummers World also in New York City, and for a third place in California. I have some work to finish right now, but since I'm recuperating my energy isn't what it was.

I don't chrome myself but send the pans off to one or two places. One place returns the pans right away, in a matter of days, but I don't understand why the other place does take so long, sometimes weeks. I started chroming many years ago, about thirty years, in the '70s, but have only the lead pans done. It's too expensive to have the big pans chromed. Lately, Rudy King does take care of that for me.

You asked about my bore pans in my basement. Mine are thirty years old. They were chromed but lost their luster. I refuse to sell them or give them to anybody because I like the way they sound. The guy who started boring pan first started that right here. His name is Denzil—I can't remember his surname. Not everybody wants the bore pan, but if someone orders a bore pan, I make it. I made quite a few that people ordered.

I'm different from a lot of people. I don't spend much time with steel bands today and have no argument with Steelband people. Pan is here and I don't see the point in asking how much further it can go. It's all over the world and I myself helped to take it to where it is. I can only see development in the area of sound, improving the overall tonality of the pan. People will continue to come up with some new invention here and there, but those they tried in the past haven't worked. We brought the pan through all the stages, from a crude thing to a musical instrument, and that's what it is today. Whether they want to come up with a six-piece section when before it was two pieces is only experimentation that might or might not work. The idea is to have something that people can readily play. The circle of fourths and fifths was a major improvement that will last. But if someone comes up with something unique to his band and it is not really useful to the market, his innovation wouldn't survive. What's the point? The orchestra, as far as I can see, is complete. We have all the sections.

While I don't experiment or haven't created any pan, not like Jules and the others, if someone asked me to make a pan based on what is already there, I can do that. I suppose I'm one of those who kept the thing going. I remember when Jules used to use the caustic soda drum and he was the only one with a whole lot of those drums, and it was years I wanted to do that, too, but never did. I couldn't get my hand on one of them. There were some good bass drums he made back then and I wanted to experiment with that, too. Then that passed. A lot of people now want to experiment with pan and good luck to them. I will concentrate on improving on what I'm doing right now.

I learned some music theory for tuning, and how to work with the strobe. But I still rely on ear for tuning and playing. Sometimes, even after using the strobe and mounting the pan on the stand to play, to me it still sounded like something was wrong. I found that I still had to please myself to get to the sound I liked. This is why I say many times that you don't really know sometimes what to do about tuning a drum except to please your own ear. So, even though I work with the strobe, sometimes it just doesn't sound right to me. I don't change the key the note is in but just tinker with the note till it sounds right to me. Not everyone does that. Some leave the note as the machine says. Not me.

In New Jersey, I helped to establish Pan in two schools, one in Red Bank Middle School. I don't know if that band is still going because I called recently and the music teacher I was in contact with is no longer there. I used to visit Philadelphia a lot when I made pans for a group there that John Gibbs of Medgar Evers started. In fact, I made a whole lot of pans for Medgar Evers when they had a band there and made some money from that, too.

Being in Steelband has not been easy. Some people probably wouldn't know about that and they are lucky. But know that as long as your name is associated with Steelband, you can expect some hardship. Back in Trinidad and here, too. It's a problem keeping a band going when you have men with bad attitudes who want to fight and misbehave. Then, you have problems with people who want you to play and not pay you. They want good sounding drums and not willing to pay for your time and labor.

Now, I just want to associate with men my age, or those who're really serious about this, like the band I helped get started, Dem Stars, a band that is just about three years old and used to practice at Utica Avenue and Sterling Place. You have no idea how many kids passed through here, first learning to play here in my basement. I've done my part, I think, in helping the movement to go forward. Dem Stars is the only band I deal with. I guess that's why they gave me that award.

I'm proud of my grand-daughter, Nicole Gibbons, who plays lead/tenor in the Brooklyn steel band, Pantonic, the winner of the 2001 and 2002 Brooklyn Panorama, and my son Carl James of Toronto's steel band, Metrotones.

The following is a short early morning telephone conversation 2002 with Carl James in Toronto on December 4.

Thank you, so much for speaking with me. Would you share the extent of your involvement in the Steelband movement first in Trinidad then in Toronto?

Actually, there was a band here in Toronto—some of the guys from Trinidad from my old band, Guinness Cavaliers—formed this band here, I think in 1972, and called it Trinidad Cavaliers. That's how I became directly involved in Steelband in 1974. Because of my father, I was always around Steelband but not directly active. I was just supportive of the movement. I became active when I got together with these guys from Trinidad Cavaliers, and that went on for about three years. Then, I got involved with another band now called Metrotones.

Do you recall who organized the band in 1972?
I think his name was Balthazar Haggard.

How did Metrotones get started?
Some guys from St. Vincent got that band started. I was working nearby and they asked me to help them with some arranging. That's how I got involved with Metrotones and have been with them until today. I don't know who the original founders of the band were.

Who is the current leader or captain?
Right now? Me. I'm the arranger and a player. We've done quite a bit. A couple of years ago we made a CD, and we still perform at the various carnivals in the area: Toronto, Ottawa, Windsor, Montreal, St. Catherine's, Buffalo, to name a few.

Are there many bands in Canada?
I don't know how many there are in all. In the Toronto area, there must be about fourteen to fifteen bands.

How else are you involved in the movement?
I'm the vice chairman of Pan Trinbago Toronto. The chairman is Cecil "Muggs" Clarke. We organized here in 1990 and I keep in touch with Trinidad. I've gone to Trinidad Panorama every year since 1979. Pan Trinbago Toronto is very instrumental in promoting Steelband in Canada. During the summer, we have a youth program that promotes youth awareness in Steelband. We have a Toronto Panorama every summer. We have a Pan-jazz—we're now involved with the Toronto Jazz Festival every summer. Robert Greenidge was here for the last one we just had.
Have you considered entering Metrotones into the WSMF?
Maybe in the near future.
How have Canadians received Steelband? Here in the United States, some men whom I've spoken with are concerned that it remains fixed or colonized in some sort of island-music, the folk-music milieu of "Yellow Bird" and "Mary Anne." Is it similar in Canada? Where would you like to see the movement headed?
I would like to see it moving beyond being exploited and colonized, to use your language. The time is long come, *long come* for Steelband to be regarded as its own orchestra capable of playing any type of music. I don't think it is accepted yet as a musical instrument, as it should. That's what I would like to see right here in Canada, and in the United States, too. It's the same thing happening in both places. Same exploitation. We need more opportunities to play, to show our versatility and give people the image of Steelband that is more than just rum and Coco-Cola. But if we only get hired for certain gigs, we have to meet the terms of that contract, and that makes it hard to make the statement that the steel band can go wherever you want it to, that it can fit right into any setting.
Are there any programs in schools and colleges?
Oh, yeah! A lot of guys here in Toronto are getting involved as tutors and teachers in the schools. The Toronto Board of Education has taken over that, I think, and is controlling most of the school programs. On the college level, York University has a program set up for students to receive credit.
Do you know which steel band first organized in Toronto and the name of that band?
Afro Pan is the oldest and the biggest band. The leader is Earl LaPierre Sr. The size of their band is about twenty to twenty-five. Metrotones has ten members.
How were you active in Steelband in Trinidad, prior to immigrating to Toronto?

I was a member of the Guinness Cavaliers in Trinidad. For a little history of the band, let me see, where to start. It won its first Panorama in 1965 and then again in 1967. Then it toured Suriname, then South America, then Venezuela in 1968, then Grenada and Tobago, and then in 1971 went on a world tour to Japan, Malaysia, Australia, Europe, and North America. But I was already living in Canada by that time. This was all under Lennox "Bobby" Mohammed, an outstanding arranger. I came to Canada in 1970.

I first started in Steelband with Big City Boys from San Fernando, run by John Wilkes of the Wilkes brothers. From there, I moved up to Melody Makers and then to Guinness Cavaliers and then to here.

Do you tune?
No. My dad and a couple of guys here provide pans for the band. There are about four or five tuners here in Toronto.

Well, thank you again sincerely, for allowing me to disrupt your morning and sharing a little about Steelband in Toronto and Guinness Cavaliers.
No problem....

10
We're Not Materially Rich: A Vignette by Jeff Narell[1]

Jeff Narell *is an internationally known pannist, Afro-Caribbean percussionist, and educator-clinician. He began studying Pan with Ellie Mannette in the 1960s.*

Narell *has recorded and performed with a diverse array of artists including George Benson, the Grateful Dead, Bobby McFerrin, and Olatunji. He has performed for four big box office films, including* 48 Hours *and* Commando. *He has composed two theatrical scores, one of which commissioned for the California Shakespeare Company's production of* The Tempest, *and won the* Hollywood Dramalogue *award for "Best Original Theatrical Score."*

As a bandleader based in the San Francisco Bay Area, Narell *has brought his musical ensembles before audiences at concert/club/corporate events across the United States, including Hawai'i. He has also acted as musical director for calypsonians Crazy and Chalkdust in San Francisco Bay Area shows, performed with Len "Boogsie" Sharpe and Shadow in Trinidad, and with Robert Greenidge and Ray Holman in the United States.*

Narell *was a guest artist on the Grammy-nominated CD in the Latin Jazz Category,* Rhythm at the Crossroads, *featuring Cuban master percussionists Patato, Changuito, and Orestes Vilato.*

In 1995, Lost Tribe Records *released* Narell's *self-produced debut CD of original compositions,* Wave of Love, *which received national airplay and was reviewed by Latin Beat Magazine as "hot World pop debut ... pure Caribbean sugar ... funky, jazzy around the edges and ready to get you dancing."*

Narell's *second CD* Voyage to Paradise *features standout performers in the Caribbean Jazz idiom including Rebecca Mauleon Santana, Ray Obiedo, Manny Oquendo, Jesus Diaz, and Michael Spiro.*

In his commitment to perpetuating the art form, Narell *has traveled internationally to establish Steelband programs and conduct clinics and workshops. In addition, he directs several ongoing Steelband programs in the San Francisco Bay Area, involving hundreds of students at the middle school, high school, and college levels. He also leads his professional group in performances under the auspices of the San Francisco Symphony and Young Audiences* Arts in Education *programs.*

Narell *has been teaching at the Meet Me in Morgantown (MMIM) workshop since 1996.*

Murray Narell and Ellie Mannette

I grew up in New York City where my father Murray was a social worker. He had an early steelband experience in the 1960s when he met a young Antiguan, named Rupert Sterling, who was living in New York. Rupert and Kim Loy (Trinidadian), as far as I know, were among the first pan-players/builders in the United States. Rupert and Murray started an extensive program for the youth, with Rupert building pans and instructing, which is how I got started in Pan. Approximately twenty groups came and were involved in the program: Blacks, Puerto Ricans, Italians, and kids-at-risk who attended as groups to be involved in something really positive. The youngsters were organized into weekly practice time slots and came with their respective social groups (gangs).

Murray made some trips to Trinidad in the 1960s and was directed to Ellie, who at the time was working for Shell Oil; had a desk job. He was an innovator in Pan but was doing pan-work only part-time. Murray had to convince him to come to the United States because of Ellie's reluctance to come due a prior experience with racism in the South. When he came in 1967, we were living in Queens, New York. Murray established him with a shop in a shared space with our steel band. Ellie built pans during the day and the band practiced at nights. He eventually got his own place. Later, Murray got him work in the schools building pans, while he continued to build pans for us. Ellie improved the quality of the instruments we were playing.

Andy and I were adolescents when Ellie first came. But even as kids he was always receptive to our presence while he worked on pan-building. He loved to share stories with us about Trinidad. I also got to see firsthand the energy involved in pan-building. As a child, I used to admire him as a very strong man with powerful arms who beat us at arm-wrestling.

I've done some work with Ellie over the years. I went to San Diego with Ellie and Kaethe George and did a workshop with them. Before that, I kept in touch with him off and on during the 1970s and visited him where he lived in New York. One thing I observed; he always tuned pans with the radio and TV on. Nothing fazed him. He had a great ear for music. He worked hard by himself, a one-man operation. I saw more of him during the 1980s and '90s, and in the early '90s accompanied him on the San Diego trip. MMIM is our annual meeting place. My first one was in '96 when Ellie invited me to do the Golden Anniversary of Pan.

No one can steal Pan from Trinidad and Tobago[2]

I want to emphasize that Ellie came to the United States as a result of Murray's vision. Murray had already experienced the effects of bringing kids to Pan and connecting them to its music programs, of bringing these programs into community outreach for at-risk kids. Murray had seen the power of Pan and its positive effects on kids who couldn't get music training, who lacked the opportunities of more privileged kids. That was the original idea, which then blossomed as it expanded into schools.

When Ellie arrived, he considered what Murray was doing and came aboard. He was ready to try something different in a different place. After he was in the United States, then the talk began that he was a traitor to the country. But I see Ellie as an ambassador who did not share with the idea, "Let's hold on tightly to what we have, 'cause this is ours, and let's not share it." His dream now is to leave the art form in the capable hands of those who will advance it even beyond his own dreams and capabilities. He has offered fifty years of trial and error as the foundation on which his students can build; indeed, he is a master teacher. His spirit has always been one of sharing. No other tuner has been able to explain all the intricacies of pan-building as Ellie does.

About the controversy, I have never felt that my family would receive any animosity for our involvement with Ellie until Andy and I visited Trinidad in 1985. We were invited to play a show at "Spectakula Forum—PanJazz organized by Robbie Greenidge and hosted by Boogsie Sharp—and the promoter called it after a calypso by Merchant, Pan in Danger, which spoke about how Trinidad was losing Pan. The show was billed: "USA versus Trinidad." The players—Earl Rodney, Boogsie, Andy, and I—all had different styles and played individual sets. Then, we had a great time during the final jam session. Boogsie was a superb host. We were featured on TV and the promoter was asked how he viewed the show. He replied that it was a war. Of course, this was for promotional purposes, but that was when Andy and I began to pick up the vibe that Trinidadians perceived us as a threat. This took us completely by surprise.

Andy can share the story of one day someone wrote in the *Trinidad Express*, "Andy Narell, Millionaire, such and such." It's true that he is famous, having played all over the world. His is a great story that ought to be documented, too,[3] but working the Jazz world is not the lucrative side of the music biz. He has struggled, too. We all struggled during the 1970s and '80s, like Ellie, breaking ground and like Ellie we've made some progress. Andy has developed this into a business and doesn't have to do everything himself. He got some breaks and doors continue to slowly open.[4]

We both have a deep respect for the art form and where it originated. We do not hesitate to brag about Trinidad, about Ellie, about all the other contributors and great players. The last thing we had in mind was to claim that we built this [instrument], that we figured this [process] out. Like we could ever try to tell that lie! There's too much respect for the art form for us to do that. Some people didn't want to see Americans play pan; however, for the most part we received acceptance, praise, and respect from Trinidadians.

I see this music as bridging people. Pan is a great gift to the world. Other instruments were started in various parts of the world and the world now enjoys them all: the violin, the guitar, and so on. So it is with pan, and Trinis can take pride that the world loves their creation.

The next generation of players should continue to take this music into the world and they will continue to find acceptance. Acceptance is growing beyond the idea and image that this is folk music played on a folk instrument. The instrument is moving beyond these images, yet my generation is still dealing with this problem of image.

Calypso is, of course, tied to Pan and just like the older calypsonians are dying—Kitchener passed last year and Roaring Lion and Shorty before him—so are the old Pan pioneers. There aren't many of them left today who can tell the story of Pan and how it came about.

My personal story is not one of as soon as I got a pan the money started coming in through the door. I, as a first generation U.S. pan-player, share somewhat of a solidarity with the early panmen in Trinidad in their efforts to gain acceptance and make a decent living out of something they loved. I, of course, recognize that life in the United States makes things a little easier for me than life in Trinidad was for the early panmen. But we all share the story of struggle. When I was in my twenties and came to California in 1970, I had one lead pan and I committed to the decision to be a pannist and all of the struggles that came with the commitment. In the '70s, not many people knew about Pan so opportunities weren't knocking on our doors. We had to create work for ourselves. We had to start from scratch.

I connected with some local guys my age that I met in Berkeley—one played Latin percussion. I got with the family and taught a couple of the young brothers how to play pan. They came to the center where I worked. I began working at community centers in Oakland, California, a sort of takeoff from what my dad had done. From among them, I got a band started. In New York, we had a group, a band that played and did a lot of shows. In California, those days were gone. My friends had all graduated from school and gone into professions. Andy and I decided we would keep the music going. We played together and separately. It was definitely a process of taking the pan, bringing it into an ensemble, and trying to find work for that, to make a living doing that, and some teaching of pan, too.

My work's evolved over the years so that now I no longer teach at recreational centers. Some schools have accepted the idea of Pan and incorporated it into their music programs. I teach at various schools and continue to give educational music presentation sponsored by San Francisco Symphony's "Adventures in Music." I have demonstrated Pan in every public school in San Francisco over the last ten years. In the '80s, I started to compose some of my own music and learn how to record. It's been a process of many years of barely having enough money to pay rent, like Ellie experienced in Trinidad. In some ways, it was harder here in America because at least in Trinidad Pan had come to be accepted as a national art form.

It's been an interesting struggle, but I've never regretted any of it because I still wake up every day with that little edge of excitement that I'm doing something that I loved and was being creative at. I love the music, the harmonizing of sound and rhythm, and to have an orchestra. I have the steel orchestra to continue to create with, and for this I'll be eternally grateful to all the pan pioneers.

I enjoy all the logistics of having and managing my own band: the phone calls for the gigs, the paperwork, setting up the instruments for the gigs and pulling them down. It can all wear you down, but the music compensates for all that. So, that's a part of the story of the early struggles we had that needs to be told.

Pan's Future

In addition to spreading the love for Steelpan everywhere I go, I hope that with my live performances, recordings, and compositions that I have contributed to paving the way for the next generations of pan-players to follow and continue to innovate and create with the instrument. Using the pan as a solo voice in Jazz and pop music, incorporating Pan in an Afro-Cuban setting, and my approach to teaching and arranging Steelband into other musical idioms other than Caribbean music and classical music, I hope I have helped forge ahead in these directions. I am inspired by Robbie Greenidge's overall command of the double second, and so on; by Ray Holman's Panorama arrangements and compositions; Boogsie Sharpe's Jazz soloing. It is my hope that we can continue to innovate and enjoy this journey in Pan and share it with people all over the world.

Author's note: the following calypso, "Ellie Man," was written by Jeff in 2003. It was sung by Crazy (Edwin Ayoung) and initially selected by BWIA Invaders and Belmont Fifth Dimension to play at Panorama 2003.[5] In all, eight bands played the calypso.[6] For the Junior Panorama competition, three bands played it.[7] It is used here by permission.

Verse 1
He was born in the Caribbean
Trinbago the land of Calypso and Pan
Where he started to pound
From dustbin to drum
Looking for that special sound
His band Invaders was the best

They came from Woodbrook in the west
His main ambition to improve the pan
This how the story began

Chorus
Ellie man Jam de pan
He making a sweet sweet guitar pan
Second too, tenor for you
He making a sweet six bass it's true

Ellie Mannette, oh
You are my hero
You give your life for
Something we all can share in
You never waver
Now we can savor
All that you done for the pan

Verse 2
Jeff and Andy in New York City
The time was the 1960s
Rupert build them a pan
They form a steelband
Jammin' as hard as they can
But there was a man down the way
Working on the pan night and day
Creating a tone that chills to the bone
Murray bring him to the U.S. of A.

Verse 3
He was strong in his heart and his mind
And hoped in New York he would find
Embrace of the art that he was a part
Pan for the U.S. of A.
Down the road he built band after band
And Pan start to spread 'cross the land
A real pioneer his mission was clear
Pan for the spirit of man and woman

11

From the Decks of the U. S. Navy: A Vignette by Franz Grissom[1]

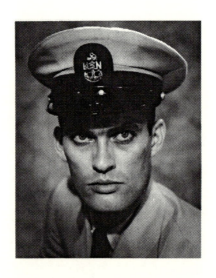

The late Franz Grissom *was the former Chief Musician and Director of the United States Navy Steel Band during its formative years from 1959 to 1965. He believed that the band's success was due to exceptional musicianship, innovations in arranging and song writing, and the immense talent demonstrated by great Navy musicians turned steelbandsmen like Thomas Oliver "Ollie" Knight, Hyland Miller, Jim O'Sullivan, Hugo Bailey, and George Hamill, to name but a few. Though the Navy Steel Band disestablished in 1999,* Grissom *was proud of the national and international roles the band's leaders and members played during its forty-two-year history in shaping Pan's history.*

Upon retiring in Nevada in 1993, Grissom *became immersed in Pan as much as possible by writing songs and creating arrangements on his Web site, writing articles on pan-related topics, organizing and playing in several bands including a civic steel band, and with his own group,* Hurricane. *His band mates were involved, with Grissom's help, in implementing a steel band program in several Las Vegas elementary schools.*

In Recognition of Admiral Dan V. Gallery, a True Pioneer

Steelband in the United States began with Admiral Dan V. Gallery. He was in command of the entire Caribbean and stationed in San Juan, Puerto Rico. The U.S. Navy had its seaplanes based at Chaguaramas, Trinidad. In 1941, the United States and Britain signed a ninety-nine-year lease for a large tract of land at Chaguaramas, in the northwest of Trinidad, where the Navy built a seaplane-base that operated submarine hunter-killer planes during World War II. The base has since been turned over to Trinidad, but in 1956 it was still in operation. During the war, much of the gasoline and lubricating oil for the aircraft was brought in by ship in 55-gallon oil barrels, and in the 1950s a section of the base had thousands of empty barrels stored in giant stacks. In a way, the Navy contributed to the growth of steel bands in Trinidad, as many of the barrels used to make early drums came from the base.

During one of his visits in 1956 to Chaguaramas to inspect the base, which incidentally was at Carnival time, Admiral Gallery was invited by the Trinidad government to the Carnival parade. He sat among the officials and dignitaries in the viewing stand in the section reserved for officials. When the steel bands came by, he was totally enchanted by the sound of the steel band and the spirit of the music and became very enthusiastic about this particular art form.

Gallery was always a man who charted his own course. He blew his own bugle and made a name for himself in the Navy in several different ways. For instance, he was the first man since the 1800s to capture a foreign warship. During World War II, he captured a German submarine, the U-505, with an aircraft carrier. This capture was big news because it was the first capture of an enemy ship by the U.S. Navy since 1815. Consequently, he received a medal of distinction and became a big hero. Admiral Dan, as he was called, also was a noted writer and novelist, and the one who introduced Little League baseball to Puerto Rico. A cultured man, he was the antithesis of the traditional Navy admiral. He listened to classical music in his home, attended concerts and the theater, and was friendly with people like Pablo Casals, Harry Belafonte, Bob Hope, and Herman Wouk. He was also something of a showman, and sometimes quite controversial in his speeches and writings. He never shied away from the spotlight or failed to lead his organization into the spotlight. He returned to Puerto Rico gripped by steelband music and approached his Navy band master, Chief Musician Charlie Roeper, and instructed him to form a steel band.

In contrast to Gallery, Roeper was a fairly typical Navy bandleader. A piano player by profession, at this point he had been in the Navy over twenty years and was well satisfied to be running a traditional Navy band at a sleepy naval base in Puerto Rico. The hours were good and the demands few. He led a band of thirteen musicians familiar only with the trumpet, trombone, and this family of instruments. Consequently, he balked at the idea of a steel band. Roeper told the Admiral that he didn't think his men could learn steel drums, to which the Admiral replied, "They *can* and they *will*." In spring of 1956, Roeper and his boys were sent off to Trinidad first to purchase steel drums and, second, to learn to play them *before* returning to Puerto Rico. Thus began the Navy Steel Band's existence.

In Trinidad, the Navy band stayed at the base while on their "learning" trip but hung out all day in Ellie Mannette's backyard. Ellie built the first pans for the band and was compensated by being able to get barrels from the base. He and his band members also gave the aspiring pannists their first lessons. Wisely, Roeper and others with piano and mallet skills learned the tenor/lead pan, then called "ping-pong"; the tuba player was assigned to basses; the trumpet and sax players got the double second pans and cello pans, then called tune booms; and the drummers were assigned to play hi-hat, called the "cutter," and brake drum. At the time, steel bands were using "thumpers," which were half-barrel, two-note, non-tuned instruments that played like a bass drum. The player traditionally put his left hand on the notes to further muffle them and make them non-tonal. Also used were half-barrel basses, which produced a low-resonance note, somewhere between the thumpers and modern-day basses.

The Navy Steel Band would not have existed were it not for Ellie Mannette and all he did for the Navy band in 1956. I don't know if Gallery met him at that time or how he eventually made connection with Ellie. Anyway, the Navy band returned to Puerto Rico, having met the Admiral's directives with pans and knowing how to play them. They knew three tunes and this is a sort of joke: one of them was "Mary Anne" and the other two were not "Mary Anne." I didn't make that up. General President Grant said that in the Civil War. He said, "I only know two tunes. One is 'Yankee Doodle' and the other is not."

With the Admiral breathing down their necks, the band members had to work in earnest. They had brought back some calypsos to Puerto Rico, the most memorable being Sparrow's "Jean and Dinah," the year's winning calypso. Sparrow was that year's Calypso King. Roeper who was a fair arranger for a military band contributed "Colonel Bogey" and "Stars and Stripes Forever" done as meringues. Belafonte was at the height of his popularity in the United States, and his sanitized versions of calypsos and other Caribbean songs with their simple melodies and easy chords were especially adaptable to early learners on steel drums. Some of Belafonte's calypsos became a part of our repertoire, also.

We were able to accomplish all this because we had some excellent players, which charted the band's direction and made it into the really outstanding organization that it was to become. In October of 1956, Thomas Oliver "Ollie" Knight arrived at the band. Ollie was music major in college and capable of playing a variety of instruments and playing them all well. He came into the band as a drummer but also played piano, vibes, marimba, baritone sax, and was a singer and arranger. He took to the tenor/lead pan like a duck to water and eventually was able to play an astonishing cascade of notes during ad-lib solos. Another notable addition to the band at that time was Hugo Bailey, a tuba and string bass player with a symphonic background who eventually played the fastest steelband basses anyone had ever heard and danced the lowest limbo that anyone had ever seen. There were also Hyland Miller, a genius on any reed instrument who became the true utility infielder by being able to play well on any steelband instrument, and George Hamill who led the double-seconds and cellos sections into playing as nearly like Trinidad steelbandsmen as possible.

Hugo, Hyland, and George all left the Navy at about the same time and, along with George's brother, formed a steel band that played at Disneyland and was a mainstay for many years at the ski lodge at Sun Valley, Idaho. Hyland and George are now deceased. Hugo is still hanging in there in Ketchum, Idaho, where he makes pans and has recently formed an all-female steel band. Ollie Knight did eight years in the Navy and now lives in Richmond, Virginia, where he is still active with steel bands and does a one-man show where he plays pan with recorded backgrounds.

To return to the Navy band: in June of 1957, after a year of playing mostly local jobs in Puerto Rico, with a few side trips back to Trinidad, the band hit the big time. They were still playing fairly basic music and were short on charts, but they had arrived and within a few months made a big splash with only three tunes: "Mary Anne," "Happy Wanderer," and "Colonel Bogey March." After a year in business, they were ready for some heavy-duty engagements and went on tour.

In late June, after they returned to Puerto Rico, Roeper became ill and was flown back to the United States. He eventually was given a medical discharge from the Navy and settled in Charleston, where he and his son taught Steelband in local schools and formed a professional steel band group. He passed away a few years later. His tenure with the Navy Steel Band was quite short.

Orders went out for a replacement for Roeper, and in July 1957, I was tapped for the job. I had been recently promoted to Chief Musician and at the time was assistant leader of the Commander Sixth Fleet Band stationed at Villefranche, France. At the time, I had been in the Navy for seven years and was a graduate of the Navy School of Music bandmaster's course. I am a percussionist, which I am sure had some bearing on the assignment.

Coming Aboard

I arrived in Puerto Rico in August, 1957, and immediately started working with the band. I had a lot to learn, having no experience with either steel drums or Caribbean music, although I had followed closely the Afro-Cuban and Latin trends as performed by Dizzy Gillespie, Stan Kenton, and Tito Puente. I had done some dance-band and concert-band arranging in prior years and I looked forward to writing charts for Steelband.

Ollie Knight had been the interim leader of the band before my arrival, and I found the band in good shape musically, other than the aforementioned paucity of charts and challenging music. Along with Ollie and others, I set to work arranging suitable material and over a period of years had a book that contained fifty to sixty arrangements that were rehearsed and available to perform at any given time, and up to one hundred more in reserve. We did full scale arrangements of classics like "Poet and Peasant Overture" and "Ave Maria," light classics with a Latin beat, and a large number of American, Puerto Rican, South American, and Caribbean songs.

We expanded our Calypso repertoire by going to Carnival in Trinidad every year and recording the top calypsos and steelband arrangements, and upon returning to Puerto Rico we transcribed them off the tape and performed them for the next year until the new ones came out. The band played these calypsos for many years to come.

None of this would have been possible without Ellie who helped to stabilize the band. First, Ellie helped me by bringing the band out of disarray into a reputable band. He went to live in Puerto Rico and worked with the men. The men, in turn, as continued to visit Trinidad annually, continued to visit Ellie's panyard. At Carnival, we played with the Invaders and pushed pan when we weren't playing. In fact, I pushed pan for Ellie.

We also tape-recorded the current road marches, recorded other bands at their panyards, then returned to Puerto Rico and transcribed and arranged all this music. Many of the road marches and calypsos became a part of our repertoire, which included Trinidad music from 1958 to '62. During those years, we also came to meet and know Sparrow and Kitchener.

But, it was our connection to Ellie and Invaders that helped to bond Ellie with the Navy Steel Band and how he became to be regarded as the "father of the Navy Steel Band." I remember everything involving Ellie because it was all so pleasant. Once, I went to his house and remember in his living room he had a new *grundig* on which he was playing a recording of "Voices of Spring," a tune that Invaders played later as a Bomb tune. He was quite sad because he couldn't stay to entertain me. He had to attend the funeral of his aunt. This was in 1958 or '59. When reminiscing, he marveled that I remember that house visit.

I continued to work to redefine the band and developed a slick show that comprised of hundreds of tunes in our repertoire because all the men could read music. Among other things, we were expected to be the band for the Admiral's social functions and as a result had a book of Steelband cocktail music. We did soft-tinkling, fake book tunes with maracas and guiros and featured several vocalists. We developed a system where we had sixteen pannists playing from lead sheets, and it still sounded like an arrangement. With the lead pan and double seconds alternating the melody, the other pans divided up the chords so they were voiced correctly and had good voice-leading. The seconds usually strummed a pattern as set by the best player, and the others then followed, although most Latin tunes or American tunes with Latin backgrounds had pretty well set and recognized patterns. The cellos sometimes strummed but often played arpeggios and bass figures. The bass players became experts at deciding which inversion of the chord to use. We didn't just do these things off the top of our heads. We spent hours and hours with chord progression books written for guitar and piano learning how to voice all the different kinds of chords in all keys.

My brief tenure was a time of frenzy of keeping a family together while keeping all the gigs: festivals, parades all over Puerto Rico, the Virgin Islands, Cuba (we played in Cuba a lot), Trinidad, Barbados, Antigua, Guyana, the Bahamas whose Carnival we attended every year, the United States, and Latin America. We played at the 1958 Brussels World's Fair, the *Ed Sullivan Show,* and at the White House. For the Fair, we played only those three tunes I mentioned earlier—"Mary Anne," "Happy Wanderer," and "Colonel Bogey March"—in ten-minute sets all day long.

Gallery passed his vein to the band, which came to be called the Admiral Gallery's Steel Band. He got a lot of publicity and mileage out of the band. It went all over the world, played at almost every military installation in the United States, in Hawai'i for the statehood for two weeks, in the "People-to-People Program"—a program designed by President Eisenhower to make friends in South America—for thirty-five days.

When we began touring South America, we arranged Brazilian and Argentinean music for the steel band to play for those local audiences. When we played in Guyana, Phil Solomon said he first saw the steel band perform during one of the "People-to-People" programs there. He was a boy at the time and remembers seeing me and the band perform. Solomon later spearheaded the whole Steelband movement in British Guiana (BG). The Minister of Education and Cultural Arts was also a steelband player in BG and helped to promote Steelband there for a little time. Then in New York, we met Murray Narell and Jimmy Leyden. We did quite a lot during those years.

I don't hesitate to say now that in our enthusiasm for Steelband, we probably didn't project the highest quality Steelband image. We were all White men playing our renditions of calypso music on instruments that were fairly inadequate by today's standard of Pan. People seeing us on TV may not have been impressed. While we meant well, we could have set back the movement a few years.

Anyway, at that time, we also did dances, and in Puerto Rico that meant plenty of meringues. On tour in the United States, we often played theaters and had a show that featured the band's music plus acts that included singers, a pennywhistle player, the Limbo dance, and, at one time, a comedian. We sometimes featured combo instruments and steel drums with a standard rhythm section. We were often booked by the Department of Defense Public Affairs Office. We were combined with the Blue Angels, the Navy Parachute Team, the Navy Trampoline Team, and various other acts such as the Naval Academy Choir for air shows.

While in Puerto Rico, I also organized the Shriners Steel Band, which as of a few years ago was still doing Shrine conventions in the United States. After almost six years in Puerto Rico, I got promoted out of the job and was assigned to the Navy band at Treasure Island in San Francisco. My steelband days were not over, however, as I had purchased a full set of pans from Ellie prior to leaving the islands. I took the pans back to the States with me.

I think Ellie left Trinidad before I left Puerto Rico. I saw him years later when he was in Charleston, South Carolina, working with Charlie Roeper's school music programs. Then when the Navy Steel Band was on tour, he tuned our pans.

In 1964, in San Francisco I formed my five children into a steel band called the Pandemoniacs. Their ages at the time ranged from age five to age twelve. My son, Eddie, played a set of full-length basses, standing on a stool, but at age five was too young to read music. He did know his colors, however; so we painted each note on the basses a different color and had him learn tunes, for example, in the key of "red." Rehearsal sounded like this: "You remember this one, Eddie; it goes red-blue, red-blue, green-blue, green-blue, red-blue, red-blue, red-blue, red."

The band had a good Hollywood agent and played shows and promotions in and around San Francisco for three years until we were transferred to Italy. In Italy, we played during the summers when the older girls were home from school they attended in Germany. Transfer back to the United States and teenagers with other agendas caused the breakup of the band in 1969. The pans were sold to George Hamill in Idaho, and I'm told some are still in use. After I left the steel-band business, I lost touch with Ellie. I think by that time he went to the west coast.

I got out completely of Steelband and tried to make a living doing other things. For fourteen years, I had little to nothing to do with music; I was a Jazz drummer for a little while. When I got out of the Navy, I decided to get out of music because I didn't like the way the entire music industry was going. I returned to music after leaving the job and pursued an interest in the symphonies as a symphonic musician.

Then, I met guys from Panyard at a convention for percussionists in Phoenix, Arizona. They were from Akron, Ohio, and were selling steelpans and recognized my name. They immediately contracted me to write arrangements for Panyard in 1995. I was playing bagpipes drums when I saw a guy playing a single drum. We struck up a conversation and I told him what I used to do. He offered to have me join him. He was Jack Cenna and his band was called One-Eyed Jack. He advised me to call Ellie for drums. When I did and spoke with Kaethe, I learned that the wait was sixteen months. Cenna then advised me to call Phil Solomon, who sent me a set of drums he used for gigs but wasn't using at the time. They were beautiful drums. That's how I returned to Steelband. I played with Cenna for about three years.

I continue to be in touch with Ellie when he comes to Las Vegas and is on his rounds to sites in the west coast that have his drums—Phoenix to Las Vegas to Salt Lake City.

Addressing Some Misconceptions

I was aware of the controversy, that in Trinidad the people and the press were saying the United States was trying to steal the art form. However, let me say emphatically that there was never any danger of the United States stealing the art form. It may be that in a way the Navy contributed to the advent of steel bands in Trinidad, as many of the barrels used to make early drums came from the Chaguaramas base. Our claim is that the Navy Steel Band was the first White steel band that did anything of any U.S. national prominence, and in doing that we brought Steelband out of the Caribbean into the United States into the eyes of the American public, as featured on the *Bob Hope Show*, the *Ed Sullivan Show*, and so on. We are the reason some universities and high schools have Steelband programs, in part, because the Navy Steel Band brought it to the United States. But we have never tried and would never have tried to claim that the steel band originated anywhere but in Trinidad. In fact, we used to do long shows that featured the evolution of the pan, giving full credit to Trinidad and Ellie Mannette, so there was no reason for those feelings.

The feelings that continue to be harbored against Andy Narell are unnecessary, and Andy Narell continues to be resented because he plays extremely well; he's a very talented guy. Even Americans resent him for his talent, not just Trinidadians. Even though he brings a rock feeling—which some people don't like—to the art form, and even I don't like its sound, Andy is an artist.

I met the Narells when I took the steel band to New York in 1961 or '62 to the World's Fair. We were playing in the bandstand all day when this man brought this gaggle of kids who sat down in the front row. Afterward, Murray Narell came up and introduced himself as the one in charge of a children's steel band that rehearsed in the basement of his house. Murray invited us to come over and hear his children's band, and I balked. After playing all day, I didn't want to go and listen to some kids who probably didn't know what they were doing. But Murray insisted. I selected some of the Navy band members to accompany me to Queens to hear these kids play on Ellie Mannette's drums that were set up in the basement. They started to play and the members of the Navy band wept. One of them said, "I quit. I can never play steel drums again after hearing this. These are nine-year-old kids." They were excellent!

Another controversy is the Navy advanced the technology of the pan. I have never made that claim. I know that Gallery approached some friends of his at Dow Chemical Company and informed them on what was being done. He saw some barrels behind the Dow Chemical plant and requested to use them. He was granted permission to use them and the drums had the Dow Chemical logo. He then asked his friends to research a method to dish-in [or sink-in], since dishing-in the bottom of the barrel is the hardest work, hard on one's ears and arms. Once that is done, the rest is a lot easier on the ears. He got the Dow people interested in trying to build a big machine that would press the bottom of the barrel down and dish-in it. Ellie is now using water pressure to accomplish the same task.

Nobody in the world was using a stroboscope to tune the pans until we did. Ellie was tuning by ear. The Navy bought the stroboscope for the Navy band to tune their own instruments—trumpets and trombones—and they then used it to test whether the drums were in tune. Hugo Bailey went down to Trinidad to live with Ellie and to learn from him to tune drums. When Bailey started to tune for the Navy band, he used the strobe. So, the Navy band was the first band, I am sure, to use the strobe to tune pans.

The Disestablishment of the Navy Steel Band

To many people's dismay, the Navy Steel Band is now history. During its life, it had ten or more leaders, numerous changes of personnel, and undergone many transitions, including moving from San Juan, Puerto Rico, to New Orleans. When it was disestablished in October 1999, at least twenty different people pleaded with me to intercede with the Navy to keep the band. I could not. It was a decision made by the Navy predicated on the amount of money it had and the number of personnel it had, which cannot be changed. People even suggested the establishment of a special fund made up of contributions to the Navy for the steel band. The reality was this: we were taking sixteen players, common players, out of other bands or villages, and making a band of steelband players out of them. This meant that the other bands were short of players. The Congress authorized a set amount of money for the Navy and the Navy authorized a set amount for the Music Program. No one wanted to pay for the band to travel anymore. The budget was limited.

The band was stationed in New Orleans, and once it played at Mardi Gras, a couple of high schools, and the officer's club, that was it. Nobody could afford to take it anywhere else or to do anything else. All the money dried up for Av-Gas, meaning military air fare. The men continued to get dressed up and to practice but had no where to go. I feel quite bad about it, but as a Master Chief who dealt with funding, I saw and understood how money trails flow or are stanched. I would love to see the band resume, but there is nothing anyone can do.

Steelband on the whole has just not had an easy time, wherever it existed. The Navy band used a two-and-a-half-stake truck for transporting the drums. Plus, the loading, traveling, setting up, and pulling down the instruments are all time-demanding. Depending on where you're going, you're looking at half a day to a full day to do a gig. Also, one had to be careful with the instruments.

The history of the steel band is one of gritty steel and determination. Working in Steelband is not for the faint of heart. In the eyes of many people, it is an illegitimate instrument, playing illegitimate music, and by men viewed as the wretched of the earth. One of the contradictions is the mainstream still wants the music to make them feel good.

Some Firsts Claims

I'm proud of some things we can claim as first for Steelband:

- The U.S. Navy Steel Band was the *first* to be made up of players not born in the Caribbean, although in 1960 a Puerto Rican native, Clemente Bobonis, joined the steel band.

- We were the *first* to write and read steelband arrangements and to play music especially written for Steelband.

- We were the *first* to appear on U.S. national television and *first* to do extensive U.S. national tours.

- We were the *first* non-Trinidadian band to tour South America; *first* in Hawai'i; *first* to record using steelband instruments mixed with other instruments (see recording *New Paths for Steelband* using concert grand piano, dance drums, vibraphone, string bass, and pennywhistle on some cuts); *first* to use electronic tuning devices; and *first* non-Trinidadian band to play in Europe.

I'm also proud of the first claims made by Pandemoniacs, the Grissom family steel band. Ours was

- the *first* all-family band in the United States with the youngest professional members ever: bassist Eddie Grissom was age five; cellist Gina Grissom was age six; on record is the *youngest member of the Musicians Union ever*, Eddie at age five;

- *first* in the United States with four female members—Gloria, Gilda, Gina, and Giulia; *first* to play extensively in the San Francisco area;

- and *first* to play extensively in Italy.

In Memoriam

Franz Edmond Grissom (MUCM, Ret.) passed away on July 26, 2005, in Boulder City, Nevada. He is survived by his wife, Raffaela "Lina" Grissom; brother, David Grissom (Cabot, Arkansas); a son, Franz "Eddie" Grissom (Oklahoma City, Oklahoma); and daughters Gloria Wade (Pahrump, Nevada); Gilda Strom (Fallbrook, California); Gina Norris (Elizabeth, Colorado); and Giulia Lewis (Watertown, Wisconsin); as well as eleven grandchildren and four great-grandchildren.

All who knew and loved Franz found him to be a loving, caring, sincere person and a generous, patient teacher—the best friend a pan-player ever had. One of the great joys of his life was seeing how the love of Pan has migrated globally. Surely, the title of Panman fits Franz. He was honored and thrilled to have been a part of Pan's history. His voice will be heard so long as the pans keep beating.

12

The Introduction of Modern Music Technology: A Vignette by James Leyden[1]

James "Jimmy" Leyden *has lived in Banks, Oregon, since 1977 where he owns a vineyard. For the past twenty-five years, he has worked as choral director and arranger with his brother Norman, associate conductor of the Oregon Symphony in the Symphony Pops series.* Leyden *is credited with helping advance Pan technology.*

Inspirations

My love affair with Steelband began in the '50s. Although I and my family vacationed in Tobago a number of times, I first visited Trinidad in 1957 while spending a week in Tobago. One evening's entertainment was a small, local steel band. The sound was fascinating, although their pans were primitive by today's standards. On our way back to the United States, my wife and I visited Grenada where we heard a very polished and well-tuned band. That's when I knew I was hooked on the sound.

But, it was not until some years later when I became a music teacher in Chappaqua, New York, that I approached the principal and requested five hundred dollars to buy some drums. After I played him a recording of a steel band, he readily agreed. I ordered the drums from Carol Drum Service, a percussion service company located in New York City. When they were available and I took them back to my school, I found that they were not tuned to the standard A-440 pitch. I took them back to Carol Drum to have them retuned. To my dismay, they told me that the builder-tuner had moved out of town and referred me to a person who knew of Ellie Mannette. In due time, I made contact with Ellie and explained the problem to him. He was able to tune the drums up to standard so I could use them with my concert band.

I stayed in touch with Ellie after that. He had some drums which had been made for the Settlement Houses in New York that were no longer being used by Murray Narell. I bought a number of these and Ellie brought them up to pitch. It was these drums which, added to the original group, became the Calliope's Children Steel Orchestra.

At the time, Ellie was using a circular chromatic pitch-pipe to tune pans, which was not a very accurate way to tune. I was using a stroboscopic tuner made by the Conn Instrument Company to tune up my concert band. This device, which has a rotating disk whose speed can be regulated, allows the tuner to set the desired pitch in alignment with the disk's vertical markings. A note is struck and when played into a microphone the vibrations are displayed on the spinning disk. The tuner then shapes the note he's working on until the selected marks on the disk are aligned. That note is then at the correct pitch.

Using the strobe and having Ellie use his tuning hammers, I was able to show him how the notes were brought in tune more accurately with the strobe than with the chromatic pitch-pipe he had been using. At the time, Ellie was not convinced and said something to the effect of, "I don't think I like that machine. I feel more comfortable with my ear and the pitch-pipe."

What followed were several lively discussions until I was able to convince him that the strobe would indeed be faster and more accurate. He would be able to see the lines moving, could change the shape of the notes in various ways, and could move the note up and down at will. This experimenting led to the concept of centering notes.

Once he was more comfortable with the technique, I explained the concept of harmonic overtones. And, though he was not familiar with the concept, he latched onto the idea and its implications. I explained that every note has harmonics, sympathetic vibrations of definite pitch. It could be the same note but an octave higher; it could be a fifth or a third above, or a ninth, and so on. It's known as the harmonic series, so named by an acoustical scientist, Helmholz.

This led us to another series of lively discussions on manipulating the note shapes differently than he was used to. Somewhat confused and finally in frustration, he declared one late morning, "I can't work for you any more!" I suggested that we have some lunch. After lunch and a time of relaxation, we resumed working with these new ideas and that afternoon he exclaimed, "I got it!" I recall him saying with some satisfaction and amazement, "Ain't that something!" Once he had the hang of it, he was off and running.

We explored the control of various harmonics and the arrangements of notes. The note on the drum is pretty much tuned north-south-east-west. The notes on any pan are, for the most part, tuned on a north-south and east-west axis. The harmonics can be brightened or dulled depending on how complementary the axis was. We experimented with putting certain intervals on the basic notes to find which ones made the notes more or less resonant. We learned a lot of things during this process, which led me to having a wonderful set of drums for our band. Ellie has since advanced the technology beyond what we had originally worked out. All in all, it was pretty exciting to see how the theory worked out in actual practice.

Tuning is a gradual process. You take one note and in effect stretch metal around and around, moving the pitch closer and closer to its final shape. When you get all the notes to that final stage and when you're doing fine tuning, you have to keep all the conceptual details in mind so that the whole pan will have a uniformed, pleasing sound. The whole process is very time-consuming.

Understanding One's Worth

Ellie and I continued to work off and on until I moved to the west coast in 1977. We had a good relationship. However, it was during these years I became aware that Ellie was being taken advantage of by the steelband players from Brooklyn, Washington, D.C., Philadelphia, and Baltimore.

At that time, he was living in Long Island with Jackie and their daughter, Julie. I lived some thirty-five to forty miles away in Westchester. On numerous occasions, when we had made arrangements to work together at my school, I would drive to Long Island to pick him up. Upon my arrival, Jackie would come out and greet me and inform me that some of the boys had come during the night, knocking on their door and refusing to go away, insisting that he must come and tune their drums for some immediate upcoming performance. When he demurred, they used the wedge, "You're turning your back on your own West Indian people." The accusation that he was turning his back on his people bothered him a great deal.

Without being privy to the facts, I observed that Ellie had become discouraged. Once, just before the spontaneous and enthusiastic recognition he received at the 1974 Regional Music Educators National Conference (RMENC), he was very depressed and contemplated returning to Trinidad. It was actually when we were on our way to this Conference that he mentioned he just couldn't deal with the financial uncertainty and the social problems that came with it. He always tried to do the best job he could but was not getting the payment or the recognition for his efforts. Too often, folks paid him late or didn't pay him at all. Many times, the boys just didn't treat him right. And, he wasn't really charging that much for his labor.

It takes many, many hours to craft and tune a quality drum. Mind you, this was 1973 to '74. What was his hour worth? Five—ten—twenty dollars? Building and tuning pan is hard, demanding work and few people have the skills to do it well.

One interesting character was Victor Brady. He was not one of those who manipulated Ellie, though, and was quite one of Ellie's better clients. He was a flamboyant street musician and a very good player. He wanted his drum to scream. "That is what I want, Ellie. That is what I'm paying you for." So, Ellie would put on all these overtones to satisfy Victor. When he performed on the street, he wore bells on his ankles and stamped the pavement in time with his playing. Many times, when interacting with his sidewalk audience, he got into—shall we say?—very lively discussions with these folks. He was a most unusual, sometimes contradictory, but very active street player on the New York City scene.

Meanwhile, our band, Calliope's Children—Calliope being the ancient Greek Muse of lyrics and poetry—was developing and receiving invitations to perform at some rather prestigious functions around the State. Whenever possible, Ellie accompanied us. That's how it happened he was with us when we gave a concert at the RMENC. He was introduced as the creator of all our instruments and indeed the creator of the first new instrument of the twentieth century. The Conference received his remarks with rapt attention and at the finish gave him a standing ovation, which in those days was a very uncommon occurrence. I think this was the starting point of his recognition in the music education world. I recall that at the reception following the concert, one of the girls in our band approached us and exclaimed enthusiastically, "Ellie, Jimmy, we're making history!" I think we were one of the very first high school steel drum ensembles in the country, so I guess we did make a little history that day.

In 1974, Calliope's Children played in the St. Croix Carnival parade. In 1975, we toured in Romania and in 1977 we toured in Russia and Poland. In none of those European countries had anyone seen or heard steel drums—and this was during the Cold War years—so it was a very exciting and sobering experience.

Moving West

Little was known about Pan in those days, when I moved to the west coast in 1977 and brought along some drums. I was able to contact Patrick Arnold, who was residing in San Francisco, and invite him to come to Oregon and make some additional drums for what I hoped would be the first steel band in Portland. The drums were made. I had radio, TV, and newspaper interviews, and put up signs advertising the establishing of a steel orchestra in Portland, Oregon. ZERO response! People out here had little or no knowledge of steel drums back then. Later, I developed a program in one of the schools in Vancouver, Washington.

Later still, the director of the Summer Arts Program for Portland State University called and asked me if I could do a workshop with the drums at a place called Haystack on the Oregon coast. I jumped at the chance and persuaded Ellie to join in and show folks some of the ins and outs of pan-making. A reasonable number of people attended, and we pounded on steel barrels and played on the pans I got from the schools for the occasion. The following year, the number doubled, and each year thereafter the number of attendees continued to increase. But as the program grew, the logistics of space, housing, and scheduling became complicated. The university eventually withdrew its funding for the Steelband program. But many seeds were sown and in the years following some thirty-five steel bands in school programs were started in the Washington state alone.

Not long after the Haystack years, Ellie was invited to teach at WVU and soon afterward he organized a week-long Pan workshop. Again, there were pan-construction, -tuning, and -playing. I joined the staff, along with some well-known Pan folks: Ray Holman, Ken "Professor" Philmore, Tom Miller, and Jeff Narell. For the most part, I worked with folks who were comfortable at reading printed music—I brought along a bunch of arrangements—while Ray, Professor, Tom, and Jeff in the various years they participated worked with those players who were more rote oriented. My hopes and energies were directed at developing Ellie's dreamed-of steel symphony orchestra, but a financial pinch and some restructuring occurred along the way so these best efforts were not realized.

For Ellie's workshops, the rote situation remains the strongest suit and has indeed prospered in recent years. I am not one to disparage the rote approach. It's a different approach to learning and playing music. I admire those who perform at Trinidad Panorama, the majority of whom learn ten minutes of very complicated music by rote. It's a remarkable feat. But it's a very time-consuming process. You know, here in the United States it used to be that when you walked into a recording studio every minute counted. You were given a piece of music which you had to be able to play in a minute or two. In the professional world of recording, time is precious and the rote process costly. Nevertheless, I take my hat off to those Panorama performers. Theirs is a different world from that to which I was accustomed as an arranger and musician working in studio situations.

In today's pop world, however, the wheel has turned. Pop artists are able to indulge in multi-tracking and unlimited studio time. Sometimes, they take as much as a year to complete a CD recording! It seems the current wave of pop musicians and singers don't really know what they want to do or how they want to do it. Ah, but so goes the world!

The Future of Pan in the United States

Most everyone agrees, I think, that how the pan is built—the technology, and so on—has to be commercialized to lower the cost and increase the availability of instruments, which would encourage and support a universal market. Mass production could be the answer. And, when that happens, the Steelband movement will really take off!

Even with this happening, it will depend on music educators—be they Classical-, Jazz-or Folk oriented—to broaden the scope of the music that will be presented in their concerts and recording. And, the school situations, because of the continuity of instruction, will provide the eventual critical mass of Pan musicians and composers who ensure the continuing development of the Pan movement.

13

Bridging Cultural Divides: Clifford Alexis's Story[1]

Clifford "Cliff" Alexis *was born January 15, 1937, and lived in Laventille—Behind the Bridge—and Petit Valley. He is the co-director of Northern Illinois University (NIU) Steel Band; pan-builder, tuner, clinician; Steelband composer and arranger. He resides in DeKalb, Illinois.*

Some of Alexis's *awards include: Sunshine Award Hall of Fame Calypso and Steelband Music* **2002**; *Trinidad and Tobago Folk Art Institute Legend of Pan Award* **2001**; *Pan Trinbago Award of Excellence* **1997**; *Percussive Art Society Special Recognition* **1994**; *Percussive Art Society, St. Louis, Missouri, First Mass Steel Band Arranger* **1987**; *Annual Twin City Black Musical Award* **1983** *and* **1984**.

First Impressions

I was born Behind the Bridge, as people call it, but didn't stay there long. The family moved when I was eleven, so for the first eleven years of my life I was exposed to some of the first steel bands because Behind the Bridge everything was Pan. People from that old neighborhood say that I heard pan in utero, and today when they hear that my life is all Pan, they're not surprised. I'm not the only one. One of my aunts who still lives Behind the Bridge can write Pan's history. She, and others like my good friend Rudy Johnson who knew Winston "Spree" Simon very well and now lives in Chicago, has seen its evolution, from its embryonic stage to what it is today.

During my early childhood, I couldn't touch pan, so I didn't start playing until around age fourteen or fifteen in the '50s in a band named Hit Paraders. I was living in Boissiere then. I next played in Tripoli and then Stereophonics. I didn't stay with Stereophonics for too long, as it overlapped with my involvement with Invaders. Stereophonics gave me my first chance at arranging, which continued with Invaders.

Invaders' tuner, Emmanuel Riley, a.k.a. Corbeau Jack, approached me one day after a Carnival. I was riding my bike near Simeon Road, Petit Valley—I used to live on Thomas Drive off Majouba Cross Road—when he stopped me and said the men wanted me to arrange for them. I'm guessing some of their men scouted the yard and picked me out. I agreed.

When the National Steel Band made the announcement, its call to organize was for each band to send either its arranger or best player. I knew Invaders was planning to send Corbeau Jack, so Stereophonics suggested that I represent them, even though at the time I was a member of Invaders. My membership in the National Steel Band changed my life, is history.

George Goddard formed the National Steel Band, and Eric Williams provided the first set of pans. That first National Steel Band was not like the one today with the members employed by and paid by the government. That was purely a voluntary thing for Goddard and us, but it served as a springboard to what we're doing now, both back home and here in the States. There's a group of Trinidadian panmen living in America whom I got to know well, all members the National Steel Band. Regarding Goddard, he wanted the best players and arrangers. Forty-four members were involved when it started, and I was one of them.

The National Steel Band's first major venture was our trip to America in 1964, when twenty-two of us came under the auspices of the Moral Rearmament[2] to attend its conference. The conference initially invited Goddard to give a lecture in Mackinac Island, Michigan. He responded, "Why only me? I have a band that can do a better job." So, the invitation was extended to the National Steel Band and included our travel to Miami, Florida, then to Michigan. That conference included hundreds of delegates from countries all over the world. So, when we played, we played to almost the entire world.

After the conference, we traveled throughout the southwest in a type of Greyhound bus, primarily because the Native Americans at the conference invited us to visit New Mexico. Our first experience with Native Americans from Santa Fe and Albuquerque was at the conference where they performed their dances, and so on, which made me begin to realize that they were normal like everybody else. Our visit to New Mexico was for one week and coincided with their fiesta. We visited some Pueblo villages and met various Pueblos. We played in the big plaza downtown. It was a good experience.

That visit made me realize fully that what we saw in the movies about the Native Americans with hatchets, and so on, was totally misrepresentative of them and their reality. They were very normal people. I was so impressed that I wanted to stay there. When I met two Black educators in Santa Fe, I inquired into this and learned that Stewart Udall, Secretary of the Interior, was the contact person in Washington, D.C., regarding the Bureau of Indian Affairs. I followed up on this only to learn that the jobs were available only for people who owed allegiance to the Native Americans. While that didn't work out for me, the response opened my eyes to the state of affairs here.

After leaving New Mexico, we visited other places: St. Louis, Missouri; Wheeling, West Virginia; and Louisville, Kentucky. In Louisville, we played on a boat on the Ohio River. In West Virginia, we stayed at a big mansion, either the archbishop's or the bishop's or someone in that position. We also stayed at various hotels, including the Sheraton.

At one destination, the Beatles were there and we played "I Want to Hold Your Hand." People went crazy when we played that song. On the whole, when traveling with the National Steel Band in '64, a very, *very* excellent treatment was meted out to us. Almost king-like in nature. I watched the crowd's response everywhere we played, and always there was a large crowd who received us well and responded to our performance with great enthusiasm. I cannot forget when we played at Oklahoma City's Rotunda, the State capitol. The crowd and the applause. This treatment made me want to return to America because I knew that Trinidad wasn't responding to us like that. Here we were, twenty-two men, and the people were receiving us the way they did. We also visited Trinidad, Colorado, and on our Independence night in August, 1964, its mayor closed down the main intersection for us to play right in the middle of the town.

Eventually, a lot of the guys became antsy and wanted to return home to Trinidad. We did, but that wasn't my choice. A few of us didn't care to go back. But the big wheels in the band had their jobs to return to and the decision was theirs. If I'd got a job or something, I would have stayed here. I learned so much from that trip.

I, subsequently, returned to Mackinac Island in '66 on a second invitation. But even before that, I always knew that I would be returning to America to live.

When we returned to Trinidad and I realized that I had a visa that allowed me to reenter America any time, I said, "Why not?" I kept that dream alive, and when I immigrated to Brooklyn in 1965, I did so knowing that I'd worked and dedicated my life in Trinidad to Pan.

Immigrating to Brooklyn, New York

During those months of biding my time until I departed for the States, I arranged for Stereophonics and was involved with them at the beginning of Panorama. I was there for Goddard's "Pan on the Move" when he was speculating on what to name the event. Someone called me once and said there's a guy in Brooklyn who is saying that he coined the term "Panorama." He didn't. The name of the event was "Pan on the Move," which was what it was called for the Carnival of '65. Desmond Chase was a member of the executive board when they were looking for a name for the event. Goddard asked them to find a name for it. At the time, there was a TV program named Panorama and Chase was familiar with it. He suggested the event be called by the same name, too. That's how the name came about, from the TV program.

At that Panorama, I placed in the top ten with Stereophonics, and another little band I used to arrange for named Joyland placed in the mix of things, too. In retrospect, had I not left Trinidad I think I eventually would have won a Panorama because I was really in my prime.

But if you'd seen me then, you would have seen me with my plane ticket for America in my pocket. The BWIA ticket was around two-hundred-and-something dollars, and my hand was in my pocket holding on to my two-hundred-and-something-dollar ticket. I was set to leave on Ash Wednesday morning of '65, with an extra five dollars in my other pocket, which is how much money I had when I landed in Brooklyn. With Carnival over, come Ash Wednesday and I was out of there. I wasn't staying another day.

What also enticed me to come to America was the story that pan was being played in clubs and I wouldn't have any trouble getting work. Lo and behold, it was a different story.

When I came to Brooklyn in '65, Rudy King helped me a lot. He's a person I would never forget. He's the one credited as the first who brought the pan to New York. He helped many people, including Ellie and many others who have settled in the States: Kelvin Hart, Junior Pouchet, Hugh Borde, and Vincent Hernandez, to name a few. We all can offer unique perspectives, neither right nor wrong, on Pan.

A main thread of my story weaves through my friend, Hugh Borde, the leader of Tripoli, and through whom I became involved with the Liberace show. As previously mentioned, I was a member of Tripoli before joining Invaders and Stereophonics. Some time in '67, Liberace had a show in Cherry Hill, New Jersey. Hugh Borde encouraged me to come to the show and meet some people, which I did. I met most of the people in the Liberace show, including the manager who was also in charge of promotions (selling records, and all of that) and invited me to help him when I wasn't busy. I accepted and through that work I met many people. That work opened doors for me.

Sometime later in '67, Hugh called and told me about a big affair in Birmingham, Alabama. He wanted me to put a band together and I agreed. But before getting started on it, I returned to Trinidad to tend to my little band there. Upon returning and forming the band here, I first called it Trinidad Troubadours, but the manager—the Liberace person—suggested the name Trinidad Steel Drummers. We complied and played around the country under that name—mainly in shopping centers—which made me learn how things operate in this country music-wise. For instance, you have to look for summer work during the summer and winter work during winter.

I've traveled throughout this country playing pan: Las Vegas; Reno; Lake Tahoe; Hollywood (where I lived for three months); Columbia, Maryland; Cherry Hill, New Jersey. Also, I got calls from various people who had heard that Tripoli was on the road with the Liberace show and wanted my band to do a job.

Regarding Hugh, his plan was to leave the Liberace show wherever it was on the road and come to Birmingham, a city I came to know well because I played a lot there during the late '60s. In the mix of things, there was some confusion between Tripoli and the show, and Tripoli left the show, which then wanted me to play some dates. At the time, my little band was playing in Vegas. But my band couldn't play like Tripoli. I must say that Tripoli was one of the best bands I'd heard at that time. People used to talk about Pan Am North Stars, but Tripoli had a wide repertoire. Their arranger was a priest named Father Sewell, one of the greatest pan arrangers. He was a Welsh man and is now deceased.

Between traveling with my band, doing some dates with the show, accepting jobs here and there, I remained busy until I relocated to St. Paul to be with the family, a story that I'll give shortly. Then, even though my two kids were very young, they still used to ask me when next I would be coming home. The sort of life I was living on the road made things difficult for my marriage. Besides, I was too set in Pan, doing my own thing, and not paying enough attention to the family like I should have. So, that first marriage suffered. My wife, an American from St. Paul, moved back there and made contact with a school so I could move there to be with her and the children, which would have worked but I was too much involved with Pan.

Relocating to Minnesota

As I previously said, I lived in Brooklyn when I returned to America in '65. I came with the assumption, based on the guys' encouragement, that we would be playing pan every night, that I'd be making a living just playing pan. Lo and behold, the biggest surprise of my life was that the men weren't making a living playing pan. They were playing pan only on weekends, or on a boat ride, or a dance, or something like that. I thought things would be like they were when we were with the National Steel Band: shows, tours, and whatnot. But that was not the case when I got to the West Indian community in Brooklyn. It was a rehearsal in a basement and a guy saying to me, "Well, you know you have to look for a *job*." I said, "A *job*? I didn't come here to look for a job. I came here to play pan."

I remember one time they took me to a job where the people were making pocket books. I said, "Oh, boy. This is a job. Okay." When lunchtime came, I told them I was going down the street to come back and never went back. Another time, they took me to a steel company. I lasted for maybe about ten minutes. I couldn't concentrate on those jobs; my mind was on Pan. More satisfying was work with a band at the time called the BWIA Sunjets, a band BWIA had sponsored in Brooklyn. I received a little remuneration for doing the arrangements, but nothing to keep me occupied, really. Then I got married and that complicated things a lot.

My first wife always talked about Minnesota because she once lived there. Her parents, though divorced, still lived there, and she wanted to return. Once in Minnesota, she encouraged me to join her, hoping that things would change. I traveled so much that the traveling put a dent in my marriage. A very deep dent. At first I said, "Minnesota? What am I going to do in Minnesota?" Not ready to settle down, I visited Minnesota and returned to Brooklyn.

I continued playing and moving around. Once, I had to play at a show in Winnipeg and planned to travel via New York State. I decided to visit Minnesota and stayed there for one night only. The other few times I visited Minnesota, sometimes my kids didn't even know I was there. I was in and out, arrived at night when they were asleep and gone before they awoke. Yet, on every visit I saw that the kids were getting older and I was not around.

Some time in the '70s, after life on the road began to be tiring, I decided to finally settle down with the family in Minnesota. This meant that I had to find something to do, but it had to involve playing pan so I brought my set of pans with me. After settling there, I constantly dreamt about Pan, always looking and asking where it could go from here. My eyes were on the educational system, because I had a vision that Pan would do well in schools, even though I didn't have a clue how to implement a program. One opening came through my wife.

She was a school teacher and someone suggested to her for me to try the Performing Arts Center, which was a part of the St. Paul public schools. St. Paul's public schools had different learning centers for students, in conjunction with the desegregation guidelines of that time. Kids from different backgrounds were brought to these centers to learn about diversity. I was hired by the Performing Arts Learning Center. That hiring started the venture into Pan and education, which took off and did well. So well that when an Arts magnet school was built, the center was closed and the program moved into the Arts magnet school. A special wing for the performing arts was built, which included space for the steel band, dance, acting, and so on. I worked in that Performing Arts high school for twelve years.

The learning centers were away from the regular school building. The kids left school and came to the various centers and interacted with each other. Sometimes, I had the junior high students from all over the city in the morning teaching them steelpan, then in the afternoon I had the senior high students. As the program developed, I think it met its goal. Then, the Performing Arts Center was moved back into a traditional school that had been built with a wing for the Performing Arts. This was an Arts magnet school and my first experience with this type of school. That was a very, *very* wonderful experience. Except, outsiders used to call us crazy. The dancers. The actors. We were all nontraditionalists, but we teachers taught the kids.

At the same time—1971 to '74—I started to learn how to tune. I had all this room and could come in whenever I wanted to, so I decided to start tuning. Shortly after accepting the St. Paul job, the school administrators told me of their desire to have pans made and wanted to know if I could make them. I told them no, but I would bring somebody who could. I invited Patrick Arnold and after he left I decided to teach myself to tune. I couldn't go to the principal every Monday morning and tell him the pans needed tuning. That's why I started tuning pans in America, in Minnesota of all places during the '70s. There I was, living in a place with minus sixty degrees weather and working in the public schools. If I were living in New York or Trinidad, I probably would never have learned to tune pan. There was a need at that particular time in that particular place for me to do this work. No one else was there to do it, and besides I wanted to learn to make and tune pan myself, to help myself out. Ellie and the other panmen were in Brooklyn and I'd left Brooklyn and couldn't reach them. Who else to get the work done but me?

I began with trying to figure out how those guys got those notes tuned. I thought that I'd known it all until I began teaching myself to tune. Then I had to persevere through the entire process. Someone said Ellie told him that we used to work together, but that's not true. I never worked with Ellie, not with tuning. I never did an apprenticeship with anybody.

When I finally mastered it, I never believed I would ever sell a pan, or that people would point out that I was making good pan. Then I started selling pans. That was good. I've been making pan for thirty-something years now. My actual life in Pan covers about fifty-three years, so to speak. My role in Pan in Trinidad was playing and arranging, and I began tuning and composing in this country. I've completed the full cycle: from playing, to composing and arranging, to building and tuning pan.

Journey to Illinois: Becoming an Academic

A few years, later Al O'Connor heard of me. I used to tune pans for the U.S. Navy and they told him of me. Al started the first university steel band in the United States. He got NIU to eventually approve Pan as a degree program. He's a wealth of information on this topic. In essence, he approached them with the idea that a kid enrolled in the Percussion Program has to learn the drum-set and all the different requirements for a percussionist: the marimba, and so on. He proposed that the requirements for a candidate satisfying that degree program could be applied to Pan, because Pan was very demanding, too: applied lessons, scales, ensemble playing, and so on. The only difference between one in traditional studies and Pan was that Pan was the specialty, the instrument to be mastered. Sometimes though, Pan studies were a little harder than what the marimba people were studying, regarding some exercises. That's the program in a nutshell. Al is the academic person who can provide further fuller details on when the program was approved, the number of graduates, and so on.

It took him two years to make contact with me in Minnesota, to visit and make arrangements for me to tune their pans. This was around 1979 to '80. A few years later one summer, we did a workshop at the University of Akron and afterward had a long talk, at which time he suggested again that I consider coming to NIU. At first, I'd resisted because I didn't want to change. I wanted to remain in Minnesota. But after that summer, I decided to give NIU a try. I came that summer of '85 and was made an adjunct instructor. In '86, I was hired and decided not to return to Minnesota and tendered my resignation.

At NIU, talk began about tenure-track, and I wondered what that was all about because the word meant nothing to me. Al explained that tenure-track meant in six years it's either I made it or not, and I could be out the door. Then, he took me around and introduced me to various people. I remember one of the vice presidents was a Black guy who advised me, "This is the plan you should put into effect. First, make up your job description detailing what the job is all about. In some way, present yourself as a faculty, because you will be teaching. So, let teaching be embodied in your description. Craft it well, then bring it back here so I can present it to the president for his signature." The president signed it and declared me hired. That job description has held up for the past sixteen years and covers what I still do today: assist with the music; help teach the steel band; tune the pans; codirect the steel band; and so on.

I was sent to Human Resources with the assumption that I was hired. But once there, I was told that I had to take a test, one that had to be found for me. I hemmed and hawed and said, "No, I'm not taking any test. I don't want to take any test." I got a little hot-headed and left but then returned and asked, "Okay, what will the test be all about?" The administrator said that it was a test from Springfield that will cover instrument-tuning and instrument-technician. Then I hemmed and hawed again and at the end of that was told the test will take me four to five hours. I said, "What?!" Anyway, I took the test because no one takes more test than us in Trinidad. Everything there is a test. At the end of it, the administrator said, "Look, this job has to be advertised." I said, "It looks like I'm making a mistake in coming here. The person who wants me here, his hands are now tied. You have to follow all your guidelines about hiring me, and all of that. It looks like I should have accepted this tenure-track thing." He said, "Well, when they have budget cuts and all that stuff, people like you they may want to throw out the door right away." Knowing I didn't come this far to face joblessness in the future, I said okay to their procedures, and he assured me that I'll hear from them in two weeks.

In two days I got the results. I opened the mail with my fingers trembling, wondering whether I'd pass and saw my score. I got an eighty-five out of one hundred. After all those hours that's all they gave me?! To certain parts of the test I responded N/A, meaning not applicable to what I do because they didn't make any sense. Those parts had nothing to do with my job: so how was I supposed to respond? What does fixing a trombone have to do with tuning a pan? So, I guess that's why I got an eighty-five. I called Al to tell him that I failed the test. He said, "You failed? Well, we might have to go to Affirmative Action." I laughed and said, "No, I passed it." He was relieved.

I was hired as a full-fledged staff member with all benefits. Some people call me professor. But as far as the School of Music, which puts out a brochure on the Division of Performing Arts because the School has its own autonomy, I'm pictured and described as a member of the school.

The steel band was formed by Al in the early to mid '70s and presently has thirty-two or thirty-three members. When I first came here, the band had seven members. It now meets four days a week, Monday through Thursday. Al, Liam [Teague],[3] and I do all the teaching. I teach the calypso repertoire and R&B, and Al does the classical. I also do the composing. My focus is on doing the part I know very well. The first time I came to this university and witnessed the teaching of Jazz, I thought that what people thought of as Jazz and what they were playing as Jazz was not really so. So, to differentiate myself from that, I called myself a calypso arranger for Pan. That is what I know well. I don't know Jazz very well, even though I studied it quite a bit when I was in Minnesota and working at that inner city school with inner city kids.

My Teachers Were Black Students

I learned from the Black students in Minnesota who taught me a lot. Imagine living in a culture that is totally different from what you knew as a West Indian and having to learn from whatever source is available. Those students taught me. We are so colonialistic-laced, that is, how we readily accept classical music, and all that, as superior. You know, kids in the inner city don't so readily accept anything like that. A lot of my repertoire turned those kids off. They weren't interested in any "Mary Anne" or "Yellow Bird," or anything like that. That wasn't their language at all. So, I had to learn while I was teaching them. I tell people that I got my education from those Black kids in Minnesota. So that today, I am not afraid of working in any inner city. If somebody from Chicago came to me with the proposal to put together a band of one hundred inner city kids, I wouldn't hesitate because I believe I can speak the language on the inner city very well.

You don't put yourself in the position that makes you look like you're above African Americans because they're Black Americans. You know some West Indian people do sort of that nonsense. I don't do it. African Americans have their own culture. They were born in this country and have negotiated and navigated themselves very well to high levels of success. Sometimes my brother-in-law and I get so angry at each other because he always puts down the Blacks here, saying they should go elsewhere. I say he can't say that because they were born in this country. This is their country, too. All this I learned from Blacks. I keep my radio on a Black station out of Chicago to continue to keep engrossed in the Black culture.

For instance, at the school here the band is mostly White and I have to teach Black music. Sometimes they're not going to get it anywhere else. I told a student once that I'd just heard a tune by George Benson, the Black guitar player. I suggested that the student buy Benson. That student, like White students in most cases, purchased the White answer to George Benson and brought that back. I always have to remind students that I didn't instruct them to buy that person but to buy George Benson. The racism is so hidden they don't even recognize their own behavior as racist. I teach that way, to play R&B music by Black musicians. I'm not impressed with the mixture of pop and R&B. Pop is not Black music of Black culture. R&B is. A lot of West Indians have to learn this difference in music and culture and why Blacks do what they do. That's a part of the issue. People don't want to take the time to learn what Black culture is. Not me. I took and still take the time to learn about Black culture, which has served me well in the end.

I've learned how to really understand. So many times, we have the wrong understanding of who African Americans really are. Sometimes, we think that as soon as they come into the classroom they come to cause trouble. We never really pay attention to their background. I was one of the few teachers who made house-visits to learn more about a student. If I saw an exceptionally talented student, I wanted to tell his parents, just as when I saw a kid was terrible I wanted to make his parents aware. Musically, I learned to understand their ideas on music, which we fail to appreciate and understand. We look at their music and their labels—that's just Blues, that's just so and so—without stopping to think that that is their makeup, a part of who and what they are. These are some of the things I learned from them.

I taught Pan for twelve years in the public schools in Minnesota before I came to NIU. I've been working here for sixteen years. In all, I've been in the educational system for twenty-eight years in this country and have taught both high school and college students. The information I've gathered is a wealth, going back to teaching in Minnesota where my experiences included administering tests to tenth-graders, which I did not mind doing because I wanted to be a teacher and see how I fit in as a panman who was allowed to do a job like that. When I grew tired of that and was ready to move on, I pointed out to them that I was not a certified teacher and shouldn't be allowed to do that. I was an educational assistant in the Arts, which they allowed, and came under the supervision of a lead teacher, and that was cool.

It's ironical, this test-taking business. I have to tell people that NIU didn't just employ me because I happened to walk in. I had to prove I was qualified. I also tell everyone that I went to school in Trinidad but never intended to take the Cambridge qualifying exam. When the time came for that, I just walked out and went my way. I attended high school in the days when you had to pay to attend high school. But my deal was that I didn't go to school a lot and sometimes spent my school fees on other things. I'm not ashamed to say that because I didn't want to take the Cambridge exams. I didn't think I could do that, come under that. I attended Belmont Intermediate for a while, then Ideal High School. A lady is here who has her PhD and went to Ideal [High School]. She and I the other day were joking about the principal who used to live on Quarry Street. But my ambition was to be a pan-person and I didn't see how the Cambridge exams would help me accomplish that. Coming to America really changed my perspective on test-taking. Now, I've done it all and I could look forward to retiring from this job, satisfied that I did what I wanted to do with my life, glad that I had this opportunity to teach at the college level, because once I arrived here I knew this was what I preferred doing. But I will always appreciate the Black Minnesota high schoolers who helped shape my perspective. We all have different perspectives, neither right nor wrong, as I said before.

To sum up this part of my experience, I began at NIU as an adjunct instructor before I was hired full time. Once I became permanent here, I tried to bring in as many people as possible to talk about Pan. I brought in George Goddard once to give a lecture.

Toward Bridging the Cultural Gaps and Building Inter-cultural Understanding

My life has been full of many rich experiences. There's a group who became public a few years ago called Mint Condition. I used to teach some of its members in high school. I'm still in touch with them. The lead singer's father brought him at eight years old for me to teach him. I used to teach in summer school at McAllister College in Minnesota. The minute I heard this eight-year-old play the drumset I wondered what part of him was West Indian. The way he approached pan-playing and drum-playing convinced me that he had to have some Caribbean roots. It turns out in the final analysis that he had some little-known West Indian roots. The Caribbean ancestors came from the Bahamas and immigrated so long ago that the family today knows virtually nothing of their Bahamaian roots. I intuited this. But that is not to say the talented ones came only from the West Indies. What I want to emphasize is many Black Americans have West Indian roots that they don't know or forgot about. Wherever they've come from, Black Americans are talented people, like anyone else.

Once, I was asked a question in Trinidad about Black kids here in school playing steelpan. They wanted to know how come they don't see a lot of the Black kids coming down to Trinidad playing pan or to learn to play pan, that they were seeing mostly White kids. I pointed out to them that the White kids were more fortunate than the Black ones. It doesn't mean that the Blacks can't play pan. It means they don't have the money to buy a plane ticket like Whites do. People come to the wrong conclusion about why Black kids aren't going to Trinidad to learn about Pan. Then, problems are on the Blacks' side, too.

I've met some kids who were resistant to Pan in high school. They didn't want to play that African music. Many things remind them of their past. The idea of a drum is too African. They don't want to embrace the idea of an African drum because they were born in America. They were born into Hip-hop, or whatever their case may be. So, how dare you bring this African thing to them? These are just some of the things to learn to bridge and help to bring an understanding that drumming is a part of the culture.

What really caught on was the emphasis that Pan was invented by a Black man. Somewhere along the line, they were told it wasn't invented by a Black man. So, to bridge that gap you have to emphasize if something was invented in Trinidad or Jamaica to help them see the part a Black man played. A lot of corrective visioning must go into bridging the cultural the gaps. Meanwhile, during that corrective process, you're trying to get them to understand through videos, lectures, and instructions that mutual learning was going on.

I always had to learn one of their tunes and play that for them to show them how to appreciate diversity. Once they realized that I was willing to learn their thing, they started to bring in their own records every day for me to listen to. That is why I said before that they gave me my biggest education. I was an adult and the only teacher in the civic center, because I went with them to hear a group they said was coming to town, another teaching moment. I so kept up with this interest in their culture that after a while my class was so well Black populated that once the principal told me I was not following the State's guidelines for the desegregation plan. I needed to have one or two Whites, or we could get cited. I pointed out that was not my fault, but then we started recruiting Whites into the class. Another lesson I learned.

With a new focus on the State's expectations, I began organizing tours for the band. I got an organization going called COMPASS—Community Programs in the Arts & Sciences—to sponsor after-school groups. I took the groups to the state fair. One summer, I discussed with the principal the idea to take the kids on a summer tour and suggested hiring a truck driver and bus driver. They would deliver the instruments to the site and when the kids arrived the instruments would already be there waiting to be set up. When they were finished performing, they would put away their sticks and return to the bus. Let someone else be responsible for loading the pans unto the truck. The principal agreed with my suggestion. I also suggested getting a per diem for them while they were on tour, which at first was greeted with skepticism. They thought I was going crazy. But it worked. It worked. Many of these kids given up for lost turned out to be engineers and lawyers. Those at-risk students ended up with me, and the rest is history.

We can do more toward bridging cultural gaps, something in which I am very much interested. African Americans lack a financial wherewithal to readily pursue Pan interests in the same way Whites do. Blacks cannot afford the buy pans and travel abroad or to local gigs as Whites can. What we need is more historically Black colleges and universities (HBCUs) affording steel bands or steel orchestras. I know of Bethune Cookman College in Florida that has a steel band, one of the few campuses to have a steel band. This paucity of Pan on HBCU campuses is also related to finances, which White schools have more of, even though some White schools have problems acquiring finances for a steel band, also. It's also sad that not many African Americans are clamoring to learn to make pan, not as Whites are. On the other hand, it's good to see that some Brooklyn, New York, schools have a steel band. One or two are in Chicago, with Clemente High School in an Hispanic area being a rare exception. What I really want is an imperative that the Steelband projects be inclusive of all voices.

I think I mentioned before that some Black musicians have said they don't want to play any African music, and until they realize the pan can play some sort of melody they can identify with, then they become all interested. I remember in St. Paul when I played tapes of classical music, they said they didn't want to do that. But if on a pan I began to teach them their kind of music and afterward brought in some classical then I found them more responsive to the classical. So, it was starting with what they were familiar with then introducing the idea that they had to expand their repertoire that worked. I also informed them that Pan had a long history, and a part of that history was playing the European classics. Once we got going, they then asked for more. If I had started with classic, no way would I have made a breakthrough. And, if I had started with "Yellow Bird" that would have been even worse. Once I started identifying with their music, playing their music, I was the biggest thing at that school.

That's one way to spark interest. We have to be sensitive to people's interests and culture. We can't just come with an instrument whose indigenous past is made to appear like it's being forced upon them. No, that's not the way. You have to start with what they know and like and are familiar with and move them toward what else they can do. Eventually, they played all types of music, including Calypso. I saturated them with video tapes of Panorama, and so on.

Once, the students wanted to know what a Chinese was doing in the band, if it wasn't an all-Black band. I had to point out to them that that was not the way things happened in Trinidad. When they saw Jit Samaroo they couldn't believe he was a Trinidadian, too. They couldn't conceive that Chinese, Indian, African could all do something together. They weren't accustomed to seeing something like that. This country has presented to them a distorted picture of how people can get along. The segregation that keeps people apart has blinded some to other cultural realities. I mean, they were *really* concerned about seeing a Chinese guy in a steel band. So, what we also need is historical truth linked to the imperative to be culturally inclusive.

We have a lot of unlearning to do first before trying to teach. We have to undo the damages of colonial education then set ourselves on the right track toward new appreciations of our cultures. And, we can't stop there. We have to emphasize music literacy.

A Call for Music Literacy

The Western hemisphere is suffering from a paucity not just in music literacy but total literacy. So, we really need a new focus on literacy, not just a focus on one thing and not the other. It's a whole literacy program we have to be developing. We're competing with an international market, with Europe and Asia and other places whose students are musically literate and literate all around. We have to have students who can compete with them.

In Trinidad, UWI is already producing students from the Creative Arts Centre who are musically literate. Now, Trinidad must build a conservatory of a broader scope that will reach more pan-players. America must make more opportunities available for students. For instance, some high school students come to a university or college and enter a program as a percussionist and see for the first time a pan. If they then want to pursue Pan and if that becomes their new interest, the program should be so designed to accommodate that. America must keep moving forward instead on going back, like the direction things seem to be going in.

All over, I'm still seeing we have this class thing in us. Back home, if you weren't living in Cascade and St. Clair you were nothing. Here, you have to have the money, and of course, talent.

In Trinidad, we built this thing on talent. I can talk about Alan Gervais, Earl Rodney, the Bonaparte brothers—those guys from Southern Symphony who were doing their thing down south in Point Fortin. They were tuning their pan, adding notes, octaves, etcetera. In fact, I can tell you that Alan Gervais made some improvement to the Invaders' tenor pan and Ellie's double second. Gervais and the guys from south used to play the Invaders' tenor pan and double second. But it was Alan who changed Ellie's double second by moving the low E up to F-sharp. I remember what event lit our eyes up.

There was a jamboree in the Oval, I think it was Christmas of '64, and the National Steel Band played. The Guinness Cavaliers—I know Bobby Mohammed very well—performed after the National Steel Band. When all of a sudden Guinness Cavaliers started playing, everybody ran over to them. "You hear dem pan?" and was asking them, "Who made dem pan?" Everyone wanted to know this new thing, this new sound. They answered, "Alan Gervais, a guy from Point." We wanted to know if it was an Invaders' tenor pan they were playing, and they said yes. That's how we found out that Alan Gervais was putting octaves on the Invaders' tenor pan. Ellie couldn't come close.

Once, Ellie wasn't getting as much work in Trinidad, if he was getting any work at all, because all the tuning was going to guys who could put octaves on the notes. I'm not lying. Later on, *the west* (see Introduction) went through their whole revolution in sound. But in those earlier days, other people were doing things, too, and they deserve credit. Hugh Borde and guys like that snatched up Gervais to make their pans. Another one was Bassman who's living in Brooklyn now and not doing so good. Rudolph Charles brought Bassman on board because he was doing new stuff, too. It's a whole lot of people who started the new type of sound, which Ellie wasn't doing. Ellie's pans weren't ringing like some other pans. We'd go to the Savannah knowing that our Invaders band wasn't going to ring like some of the other bands. I'm not betraying anyone because I'm still an Ellie fanatic.

Ellie came to America with the help of Murray Narell, after Vincent Hernandez recommended him. Patrick Arnold and others came later and there with Ellie learned some of the new things about tuning. I wasn't a tuner then but remember that Ellie was worried when he learned about tuning with strobe. Then, the others followed him using strobe, and now he must be credited as the first Trinidadian to do that. But he must also give others credit, too.

Another of my experiences revolves around the WSMF. Trinidad had a rude awakening at the last WSMF when all these bands came and nearly tore them up. We [NIU Steel Band] were given a raw deal, but as a Trinidadian I could deal with it. The day after the Festival and the news came that we placed second, we were in Phase II yard, where we rehearsed. I'm a good friend of Boogsie Sharp and said to him, "'Boogsie,' you're something else." He said, "Cliff, I couldn't let these people down. A week ago, they came to me and asked, "'Boogsie,' you're going to allow this thing to leave Trinidad?" We were having this conversation because when I got to Trinidad they told me that the Festival would end up with eight Trinidad bands in the finals. I responded, "Well, if that's the way all yuh see it." They said in return, "Where all yuh going? This band only here because of you, but all yuh going to get licks, too." And, I said, "That's okay." The results were four foreign bands and four Trinidadian bands fiercely competing for top position. Pan has been going in this inter-cultural direction for many years now.

Because of 9/11, I don't know yet if we're going to this year's Festival. If we go, Trinidadians must understand that those from abroad are confident in what they know, do, and bring to Pan. Trinidadians must accept that if the Festival calls for foreign judges and a foreign band wins, such is because these guys are very good now. Look at the bands from Switzerland and Finland two years ago. Prior to 2000, their tuner *and* arranger would have been Trinidadians. Now, no such thing. They came with their Finnish tuner and arranger and their Swiss tuner and arranger. And, they were proud of that. Of course, in Trinidad they told me I'm selling technology because I'm tuning Pan and arranging and composing for an American steel band. They pointed, "You, you!" And I said, "Okay, okay." But the state of Pan today is: Pan is not for, by, or of Trinidadians only.

Many years ago, people used to say once Pan gets into western music and they [westerners] started scoring it, watch out. And, it's true. Now, if NIU Steel Band goes to the Festival this year, we won't be able to play a note until August 28 or so. When we went last year, we had to get there for October 13. I went to Trinidad and made all the bass, and we only started rehearsing August 29. We came in second; whereas, a lot of those bands rehearsed for weeks and months ahead of time and did not place. That's not how music education should be. You shouldn't be spending months at a time rehearsing one tune. You don't want to stand in a panyard and learn two to four bars a night. That's not Pan anymore.

I'm a strong advocate that everyone should learn to read music. Even as I say that, conjunctively, there is still that reality of some individuals with no formal musical training who could walk in a panyard and have such a natural ear for music that they could learn a tune as well. We don't want to lose that either. However, if those individuals have to compete in America for really good jobs, they have to be very, *very* literate musically. They must be like Lennard Moses, one of our own graduates who used to play for Desperados Steel Band, and now is head of Percussion at Central State University in Xenia, Ohio. A very astute person who came from Laventille, he did his high school work here and got a scholarship to Central State then came to NIU for his master's. He has a good story, too.

One of my most valuable experiences is formally learning music. No ifs, ands, or buts about it, I came to NIU not knowing where middle C is. If I didn't learn where middle C is, I don't think I'll be here. I was learning music before I got here but it's here I mastered music literacy. To succeed today in Pan, you can't escape or hide from music literacy. You'll just be destroying yourself without it.

For instance, when we've invited Pan guest artists from Trinidad, they would ask for a certain amount of money to cover airline fare, ground transportation, hotel, and daily food allowance. They would arrive on Friday and attend a couple of rehearsals. Rehearsals would include say three calypsos, one of which they would have to improvise. The Boogsie Sharps and Robbie Greenidges would know what to do. We would also ask them to play a solo or two on stage. They would perform at the Sunday concert, collect their remuneration, and depart on Monday morning. On the other hand, if the Percussion Department hired a guest artist for the same money that guest artist would come in on Thursday and hold master classes. We could ask Andy Narell because he has a degree in music and would be able to handle the students. We can ask only a few pan-people from Trinidad to do that. One such is Liam Teague who studied here at NIU. He usually visits as a guest artist at different schools, and because he's a trained musician the schools send ahead all their music so when he arrives he can assist that band. The guys who can't read music can't help out like that. One last example is if a commercial jingle comes up and we hired one a guy who can't read music, he'd have to ad lib his way through it, whereas a trained musician wouldn't.

A story to crown this is about a kid just the other day who went down to Trinidad and told them he can play pan. He played pan, the drum-set, the congas, and everything that was percussion in nature. The pan-guy probably would have needed somebody to play it for him first to hear how it goes, then follow suit. The call for music literacy also has a lot to do with recording. Nobody in a recording studio is waiting for people to have to hear what something sounds like first then follow suit.

All these young people, who say they're coming to America because they're professionals, must understand they're not professionals unless they can do these things I was allowed twenty-eight years to experience these differences myself. Consequently, I can pose this question regarding my own work: am I a Jazz musician who can teach and play Jazz? I thought so, until I came here and met a guy teaching an introduction to Jazz and came to realize that I really didn't know anything about Jazz. I thought I knew but didn't. So, that's my argument. People have to know the academics, business, as well as have formal training in Pan. That's the only way to compete on a professional level.

When I first arrived at NIU: at first, I didn't even know what they meant when they said a percussionist. I thought that a percussionist played a drum-set only. I never believed a percussionist wrote music until Al asked me if we had a tune written by the drummer. I asked, "The drummer? He writes music?" He said, "Yes." That's because drummers also receive a full education. That same drummer would be able to play rap music, in the wind symphony, wind ensemble, orchestra percussion, and if he wanted a job in a symphony he would have been already trained to do it. These are some of the things I had to learn, how the different segments of training come to bear. I gave a lecture recently and said, "I've now begun to understand what a trained musician is."

Someone with training can more readily understand different learning styles. Sometimes, when a student was resistant I wondered what was wrong with him until I realized that nothing was wrong. He had been trained a certain way and was approaching his music from that vantage point, which was different from mine. With a little explanation, things became clear to him. Now that I'm a trained musician, I'm better at these things. Guys come here and want to teach tunes and they take something within the diatonic scale of eight notes and go to four low notes playing, "Dah, dah, dah, dah," going up and down. The untrained person would have trouble doing and understanding that. He has to learn the diatonic scale in the context of one through eight, and not go one, two, three, seven, eight, five. These trained guys go to Trinidad and play, and some people think they don't understand what's going on. They very well know what's going on. Rhythmically, they might be a little off. Musically, they know exactly what's going on. These are some of the things I had to learn, come to understand who and what they are. From that standpoint, it makes my day a lot easier.

I cannot now go to teach any steel band where I have to hold the sticks to show them anything. For sixteen years now, I've been dealing with scores. I have a person who writes all the music for the band and the band goes from there. If I had to hold a stick and count and tell the kid you're coming in on beat one and the other one over there he's coming in on beat two, I'm going to faint. But that's the system I came from. I could learn within that system. I'm not afraid of it. But fellas like Liam Teague who grew up in panyard run from that now. They want to see the music. If you go to a band like that [musically illiterate] and dealing with a hundred bars of music, you can focus on eight bars a night. But with a band where they know music, though they may not know the rhythm, you can get them playing twenty to thirty bars of music, and you know exactly which bar will need fixing, more work. You can point them to the exact bar, and because they can read, they can go straight to that bar and work on it. You can't do any of that in the regular steel band in Trinidad. You have to do these nights when you go to three, four o'clock in the morning. I have a niece and I tell them don't send her to any panyard that she has to leave at two o'clock in the morning then to go to school later that morning. Eh, eh! No!

One of the problems in Trinidad with this arrested state of development is finances, similar to here in the United States. The at-risk students I mentioned earlier are a good example to use. The teachers used to say to them, "Go and play steel drums because you can't do Math, or whatever else." I took those kids and said, "Look, this is a musical note of four beats. This is a square that makes four parts. Divide the box, divide the note." The kid said, "Aw. That's what it is?!" Some of them didn't know how to find the center of a drum. They never heard of diameter by *Pi*, or circumference or whatnot. Since I've been teaching pan-tuning here, I've met some college kids who can't find the center of a drum. Making pan is a lot of Arithmetic. It's not a joke, you know; it never was. Now, we've come to understand that making pan is a definite detailed science, with students who are grasping it all. I have students who learned to tune here in America asking me why I'm allowing tuners from Trinidad to come to America now that we are having our own tuners in this country. This is how pan-tuning has developed and will continue to develop, with science and literacy.

Pan, Technology, and Tautology

Pan is changing. It is and always was a musical instrument that continues to improve in technology. This instrument is not a novelty anymore, and the Trinidad government needs to pay closer attention to what Trinidadians have given to the world. Pan is everywhere. I've been to Singapore, New Zealand, and Taiwan, too, many times and seen how Pan has impacted their various cultures. Our steel band was in South Korea playing during the World Cup. There are 258 steel bands in Switzerland, and the Swiss are conducting research with University of London, as I saw recently on the internet. That calls attention to the fact that we don't know the exact number of steel bands in Britain, Sweden, and the many places around the word where so many people love Steelband.

Everyone in Pan has heard of the brouhaha there in Delaware with the guy and the stainless steelpan. The man only patented a process that can produce a pan made of stainless steel, shiny and looking beautiful. When you see the product, it's frightening to see where the technology is going. That somebody can do that. He is trying to do it the hydroforming way: taking this stainless steel which without much carbon is very malleable, and because of the ductility it wouldn't split; then specially pressing it out and using nitrogen to bake it for some hours; and then using the electro-plating process that produces the material at a specific thickness. But all those specificities go to tuning, which still point to the original knowledge of pan-making invented by Trinidadians. Then, there's still a problem with tuning pan made of that material, which may not be a problem for too long. This type of evolution is what Trinidad needs to pay attention to. Not look to sue the man and create this big controversy that died down just as quickly.

Instead, the Trinidad government should know that Trinidadians shouldn't have to come to the States, not now or in the future, to see how to sink a pan. This can happen if this thing continues to evolve the way it is. They should know that this man cannot take over Pan, as some Trinidadians worry. If they knew Pan history well, they'll also know that this same process isn't even original of this man. Enough people know that some fellas in Trinidad tried to do the same thing years ago, the same hydroforming process, but the government didn't support them financially. The story goes on and on like that in Trinidad. Trinidadians try to do something and they don't get enough governmental support. Not so in this country and all over Europe where it has become a respected instrument and the people investing a lot in R&D.

Some Trinidadians also have their own retarded way of thinking. Back in the days, some tuners didn't like people to just walk into their panyard and see what they were doing. Depending on who you were, if you had a pan to tune they met you at the gate, took your pan and told you when to come back for it, so you never set foot into the yard to see what they were doing. They so kept secret what they were doing that a lot of people never saw how to sink a pan. Now, quite a few of us who know how to do that are living right here in the States and willingly sharing this knowledge. We have to. And, we do this not because we think anyone is trying to steal Pan. No one can steal Pan. All people can do is advance the process of building one. We've sunk the concave and used the six-pound sledge and four-pound hammer, and the time came for a better way to do that. The time will come for a better way to do everything.

Some Trinidadians, however, still see this as "we t'ing" that was made in somebody's backyard. They fail to understand how labor intensive this work is and how to value this labor. When a Trinidadian calls and asks me to make him a pan and I tell him the cost, he then says he's not paying that much, and look at what Pan has now come to now. That attitude is very demoralizing. That kind of attitude fails to give Pan the credit and respect it deserves. A right attitude begins right there with respect. Charity, in this case respect, begins at home. Right there in Trinidad. When we go home for the Music Festival, they shouldn't be looking at us and saying, "Wow! This is how a steel band should be run." But how are they going to get there? The government and the people still have that colonialistic attitude, rooted in the fear of change.

In Cuba, and I'm not a Communist, some of the top musicians in the world are from Cuba and don't need any prerequisites to get into any music school. If you see some courses established in Trinidad, they have some prerequisite or another. It's some passes in this and that, and, therefore, the guy who hasn't all of that gets shut out again. We pay all this attention to education, which itself is not bad, but don't give people without it a break. You find that what should happen is the people who don't have these prerequisites for university courses should be given another chance through some other means. All these great musicians from Cuba didn't attend any college we know of. They attended a conservatory of music in Cuba and graduated. This is what I'm looking for. That type of assistance for the people and more government involvement. And, if not the government itself, Trinidadians should establish places where people can go to hone their skills, so that when they're finished and want to call themselves professionals, they're true professionals. We shouldn't have one Boogsie Sharp for five years and when he's gone then another has to be trained. We should have several Boogsie Sharps. In this country, there are several whoever-they-are from the east, west, north, and south. That's what I'm saying. Trinidad shouldn't only now be talking about establishing Pan in school curricula and in training colleges, as was reported in the Trinidad newspapers yesterday. All that talk is so late, too late. Other countries are already ahead of Trinidad.

I think that some people want to move Pan forward but subconsciously something is blocking them. If you look at St. Croix and St. Thomas of the U.S. Virgin Islands, and you listen to the budget read by the legislature annually, and see four hundred and fifty thousand dollars given to Steelband, what would you think of Trinidad in comparison? Places like Grenada and St. Vincent are regarding Pan more highly than Trinidad. You wouldn't find Pan on the Trinidad legislative budget. You would always find the organization begging for some subvention. Sometimes, I wonder what we Afro Caribbean people are thinking. For instance, I wonder what these guys have got out of their studies, why they haven't returned home and changed some ways of doing things. Instead, they fall back into the thinking of letting things go along the way they are. This is very disturbing and for my own sake, and hopefully to help others, I have to speak out.

I didn't want to be anything else but a panman in Trinidad. All I was saying was, "Give me a job just like any other civil servant with a salary." In that case, I could buy a car just like one of those guys. But when I said to them, "I'm interested in Pan," their attitude was I didn't deserve a car. I had to go to some university or work in the Red House in order to afford a car. But in this country, I'm just like everybody else. All I wanted was a job in Pan and to be respected just like everybody else. I didn't want to kill anybody for money. The same car that some civil servant was driving, I should be able to drive too. It should not have been about who your cousin is and your mother is. If I wanted to buy a car from the job I have *in Pan,* they should have afforded us that. Trinidad has just paid lip-service to a few people but, on the whole, it's not there for the average panman. Then, they get real angry when other people are making progress, improving things in and for Pan. Real angry.

The last time I experienced this anger was at the last Festival when they told me they're not ready for people like me yet. We were there and they were saying, "Who dey t'ink dey is?" The common people with a certain amount of ignorance still exist there, you know. "Who tell dem White people dat dey could play calypso?" Well, there's a rhythm written for Calypso they could learn. You were born with the natural rhythm, and it's great. But that could be put on paper. This is the literate society in which we live. The books and the literacy. This is what Trinidad fails to realize. Our students were there with music stands and they were saying, "Dey come down here wid music stand. We doh need no music stand." Well, that's what literacy is. You're reading everything. You don't need a music stand but you're taking months to learn one tune that a literate person will learn in weeks. They don't look at it from that standpoint.

From the colonialistic mentality, you can still see vestiges of the same Black people who wanted Dr. Williams—and whoever else—to change all of that, and things still haven't changed. The government still hasn't built a venue for competitions. Imagine, you go to Trinidad to compete in this world festival, rain falling on the pans, and no proper place to perform with convenience. Why not? Nobody wants to go that mile for Pan. Trinidad should have a performing center for a competition to take place without rain soaking competitors. The organizers bring in foreign students who aren't accustomed to that, who have to get cloth and paper towel to keep wiping the rain off their pans so the competition could take place. Yet, everybody's making a promise, "Yes, we have to build a hall." Meanwhile, other members of society are saying, "Wha' more pan-people want?

Wha' dey want?" They're looking at it from the outside and not seeing what's really going on. I made such a fuss about all of that then, and now that I've said this, if I returned to Trinidad they'd probably kill me.

A Vision for Pan

Our band is sponsored by the Trilla Steel Drum Company. The man who pays for these students from Trinidad is Mr. Trilla of Chicago. I spent nine years there. One day, he met me on the sidewalk and gave me a card. He introduced himself to me as owning this company. When he wanted a band, he called and we had a long talk. From that talk, I invited him to come and hear our band. He promised to come after he returned from Italy that Saturday night. The concert was on Sunday night. He came. When the concert was finished, he asked, "What can I do to help?" I pointed out to him Liam Teague and said he needed money to finish school. He invited me to come and talk to him about it. Al and someone else went with me and we discussed the full cost with Mr. Trilla. He gave us the full amount and Liam got to complete his education. When that money ran out, we went back to him and named the amount we needed. A large amount. He said that was not a problem. He continues to pay for the students who want to come and get their graduate degrees. The grad school pays for their tuition and the Trilla fund covers the other expenses. That's how the Trilla fund was established. He's been supporting us since the early '90s. He also supplies all the raw materials. We don't have to buy drums. I just got him to send some drums to Trinidad, too.

Now, why should the land of Pan have to rely on drums from abroad? Trinidad should have a company there making the drums for the instrument. But they're not doing anything like that. And, because I make noise, they say it's because I'm living up here and only talking. They quick to say, "He just went to America and come back now playin' like he big." But that's not what it is. We were allowed to venture into this society and see how things work. We only want to come back now and offer what we learned to help make things better for us, our people. That's all I'm trying to do. I'm not trying to take over anything.

I make this argument out of respect for what Pan is. You have Panorama and the Savannah is full of people, yet they hardly want to give the pan-people their money when Panorama is finished. Pan-people still have to be on their knees begging them for their prize money. They take all the choice seats in the Savannah, so they really can't make as much money as they should, yet they come in and drink and have a good time for Panorama. After Carnival, you see them in their suit and tie and in their Mercedes, and they don't even want to look at you. I'm referring to those considered the big wheels in Trinidad. The organizers are themselves suffering. The president of Pan Trinbago is a good friend of mine, and I relay to him the way I see things, how they run things there. You have this competition where they're selling tickets but giving away complimentary ones. How are the organizers going to make any money? Every thing in Trinidad is a complimentary ticket. When I go to Trinidad to any Pan contest, I buy my ticket. They wanted to give me forty tickets, wanting to know how many members in the band. I say to them, "Who these people know in Trinidad? Why you want to just give them free tickets so? Keep the tickets and sell them." All this complimentary, free-for-all-who-supposed-to-be-important is bad business. These are some of the things that are still wrong.

Since during the O'Halloran days, the Robinson government was supposed to have given $7.5 million, and only this year the organizers got the rest of it. The first time they gave them $3.5 million but put into the Pan Vest trust fund, so that the organization didn't have access to it much less spend it. A lot of the men in Pan Trinbago like Patrick Arnold have their college degrees, so they are not unlearned and know how to manage affairs. It's not like years ago when you had to pay for your secondary education and only few people could afford to go and a few people knew how to manage affairs. Yet, the government is still treating people like they're illiterate and unlearned. All right, that's that.

Technology continues to grow, which is coming to the fore at the conference on Science and Pan. The next time I go to Trinidad, I intend to say something to them about that conference in regard to who's being excluded and how.

It's ironic that when we went down for that first WSMF, I brought those guys to meet my students and introduced them as the guys who taught me the first strums on a pan. There they were, not playing anymore but still they were the ones who taught me. This goes to what I was saying before about the lay person and prerequisites and the whole literacy thing. These guys have these workshops and they talk completely over the head of these tuners. The tuners don't understand that lingo at all. Which of those older tuners know the meaning of the word "torque"? What you mean by the torque of the note? How useful is that to me if I don't know anything about torque? You can relate to a car engine and the torque of a car's engine, and there's compression. If you try to relate that concept to the tightening of the note, he would understand you better. Leave out words like torque and compression. What tuner from say La Brea will understand talk about the compression of the note and the nodal? Use language the men understand. There's still a layman term for all that, and the scientists at the conference refuse to come across in this way. They're using too much big language. You're telling a guy about ductility. Tell the guy that ductility means you can stretch the material without its bursting, and the guy will say, "Aw, okay. I know what you're talking about." But what you mean when you come saying ductility and only you know what you're talking about? Maybe in the Physics lab here you can use that language and everyone will know what mean. But in the real lab, the lab of the Trinidad panyard, you have to use language the men know and understand. Stop wasting the men's time! My time! I understand that now they looking to have a conference that will include tuners who can relate to these men, to the average tuner. That's what I'm about and talking about! We can meet in a workshop and talk in ways that these guys can understand what's going on.

Another thing is: all these different scientists want to be involved, but, on the other hand, they're not taking time to learn how to deal with a few men who invented the instrument. Instead, they want to deal with just one pan-tuner. They go and work with one tuner and think that's enough. No. Work with several tuners and really learn from all of them. They can't learn everything from just one tuner. That's not what the entire tuning process is all about. It's like the history of Pan. A lot of people were doing things and not communicating with each other. If they want to advance now, they have to work with a lot of people and not repeat the same old colonial hierarchy that is restructuring itself. It's happening again to exclude those who don't know the language from those who're claiming they know. And, I have a lot of problems with this. These are some of things I have learned, and this comes from my dealings with those St. Paul urban kids. You have to relate to people on their level first then bring them to the place they can be. Some day, I intend to write about these things myself so I don't die with this knowledge....

To give an overview of Pan's growth in the United States: it developed around more than just Ellie Mannette. Before Ellie, Murray Narell started these youth bands all along the lower east side of Manhattan, in New York City in the late '60s. Later, I started to make pans and people learned that I was at a school and making pans for different schools: University of Akron, University of Illinois—I started those bands. Then, before I moved here to NIU, I was teaching here as well as at the University of Western Illinois. I made all those pans, some of them I don't recall now. What Panyard is doing now Murray Narell did in the late '60s. I turned to tuning also with the intention of eventually starting a business with my good friend Patrick Arnold, who was going to move to St. Paul, Minnesota, but it never happened.

In the meantime, I used to put out correspondence, advertisements in a magazine called *The Instrumentalist*. If you were a band teacher in high school, you received that magazine. From that, people started to get to know about me. A high school in Connecticut I started making pans for then turned to Ellie. I made pans for the University of Hartford's School of Music, made their first instruments. So, it's a few bands I got started even before the other tuners came aboard, including Ellie. The truth of about Pan in the United States must include that I was one of the first to do things like that. I'm not saying I was the only one because there was also Kim Loy Wong who lived in Brooklyn, New York, at the time. He had a space at the lower east side Manhattan settlement, too. He benefitted from the Harry U Act[4] that allotted money to projects like the Manhattan settlement. That Act afforded programs in Harlem to start up and allowed the guys to ship pans all over the country. These programs came under a catchy slogan, whose name I can't recall at the moment. So, I was one of that group making instruments for school before Panyard and others got going.

I held some of the first set of workshops every year at the University of Akron, which started around 1980. Those were big workshops for that time and included twenty to thirty people. Al and I used to do them, and we had a standing agreement, which ended when some bad politics began to filter its way from—. So, Ellie is not the first to have his annual Steelband workshops. I also held workshops in Arizona with Jeanine Remy and also in OshKosh, Wisconsin. Now, with all that I have to do, I don't have the time to hold workshops. My vision is to do things on a larger scale. I want to see a place teaching this trade on an ongoing basis, not just in a two-week workshop. I don't want the headaches of a short-term arrangement that the school doesn't invest into. The school will do all the logistics—give the facilities to do it—but you must break even without depending on them financially. There's no money for them to give with the way things are today, so that you have to generate your own income, your own funds, through the workshop's registrants, and so on. I don't want to be involved in that sort of carnival and the price you have to pay. Granted, you have to start somewhere. But you have to have a vision of something better.

What bothers me is the illusion that you can make a tenor pan in a week, or that you can learn to play pan in a week. Then, when you get there you find it's a different story. I prefer to remain in my corner here and do what I'm doing well. I want to make pan, arrange music, compose music, and develop my wealth of confidence in what I'm doing. Sometimes, I probably come across cocky but that's not it. I've just invested so much time in this that I can look at a glance at what someone is doing and suggest ways to make things better. For instance, a guy was recently in my shop and I could tell from the shape of what he was doing he had to do it over. Years before when I wasn't as experienced, I would have had him throw the pan out and start from scratch. Now, I can tell from the concave shape of the pan just how to fix things. This knowledge comes with experience and the confidence such inculcates. Being at NIU has given me this understanding, this discipline, this awareness of the regimen that Pan education demands. Where I'm going with this thing, well, that will be history....

Rising Sun Steel Band, ca. 1947
Front (l. to r.): George Roberts (band master), Reynold Lohar,
Dudley Smith, Percival Thomas, Robert Greaves
Back (l. to r.): Glen Bernard, Albert Jones, George Armstrong,
Patrick Antoine, Horace Toussaint

Bore pan

Destiny, Desmond Bravo
great-granddaughter, 2003

**Elliott "Ellie" Mannette in Trinidad,
radio interview, 2001**

Geoff Hohn and Cassie Kelly, 2001

**Harold Headley, Ellie Mannette,
Robert Greenidge, 2001**

Solomon Steel Company

Registrants, MMIM, 2001

Robert Greenidge and Carolyn Hendricks

Ray Holman, demonstrating early pan at MMIM 2001

Pan Stars, 2003

Sons of Steel, 2001

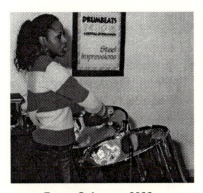

Fauna Solomon, 2002

Tom Miller and Ellie Mannette, 2001

14

Launching an Academic Program: G. Allan O'Connor's Story[1]

G. Allan "Al" O'Connor *earned his Bachelor of Music Education degree and Performers Certificate from the State University of New York at Fredonia and his Master of Music degree in Percussion Performance from the University of Illinois. He was appointed Head of Percussion Studies at Northern Illinois University (NIU) in 1968, Assistant Chair of the School of Music in 1983, and Associate Dean of NIU's College of Visual and Performing Arts in 1989.* O'Connor *retired from the Associate Dean's position in 2000 and remains on the NIU faculty as co-director of the NIU Steel Band.*

Rising to Challenges

I was first introduced to Steelband when I was a graduate student at University of Illinois from 1965 to 1967, majoring in Percussion Performance. At the time, the university had a reputation that was primarily focused toward experimental music. So, just before I graduated the last thing I did was play a piece that one of the faculty composers had written that had four very large, multiple percussion setups in it—fifty instruments per player, or something like that. In each set, there was a steelpan. It was the first time I had ever seen one, for the composer had rented them from a drum shop in New York City. Today, I know they were not of a very high quality, but at that time I had to figure out what kind of sticks to use on them, as well as other challenges related to dealing with something new.

Gradually, I became interested in where the instrument came from, how it was made, and everything about it. I graduated the same day I learned it was of West Indian origin. The following month, I got married and my wife and I decided to work in our school districts throughout that summer to save up money for our honeymoon in the Virgin Islands. We went in August of 1967 and at the hotel where we were staying, maybe that Thursday night, a twenty-piece steel band for entertainment was brought in. The first time I heard that band, I knew that I had to have one. It absolutely blew my mind. The name of that band was The Bill Bass and the Royal Tones. I got to chatting with the bartender of the hotel who happened to be from Trinidad, and he said he knew one of the employees who built pans. I ordered an instrument and he made it for me in about a week. I then brought it home, taught myself to play, started buying records, then got hired the following year at NIU. I started here in September of 1968 as a Percussion professor, and I knew that I wanted to make a steel band part of the Percussion curriculum. I started hunting for instruments, and it took me about five years to find a set.

I located the instruments through a student who was studying Percussion at a very small college about forty miles north of here. Its program didn't have a full range of faculty, so whenever a student was admitted without a faculty with whom he could work, the student was allowed to work with a faculty at different school. This student used to drive down once every two weeks and study with me. He just happened to mention one year that he and his parents were going on a vacation to Aruba. Seizing the opportunity, I went to the chairman of the Music department and asked if I could get an advance, in case he found anything while there that he could buy. The chair gave me five hundred dollars, which the student was to use toward purchasing what he could find.

Lo and behold, the following week he called and said he had found them, a set of instruments a guy was willing to sell and ship up here for that amount. We made the necessary arrangements, and when they arrived at O'Hare Airport I was notified to come and pick them up. At the airport, while trying to clear through Customs, the Customs agent had never seen one before and couldn't find any category for them in the book. So, he wasn't going to let me take them until we got some verification. Finally, after about an hour of haggling we decided to call them bongo drums.

I started, as I said before, with listening to records, teaching myself to play, and transcribing arrangements off the records. We eventually debuted them at a Percussion Ensemble concert in 1973.

There were other programs at the university where people who were teaching music in the public schools could return and take extra course work so they could enhance their salary. During that summer, I demonstrated the steel band for a class of music teachers who were pursuing their interest in steelband music. At the end of the demonstration, one of them approached me and asked, "Would you like to bring your group to my school to play for my students?" I said, "Sure, that would be something that might be enjoyable." It turned out when we got there that it was a middle school with fifteen hundred kids in the auditorium waiting for us. I said, "My God, what's going to happen now? This age of school kids is the hardest to deal with. This is going to be a disaster." It turned out that they absolutely fell in love with it and were screaming like girls used to do for Elvis. I said, "Maybe, I've got something here."

We decided then to turn the steel band into a separate entity and make it a separate course above and beyond the regular Percussion curriculum. We established a regular rehearsal time every day of the week for an hour. The students all read music and we did it all by writing the parts on paper and people taking that instrument and learning the music.

Because I'm originally from the east coast, I had a lot of connections back there in the schools. We decided to start doing a week tour after the academic year ended in May. We went back there probably four or five years, playing in public school assemblies during the day and the kids going into New York City at night. Once, we played for a soccer half-time game at Yankee Stadium when the first U.S. professional soccer league played off against Pélé's team. It was really quite enjoyable. We made enough money from those performances to actually establish our own independent revenue source. I've run this program from then to now without any money from the university's operating budget. We generated it all ourselves from performances done around here or on tour or things of that nature.

Soon, I began getting calls from West Indians who heard I had a band here and wanted to know about it. They also wanted to give me the names of other people in Steelband and whatever material they could, which I might find useful.

Then, around 1977, I think, I went to hear the U.S. Navy Steel Band perform in a high school nearby. I heard their instruments and recognized they were a much higher quality than ours. At the end of the concert, I went to the leader of the group and asked him where he got his drums. He said, "I'm not really sure. I think they were made by this big guy named Cliff [Alexis] who lives in St. Paul, somewhere." It took me a year and a half to track Cliff down. When I finally got to talk to him, I said, "I've been doing this for a while. We're going to be playing in a concert very close to where you are in a couple of weeks. If you can come down, I'll like to meet you."

Sure enough, he showed up and noticed right away that our instruments weren't as good as the ones that he made. I discussed with him how serious I was about this and my willingness to learn everything about maintaining the instruments and everything else. I shared that I was going on a sabbatical the following year and would like to be able to come up to St. Paul and study with him. He agreed, and I went up there every two weeks for a couple of days and returned home and practiced what he'd taught me. I realized after that semester that I would either have to devote my whole life to this, like he did, or else not try to do it because you can't be half good.

Meanwhile, I decided to try to raise enough money for Cliff to gradually replace our instruments with his, two at a time, over the following four or five years. We did that, and then he came down to tune them once a year. During that time, we became pretty close friends. We seemed to be on the same wavelength. He'd asked me, "In return for me giving you these tuning lessons, I want you to teach me to read music." I said, "Sure, that's no problem." Then, he traveled to me to learn to read music for two months before saying, "To hell with this."

During our conversations, I learned he'd come to a turning point in his full-time job in the St. Paul public school system, where he was in an Arts magnet school for problem-kids who were sent to him. He had to make a unit out of them, which he did, but the time it took in dealing with those kids was really incredible. He'd start working at seven o'clock in the morning, teach school the whole day, then work on his instruments at night. By this time, his reputation had grown to the point where he was known all over the country. He was getting calls from people to make instruments and had found himself backed up probably five or six years in commitment. I said to him, "Why don't you do this?" (He's a diabetic and has to have health coverage.) "Take a leave of absence from the public schools for a year so you can continue to have your health coverage, and come down to NIU"—I was able to arrange a half-time appointment for him—"and see if you like this level. This will basically free you up from all that public school work, and you'll do nothing but work on pan. You'll help me lead the band and keep the instruments in tune, and whatever else is necessary."

In 1985, he came and never left. I was able to raise his job to full time—he's in the civil service system and not on the faculty. I did that purposely because of the budget situation fluctuates from one level to another. If he was a visiting lecturer, or in some such position, that position would put him in an immediate catastrophe if there were a budget crunch. But once you get into the civil service system, they can't get you out of there with a crow bar. His title is Instrument Technician Steelpan IV, the highest grade. He is basically treated like a member of the faculty, but he doesn't have to deal with all that tedious committee work and other stuff irrelevant to his work. He works on his own.

Meeting a Pan Virtuoso

The next probably significant step was when Cliff and I were invited by Pan Trinbago in 1989 to observe the School Steelband Festival. We went to Trinidad and they gave us—we weren't actual judges but were in the audience—some judges' sheets and asked us to fill them out. They wanted to compare them with what the judges said. We listened to the groups and filled out the sheets.

Now, at the very beginning before all the bands play, there's a solo competition. I heard this guy Liam Teague[2] who just absolutely blew my mind. He was sixteen years old at that time. He composed a long piece, which was really a mature composition for him to write at that time, then played it like nobody's business. I didn't get a chance to talk to him much at that time, but about two years later I got a letter from him begging me to help him. He was just stagnating in Trinidad. He described that he played the violin but not good enough to get into any of the European conservatories. He asked me to do anything to help him. I decided to try to raise some tuition waiver funds for him, because he was considered an out-of-state student and a foreign student whose tuition was more than triple. It would have cost him twelve to fifteen thousand dollars a year. A woman named Joy Caesar who worked at Citibank in PoS got the bank to invest in him and started a fund for him. Between that and what I was able to generate at the university, we were able to offer him something that wasn't going to last longer than a year. We agreed to get him up here and then see what happened. He came.

Meanwhile, Cliff continued steadily working on his instruments and needed a supply of barrels. He'd contacted a company in Chicago, the Trilla Steel Drum Company for his drums. One day, when he was picking up his order, the president came out because he had heard talk of this guy, Cliff Alexis. They talked for a bit and Cliff invited him to our concert that April. Because he was returning from Italy the night before the concert, he promised only to see what he could do.

What usually happened at the end of concerts was people who had come for the first time mobbed the stage to look at the instruments, and we would try to keep them from banging them with their hands, and so on. During all that running around at the end of that concert, this guy came up and put his hand on my shoulders and said, "I'm Lester Trilla. How can I help?" I exclaimed, "Oh, my God!" We talked for a little while and I said to him finally, "The primary concern I have right now is trying to get Liam Teague through school. The university has committed some money which is supposed to decrease year by year, and the funds from Trinidad because of the foreign currency exchange rates were just enough to help him through his first year." He said, "Don't worry. I'll take care of everything." He paid his tuition all the way through undergraduate school.

After graduating, Liam decided, with my coercion, to stay and get his master's. It was obvious to me that this young man was going to be a major talent, and he really didn't have enough musicality or maturity to go it on his own. He stayed two more years and did an absolutely outstanding job. You must know about the concerto one of our faculty wrote for Liam, who was playing at a Convocation, one of the recitals that the School of Music holds. This composition professor, who is a fairly well-known composer in this country, heard him and was just dazzled by his technique. He said, "I'm going to write you a concerto." He did it over the following summer.

At this time, the second best professional symphony in Chicago, called the Chicago Sinfonietta, was establishing ties with NIU. For instance, when they did a piece for orchestra and chorus they would use our chorus. We presented this concerto to the conductor who was just knocked out. He has a reputation for really trying to do different things with an orchestra program to bring in bigger and better audiences. So, Liam premiered this concerto in Orchestra Hall in Chicago, and the reviews were just stunning for him. The conductor also conducts the Czech National Symphony in Prague and brought him out there to do it. Liam's now played the piece probably fifteen times in various places around the world. Another composer has written him another one.[3] The names of the two composers are Jan Bach, the first one, and Joey Sellers, the second. The conductor of the orchestra was Paul Freeman. Bach's concerto is called "Concerto for Steelpan" and has two movements: "Reflections" and "Picada." Sellers's piece is called "Three Movements for Steel Pan," but I don't remember the names of the moves.

After Liam graduated with his master's, he returned to Trinidad but he really wasn't able to do enough to be a full-time musician. There just isn't enough work there. So, we talked about the idea of getting him on the faculty here since at that point Trilla's gift was increasing. He continued to give funds to support Liam and even improved it. Since my first meeting with him, he has given us quite a few hundred thousand dollars, and the money is still coming in. This is money primarily for scholarships for students mostly from Trinidad, but we've had students from places like Grenada and St. Martin.

The program is set on various levels: Priority I is given to West Indian students; Priority II to minority students in the United States; then finally White Americans are Priority III. The allocation of funds was such that if we had a year when Priority I and Priority II students were not in the application pool, then we would go to the third category. But we've never gone to the third category. Actually, we're backed up for three years with students who've expressed an interest and auditioned to come here, and we just don't have enough money to fund them all. The check I get from Trilla every three months, though generous, is not enough. I use the money as I deem appropriate, which I put all into scholarship money.

The Academic Program

The program, the first of its kind, began as an undergraduate one with general requirements for a Bachelor of Arts degree in Music. The way that is structured here is: there's a core set of requirements that all music students must take: four semesters of Theory and Ear Training; three semesters of Music History; a minimum of eight ensembles, one every semester; and, private study every semester. In Liam's case, what we basically did was: for the private study his lessons were made one hundred percent Steelpan as opposed to Percussion, and the steel band was his ensemble requirement. Then, he took all the other required courses all students took. There's also a fairly large amount of electives from which they can pick and choose pretty much whatever they want. He's taken a lot of Jazz improvisation and Jazz theory for those classes, and has gotten very much interested in it.

We primarily focus on graduate students. The reason for that is at the St. Augustine campus in Trinidad there's now a Pan program that leads to a bachelor's degree. We encourage the students to go through that program, even though it's more musicologically oriented than performance oriented, and then apply here as a graduate student. We can then offer them an assistantship, which pays them a nine-month stipend for a certain amount of money. The graduate school then picks up their tuition. This makes it easier for us to bring in more students. They normally complete their degree within two years and graduate. What we've done now is to develop a Pan major. Students earn a Master of Music degree in Steelpan. It involves private study, which Liam teaches, the steel band counts as their ensemble requirement, and then a seminar class with Cliff on whatever topics he emphasizes that semester. They then take the regular requirements for a Master of Music in Performance—a music history class and a research class—all to help them in their future professional lives, if they chose to go that route.

We now have either seven or eight students in that program. Cliff, Liam, and I do the steel band at various times because I am semi-retired. I used to be a Dean of Students for Art, Music Theater, and Dance, which is what I'm retired from.

The university has retained me for the past four and a half years from the time I left to continue to work with the Pan program, because the ultimate goal is to turn this over to Liam. So, I have all this time to mentor him.

As a faculty member of sorts, Liam is getting support from another foundation in Wisconsin through a very wealthy family who supports their foundation. The way that connection came about is that I teach at a music campus there two weeks in July every year. I've been going there for twenty years. About six years ago, I got a call from this woman in Fort Wayne, Indiana, who runs a summer program. She said, "We're going to emphasize the Caribbean this year. Can you help me out with anything?" I told her about Liam and asked her what she thought. She said she knew someone who worked for American Airlines and would try to get him a ticket. Sure enough, she was able to do that. I asked her whether it mattered when we arrived, because I had something else I wanted to attend. She assured me there was no problem with that. When we finally got there at the Wisconsin camp, he just absolutely knocked everybody out, as he always does. We have something there that we now call the Liam Cam. A camcorder is put behind his shoulder that records how his hands move around the pan because he plays so fast.

The university told me that the only way we can get him on the faculty is if we generate his salary externally because it doesn't have another position in its budget. So, this family and Mr. Trilla are paying his salary. It is supposed to be like that until I leave, because the money the university is giving me will become the basis of his salary.

The first person to graduate from the program, that honor belongs to the person Cliff wound up marrying. She was one of the high school students he brought from St. Paul, a very bright and talented girl who was from a not-too wealthy family. She and another friend of hers whom Cliff thought were the two best players in the band he had there were granted minority funding to attend school here. They were the first two. One graduated in the 1980s; the other one didn't.

The World Steelband Music Festival

I was invited to judge the Music Festival in '92 and again in '98, then we went for the festival in 2000. That was quite an experience! The way the Festival works is this. The normal selection process is a test piece, a calypso piece that cannot be from the previous Panorama, and a tune of choice. You can choose anything, and ninety-nine out of one hundred competitors choose a classical piece. Our NIU steel band didn't do that. We prepared the test piece, which was awful. But Cliff composed a calypso called "Pan 2000," and then we did this piece that I had one of the percussions professors write for our first tour in Taiwan in 1992, called "Wood and Steel." It uses a Ugandan xylophone called an Amadinda xylophone,[4] which is about six feet tall. It has twelve keys, I think, and is played by three people.

He wrote this piece for the steel band and this instrument that combined them and had them play separate parts at one time or another. The piece starts off very slowly then the steel band fades out and the xylophone does the traditional Ugandan music. When we got to that, that's when the people started to really go nuts. After that was going for a while, there was a bunch of what is called metrical modulations, a way to double tempo as the music gets faster. By the time it got through three or four of those, the tempo had sped up from what it was in the beginning. Then, when the band came back in, it played at a very loud and rapid rate with the xylophone. That's what brought everybody on their feet.

Another thing I was quite somewhat amazed about was what Cliff and Liam both do as Trinidadians. Each time that you play a calypso piece at each level of the competition, it usually changes a little bit, but none of the bands did that. They played the calypso the same way every single time. Each time we came back, however, we added two or three different sections. The Europeans were furious. We weren't supposed to do that, they complained.

Ultimately, the whole thing was resolved. A letter was sent to Patrick Arnold, the president of Pan Trinbago, saying that one of the judges, Eugene, was a student of mine. They actually had it wrong. We went to two different schools in Illinois. My school is about 150 miles north of the University of Illinois's main campus. He attended there to get his doctorate in Percussions, and he obviously got very interested in Pan and knows Cliff very well. Of course, Cliff built all his instruments, and he is now a professor at Humboldt State University in northern California. And there was Ann Osbourne; I had judged with her several other times. So, I can see in there the sort of anger they got that they could feel something was dishonest, but both of those people are of the highest integrity. Eugene even told me that he had to be extra critical of us because he knew what everybody was saying.

But that's not why we didn't win, and I didn't see there was any problem with the judging. I think there's no question that the band that won deserved to win. They were *really* good players. I was disappointed, however, in some of the preparations of the Trinidad groups, to tell the truth. After judging them twice, I came to know what to expect. One band, I thought, selected a really lousy calypso piece to play, and the judges probably thought the same thing. Things like that happened.

Other Achievements

The Percussive Arts Society holds an international convention in the United States every year at various locations. There's always something about steel bands included. Our band has done more of those than any other group in the country. The year 1994 is notable because we shared that convention in Atlanta with Ellie's group, our band and the WVU Steel Band. We arranged for the Society to present both Cliff and Ellie with an award for their accomplishments in the development of the instruments.

Going backward, another significant event was in St. Louis in 1987, when the first mass steel band in the United States was put together. There were 105 players. To prepare those who were able to raise their own money to come, we sent them a tape-recording of how the arrangement of the various parts should sound. When everyone arrived, because there were so many things going on throughout the three-day convention, it was very difficult to find a room or time to rehearse. Our program was slated to be on Saturday morning at nine o'clock, I think, and our rehearsal time was at one o'clock that morning before. We had to go into the room at one in the morning, and since we were the first to perform we could leave everything set up. It was a matter of saying, "We're gonna start this off and if it doesn't work, we're screwed." But it all came together just fine. Quite amazing! We sight-read all the arrangements for that.

We brought Boogsie up as a soloist, and schools from all over the country participated. They came form Indianapolis, Indiana, and Knoxville, Tennessee.

Also in 1987, I was invited to start a steel band at the National Institute of the Arts in Taiwan. I went for a semester and put on a performance. The professor of Percussion had his own professional Percussion ensemble, which was a very, very good group. I told him that I would try to nominate him for an appearance at the Percussive Arts Society's convention that was slated to be in Philadelphia in 1990, I think. I was able to get him and his group here, and in return he invited us to bring the steel band to Taiwan, which we did in 1992.

We played about eight or nine programs, and the coverage and the people's response were just astounding. We did one in the Chiang Kai-Shek Memorial Square, and there had to have been ten thousand people there. Ours was the second steel band to be in Taiwan, and they said the first band wasn't very good and people didn't really like it very much. That first band gave them an idea of what it was like, but our appearance was much more impressive. They invited us back in 1998. In '92, we did the northern half of the island and in '98 the southern half. Taiwan now has a steel band at the National Institute, which I started, and one that the Percussion professor put together for his own professional ensemble.

Last May, we were invited to South Korea for the 2002 World Cup. The Seoul Municipal Government paid every penny of our costs. It was amazing! We didn't actually play in the stadium. The city had a festival organized for the people who were attending just for the fun of it. They invited one musical group from each country that had a team in the tournament. There were about thirty-two groups there, all very different and all based on drumming of some kind. It was called the Festival of the Drums. There were seven venues set up around Seoul, and afternoon and evening performances in each one every day. They told us to prepare twenty to thirty minutes worth of music—each group was supposed to do that. Then three groups would make up a full performance. So, one day we would be playing at the National Folk Art Museum with Senegal and Germany, and the next day at other venue with two other groups, and so on, in rotation. The great thing about that was all the people got to hear all the groups. We all stayed in the same hotel, and it was fantastic. It's the cleanest city I've ever visited.

Korea now wants me to return and start a steel band. I don't know if I'll be returning because I'm getting sick of those plane flights. I think I'll refer someone else to do that. The person who is leading the band at the National Institute in Taiwan is a former student of mine. She fell in love with Taiwan, is married and has a family over there. They could fly her to Seoul. That would be easy. It's about a four-hour trip.

There are some bands in the mainland China and Japan. There's a Chinese musicologist on our faculty; his name is Kuo Huang Han. He knows where the bands are in China.

Steelband continues to grow rapidly here and throughout the world. For instance, right here in the United States it's just amazing. At least once a week I hear about another band some where that I didn't know about. There are hundreds of them here.

In regard to Trinidad, the thing that I see needs to be dealt with there is that they've got to get out of doing the same thing every year. It's very difficult for anyone trying to experiment with moving the calypso arrangements into some uncharted territory because he'll get criticized for it severely, both by the people and by the judges. I think they could see that it's possible basically from what we were able to accomplish at the Festival, which was a total surprise to me. Many of the groups both in Europe and in Trinidad had been working on that music for a year. We didn't have our first rehearsal until the last day in August. The thing that made it possible to put that all together like that was the fact that everyone read music.

Also, when we came to rehearse the additions that we wanted to put into the arrangement, Cliff and Liam would go off some place. Cliff would tell Liam what he wanted and played those notes, Liam would write them down on a piece of paper, pass the parts out to everybody, and usually we would have it learned in a couple of hours. We were at Phase II's panyard and a lot of them were standing around in disbelief, 'cause they weren't in the Festival. They said, "Man, that would have taken Boogsie all night."

It's always been true in the history of music for every instrument that there's got to be room for tradition and room for experimentation and expansion. If not, it's going to lose its popularity. It's sort of similar to what's happening to a lot of symphony orchestras in terms of losing their sponsors and audiences, because they keep playing the same pieces year in and year out. The same classical, romantic music. This is because primarily the people who have the money to support the groups want what they like, which is that sort of music. But they're shutting out all the other people where the audience is concerned. Pan is a versatile instrument that plays all types of music, but it's moving in that direction toward stagnation, unless the people become open to the idea of experimentation toward expansion....

Author's note: O'Connor concluded our conversation with the following highlights of additional achievements:

- He has received four grants from the United States National Endowment for the Arts to support various artistic endeavors and was twice nominated for Fulbright fellowships by the Council for the International Exchange of Scholars.

- As a percussion soloist and conductor, he has premiered over twenty-five compositions for percussion solo or ensemble.

- He has written more than seventy arrangements for Steelband, some incorporating other acoustic and electric instruments as well as the musics of West Africa and T&T Tamboo-Bamboo.

- His arrangement of Aaron Copland's *Appalachian Spring* was performed by "Our Boys Steel Orchestra" of Tobago at the 1988 Music Festival held in PoS, Trinidad.

15

A Thriving Family Business: Philbert Solomon's Story[1]

Philbert "Phil" Solomon *was born on February 26, 1946, in Guyana. His wife, Marilyn, and daughters Janera, Jonnet, Leigh, and Fauna are integral parts of the family business,* Solomon Steelpan Company. *His musical accomplishments include some original compositions, which include the song to the national hero of Guyana,* O Martyr to Cuffy We Sing. *He has written for the Guyanese newspaper (1972–74). Some of his awards include: Lifetime Achievement Award (2000), Music Educators National Conference; Governor's Heritage Folklife Program (Pennsylvania).*

Pan's Background from a Guyanese's Perspective

To my knowledge, Steelband originated among the people who lived in the British Caribbean: Ellie Mannette, Kim Loy Wong, Tony Williams, Neville Jules, and Bertie Marshall.[2] Jules started making a larger pan and had a whole band of the larger pans, though it was not the 55-gallon drum. He used cans around the

30-gallon size, the caustic soda barrel, which made a very good sounding bass because they were thicker and bigger than the cans. They used these barrels for approximately ten years both in Trinidad and Guyana. Some people say it was Kim Loy who first did it; others say Jules; and others say Mannette. I know that Ellie made smaller pans before he made the big ones. I saw them.

I got involved in Steelband when I was twelve. I'd seen the small drums and first made a tin can when I was about seven. I played songs from the radio on it. At twelve, I got involved with the caustic soda barrel, and when I was fourteen I joined a group that was just starting and they had the full-size drum.

People ought to have a vision of how the government operated—in relation to how the kids descended from slavery were learning in the face of poverty—to understand how in context this development of the steelpan came to be. Steelband is the greatest collaboration of the West Indian people that has existed, without the people even talking to one another.[3] Nothing else reflects this collaboration, this togetherness, this one-mindedness. At the same time the people in Trinidad were making these steelpans and trying to get sound out of these drums, people were doing the same thing in Antigua. And, none of them actually knew they were doing the same thing at the same time. When it comes to history, I don't like to get too bogged down in the details. But I know about this stuff and what was going on around the Caribbean because I was commissioned by the Guyanese government in 1968 to study Steelpan. I traveled to all the islands, visited the bands, and talked to the players.

When you look at the history, the first steel band and its recording in the world was from Antigua. That was in the late '40s to early '50s. [*Note*: Kim Johnson has written that Casablanca made a recording in 1947 and TASPO in 1951. See his article, "With Music in His Blood," *Trinidad Guardian*, April 21, 2003, that suggests that Casablanca may have been the first recorded steel band.] Trinidad had the steelpan but didn't have a band. Guys were making lead pans, the ping-pong, but they didn't make a band. Antigua formed the first steel band and made a record of steelband music. They had two bands that grew out of one big band: Hell's Gates and Brute Force. They made records, 45s, and put them out before any other country. This is why I don't like to get too involved in the history, because it's too controversial and people get too upset when you make statements of this sort. I don't blame them for getting upset because they are dedicated people who love what they're doing. They want to be the first, the only, the original, and then they hear that somebody else already did it and get upset. They exclaim, "What?! That's not true! That's a lie!" It may be true or not. I know that Antigua is true because I had the record, so I know it existed. I no longer have the record because back in those days we didn't take these things seriously, as some do today. Somebody asked me for it and I gave it to him, and that was the end of that. Most of my stuff I gave away: lent to people, gave to the Guyana National History of Art Council. I have some of this written down and in memory.

Guyana is the second largest Steelband place in the Caribbean. Three places are really responsible for the birth and development of Steelband: Trinidad, number one; Guyana, number two; and Antigua, number three. After Antigua got into it in the early days and made those records, I don't know what happened because I didn't live there. But it just died after they got off to a good, early start. There's a guy from Antigua living in Florida who tunes pans, Tom Reynolds.[4]

Guyana got involved seriously in Steelband after Jules and his boys visited Guyana. They were banging on tin cans and caustic soda drums, and so on. Two brothers, the Gundadin brothers, who lived in the city went to Trinidad, got a pan and brought it back to Guyana, around the late '50s. People saw it and were impressed. Men started picking up hammers and trying to make a pan like it. A guy named Hercules was successful in making and selling these drums. He wasn't interested in making a band; he merely made pans for individual people. When Jules and his group visited and performed in Market Square, people heard what this thing could do. It took them by storm. It was the first time they heard a bunch of guys play these things at one time. After Jules left, within a year we had three or four bands. Guyana got very serious into Pan in the '60s.

During the early '60s, we had twenty regular size bands and five large road bands of over fifty people each playing in them, and six small combo bands. Then, we formed the Guyana National Steelband Association (GNSA), and the president of the GNSA was the speaker of the House of Assembly. We went on to form a national steel band, which was sponsored and paid for by the government, and around the national steel band we tried to organize Steelband. Most of the achievements we know of today, like Pan Trinbago, were done first by Guyana, which set the pace in organizing.[5] The bands in Trinidad sounded better, their pans sounded better, and their arrangements were better. They took the pan itself more seriously. But we were more into organizing, forming associations, getting the panmen paid, and having the pan played in church.

When Trinidad got its Independence, the first steel band to play its national anthem was the Guyana National Steelband, which was invited to perform in Trinidad. I was a little too young to go, fourteen at the time, and my parents didn't allow me to go. I was actually dropped as a member of the band because of how good I was. But at fourteen, to go out of the country my parents said no. I remember the band learning the tune, and so on. Back then, we didn't think of this as making history. Then, the band went to Cuba for about seven weeks and performed. We had a very vibrant Steelband culture, but it all came crashing down in '64 after Burnham[6] took over.

When Burnham came into power, the first thing he did was scrap the national band. He said it was ludicrous for Steelband people to be paid by the government, so he fired the national band. The national steel band had a venue for rehearsal. He took that away from them and called it the National Service Centre. He dismantled the whole Pan thing. The men got frustrated, got other jobs, and the band just went downhill from there. When that happened, most of the older guys quitted. Cedric Williams, a top tuner, opened up a food stand and quitted Pan totally. That's where I came in.

At that point, around '66, we'd just got Independence, I decided that I would really get serious in this thing and try to keep it up, not make it fall because I could see how it was disintegrating. Every day, you could hear the people talking about how the band broke up. So, I talked with Roy Geddes and Calvin White and formed a group. We became the three musketeers who took the whole Pan movement on our shoulders. We kept the organization and association going. We became the three top pan tuners and steelband arrangers, and our bands were the three top bands of the country. This continued until I left the country in '84.

Before leaving, I was made the Steelpan program director for steel bands in schools. We got some instruments into Bishops High School, St. Rose's (a girls' school), and the college. I was also the organizing secretary for the steelband association. We tried to keep it up pretty good. In '72 when we had the Carifesta, the steelband association organized for a visiting steel band from Trinidad, and we had Tony Prospect come over and do our adjudicating. But the pressure from the government was too much, and we always had a problem with finances. The government could never find money for the instruments.

Eventually, I broke; that was in '75. I decided that it was just too much work and I wasn't getting anything for it. I quitted and started a new group called the Sound Waves. We got sponsored by the Pegasus Hotel and became the Pegasus Sound Waves, which lasted until 1980, and after that I was in charge of the police force steel band till '84 when I left Guyana. I made a total of four steel bands: Pegasus Sound Waves; Bell Boys; Atlantic Symphony; and, the Guyana Defence Force Steel Band, the police force steel band. I also made three bands in New Amsterdam.

Roy Geddes got sponsored by the Tobacco Company, so his band became the Tobacco Company Silvertones. Calvin White got sponsored by the Bauxite

Company and his band became the Demba (for Demarara Bauxite Corporation) Invaders. Once that happened, everyone started going separate ways. Because of my abilities and talents, I was able to make a successful career, a very good business, out of the Sound Waves. We became the top band in the country. We did classical concerts and a variety of other performances. We played over three hundred times a year and made a lot of money. But the Pan movement went down and there was no more growth. We were the people who were building, making, and developing pans in the country, and once we stopped then that was the end of that. The government wasn't going to spend any money on Pan; it wasn't worth their while.

I came to the United States in 1984 and settled in Pittsburgh. My success in Guyana and now here is attributed to my abilities as the only tuner, arranger, and player who could read music then.

Most Valuable Contributions to Pan

I taught myself to read music over the course of two years. I started studying when I was fifteen, using the pan, and when I was seventeen I could arrange a classical piece for Pan. I not only played with a steel band but played solo steelpan with a Jazz band and with the top musicians. I did classical concerts with the top musicians in the country. So, I was well prepared when I came here. I could make a pan, play a pan, and teach a pan. I could arrange and read music, play Jazz, so I had all the skills necessary for success in this field. As a matter of fact, that's why I came to Pittsburgh, because Pittsburgh didn't have anything—no steel band at all, which was ideal for me. I didn't want to be in New York with all those other guys who were talking only about whose pan was better, and all that nonsense. I didn't want to get caught up in that. I made that decision before I even came to the United States.

In fact, I went to Nassau, Bahamas, and tried to do the same thing that I've done here and talked with the government, but they weren't interested. Coming from Guyana after being the program director for schools, and so on, I had a definite plan, which was to establish Steelpan in the educational system. What I found when I got here was that tuners from Trinidad like Kim Loy and Cliff Alexis[7] had their own interests and ideas. Alexis got involved in a university where his future would be solid. Ellie Mannette was probably looking for the same thing at WVU.

Here's something that isn't well-known. I was first offered the job at WVU because I was right here in Pittsburgh, a mere fifty minutes away. Someone told WVU about me and they called me for an interview. They explained to me what their plan was, but their plan didn't coalesce with mine. When I explained to them what my plan was, they thought I was crazy—the plan to establish Pan in the educational system, starting in Pittsburgh, spreading throughout Pennsylvania, then branching out to other states. They told me I could not do that. Their idea was for me to join their program, serve it well, become a part of them, but not do anything outside. This was in the early '90s.

I suggested to them to try Ellie Mannette or one of those guys, because Ellie was about twenty years older than me and might be looking for some place to settle. They said all right and went out looking. Then, I heard they talked to him and he said yes. I continued my plan to get pans in schools and establish a business, and started the first steelpan manufacturing company in the United States in 1990. Of course, at first it was laughed at. But all that is changed today. I went on to register it as a business, had a price list, model numbers for the drums—established the whole operation as a business. I'd done this before and was familiar with all these procedures.

Here in Pittsburgh, because there were no bands in schools or anything, I started with soliciting the nearby schools, sometimes giving them a free pan to start with. When they eventually saw it was a good idea and good plan, they started the program. Now, I have eleven schools with a Steelband program in Pittsburgh alone. In 1992, I was enlisted into the Folklife Commission of Pennsylvania as a folklife artist for Steelband music. This commission was created in 1980 and got official recognition in 1982 by Congress. It's a state-wide program that includes every artist/e that is successful in bringing their art from another country into Pennsylvania. Once I was enlisted, I became known state-wide because this list is sent to every school, every organization in the state, and I started getting calls from people. The next thing I did was become a member of the Arts Education Program in Pennsylvania. My photo was included in the publication of this Program, which includes photos of all artists/es in Pennsylvania. Every school receives this publication and the calls increased.

During the late '80s, the calls became frantic and I was running day and night, establishing resident programs in schools. Because I'd got my business started, at every school I visited I solicited the purchase of my pans, and my business began to pick up. The orders began coming in rapidly, so that in 1993 I removed my name from the program. I couldn't do that anymore. I concentrated on establishing the business of putting steel bands in schools. I went to Harrisburg, Chambersburg, Coatesville, Media, and other places. Today, we have twenty-three programs throughout Pennsylvania—which I think is more than any other state presently—in high schools, middle schools, colleges, and universities. Then, I became nationally and internationally known when I was featured on *Mister Roger's Neighborhood*. After that appearance, I began receiving calls from California, Ohio, Michigan, Idaho, North Dakota, South Dakota, to name some places.

Soon, I began to run out of space so that five years ago I moved in this building, a 3,000-square-foot building, where we manufacture, tune, and sell our products: pans, cases for the pans, stands, mallets, and all accessories. We are a complete steelpan production business. Right now, I don't go out to the schools anymore. They bring their instruments to the company for retuning, repainting, or whatever they require to enhance the appearance and sound of the instrument, which I complete within a week.

Throughout the years, I've probably made more steelpans than anyone else. Most of the pans you hear on the radio were made by me and my company. Ellie's and Andy Narell's[8] pans may be used, too. One of the problems people have had is that the pans sounded good in a steel band or steel orchestra and in gigs. But when they were recorded, the sound wasn't as good because, as I discovered, the pan itself had a lot of extra noise that caused bad recordings. The microphones were so sensitive that they picked up every little noise that was heard during a playback. So, in 1990 I came up with a new technique of making pan, which I call the Grooveless System^{TM}.

We don't put the grooves into the pan anymore, which make the notes much clearer and with a lot less noise. Once people began using these grooveless pans for recordings, they could hear the difference. The sound was great. This is why my pans for recording became more in demand. The grooveless pan eliminates the extra noise, the sympathetic vibrations. The groove, when it puckered in some areas, the pucker caused a harmonic report or micro-tone in that area that is irrelevant to the particular note.

The bore pan[9] still has grooves, a border line. I once considered that idea of the bore pan, but relying on my knowledge of physics I saw that it was not the best idea. The pan is a two-dimensional instrument, similar to a bongo or conga. When you hit the top, it makes a sound at the top and another sound from the bottom, which is not the same sound. All skin drums do that.

We don't put the grooves into the pan anymore, which make the notes much clearer and with a lot less noise. Once people began using these grooveless pans for recordings, they could hear the difference. The sound was great. This is why my pans for recording became more in demand. The grooveless pan eliminates the extra noise, the sympathetic vibrations. The groove, when it puckered in some areas, the pucker caused a harmonic report or microtone in that area that is irrelevant to the particular note.

The bore pan[10] still has grooves, a border line. I once considered the idea of the bore pan, but relying on my knowledge of physics I saw that it was not the best idea. The pan is a two-dimensional instrument, similar to a bongo or conga. When you hit the top, it makes a sound at the top and another sound from the bottom, which is not the same sound. All skin drums do that. The top and bottom produce a different sound, if you listen carefully. A trumpet is a one-dimensional instrument. When you blow that note, that's what comes out of the instrument. So, if you drill holes into that drum and create air to come through, then you diminish one of the dimensions and it becomes a one-dimensional instrument. You would have more of a piercing sound like a horn, which is not very good for the instrument. After studying that concept, I decided that boring the pan, putting holes into it, was not the best idea for the instrument. The bore pan originated in Trinidad in the '70s. [*Note*: Vincent Hernandez's story suggests otherwise.]

The grooveless pan has no lines. We mark the area then shape the notes with the hammer from that mark. When you groove the pan, you have to hammer the groove out to some extent so that it doesn't affect the note or make the note sound as though you're putting your finger on it. During that process, the note cracks. In most grooved drums, you'll see the crack or a welded area. In my pans, there aren't any cracks, welding, or grooves. That's one advantage of using the Grooveless System™. Another advantage is over the years as the pan ages, the first part to crack is the groove. First, there's a hairline crack, which begins to affect the note. Now, if you try to weld the crack, the original sound is distorted. The Grooveless System™ extends the life of the drum, the pan. Another positive is because you're not grooving anymore, it cuts down on the time to make a pan by about two hours. To every three drums, I can make four. Six hours of not grooving frees my time to make another pan.

I've done other things both musically and businesswise to make the production of the pan a successful business. One needs to have certain mechanisms in place to make a business successful. I established quality control, for example. All my leads are very similar, so similar that you wouldn't know which one to choose. They are all good. Another pan-maker, making three leads, will produce a very good one, a good one, and a not-so-good one. That pan-maker cannot consistently follow through on his production of a similar quality instrument. With my pans, you don't have that problem because my method maintains consistency. I've been able to reduce the length of time of production from the raw material to the finished product to one-fifth of the original time. And, that is very good for any business. Once you can make the product quicker, you can sell more.

I've also paved the way for what might be in the future a mechanical process. If anyone were to come up with the idea of a machine to manufacture these pans mechanically, my method would be perfect. For example, when I make a six-piece bass, I have one pattern for all six drums, the processing and marking. When they're done, I tune one drum to a C, then another to the C-sharp, then the other to the D, then the next to an E, then E-flat, then F. I have the perfect drawing that allows me to do this. I just need one drawing for all six drums. All other pan-makers have six different drawings for each drum. I use the same process to make a double tenor, as another example. When I make a double tenor, I sink the two drums and then use one pattern for both drums. When that is done, I first tune one to F and then the other to F-sharp. I've cut every process down to a minimum time.

Another concept I've contributed to Pan is the synchronized designs of the steelpan, a concept I first came up with in 1970. Synchronized designing is the complete design of the lead pan to the bass pan, in which every pan is synchronized, similar to the way a guitar or a piano has a pattern, so that each steelpan has a perfect pattern. These patterns were sent to the National History in Art Council, headed by Lynette Dolphin. Copies were made and sent to Trinidad for review and evaluation. The reports were most of the bands said it was the best thing they'd ever seen and the person who did that must be a mathematician with everything being so perfect. But they disclaimed it saying that cannot work for Pan; it's too perfect. So being a tuner, I made drums from those patterns, from then until today.

What has happened through the years, I learned that when I sent my portfolio that included a documentation of these patterns to a school encouraging them to start a band, when they reviewed the patterns of the drums and their designs, many times they made a decision based on this information. I was able to win over the competition based on my patterns because they make musical sense. Any music teacher looking at these patterns will see the G and G-sharp together, the F and F-sharp together, every thing in perfect balance. I came up with this idea after visiting the bands in Trinidad and observing everyone having a different design, except for when the same person made the drums. For example, a Bertie Marshall double tenor in one band was the same as a Bertie Marshall double tenor in another band. But the designs from one tuner to another were all disarranged musically. The notes were basically placed where they could sound best and not how to best access them.

I came up with the idea of synchronizing these designs based on Bach's idea of equal temperament. What I actually did was take the twelve notes of music and divide them equally among the number of heads or barrels used to make the instrument. For example, if you would use three drums to make a triple, then you take every three semi-tones. So you will have a C, then an E-flat, then F-sharp, then A, which then will lead you back to C. I discovered that was a diminished seven-chord. So, I made one diminished seven-chord from C, then took the same pattern and started with C-sharp, then using the same pattern started with D, and I got three drums with the same pattern on all three drums in the same fashion. After you set up the instruments to play, all the chords, arrangements, and the sevenths and ninths and thirds sounded very similar to one another. Every note was in a synchronized pattern.

Two companies currently are established as companies, Panyard Inc. and mine.[11] I established mine first in the United States, then Panyard Inc. came to me and said they wanted to start selling music. I contributed to that and I suppose helped them get their own company going. While individuals like Ellie Mannette and Cliff Alexis are making pans in big demand, Panyard Inc. realized that it had to adopt the synchronized design or else it would not succeed as a business. Panyard Inc. and my company are the only two using this synchronized pattern right now.

My business is succeeding with five employees, and I am in the process of establishing steel bands in community areas and churches. My oldest daughter is in charge of the outreach program. She's also responsible for going into the community and talking to leaders, getting funds and financing that allow us to establish the program. We have people who will go to the sites and teach and train the players. Within a year, we can prepare a band of children to play at any cultural center or concert hall. My wife and other three daughters are involved in various aspects of the business.

Tell the Story of Steelpan Well

What people need to understand is the steelpan was created out of a marriage. It is the off-spring of Africa and Europe, specifically England. The combination of those two, the African heritage and the European way of life, produced people like me. I look like an African but I am an Englishman. I was born in British Guiana. I was brought up to be a British subject. I know everything about England that the average Englishman knows and very little about Africa, so I became an

Afro-European. And, the only person who could have made a steelpan was an Afro-European. It's the only drum in the world that can play a tune or melody. If you understand and believe that, then you can write a book and communicate to other people what this thing is all about. All the other stuff about this pan and that pan is all flowery. It's like in everything else—the myths and stories, and so on, of everyday life. If the pan was not created at the time it was created, it would not have existed today. No one person could come up with the idea. It had to have happened at a certain time and at a certain place and by a certain people.

The Caribbean was also known as the New World inhabited by new people. It gave birth to new nations that produced cricket champions, soccer [called football outside the United States] champions, and boxing champions. We created things that only we could have created.[12] Some of the foods we have in the Caribbean couldn't come from anywhere else. Some of these things couldn't come from Africa, Europe, Asia, or China. They had to come from the Caribbean and these new people who created new food, dress, and music. And, they were created to be sent into the rest of the world and become a part of the whole world. They weren't created for us to keep at home or be made like and unto ourselves. The Spanish created the guitar and let it loose into the world, so that today we have the Mighty Sparrow's music and calypso, the calypso being made by a guitar and a man singing. We now have to understand this metal, steel, and how we were able to use steel to create this instrument. The steel drum possesses the necessary things to make this instrument sound the way it does.

Let me make a point about Jazz. It is also necessary for people to understand the difference between Jazz and Steelpan. Jazz is a musical form that came from the African Americans but it doesn't have an instrument. The pan is a musical instrument that was created by the people of the Caribbean and has been proven throughout the years that it can play any music. The problem we have with Jazz staying alive is that it doesn't have an instrument that composers can write new Jazz pieces for, like the way Chopin did for the piano. He sealed the piano when he wrote all those pieces for the piano. You can play Chopin on a pan, a violin, or any instrument. But the music was written for the piano. Jazz doesn't have an instrument. We're borrowing instruments for Jazz—the piano, the saxophone—and what that does, it creates a situation where the performer is the one that is being depended upon. Nothing else. Now, even if Chopin didn't play any of that music, it still would have been established because someone else would have played it. Jazz isn't like that. You have to be a Jazz great, a Coltrane, or nothing would happen.

The way the world works, each generation looks at something else, so if you don't establish it, it's going to be lost. I expressed this opinion at a panel discussion on a radio program, WDUQ/NPR, to some Jazz people and they were upset. I maintained that we would lose Jazz like we lost other musical art forms. But when you establish it with an instrument, like Piano Concerto #1, there is no other way to play that piece. Pan wouldn't suffer from cultural stagnation if we follow a similar path.

I didn't pioneer this thing, but I've got a lot to do with how it developed since I arrived. Cliff Alexis is one of the people who started what I came along and continued. But the problem with Cliff—and anyone who has Cliff's pan will tell you—is that his pans sound very good, but it takes forever to get them. That's because he's got a university job he has to do. He makes his pans on weekends and when he has other spare time. That can't work. He's made quite a few pans for people in schools. As a matter of fact, most of the pans I've seen in schools are Cliff's. So, he seems to have been concentrating on the same idea I have, but he probably wasn't willing to go out there and rough it like I did. He wanted to have a secure base to work from. But you can't serve two masters at one time. I learned that from refrigeration. I had to give that up if I wanted to do Pan, with no regrets. It was the best decision I've ever made.

I make pans with my name on them, and I would never see a refrigerator with my name on it. As a matter of fact, I once built a freezer for a butcher in Guyana, built from scratch with galvanize and other scrap material, and delivered it to him at his shop. It worked really well. He asked me, "Where's the name? There's no name on it. Put Solomon on it." One of the market constables saw it and reported it and caused a big problem. I got a letter stating I needed a license to do that and to cease and desist from building any more, for which I needed a license from England. I was to be a typical subject of the queen of Britain who did things according to the queen's way. I understood that's the way things worked for British colonial subjects in the Caribbean. No one can tell me that about the pan.

For this reason, I don't think that I'm functioning on the margins of Pan in the United States. There's no tuner from Trinidad who could come here to the United States and rival me in my domain, my market. For example, every year Trinidad Pan Instrument Limited, the largest pan company in Trinidad—I think run by Neal and Massy—sets up yearly at the convention held by the Percussive Art Society. They display their instruments. I don't go to the convention but get more sales than they do because their instruments don't fit into the U.S. school system. A few people have bought them. One girl from Central Michigan University bought one and took it up there to play in the band and they didn't allow her to play. She eventually sold it and bought one from me. I have what the schools in this country want. Everything. The design of the pan, the style of pan, and all the accessories.

Now, if I try to compete with Panorama, I'll probably lose. I have no involvement in the Brooklyn Panorama; I have no connections. I've made pans for individual players and groups. Apparently, when the pan was transported from Trinidad to New York, the intention was to transfer the Trinidad-style steel band to New York. That is something I'm against. I don't think we should try to force our way upon others. That's our way: Carnival in Trinidad, Mashramani in Guyana, which are our things. I have nothing against them; I think they're great. Even the Labor Day festivities in Brooklyn, I think that's great, too. But that should be for us. If we want to put Pan in the United States, it should be in a way that the United States would benefit from what we're doing, not us. We're not the majority here; we're the majority back home.

So, the bands I've created here I don't encourage to play "Yellow Bird" or "Mary Anne" and songs like that. Some do play them, which is fine. If they want me to, I'll even teach them these songs, but I don't encourage them. I encourage them to play what they want to play—"Yankee Doodle," whatever pleases them. I enjoy more when they play "America the Beautiful" and "Camp Town Races" than when they play "Yellow Bird." They cannot play our songs the way we play them and we cannot play their songs the way they play them. We enjoy each other more when we play our songs best.

My vision to establishing the next phase of Steelpan in the United States is similar to the way the piano or violin came to be established. Let the people play their style of music. I don't think that's the vision of the Brooklyn people in the movement. So, we have totally different visions. I talk with them on the phone and they call me "the professor and the doctor." But I decided that I don't want to be involved with Panorama. I was involved with that for twenty years. I was the tuner for Laventille's Savoy and played in Trinidad Panorama. Every year in Guyana I won the Mashramani Competition, which used to be Carnival but the Guyanese decided to change the name. We wanted to be different and didn't want to use Mardi Gras or Carnival used in Brazil and Trinidad. So we came up with the word *Mashramani*, which means celebration, and has its roots in a native South American language.[13] Every year at the same time as the Trinidad Carnival, we have Mashramani, including a Panorama competition.

Bertie Marshall, who I used to live a block away from, and those other earlier guys are very good at making the ringing Panorama-style sounding steelpan. I used to make those types of pans myself. But they take too long and too much work to get that done here, and that style is not needed here. The people's tastes here are different from Trinidad's. Americans like softer tones, Jazz and Classical, and so on. Panorama music wouldn't catch on because the majority of people don't like the ringing sound. So, if you want to put pans in schools, it has to be put as a tool, just the way you put books and other instruments, and integrated into the curriculum. That's the way I'm doing it. I'm not putting out pans for the schools to go and play once a year at Panorama. I want pans to facilitate academic learning and academics studies. That's a part of my vision. That's also a part of telling the story of Pan well.

Now, I have to be honest with you and let you know that I wasn't too sure I wanted to continue to do this, talk about my role in Steelpan and what I knew. But after our first conversation and I recalled Antigua and the fact that that part of the story isn't very well known, I decided that I would do this because people ought to know about this, have the broader picture of what was going on back in those days. Today, we have this controversy about Antigua having the first steel band and first steelband record, and Trinidad saying they had this and that first. The second reason I decided to continue our conversation is I wanted to let you know that I'm speaking with another woman who is in South Dakota who is also researching the story of Steelpan. I didn't want you to be surprised when her story comes out and you didn't know, or you wondering who said what first, and so on. But the fact that you and this woman are researching the story of Pan and probably doing the same thing is like what was happening back when the pan was being invented.

A lot of people were doing things that other people didn't know about. Take, for example, what I'm doing here. A lot of people in Pan don't have a clue what I'm doing here. Back in those days, a lot of people were doing the same thing and didn't know about each other. So, to say who was first and so on will always be a problem. About four years ago, I saw Panyard's catalog, and they had the design of a pan they called the synchronized design. They're saying that it's their design. Yet, it is the exact design I had since 1970. Unfortunately, I didn't patent it. But the concept is not unique to music.

Panyard's people are also musicians who studied music from an Akron university. They probably saw the same thing I saw. As I think about it, they have no idea that someone already did that same thing some thirty years ago. They were bold enough to print it as their new design. It doesn't bother me really, because I know that in the future all pan will be designed like this. People will also stop grooving the pans, too. That's going to be the modern pan. I've been making the synchronized pan since 1970 and the grooveless pan since 1990. I'm not worried about the fact that I didn't patent my design or method. I'm happy to see that things are moving in the right direction, my direction, and in knowing that I've been doing the right thing all along.

Musicians understand that music is the art of combining sounds and tones in rhythmic, harmonic, and melodic forms to affect the emotions. Music is the art of putting all these techniques together. You compose in your head then write down the composition on a sheet, which becomes a birth certificate of what was in the head, the proof of what you heard in your head. The reason we don't have a lot of great composers today like Beethoven and Mozart is that some people don't understand how sound, tones, etcetera, all parts of one process work.

I mentioned before that Burnham killed Pan in Guyana. On the other hand, in my opinion, Dr. Eric Williams was one of the few people in the Caribbean who had the insight to see and understand the potential of Pan. He's a big part of the story of Pan. He really did understand this thing. I remember him visiting Guyana in the early '60s and was greeted by the national steel band of Guyana at the airport. I was there. He said to the band after they performed, "You guys should really try to continue playing. This is the Black people's piano." I remember those words. What Dr. Eric Williams did for Pan is what no panman could have done. He set the stage: the rules for sponsorship, assistance, and the development of Pan in different parts of Trinidad where there was no pan. He initiated the whole program for developing Pan as a national pastime, if you want to call it that. Burnham hated Steelband. He didn't like Steelpan and said it was a joke. And, when he got into power, he made good his intentions. That was the difference between those two political leaders and their vision. One built and the other destroyed.

What I'm saying is: there were things the panmen couldn't do, and that's what Dr. Eric Williams did for Steelband in Trinidad. People call names—Bertie Marshall, Neville Jules, Ellie Mannette—men who contributed directly to the development of the instrument. But without Dr. Eric Williams, Pan would have been just another little something in Trinidad, like it is in some countries today. It wouldn't have become anything big. He's responsible for giving Pan that national recognition, more than any other person. Some people may even say George Goddard did a lot. Everybody did his part, including some who were not panmen, like musicians as Anthony Prospect who arranged for bands. Panmen couldn't read music back in those days. Musicians came in and took charge of the music so that the bands could play classical music. But I'm talking about what on a large scale people did who had political power and were in jurisdiction that the panmen had no power or control over. Had these people made certain decisions, there would have been no Pan. They could have squashed the movement. But they didn't. This is why I say Dr. Williams is the main person responsible—I would even say the sole developer of Pan in Trinidad. He fostered a national interest in Pan by promoting a positive environment for it. Today, when you look at Guyana that had begun to rival Trinidad as the only place rivaling Trinidad in Steelpan with almost fifty bands, Guyana now has only two bands. So, the effects of what Burnham did were long-lasting.

What Williams did can be seen today as the mirror opposite of what Burnham did. One was positive and one was negative. People may say that Dr. Williams was not a panman, and those in political power were not panmen. But you didn't have to be a panman to help develop Pan. Without the assistance of these key people, Pan in Trinidad would not be what it is today. So, when you're calling names, you have to name all these people outside of Pan as responsible for doing a lot for Pan. Most of the panmen focused on Spree Simon who invented the tinpan and Ellie Mannette who invented the lead pan, and so on. They tend to think that because these people did these things, Pan is where it is today. For example, one tuner told me, "Ellie Mannette is responsible for the kind of pan we play today. He's the first man to make the full-size pan." That may be true. But if Ellie Mannette couldn't find a place that would accept what he did, it would be null and void, without meaning. It would have died like many other things that people have invented and done that we don't hear of today because nobody was interested; or it was specifically killed, like Pan was in Guyana.

There're so many people in Pan and outside Pan who contributed to its growth. You probably heard some names and not others. Let me provide my list. In Guyana, a guy by the name of Marsden "Patsy" Adams was one of the greatest pan-players in the world. He could be compared to Boogsie Sharpe, Robert Greenidge, or any name you call from Trinidad. He was a composer, like a Mozart. He was also a tuner and made his own drums. But today, when names are called, you don't hear his name. There's another pan-player by the name of Cedric Williams. He was a top tuner in Guyana, and during Trinidad Carnival time he went there to tune pans for Kentups, I think was the name of the band. You never hear anything about him either. His nickname was Pemia. I think he was also a tuner for the National Steel Band in Trinidad. These were guys who did a lot for Pan during their time. Many Williamses were associated with Pan: Anthony Williams who everybody knows, Leroy Williams, and Cedric Williams. So many people helped Pan through its rough times, from those who created it to those who kept it going. But the time has come for us to make it a universal instrument for the world. It's a gift that was given to the world. We just happened to be the conduit, the people through whom this gift was channeled. We may have created it: but who created us? That's the type of interest I have in Pan and its story.

I've got awards in Guyana, which I refused. For example, I was given a trophy once for the best arranger, and I didn't even show up because the people who were giving me these things don't know anything about what I did. They were just giving me this trophy so that they could look good. So I refused to accept it. I saw other people get medals; some of these people can't even tune a steelpan, arrange a single note in music, could hardly play. Yet, they got some medal or something for Steelpan. Other people who got medals for Pan made only one or two bands. They've stagnated Pan and are not doing anything that would allow Pan to grow or encouraging people to make drums for Pan. I came to the United States in 1984 and have made thirty-five steel bands since I've come. I've also made over three hundred single pans for individual people. I don't consider myself the greatest or the best or doing more than anybody else. I do what I'm capable of doing and will continue to do that to the best of my ability.

I know there are people who are saying, "Solomon? He's no good tuner. He's a mediocre tuner." All that sort of foolishness. It doesn't matter whether a guy is mediocre or the greatest. What he does with his skills is more important than the skill itself. If I made a pan for you and it's not such a great pan, and you became a great player, that's what people are looking for. People can always go to the king of pan-making and get the best pan, but then it all depends on if and how they can play. So, I'll provide you with a pan, regardless of what people consider its standard is, and it's up to you to become a great player. The pan is just the opportunity. We have people today playing violins. Now, a Stradivarius violin is approximately two hundred and fifty thousand dollars. Who can afford to buy a Stradivarius violin even though they love this violin? They start off on a Yamaha or a mediocre violin. What's wrong with that? Nothing. But when people start talking foolishness, then you have to realize what you're in this business for. I'm not in this business to be talking about who's better than whom, who's the first, who invented what. That's not what's important to me. I've done quite a few things to promote Pan.

For example, wherever I've lived and gone there was Pan. I went to the Bahamas some years ago and there was one steel band. When I left, there were three. I was there for about three months and in the space of that time I made two bands. I came to Pittsburgh and first lived in Oakland for three months. During that time, I established a steel band, a five-piece band. Then, I moved to the South Hills where I live now and here there are three steel bands: Keystone Oaks Middle School Steel Band, Keystone Oaks High School Steel Band, and my own group, Steel Impressions. So, wherever I go, you will hear steelpan. I'm not going to keep it in my house or to myself. I'm going to make sure the school in my district plays steelpan. Whatever I have to do, whatever it takes I'll do to accomplish that goal. If they say to me they can't pay me for the drums, I'll say fine; I'll still make them. I'll still try to get paid for them, but if I can't I'll still make them. That's what I've been doing for most of my life. I came to the United States with one intention: to help develop Pan in the United States. It doesn't matter to me who's making and who's tuning. I'm not interested in that.

Pan's Future

We definitely would need people in authority, like Eric Williams, people in power to have the vision of Pan's future, people who share the vision I have. The steelpan is the newest family of musical instruments to be invented. We have the violin family called strings: the first violin, second violin, viola, cello, and bass—all one family all made the same way, from small to big. We have the woodwinds, then the brass family. Now, all these family of instruments can play pieces all by themselves. The brass family is the most difficult, especially when it comes to the bass. It's very difficult to play bass lines on a tuba. Now, today we have steel. The family of steelband instruments is supposed to take its rightful place, like every other family in the orchestra to reflect the world we live in.

You see, the symphony orchestra is the largest entity of music assembled to reflect the world we're in. And, they try to include everything in it: the flute, the bassoon, everything. So, when you play a piece you can portray the world in that piece. Now, let's say today we had a great composer like Mozart and he was writing a piece and called it "Today's World." How could that piece not have a pan in it? It wouldn't be accurate. One hundred years later someone listens to that piece and notes that it was the year 2002, and there's no pan. That person doesn't have an accurate picture and wouldn't dream or even think that something like the steelpan was in existence then. We would never know that there was a violin if it wasn't included in the symphony orchestra. Because it was included and made a part of the ensemble, everyone knows about the violin and what it does. You can go off and play your solo violin, if you want, and only those who are there would hear and know about it. But things changed for the violin when it moved into the large ensemble of the orchestra and played worldwide. Then everyone knew, what has to happen with Pan. People playing the pan still are somewhat in isolation. But the pan is supposed to take its rightful place in the world of music, like every other family of instruments has done. And, we would need people in power, people with vision, and people with that basic understanding to assist the pan to make that transition.

My specific vision is that this will happen, maybe not in my time, I don't know. But it's going to happen. The steelpan, you must understand, is going to be the next big revolution in music in the future. There's no getting around that. Some people are already tired of the piano and violin. Pan will take that place and become the new music, new revolution, new combination—people will be combining pan with viola, pan with bassoon, pan and brass, pan and strings, pan and piano, and so on. That is what will be happening in the new ensemble. Everything is pointing in that direction, whether people like it or not. It doesn't matter. It is inevitable.

The pan doesn't need anything to play: no batteries, no electricity, nothing. That is an advantage, which is what has helped the violin family and other instruments that need only human energy. Pan has got a color and a tone of its own. It sounds like nothing else, and nothing else sounds like pan. Another advantage. If you invent a new instrument that sounds like a piano or something we already have, it wouldn't make it. That's what is happening to the keyboard. It sounds like everything else and doesn't have a sound of its own and wouldn't go forward. Pan has everything that the violin or the woodwind or brass has. So, there's no way the pan will not get to that level. The only question is how long it will take.

In the United States, there are now three pan companies: two are doing synchronized pans and one isn't. In Trinidad, there's very little synchronizing. With the lead pan everyone is doing the fourth and fifth style, so you can call that synchronized. Some bands have synchronized bass pans. I haven't been to Trinidad in over ten years, so I don't know exactly what they're doing and how they're developing, whether they're moving toward synchronization. As far as I know, based on the pans that come through here for me to re-tune, I have two pans here made by Gupee Brown about three months ago, brand-new; they weren't synchronized. Most likely, they're all still making pans after the first generation style. One of the problems they have in Trinidad is the difficulty in changing, because so many players have been playing the first generation style of pans for so long. Now I come and give them something new, they aren't going to accept it. Change will have to come gradually.

Today's Women in Pan

I'm encouraging my daughters to learn to tune. If one of them learns to tune, she will probably become the first successful woman pan-tuner. Right now, they're very involved in the business. Janera, my oldest, is responsible for the outreach program. She establishes programs in the schools, which I used to do. She took that over once she graduated from the University of Pittsburgh. She drafts the proposal, contacts the person in charge to arrange a visit both to the school and for the school to come here—she arranges all that. Jonnet is the business manager and accountant. Fauna is responsible for marking the drums, making the mallets, and has her own machine to polish the pipes for the stands. Leigh plays and is actively involved with the band. She can play any instrument. She is more of a pan-player, a pannist. My wife does all the advertising and promotion. She prepares the brochures. But my daughters keep the business going. They can do everything, except tune a pan.

I taught them to do everything, not only in the business but in life. I don't separate tasks according to gender, and all that nonsense. So, I taught my daughters to do their own car repairs, wire electricity, and fix plumbing. They know how to change oil and flat tires. They can do more than just change a light bulb or a leaking faucet. Yes, I have taught them how to stand on their own two feet because you never know what will happen in life. And if I had boys, I would have taught them how to cook a good meal, too. None of that running to Burger King and McDonald stuff. I would want them to know how to make that hamburger themselves. So, my daughters can cook and do anything a man can do around the house. They are well-rounded human beings.

I'm thankful for my life and for their full support. They've always supported me in everything I did. At times, things were hard—getting the business started after leaving Guyana then Brooklyn and then settling here in Pittsburgh. But I have little to no regrets about anything.

Pan as a Bridge between Cultures

What I've also discovered recently—I get this music magazine every month—is that the entire music industry is being driven by CEOs and companies that push an instrument. The industry is not being driven by the love of music, like it was before. They force this upon the schools and made them buy these instruments, make them have a marching band, all for their own profit. Fifty-two percent of musical instruments is now being imported, while forty-eight percent is made in the United States. So, it's now strictly a money thing with most of the instruments coming from Japan. Every drum-set is now made in Japan and Taiwan and none made here in the United States, including the American brands. I think they're actually killing themselves, which makes a wide opening for Pan. Pan can walk in and fill the gap.

The one thing I'm working hard to see happen is Pan filling the gap between the symphony orchestra and young people. Throughout the years as the older generation dies out and the young people become matured, the audience for the symphony orchestra is becoming nonexistent. So, the gap between the two generations is very wide. If you asked a kid on the street who was Beethoven, he would say it was a dog or a movie. This young generation not only doesn't know much of anything, they also are not interested in hearing any classical music or symphony orchestra. But the steelpan is the perfect tool to bridge the gap. You play Classical, Calypso, Reggae, Jazz, R&B—everything. So, right now in the schools that have steelband programs, those kids can tell you who is Beethoven and Mozart, and they can also tell you who is Boogsie Sharp and the Mighty Sparrow. The regular kids cannot tell you that. Even those who take piano lessons and talk about Chopin or violin lessons and know about Paganini, they don't know who is Sparrow or Kitchener or Boogsie. They have absolutely no idea who those people are, or about Desperadoes. The pan then is a wonderful tool in closing that gap because you are capable of performing all types of music.

What I'm saying is that Pan is standing in the cultural gap with one hand stretching back into the past with knowledge of the classics and the other forward toward the future and knowledge of the contemporary and where music is going. Bands play Boogsie Sharp at Panorama then play Mozart at the Festival. These kids are familiar with a musician from way back as well as one alive today and their related instruments. The people in the marching band don't have that exposure. They play Sousa, and that's it. I'm hoping that more people understand this and look to include the steelpan in their music curriculum. That's what I'm working on right now, trying to encourage and move Pan in this direction.

My argument is that Europe and White America ought to have a more vested interest in Pan. Pan will retain the knowledge of all music. It will eventually keep all music alive. Because I'm in this I can see this developing trend. The symphony orchestras will not be able to financially keep playing. Three symphonies have closed down in the last three years. Baldwin piano company has closed. They just sent me some stuff trying to sell some equipment. But they don't have anything that I need. That is what's happening and I don't think people understand this new wave. The piano store out here where I live has a big liquidation sale sign up. They're going out of business. All this in spite of all the efforts made—for instance, as in the movie *The Piano*—to revive the interest of this. Who wants to be playing something that needs a special truck to haul around? You want something you can pack into a case and take out yourself. The violin is not as much trouble as the piano but it's not very versatile. That's how the pan without too much effort is taking over.

I have so many kids whose parents are buying for them a lead pan and they play in bands or in their own gigs or in concerts and performances. They're going all over the place. They just tote their pan in a case and when they arrive, set it up on its stand, play, then pull it down and put it away in the case, and leave. No hassle. That's what modern living is about.

I don't understand why it's taking so long. I have different assumptions and related conclusions, and I think one is where the instrument came from and who invented it. It fits all the modern criteria of convenience and mobility, and it plays enjoyable music. But more so, I think that the pan is supposed to be integrated into the community of musical instruments, which is the symphony orchestra. If that is done today or tomorrow, it will breed new life into the symphony and sustain it. From the time the symphony was formed, the different family of instruments was incorporated into it—the woodwinds, the brass, the strings, and so on. The original symphony didn't include the percussions, but when they were added to it they brought a new life into the symphony for a period of time because they brought a new sound, a new life to the old music. The timpani, as well as other drums and percussions, made the music appealing to a new set of people because even the old symphonies sounded fresh.

Imagine now putting an eight-or ten-piece steelpan section into the symphony and playing one of Beethoven's symphonies. That steel sound in harmony with the strings and brass and woodwinds would definitely be a new thing, a new sound, with a new appeal. The orchestra would breed new life and bring an entire new generation with their interests and accomplishments into it. People will return to the symphony orchestras to hear what they sound like with the pan. But they don't have this vision so they don't think this is the answer. If they studied and understood history, they would see that a dull moment or a lull signaled the time for something new to bring new life into that moment. And, we have the instrument to do that, but it's not being utilized.

Sadly, some people would prefer that the symphony died than to include the pan in it. They say it's degrading, and all that nonsense. One guy has told me that the steelpan is not a musical instrument. I responded, "That comes from the perspective that black men are still boys." He just walked away; he had nothing more to say to me. I have an answer any time stuff like that comes up. People need to understand that I feel the same way about the pan they do about their instrument. No different. I represent and stand for it just as they do theirs. It's a shame the world has to suffer a musical travesty because some people feel that the pan must be kept in its place. But not for long. They're just delaying the inevitable. I'm confident that the world will not be denied the beauty of what this thing is. And, as long as we keep doing what we're doing, perfecting the instrument, everyone will see that this is exactly what they did. Like them, we're constantly working to improve the pan and its production and getting it into the marketplace. Once we keep working at our art and trade, then it will happen.

16
Breaking Class and Genre Barriers: Othello Molineaux's Story[1]

Othello Molineaux's *Accomplishments*

Publication

Beginning Steel Drum (Belwin-Mills Publishing Corp., 1995)

Honors

Black Music Month's Vanguard, 1991; cited in the Japanese Jazz Encyclopaedia; nominee for the best band in the Jazz-Rock category in the Carbonell 1979 and 1981 Music Awards; tenth place, International Music Poll, Miscellaneous Instrument Category; Commendation from the Ohio House of Representative, 1987.

Musicians Played With

Jaco Pastorius, Herbie Hancock, Hubert Laws, Dizzy Gillespie, Pete Minger, Toots Thielmans, Monty Alexander, Art Blakey, Ira Sullivan, Peter Erskins, Ahmad Jamal, McCoy Tyner, Randy Brecker, Bob Moses, Joe Zawinul, Bob Mintzer, Jack Dejohnette, Howard Johnson, Peter Gordon, JJ Johnson.

International Festivals

Jazz Festivals from 1979 to 1994: Fort Lauderdale, Palm Beach and Sarasota, Florida; Detroit, Michigan; Los Angeles, San Francisco and Hollywood, California; New York, New York; Athens, Greece; Berlin, Germany; Vienna, Austria; The Hague, Holland; Toronto and Montreal, Canada; Milan and Rome, Italy;

Luzana and Montreaux, Switzerland; Stockholm, Sweden; Pori, Finland; Copenhagen, Denmark; Antigua, West Indies; St. Croix, U.S. Virgin Islands; Trinidad and Tobago, and Jamaica, West Indies.

Television Appearances

Channel 6, Trinidad and Tobago; Japanese National TV; CBS This Morning; The Mike Douglas Show; the Cable Satellite Network. Also performed on the soundtrack for "World of Difference" TV show, Miami, Florida.

Discography

It's about Time but Eventually Happy Talk (1993)
Jaco: Word of Mouth; Twins I, Twins II, *with Jaco Pastorius*
Chicago X, *with Chicago*
Ecstasy, *with Michael Urbaniak*
Marilla; Ivory & Steel; Ivory & Steel Jamboree; Caribbean Circle, *with Monty Alexander*

Concert Hall Performances

Radio City Music Hall; Avery Fisher Hall, Greek Amphitheatre, Left Bank Jazz, Royal Oak Theatre, The Savoy, Dorothy Chandler Pavillion, Ontario Place, and others.

Clubs

Blues Alley; Village Vanguard; The Blue Note; The Bottom Line; Keystone Corner, Jazz Showcase, Fat Tuesdays, The Bijou Club, and others.

The "Gaza Strip": Initiation into Steelband

I was born in Longdenville, the youngest of four children, to the headmaster and headmistress of Longdenville Government School. My parents then moved around and worked at Cunupia, New Grant, Arouca, and San Juan government schools before my father retired and the family moved to St. James in 1950 when I was ten years old. My parents were also musicians: my mom was a piano teacher, and my dad played the violin. I grew up with the sound of these instruments in the home and, in fact, received piano lessons from my mother from an early age. So, prior to moving to St. James I didn't have much exposure to Steelband.

When we moved to St. James, I was already attending QRC and then later attended Fatima College. I don't remember if, when we moved, Tripoli was already there, or if shortly after we came they moved in next door. Anyway, we ended up living next door to Tripoli Steel Band. At that young age, I often looked over the wall and observed the men tune and play the pans. After observing the tuning process, I decided to try my own experiment. Not having access to steel drums, I got eight Kiwi shoe polish tins and burned them and then tuned them into a major scale. This done, I climbed up on the wall and laid out my "drums," proudly presenting my invention. That's how, at ten years of age, I formally introduced myself to the guys. They were pretty impressed.

There was also a fledgling Tripoli band, if you will, that practiced in the Tripoli yard. They were teenagers, closer to my age. I was not in the band but went over and hung out and played on the pans. They realized my aptitude and provided me the opportunity for my first public appearance and first embarrassment. Totally. The band had practiced for the Music Festival and the same afternoon of the competition asked me to learn the bass part because their bass player was unable to make it. I accepted the challenge and learned the two tunes between four o'clock and six o'clock. The competition was at eight o'clock that night. Very excited, after the rehearsal I went home and informed my parents then got dressed and went up to Roxy Theatre. The band took the stage. Lights. Camera. Action. The tune was counted off. I couldn't play. I was confused because something was terribly wrong. The whole performance was a disaster as I struggled to play. Afterward, I discovered that my bass pans were set up incorrectly. What an initiation!

About a year later, I really began experimenting with tuning but doing this with my contemporaries. We were all going to college, hanging together and moving in the same circle of friends. We formed a little stage-side band[2] and I continued to experiment with making pans for the band. When we started to play, because I was one of the better players the word began to get around and the people in St. James came to know about my abilities.

A couple of years later, there was a riot between Invaders and Renegades, and because of Invaders' involvement all the West was drawn into it. At the same time, the Tripoli band was playing at one of the clubs on the Wrightson Road "Gaza Strip." It was called the Gaza Strip because of the many altercations that took place there. Invaders really would have preferred not to fight, as the men were tired from previous hard-fought battles against Tokyo and Casablanca. So, their half-hearted desire to fight resulted in Renegades goading them into battle. Some other older Invaders and Western heavyweights joined to affect some damage control. One of the first things they did was to order Tripoli not to return to their gig. Since they were not coming under any fire from Renegades then, they thought that Tripoli men were acting as informants for Renegades. I guess the Invaders heavyweights were looking for scapegoats and targeted Tripoli who obeyed and didn't return to their gig.

Cecil Borde, the youngest boy of the Borde family and a member of Tripoli, also hung out with us because we were younger and had all the girls. He informed us about the gig being open and we jumped at the opportunity. Cecil, Tommy Crichlow, and I were excited. We considered ourselves to be professional musicians who played from 7:00 PM to 5:00 AM and enjoyed wine, women, and song. But we were kids, still in short pants! Now, we had the chance to play on the Strip!

That gig brought us into the company of a few greats, the cream of the crop like Kelvin Hart, Emmanuel "Corbeau Jack" Riley, George Bruce, Arthur Kennedy, and Gerald Forsythe. I was much younger than those guys, but being a piano player my harmonic concept was more defined than those guys, who were just incredibly talented. Gerald was also a piano player and as musicians he and I related to each other in a special way. We became inseparable. Later, when he was hired as Invaders' arranger we went in together. That's how, even though I had my own band with my college friends, Invaders was the first major band I became involved with. My involvement with Tripoli the year before was quite marginal.

Wonder Harps

My band was named Wonder Harps, but at the time we hadn't named it yet. We just had some pans at the house. I was with Invaders for almost two years, which was really an incredible experience for me. Invaders was like a family. I had heard about the violence of the culture from my bigger brothers—those times were rough and St. James had about nine bands, all *bad-john* bands, so to speak—but my getting close to all the major players and the riots is something I cannot forget. I wasn't involved in the riots, per se, but was a player and hung around with the fighters like Ellie, Ozzie, and Peacock. I was exempt from the fighting because even the Renegades guys came to know me as a good player. Goldteeth, Renegades' leader, poked fun at me and said things like, "Yuh mother know you out here?" "You kiss yuh pillow goodbye?"

After the '57 Carnival, I saw it necessary to form my own band. I did that in '58, and for two years my band came out of St. James, which was when the band was named Wonder Harps. I was the band's complete package: tuner, player, arranger, and promoter. One of the reasons I think the band was allowed to happen was our parents didn't really think it was possible. They thought we were just fooling ourselves because the idea was so far fetched. Though they didn't really believe that it could be done, they didn't stop our efforts. I think my parents were aware of my ability and also my leadership instincts and skills. So, the prevailing mother's attitude, "Doh follow dem boys!" was not applicable in my case because the boys were following *me*. Parents' simple rationale for letting their kids play was that since there were so many high profile kids involved then it was all right. I was the son of retired headmaster, Mr. Joseph Molineaux. There were Winston Maynard, son of Mrs. Olga Maynard, the headmistress of Tranquility Girls' Government School; Lenny Roberts, son of Inspector Roberts of St. James Police Station; Terry Saunders, son of Inspector Saunders of Glencoe; and, Len, Patsy and Ann Barnes, kids of Superintendent Barnes. That's just a few of us. The actual steel band was about thirty to thirty-five, which was big in those days and an acceptable size.

One J'ouvert morning—we played in a fête west of St. James in Cocorite at the Aquatic Club, one of the major venues for Carnival fêtes at that time—we were returning home then to head into town. We had some really little people, a few ten-year-olds and the majority of the rest were teenagers, which was unheard of at this stage. When we reached my street, the home of the band, all the parents were there waiting for us, demanding, "Where do you think you are going?" We said we were going into town where all the bands were. I think that was when they realized what they had allowed in granting us permission to go that far up to that point. I don't think they believed it was humanly possible for us to go into town. But bands weren't considered real bands until they went into town and were accepted, so going into town was the rite of passage. It was truly remarkable that the concern they showed for our safety in venturing into town was eclipsed by the pride we saw in their faces. And into town we went!

One of my main reasons for bringing out the band was to address the prejudice that existed in movement, the adverse feelings that society had toward pan-players and the whole Pan culture. That was the governing thought behind my effort. I'm actually surprised today when people tell me that in the '70s and even the '90s their parents were objecting to their involvement in this. I guess after '58 I stopped thinking in those terms because I thought I had broken the class barrier. Boy, am I wrong that change occurred then! But I think I started a beautiful metamorphosis.

I was motivated in the first place because being in Pan was not supposed to be proper. My contemporaries went along maybe because they wanted to know how to function or socialize with people on the street. But I was comfortable with this socializing. I wanted to bridge the two worlds because I saw the magnificence of the instrument itself and was completely encompassed by that. I didn't see any reason for young people to be barred from exploring the possibilities of the instrument. So, I was successful in the beginning to break down the barriers by getting the middle-class kids to participate in the Steelband movement. We did that for two years and then I lost interest because that was really the issue for me.

The next year most of the guys in my band went with some other friends of ours and started a band in the yard of the superintendent of police, Superintendent Barnes, the highest Black officer in Trinidad. My best friend Len, Barnes's son, was their leader. "A steel band in Barnes's yard," I thought, and saw the band being there as a major accomplishment. I had accomplished what I set out to do.

The following year, the whole Tripoli band walked out on their leader, Hugh Borde, and there was no Tripoli band. They went off and formed their own band, which happened a lot back in those days. So, after having stayed out for one year, I regrouped Wonder Harps in '61 and joined with Hugh Borde to play in Tripoli to help the name Tripoli stay alive and on the road. We also had quite a few girls playing on the road. And, although it may not have been a first in Trinidad, it was certainly a first in St. James. So, we came out as Tripoli that year to help Hugh Borde survive his crisis. I suppose that was another one of my causes.

After that, I arranged for a couple of bands. Then, I played for the Carnival with Silver Stars for a couple of years because I really respected and enjoyed what Junior Pouchet was doing as an arranger. I adored Ray Holman, but Silver Stars was nearer my home. I also arranged for Starlift of Tobago. Then, I went up to Laventille and arranged for [Love] Serenaders, a feeder band to Desperadoes, for a couple of years. I later did East Side Symphony in San Juan. Both bands competed in Panorama after it started in '63. All this time, I continued to work with my music band.

I left Trinidad in '67 and went to St. Thomas as a piano player contracted to the V. I. Hilton Hotel. I arranged for a steel band there that needed an arranger and met a couple of Trinidadians. This was the first time I was out of the country and saw Trinidadians functioning as pan-players. The fact was: they were not being very professional about their work or did not know what they were doing. Most Trinidadians who left home at that time would have been spoon-fed bandplayers from some band. So, because of national pride I got involved again. I was very embarrassed because they were not representing themselves and the instrument well, not with the sort of dignity that I felt Trinidadians should be demonstrating.

People from the birthplace of this wonderful instrument could be more professional in their approach to the instrument and how they conducted themselves. I still didn't know at that point that I would be dedicating my life to the development and acceptance of the instrument and to preserving its ethnic significance. I thought then I would just show them how to do things and continue with my piano-playing. Then, there was a radical shift in my priorities and I became really involved, and here I am today. I eventually stopped playing the piano to immerse myself completely into the instrument and to bring an intellectual approach to it. It was such a unique instrument. I realized that as a conventional player in order to be a spontaneous player, I had to really immerse myself in the instrument. So, that was the big sacrifice I made when I stopped playing the piano.

I had to unthink, meaning not think conventionally as required when playing a conventional instrument, because this was so different. I saw it was necessary to have the intellectuals take a look at it, as opposed to tourists. Up to this point, only tourists were looking at it and saying, "Wow! This is such a lovely sound!" A sort of romanticism was attached to it. The fact was: here was an instrument with the musical staff but with no logical coherence. There was no finger interplay, which is so important for the production of different musical sounds. This instrument was played with both hands equally for striking the desired notes. I recognized a very strong physiological significance, similar to how the brain coordinates two functions, as when we begin to learn to walk and talk—when walking you take steps and maintain balance.

When playing a conventional instrument, the brain coordinates two functions. In the wind instruments, there are two functions, the breathing and the note positions. In string instruments, the fret positions are of one hand and the sounding action of the other. With the steel drum, the two functions that are incorporated into a fluency that comes from practicing and becoming familiar with one's instrument are not there. So, although some degree of freedom seems to be lost with the absence of finger interplay, to be as spontaneous as a conventional player you have to make your own rules, and being a radical—I couldn't be happier—I relished the freedom. This was the most intriguing characteristic of the instrument. It gave the player the freedom that allowed other freedoms to exist.

It was in St. Thomas that I was able to start the real drive to have a steel drum program in the schools. St. Thomas has had a program in the schools since 1973.

From St. Thomas, I moved to Miami and hooked up with the University of Miami's (UM) School of Music and did workshops and forums there. I found this was necessary because back then the guys who would have come out here were not guys who would have represented the instrument properly or even relate to music on that level. Students of music would have tolerated it because it was a new instrument and would have wanted to see what this guy had to offer and to try to understand what the operational features of the instrument were. But there would have been no rapport worthy of that acceptance given to one musician from another musician. So, I worked very closely with UM to accomplish a credible rapport and build a network while working with my professional band of all UM's students.

I met and played with great musicians and it is documented that "Ivory and Steel," which was recorded with Monty Alexander in '79, was the first successful commercial Jazz record using a steel drum. I had already recorded with Jaco Pastorius in '76. He is said to be the greatest bass player of the twentieth century. He revolutionized the bass and was bigger than life. Sadly, he died too soon. He is spoken of with the same reverence as the great musicians of previous centuries. His influence could be identified in almost everything we hear today. To have the pan connected to him and his work is of profound historic significance. I also played off and on with Ahmad Jamal for about eighteen years. He is known as the "piano player's piano player." He is also one of the great players of the twentieth century. I do believe that to be friends with, and to have played and recorded with, these two musical geniuses was not coincidental but part of a divine plan, and an association that the pan—this incredible innovation—deserved.

I've seen the whole Steelpan phenomenon just escalate. It's incredible to have witnessed this. I don't think Trinidadians realize that the reason they are as proud of the instrument as they are today is born out of the struggle to get it where it is. A part of that struggle was to have recorded in this medium. I have seen it blossom more and more and also how Trinidadians developed that sense of pride in and for the instrument. It's really incredible to see where it has reached, how far it has come from.

Travels Abroad and Major Contentions

Jamaica is a wonderful place. Jamaicans and I share a mutual respect; they are very respectful of the instrument and our culture. Quite a few Jazz festivals are there. I have an open invitation to the Ocho Rios Jazz Festival and go there whenever I can. I've also been to the Jazz and Heritage Festival in Montego Bay a few times. I've traveled extensively for over thirty years and have done most of the major Jazz festivals in Europe, Japan, and the United States, as well as many of the smaller festivals in France, Germany, and Switzerland. I've taken the pan all over the world. I've been to the Middle East and South America, and even to festivals in Iceland!

My response to the controversy revolving around Japan's technology that threatens to displace Trinidad in the development of Pan is also controversial. I think we Trinidadians are very paranoid because of insecurity. We should have assumed a leadership role in the evolving Pan-world a long time ago. We have the scientists and we certainly have the money. I think we underestimated what it takes to be on top of this potentially lucrative million-dollar industry.

It takes vision, assertiveness, an innate love for the instrument, cultural literacy, and most imperatively, government subsidy. Naming pan as the national instrument is certainly not enough. We could have started years ago an international pan-tuners guild that would have focused on the technology, education, quality of instruments, and networking, which all collaborated and coordinated would have created a trillion-dollar industry. These countries with which we are now concerned are making progress because they love and respect us for the gift we have given the world. I only wish we could love and respect ourselves as much. Then, we would not be whining and complaining as we do.

With all due respect to Pan Trinbago, I know they are doing the best they can. But the movement has become bigger than who Trinidadians are, and the organization should be made up of lawyers, physicists, economists, accountants, engineers, and most definitely trade unionists. I think this will give it some credibility that speaks to integrity. We have nations with billion-dollar industries to deal with. Other countries are just taking the instrument to another level by doing things that we are not doing for ourselves. The first commercial outlet where we could buy accessories for the steel band is in America and owned by non-Trinidadians.[3] We tend to follow what is happening out here and that gives us that sense of insecurity, and why we grumble about who is doing what and taking what from us. The saying, "Locking the stable door after the horse has escaped," seems to be applicable here. But I'm very optimistic.

Some of our historians all say that the pan was born when the Americans left their oil drums there. I think that historical inaccuracy diminishes the pan's ethnic significance. Pan is the spirit of Trinidad! It is the heartbeat of the nation! We were getting different tones from bamboo and other pieces of percussion long before the Americans came and left. And, with the Tony Williamses, Ellie Mannettes, Rudy Wellses, Dawn Batsons, Earl Rodneys, and Robbie Greenidges of the world, I think a light is at the end of the tunnel for Pan's future. We eh have to *fraid* nobody!

This fear, I think, is what led to our overblowing the issue regarding the couple of guys who patented a process, which sent Trinidad into an uproar about the whole thing.[4] The idea is not to complain but show the world what we can do. Have all our processes in place and when people come, whether we officially invite them or they come to visit on their own accord, they can see what we have done. We have the opportunity to make new marks in history.

Our history is different from the African Americans'. We had a little more freedom to use the drum to communicate, to send our messages back and forth. And, we didn't have to be afraid that a house-slave would betray us. That was where our level of trust originated first from, that level of respect for what we were doing. That cat knew that nobody, *nobody* would give away the plan to escape or rise up against the master. That level of trust began to break down after Emancipation. When you think about that level of trust, it's a fascinating thing. To move from that level to the insecurity that now exists is something we should really study. We're so insecure that we're seeing theft where theft is not occurring.

To address the patent brouhaha. People need to understand what the patenting process is about. If you don't patent a process you started, you stand to lose it. If you do, you cannot bring the argument to the table that you started the process but didn't go through with it. That's the reason things are patented in the first place, to avoid these things from happening. All the two Americans did was patent a process that was not the same but was under the same school of thought. But this whole paranoia is what Trinidadians are all about. The collective energy of Trinidad is like that—very, very paranoid. They want to ban people from coming. They used to not let them into their yard. Now, it's some of these banned people who are helping spread and advertise our culture and the instrument. That's all people are doing.

I remember about Antigua. You know that in the music world you're known by your recording and as a newcomer you become known by your first recording. Antigua recorded before we did. [*Note*: Kim Johnson has written that Casablanca made a recording in 1947 and TASPO in 1951. See his article, "With Music in His Blood," *Trinidad Guardian*, April 21, 2003, that suggests that Casablanca may have been the first recorded steel band.] So, there is the possibility that they could have started Steelband first, and that is beside the point I want to make here. I remember when their band came to Trinidad how our insecurity surfaced. Antiguans came to Trinidad to Cook Recording Company. When they came, we laughed at them; this is how Trinidadians are. We talked about and made fun of their pans because the tops of the pans were painted. We used to call them small-islanders, because we were a big island and felt superior because of the difference in island-size. So trivial. This is why I don't think it inconceivable that since Antigua recorded before us they had Steelband before us.

Who knows where it really started? Even in Trinidad we don't know whether it started in Gonzales, John John, or the south. Now, we have all this talk about giving this and that person due credit. You have to realize all this has happened, this clamor for due credit, because of where the pan has reached. Ellie Mannette in 1967 had almost given up when he fled from Trinidad. He didn't even go back for his mother's funeral. But it's because of where the pan has reached that Ellie Mannette has been elevated to where he is. It's just like TASPO. Because of where the pan came from, nobody really documented or was proud of those achievements, and now in retrospect they're documenting TASPO.

I saw in 1998 when "Patsy" Haynes died in New York City it was not a big deal. Four years later, "Boots" Davidson died and there was a brouhaha because in four years Pan grew so much.

I know Tony Williams. Every time I go back home, I go to see him. I was in Trinidad last year for the Wee-Bee thing, and they were arguing about where Pan started and talking about Tony Williams as the greatest and all that sort of thing. I had just come from visiting Tony Williams's house earlier that day. Both he and his wife are very ill, and those cats were talking about him but were not even trying to help him.

Tony Williams, in 1979, already had health problems while in the Princes Building where he was keeping all his tuning equipment and other stuff. He had stopped beating [pan]. Then, that building burned down with all his instruments. He has never tuned since. They ain't tried to help him. Now, we're hearing about how great he is and he never got his due. I've seen it happen.

I remember the days when I was alone in the 1970s and performing at the Village Vanguard without support of my fellow Trinidadians living here in the States. One panman actually gave up his pan to go looking for his roots in this little African drum he was beating in his basement. The craze at the time was Osibisa.[5] Recently, in the 1990s he wanted a steel drum. More than twenty-five years ago he didn't have time for it. He's returning to his roots because of what is now happening, because of where Pan has reached. It's because of the efforts of the people who have brought it to this level you now hear talk about Andrew de la Bastide this and that, when this thing little mattered before.

Trinidad society never had that sense of cultural heritage. If we had that from the beginning, it would've been cool. They're now trying to scramble and do this and have these associations because of the grind that people like me have made. So, to say that they persevered: persevered what? What I'm trying to tell you is that nobody persevered. They went along with it, as I told you when we spoke informally.[6] How could they be persevering when they started to *mash up* pans years later, and before they never used to do that? The respect for the instrument and the art form waned and kept waning. In the beginning of the rioting days, they never *mashed up* drums. Twenty years later, they started disrespecting the drums that much that they started destroying them! So, there was a period when nobody was fighting for the art form. The disrespect began before people started to really do stuff out here [in the United States]. It's when word trickled down about what was happening in America that Trinidadians sort of picked up on it and started to have pride in where Pan came from.

If you look at the state of Trinidad today, it's the same thing that's happening. The young people don't respect the older guys. Today in Trinidad, they cannot. They don't know how to. So that same thing you're speaking of, the fact that people persevered and none of them got their due—well, you have the Tokyo people right there in Trinidad who aren't getting their due, still. They're in another steel band. They were put out of Tokyo by the young people who never learned about and grew to respect tradition and heritage. There was a generation or two of people who never grew to respect what this really was. They just don't care that Tokyo is sacred to the tradition, one of the places the whole thing was supposed to have started. The Invaders' experience is also one to be respected, taken sacred even, and they don't see it that way. These young people don't have a clue to any of this.

I've seen in Japan how the young people have a reverence and respect for their older people. If a young Japanese saw an old bent woman, he would know that she spent years in the rice fields and it was those years that bent her back. He wouldn't laugh at her, and nobody has to tell him this. He would be willing to carry her load for her because he knew what she has done. This is what our young people today lack. They can't look at what we have and treat it with respect.

This disrespect stems from cultural illiteracy. We have to be taught to value what is important to us. There was a time the men just fought and hurt each other but didn't touch the pans. The panmen protected the pan and that sort of destructive behavior was unheard of. We saw a deterioration of respect for the instrument by some younger men who didn't care about people's labor. And that spirit is still there.

I've seen the transition. We've gone from men who at the Royal Albert Hall and didn't know how to behave in that world of classical music to some improvement. Once, one man hit a conductor. Another time, North Stars went to Carnegie Hall with Winnifred Atwell and were treated so well with limousines and hotel that they thought the treatment incommensurate to the money they were getting. They grumbled, "How wid all dis nice hotel an' limousine, we only gettin' dis? She robbin' we." And, that was the end of that liaison, that Winnifred Atwell-North Stars thing. That performance was even recorded, and it's the most wonderful recording of Steelband you could hear. Later in Australia, she was so proud to have a steel band with her. All that ended because we were ill-prepared. We have a history of a lack of proper behavior. I think we are just culturally illiterate and behave accordingly.

Maybe, that is what's shaping the whole controversy around the name of the instrument. I've been out here commercially for about thirty-five years. I've established the instrument, got it written into the Japanese Jazz Encyclopaedia, and have been promoting the instrument, marketing it. I'm a steel drummer and I've marketed it as a steel drum for the last thirty-five years. It's in the Japanese Jazz Encyclopaedia as a steel drum. I see a reason to having that connection to the instrument as a drum, because although the thing originated in Trinidad, we have to have some connection with Africa. Apart from all those reasons, recently since they got all this pride in the instrument and carrying on and naming it the national instrument, they decided—apart from all that's happening, whether they're aware of all that has happened out here—to rename me a pannist. This is hurting them more than anything. This is bad marketing strategy because you don't change the name of a product in midstream. That is disrespecting the work that everybody has done to bring the instrument and the respect of the instrument to this level. It's confusing to people. And, they're very adamant about it. Somebody sent an article on me to Trinidad and gave it to a reporter. He changed the word. They just made up this name because they think they just have to have a nice name for it.

Pan is a vernacular word, our word, and it's great. We can use it, and do what we want with it. What really interests somebody about somebody else's culture is the thing they don't understand about the culture. Now, I have to explain to people all over the world what the difference is. The ironic thing about it is nobody, none of the players in Trinidad, is on the market here. Yet, they want to expound this thing now and say people are taking it from them. They want to be in control. As somebody said in the papers, they don't want anybody to name their thing. I'm a Trinidadian and I know what to name our thing. I call it steel drum because when I left Trinidad that is what it was. The fact is: it's gone too far; it's been marketed; it's been documented. If you try to do something else, you're just hurting yourself. So, we don't even have the foresight to know that is something that shouldn't be done. We are our biggest enemies and now looking for scapegoats to blame other people for what is happening.

Class Demarcations

Imagine, I lived four miles from John John. St. James is about four to five miles from John John and I didn't even know about Andrew Beddoe. We lived in separate worlds because of the class thing. People also need to know about City Kids, 'cause they were young guys, too, some from the Belmont area who came up around that time. What was their genesis? They were really kids, little guys, and they were good. We need to know about that! [See Albert Jones's narrative for his authoritative account on City Kids.]

People also need to know the true story of Invaders and Beryl McBurnie. I was in Invaders so I know this first-hand. Beryl McBurnie is being historically spoken of as somebody who was a friend of the steel band, a friend of Trinidad culture, or something like that. Beryl McBurnie brought Invaders into her Little Carib [Theatre] to play for her dancers: the Bonnie Morriseys and Annette Dollys—those nice-looking girls. From the outside, one would tend to believe that she was a friend of the instrument because it appeared she was helping Invaders. The truth is: we had to clean the toilets before we played, and she didn't want the panmen to speak to these girls. I don't think even Invaders realized the real reason she had Ellie Mannette tune pans for the Girl Pat Steel Band.

Ellie probably didn't know the reason for propping up Girl Pat. Girl Pat came out of Beryl McBurnie really not wanting Invaders to socialize with the girls. She didn't want any intermingling because Girl Pat was really Little Carib girls. I saw this. My music band used to rehearse in Hazel Henley's house later on, years after. Again, it was confirmed that Beryl McBurnie wanted to keep the panmen distant from the girls. She had Ellie tune pans for them to have their own band so she could sever ties with panmen. I don't think Ellie ever saw it that way. He got this job to tune for her, and he was happy to say, "Oh yeah, I tuned for the girls, and so on." So, with all due respect to all she did for our culture, the underlying cause for Invaders' involvement with Little Carib was another story.

This thing came from the ghetto and we were really repressed. I was just telling somebody the other day, "Look at it, eh. We were on the ground, and the upper class society people were on trucks, with their little masks covering their eyes while they played Mas on trucks. Now we're on the trucks and they're on the ground." We're on the trucks! They've taken the power away from us. That should not have happened. When I think of the power Wonder Harps had on the street, like Invaders going into town and having a whole community, the entire Woodbrook being responsible for the safety, our safety as we went into town then went back home, the whole thing was incredible. The music that was born out of that intense energy was incredible. Now, you look and see twenty guys squeezed up on a truck and playing, and somebody like Poison taking like five hours to cross the stage, and that is what has taken over Carnival. That is what it has come to! I have a big, big problem with where Trinidad's school of thought is.

I got involved because I saw my middle class was not really interested. Some of us may have wanted to rebel against our parents and hang with the bad guys. Others couldn't really because of the reputation the men had for carrying knives and not hesitating to use them. Some attending college may have wanted to hang with steelband guys but weren't allowed to. You had to be rough to be able to do that. But with the love I had for it, I had to explore all this. The Invaders thing for me was a real experience when I was sixteen and hanging with those rough guys.

What I really want to say about where the instrument is now is this. It's single individuals who have brought it to where it is and not people playing "Yellow Bird" and a couple of classical pieces to a captivated audience. Single individuals played and showed the intellectual side of the instrument, and that is a lot. A lot of people were playing the instrument here in the States long before Trinidadians were. People from St. Kitts and Antigua are some people whose efforts brought Trinidadians aboard to see that they have to take this thing seriously themselves.

The next thing is the level of respect. We know that Invaders didn't exist at the very beginning of the history of Pan but arrived shortly thereafter. Tokyo, evolving from an earlier John John band, had to be at the genesis of the movement. We have to respect these men from those days. We should have shrines built in those three yards: the early John John band, Tokyo, and Invaders. Equally to be respected are men like Neville Jules and Ellie Mannette, even though these two men will never agree on the facts. Forget that! Jules will never admit to what *the west* (see Introduction) has done and Ellie to what Jules has done. The fact that they will never agree shouldn't really matter. What matters is that they both made invaluable contributions to the instrument and ought to be respected for what they did.

Then, there's Oscar Pile. He's probably the oldest living guy in Trinidad in Pan. I think he's eighty-four years old and was around during the tamboo-bamboo days. Remember, the tamboo-bamboo thing predates the steel band. A story on Pan that doesn't include Oscar Pile is incomplete. He's to be honored, too, given his due credit. So many men who deserve so much and have received so little, if anything at all. If Trinidadians really knew and respected this on a daily basis, they would see a change in Trinidad. We have a lot of work to do....

17

New Wine in New Wineskins: The Last Social Experiment: Leroy Alí Williams's Story[1]

Leroy Alí Williams's *every innovative endeavor is toward making Pan as accommodating as possible worldwide. Hence, he is proud of his pursuit toward completing his dream of producing the single drum that can replace the double and triple drums of some sections. He hails his accomplishment as one that can move Pan one step closer toward standardization and is currently preparing to market his innovation. His spiritual vision for Pan's future is for its inclusiveness of all peoples.*

"He's One of Us"

I was born on Parshley Street, Sangre Grande, in 1946 and lived in several parts of Trinidad: Santa Cruz, San Juan, and John John. I think I have a pretty interesting beginning in Pan; I've had some heavy downfalls, too. But I love the whole involvement—working with individuals like Ellie and others who there're no words to describe their ability to teach and inspire. I think that has been my greatest experience in Pan.

I first began playing in '59 while living in Laventille on Desperadoes Hill. At that time, Desperadoes was a road band with a stage-side band,[2] also. I began experimenting with playing pan a little before that, when I was thirteen going on fourteen. One day, I found an old drum that belonged to an old band named Kentuckian. The drum was an antique, really old. I took that drum and decided to play the first half of a song that I liked. I can't recall its name right now, but I know that I just wanted to play pan itself. After learning the first half, I decided to learn the second half. I continued doing this until one day my mother, her name is Mary "Molly" Williams, looked at me and said, "All that music and drum is all right. But you know we're moving from here pretty soon." She had bought a house up on the Hill. She said, "You're going to leave that drum here."

My mother, who is everything in my life, had rented that house, the first house I lived in in the city. My mother moved into the city when I was four to five years old and left me with my godmother in Sangre Grande, while taking my sister and little brother with her. When I joined them about a year later, they were living in the house that was Spree Simon's father's house. I think "Spree" was born in that house. I came into the city and went straight to John John. My mother eventually had a very keen love and interest in the whole culture of Trinidad, especially Pan, and became fully supportive of everything and everyone in Steelband. She probably always was.

She also came to know Ellie Mannette. She used to work in a restaurant that he frequented and used to talk about the way he dressed and decked himself out as a *saga* boy, you know. When she called that name Ellie Mannette, it was with a reverence that was normally reserved for when she used the word Jesus. That touched me all through my coming up because she always talked about Ellie, Kitchener, and all these people of our culture with such reverence that it registered in me to some degree.

After moving into our new house, we realized that a band practiced in the yard of the house behind us and the men came through our yard to get to the road. It turned out that one of them was the leader and arranger of Desperadoes. This was before Rudolph Charles's time. This man was Donald Steadman, the music director. These men were all so nice my mother couldn't resist them. Steadman was a perfect gentleman. So, I started playing with the band. They gave me an unfinished drum, which I decided to try my hand at finishing it, tuning it. That was how my interest in tuning began and never stopped. Later on, I became the leader of that band, the tuner and everything.

That band was named Serenaders, which we renamed Love Serenaders. It was a great little band. In a way, we never had good management and that sort of thing. But whenever we reorganized and went to Carnival and Panorama, and whatnot, we made an impact. It's that band Desperadoes got its players from, because guys came into our band and played for one or two years then moved on to Desperadoes. So, Desperadoes began to regard our band as their nursery and called us so, their nursery. Growing up on the Hill as a panman was another great experience of my life.

After Rudolph Charles became leader of Desperadoes, we came to see that he was a very competitive individual. I mean, he's a warrior where Pan is concerned. I am also a warrior, and he and I began vying with each other for supremacy, I would say, for best pans and beaters. My band never quite made it up to Despers's standard because they had much more going. They had the government's support; Eric Williams used to visit and so on. Later, Rudolph and I came together while I was developing as a tuner. He, as a more outgoing person, had seen every tuner in the country. He brought back information he had garnered from these tuners to me and encouraged me to keep on working. Eventually, he said to me that I would definitely become the number one tuner in the world. Another time, he said that I would be better even than Ellie, which I never took seriously. I'm not in competition with Ellie. Ellie is the greatest teacher and inspirer of all time where Pan is concerned and also a very giving person.

You know, you walked into a lot of pan-tuners workplace and they stopped working. But Ellie didn't stop working. He began telling you what he was doing. That's just what he's been doing from the beginning and still is.

I met Ellie through Gerald Forsythe, one of his associates who was a tuner and a member of Invaders. He was tuning as well as Ellie and was a great musician as a piano-player, pan-player, arranger, and a great sportsman, too. In 1961, we got him to come up the Hill and arrange for Serenaders. In 1962, he took me one morning to meet Ellie. We walked into the yard and Ellie was working. I don't think Ellie even looked up or made eye contact with me when I first arrived. He was tuning some pans and I was admiring some others: the workmanship, the tone, everything. It was so beautiful. At that time in 1962, Ellie was the top tuner in the world, although I think Tony Williams was also doing great work, he wasn't as public as Ellie. We visited for a while. Forsythe and Ellie talked while I walked around the yard, which to me was the Mecca of Pan.

While walking around the yard with my hands behind my back, I had the feeling, "Hey, this is really your thing, man. You're the man, here. It's not Ellie." I was saying this to myself and I hadn't even made my first drum as yet, so I wasn't being rude. It was just this feeling that came over me that this was my thing and I would take it further than anyone, even Ellie.

When it was time to leave, Ellie finally looked up at me and said to Forsythe, "You better keep an eye on this man, you know. I think he's one of us." That was my first meeting with him and being officially endorsed into Pan. A couple of years later, he invited me to play with the band and work. He didn't hire me. He just wanted me around. I could do a little work or not; it didn't make a difference. I remained with him for two seasons and then he left Trinidad.

Before coming to the States, I went to the Virgin Islands in '68 and lived there until '70, then left during that year and returned to Trinidad. I stayed in Trinidad until '72 and then joined a cruise ship with Othello [Molineaux], a buddy of mine, and others. We were on that cruise ship for three months then it docked in Miami. Some of us went to Atlanta and stayed there for six months; then Ellie invited me to come to New York. This was in 1973. I went to Brooklyn and he was working on Delancy Street. I visited there every day for about six months. It was a community-center sort of environment where he had workshops. A band was on the premises. Later, I branched off on my own and went to New Jersey. But his teaching—his ability to share information that I didn't begin to understand until ten, twelve, fifteen years later—was truly phenomenal.

At War with Those Bent on Exclusion

One incident that puzzled me a few years back excluded Ellie. It had to do with talk in Europe among the foreign tuners about standardizing Pan, which is good in some ways but not in others. I went to a convention in Trinidad in 1988 and tried to talk about what I was doing. I'm still doing the same thing right now. There ought to be a record of the convention. I laid out what it would take, calling upon the government to supply the machinery for drum-making, finding the experts who would work to manufacture the best possible materials, and things like that. But none of the panmen echoed it. Not one of them supported me. I was so dismayed. People were just sitting there like, "I wonder when he's going to be finished." You know, no response whatsoever. Then, this body of foreign tuners presented their information on what they called the standardization of Pan.

The move to standardize was a good one but their motives were not. The people they excluded from the talk was an indication that their motives were commercial, which to me was indicative of why they hadn't invited Ellie to that conversation. That's a conversation that everyone should have been invited to, and it's a shame that some panmen were excluded. But then, we should have already standardized the instrument and not just talking about standardization at that time, which grieved me. Since living in America, I've traveled throughout the country and seen some of the Indians' [Native Americans] experiences. So many of them look totally subdued, totally sad, enough not to function. I sort of related that in a way with Pan, and how we've joined these Indians in mourning. It's really grievous, the threat of others taking over and controlling the future of Pan in terms of technology.

I lost a girlfriend who thought I shouldn't *bad-talk* Trinidad. But I'm not *bad-talking* Trinidad. The government didn't give any guidance to us pan-tuners, yet we've succeeded in inspiring the rest of the world, you know. Untrained as we were, we've brought Pan to being the greatest success story of all time coming out of the West Indies. It's not even like the West Indies Cricket Team, which is comprised of some of the greatest cricketers of the world coming out of the entire Caribbean region. Pan came out of Trinidad and blew everybody away to the point that the rest of the world wants this music. But the political leaders who should have known better never really gave any good direction. I look back now and realize that if anyone was looking for direction from them he was foolish, because those leaders needed direction, too.

I remember there was a big controversy in Trinidad once about some doctors and lawyers who had returned from abroad, and having picked up the game of golf wanted to play golf in Trinidad. Most of them were Blacks and Indians and lined up to get into this White golf club, and the people showed them they were not wanted. What I couldn't understand was: how in their own country, as a body of educated professionals, couldn't they have the insight to open their own golf club? Maybe they had the idea but lacked the wherewithal to pursue it. So, if they couldn't pursue their own interest, what could they offer us?

Still, if the leaders had taken a real interest in this thing that has taken the world by storm, Pan would have been standardized by now. We would already have had a factory making any kind of drum with any kind of material. We would already be exposed to a dozen varieties of compositions of metal, long before the rest of the world who is now experimenting with these ideas. True, traditionally America is the place where a whole lot of stuff has developed. I mean, many ideas were brought from Europe and finished here. American ingenuity is not to be messed with, their science and engineering, the blessings from God that Americans have received, along with the free and cheap labor of the Black man.

When I pause during the day to reflect upon the story of Pan, I see it as a microcosm of the story of the whole earth. It saddens me that at this time a bunch of foreigners is setting out to present to the entire world a standard set of pans. And, it is very sad they hadn't included Ellie Mannette in that forum. They hadn't invited Neville Jules, who is the father of all panmen, to be present. It's a lot of disrespect. That's why when a few days ago a tuner called me and asked me if I wanted to do some work from some American company that was sinking drums and giving them to tuners to tune I said, "No! I'm at war with these people!" I hope God gives me some more time to finish what I have to do in both my professional and personal lives. I don't want to die a sad panman, having come here with love and inspiration and goodwill, to be ripped off like everybody else has been ripped off. This is why I'm trying my best to complete my catalog to present my work. I plan to take Pan as far as I can.

My big problem with the foreigners who want to standardize the pan is that they give the impression that Trinidad doesn't matter any more, which is ridiculous. In a way, they're right because we ourselves should have had the respect and foresight enough to standardize the instrument.

I was away for six years and just returned home for a while and got to realize that every year they held a convention about standardization and then didn't standardize anything. It was all talk and money. They got the money to do it then merely went through the motions. In a way, Trinidad has done more damage to the Pan movement than anybody else.

The Instrument of Civilization and the Perfect Musical Instrument

The idea of the cycle of fifths in which the tenor pan is designed is one of the just perfect things that has ever been invented. There are twelve notes in music and every note is in the same environment as every other note. Now, music is numbers, so let's say you have the note "C," which is set between "F," which is a fourth of "C" and "F" is between "G," which is a fifth of "C." So, "C" is in a five-four environment and so is every other note in an unbroken circle. Even that idea can be taken beyond music because it is a symbol of balance: five-four-five, five spiritual and four materials. In musical terms, this is harmony, an unbroken circle of harmonic clusters, as I like to call them, that makes this instrument the unique one it is. No other instrument is arranged in a more perfect circle.

Apart from being the instrument of the twentieth century, I think it's the instrument of civilization. You can read so much into it. I can sense almost every day as I work on one of these pans something different every time. So much information is there, so many symbols. I'm not surprised it has come to what it is now. I am surprised because we used to think we loved Pan in Trinidad more than the whole world. That is the great surprise. The whole world loves Pan because of what it can come to mean everybody.

So far, what I've done is develop a standard setting for all the instruments. The tenor pan is made in the cycle of fourths and fifths. Using bigger containers I have made other sections also in the cycle of fourths and fifths. In this way, if one can play a lead pan he can also play the double second pan, because it is set in a similar cycle, and he can also play the double guitar. Both of these pans I have made into one drum, as I have the double tenor. It's like playing the higher scale of the piano and the lower scale. You play the same thing. I am trying now to build a stock of these pans, which I will advertise in my catalog. I'm also approaching more range on these pans, which I don't think any other tuner has done. Plus, I am scribing around every note.

I've been working on developing the single big pans for at least ten years. But I started scribing about twenty years ago. Scribing is putting two lines around each notes. I brought this technique to Pan, which Ellie complimented me for doing. When he saw one that I made, he called me, which was the last time we spoke on the phone. He said it was the best piece of work he'd ever seen. What he meant was the workmanship. The drum itself wasn't a great quality tone, even though it's still being used. I approached thirty-seven notes, and they were playable because of scribing the notes. This was on a soprano fourths and fifths. That's the pan I made for Jeff Narell, Andy Narell's brother. So, I've done this type of work, but the demands of living so often pulled me away from it, you know. I'm getting there, though, and hopefully by the end of the year I'll have that catalog ready and in circulation. By that time, I also hope to have taken the instrument to Trinidad to present in a show. Only a few tuners know what I've been doing, which I'm happy your work will make public. [*Note*: both the pans and catalog are now completed.]

The tenor basses can also be reduced to four drums and put into a cycle of fifths, too. The basses have already been in the fourths and fifths over the years. What really inspired me years ago was when I noticed that the leads are fourths and fifths, the high end, and in the low end the basses are fourths and fifths. I realized that we only had to fill in the middle sections. I eventually found a company in Ohio to make the bigger drums for me. I also just found a new company here in California. I plan to visit them to see what they can do for me. I still desire a little more than what I'm getting right now by way of material, and so on.

Inspirations

My inspiration to take the instrument as far as I can first began with doing battle with Rudolph Charles and then with those people from the west who came and helped us: Gerald Forsythe, Corbeau Jack, and Ellie. Musicians like Rob Greenidge, Clive Bradley, Beverley Griffith, and Othello Molineaux, first of all. They all inspired me. Later here in America, American bass-player named Jaco Pastorius became very inspirational to me. He had Othello and me play on one of his first recordings.

He became really fascinated with the steel drum and decided that in five years we would put together a band just like the one he used for his recording: three or four steel drums—we only used two for his recording along with an electric bass and other conventional instruments. He thought that would be a sample of instruments the world would want to see. He was the greatest bass-player of all time. He didn't even have to think about what he was doing because he did everything by inspiration. He invited me to move to Florida and the plan was to work with him for five years. He had a commitment for five recordings over five years for a company, and on the sixth year we would make what we called a *Holiday for Pan* album. We actually recorded it and were in the process of mixing when he died, and that was the end of that. What a loss!

In a way, we are still continuing that movement, Othello and I. Othello has been playing internationally. I consider him to be one of the greatest soprano (tenor pan) players of all times. He is on the international Jazz circuit. He also plays with Ahmed Jamal and Monty Alexander. People ought to know of him. He's the most senior Pan musician, as far as I'm concerned. When I listen to him play, I'm inspired to go further, to make pans at the level that he is playing.

In a way in relation to Jazz, he and I are responsible for what is happening in Pan today. I remember the first night when we were finished recording the first tune with Jaco Pastorius—Herbie Hancock was the pianist—Herbie went to the phone immediately and called Miles Davis and said, "Miles, there are three men here you should meet. There's a bass player with no shoes playing the bass like you never heard it." Now, to say to Miles Davis, the top Jazz-man of all time, that there was a man playing the bass like he Miles had never heard it was brave. He continued, "And Miles, there are also two steel drum players, and one of them who makes steel drums is playing, too, and the instruments are in tune. I think I should bring them for you to meet." Miles said, "Yes." But Miles hadn't seen anybody in seven years, hadn't come out of his house in seven years. You know, he was very reclusive in those last years. We didn't go. Miles didn't really want to see people at that time. I share that to give you an idea of the kind of reception we had. Later on, we went on to meet a lot of the really great Jazz musicians in the country.

That was the sort of atmosphere I grew up in and later experienced, one in which I wanted to learn and having people willing to teach. People who shared willingly. I believe that in that way the whole country was behind this: the people, the government. But some of those people didn't really do as much as they could. In fact, sometimes when the government officials came to visit the bands they acted like they were more *bad-johns* than the *bad-johns* themselves. They wanted to be rougher in manner and speech. I could understand even that, too. The Pan movement is a powerful one. The panman is a powerful man.

I have a little vision of myself as being inspired by Kunta Kinte himself. A great story, Alex Haley's *Roots*. You know that Kunta was on his way to cut a log to make a drum when he was apprehended and brought here. He didn't get to continue that tradition, but other drummers were able to, both here and in the

Caribbean. That drum—you know the history—the colonials' suppression of that skin drum eventually caused the rise of the steel drum. That goes all the way back to Jesus and what He meant when he said if they take something from you wrongfully you will get more. The skin drum was taken from us during a time in history and the way things turned out we got another drum. But this time it was to be a very "wicked" drum, as we used to say back home, because it has multiplied and spread across the entire world in a wonderful way. This is the path we're seeing these days, one similar to Kunta Kinte's story. One of the greatest stirrings that has taken place here in the Western world is *Roots*, which has caused every *tout moune bagai*, as they say, to look for their roots. It's a mystical thing, not that I know fully what mysticism is. But if there's anything mystical about our modern experiences, *Roots* is one; the second is Pan.

This is why, though I feel quite under the weather about what is happening with the pan, I'm not going to give up. I intend to present the most sensible ensemble of instruments. I'm going to take this to the max because the cycle of fifths is the max. So far, we've only scratched the surface. What I'm also doing is putting together a book on how to play the fourths and fifths. I've read all the books out there and no one has approached the instrument as the orderly instrument it is. The current books explain only how to play this scale and that scale. One of the most important things in playing an instrument is to know what pattern to follow. Take, for example, the piano. We know which finger to use to play which note in which particular key. You don't just throw the fingers any where. Even the guitar players—and other instrument players—know if they're playing in the key of G to use the left middle finger, or something like that. The pan is similar. Why this is important is: if you learn to apply the stick to a particular note when playing a particular key, your physical approach to the drum would become automatic. When you begin to play, you wouldn't have to be negotiating whether to use the left or right hand. If you don't have a plan or a pattern and always use some random process, that negotiating process occurring in the brain never becomes learned.

You see, the brain forwards the right hand or left hand to a particular note until the process becomes automatic, and you can play the pan with your eyes closed, eventually. I know the human brain is big and we're not using all of it, by far. But if in your playing you have negotiated the physical movement, then the emotional part of the music can come through. I think we can separate the two, the physical and the emotional. But it's that emotional part that must be given your total focus. After you learn to play, playing becomes automatic. When you look at a sheet of music your hands already know where to go without your taking your eyes off that sheet. This is how any piano-player can pick up any sheet of music and play. This is the type of training I would like to take back home, or wherever I am welcomed, and teach. I wish to set up players at this level. In a way, the standardization of the instrument is very, *very* important because it would move us toward accomplishing this.

Once I've completed my new ensemble, I think it would be accepted and I hope to write a book that describes this process. Presenting the double pans as singles will be used because people can already play them. I invited Boogsie and had him play two of my bigger ones, which he did without thinking because they're standard. What is going to happen for standardization to become complete is the development of players who are willing to adopt this proper pattern of learning the instrument, this system that is much easier because it is more natural to the way we learn. I have a few students who are learning this pattern. I don't allow them to learn to play a melody because the hand does not yet know how to play. They begin with playing only the exercises, and that takes about four to six months. All my students eventually run away because they want to play. They want to short-circuit the learning process. But I'm persisting and I want to eventually present my method in a formal way where people will know this is what they've come for. They're not coming to play pan or just some particular tunes. They're coming to learn to be musicians, and a musician must know his instrument.

The other part of my book would be on how to play the fourths and fifths. I think these instructions are equally as valuable as the instrument. I hope I can finish my thing and take it to Trinidad and present it formally. Then, the Pan world can do whatever they want with it.

Neville Jules and Albert Jones are two men I respect greatly. In spite of what men like them have accomplished, something seems to be holding us back, preventing us from moving beyond what they've done. Speak to one hundred of us and we will tell you we should have already standardized the pan. But no one has made a step in that direction. I've made the step. I have the instruments as proof. I've spent about four thousand dollars I borrowed toward making a slightly bigger single pan and I have three of them here. I have the different pans, even though I've never had the entire ensemble together at one time. Hopefully, by the end of this year I would have that. I have some at the chrome shop right now.

I think this is something I was meant to do, because I have started the process and accomplished what I have. While I greatly admire Neville Jules, who was a great inspiration to me, and Ellie Mannette, and all the other great tuners, I think that they have taken the instrument as far as they could. Even though Ellie has the resources and the backing of communities and governments, to some degree, I think it's men like me who will take Pan to the next level. I may be bridging the first and second generations of panmen. Really, we're still in the infancy stage of the instrument and its development. But we have to hurry up and do the work. A part of that is to stop all the talk and get down to business. Too many conventions have come and gone and it's still only talk.

Cultures in Collision can Collude: A Spiritual Call-to-Action

Our government is the chief offender of all talk and no action because it has merely taken over from England and promoted the old colonial ideas. Some where among those higher-ups I know are people who love Pan and think real highly of it. But there's an inferiority complex that still controls them. I see the way they listen to music and buy records. They still think the foreign, conventional instruments must be put above Pan. What they don't see is that Pan is not an ordinary instrument. It's a medium that can accomplish any number of ends.

A while back, I got to thinking how the American pan-people who are inspired to their throat with this thing went down to Trinidad, to the Mecca of Pan, and were welcomed. Those guys showed them a good time—you know how Trinidadians are welcoming and hospitable—and greeted the Americans with love and friendship. It wasn't anything commercial for Trinidadians but social. These men were given nice parties, great food, introduced to good friends, and all that. But the Americans didn't go to Trinidad for that. They went for the pan. They returned from Trinidad only to talk about the low work ethic of Trinidadians and panmen, the low standards of living, the addiction and begging on the streets, and people with a typical third world country mentality. That is what they came back here reporting. The same people who inspired them and gave them gifts and stirred their imagination, they came back to America to *bad-talk*.

Trinidad didn't see these people being there for any commercial intentions. They weren't formally invited to come and see what was happening in Pan and how to set up business relationships. They went down there on their own and Trinidad received them in that spirit, as people who were visiting for social reasons, and were invited into the Pan world because Pan is a very social instrument. I know others were invited to establish good political relations, too, and were treated accordingly, but they weren't invited. That's the sort of thing that breeds ill-will. If the people who became friends through Pan continue to be friends, then Pan is a success. We have to let the foreigners, not just the Americans, know that. They have to know point blank that their own bad manners will not, must not, pass unnoticed, not when they themselves behaved like vagabonds with their *bad-talking* Trinidadians.

I have a tuner-friend in Arizona; he's a warrior like me. He knew what was happening with them. So he set up a friend of his to call this company,—, to order some drums. He ordered some accessories and told them that Ancil Joseph was going to make the instruments. The people of that company *bad-talked* Ancil, Ellie, and everybody else in Pan. Ancil can't do this; Ellie can't do that. These are the very people from whom they got the knowledge to set up their company. This is something that has been happening over and over right here in America and other parts of the world.

You see, this material thing is what has led the world to destruction. It's already documented that materialism has led the world to many wars. In America's case, they've taken over where the British left off. They go somewhere, are treated well, take what they feel like taking from the so-called third-world countries, then return to America to put down the people. I speak about this visit and their response because I don't believe we should let this one pass, especially when Pan has been used so much to build good social relations, as a sort of social experiment which we must not let fail. We in Pan have to be the example that this thing cannot fail and we have to remain friends amongst ourselves. Those Americans I've been referring to must see that there is this social aspect to Pan that was built on good relations and feelings of good will that we are not allowing to be destroyed because of materialism. If we can preserve this successfully, I'm sure we will be more of an inspiration to people at all social class levels, not only in Trinidad but all over the world, if we do the right thing where Pan is concerned.

The thing is not to sell more pans than Trinidad or think you can make a better pan than Trinidad, because I doubt that. No one can surpass Ellie, or me, for that matter. There's Bertie Marshall that they can't surpass either. The thing is to show people, to warn them not to go in the wrong direction because this was a social experiment. I mean, every thing that God put on this earth, every thing that He has inspired by putting it into our minds was first for our individual benefit, then for those around us, then for the large world. But the way these people are bent on materialism, on trying to outstrip us from everything we bring to them, the way they behave, you have to wonder whether they are believers. Of course, not everyone will receive what I'm saying because this spiritual-social approach to Pan wouldn't make sense to those who only want to make money.

Wayne Bailey is another person who inspired me, and having been so inspired I have to talk about what's on my mind, about wanting the right thing to continue to be done to inspire the rest of the world. I'm arguing for what is right and better toward improving human relations. I don't think it's just America and Trinidad but the world community that must find a way to live more harmoniously. Allow these experiences that bring us together to be kept sacred. These people who are violating the pan in that respect are violating us, too. Again, it is not so much for our benefit that we want to call bad-behaving Americans to order and accountability but for theirs. They're the ones who are violating trust and friendship once more. They should not be allowed to pass through that tunnel unnoticed. They won't have a warm reception when they come out at the other end. And, I think it's our right, our duty as intelligent people here and now, and not just as Trinidadians to say to them, "What you're doing is wrong." The way I look at things is not just as a Trinidadian. I have a citizenship there and that's it. I see myself as a part of this whole world. And, whatever has been put into my hands I don't want to go to waste, and this is my business, too.

You know, the things that I have done, the depths to which I've focused on what I'm doing and my belief in it have made me come to realize that it's my beliefs in the pan movement that are most important. Some of the things have happened—some stories too long to include here—can only be explained as supernatural, miraculous. A quick story is on how Love Serenaders, my little band, was cheated out of qualifying for Panorama one year, when everyone was so sure we'd qualified. Three months after Panorama, a friend brought me a piece of paper that showed the actual scores of the judges. The scores showed that we had placed higher than Jewel 22, but Jewel 22 was announced as having qualified. Jewel 22 was owned by the president of Pan Trinbago at that time. Do I need to say more?

Even an article in *The Punch* praised our playing above all the other bands, describing our pans as sweet. He used a whole paragraph to describe us while giving only a sentence or two to all the other bands, including Despers. You know, the whole time I was home I was so shocked by the whole injustice that I didn't stop to think about this newspaper reporter. It's after I returned to the States that I came to realize I should have gone and asked the reporter what he felt. Why did he write the way he did? I knew that we had been cheated and then came to find the evidence of it. Knowing what he felt would have made me feel better then. Anyway, when things like that happened I got new courage to go on. I know that there's a Higher Spirit involved in this movement and also the good works that we undertake are multiplied and returned to us one hundredfold.

Some of what shape my beliefs comes from living in John John, which was a great place for me, despite the violence in Pan. We had Spree who left the country for a while and traveled abroad, and my mother regarded him as an ambassador. The whole community respected Spree greatly. He was like the mayor, the governor of Trinidad to the community. I don't believe that I ever saw him except maybe during my very young years. I really don't remember knowing him, and I knew all the other guys in Tokyo. I don't recall him until 1980 when I was in Trinidad and he had returned home.

He'd come back home but not to the awards he should have got for what he did. I mean, he didn't even receive the respect from the Ministry of Culture. He was working in Special Works, doing what I don't know. But he ought to have been given a prominent place in culture. I remember when I first saw him I couldn't help but say to myself that he was a good-looking man, with a sort of stateliness about his appearance, quiet and dignified. Whatever honors he's receiving now, though too late for him to appreciate, he deserves.

Regarding the violence, I can recall how those older men protected us little ones from danger. I remember once when fighting broke out, those men got us into the center of the band and made sure all of us made it home safely. Each man took two or three of us and escorted us safely home. We never got a scratch. That was the kind of community spirit we had, with everyone looking out for each other. That was the great part of growing up in John John, which outsiders didn't know anything about. We looked out for each other and lived in that "it takes a village to raise a child" spirit.

We shared everything, too, so that people didn't go hungry or without clothes. People didn't have to rob people, even though today drugs are causing that. We had that what-I-have-is-yours-and-what-you-have-is-mine way of treating one another. It was a strong community and people worked hard, very hard. The steelband violence overshadowed these things about our community and the ethics the big people instilled in us. But if you look at what good things have come from the Hill, you have to know that good things must have been happening. That too was a microcosm of what is happening in the world, just like today. More good things are happening than bad, but bad news is what makes headlines.

Just like John John had a lot to offer Trinidad, now Trinidad has a lot to offer the world, if people know how to behave toward one another. Trinidad has given Pan to the world, and Pan can bring all cultures together. So much so that, if there were to be an international flag, the symbol of the pan is to be on it. The essence of Pan is the joy of life, what everyone craves for, to live a life of joy.

New Wine in New Wineskins

In closing, I want to emphasize that Pan as a social experiment cannot fail. The whole world will eventually be looking at this thing and us. I hope they will see that we are working things out. We have to pour new wine into new wineskins, as Jesus said, to preserve this new thing God has given us. Pan is this new thing and if we deal with it in the old ways, the whole thing will blow up in our face. I think the movement is a metaphor on many levels as we try to figure out how to live harmoniously. We can't keep going back to the same old ways and expect things to change. If they didn't work in the past, how we expect them to work today? We have to find a way to live better, live harmoniously. Learn from this instrument born out of intelligence. We are all intelligent people.

18

Trying to Make a Dollar: A Vignette by Trevor Stubbs[1]

Ras Trevor Stubbs *(b. 1961) attended Tranquility Boys' Secondary School and John Donaldson Technical Institute before immigrating to the United States in 1989. He is a current member of Terrance Cameron's steel band, Steel Kings, and formerly a member of the Frank Clark Kids Steel Band, the Julia Edwards Dance Troupe (the band), Invaders, Starlift and Phase II steel bands. With Phase II, he had the opportunities to tour the United States and Europe throughout his pre-adolescent and adolescent years.*

Upon settling in the United States, he has conducted Steelband workshops and performances at Syracuse University, Brooklyn College, Borough of Manhattan Community College, Columbia University, Villanova University, University of Pennsylvania, Pennsylvania State University, and others throughout Florida. He developed his pan-tuning skills under Rudy V. King's apprenticeship and formerly worked with Mannette in WVU. He notes that he may be the only Trinidadian of his generation tuning pan in the United States.

Note: Trevor approved of my retaining as much as possible Trini Creole, grammar, and linguistic speech patterns I saw fit. Thus, for language and cultural authenticity, I preserved Trevor's narrative as close to the original as necessary. My decision to present Trevor's story in this way goes to the fact that many Trinis are proud of their biculturalism, of being able to straddle both First and Third World consciousness, and that such is reflected in the way they choose to speak. Also, my First-Year Writing Program students of Temple University frequently beg me for examples of Trini language. Here's to accommodating them, with pleasure.

A Second-generation Invaders Panman

I was introduced to Invaders and Pan music by my uncle. They used to call him Ralph but his name was Elmond Stubbs. I remember him carrying me to the Invaders panyard when I was very young, and from the first time I heard the music I was very fascinated with it. I couldn't play at the time because I was too small. Not till I was about seven years old I got my real taste. What used to happen was the older guys didn't want anybody to play the instrument they were playing. So, I used to wait until one of them left their pan to go and get something and grab that opportunity. If it so happenned that he left his sticks in the pan, I would use them and play the same song they were just playing. When they heard me playing, they wanted to know where I came from, who was I was.

When I could, I joined a kid's band named Frank Clark Kids. We used to play a lot in schools because we were still in primary school. I went on a lot of trips with that band. We had a contract every summer to play in Orlando at Disneyland. At that time, it was Disneyland not Disney World. We used to spend the entire summer and then come back on time to go to school. So, I really started playing pan professionally from a young age.

During that time, once while in Invaders yard, the captain come and ask me what I doing in the yard, and said that I wasn't supposed to be there. I answer that I come with my uncle. The captain then let me stay because of him. After that, I got more opportunities to really play.

When I first went into the yard and eventually joined the band, another guy who was about a year or two older than me was already there playing, a'ight. His name was Rogers. He started off playing the bass. He and I were the two youngest members in the band. I started playing with Invaders around the same time I was making trips [abroad] with the Frank Clark Kids. You have to remember that after Carnival not much was going on. After the Lenten season, nobody was playing pan until later in the year. So, we used to practice until Lent was over toward making these overseas trips. This was in the '70s. We made these trips every year for about eight years. We played in hotels and around the whole compound at different functions. I stayed with the band until '74.

When I joined Invaders, I started off playing the lead pan and left when I first heard Phase II. I fell in love with their music. That music grips me. It took me away from wherever I was. It was when playing in Phase II that I started to get more versatile in playing the other pans. I stayed with Phase II until I left home in '89 and came to the States. With Phase II, I toured Japan, Martinique, Guadeloupe, England, Switzerland, and was basically traveling a lot from a tender age, from a small age.

"Kidsploitation"

After I came to Phase II, the Frank Clark Kids band *mash up*. We had got to realize that Mr. Clark wasn't really paying us what he was suppose to pay us, and we were getting robbed. Sometimes we got paid and sometimes we didn't. The band *mash up* around the time we were playing at the Holiday Inn, which had just opened in Trinidad. We got the first contract to play there, and we played at the pool side every Saturday and Sunday.

Then, I joined the Julia Edwards Dance Troupe—another guy and I—and played pan with the drummers, a'ight. There was a show we used to put on with the pans and the drums before the dancers came on, and all that.

We also did shows in the Hilton Hotel every Wednesday, Friday, Saturday, and Sunday. It was also around that time I first started traveling to Japan with the Julia Edwards Dance Troupe. We traveled to Japan for six months, came back home for two weeks then returned to Japan for another six months. It was a routine that I did for about three years.

All this time, I was still in school. I useta get time off from school to perform. Sometimes, it [the tour] useta run into the holidays, so it wasn't really that much time off from school. Then, when I joined Julia and dem, I had only one more year in school. I was going to Tranquil Secondary at the time. At the time, Tranquil was called Tranquil Intermediate. We still useta wear tie, an' all ah dat. So, things started up for me with the Frank Clark Kids, and that gave me the opportunity to play. Then, while going on to secondary school, I went with Julia and dem, and then to Phase II.

Looking back at those days, I feel if I was paid like I was supposed to, my life today would be so much different. I would be doing much better now. Yuh live an' learn.

Second-generation Violence

You must remember that Pan was still in its primitive stage when it still had a lot of fighting going on at the time. Sad to say, when I started in Pan it still had a lot of violence, but it was starting to mellow off a little. I witnessed a lot of violence right there in the yard and on the streets.

My take on the violence was that basically certain people didn't like certain people. At that time, you couldn't leave one band and go to anot'er band. Some guys were brave to actually still pass by a band, and that would cause some conflict, yuh know. Some people were still arrogant and ignorant at that time. You found a lot of that going on, too.

When I joined Invaders, I remember there was a time the band couldn't go into town at Carnival time because of the rivalry between the bands. Then they decided to do away with that and to start back going into town. That caused them to get into a lot of battles. A lot of stupidness.

Life in the United States

When I came in '89, I began playing with a band called Moods. I first came up here with Phase II in '88 after we won our second Panorama. While here, we did a show for the mayor [of New York City]. There was a summer tour of bands playing at different places all over New York, and we played for the mayor then. During that time, I came to know Climmey, the manager of Moods.

After Phase II returned to Trinidad, I came back with a guy named Sydney Joseph to start playing with a church band in New York. The band eventually *mash up* and Joseph wanted to send me back home. I told him I was not going back home, and that's how I ended up staying here. After that, I started hanging around Moods and started playing with them, doing gigs all over the place. Then, I left and started playing with a little conga side that had drums and pans. It had a drummer, a guy playing bass, and I played with them, doing school projects, visiting colleges and doing shows an' t'ing.

Later, I *bounced up* with Sydney Joseph again, and I brought him into the conga side, the band. Somewhere along the line, he and I couldn't get along. Then, I got this call from Open Minds in '91. I came down here to Maryland with that band and stayed with them for five years. We traveled between Maryland and Florida, going back and forth. Then, that band came and *mash up* because of different conflicts. That's a long story. Buh is de same ole story ah men who *kyar* get along.

After that, I went back to New York. While in New York, I got a contract to go to Israel to play on a ship for six months. This was in '96. When that contract was up, I decided not to go back. They called to come back but I didn't go because I just didn't want to do that again. I alone was playing pan, along with a bass player, a drummer, and a keyboard player. I and the bass player useta sing in the band. After we come back, they call me to go back with them, but I decided I wasn't going back. I decided to go back to Moods.

They had these winter jobs they were doing, going into schools playing. Then, Moods came and *mashed up*, and from that we formed our band name Utopia Band Soul. You hear 'bout it? I was one of the founders. Basically, all the pans they have I made them. The bass, the four-pan, the guitar pans. I also made pans for Metro, Sonatas, and Pantonic, who just won Panorama last year. People are now seeing my work and liking it and wanting to get pans from me.

I learned to make pan from Rudy King who I hooked with just before forming Utopia. I met Rudy through playing a gig with a guy by the name of Peanuts who useta play the second pan—a very good player, too. He had this gig and called me to play with him and call Rudy to play the congas. That's how we and Rudy met.

Rudy's telling me now that when he first saw me, he didn't know what to picture. He didn't know what I coulda played. What he was saying basically was, "I going out playin' wid guys who doh know de pan. T'ey doh know what to do. When we call songs t'ey won't know what to play." That sort of thing is behind the idea of not knowing what to picture when you meet someone like me for the first time, yuh know. But he was actually surprised when they start calling songs and I was just playing. We actually had a good time. When we were done playing the first set now, he ask Peanuts, "Whey yuh get t'is guy from?" Peanuts say, "You doh know Stubbs, man? I know him a *long* time now." And, that's how we began to get close. Then, he invited me home by him one time, and I got to realize that this man in Pan for a *long* time, almost from the time it got started. He started showing me a lot of things and I got a lot of interest in what he was talking about.

One day, I went to him and said, "You know what, Rudy? I am ready to start to make pan, man." He say, "You really serious?" I say, "Yeah, man." He say, "Well, for you to do this work, you have to have tools." He was telling me straight, "I not going to let you use my tools." I say, "Well, okay." So, I took my credit card and went to the hardware with him and started to get all the tools together, and that's how I started off making the pan. That was '97, going into '98.

I was ready now to start to try a lot of different things. Yuh know what ah mean? I actually tried something already, here. I made a tenor pan out of two drums, where you have the sharps and flats on one side and the natural notes on one side. I don't know what the outcome of that pan will be. I never even try to play it yet. I just know it's there. I'm going to continue making pans for all those different bands in New York.

I kinda *graffing over* a lot of different things, too.

Making a Dollar Any Way I Can

I don't play only with Terrance [Cameron]. I play with all who call me to play. Right now, that's what it's all about for me, basically. Trying to make a dollar to survive. That's how it's been for me up to now. I still do a lot of stuff with Utopia, a lot of gigs. But I left the band because I was trying to make a certain breakthrough, and the band wasn't ready for what I had in mind. I wanted to do a CD and some other things they weren't ready for. That's the problem with most Trinidadians. They don't look ahead to see where this thing can go: yuh know what ah mean? They too full ah fear an' suspicion. They don't want to learn to read music. They don't want to try things to enhance their awareness of the instrument's versatility. In the long run, they're only holding back themselves and where they could take this thing. Trinidadians still have a long way to go....

Author's note: I met Trevor in 1995 when he was a member of Open Minds. The band was filling its annual summer engagement at Schaeffer Canal House, Chesapeake City, Maryland (now closed for reconstruction due to storm damage). Trevor provided me Terrance Cameron's contact information, Terrance being a longstanding pan-builder-tuner who outfitted Blaksilvah Steel Band, my family band.

19
When Behaviors Eclipse Talent: Ruth and Terrance Cameron's Story[1]

Terrance "Muggs" Cameron *is a pan-builder and tuner, and the owner of Steel Kings, a steel band based in Philadelphia, Pennsylvania, his home city. Originally born in Soubise, Grenada, he grew up in Trinidad and was attracted to Pan during his adolescent years.*

*His most notable grant is a **2000** Pew Grant.*

The following truly delightful interview was conducted at the Cameron residence in Philadelphia and points to the challenges of working with men who had little to no vision of themselves in relation to U.S. culture and society.

Ruth Cameron's *perspective from the vantage point of an African American, a woman, and the manager of Steel Kings underscores the role that racism and intra-cultural sexism played in defining the band's public image, and how she survived it all based primarily on her love and commitment to Pan and sense of humor.*

From Apprentice to Philly Icon

I fell in love with Pan in Trinidad as a little boy and always dreamed of playing, but my parents did not want me to get involved in Pan because of the reputation of Steelband and the stigma attached to it. I was about sixteen when Carl Greenidge from San Juan got me involved. I started playing with his band. He was making pans for the band at that time. He was the first person I saw making pan in Trinidad. I also spent a lot of time with Stanley Warner. He was from Second Street, San Juan, near to where I went to school, San Juan Government School. I used to go there after school and watch him, to learn from him. I stayed with him for about five years learning to make pan.

My opportunity to be on my own came when the parents of some kids living on the street where I lived bought pans as birthday presents for their children and wanted me to teach the children and tune the pans. I did that and we formed a small band. Somebody from the Sonnets heard us and wanted us to play with them for Carnival. Stanley encouraged me and I started making all my pans for Carnival. I did that for about three years. I was about twenty-two, twenty-three at the time.

I made my pans in the panyard where the band rehearsed. After a while, my reputation grew. People wanted me to make pans for them and their bands. I started working for Silver Stars and Tripoli and then for people from all over Trinidad. Then came [San Juan] All Stars. The person who made their pans was on tour with another band, and Stanley recommended me to All Stars to get that job of making their pans. He also recommended me to other bands, and when he started to travel he had me take over his jobs. He went first to the Bahamas, and when he decided to leave permanently, he recommended me to most of the bands.

I came to the States on tour with All Stars in '78, and when the tour was finished I was supposed to return to Trinidad. Actually, I came six weeks before the rest of the band to prepare the pans. The band was to play at Madison Square Garden. Earl Harris was the promoter and arranged for bands to visit the United States. When the tour was finished, I found there was a need for someone to make drums, and the news began to spread that I was here and could make drums. People in Boston and New Jersey contacted me. Joe Lendor, originally from Santa Cruz and living at the time New Jersey, wanted to start a band and invited me to stay with him. He's now back in Trinidad. I accepted and when I was finished some people in Philly contacted me in 1978 and asked me to come and get them started. In 1979, I moved to Philly. I liked Philadelphia and decided to stay. To the best of my knowledge, I was the first pan-maker to establish Pan in Philly.

After leaving All Stars, I became involved with the Folklife Association, which was funded by the Council of the Arts, and through this organization some information on me was published. I worked closely with them but still maintained contact with All Stars. I returned to Brooklyn and stayed there for three years making pans for the Brooklyn bands. I then returned to Philadelphia in 1984, and the National House where the Folklife Association had its office wanted a steel band for their seventy-fifth anniversary. There still wasn't a steel band in Philadelphia at that time. They knew about me and contacted me in April for the event in September. I assured them that I would have a band by then for their occasion and used that opportunity to form my own band.

I got some old pans from a band in Baltimore—I didn't have enough time to make pans for my new band—and put my group together with their old pans. When I started there were seven to eight members. Today, my band is much smaller and it's no longer all pans. Back then it was all pans. Today, I have a couple of pans played by myself and Trevor Stubbs, a keyboard played by Dwight McIntosh, and a guitar played by Rich Simmons. The band has changed with the times. Personally, I would like to have all pans, but with the type of work I'm doing, it's easier to get around with a smaller group and less pans. But I always loved an all-pan band. My band, however, has a good reputation and some fame in this area. For instance, we've played at the baseball All-Star game, one of the biggest gigs, in 1987.

My band did a lot of things. We've played at a lot of colleges.

Before me, to the best of my knowledge the spread of Pan in the United States started back in the '60s when Liberace had a steel band on tour with him. The band was from Trinidad and headed by Herman "Rock" Johnson from St. James. He recently passed away. I can't recall the name of the band. This band broke off from Pan Am North Stars and formed their own band. In the '70s, Kim Loy Wong's band also toured quite a bit. As for my band, I worked a bit with the Pennsylvania Council on the Arts (PCA) doing tours with them. I was in Ohio when someone contacted the PCA—I think it was Cuyahoga Arts Festival—and invited me to play. My band also does all sorts of gigs: weddings, christenings, whatever the occasion is. I'm still playing for the baseball teams. I do the pre-game show and have been doing this for about twelve years.

One of the problems I've had over the years, though, is keeping the same players in the band or even keeping members committed to staying with the band.

That's the reason I'm now down to two pans, a guitar, and a keyboard. The guys come and play and then want to branch out on their own. A lot of the Philly bands now formed are by guys who started with me.

Wandering in the Wilderness

Personally, my experience has been positive. I haven't run into any major problems. Not anything to deter me. My biggest obstacle was the players themselves, their personality differences. I had to keep a close eye on them a lot to make sure these personalities didn't develop into any major clash. Nothing like what used to happen in Trinidad when bands clashed and the violence that resulted. It never came to any thing like that. It was mostly who didn't get along with whom, and then sometimes not doing simple things I asked them to do. For example, when going out on certain gigs, you had to dress the right way. I would let them know this ahead of time and some would turn up dressed inappropriately. I would also let them know what sort of behavior was expected because we had to carry ourselves in a certain way. These men who wouldn't cooperate, I had to ask them to leave the band. What they couldn't see was that we weren't just promoting Pan, we were promoting ourselves, the business of Pan, and everything associated with Pan. Some of these men just didn't understand this. They just wanted to play and that's how far their vision went. Play, get their money for the gig, and nobody tell them what to do. These were experienced panmen. I've always worked with men who already knew how to play, mostly men from the Caribbean, from Trinidad.

Ruth: Terrance is being too nice and polite. Some of those men's behavior was atrocious and their attitudes were appalling. They came with the attitude that no one could teach them anything, tell them anything, and whatever we told them they were determined not to cooperate with. We tried to prep them for gigs, to let them know that the people followed a protocol regarding gigs and band players. The men would arrive at these places, put their feet up on furniture, and smoke and drop the cigarette butts any and every where. When I tried to explain to them that such behavior was unacceptable, they became belligerent. Behaving like they were God's gift to America, or something. Men like that we had to let go at the end of the gig.

One of them, and I don't have anything about dreads, refused to remove his hat for this special gig. Had this big hat with his dreads piled under it, which I told him didn't look appropriate for the occasion. The hat, that is. Would he listen? Some men just refused to accept that people have certain expectations when they hire a band—attire, behavior, language, the whole package. White pants with floral shirts in the summer and dark colored pants in the winter. They'd show up in anything but that. Very unprofessional and arrogant. They were so arrogant, they even got cocky with the man who was signing the check. "I don't give a damn who you are." This was after the man reprimanded one man for his inappropriate behavior. It was frustrating. They felt like they were doing people a favor, not realizing that no gig meant no money. When they realized that we had let them go, then they had an even worse attitude. They just didn't understand how business works in America. People don't care where you come from. All they know is they hire you for an event and expect you to rise to the occasion. Sometimes, we had to pamper them along, hoping that they'd get the picture and come around. Sometimes they did; sometimes they didn't. They were generally of a low-class mentality, very uncouth and with little to no aspirations.

I'd ask them, "Where do you see yourself ten years from now?" They'd answer, "Not doing this for sure." Well, they were right. Some of them are now hanging around street corners with nothing to show for their talent. No good to themselves or society in a land of opportunities for them to make something of themselves with this instrument and music that all sorts of people just loved and were paying us quite well to hear.

Were it not for the attitude and behavior of these men, Pan could be much further along. How could we accept gigs without thinking of who would embarrass themselves and us? They didn't get it that these were business opportunities. So, that's why the turnaround in my band has been so frequent. But it's not only me who had this problem. Band leaders, band managers, and band owners across America—Florida, Brooklyn, all over—have the same complaints about these types of men.

Ruth: Some of the men it's as though their minds stopped when they picked up the sticks. Pan has grown but these men haven't. In fact, they acted as though they never grew up. They only thought about themselves in the moment. They never thought that what they were doing was affecting the money flow. Then, they'd call me and complain that they didn't have food or money to pay the bills or money for clothes, and so on. They'd always come late to rehearsals with the same attitude—that they were doing Terrance and me a favor. Terrance would say, "Are you ready to rehearse?" They'd respond, "No." They were very content with being mediocre and mediocrity. They were so negative, and like everything the negativity rolled off. Sometimes, they even arrived late for our departure for gigs. We'd tell them to get here by three o'clock. Three fifteen we'd call and they'd still be in bed. Then, when they got here they'd demand food, because they were hungry. Obnoxious.

Take the hat, the knit hat that was about eighteen to twenty-four inches high, in temperatures of over ninety degrees. At this one gig, I was asked specifically to speak to the wearer of the hat, that it wasn't appropriate for photo-taking because he was blocking anyone and everything behind the hat. The guy just wouldn't hear it. Didn't want to hear any criticism. The man who hired the band was upset, and so was I.

This was a well-paying gig, and the people loved, just loved, the music and would have hired us again. But how could they when this guy refused to remove his hat? Couldn't see that he was biting off the hand that was feeding him. If someone who was paying the amount of money he paid us for that gig told me to jump, I'd ask him, "How high?" You understand what I'm saying? But not these men; they just didn't get it.

Sometimes, some would show up wearing wrinkled, unkempt clothes that looked and smelled like they slept in them and refused to change, and I would be expected to deal with being embarrassed. To deal with their saying if people wanted them to wear a different shirt, let them buy the shirt. Maybe I would deal with it once, if they showed up for a gig dressed inappropriately, and try to make the best of the situation—lend them a shirt of Terrance or something. But not a second time. That man would not get another call from me for a gig. What they couldn't understand was that with the amount of money they earned on gigs, they could more than afford to buy appropriate shirts. I always had to be on guard, never knowing what to expect from their low-class ways. All of this had nothing to do with whether they were educated or of a high class or not. These were men with just bad attitudes. It was all about attitude.

Attitude is costly, and we had to make good on our end of the agreement. If anything was broken or damaged because of their lackadaisical manner, the band had to replace it, which cut into how much we earned. They didn't understand that either. They didn't understand and didn't want to hear anything.

They just didn't understand that this was a business, and when people hired you they expected you to dress and behavior in a certain way. You are doing a job. I told them every time they had to present themselves well. We sometimes arrived at places and the caterers were looking better than them. I told them this, too, that even the caterers were better dressed than them. That didn't work. People looked at these things and passed judgment. All this have hindered the progress of Pan. Pan itself is magic. It doesn't take a lot of playing to reach people. Just the sound of the drums would take us ninety-five percent of the way.

The new generation of pan-players holds a greater promise. The new panman is coming with a degree in music and generally has a better, more professional attitude. This new generation of panmen also has a lot of love for the instrument and is well educated. This dynamic combination will take the Pan to the next level, not just to the professional level but just into more into schools, colleges, and universities, toward becoming more established as a mainstream musical instrument in American society.

Ruth: I've said numerous times that this thing should by this time be much further along. Having been involved with Pan for eighteen years, having been in the business this long, I could see what the hindrance is, where the problem lies. Some of the younger generation who has already disassociated themselves from the type of men I've been talking about have to persist in a positive direction. They're already serious and focused; they're professionals; they're business-minded; they want to have good, clean fun with what they're doing; and they want to be respected. They are conducting themselves accordingly, too.

But it's hard to forget what these men put me through. I had to fight them long and hard without losing my self-respect and eventually getting their respect. I refused to back down. So, I came across as the hard, tough one while Terrance who was too quiet sometimes let them get away with some things. But I couldn't afford that. This is a business, too. Some types of behavior can hurt one's business. I can give many examples, in addition to what I previously stated. This next one is similar to the one with the eighteen-inch knit hat.

We were at a big fund-raiser. People were dressed in their Sunday-go-to-meeting outfits. A black-tie, Saturday night affair for which the people paid about one thousand dollars for admittance. The élite were there. I was standing in the corridor next to the Cadillac showroom floor speaking with the gentleman who organized the affair. We were talking for about twenty minutes, with him telling me how they had provided us all with our own dressing rooms—offices converted into dressing rooms for the occasion. Some of the guys needed to change because they didn't plan to perform in their travel wear. We stood there talking while he went over all details with me when I noticed him looking over my shoulder. Then, abruptly he said, "Okay, Ruth. Look like the guys would be ready to start in a few minutes. Let me go."

I wondered what the heck that was all about, why the abrupt end to our conversation. So after he left, I turned around. One of the guys was standing next to the drums, in his boxer shorts, *pulling up his white pants.* The band was wearing white pants that night. He reached over in his boxer shorts grabbed his white pants and began pulling them up. The guests had already begun to arrive. I thought I was seeing things. He had no respect for me, the only female there, while he stood there in his underwear. I asked Terrance to say something to him. When Terrance did, his attitude was, "Wha'?! Wha?! Ain't nobody back here." He didn't see anything wrong with his behavior. This was a guy about forty-something. No kid. At his stage in life, he should know better, that he couldn't just walk in there and start getting undressed while a woman was standing there. He decided that he wanted to get comfortable right there. That behavior, to me, is not normal. Neither was when one of them spat on the spotless floor, like it was no big deal to spit onto a clean floor.

Another guy got off the van one day. We were playing at Neiman Marcus. That's upscale, too. Not some small plaza, street-front store. He also came out wearing his boxers and thought he could get away with it. He was walking into the store, unloading the equipment, in his boxer shorts!

But the most atrocious behavior involved a glass table at this country club. We got to this other upscale gig and the host expected us to use the dressing room, help ourselves to something to eat, and be comfortable. I was inside when someone came to get me to go out and talk to the men. When I went to see what was the matter, well, some men had had their fill and one or two had their feet up on the glass table. I couldn't get out there fast enough to them. My knees were shaking. They had messed up the people's table arrangements by digging into the food, before *the guests arrived. When I asked them how they could do that, they answered the people told them to help themselves. I said, "But that was to be* after *the gig not before, and* after *the guests were gone or were leaving. This event is for the important guests. We are hired to do a job." Do you know how they responded? That my sort of attitude was massa day ain't done and as far as they were concerned massa day done. They failed to distinguish, however, that they were there to do a job and were getting paid. The food was offered out of courtesy. When the members of the country club began arriving, you could see them looking at the men wondering whether they would get mugged at the country club. We were the only Blacks in the area and these men were tossing their cigarette butts onto the landscape, too. One was smoking a marijuana joint right in front of the person who hired us. What give them the right?!*

There they were, behaving like they were the owners of the place. Such nasty attitudes. When I tried to explain to them what they were doing was wrong, they didn't get it. All they knew was they weren't bothering anybody. Their mentality was, "So wha' happen? We kyar *sit outside, now?" They couldn't understand first of all that they couldn't go to people's place and make a mess. No one else was smoking and the grounds were clean. These were grown men of over forty behaving worse than children. It's like when they picked up their sticks to play they stopped growing. They were like social retards, completely lacking in social graces. They never looked around to take their cues from others.*

I came up in a rough environment, too. But I had enough sense to look around and see things. If everyone was using the fork on the left, then I'd use the fork on the left, too. But their attitude was, "I don't have to use a fork. I'll use a spoon if I want." Never mind what the spoon was for. They even picked up their food with their fingers. I could write a book on these men's behavior. They just never understood that we're in a fish-bowl. Many times, I simply shook my head and walked away. Another time at another country club, one of them who was a vegetarian was so obnoxious in his loud questions: "Does this have any pork in it?! I can't have any of that stuff. I'm vegetarian. I can't have anything with meat." As obnoxious as they ever come! The people were looking at him like, "Why didn't you bring your own sandwich, then?"

Another time, I also couldn't understand how on our way to the gig their hair would be neatly combed and by the time they came out of the dressing rooms—those who used them—they would be wearing this little thing all balled up, like they rolled it around on the floor before plopping it on their head. Ready to pose for pictures, as if to deliberately irritate me! "We're taking pictures today. You know that?" "Yeah! But I don't feel like combing out my hair, so I put this on." "Your hair was already combed, and this is not unacceptable." One of them came out once wearing a big, white fur hat. What was wrong with them?! Then, they tried to intimidate other people, being angry and nasty and barking like dogs at people, "Woof! Woof!" They had gruff, course manners. Their attitude was, "We got something nobody else has." But they will lose it; they'll lose it.

As you know, everyone is looking seriously at Pan now. Mainly the Caucasians. They're examining this thing inside-out, upside-down and seeing where this thing can go. They're conducting themselves properly, answering questions clearly and concisely, and before long, this thing is entirely in their hands because we didn't know how to hold on to it. Come on, know your pan but know your business as well. Know where you want to go and how to get there, and what you should be doing to get there.

No one will argue that this is an excellent instrument. But to move to the next level, you have to have people whose mannerisms, attitude, and behavior complement the instrument. You can't have men showing up wearing unkempt clothes and when you get to these upscale places behaving with such lack of respect. Lots of lack of respect. Foul mouths.

Some say that this is a male-dominated thing. Has been a male-dominated activity with women only recently coming in. So, some of them had the attitude that a woman can't tell them to do anything. But I held my ground and demanded they respect me. I wasn't going to take that sort of sexist you-know-what from them. I'd seen how they behaved at gigs when those White women, a little tipsy from a little too much drinking, came up to the band to tell them how much they loved the music. You know what they said, with the mikes on so everyone could hear? All sorts of remarks about their behind and whatnot. Once, another woman had to approach them and let them know they were being rude, sexist, and plain disrespectful. Many people have probably said, "I would love to have a steel band perform at my event but—." They probably changed their mind after seeing or hearing how those men behaved.

For Pan to get ahead, because of these men's reputation some people may demand a rigorous screening process because you are known by your reputation. People come to know what to expect based on how you behaved, what you offered in the past. They know what you're bringing but not what is going on behind the scene. So, you always have to be able to bring a certain presence to what you're doing. You can't leave anything to chance. You go to a private home and someone shouldn't have to ask you to get off the banisters.

We were at this large home once, and one room had about five steps leading up to another area of the house. The guests were arriving who had to use these steps. With these men lounging on both sides of the banisters, the guests had to go through them. These men shouldn't have to be told, first of all, this is not your home and you are to remain in the designated area where the band is playing. These men were sitting on both banisters and others roaming through the house like it's theirs. The people then came to me, the one they contacted to hire the band, and complained. I then had to go and talk to the men who didn't take anything from any woman. Their behavior was the same every where—in people's homes, in clubs, in hotels. I hate to have to even keep saying this, but you must understand that we were a business based on referrals. People got to know us and felt comfortable referring us to friends, family members, their companies, on and on. That one incident shut down the possibility of many more jobs.

I shouldn't have had to be policing and controlling these men's behavior. All I should have been concentrating on was building the business aspect of the band. At this private home, the people were Jewish with White guests. Why should their guests have to pass through these five Black men their hosts hired, lounging on the steps? You could see it on their faces. One man had the nerve to ask a guest gruffly, "Wha' you want?" The hostess then had to make it a point of telling the men they were to stay in their designated area. That was another incident that was totally embarrassing for me. It left a bitter taste in mouth, and it should never have been. Those were grown men, adults who should have more sense. It was like going into someone's private swimming pool without permission. You just don't do it. Know your place. Now, if it were me having an affair the following year and really wanted a steel band, when I called you I would want to know if you were bringing those same guys. I would be asking, "Is there any way you could tailor it down to two? The two who were so polite and well behaved and weren't so obnoxious and offensive? The two who didn't act like they owned the world and were really a pleasure?"

This is now the year 2002, but a lot of things are no different racially, economically—no different than they were ten, fifteen years ago. When you walk in, don't forget that it's only because you have something they need, and you're not there to get more than they are willing to give. You're not best friends, or even friends for that matter. They tolerated me and Terrance and what we had to offer. If that weren't the case, I couldn't get a job in a heart-beat but for what I have to offer. It's no different than being at the workplace. You're there because of what they need—your skills. That's all. But the racist thing hasn't changed.

One cute incident was when we were on a stage rehearsing at another country club. We were there among all White males—your basic country club. The cooks, custodians, servers—all White. We finished rehearsing and I went out and passed by this table—apparently this group of people had arrived early and one of the members whose membership counts probably let them in. As I passed by, they were eating and their mouths stuffed. They asked me to get them some more rolls from the kitchen or a pitcher of water. I knew that they were trying to be clever and answered, "Oh, just leave it there. Leave it there." While they were praising the food, "Oh, did you see the shrimp and the lobster?" "It's going to be nice here." And so on. Then I forget them, trying to be clever, and went about my business.

Later, when we were performing, they each had to come by the stage to get to the area where all the seafood was set up. On their way back to their table they had to pass by me. Seeing me, they pretended to exclaim, "Ooh, I thought you were—. I'm so embarrassed." Each one came by and made the same remark. When they were sitting down, I went over to the table, looked around, and asked one man, "Are you a member here?" "Maybe." "You're not a member here. If you're a member you would know there are no young Black females working here. So, I don't know if that was your idea of being funny. But I enjoyed the humor. So, you all have a good evening." They responded, "Oh, I'm so sorry. I thought you worked here." No, you did not think so. I know you know better than that, is how I had to respond to that sort of thing.

You have all sorts of people coming at you with their various racist attitudes, not to the same degree like it used to be before. But the attitudes are still there and you have to be ready to deal with all of them. It was racism from the outside and sexism from the inside. Those were some of the issues as band manager I had to deal with.

From my perspective, these are some things that have hindered Steelband. I'm not saying my eighteen years weren't good ones. The music of the band is pure enjoyment. Some of the people we met were a joy. The audiences have been so receptive to us and the music. We've played at some private events that we still can't disclose because we signed contracts accordingly. I could name names that would surprise people when they hear who hired us for gigs. So, being involved with the band has brought some rich rewards. The problems have been within the band itself, the tension and upheavals, and all I've been talking about. If the mentality of band members is anything like it was in the past, we're fighting an uphill battle.

The future calls for more than excellent pan-players. A lot of the men who came through our band were just that: excellent musicians, period. It stopped right there.

When it came to being humans, they left much to be desired. No real discipline. Their attitude was, "We liming; we taking it easy." *That's nonsense. Some of them were even grandfathers and behaved like little boys. When you listened to their level of conversation, right here in this house, you'd swear they dragged their street behavior all the way from the Trinidad ghettos to this house. What a shame!*

All in all, we've had more good times than bad. It's just that those bad times are unforgettable. The proof is in the pudding. I never missed a gig in all those eighteen years.

Another thing about some of the men, they thought by not going out on a gig they were hurting us. They soon came to realize that someone else was always there waiting to fill in for them. Terrance used to warn them that he wasn't solely dependent on them. He knew how they thought and made it clear to them that he wasn't allowing them to corner him. He was in this band for the business as well as the pleasure.

The pan itself is a beautiful instrument. Everybody loves it. The movement itself is already changing, as I already said. A lot of young people, educated and talented, are getting involved. I was in Delaware just this past week, taking some drums to a private school in Claymont. A guy there is doing a residency and working with some fifth-and sixth-graders. You should hear them play and see their enthusiasm. The way they play the pans is a joy to see. So, there's a lot of hope. The school was predominantly white with a few blacks and a mixture of girls and guys. The whole concept of the pan-player has changed from the days when it was only men. The new generation of players will continue to be diverse. Somewhat like your own band and what you experienced.

When I formed this band, I knew what I had to do and what I would be dealing with, so I was always almost six months ahead of them in planning. Some of them left me, branched out to form their own groups, which lasted for some months to a year or two, because they couldn't get along with one another. They thought I was the problem and they wanted to branch out on their own. But they couldn't stay together. In my planning, I had a line of men to fall back on, men from all over Trinidad and some who were also already living in Brooklyn. They knew about me and contacted me, looking for the chance to play. I had a long list of panmen looking for work.

Ruth: We've seen many of them come full circle. They came to Terrance looking for work, he offered them the opportunity, then they developed this attitude of not needing Terrance any more and took off to try to make it on their own, only to realize that it's not so easy. Then, they come right back here to Terrance, admitting that this is as good as it's going to get. "Okay, I'm back in the city. If you have anything, don't forget to call me." But in the beginning they couldn't wait to get away. They wanted to go and play what they *wanted to play. Would argue with Terrance, and Terrance with his easy-going nature would have to insist that they weren't here to please themselves but to please, to entertain, who hired the band. "Buh I doh want to play any ah dat dead stuff." Guess what? That's what you're going to play because that's what the people want. That led to another thing.*

If they brought their pan with them, they took it and left, which is why the band now has a keyboard and a guitar. At a gig, some of them with their attitude, all huffed up, would say,"Where are we? I want to leave here." And, they don't even own a bike. Didn't even know where we were or how we got there because they went in Terrance's van. That was another kind of attitude they'd had. Take their pan and leave.

I've been the percussionist for the band for all these fifteen out of the eighteen years. It was so much fun and enjoyment. It made putting up with those men worth it. I also did all the bookings, the administration, the finances, everything. It was quite stressful. But I enjoyed it, which is why I couldn't understand those men. All they had to do was show up dressed appropriately, behave well, and play. Sometimes, Terrance even picked them up at their home and dropped them off. They had it made. Picked up, dropped off, and paid well. Meanwhile, it was my headache to take care of the contracts, all arrangements for when we got there, that the place the band had to play was right, then play, too.

I don't think I was paid enough for all my headaches. When I became ill, my doctor gave me an ultimatum: either to slow down, or keep on going and kill myself. I had to slow down. But I could have kept on doing this until Terrance got tired of me and kicked me out the band completely. I have to figure out how to ease on back into the band. In all honesty, everyone that has left the band has in some point in time tried to get back in, and some Terrance has let back in. He lets them burn themselves out until they come up with some new excuse to leave. But I've really enjoyed these eighteen years: the places we've gone; the people we've met; the courtesies that have been extended to us have. They've all been very good. I've tried to make the experience as powerful as the music. I did my part to try to make it worthwhile, to make the men work.

A Multicultural View and Pan's Future

The Pew Grant is awarded to artists working in Philadelphia and the Philadelphia vicinity. As a pan-maker, I was working closely with the Philadelphia Folklore project. These folks encouraged me to apply for the grant in 2000, which I won. That was my second application. The first time I didn't get it because the category to which I applied didn't fit. The second time around they changed and had a category for folk artists in folk and traditional arts. So, that's the category into which I fit and then won the award. I also received a fellowship/grant from the PCA to do apprenticeships. I also received awards from the City of Philadelphia.

I'm also working with Bartram High School. I've made their pans as a part of their folklore project. I'm there twice a week giving instructions. I used to go three days but this year with their smaller budget I'm there only two days. The band goes to other schools and also performs at Bartram High School's own programs. A coed band.

Pan is spreading across America and the entire world. In the early days of Pan here, mostly people from the Caribbean were playing it. Not any more. Everyone is getting involved with Pan. Even with the pan-making, Pan has gone from individuals making pans to companies making pan and pan accessories. In Trinidad, we have the same thing—pan factories devoted solely to Pan. Many people like me are making their living solely from Pan. Some people make the pan and subcontract to tuners. So, the movement is going in that direction, along with other innovative ideas for Pan's future.

I was talking to Leroy Williams [see Williams's narrative], another tuner who worked with me in my early days. He was my apprentice in Trinidad, sometimes doing work for me in Tobago when I couldn't go. We were talking about how in the future we will be having different size drums and drum heads. Instead of having a pair of double seconds, we will have one drum with all the notes. Williams, in California, is developing that technology himself. He has the vision of seeing all the notes on one pan, so that we will no longer have a triple guitar, double second, double tenor, maybe even a six-piece bass. When he accomplishes that, he will be making a major innovative contribution to Pan. I devoted some of the money from the Pew Grant to that research. I would like to devote some more time to such innovative ideas.

One of the things I'm seeing is that in America we can develop these ideas. I don't know how easy it will be to sell them to Trinidadians back home, where they have these huge one-hundred piece bands. But here in the United States, the situation is different. We're moving around a lot more and we have to find ways to make this moving around and setting up to play easier. It'll be much easier to have one pan instead of two, three, or six. We have to try to make bands producing the same sounds as small as possible. In Trinidad, they have nine-bass and twelve-bass sections. Here, the most I'll want to have in my band is a six-piece. If we can reduce that to three or four, that'll be even better. This is, what I see, will help Pan advance more rapidly into the future....

20

The Classical and Academic Business of Pan: Dawn K. Batson's Story[1]

Dawn K. Batson is an Associate Professor of Music at Florida Memorial University (formerly Florida Memorial College). Of international repute, Batson has judged Trinidad and international steelband competitions for many years. She holds the distinction of being the first woman ever to conduct a steel orchestra. She writes original scores for Steelband and dreams that one day the body of original material for Steelband will be extensive. Even more passionately, Batson envisions a Pan industry mobilized to help effuse the Caribbean with a strong, stable economy.

Women in Pan—A Force with which to Reckon

I first became involved in Pan through my mother. She was one of the first persons to have pan in schools in Trinidad. Her name is Esther Kasiluddi Batson. She taught at Arima Government Secondary School and had pan in the classroom there. Very often, she used me as a kind of guinea pig to combine pan with violin or pan with piano, or whatever combination. This was in the late '60s when I was about eight to nine years old. I was involved in Barataria Best Village and we toured in '77 with Despers. That was my first exposure to a band on tour, a band of men with great expertise. My interest was heightened then.

When I returned home with my undergraduate degree, I accepted a music teacher position at Trinity College where we formed Wood Trin, the school band, which played with Invaders, and was the first time I played with an actual steel band in Panorama. Ron Reid was the arranger that year and we came first. Then he left, and for the next Festival I did the arrangement and we came first again. At the same time, I became involved with Pamberi Steel Orchestra and did their classical arrangements for the Festival, "Rite of Spring," which did very well.

For the following Festival, we performed "The Flying Dutchman." I also worked with a number of different bands: Renegades as their conductor in 1990 and accompanied them to New York for the Unity tour and other performances, including at Giants Stadium and other large venues in New York; as Pamberi's conductor and musical director for their six-week tour of Europe—France and Italy—in the early '90s; as a guest violist and soloist with Melodians in London, with the steel band accompanying me; and, with Wood Trin who traveled as the champion school band for international performances in Germany, New York, and other places.

What I found when traveling and working with bands is that you have to have a lot of knowledge of contracts. In touring, you need to understand the business side of music. So, I attended the University of Miami (UM) and completed my master's in Music Business. After completing the master's, I decided to go on for the doctorate in International Affairs and Music, focusing on the economic advancement of the steel band—my dissertation topic—and used Steelband as an economic force in Trinidad and Tobago.

To facilitate my work, UM hosted a series of conferences titled "Pan into the Twenty-first Century," the first in '94, second in '95, and third in '96. I brought in a number of different persons in Pan to discuss where we were going in the twenty-first century: Bertie Marshall discussed tuning; soloists conducted featured workshops; and, other Pan greats included Robbie Greenidge, Len Boogsie Sharp, Earl Rodney, and some younger members such as Arddin Herbert. I always brought a few of the younger pannists to participate: Gerard Boucaud; Elthron Anderson; Nigel Williams, who is now one of the top people in Panazz; and, Sheldon Webster, who is now at Berkeley School of Music pursuing his Music degree. We also formed a link with Mike Kernahan, a.k.a. Big Mike, a tuner, arranger, and band leader in Miami and an original Tripolian who toured with Liberace, with the band called Trip Williams. Big Mike's band is called Twenty-first Century Steel Band. UM formed a link with his band and the steelband program I started while attending UM. This link allowed us to tackle the more difficult pieces and explore the area of the combination of pan and Haitian and African dance, and so on.

At the conclusion of the last conference in '96, I found there was a greater need for more educational opportunities for young people. So, I accepted a position at Florida Memorial College (FMC) [now Florida Memorial University], a historically Black college, as an assistant professor of music. At the time, they were just revamping their music program, trying to decide whether to dump or restart it. Dr. Kingston, the chair of the program, and I spoke and together we implemented this program for pannists from around the world, specifically Trinidad. At that time, UWI had not yet started its program for pannists who wished to pursue formal music studies and music theory. When I was in Trinidad, I taught adult music classes through the Ministry of Education, another area in need of this sort of education. In FMC's program, scholarships are offered to Trinidad pannists who are technically capable of developing their techniques. We started the program with two students, Kyle Hill, the former vice-captain of Phase II, and Gerard Boucaud, who was responsible for taking Arima Senior Comprehensive to winner's row for the school music festival and was also a member of Wood Trin. Both of them majored in Pan and both graduated last year, the first graduates from the program.

Gerard graduated with a 3.8 Grade Point Average (GPA) with two degrees: a Bachelor of Science and a Bachelor of Arts in Music. Carl's GPA was above 3.5 with his Bachelor of Arts in Jazz Studies. I'm proud of how well they both did. After starting this program, I assisted in starting a program called "Something Positive" in New York. It is led by Cheryl Byron and Michael Manswell for youth pan soloists to compete for a full scholarship to FMC. Freddy Harris Jr., the son of one of Trinidad's top guitarist, was the first winner. He graduates this December. Also, from Trinidad, we have Kenrick Noel who was active in the school movement. He graduated this past semester. So, FMC's program has grown through these initiatives, and the number has gone from two to thirty. In 2000 at the WSMF, we participated in the ensemble category, which requires fifteen or less. We took part with fifteen members and won that class, the first for a band outside of Trinidad. The band comprised of all Trinidadians, except for two Bahamaians.

The program has thirty members who are not all Music majors. Ten are Music majors and the rest are Music minors. The students are using the steelpan itself as the major instrument, which overcomes the problem many pannists faced. When admitted into a traditional Music program, degree candidates had to become proficient in the piano or the violin. Of course, if you studied an instrument that was that program's focus, to switch at a later date takes time and is difficult. Here at FMC, the students use the pan as their focal instrument, study arranging with Melton Mustafa, the person in charge of Jazz and very well known in the Jazz circle, and also complete a study of the history of the instrument.

Also, they study the other requirements of the traditional degree program, so that they are well rounded. Some candidates enter the program with some theoretical knowledge, and others enter not having a strong theoretical background.

All start with Theory I and continue through to very difficult Jazz theory. They study Conducting, Small Ensemble Arranging, and Computer Music. Their favorite part of the program is to learn how to score the music. We participate in the Miami Panorama every year and have the students do the arrangement, which they have to score. To help them advance in this and other areas, two of them have done internships. I'm the chairman of the board of Trinidad and Tobago National Steel Orchestra (TTNSO), which is where the two have completed their internships. Through TTNSO, we're working on developing a body of music for Pan in Trinidad.

I became chair of TTNSO in 2000. The organization was formed in 1998, but they didn't put the board in place until 2000. During these last two years, we've been trying to get contracts for the players. I've also started an associate's degree program in Performing Arts, under what is called COSTAATT, the College of Science, Technology and Applied Arts of Trinidad and Tobago, under the seven technical colleges in Trinidad. We're the arm for the Performing Arts. The members of TTNSO take part in the associate's degree program, and learn to read, write, and arrange. Next semester, they will learn the basics of building and tuning.

We also have members of the community who participate, which makes TTNSO thirty strong. About fifteen members enrolled in the associate's degree program are from the community. It just started and completed its first year, while here at FMC we're approaching our second year. We're looking forward to having some graduates next year. Then, they'll take that back to their communities because they're scoring, writing, and reading. Recently, they worked with a composer from South Africa who was based in Toronto. He's the musical director of Ensemble Noir. He was commissioned by the Emancipation Committee to write a piece for Pan. I worked with them and went along with Bebe and Jit Samaroo. We were able to work with them because their reading was so much easier. He was able to come in and work with them and conduct the piece. He was very impressed by the musicianship of the players. If it sounds as though I've blended all these programs into one, that's because for me they're all combined. I cannot separate the one from the other because of their educational focus, which is very important to me. Trinidadians have the talent. We have the oral tradition. To move to the next step into the different areas we must go, we need to have this educational base. So, for the two years that I've been working here, education is strongly impressed.

Apart from these time-consuming programs, I've continued to serve in other areas. For instance, earlier this year in May I judged the finals of the European

WSMF, which was held in France. I had attended the first one held in 2000, and found that this year the Europeans have really improved during the period of time. Twenty bands participated in the Festival but only ten of the twenty competed. One of the requisites of their competition was that one of the pieces had to be an original piece written for Pan, scored for Pan. So, there again the body of material being written or scored for Pan is growing. My students are doing this; members of TTNSO are doing it; the Europeans are doing it; and I myself am doing it. The piece we did for the Festival we won, I wrote that. It was called, "Black Holes Do Exist."

I had the idea for this title following a particularly difficult rehearsal when nothing seemed to have gone well and we were all very frustrated. I needed a way to motivate us at the following rehearsal. During the two following rehearsals, the idea came to me, this analogy of the black hole, a place of energy into which we are vacuumed while we deal with the maelstrom of our emotions. Then, we emerge from this hole and find the rest of the world has continued about its business. It became clear to me that black holes do exist but we don't remain in them. We emerge with some sort of perspective about ourselves, what we've gone through and why, and how to go on. This is what I wanted the music to captivate and convey.

My mother is such an inspiration to me. She has produced many operettas and used the pan as the accompaniment instrument. She also always had the pan in the classroom, as I previously said, and helped different bands arrange. She still judges Panorama, having been a Panorama judge for a number of years. She's a music teacher, teaching piano, violin, and wind with my aunt, her sister who is also a music teacher—the whole family is into music. My aunt started one of the first steel bands in church in Trinidad, St. Columbus Church. She allows my mother to run the program. They run not only the first steel bands in church, but they all read and teach the reading skills through the learning of the hymns. The hymns are very effective to teach reading because they have a four-part writing, which makes it easy to marry the different sections of the steel orchestra. Each section is learning to read on a cleft that would be most comfortable for the arrangers. So, Mummy—she is retired now—is judging and has the church program. She has her students, and when there is a Caribbean Steelband festival she judges for that. She went recently to St. Lucia and is in Grenada this week for the Grenada Panorama.

Mummy has always been a proponent of Pan. While for many people it is difficult perhaps to get into Pan, I've never had that problem because she gave me that freedom. I had more problems outside the home. As soon as I went to Bishop—I attended from '71 to '78—and at the same time used to attend Best Village, the teachers told me, "Why are you involving yourself with Best Village?" But they were very happy when I played piano for the Music Festival and for the choir. The stigma was in the association with Pan.

I remember that once when I went on tour, one teacher didn't speak to me for that whole semester because she felt that I shouldn't be wasting my time with that. For my mother, there never was such an issue. She never denigrated Pan or people in Pan. She taught me to believe that once you deal with people respectfully, the entire community is elevated. So, I've dealt with Phase II and many bands of one hundred men and women with respect. I've found that pannists are very perceptive, and if they see that you know what you're talking about, they will show you that respect. But they give short shrift to someone who speaks but doesn't know what she's speaking about. Once you give them respect, because they *are* talented musicians who are capable of doing fantastic things, you will have no problems. I've never had a problem in terms of discipline in the Pan world.

A Bright Future for Graduates

There's a growing Pan culture in the U.S. Gerard, one of our first graduates, worked for a year at Mast Academy, a high school in Miami. It's a magnet high school geared specifically for those who are interested in science. Their music program is shaped totally around the pan. Instead of having the normal orchestras and so on, they have their steel band for each of the classes. He was there last year. When they held the second youth steelband festival in Miami last year, they took part.

With Gillian Daniel of Miami-Dade Cultural Affairs Council, we started a program from some workshops I did. From that, they've started Steelband programs in a few of the schools in Miami. Gerard has been doing that and teaching. Kyle has been performing. He wants to get into music scoring for the movie industry, incorporating the pan. So, he's working on that. Kenrick is waiting to hear from NIU, where he wants to pursue his master's. So, the graduates are all doing something productive.

I get calls all the time from people all over because more schools are trying to get pans into their schools. They've come to realize more that this is an instrument that works well with people of all cultures in terms of improvement in memorization skills and motor skills. Pan has worked extremely well in these areas. This is why a number of schools are now incorporating it into their music programs. So, I'm getting more offers for students than I have student graduating. And, this is the primary reason I started the FMC program. I realized a number of opportunities were going to non-Trinidadians only because many of our nationals did not have the degree.

Looking beyond Trinidad, I've now started a program in Antigua, because Antigua was one of the early proponents of the pan in the early 1950s. I'm working with one of the steel bands there, one of the oldest steel bands in town called the Harmonites, to develop their musicianship. So many young people are involved in the pan that they need the formal education. It's one thing to have the talent; however, access to opportunities is much greater if you are qualified. And, I don't apologize for focusing on people of the Caribbean: Trinidadians, Antiguans, Bahamians, and so on. Right now here in Miami, I have a number of people from all over the world who are very interested in FMC. However, my focus on the Caribbean, especially Trinidadians, is because pursuing studies in the States is very expensive. The only way prospective students can do this is through scholarships. I keep in charge of scholarships for the Music department here at FMC. I circumvent the question of discrimination by reiterating that FMC is a historically Black college whose targeted student is Black and African American. The fact that we have a pool of talented applicants who just happen to be Trinidadians then doesn't make what I'm doing an issue.

There haven't exactly been many African Americans in our music program, which I hope will change. When I first came here, the institution didn't have very much knowledge about Pan. There was the African American tradition, as well as Gospel and Jazz focuses. Now, the school understands and supports the program, even though the African American membership of the band can be stronger. Those members who are interested, even though they know Pan is of Trinidadian parentage, are focusing on Jazz and I think see the connection. The battle that has been fought and won is the realization that the soul of the music is theirs, the soul of the music in Jazz and so forth all basically comes from the same place, that it was an outpouring that produced all the Black music art forms in the past and through today, everything. Now, small groups of steelpan are being used in everything from hip-hop shows to other things around campus, which I support and the school supports.

My dream for Pan is to see concertos written for the instruments, for which actually there are already a few. I take the position that pan has its own distinct sounds with its own nuances. I can see steel orchestras forming their own literature, creating a niche similar to that of the symphony orchestras, where music is written for the steel orchestras and then you incorporate other conventional instruments with the steel orchestra, so that it stands on its own. We're getting into the mainstream in that you hear it more in advertisements and the stigma of it being a "Yellow Bird" instrument is slowly being removed. That's one thing I like, and I think that it's moving in the right direction.

In terms of education, I can see it being integrated into the school system with increasing frequency all over the world. It's in South Africa in some of the schools; it's extensive throughout England; in Switzerland there are over 140 steel bands. It's moving rapidly into mainstream U.S. culture. However, in terms of the body of literature for the instrument, I'd like to see a whole lot more written for it and about it, which will happen. It's only a matter of time. Currently, here in the United States, you can purchase a beginner's book for the individual sections of pan, which we're continuing to work on. In terms of research and development, people are working in that, even though I don't think we'll see any major changes to the instrument itself. Maybe, there'll be changes perhaps in the way it's manufactured. We have those people in Massachusetts who've been working on that. Other people internationally are working on R&D on the instrument, and I think it's all toward manufacturing it on a large scale, because right now the demand is greater than the supply. I can see people working on that, which is a market question. And, when it comes down to the market, when the demand outweighs the supply then you're in a very good industry.

In regard to the economics of Pan, while working on my dissertation I found that I could develop a plan for the use of the panyard as an entire economic system. Because panyards all over Trinidad and Tobago are in the communities, you already have the infra-structure there. As a part of the community, there are people with varying skills who form this economic base: people with computer skills, literacy skills, welding skills, a slew of skills that form the basis for manufacturing and production. From these skills as a starting place, Pan plants can be established all over the country as effective inroads and means of empowering the people economically.

The product is the instrument; the product is the music; the product is the players. These ideas, this argument shaped my dissertation, which is not published. I'm thinking of revising it for publication but haven't got around to it yet. I'm so caught up in what I'm doing right now that I don't think I'll ever have the time to revise and edit it for publication. I see all these vibrant young people who are going to be very successful, because of their exposure to education as well as their involvement in Pan at a very intense level, and they are more important to me than publishing. The future of the instrument looks very promising. Some very progressive young people are coming up, so I can say Pan is not in danger. We, in academia, have much work to do, much collaboration. I'm just excited and loving where I am and what I'm doing. Can you tell?

21

We Can Move Forward as a Literate People: Lennard V. Moses's Story[1]

Lennard V. Moses is an Associate Professor of Ethnomusicology at Central State University and a graduate of Northern Illinois University (NIU). His perspective on orality versus literacy and the role that Pan and Calypso take in the world's panoply of cultures is provocative and engaging. Moses's voice resonates with all the narrators, as well as Derek Walcott's essay, "What the Twilight Says: An Overture": "Stamped on that image is the old colonial grimace of the laughing nigger, steelbandsman, carnival masker, calypsonian and limbo dancer" who "are trapped in the State's concept of the folk form ..." (7).[2]

Pan as a Confluence of Traditional Arts

I was born and grew up in Laventille Hill, about a mile or less from Desperadoes band. It was an incredible experience in that when I went to bed at night, I would hear the men practicing, which went on throughout the night. As a little boy, I used to play around with a little pan at home, and later learned that one of my brothers, Lance, had a little steel band. His nickname was Farmer Brown and he was my protector of sorts. My parents had sixteen children, of which I'm the baby.

I joined Desperadoes officially around 1971 to play percussion and played miscellaneous percussion: cowbell; scratchers; officially, the congas; and eventually, the drum-set, the main percussion. Unofficially, I used to play around the panyard on the tenor, double seconds, double tenor, cello, and bass, eventually. Rudolph Charles, the captain for my first Panorama, was one of the first ones to recognize my abilities and gave permission for me to join the band. I was only fourteen when I went on tour with Desperadoes in '72 to London, England, and performed at the Royal Albert Hall. I was also a member of the Frank Clark Kids Steel Band and went back and forth between Despers and the Frank Clark Kids for about three to four years, I think. Those days seemed like forever. I was a member of the Frank Clark Kids band when it recorded its first album. Radio Trinidad should have a copy in its archives. I know it's listed among the discography of steelband music of Trinidad, which I was happy to see once when I was looking through it. At the same time I was in two steel bands, I also used to play drums in the Best Village competition and used to practice in the community center with six other young fellas. We all went off in separate directions as young adults. That's how I grew up basically.

The incident that caused me to set my sight on the United States is this. When I was in Miami, Florida, after a performance, an old woman asked me if I could read music and I said no. She planted a seed that became a driving force for me. After returning from tour, I decided I wanted to learn to read music. At that time, nobody was reading because we came out of the oral tradition, but I wanted to learn to read and write. I was seventeen when I left Trinidad in 1975 and came to Miami, Florida, where I lived before moving to Philadelphia, Pennsylvania. I never finished high school in Trinidad because of all the traveling with the bands. I finished high school in Philadelphia in one year. I was always interested in learning, but not particularly interested in school itself. The vice president of that high school in Philadelphia is an alumnus of Central State University (CSU), where I'm teaching at now. He heard me playing music on different instruments and approached me to talk about my plans for college and university. At the time, I didn't know you could get a degree in music. When he mentioned that, I thought he was joking. That conversation led me to think about a college career and I applied and got into CSU. I completed a Bachelor of Science in Music Education. It was a tough transition because I was no scholar in Trinidad and had to adjust to this rigorous program here. In Trinidad, I was more interested in music than in school but learned a lot of my music in the streets.

At CSU, I performed with different groups, not all pan groups. I was in a concert band, a Jazz band, and a marching band. When I was finished there, I went to NIU for my master's and received a graduate assistantship to teach there. They had begun a new program that focused on world music. So, while I was a graduate assistant pursuing Western Percussion Studies I was teaching Steelband, African Ensemble, and Latin American Music. I wrote and published a composition for the band named *Kaiso*. When I say published, I mean it was recorded by NIU's Music department. I've published some soloist pieces for Pan in an attempt to include the pan in the music repertoire. The only way to be included in the literary tradition and move away from the oral tradition is to publish. So, I've published two pieces for the tenor pan, as well as a book called *Fundamentals of Calypso Drumming*, which includes a tape and an annotated bibliography on the history of the music of Trinidad. That article was published by the Percussive Arts Society, and I'm now working on some other stuff, since this desktop business makes self-publishing easier.

Also, while I was in grad school, I was offered the opportunity to return to CSU and establish a Percussion department. So, at the end of my tenure at NIU I returned and established a program here. We also have a steel band here as part of the Percussion and World Music programs. From that time, that's what I've been doing, along with being a guest artist at different universities, presenting the history, the culture of music from Africa and the African diaspora. Of course, I teach western musical instruments, the fusion between both cultures and their instruments. I also teach classes in Ethnomusicology, Global Music Appreciation, Music Theory, and all applied percussion lessons. Wilberforce University is another university I've been an adjunct at, as well as at Cedarville University. So, in all I've taught at Wilberforce, Cedarville, NIU, and of course CSU where I've been teaching for nineteen years this coming December.

When Oral and Literacy Traditions Collide

There's a firm here in Dayton, a Human Resources Development consulting firm, which I used to do some music workshops for. Those workshops focused on the strong, powerful oral tradition of Trinidad, which has both its advantages and disadvantages, as does the written tradition. I pointed out the differences between music interpretation in the oral tradition in contrast to academic music interpretation at the university. Here, you have to deal with cognition, and how people hear things and understand the art. In contrast, the things that people do naturally don't cause them stop to think about in a scientific way. So basically, I drew attention to the differences and started with pointing out that all cultures, even those today that are grounded in the literary tradition, began in orality. When it came to western art, non-western music in particular, the music of Trinidad's subculture, as they have called it and some still do, aural learning was the more dominant force and grew out of an oral tradition, which is a different kind of learning style from the written tradition. Basically, I wanted to utilize both traditions.

In the oral tradition, the written word is not essential. What is essential is the understanding of whatever it is that is taking place. Basically, you learn by listening, observing, imitating, and participating. There's no actual visual reading of anything that is happening. When you relocate someone from that environment to one where he has to receive information primarily through the eyes and read and interpret, that is a different type of learning process taking place. That type of learning is dealing with cerebral comprehension that does not incorporate movement or attitude or disposition of individuals. It's learning reduced to a type of mathematical approach: one plus one is two, which is a more static approach.

The other type is more holistic. You're learning with your whole being. Your mind, ear, and eyes. The eyes process information faster but the ears remember it longer. Your eyes grasp quicker but ears remember for a longer time. That's why some of those guys could have played entire symphonic works entirely by ear and people were, and still are, absolutely amazed. That entire aural culture facilitated a keen memory. The number of times they rehearsed by ear the different parts of that symphony made the music a part of them. If you process that music with only the eyes, the music does not have to become a part of you because you are merely looking at it and reading it off a page to play it. That is why the music literally sounds different.

If you listen to someone who reads play versus one who walks up and plays from memory, like Boogsie Sharp, you hear something different. A lot of people have been trying to figure out what that element of difference is. The ethnomusicologist has come up with the terms used by the person who plays from the inside-out and the outside-in; meaning, one who performs within a particular music culture as opposed to someone who comes from the outside and tries to learn that music culture through written notation.

One of the ideas associated with this is the looking down upon the oral tradition, in a sense. If you notice that in the western culture the written text is exalted. One can possess tremendous information and knowledge, but if it is not written down somewhere no one takes it seriously. This attitude has prevailed for who knows how long. With the entire Pan culture coming from this oral tradition, at first no one really took it seriously until people began to recognize that the guys were playing music exquisitely. They further began to recognize the extent of science, math, and all sorts of technology involved in the creation of this instrument. But because these men weren't writing books and publishing them, people weren't really taking seriously what they were doing. The irony of the way this thing developed and stands today is that you cannot write a book about it unless you've plucked the information from the oral culture first, like you're doing. The whole process of pan creation began within an oral culture, which western culture disregards. For instance, when is one considered educated? After one has earned a degree. The problem with this is: prior to the degree one knew so much, like panmen such as Cliff [Alexis].

Cliff lectured on Acoustics at the Convention of Metallurgy and Acoustical Engineering. Cliff is a panman who discovered some things after working forty-something years with a hammer about sounds and the dimensions of tone that he couldn't have discovered by reading about them in a library. The challenge is now to bring academia to recognize that the oral tradition is not to be despised. A lot of what people end up studying began in orality and they need to have regard for this origin. Arrogance in academia lends to the forgetting that the origins of what is now considered authoritative did not begin with someone who was considered educated, according to academic standards. Right? There needs to be humility in the way the academics deal with themselves in relation to the entire Pan culture. So many panmen have no idea how to converse on the academic level because they're not of that world. I'm here by the grace of God and now can speak from both ends of the spectrum of both worlds.

Understand that I am not taking a position of oral versus written tradition. I'm talking about avoiding the extremes because within both traditions are limitations. For instance, in the oral tradition even though you learn a piece of music very well aurally and it may take a longer time, beyond that culture that music is very hard to export because it cannot be massed produced. Put that music to score and it can. So, the written obviously has its place, which is not to be discounted. But it's the attitude I'm addressing here, one that says one is superior to the other. My approach to teaching is to start at a place with my students without the use of any written music. My focus in that is teaching them to hear because the music begins with the ear first. So, I begin with training them how to hear, to listen, which is hard for students who are used to taking notes and reading. They want to write everything down. Get straight to that printed text. They're so afraid they'll forget what they've heard, which is in sharp contrast to what the oral tradition does in literally developing memory. You *have* to remember whether you go on tour with the steel band or go to a performance at the Music Festival. You have to do it all by memory, because you cannot go there and pull out a piece of music and read.

Many times, people argue and discuss toward justifying the validity of the literary document. This whole oral/written tradition has been an issue with scholars for a long time. Interestingly, the scholars I've read who've published on this matter have not come out of an oral tradition themselves. They've merely written about something that was an issue to get a perspective on it without having experiencing it for themselves. In my case, I just wanted to learn to read music and wasn't at all interested in all the other superfluous learning that came along with the degree. Nevertheless, it was a good opportunity to learn about all those things, which in the end was useful. Now, I can see how the entire culture was already an interdisciplinary one. The pan-player was usually the builder, tuner, arranger, the one who did everything, like Cliff. He writes, arranges, tunes, builds, and everything concerning Pan, *except* to sit down with a pencil and write about Pan. Someone from the outside would look at him or the older panmen and says he needs someone with whatever. Fortunately, people have recognized the value of a man like Cliff, which is why he's at NIU. He is a wealth of knowledge even though he wouldn't sit down and write what he knows for someone else.

Another example is Austin Wallace. He is one of the most profound pan-tuners. He lives in New York. I traveled with him to London. The knowledge he has is amazing, but he, like the other panmen, had no need to make this knowledge applicable to anyone outside the culture. He never saw the need to develop a written pasture for his work. Why should he? He lived in a world where everyone understood intimately what he meant: so what was the need for him to communicate outside that world? It's when someone wants to take it from that level to another, then writing becomes an issue. The men themselves had no need for books, and since people did things based upon needs, the men lived outside that necessity for writing. I tell you, all of us in the steel band understood each other. We didn't need a book on strumming when we understood and knew all about that. So, these men laugh when they hear someone has written a book about strumming. Who needs a book about that? They want to know. It's almost comical to them, especially when you then try to introduce that book into their community. They think you're plain crazy!

Books also go contra to a community seeped in an entire oral culture that teaches based on proverbs. For example, "If you have one eye, don't play in the sand." That proverb carries enormous implications. Sometimes, an entire lesson is conveyed in two words. Someone from the outside looking in would wonder about the significance of proverbs or just those two words. So, when you ask someone coming from this strong oral culture to write, he must have some problems. If you ask a panman to write about the pan, he's so accustomed to speaking in terms of metaphors and these proverbs, he'll give you a metaphor or proverb and expect to understand what he means.

Here's an example. If you wanted him to describe the movements in the steel band, the rhythms of the band, he might take you all the way down to Carenage to a river there that flows out into the sea and describe a boat with three men sailing down the river into the sea. He might tell you to listen to that rhythm of the water and notice that it's not the men moving the boat but the water itself, the rhythm of the water, the flow of the water. From that picturesque description, he would expect you to grasp an image of the steel band, and from that image make the connection to how rhythm carries momentum and how you ride on that momentum. He would speak in these metaphors and symbolism and a lot of other figurative language to describe things. When you walk into the panyard, you'll find no one there using written notations or giving instructions such as change from B to B-flat. Instead, you would find them using figurative language. My audience generally responds positively to these explanations because they can also understand these concepts. Very interestingly, these are people who grew up in the literary tradition—there may be one or two Trinidadians in the audience sometimes—who can relate to what I'm saying.

In Trinidad, the crowd at the Calypso tent laughs as much as they do because they understand that oral tradition of metaphors and shades of meaning behind the lyrics of the calypso. Even the educated enjoy the calypso because of this. I use a similar point of reference to make my own points when I'm speaking to a less academically-inclined audience. But when I'm speaking to an academic audience, I use terms that more quickly convey the same points, and they too can relate to this approach to communication.

I integrate all this into lectures, classes—all my teaching. I don't see any fragmentation in any of this. To put this another way, when I'm teaching World Music or an Ethnomusicology course or I'm directing the two ensembles—the steel band and the percussion—or dealing with a private student, I still use that same approach to convey the idea. I'm not using a different methodology. I've simply changed my language that still addresses everything. I see it not as teaching music but as teaching the student who is learning the music. My focus is on the student rather than the music. So many times we teach a subject when we should be teaching the person, who when she learns will then practice the subject. This is why we emphasize the panwoman because the pan in itself is nothing. The information must be in and coming from the panwoman who will do the rest.

I find that in the written tradition, the subject is separate from the person who then tries to study the subject as this abstract thing—a separate entity—and then look for ways to apply it. I'm arguing here for internalizing learning, which is fundamentally how everyone learns, not the other way around. People cannot express meaningfully something with any level of conviction unless it has become a part of them. That is why when you listen to some pan-players you can hear something that is coming from the inside of them. You can hear they really know what they're playing. So, even though a technique is involved in the playing, the initial approach is not in the technique. These guys go straight to the actual music with their objective being mastering that music.

Take language, for example, and the little child. We don't teach that child technique; we simply talk to that child who absorbs so much before we realize it. Then, we progress to proper English, the books, the techniques. I use the word "proper" deliberately to suggest that there's this notion of the improper. Now, that child would have been understanding speech all along, which made perfect sense to him. Based on the terminologies we use, we have in place ideas of what is superior and inferior in approaches. So, when we try to get a panman to explain the pan he might start off talking, "Well, yuh know actually, boy, de way we useta play," and the people might look at him and say, "You know, he just cannot articulate the art," not recognizing that *is* the art. He is expressing himself according to the confines of the art and the culture that gave shape *to* the art, which has nothing to do with proper language or superior approaches, according to academic standards.

So many times people go in with such preconceived notions and prejudices that the panman instantly recognizes the attitude and shuts up. He says, "So, yuh wan' me tuh talk about de pan de way *you* talk? I *kyar* do dat." Do you see what I mean? He gets vexed and walks away. In order for us to understand the panman, we have to become like him and not try to get him to become like us. If I try to make him become like me, what is the point? I'm trying to understand him and his art and world. So, if you go in with your prejudices, you are already resistant to what he has to say and you don't really get to know what he knows. This is what people also don't realize. In trying to make the panman into what he's not and what's he not even interested in becoming, they are losing a whole lot. What he knows is not in any book: so why try to make him read a book that he's not interested in? The book is not his art or how he conceptualizes or thinks about what he's doing. He laughs at you when you come telling him to read some book, or he gets really vex.

However, today's pannist has more responsibility. He needs to know the music, the cultural history, an interdisciplinary approach, as well as the economic reality of the art. For instance, at NIU there are students who major in Pan. A very exciting idea. But here's one of the challenges about that. Yes, they're majoring in Pan. But after they get a degree in Pan, where do they get jobs? Where do they go from there? For instance, if while at NIU my specialty was violin or trombone, when finished I would have a Music Education degree and could go into the public school and teach. The disadvantage of having a degree in Pan is there is: no institution established to accommodate the person with this particular training when he's finished. This is why when I went to school I entered as a percussionist. So, upon graduating I was qualified to teach in any public school in America and the Caribbean. Right now, what is the value of a degree in Pan? I think students ought to major in Percussion with an emphasis in Pan. In that way, your Music Education degree allows you to still do all the percussions: the snare drum and other instruments. But with where Pan is at the moment, we don't have a place for graduates. I'm talking about the reality of my own work and what happened with me. I didn't realize I was setting the pattern for other students.

Today's panman is coming out of a legacy of not just Pan but a culture that has developed from, of, and beyond Pan. He is moving into a whole new environment with its particular demands. When teaching Pan today, we still have to recognize this oral tradition from which Pan emerged, and use both the oral *and* written traditions. Also, today's pannists need to understand the cultural history of the pan. They have to learn not just music but more than music, and those teaching have to do the same. They have to teach Caribbean music history along with the pan. For instance, if you're teaching western music history, then you're talking about a literary course. With the pan, you have to teach it within the context of an historical perspective. If you're studying the violin, you end up studying Paganini, Strauss, and Vivaldi—the cultural icons of the violin. You bring the pan into studies within its cultural context, too, and deal with its history. So, we absolutely need the biographies of these men who gave birth to this instrument. And, this is another reason I'm excited about what you're doing. We need to study how this thing developed, how its performing practices changed, the role that culture played in these developments, and all that knowledge. So, that the pannist today receives knowledge about Pan similarly to the violinist student in a university today studying the violin. Today's pannist needs to have that background in terms of what they're doing.

Pan, Spirituality, the Politics of Economy, and the Community

If you look back as the panman's response to people trying to make him into what he's not, you'll find that his response goes all the way back to the bible. What did Christ do? He came and became like man, like us, *first*. In contrast, look at the missionary pattern. The missionaries went to places and tried to make the people become like them instead of becoming like the people first. That is man's way. He goes in with the attitude of making other people become like him, and when they do then those people have risen to whatever level, whether intellect or what. That misses the whole point of getting to know where the other man is coming from. I see that this attitude comes from either naïveté or disrespect or lack of understanding or plain lack of recognition of the other person. Everyone responds positively when someone takes the time to understand him. So, when this outsider tries to talk with the panmen, they turn away from him as someone who doesn't know what he's talking about. Ironically, they turn toward someone with better book sense, someone who understands this biblical principle of becoming like the person you're trying to understand. The panmen see through all the social biases of the outsider and dismiss him.

What's interesting about Pan is that many pan-people didn't think of their art and work in economic terms because everything was so spiritually oriented. For them to appropriate economics to their art was a somewhat unnatural thought. Now, from the European perspective, the first thing they think about is how to make money from something. These are two very powerful differences in world view regarding perspectives on art and music. These ideas, these sorts of things have seeped into the Pan world, negatively affecting those guys in Trinidad who didn't think about money in terms of what they were doing. Some of them today still don't. The older men just wanted to play pan, and the music became a social and philosophical mode of expression, carrying some deep undertones along with major disagreements on the way things were done. All these thoughts I try to incorporate in my lectures and presentations so that people can see the line that has been established from West Africa and what is considered the New World in terms of music.

Regarding the philosophical approach that the individual took is how this philosophy is linked back to West Africa, as I understand it. People didn't use to think in terms of the individual so much but more in terms of the whole. Their idea was the whole thing. The idea of virtuosity and the separation of people didn't basically exist in their concept. Their focus was on the group and group activity, hence, the now popular saying that has caught on here about it takes a village to raise a child. The people did everything together for the people. Western European influence brought the recognition of the individual. From then on, you had those two extreme ideas, which in turn were taken to their own limits. You had the individual who felt he didn't need the community, or you had the individual so stifled by the community that individuality was totally suppressed.

This is not to ignore that among some Trinidadians a type of secrecy surrounded the pan, which is antithetical to this communal vision I'm talking about. One of the things that has happened is this whole idea of the secrecy was based upon the new tradition that was beginning to flourish. How does a guy maintain his position, his uniqueness within that new community? Because, they were still human beings with this need for recognition, if a man knew something that others did not, he then became something special to that community, like Rudolph Charles was to Laventille. He became an important figure in the community and the community rallied around him because the community had something to gain, too. In terms of Rudolph Charles, he and they believed that he had and knew something others did not. He had more social clout and he may have known how to speak with others outside the confines of the culture to bridge the gap between the sponsor and the band. He could communicate with both the Trinidad élite and the man in the street and bridge the gap between the two. He could talk and do business at the same time. He became a good representative for and of the community.

I think another aspect of the secrecy had to do with the Bomb competition. The guys practiced at three o'clock in the morning with their fingers to keep secret the new Bomb tune, which was part of that tradition. Everybody kept secret what his band was doing, and if someone else came hanging around to see what he could find out, he was chased away immediately. It was almost like a musical warfare. This was in part to protect the community. So that when Desperadoes came out with "Canon in D" (I think it was "Canon in D"), they had this element of surprise and they dropped their bomb. In addition to that, among the men themselves were internal rivalries. Like in any culture or society, these rivalries were based on people who wanted to establish a position someone else already had or someone trying to hold on to his position. The younger men were coming in with their new ideas and created tension among the older men who saw the younger ones as threats. The older guys had the secret technology of the early days of Pan while the younger guys were more experimental and revolutionary. In retrospect, I think it all boiled down to the issue of respect.

A lot of people who were in the Pan culture, their own society, did not respect the panmen. That became its own tradition, too. So, having found something that the society recognized, the men were not about to give that up because they were beginning to be considered as socially acceptable. This was one of the fallacies of what happened in Trinidad. You know that the panmen were historically considered at the lowest level of the social stratum. Even men like Ellie Mannette society didn't expect anything from. Society had no expectations of these people. They were considered illiterate because they weren't going to school and were considered backward and wayward—all stigmas. Ironically, it was from this subculture that most of the richness of what is now Trinidad culture came.

After colonialism and all that it bred, the colonizers having educated the people they wanted to educate, the educated people took on the attitude of the colonizers toward their own people. Suddenly, we had Trinidadians who were looking down on panmen until they became socially acceptable, which meant when they could put on a suit and play Mozart. When the men began doing these things, they began to gain respectability for and through what they did. By that time, they weren't about give that up suit of respectability, even if that meant not divulging the secrets that helped them earn this respectability. It was a sociopolitical move that was taking place at that particular time in Trinidad's history.

All these issues inform on the attitudes of the older steelbandsmen to help us understand what they were battling against. Their main battle was against *the* society, which any born and bred Trinidadian knows as fact. You couldn't go home and say you were marrying a panman. Home would say, "What?!" That whole social culture and mentality kept the men on the fringes of society. Now, pan has emerged as this powerful instrument of the twentieth century and the mentality of the élite is a readiness to embrace it as our thing. This understandably vexes the panmen who suddenly find that they're okay now. I don't know the whole nature of what happened with Ellie, but I can tell when you meet the older panmen they still carry those things within them. They remember how they were treated. That's one of the challenges we all must face.

Pan is now in universities with people like me teaching and lecturing about it, and in many cases panmen are no longer standing on the sidelines. They are now a fundamental part of the society. Some mentality still has to change to catch up with that because not everyone in Trinidad is all-embracing of Pan as the national culture. That aside, the panmen still remember all they suffered while living to see what Pan has become. So, people have to understand that panmen were eventually accepted not just because they were people, but because they had to *prove* themselves worthy of acceptance and acceptable. Pan music was their means of gaining acceptability.

Lecturing on the Culture of Pan and Calypso

I've generally been well received, both at past workshops and now as a lecturer. Many people a lot of times are fascinated by what I'm saying. They're very interested and many of them agree because of the practicality of the argument. They find that a lot of learning is taking place right there among the audience because I'm not teaching from a purely academic perspective but from what I call in a proverbial way, similar to the example I used before.

My work now involves an interdisciplinary approach, you see. There's the music, the culture, the history, and the pedagogy that tie it all together. One of the things that has happened, when examining cultures still tied to an oral tradition, is how in the past people entered the culture and simply transcribed a piece of music without regard for the social fabric in which that music is produced. So, much of my work is on teaching the history, the music, the people, and their culture, and what that piece of music means to the people within the context of that particular culture. It's not then just music, for a lot of the music that has emerged from the African diaspora is more than music. It's music *and* drama *and* art, not as fragmented as one is led to believe, but all intertwined into the social fabric of the people's culture.

That social culture is linked to a strong sense of community, which I was talking about before. People who have never played a pan in their lives cannot understand what it meant to be a member of Desperadoes. One was a member of Despers not just for the music but for the association, for the fabric of what held the band together. The one pushing the pan or carrying the flag was just as loyal as the one playing the pan. Everyone identified himself as being a member of Desperadoes—pan-pusher, pan-player, or flag-waver. That came about from the sense of the origin of community.

You see, the steel band was not just established as a steel band but as a representation of an entire community, as suggested before. So, when you looked at a steel band, you were seeing an entire community's participation taking place, which was a very powerful force. Remember also, a lot of music coming out of Africa and of African origin is based on the concept of communal activity. That's why we have Desperadoes, Renegades, Tokyo, and Casablanca all designating not just a band but their entire communities, and all the praises and curses that came with that association. Steelband involvement was a communal activity. This is why I cannot separate the history from the music and must demonstrate both in my workshops. A large part of that history is rooted in West African drumming that survived the Atlantic slave trade and regurgitated in the Caribbean through the various instruments.

In my lectures, I also link drumming to the instruments played by the Caribs and Arawaks who were there on the island before the Africans arrived and demonstrate that. I use the conch shell and the four-hole flute. From that, I proceed to the instruments used in the Parang festivals—I used to play the quatro in Parang, which came out of the Spanish tradition. I demonstrate that, too. (I also once played tabla drums for an Indian dancer at the Penthouse in Trinidad and demonstrated that as well. Back then, when doing all those things I had no idea I was already an ethnomusicologist. I was just doing something I liked.) I then show how the tamboo-bamboo was simultaneously emerging along side some of these instruments, and how tamboo-bamboo gave way to the pan.

There's no question that Pan of itself is an Afro-Trinidadian creation, which takes into consideration that that culture was of Africans in the first place. The musical conceptions brought to this new instrument were African-inspired, and if you take the pan back into its historical significance you'll find it has its root in that rhythmic culture. It began as a rhythmic instrument that then became one able to produce a melody. A melodic instrument with rhythm, if you see what I'm saying. In terms of Black art, rhythm is the driving force. So, Pan evolved not so much as a point of convergence—the meeting of the African, Spanish, and Native Caribbean arts—but of synthesis, a synchronization of sorts. It's a new genre that developed out of the fusion of all that took place. You cannot then just analyze the music in terms of its past but also in terms of something that was being newly established, and this not out of any pure race or pure culture toward any pure musical form. The form, the pan itself, is already considered by scholars as the newest instrument in the history of world music. A revolutionary type of thing. A hybrid thing.

During my lectures, I also try to keep in focus how Africa and the New World have suffered from what I call scholastic crimes. People have written things about Africa, the Caribbean, and the Black culture that were not at all truth but, nonetheless, were accepted in the academic community and taught for a long time. I'm referring as an example to the terminologies that were used for descriptions. Any thing that was not European or western European was not good or savage or backward, and on and on. When you read the bodies of literature describing things African, you'll find words used, not in any vindictive sort of way but out of ignorance. The writers themselves didn't have any sort of grasp of what was really taking place among those of the so-called subcultures. So, you find that some scholars have erroneously stated that nothing that came from Africa remained. They thought everything was wiped out by the slave trade. After Emancipation, they then realized that the culture survived in the people's mind and was given a rebirth in ways that people could see, such as movement and dance and what was especially wrapped up in language. So, much of the music was linguistically controlled. Within the language, the rhythm, and these expressions is the idea of the art. I'm getting here at the calypso and the steel band and how they're linked.

The calypso has its origin in West African extemporaneity. The sort of improvisatory, satiric approach of the songs that was the people's ways of conveying ideas and subtle messages to their neighbors. The calypso came out of the chant world tradition. The chant world was when the people sang while burning the cane and other such activities. All those ideas, when you look at them, shaped and produced the calypso singer we have today and are heavily African-oriented in terms of the manner of musical expression. A lot of it is in the cosmology, too, the way the people perceived the world and saw things. Much of African tradition and culture is deeply spiritually rooted.

I've spent years dwelling on these thoughts and welcome this opportunity to share them. We've underestimated arrogance, that looking down mentality, and the effects of this attitude. We haven't given enough thought to how those of us who've received formal education come across to the very people who own knowledge and information we want. We are going to them because they have something we don't. The first thing we must realize is we don't have their experiences. In my case, I have some of that experience. I was raised in it and able now to offer this insider-outsider view. So, when I'm doing the workshops, I can laugh from both sides, and some audience members do, too.

I can be of the perspective of the panman who sees an academic coming and understand her intellectual world in which it is important to have a theory, develop the thesis, argue the points of that thesis, articulate, and all of that. However, the academic trying to communicate in the world of the panman must understand that he is a practitioner. The practitioner has a low tolerance for theory. His response is, "I doin' it a'ready. Wha' you doin'?" So, in my workshop I try to balance this practitioner approach with the theoretical toward unification. I try to give validity to theory but not to the extreme that it poses a disadvantageous threat to the practice. This is why I use the lecture-demonstration approach, with the one complementing the other. Far be it from me to write a book like that guy who wrote a best-seller on children, only for the public to learn he never had a child. Because I'm into perspectives, into how people look at things and hear things, which is so often different from my own, I keep focus on these differences.

The panman's world is a different one. It's a world born out of colonial repression and a constant struggle for things that were granted freely to everyone else, namely, respect. For the panmen, their thing wasn't, "Give us more money." It was, "We're a part of this society and you're saying we're not." We as panmen simply tried to demonstrate that we were part of society.

I see a similar thing happened at first with the Jazz musician. If you go back and look at all the older Jazz musicians, you'll see them performing in suits. They looked to command respect by bringing respect to the art and so be a part of the cultural fabric. So, we have these sociocultural aspects that were taking place, and music became a force, a weapon of sorts, that could be used to resist the oppressor who couldn't perform in this cultural arena. The oppressor couldn't perform the art or take it away. But then, we see a type of exploitation that began to flourish around the art, too. Exploitation left and right took place in the early days. Not too long though, the men began waking up and saying, "Wait a minute." Similarly, I was exploited in my own work.

A guy came to Trinidad, before the band went on tour, with a big video camera. It was the first time I'd seen such a big camera. He was taking all these shots of me playing under a donce tree. I suppose now that it was a great shot of me, a little fella playing pan under this donce tree. Years later, when I was in Miami, Florida, and having some breakfast, I looked at the TV and saw this BOAC advertisement, four nights-five days and so on, and there a shot of me was playing across the screen. The man sold the footage. I was so surprised. Of course, back then I knew nothing of what I know now. I didn't know or understand the business and ethics like I do now—the legal implications and ramifications of what was done to us. So, in addition to what I was saying before, I see there must be an integrity and honesty of the people who come in from the outside to try to learn about this experience, even when such applies to me. I will tell you that this is another reason I'm very excited about what you're doing.

I think there's a mood for this work and the story needs to be told in writing, because the story has already been told orally. But in so doing, these insights need to be recognized when talking about Pan and the Pan culture. Of course, the people themselves are not without fault. The panmen, sometimes their behavior and conduct were based on their choice. True, conditions can be forced upon you but you choose how to respond. Even so, we still ought to see the balance in this, too. If someone has to work hard to gain what is already a given, a natural for the rest of society, if I have to gain respect, why should that be? I am already a human being.

I can recall that people from Laventille couldn't say they were from Laventille or else they wouldn't get a job downtown. You could say you were from San Fernando or Arima, which sounded good. When I tell people where I'm from, they're absolutely surprised. A Laventille boy teaching at a university?! It floors them! When I encounter that response, it tells me what the expectations of people still are. That response is coming from those who expect nothing good to come from Laventille people. I believe that is why Trinidad is still not investing politically and economically in places such as Laventille. Ironically, some of the greatest cultural contributions to the country, and now the world, have come from these places for which there were and still are low or no expectations.

Toward the Institutionalization of Pan

The instrument has already been institutionalized as a percussion one. The first TASPO group was under the auspices of the percussion, which is why they were called the Trinidad All Steel *Percussion* Orchestra, my emphasis on "Percussion." I can say to those who claim that pan is more than just a percussion instrument that they need to look at history for their contribution, their experiences in Pan to really know what they're arguing about. I can not but wonder whether they are so arguing from merely a theoretical perspective. When someone makes an argument, the first thing I want is for it to be validated by their own experiential knowledge. The things I've shared here are what I've dealt with, what I've done. I've gone through the educational system in this fashion. Toward the end of my training, I was offered the opportunity to come into the university as a Percussionist instructor not as a Pan instructor, and pan is a percussion instrument, the percussion being the largest area of musical instruments.

The percussion family includes pitch and non-pitch instruments. The pan is an idiophone because it vibrates within itself. It is within the percussion family. The point is: every steelband-player, every pannist is a percussionist and people ought to market themselves as a percussionist who specializes in Pan. We can look at it from another perspective.

I went to Akron University and was approached by a student who was majoring in Percussion, earning a BM in Music Education degree with an emphasis in Percussions. All the degrees are set up like that. One can earn a BM degree with an emphasis on the trumpet or French horn or clarinet, and so on. Here I am, now to teach him something in the percussion family that's not included in the traditional percussion program. I teach him the congas and the pan, as percussion instruments, because the only way you can take a pan into the university is through the Percussion program. The schools of America do not recognize the pan as anything other than a percussion instrument. However, this is a total percussion instrument in that it carries with it melodic and harmonic properties as well as rhythmic properties, somewhat like a piano.

This brings us to the issue of how we define the instrument. In my opinion, the question on whether the time will ever come for us to define the instrument—regardless of what American or world culture says, whether or not for anyone's own economic purposes—is irrelevant to Pan's history. Number one, western definitions will not negate the fact that this instrument emerged from the Afro-Trinidadian tradition long before any label was attached to it. We're looking basically at an instrument that did not need someone to come by and say,

"Okay, this is what it is." It's an instrument of itself and carries its own weight and validity. The fact that you pose the argument *vis à vis* a Western imposition upon this instrument already implicates your level of Western education, your ability to engage theory and discourse.[3]

For example, one must see the broad family of percussions, which includes the piano and its similarities to the pan. The piano is a string instrument that you have to strike, also. If you look at the Greek root of the word, it means to strike. We're talking about objects that we strike and produce a sound. When you look at these root definitions and the terminology, apart from all cultural impositions, we cannot ignore that we have to strike the pan. There's a whole category of instruments world wide—besides wind, brass, and percussion—that includes the idiophones and the membranophones, that points to Africa. Africa had so many instruments that musicologists had to come up with a broader categorization, which is useful for communication in the written tradition to convey sound.

I do not use the word "steel drum" when I speak. I use the word "pan." When I'm asked whether I play the steel drum, I answer I play pan. I teach my students that this is a steel band and pan is its instrument, and I emphasize that is the traditional term used by the people. I choose to maintain the traditional term. By implication, the drum means a non-tonal instrument that cannot play melody. Right? I see that the pan is a distinct member of the percussion family. What I'm dealing with is the membership of the instrument. It cannot be classified as a wind instrument or strings or brass. It fits well into the membership of the percussion family, which is my point. I think that will help anyone in terms of understanding how it fits into a program that is economically desirable.

Here in America in the Percussion Department, the pan will always be recognized as a percussion instrument. With that recognition, someone can attend college or university with an interest in Percussion and emphasis on Pan. His degree will be of similar value as anyone whose emphasis is in Jazz/drum-set. Of course, he will take other courses. If you isolate Pan without showing how it fits into the socioeconomic scheme of things, you make it difficult for people to make a living, until Pan is accepted nationally as its own separate degree. People already recognize the percussion, yes. I'm harping on the political reality of the situation.

Here's a good example. I was a guest artist at Ohio State University last quarter. When they called me in, I told them I was doing a djembe drum solo. The djemba drum is from Senegal. One of the reasons they called me in is: I was teaching Percussion, Non-western and World Percussion, and the hand-drumming culture, which I came out of, you see, and I can still read and interpret western musical notations. They needed me to do what I was doing while still following along with the written music. But there wasn't anything written for me. My entire section was totally improvisatory. They needed to know that when they needed me to follow the music, I was able to do that too. This came from my percussion education, not just the drum education.

I think one of the intense dissociation with the drum is that there was a law against drumming, not only in Trinidad but the entire western hemisphere. This goes all the way back to the days of slavery. The drummer had a stigma that sometimes disallowed people from associating with him and the drum. Coming out of West Africa, the drum was a sort of speech surrogate and used in the Haitian Revolution. When the imperial-colonial authorities recognized the people were using this instrument to communicate, which to me is a fascinating thing, they outlawed the drum. They couldn't understand this speech. That was one of the problems associated with the drum. The other problem was the drum was seen as some sort of symbolic god, or something of that sort, from a religious perspective. The drum had these major problems against it.

In a similar way, the drummer's image is still one received with ambivalence. For instance, a guy walks onto the stage and plays Chopin and he is roundly applauded. "Beautiful," the audience says, "a talented musician-artist." Another guy immediately follows and sits down and plays a Senegalese drum, and the audience goes, "How nice," or, "That was not nice." The next guy walks on and plays an Indian tabla and the audience says, "That one was okay. But let's get back to the music." The audience doesn't know that it takes about ten years to learn the ragas on an East Indian tabla. *Ten years* to learn the different ragas. They have an incredibly complex theoretical system in terms of performing Indian music. With the Senegalese drum, every rhythm basically represents the dance, the sound, and the specific time. They have all these cultural implications. But if you ask the person in the audience what the Chopin music is related to, he may say that is a piece of music. It's the not knowing of all this that lends to the attitude of my music is superior to your music.

Behind it all, you find a certain disposition toward African art and music burnt deeply into the consciousness of many people. So, when they hear the word drum and drummer they recoil. If it came from Africa it cannot be good. The backward African. The African savage. I'm not trying to romanticize or deromanticize Africa. Africa is like any place else, with beauty and ugliness. My point is: if we're interested in extracting from the cultures the best of what their people had to produce toward recognizing their benefits, then we cannot generalize about Africa in any way. This tendency to generalize about Africa was handed down and goes against the institutionalization of anything African.

The panmen were generalized about. If you were playing pan, you were uneducated, backward, ghetto, a jailbird. As anyone knows, that wasn't the truth. Much earlier than we think those college boys from QRC became involved in Pan. It's when they started getting involved in Pan then society started looking at us differently. Here I was, doing the same thing for so many years, and it's only when a guy attending one of the élite schools got involved that what I was doing was worth attention and respect. I'll stop there in terms of that and only say that that contributed to the underlying tensions the older panmen began to experience. They felt that sort of thing more than my generation did.

The thrust toward institutionalizing Pan, then, is against these backdrops. We have to deal with all of it. The African drummer. The Trinidadian panman from the ghetto. The panman who valued aural/oral learning in an oral culture. After all, westerners, even Trinidadians, must be open to various experiences. They have to seize all the advantages of a world music culture. Everyone needs to move beyond the idea of thinking you're a real musician if you can read, without understanding that this guy over here, for example Boogsie Sharp who is a genius, is a Paganini, and is not recognized by the people who need to recognize him as such. This knowledge is vital for the next generation. They need to know and understand this inventive and creative process that these brilliant men possessed and treasure it all.

22

From the Rawness to the Beauty of Steel: A Brief Biography of Elliott Mannette[1]

The awards and distinctions of Elliott "Ellie" Mannette *are many. Listed below are just a few:*

- *Hall of Fame, International Conference of the Percussive Arts Society,* **November 2003**

- *Institute of Caribbean Studies Caribbean Heritage Awards,* **November 2002**

- *Honorary doctorate, University of the West Indies, St. Augustine,* **2000**

- *Chaconia Silver Medal, Trinidad and Tobago,* **2000**

- *Appreciation Award, Pan Trinbago,* **2000**

- *Founder/CEO, Mannette Steel Drums, Ltd.,* **2000**

- *National Heritage Fellowship from the National Endowment for the Arts,* **1999** [2]

- *Featured instruments used by BWIA Invaders on BWIA Airline advertisement,* **1999** [3]

- *Artiste-in-residence, West Virginia University,* **1992** *to present*

- *Head, University Tuning Project, West Virginia University,* **1992 to 1999**

- *Humming Bird Silver Medal, Trinidad and Tobago,* **1969**

- *Pegasus Award, Trinidad and Tobago,* **1962**

Forging a Man of Steel

Reveler. Warrior. Innovator. Ambassador. Rudolph Charles calls him Maestro. Other friends call him Cairo, named after his mother who was a LoCairo [a native Caribbean] and a most positive influence in his life. Still others call him Skip, the short for Skipper or Captain. The names are some of the hats he has worn at various stages while living in Trinidad, and of which his famous red cork-hat became symbolic. Describing its significance to Mas, Steelband, and Carnival he says:

> I had a red cork-hat with the name "Skip" on it. I would wear this red cork-hat and beat the iron to start up the band on J'ouvert morning. Every year, the boys would paint that hat a different shade of red. Eventually, it must have had about twenty coats of paint on it. Even the lining of the hat was eventually worn out, so that they reconstructed a wire lining for the hat. Hundreds of people would line up outside my house, or sit on the ground or on a fence, or all over the Oval grass, all waiting for me to come out wearing this hat, which signaled that J'ouvert was about to start. Everybody would get into position so that once I struck the iron—one, two, three, four—the band would start playing. And that was the start of J'ouvert. After I left [Trinidad], they say the hat was hung on the breadfruit tree and remained there for quite a few years before it disappeared.[4]

Throughout those turbulent Trinidad years, he tried to live peaceably whenever possible, which did not preclude all the times he had to defend his honor, even when the violence and aggression threatened to jeopardize his dreams, to take his life. Never once during those years he dreamt of wearing the hat of a peaceable teacher with a beautiful private office in his large pan manufacturing plant in Morgantown, West Virginia.

Thirty-three years separated Woodbrook from West Virginia. However, no geographic distance could erase from memory the violence of his early years in Pan. One incident that set in motion the most terrifying chain of events remains etched—.

He emerged from the court house, cleared of all charges, and paused while his eyes adjusted to the early afternoon sun's glare that magnified the brightness of every thing on Abercromby Street, PoS. Office buildings. Bustling traffic. Men dressed in business suits, carrying briefcases, and looking like they belonged in town, going somewhere in life. Unlike him. He carried a knife tucked into the left side of his pants' waist for protection. But the knife so far had taken him only as far as the court house to face one misdemeanor charge or another.

He looked warily up the street, scanning it carefully for signs of the John John gang from Casablanca Steel Band. He knew that they were out for revenge, determined to finish what started since he had come out with his barracuda pan some time before. He had named the pan "barracuda"[5] because it was so exceptionally good it was *bad*.[6] The piranha of pans to be revered and respected.

Pan, the invention of an island surrounded by the Gulf of Paria whose waters were infested with piranhas, the Caribbean Sea, and the Atlantic Ocean.

The barracuda was a curse and a blessing that demanded a costly price. The first foreboding of its Janus-sided awards came after Oval Boys began to take a lead among the early steel bands, which began the rivalry between the bands from the east and the west. The intensity of the rivalry kept escalating and he saw the barracuda as a curse. The blessing, on the other hand, came in the many girls who flocked to him. PoS's most attractive young ladies wanted him to escort them to this or that dance. To this movie or the other. His name was associated with badness, boldness, talent, good looks, creativity, intelligence, high color, and living in the right neighborhood.

When the John John boys had got a hold of the barracuda during a clash of bands the night of the V-J Day celebrations in August into September, 1945, he was merely minding his business doing what he loved best—playing sweet music on his barracuda. Oval Boys was coming up Charlotte Street when Casablanca turned onto George Street and headed toward them. He was playing at the back of the band and did not know what was going on up front when the rumble flowed to him, "Fight breakin' out!" Then followed the clackety-clang of dropped pans, the scamper, and the panicked shouts, "Run! Run, fuh yuh life!" In the mêlée, he had dropped the barracuda and run.

The next morning, the bait came that his pan was hanging from a tree by the roadside in John John, and if he wished to have it back he had to come and get it himself. He was no trout for them to catch. They could keep his barracuda. He would build another pan. One that surpassed previous imagination. One so big and sweet it could not ever be lost or stolen from mind or memory. In 1946, he accomplished this dream by bringing out his big pan for the Skinner's Park competition, which he won.

Since then, every where he turned someone or something threatened to destroy him or his dreams. And, he seemed to be always going to court for incidences like the petty one that had brought him there that morning to face charges for disorderly conduct and disturbing the peace.

One night he and Norma Callender,[7] his current main girlfriend, had emerged from Roxy Theatre and were headed for the Diamond Horseshoe Club to dance till *fore-day morning*. Loitering across the street waiting for him was the John John gang. The looks on their faces signaled big trouble. Barong was wearing a dark scowl. Low Low (so called because he was short and thick) was looking simply menacing. That I-come-out-for-yuh-blood-tuhnight look. And though he was short and heavy, he crouched and moved as swift as a tiger. Pounced as quick and sure as one, too. The seeming nonchalance of Little Drums, Black Boy, and Bake Nose (Neville McLeod, called Bake Nose because of his flat nose) masked that they could and would land some painful blows.

The last thing he'd wanted that night was any wrangle of sorts with them. Not when he was with his lady and dressed in his fine white suit with a black shirt and black kerchief in the breast-pocket next to his dark shades, and finally his pointy-tipped black-and-white shoes. He looked and felt like a movie star in his striking black and white image, topped with a small brim white hat with black band. However, his attire became the butt of their jokes and foul obscenities. They called him a forced-ripe Clark Gable and derided every article of clothing he wore, from his hat to his shoes. Then, the derision stopped and their voices became ominous as they advanced boldly, powerful in number as they taunted and cussed him. His boys from Oval Boys were no where in sight. Norma had disappeared. Good for her.

Sighting a Solo truck delivering sweet drinks (soda) at a shop on Green Corner, he darted across the road to the truck. With his back to the truck and facing the lowering approach of the gang, enraged he yelled and taunted them in turn, matching their language and bravado. He dared not back down. More than his reputation was at stake. He saw his life flash before his eyes, again, and knew intuitively that if he died at that moment all his dreams and hopes would come to naught.

Something fierce rose up in him and he began pelting them with the bottles. They paused in the face of his fury and looked at each other uncertainly, momentarily. Then, Low Low tiger-like sprang ahead of the rest. Without removing his eyes from him or the others, unflinchingly he reached behind his back and peeled the bottles from their cases stacked in a V-shape. Right hand-left hand, rhythmically and methodically, bottles flew rapidly into his enemies' faces, who paused or dodged the missiles that slowed them from reaching him. By the time he was done, the truck was empty of its bottles, their carbonated content bubbling merrily in the street, creating an evanescent twinkle of bubbles mingled with glass shards reflected from the street lights. The scene a mockery of his rage that did not dissipate as quickly as the gang had beaten a fast retreat.

The wail of the police sirens approaching from the bottom of Duke Street finally registered, but he had no energy or desire to run, as his enemies had. With his palpitating heart returning to normal, he dried his hands on his kerchief then patted the blots of sweet drink splattered on his pants then adjusted his hat after he straightened up.

The two policemen recognized and hauled him off for disturbing the peace and disorderly conduct, despite his protests that he was defending himself against the John John gang. "What gang?" One constable taunted him. "Is ghosts in de place yuh talkin' 'bout, or what? Ent nobody here but you and yuh shadow," he laughed at his own tasteless joke as he propelled him roughly toward the police van. He was all too familiar with the jeers of these men who represented all the colonial authorities and all of society who had branded panmen as hooligans and *bad-johns*. Noisemakers with no purpose in life but to beat pan, fight, maim, and/ or kill each other.

He'd spent a sleepless night and all morning in a holding cell. Dank and pissy-smelling. Obscenities scrawled on the walls with dried feces. Crawling vermin by night. Flies and cockroaches every where by day. More symbols of mockery of his dreams to make something of his life. Would he ever move beyond this cycle of wasted hours in jail and the court room, wasted energy fending for his life, then returning to the fragments of hope in steel in this colonial wasteland?

Would the men ever move beyond the crabs-in-a-barrel syndrome toward him that had begun to surface after his winning the Skinner's Park competition?[8] Would he ever be anything but a panman who refused to be a panman because he couldn't bring himself to identify with *the east,* particularly in matters of attire? After all, he was a *saga* boy.

For his court appearance that morning, he wore a grey suit, matching shirt and tie, spit-polished grey shoes, and a knife tucked into the waist of his pants. He sat around all morning while waiting for his name to be called, and made most of the time pondering his dreams to improve the pan. He answered when his name was called, answered to the charges brought against him, and smiled slightly when they were all subsequently dropped. Once more, through the human intervention of someone in authority who had taken a personal interest in him, he was a free man. Lady Luck continued to be in his favor at the moment, he thought. Still, he'd wasted another morning that could have been spent building a pan.

When he emerged from the court house that early afternoon, only Norma was there on her bike, and again he thought himself fortunate. No John John gang member in sight. He and Norma walked toward Duke Street while he reassured her that he was all right. Nothing to worry about.

He liked Norma. About five feet five inches tall and very slender, she was a contradiction. Athletically built and always riding a bicycle, she always wore very attractive clothes—bright colors that complimented her dark, smooth skin—and lots of jewelry. Always she wore a different attire every day. When she smiled her entire broad face radiated an inner light she possessed. In plain words, he admired the way she dressed and carried herself, on and off her bike, and couldn't treat her with the same cavalier attitude with which he treated other women. In those days, who heard of an attractive young woman biking all over town?

He liked best that she was always positive and encouraging him to pursue his dreams. She wished him to give up fighting, too. To stop walking with a knife, because those who lived by the sword died by the sword. She loved to quote sayings she'd picked up from somewhere. She was very intelligent and appreciated not just *ole talk* but thoughtful discussion on what was going on in the world, something that she could not enjoy with her boyfriend, Joebell. He enjoyed going to the movies with her because afterward they had thoughtful conversations about what they had seen.

She was unlike other women also in her daring. She worked at a laundry on Charlotte Street, but not because she did not aspire to improve her status. In fact, she already had. For Negro women to hold a civil servant government position in those days, they had to be born into the right family. Otherwise, they were maids, washerwomen, or other menial workers. Norma refused to work in anyone's home and found more dignified work at a laundry owned by a Chinese man.

However, she was like the many other women who doted on him, did not want to see him get hurt, and couldn't understand why he, a man, must carry protection during those days of senseless violence.

While they walked and talked, he cast a wary eye around him. A little voice kept warning him to be utterly careful. The John John gang knew he was in town to keep his court date and surely would be looking to finish what they'd started on the night of his arrest. Then, he saw approaching *badjohns* Mastifé[9] and Skipper. Though not gang members but enforcers, they delivered messages or news from one band to another, one enemy to another, if and when necessary. He tensed. What now? When they were directly in front of him they paused and Mastifé said authoritatively, "De others comin'. If yuh want to live, you better get de hell outta here." Skipper commanded, "An' damn fas' too." They resumed swaggering up Duke Street. Ellie blanched then recovered to reply to their retreating backs, "I not *fraid* and not runnin'. Let them come." Then upon turning around, he saw the gang—Ossie Campbell, Barong, Patsy Haynes,[10] Low Low, and Oscar Pile—coming from the direction Mastifé and Skipper had come. Despite himself, he swallowed nervously. "This is it," he thought. "Brace yuhself, man. Yuh fighting a one-man war today." He looked around for any security in a wall or vehicle that he could back up to and face them. Nothing but he and them. He breathed in deeply and exhaled, ready for them.

When they were within close range, he stepped back to the edge of the pavement. Norma rode off to a safe distance while they surrounded him. Calmly, he drew his knife. All senses alert, he turned around slowly so that he was facing them one at a time, knife steady. Nothing betrayed his dry mouth and pounding heartbeats.

Then, he felt a *cuff* to the back of his head that sent him reeling forward. He fell toward Ossie and Oscar. Closer to Ossie, his arms went around him in a hug to support himself. But instead of just hugging him, he drew the knife across Ossie's back, slashing it and causing a deep, gaping wound. Blood gushing, as Ossie stumbled away in shock, Ellie stabbed him in the back then shoved him to the ground as he withdrew the knife. He then quickly turned around to deal with more attacks, but his attackers were already running in every direction.

He ran behind one of them, the one he thought had *cuffed* him from behind, who was running along Duke Street. He shouted obscenities at him and for him to stop for a taste of his own medicine. He chased him pass the tailor shop owned by John Sargeant, his tailor, who was standing in the doorway with mouth agape, having witnessed the entire violent altercation, but he barely noticed him. He ran pass other terrified-looking pedestrians who had pulled aside to make a clear path for them, into a parlor at the corner of Duke and Abercromby Streets, and up the stairs following the pursued. He mounted three stairs at a time, caught him, and stabbed him twice in his back, then rushed back downstairs. He would wound them all, one by one, kill if he had to. Outside, his blade dripping blood and eyes wild with rage, he scanned the street for the rest and began racing wildly to find them.

Only when a woman's voice screaming, "Oh Gawd! Oh Gawd! Is murder in de place! Murda-a-h!" penetrated his consciousness, he stopped. Glancing down, he saw his grey suit was all covered with blood. He looked around and vaguely registered that two men were wounded badly enough to need immediate medical attention.

Seeing a guy on a bike coming toward him, he tucked the knife back into his pants' waist, knocked the cyclist off his bike, jumped on it and pedaled furiously down Duke Street toward Marine Square, pass the Electric Company, pass the cemetery, and toward Woodbrook. He headed straight for Oval Boys' hang-out shack located at the corner of Lewis Street and Wrightson Road. He knew he could not go home in his condition. No explanation would erase the shame and disgrace on his mother and father's faces, Lala and T, respectively. He could not bear to see their pain, shock, horror, and disbelief that their son this time had crossed the line and may have murdered in cold blood. T had never approved of his involvement in Pan because of the panmen's reputation for hooliganism, for being the worst of *bad-johns*. He feared his son would end up in big trouble, and that day may have proved him right.

In the safety of the shack, he sat down, breathing heavily. The enormity of his actions slowly sank in. He had stabbed two guys, one of them cut deeply. He knew that. He closed his eyes and leaned his head back on the rickety wall, taking deep breaths to regulate his heart rate. Quickly, he opened his eyes again. His inner eye kept replaying the stumble into Ossie. The sickening sound of the slicing of flesh. The squirt of fresh-smelling blood, like the ocean. The stab. More blood. His quick, furious turning around to stab whoever else dared to attack him. The quick chase of Barong, his mind now registered, as he pursued him into the shop and up the stairs. The two deep stabs. The return down the stairs. The woman's terrified screaming. Finally, the getaway on the bike.

Over and over, his mind replayed the incident. He groaned and lowered his head into his bloody hands. Why him? Why couldn't they leave him alone? Why were they out to kill him? For what? Always forcing him to defend himself. So many times in the past he'd come face to face with life-or-death struggles. But this one was surely the worst encounter. He closed his eyes again to blank out the incident and then just as quickly opened them. This was hell, for sure.

Around dusk, he heard a soft knock and an urgent whisper, "Ellie, Ellie? You there? Is me. Audrey. Ellie? Open the door." Audrey, his closest sibling and confidante, of course knew where to find him. He was not ready to face anyone. Not even Audrey. He was unmasked in this most vulnerable state and covered in blood. For the first time in his life, he truly felt afraid and couldn't disguise it. Again came her urgent knock and whispered entreaty, "Ellie, open the door, please." "Go back home, Audrey. I doh want to see nobody." "I staying right here till you open this damn door. You open the door right now, yuh hear me, or I'll kick it down!" she commanded more loudly and authoritatively. "The yard is swarming with police. They say you killed a man in town in cold blood." When he heard that he opened the door. Did Ossie really die and he was now, *for true*, a murderer?

She came in and demanded to know what really happened. She was in no mood for any *nancy-story*. He explained weakly, "They jump me, Audrey. They surround me, and one of them *cuff* my head from behind. I fell onto Ossie and that's how he got slashed. The rest was from instinct, from defending myself. I'm always defending myself. You know I couldn't kill anybody just so."

"I know, I know," she reassured him of her loyalty. Then, she noticed his appearance and said gravely, "Lord, what a mess! Look at you! Covered in blood! You need some clean clothes. Pray Lord that worse don't come to worse. Lala and T sick to death with worry. Everybody worrying."

"How you know where to find me?"

"Somebody saw you come in here and told Doris. I don't know who it was. As soon as I heard I came. Lala and T don't know I here. We *fraid* to tell them because they might tell the police. When we know what really happened and how Ossie Campbell doing, then we could say where you are. I only relieved yuh not hurt."

"I all right. But I had to defend myself, Audrey. It was either them or me. I feel they were really out to kill me this time." His voice trembled, despite himself, and he felt on the verge of tears. He swallowed the aching lump in his throat and continued, "From the time I wake up this morning, something tell me big trouble coming. Ossie really dead? I can't believe that."

"Nobody believing it, but that's the talk going around. We just waiting to see."

"How bad they say he wounded?"

"Real bad. His whole back ripped open and you could see his lungs, they say. Norma say is blood all over the place, flowing like a river. That poor girl! Lord, Ellie," she moaned and shook her head despairingly, "and things were beginning to look so good for you and the band. And, I so damn proud of you. All of us so glad to see you making good for yourself. Now this! What go happen now?"

"How you expect me to know that? Leave me alone, nuh." He was not really dismissing her. He was simply scared beyond relief and impatient of any question for which he had no answer. He did not really want to be left alone to imagine the worst either. If it was true that Ossie was dead, then he was surely to be executed, and prior to his execution be whipped with the cat-o'-nine tails like some dog, because the authorities were talking about bringing back the whip to try and bring the *bad-johns* under control. Maybe, they'll start with him.

Sensing his withdrawal and after offering some more comforting words, Audrey finally left, promising to return as soon as she could. In the shack's quiet and growing darkness, all he could think of was he would be whipped like a dog then hanged. Then, a thought occurred to him, "If they will execute me for this violent crime, then all those men who beat me up, some with bottles all over my head, like Charles Samuel and Bad Man, I swear right here, right now, I taking out all those guys who beat me up. One at a time. As soon as it get dark, I going to hunt down those men and take them out, one at a time, starting with Charles Samuel and Bad Man, right here in St. James. I going to *laywai'* them down by the club. If they're going to charge me for one crime, they may as well charge me for all the crimes." Let his infamy be emblazoned across every newspaper's front page. He'd be damned if he cared.

The cycle of violence and revenge, the course of human history which began who knows when, now engendered the lives of panmen, now dominated his thoughts. Even while he plotted his violent ending, he wondered what had made his behavior so vicious. Surely, this was not his true nature, his conscience penetrated his consciousness. He was a man who defended himself. He was never one to start a fight for the sake of fighting. If only the social conditions over which he had little to no control were different for men like him, surely society would see a different man, one who merely wanted to pursue a dream that compelled him toward some unknown future. Yet, he had control over his response. But when the promised vehicle seemed to be the vice-clap that was plunging him to his death, what was his way out? His hope? He moaned despairingly—.

The Early Years: The Oval Boys

He was born Elliott Anthony Martin (named after St. Martin) Mannette on November 6, 1927, to Emelda and Sydney Mannette in Sans Souci, Toco, a town settled by those from the francophonic islands—Haiti, Martinique, and Guadeloupe. His father's family came from Martinique, and his mother's family from Venezuela. He inherited his light complexion, good looks, and curly hair from his mother. His parents' relatives and friends called his mother Lala and father Pappy or T: the children did likewise. He was the sixth of nine children: Lionel, Rufus, Phyllis, Audrey, Doris were those older than he; those younger were Oswald and Vernon, nicknamed Birdie; and a half sister, Rosalind.

When he was five, the family moved to Agra Street, St. James, then to Damien Street, Woodbrook, probably to be closer to his father's family-owned property in Bournes Road, then finally to 147 Tragarete Road.

He was six when he began attending Akal School in St. James. Similarly to his siblings, Lala dressed him immaculately every day for school. This made him a favorite among his teachers—Misses Byam and Griffith—who appreciated children coming to school clean, well-dressed, and eager to learn, all of which he was. He took to his books, as they say, and progressed from one standard to the next, distinguishing himself as a bright boy, excellent at Arithmetic, History, Geography, and later on the sciences.

He fed his passion for learning by avidly reading encyclopaedias—*Encyclopaedia Britannica, Viking Desk*—and other works of nonfiction, which his father had purchased from door-to-door salesmen and shelved on built-in shelves in the walls of the living room. When he tired of the encyclopaedias, he studied atlases and maps, memorizing the names, places, and rivers of various countries. His favorite history topics were the pirates and sea warriors, specifically Sir Henry Morgan, Horatio Nelson, and Black Beard.

Before long, he advanced well beyond his classmates and when tested for secondary school, he did well enough to earn a scholarship to Bishop Ansty High School for Boys. One other classmate posed him competition, a girl named Irma Jarrett. She was also very bright, especially in English and Spelling. She similarly earned a secondary school scholarship for a girls' school. However, he was no bookworm.

His extracurricular interests included football, track and field, and swimming. He excelled in long distance running and swimming. He learned to swim when he was about twelve years old and hanging around intrepid boys who knew where every large stream and connecting pond nestled in their neighborhood. A favorite was the stream between St. Clair and St. James, whose pond called Sandbox was surrounded by trees and overhanging vines. The boys loved to swing across the pond on the vines, with the more daring ones releasing the vines midway across and dropping into the water then swimming to the other side. Having never been taught to swim, he did not dare swing on the vines less he accidentally let go and fall in. One day, standing on the bank of the pond and enjoying being a spectator of the other boys' exploits, he was suddenly shoved in. After surfacing, he swam easily to the bank and never stopped swimming after that. Later on, he loved biking, wrestling, and boxing. All in all, he had a pretty uneventful childhood.

Though very industrious, Lala and T were lax in their discipline and left him to chart his own course, which he began as a pre-adolescent. Having been christened as a Roman Catholic in St. Teresa Church, he attended Mass and received Communion there, and because he liked to go to church he decided one day to become an acolyte, simply because it was something to do. However, he gave up being an acolyte and stopped attending Mass. Church and its rituals held no compelling meaning or interest for him. Instead, the sounds of the island were calling. He was eleven going on twelve when he found he could no longer resist.

He became aware of the Alexander Ragtime Band[11] before he was even ten years old, the images of that yard shaping vividly his pre-adolescent and adolescent years. He recalls:

> I heard about the Alexander Ragtime Band from around Woodford Street and Tragarete Road, in a yard they called the Big Yard. But I was too little to go up there. That was 1935 or '36, I think. I remember one day I ran away from school and went up there. I climbed a tree to look over into their yard and saw some men stickfighting.[12] They were singing, and dancing, banging on their pans, and beating each other up with the sticks. I was so excited to see this thing that it drove me crazy. I wanted to climb down the tree and go into the yard, but I was too young. They wouldn't have wanted a little boy like me there. And, that also drove me crazy.[13]

These same men on some occasions dressed like pirates with sashes around their waists, some in torn clothes, others in various costumes, all fighting, jousting, and "dancing like the devil."[14] He found it dynamic in some ways—the ten to twelve different moves interwoven with various highly complex rhythms. Those men were obsessed with what they were doing and had obviously mastered their techniques to the point of being professionals. Today, he observes that current dancers will have to work quite intensively with these men to learn and master their dance and rhythm forms. These rhythms were constantly changing from one moment to the next even while the men were performing. The clacking sounds of the sticks, the accompanying beating of drums, and the fire-dancing all reverberated throughout the neighborhood, and the neighbors complained about the noise. The boom of the bass kettle drum, the most important rhythm instrument, could be heard for miles. The men wrapped their hands in towels to produce the sound. He was also most curious to see the instruments that produced these sounds. Finally, the desire to see first-hand overcame the fear of being caught trespassing and dealing with the men's wrath. The pleasure being worth more than the risk, one day he dared and states,

> ... after they were gone, I climbed down the tree and went into the yard to see their drums and saw their convex shaped. Then, I climbed back over the fence and went home. I went straight to my father's yard to look around to see what I could find. I wanted some pans I could use to make the same kind of drum. I continued to look around the Oval[15] and found paint tins from after they'd painted the tracks, and some grease barrels. And, through trial and error, I began to experiment with these tins all by myself. Every time my father heard me banging and so on, he would grumble, "Leave the drum alone." And I would leave it, but every chance I got I would poke at these drums.
>
> Then, I got Francis Wickham, Kevin Dove, Joe Ryan, Stanley Hunt—all those guys living right around the neighborhood—and suggested that we got together and form a band. Before long, a bunch of other little guys started coming around and that's how we formed the Oval Boys.[16] We used to hang around the Oval all the time fielding cricket and helping clean the fields.[17]

Thus, he launched his panman career.

Soon, his father's backyard was transformed into a panyard. It was a place and time for harvesting the complex, dynamic sounds and rhythms that became a source of inspiration for a future these men possibly could not begin to envision. Meanwhile, the sights and sounds of Alexander Ragtime Band's yard continued to fascinate him, for the older men continued to experiment with Pan's development and he remained most fascinated with the drumming. Hence, his adolescent years were shaped by this fascination and desire, and what he observed the men continuing to produce.

Some time around the late 1939 to early 1940, he saw the first four-note pan played by a panman named Granville and then another one played by Sonny Roach. Granville, originally from St. James, was playing in Point Cumana at the waterfront. Sonny Roach of the Sufferers around the same time was playing the convex four-note pan in Bournes Road. Shortly thereafter, talk was abuzz that Winston "Spree" Simon of John John dented the convex top and got a pattern of three to four consecutive notes on that convex surface.[18] Prior to that, the rumor was Spree had lent his pan to Thick Lips who while beating the thin surface of the pan with a broomstick or broom handle, the top began to sink into the concave shape. Spree then took a broom handle to pop back up the sunken surface. By popping it out, he accidentally came upon this idea of the popped up note. This event happened in 1938.[19]

Though he never saw Spree's pan during the four-note pan period, he did see Granville's and Roach's pans. Also, he notes that Spree was first to make the convex four-note pan and played "Mary Had a Little Lamb" on it has already been historically established. With no wish to contest history, he observes that no one really knows who was first to do anything,[20] or exactly what day and year events occurred. Rather, these contentions resonate today among those who have the luxury of history upon which to cogitate. The early panmen and innovators simply followed a desire to create something that was born out of nothing else like it. Unnamed, undefined, and unique.

Mannette particularly was trying to find something to emulate the sound he had heard in Alexander Ragtime Band's yard. He says:

> My quest for emulation and what I and the other men were doing was not an invention. No one said one day that I will invent an instrument from trash cans that could play music and rhythms. The steelpan was born out of the trash can being used to play a rhythm. Other sounds by accident were added from the same desire to create rhythmic sounds and the desire for expression of internal rhythm, then later the additions came about.
>
> In the Woodford Street area, Ford Alexander formed the Alexander Ragtime Band, a bamboo band. As the story went, one day in 1935 when a mêlée, a fight, broke out in PoS and his boys scampered for cover, he picked up a trash can and beat it rhythmically to call his people back out of hiding in people's backyard and behind fences. The fight broke out about two miles away from his residence. Beating on his trash can, the sound drew his members out, and they joined him by picking up trash cans and beating them to draw out the remaining members. So, all the way home there was this beating on trash cans instead of bamboos. That is how I heard the story of how the trash-can rhythm started, which became the roots of the steelpan. The following Carnival, '36, the men looked for trash cans instead of using bamboo, because the rhythm of the trash can was so much louder than the bamboo. Then, other bamboo bands started to follow suit.[21]

After seeing the four-note pan with its convex shape, Mannette with his friends did what many other panmen in desperate search for tins, cans, and pans did. Whenever they came upon trash cans left at the side of the street for the trash collectors, they dumped the trash into the street and took the cans back to his father's backyard to experiment in pan-building. Soon, the people began to chain their trash cans unto their fences and gates, which did not deter them. They began walking with saws to cut the chains and then dump the trash into the street. Undoubtedly, this disregard for others' property or sanitation helped define their image of being worthless and good-for-nothing boys. Later, after they realized that those cans were not worth the trouble, because a couple of hard knocks with sticks to produce sound caused the bottom of the cans to tear, they began looking around for something harder than trash cans. They found them in the steel containers and later in the sweet-oil drums.[22] Hence, by 1939, either by accident or deliberate intent, the pan arrived.

Every day, he continued to scour his father's backyard, the neighborhood, and the Oval for pans. The Oval was the place for sport activities: cricket, football, tennis. His father's yard was right across the street from the Oval. Whatever he found, he took to a spot that became his secret yard. A big saman tree shaded the Oval's Grand Stand and bleachers. Under the bleachers in the shade of that tree, he conducted his experiments, hammering and pounding like he heard it was done. This he continued for about two years before introducing his first pan to the boys who scoured the neighborhood for pans with him. Realizing its success, he was encouraged to build more pans toward the formation of their own band shortly thereafter. During this time, he was attempting to build the four-note pan similar to Granville's and Roach's. To the contrary, he could not. He says,

> I tried to do the same thing but just couldn't get my notes to play. That was when I pushed my surface down and made the concave instead of the convex pan. When the others first saw it, they made a lot of jokes about how I made a baby's bath pan. "Wha' yuh makin'? A baby's bath pan?" I remember one night I went to Rialto Theatre with Neville Jules, Fisheye, Bully, men from All Stars. They weren't called All Stars then but Red Army.[23] All of us were at the Rialto for a steelpan contest, and I had my pan turned face down. They all gave me jokes about how I made a baby's bath pan. I had the concave shape with the notes dented upward. But how Sonny Roach, Neville Jules, and Granville had their convex shape pan with the notes pushed up, too, I just couldn't do it.[24]

His "baby's bath pan" made an impression, and when others began building pans, they soon found it was easier to build the concave pan. Shortly after this incident and some time during 1940 to '41, the Oval Boys came into existence, their name deriving from the boys' activities around the Oval, as previously stated. They fielded cricket balls just for the fun of it, and sometimes got two shillings at the end of the week. Because they worked at the Oval, they were already considered the Oval Boys. So, when they formed their own little band, they so called themselves and soon became nuisances to those neighborhood people who could not tolerate their noise. These people chased them away or took their pans away. They then regrouped and found more pans to shape into instruments. Each new pan brought an improved technique and better sounding instrument, which caused them to be regarded as a challenge to the older bands. Apparently, the men of the bands from Laventille and Behind the Bridge saw this band of little boys from the Woodbrook area as upstarts, which marked when the rivalry first began and then intensified. Mannette states:

> ... One day when there was a contest in the Oval, there were other bands, including Jules's band. We started at the back and walked around the perimeter of the cricket field where people rode their bikes, and came around to the Grand Stand. We won that contest. It wasn't an elaborate contest, not much to win. But we won that contest. The other bands got jealous of that right away and that started a little conflict. But the real conflict started up in Tunapuna, where there was another contest and we won again. When leaving that contest, coming down a dark back alley some of the boys attacked us.
>
> Later on, when we became the Invaders band, the conflict continued and the Invaders boys fought back. We weren't going to take anymore. I was one of those fighting back because I wasn't going to take any of that, too. We fought back against John John, Casablanca, Renegades, which wasn't Renegades at the time, a band from San Juan, and another from Belmont. That's when the trouble started. There was another band from Behind the Bridge called Bar 20. Then, there was All Stars,[25] which used to be called Red Army, and the St. James Sufferers from Bournes Road.[26]

Thus, the pattern of violent behavior that would dominate the Steelband movement for many years—the pattern of those in authority seizing pans and forcing the men to find and/or steal new ones; the rivalry among the men, which more often than not ended in violence—was born out of the men's competitive spirits to be regarded as the best band, primarily.

Even in the pan's birthing stage, the men were already locked in the struggle to win, to be viewed the best among themselves and to challenge any one who held first place. During these early days, they were not yet competing for awards or money. Such came later, after the men organized toward setting their own course via the steelband association and competing in Music Festival and Panorama.

With the birth of Oval Boys at age fourteen, Mannette began determining his chosen path and Lala and T left him free to follow his devices. He continued to pursue his dominant thrill of Pan, which was linked to his fascination at the sight of men who stick-fought exquisitely and drummed magnificently.

He was also magnetized to the sight of a bamboo band coming up Tragarete Road with about five hundred to seven hundred people waving tree limbs, which from the distance looked like an entire moving forest, as he describes the scene. Stick-fighting and the bamboo band—two images etched indelibly in his memory—completely changed his life. No matter what people and his father said, he knew that he had to master what the men were doing in that backyard and one day be a part of a similar Mas band.

The Mind of an Innovator: The Creative Years

Guy Claxton, professor of Education and Psychology at Bristol University, writes that the source of creativity is a combination of inspiration and evaluation. Creatives allow ideas to come to them when in a state of reverie then craft the ideas into existence.[27] Certainly, this process applies to Mannette to whom some of his later innovations came through dreams. While he cannot recall specifically how the idea for his first innovation came to him to build the concave pan with raised notes, not as specifically as he can recall the later ones, he knows what he did was in an attempt to better control the sounds and pitches. Incidentally, what he was doing coincided with the years 1941 to 1944, which began to bring a better understanding of the pan in relation to sound and pitches, and the beginning of the manipulation of the "bumps" for improved sonority.

The term ping-pong was introduced during these years, and he credits Eddie Myers as having built the first one. The ping-pong was a larger pan on which one could play a melody. Prior to the ping-pong the pans were used primarily for rhythms. The transition to the ping-pong occurred almost simultaneously with the burning of the drums, which process accidentally came about. He recalls:

> At first, the drums weren't burned. One day, after finding a drum whose bottom was crusted with asphalt, after trying all methods to remove the asphalt—washing, scrubbing, scraping, kerosene, and gasoline—it couldn't be removed, someone suggested that they try burning it out. After burning it out, when we went to play it we recognized that the sound was different. And, we were quite surprised. We decided to burn another one out and see what happened, for the heck of it. When we tried that one out, we immediately recognized that the texture and tone were better sounding. This, too, came about

by accident. No one sat down and thought up the idea of burning the drum for a better quality. We weren't thinking that way.[28]

It was during these years, 1943 specifically, he wrapped his stick with rubber, yet another innovative idea that simply evolved. He states:

> At the time, we used hard sticks to beat the rhythms, which created harsh tones. I desired a softer tone. First, I tried using the branch of the Black Sage hibiscus hedge. But this frayed too quickly. Next, I tried the coconut or cocoyea branch by stripping the smaller branches and cutting them down to a desirable length. But the tips of the cocoyea branch curled with each strike unto the pan. The broom handle was too hard to satisfy. So, from the inner tube of my bicycle I cut out a piece of rubber and wrapped the end of the stick. Immediately, everyone recognized the better sound the rubber-tipped stick created.[29]

Who introduced the idea of the rubber-tipped mallet and when is one of the controversies in Pan, which Neville Jules's narrative addresses toward answering the call for the truth of Pan's history. All the various arguments actually attest to the fact that this time was pregnant with creative ideas that flowed freely from one source to another. The effusion of these ideas into a community that gave little pause to who was first is further testament to how spontaneity as both a cause and effect of the creative energy of a moment is generative. Mannette iterates in response to the controversy that the focus today should be in developing the pan. The emphasis should be in putting into process an evolutionary pattern, such as existed during the early days of Pan when it was being born out of a recycling process among people who were themselves being recycled for one of life's grandest purposes. Back then, the men focused on making an instrument that would produce the sweetest music humanity has ever heard, according to the Pan world. Today, the pan ought to be evolving toward its perfection.

Mannette's definition of the historical process comes from his intimate experience with creating new pans. The following account provides a window into his own unique creative process that confirms Claxton's assertion in regard to the source of creativity:

> Great ideas live within a creator. People are born geniuses, which then comes out gradually and develops with lots of hard work and effort. Sitting over the drum day in and day out, I used to wonder how to make this right. I used to see the vivid picture in my mind of what the drum looked like and hear how it sounded. Yet, I couldn't get it to come out like I was seeing or hearing it. So, I

> would sit over the drum and ponder this long and hard, trying this and trying that, and going damn crazy with frustration when it didn't come out right. I was sixteen, seventeen, and eighteen around this time when I would fall asleep over the drum and my father would awake me. It was an obsession, as I was haunted by the question of how to do this and get it right. I couldn't think of anything else. It was a mental affair. So, I fell asleep over the drum, many times out of frustration and nervousness stemming from anxiety, which produced cold sweats all over the body, from head to toe. That sort of anxiety drives you to the edge of a nervous breakdown, which then produces a deep sleep.
>
> All the instruments I gave birth to, I went through the exact process—seeing it in my sleep, pondering day in, day out how to produce it, the nervous anxiety that drove me to the edge of a nervous breakdown, and then deep periods of sleep. An incredible intensity drove me on. It wasn't easy. All my seven sections—the guitar,[30] the double second, and the lead, all—I went through the stages of dream, trial and error, of remembering the mistakes and avoiding them so as to get it right the next time, pondering what and how to do it, the nervousness, and then finally what I saw in my dream, the pattern and design. I'd awake from those periods of sleep, those where I fell asleep in the yard, and go home. All the way home, I'd ponder about the drum. On my way to work, I'll still be pondering how to bring this dream into creation.[31]

The above quotation gets a little ahead of Mannette's story and the story of Pan's evolution; however, the insertion here offers a remarkable account of the feverish burning associated with the intensity of labor and creation. "It wasn't easy" to create this hybrid musical instrument which did not exist before in all of human history, the panmen reiterate. To have no pattern or design to follow but rather be driven by an unnamed, unidentified, unrealized Muse was their source of inspiration.

One is not stretching to comment that history's unfolding events of those years occurred without parallels and in two extremities, as Mannette himself has observed. He has stated that in Europe one man was leading an army into unleashing unimaginable human atrocities on millions of people of various creeds, ethnicities, and moral/immoral imperatives, while on the other side of the globe a different army of a few front-line men were creating an instrument that would bring healing through music. Germany and Trinidad: two unlikely countries whose citizens would leave sharply contrasting indelible marks on the twentieth century, one much more quietly than the other.

The 1941 to 1945 war period can be described as the panmen's incubational time. These were the years when the pan was outlawed and there were no parades. There was no Carnival in Trinidad from '41 to '44. According the Earl Lovelace, similarly in 1919 the government "passed a law outlawing the Spiritual Baptists of Trinidad. They outlawed the beating of drums, African drums. There was a lot of outlawing of African customs and so on in colonial times here."[32] Thus, the war years simply brought another outlawing of a culture emerging from the African diaspora.

One official reason the government used to outlaw and preclude any street parades or any multitudes on the streets was supposedly safety during the time of war. German U-boats, in search of oil for their ships, had surrounded the oil-rich island. The war thus heightened everyone's fear of German aggressiveness. Pan music served as an escape mechanism from this imminent threat of a German invasion. Mannette recalls that some activities were allowed to go on, such as contests at Skinner's Park and Queen's Park Savannah. The Oval Boys, Hell Yard, All Stars, Syncopaters, Renegades, Tripoli, St. James Sufferers, Crossroads, Casablanca, and others, were all in competition during this time, which allowed for the instruments to evolve.

According to the chronology, another significant change also occurred during this time: the name Oval Boys was changed to Night Invaders. Mannette narrates that based on the Normandy Invasion of 1944 on D-Day when the Allies attacked Germany, and also based on the British attack on Rommel in the desert (Erwin Johannes Eugene Rommel "The Desert Fox"),[33] the boys decided to adopt the name Night Invaders for their band whose members were growing from boys into men, and because the invasions occurred during the night. Other bands were similarly adopting new names: Casablanca, Tripoli, North Stars, and Desperadoes, to name a few. The Oval Boys identified themselves as young men who invaded the Pan world of these older men by storm and redefined the development of the instrument. During this time, the instruments really began to evolve as a result of these contests held in PoS and San Fernando.

Mannette delineates the results of his own experimentations as follows. He made the first concave pan in 1941 with two to three notes, of no particular shape or grooving. It was just sunken and dented from the underside with a broom handle or a wooden object. He also followed no particular pattern or design but simply made this pan and all subsequent ones from the 18-to 20-gallon drum. He was trying to make pitches, to get as many as he could onto that surface. As stated before, prior to this innovation the top was convex with concave-sunken notes, and he could not get any consecutive pitches from that convex top. He found that with the new design he could better control the humps. He also was not looking for any definite positioning for the pitches either and randomly placed the notes any where he could.[34] For this contribution of the concave pan to the development of Pan, he stands proudly. While history may be uncertain of who first brought out the three-to four-note pan, no one can disclaim he was the first to sink the pan and pop up the notes. Time has since proved that the sunken pan is better for manipulating the arrangement of the notes. Soon, others were sinking their ping-pong pans, too, the name for the instrument beginning in 1945.

Debuting in the early '40s was a pan called "'round-the-world" because the notes were placed in a circle. This pan had three or four notes, which were not designed after any specific pattern or chord. They were placed according to what the men heard and wanted to capture on the pan to play a particular melody. Other pans were the doo-doop, a single-note pan; the bass kettle, two notes; and, the boom, one note.

Wishing to avoid not giving credit to whom it is due, Mannette prefers to cite 1943 to '44 as the time the men converted the convex kettle drum to concave and created two notes and a rhythm, called contrary beat, for that drum. In 1945 to '46, they came up with the tune boom, a biscuit drum played with one's hand. This also had a convex top, which they sank down and placed five notes on it. This was the precursor/ancestor of the cello pan, though it was not called cello then. He mis-credits Ollivierre, also called Fisheye, for making the tune boom.[35] Ollivierre was from the Red Army band.[36] According to Mannette, after Fisheye left Red Army and joined Invaders and brought his tune boom with him, Mannette saw and copied it.[37]

In 1944, Mannette developed the nine-note pan from the sweet-oil drum that came from Laventille. He called it the barracuda, the "baddest" ping-pong pan in PoS at the time, as previously stated. When Carnival resumed in May, 1945, after Germany surrendered on V-E Day and the government allowed celebration for the victory over Germany, he used his barracuda for the celebration. Later that year, during the V-J Day celebration of the Allies' victory over Japan, as previously stated, the band left Woodbrook that night for PoS. He was carrying his barracuda in his hand when the fighting began, and he dropped his pan and ran. The lost of the barracuda led to the decision to build the big pan in 1946, which he introduced at the Skinner's Park contest. He describes that deciding moment for building his big pan:

> ... With no pan to play and wanting to take part in the next year's contest, I decided to build a big pan and told my friends so. Everyone said it couldn't be done, and even if I did it would be too big and heavy to carry. But I'd decided

that I wasn't going to build that drum [the ping-pong] anymore. With the barracuda gone, I had to build something else. There was this piece of old, old pan that was sitting around in my father's backyard that was perfect for building the bigger pan. I took it back to the pavilion near the Queen's Park Oval right across the street, down in the back by the big saman tree near the Bleachers. I was trying to get a little darker stock, so day after day I would beat on it. It was kind of like in secret, except for the older guys, the groundsmen—Brandon, Ellis, Harold, and Pierre—who cleaned the Oval, cutting the grass and keeping the grounds clean. They knew what I was doing. It was during that time I decided to enter the Skinner's Park contest in San Fernando.

At the time, I was working at a machine shop and learning the fundamentals of pan-building, even though I was unaware of that at the time. I was learning about drilling, bit-cutting, welding, tempering, freezing, and plumbing—the techniques of black-smithing. I bought a two-pound hammer and with a raw barrel went to the back of the Oval pavilion and under the big saman tree and under the bleachers and worked daily on the drum. No one, except for the groundsmen, knew that I was actually building it for the Skinner's Park contest. When it was time for the contest, I took the pan down to San Fernando, and the nation saw the big pan for the first time. This was in 1946.[38]

Other big bands were competing, about ten in all. I was contestant number seven. I took the pan onto the stage in a brown crocus or burlap bag used for sugar. That was the first pan case of all time. The crowd, you could hear their speculation at what I was carrying onto the stage. I sat in a chair, perched the pan on my knee with one hand and with the other played Brahms's "Lullaby and Goodnight." Everyone was enthralled. It was a dynamic effect and they were delighted. Of course, I won the contest and was the talk of the island the next day. The next day, Sunday, in my father's backyard a crowd gathered to hear this drum, including Radio Trinidad.[39]

After he played for the crowd, Radio Trinidad invited him to play on the Auntie Kay children's program[40] the next Sunday morning, the first time the sound of the big pan was to be aired on national radio. He selected for that performance a part of Schubert's *Ave Maria*. That performance became the catalyst for his determined concentration on developing the instrument, and can it be recognized as the moment of conception that set in motion the birth of his following innovations.

What preceded can be viewed as his and the men's inspirational years: the appearance of the four-note ping-pong around the end of the '30s and into the early '40s; his introduction of the concaved pan shortly thereafter; the barracuda's public appearance in 1945 then its theft; then the big pan in 1946. These years indicate how the panyard continued to be a place of inspiration and innovations, and of where melodies were beginning to be played. In 1946 to '47, things then began to change even while the men continued to use the convex top to create their pitches for the convex boom pan, the convex kettle drum, and doo-doop bass pan.[41] Meanwhile, Mannette was himself honing the mechanical and elementary engineering skills he had developed on various jobs as a machinist, beginning with the first major job.

He first worked at the age of nineteen for about three years at Robinson Engineering, which was first located at French and Richmond Streets before it relocated to Edward Street. Robinson knew his sister Audrey and also knew him to be a bright young man, so he offered him the opportunity to learn the trade under his apprenticeship. He left Robinson Engineering and went to work for Acme Engineering located in Sealots in the Wrightson Road area and remained there for three to four years. His friend, Sidney, who was working at Acme as a foreman and knew him to be a conscientious worker, suggested that he come and work at Acme and earn more money than he was earning at Robinson. At Acme, he became acquainted with a very good machinist who left to work on the U.S. Navy base in Chaguaramas. Impressed with Mannette's skills as a machinist, he got him a job on the Navy base. All these jobs provided him with the foundational skills necessary for pan-building and tuning: hammering, tempering, welding, and black-smithing, among others.

When in 1946 he had decided to pattern the big pan similarly to the one used for the ping-pong, he was desirous of an instrument on which he could play the classical music and had set about developing such. The spot under the saman tree that stood near the bleachers in the Oval became one site of creativity, what Lloyd Best might recognize as one of Limbo's nuclei, as first mentioned in the Introduction of this work. To reiterate, Best defines Limbo as a place where "first imagining, and then creating or inventing, clear space and passage, where before there was none."[42] Months later, Mannette transferred his activities to his father's backyard, but for the time being the saman tree marked the site of his creative energies.

Having persisted in building a big pan and introducing it in 1946, after the contest he returned to improving it. Returning to his spot under the bleachers, every afternoon after work he hammered toward the materialization of his desire. Shaded by the bleachers and the saman tree, he worked with a two-pound hammer trying to sink the drum and noticed that the more he pounded the harder the surface got. He was unaware at the time that he was hardening the surface to the point of breaking it. He eventually sank the surface to four inches and when it refused to sink any lower he stopped. To this surface, he increased the number of notes. For instance, to the whole notes, he added an F-sharp, for he realized while playing a song on the barracuda that some notes were missing. So, his desire was merely to build a drum to include the notes he heard in songs, and in the process he sometimes built an entirely new drum just to include a single note. As the process continued to evolve, he built another pan to include the B-flat, high E, high F, then the high G, until he achieved fourteen notes.

However, in building those new pans and placing the notes randomly, he was unaware of the conflicting sounds this positioning caused, which today's musicians such as Tom Miller call unsympathetic vibrations.[43] Not knowing any better, he was simply adding notes to complete the melody of a particular song he desired to play. One such instance was when playing Rubenstein's "Romance in E-flat,"[44] he discovered that that note was missing. This building method shaped by non-prescriptive necessity and knowledge of music theory was how he determined to add any note. Between the years of 1946 and '47, he added to the notes just mentioned C-sharp, E-flat, and A-flat, simply by scrapping an old pan, stealing a drum or pan, and beginning to build a new pan all over.

This rapid building process was taking place generally in panyards throughout the country, as previously mentioned, and as Trinidad journalist Kim Johnson's extensive interviews with Pan pioneers and their stories published on the *Trinidad Internet Express* inform. All these accounts point to the pan's evolutionary process toward the making of an almost complete chromatic ping-pong pan, though Mannette, and most likely the majority of the panmen, was unfamiliar with the term at the time. He knew only that there were notes he desired to be in place and he put them in wherever he could. Such was his first complete ping-pong.

In 1947 to '48, he introduced the single second, a pan to play the second part and recreates that process briefly: "The single second was developed specifically to create a second voice, an accompaniment to the lead pan in a lower voice. That pan was sunk about five inches deep. The skirt length was about eight inches. The pattern for the single second was used from late '47 until 1950."[45] Following the single second, he introduced the single guitar in 1948. First, the single guitar was called the *grundig*,[46] named after a record-player from Germany—a German-type radio, which had a good bass sound to it and allowed the music which came from it to be deep and beautiful sounding. The name "guitar" came about later when after the men started playing the *grundig* it sounded like a strum, according to one person's observation. When he began experimenting with the guitar pan, again he was trying to match the sounds of the orchestra—the low sounds of the timpani and the bass—instruments of low tones. It started with a C, D, E, G, and F, and another C. Its skirt was fifteen inches long and its surface was sunk about five inches. The sinking depth of all the drums was about the same because he could not get it any lower. Therefore, he was not creating different depths for different pans.[47] Rather, his focus was on trying to make pitches and to get as many as he could on the surface of the sunken drum. It was around this time the transition was made to the sweet-oil drum.

All this time, he used one hammer to tune all the drums, grooving was done with wooden wedge, and grooving as it is known today with the first 55-gallon drum was done with the chisel. Today, he uses a range of hammer sizes and readily admits that the first person he saw work with a different hammer, a shoemaker hammer, was Rudolph Charles. The song "The Hammer" was written for him.[48] Pans began to be sunk deeper with the use of the heavier hammer, with the men first using the four-pound mall instead of the two-pound mall around 1949, which allowed them to strike the surface harder and sink the bottom to about five to six inches deep. They also discovered that notes could not be tuned when the segmented area was too small and the hammering technique was not right, which caused metal fatigue from excess hammering. They learned that the larger the segmented area, the easier it was to get a pitch to drop. The negative to this was a note can only move four levels comfortably.

For example, C can move to E, F-sharp, and possibly G. When the pan is extended too much over that size, the result is too much metal for the note to respond correctly. If excess metal was in the area in which the note was created, then the result was metal-tones, or overtones, to that particular note. Thus, the G note, for example, was required to be only about five inches wide. If the G required a six-to seven-inch area to be created, then the two inches of excess metal caused overtone problems for the fundamental of the note. The excess metal on steel, even with harmonic fifths or fourth tuning, caused too much metal tones that created distortions, which could not be controlled. These distortions interfered with the harmonics of the notes. Therefore, the result was all the hammering around the fundamental note created high sounds that interfered with the fundamental note, so that none of the harmonics of the fundamental note came through clearly.

Likewise, if one decided to build the low C on the cello, which is fifteen inches in diameter, and decided to make it only eight inches, then there was no way to get the low C down. The tuner could try to beat it up and down repeatedly to loosen it, so that it barely dropped in pitch. So, one had systemically to define the right size for each note.[49] This process took many years to determine and the men built hundreds of drums before they realized what was required in conjunction with what they were looking for. As originators with no pattern to follow, they did not know when they had reached the tone as it was supposed to be. They could only refer to their mental images and their previous failures. Mannette believes the men experienced many trials and errors before arriving at what they envisioned both mentally and audibly.

While the other men were experimenting and creating the two-and three-note kettle drum, both to play different rhythms, Mannette introduced the Invaders lead pan, the nine-note, ping-pong pan made from a 35-gallon sweet-oil drum. On this pan, he created the scale all from ear, which included all whole notes and the high D. The pan was a challenge. The notes were not placed in any particular pattern and so they clashed and could not be tuned properly. They created distortions because of their overtones. Then, he tried scattering the notes, which was a little better. He acknowledges that the person responsible for taking the lead pan to the next level of notable achievement was Anthony Williams, who in the late 1940s introduced what became known as the spider-web pan, designed in the cycle of fifths. Following Williams's innovation, the men adopted Williams's design, which still dominates the arrangement of the notes of the lead/tenor pan.

Mannette iterates that at this time no one was collaborating. Every creation was kept secret to that creator. If one happened to see someone else's creation, if it were better than his, then he tried to emulate it. However, no one was disclosing his art, and no one readily admitted that the other was better. Such admittance began with the arrival with the big pan, he avows. It was then the men began inquiring on how and how not to tune the big pan to achieve the Invaders' sound. Thus, some knowledge was reluctantly shared, spontaneously borrowed, or inadvertently relinquished, and the pan's versatility grew in fits and starts. The range of notes expanded from fourteen to twenty-two around late 1947, while the background drums were still being used for single or double notes, as well as for rhythm or accompaniment. The single second to play the second part was developed late 1947 into '48, and the melody pan with the low B, the note below middle C, was created around this same time.

All the while, the men had these other pans—the single second, the single guitar, the ping-pong—they had no pan with bass notes. He offers that they had the boom bass drum, until Neville Jules came out in 1949 with the caustic soda drum, a large, galvanize garbage can light enough for the men to hang around their shoulders. From this light can, Jules's innovation, came the bass drum with low notes, which included G, A, C, and D. The caustic soda drum was unlike today's pan. A little smaller than the 55-gallon drum, its concave depth was somewhat shallow, about three inches. Used until the 1950s, because of its light weight the men proudly marched through PoS with it. More important, it is noted as pivotal in launching the beginning of the full orchestra, with Mannette beginning to build the caustic soda drums, too. He further observes of this time that,

> While we were developing the pans, we had trouble in separating tones; meaning, we had trouble separating the overtones from the fundamental note. Keeping related tones or close tones from ringing into each other. One thing we did was scatter the notes, almost jig-saw puzzle-like, to see if we would be able to better tune the notes. It was deliberate, keeping the notes away from each in a criss-cross pattern.[50]

All in all, the big pan, the *grundig*, the caustic soda drum, and all the new additions grew from the men's search for a full harmonic relationship between the sections, even though they did not use any particular technique or specific plan to realize this goal. They were just looking for a fundamental low note. They were being guided by an innate spirit of competitiveness, a keen ear for music but a lack of formal musical training, and a desire for an instrument on which they could play all types of music, as the following section engages. Their spirits were infectious, both of the men living in the north as well as those in the south. Then, the year 1949 brought another novelty to the movement.

Kim Johnson's interview with Belgrave Bonaparte reveals that much activity was also happening in the south. Bonaparte demonstrated that steel bands could play chords and harmonize their sections. Southern Symphony, with talented musicians and tuners such as Earl Rodney, Alan Gervais, and Lincoln Noel, introduced playing with three sticks. Mannette heard for the first time a pan playing a chord when Invaders was invited to La Brea. As Bonaparte shared with Johnson:

> "We start to play 'So Deep Is the Night'. First time Ellie Mannette hear pan playing chord, [he] fly upstairs. He say he have to meet me. And then he ask: 'How you do that? How you do that?' I tell him.
>
> "I say, 'Well, I always had my musical knowledge so I used the scale from C from this pan, and I gone with C from this one, going down in the other pan.' That is how the second pan and guitar pan and all them thing come out. Is the first time they ever hear that. That time I experiment and bring out all that already in La Brea."[51]

Sound travels expeditiously across an island that is 1,981 square miles (5,130 square kilometers). The wind bears many ideas. Not only Mannette but all panmen throughout the island were being affected by each other's creativity and knowledge.

The year 1949 then became a major turning point in Mannette's life in another way, also. Not only were the panmen aware of his innovations, word was beginning to spread of what he was accomplishing and reached the ears of those actively promoting Trinidad art and music cultures. Edric Conner, a singer of classical music, Beryl McBurnie,[52] one of the Holder brothers, either Boscoe or Geoffrey (he cannot specifically recall), and other influential people recommended him for a music scholarship at the Birmingham School of Music in England. His nomination was submitted to Governor Sir Hubert Grant, who referred the matter to the Ministry of Education and Culture, and he was approved. The scholarship earned him an invitation to the governor's house where Sir Grant himself delivered the news to Mannette, acknowledging his earning the scholarship was based upon his creation of a musical instrument for the nation. Thus, during the latter part of the 1940s, not only was Pan decidedly on the move but Mannette was one of the men at the helm.

The steelband association also had already come into existence by this time, with the men themselves beginning to take responsibility for Pan's development and their own well being, as Albert Jones's narrative chronologizes. Additionally, the island began to be saturated with the sound of pan music—of the ping-pong and the big pan. Even so, the quality of the instruments was not very good because the men could not create anything substantial at the time. They struggled with their limited knowledge of steel and sound to do the best they could. Then, 1950 arrived and brought more activities for Mannette and the movement with the formation of the Trinidad All Steel Percussion Orchestra (TASPO).[53]

The Middle Years: A Perspective on the Violence and TASPO's Positive Influence

The road to TASPO was coated in blood and violence.

All the while the men struggled to improve their instruments, the violence and its repercussions continued, intricately interwoven with their artistic endeavors, their emerging art form, and the right that all people take for granted: the right simply to be, and be left alone while getting on with being human. They were men compelled by the longings of their heart toward the fulfillment of their heart's desire. Hence, they fought fiercely with each other, the colonial authorities, their neighbors, and their loved ones to bring into reality what was born of their consciousness, their emotive intelligence. They were not always undaunted when it seemed like all nature and society were against them, not knowing or caring or willing to understand what they were struggling to accomplish.

For Mannette, the 1940s were turbulent years, as well as for the other band members who met each fight head-on. In addition to the two stories that frame his biography, Mannette returns to the very painful experiences, still attempting to contextualize the violence toward coming to some understanding of why men choose violence over peace. He reminisces:

> The rivalry and the clashes between the bands were for no particular reason. We were all beating the same rhythms. Sometimes, one guy would have a girlfriend and that might have caused some jealousy. But how the fights really started, I don't know. I was a part of it, and I have no regrets. I never have regrets because these were things that took place within the interest and code of the art form. These were the difficulties and obstacles in the way of the code of the art form.
>
> There were also stories of stealing drums from the Navy base and the time I stole one from Maraval Road. I remember when I stole one and got my backside *planassed*. I stole one and jumped over the fence, and while running with it I stumbled and fell, and the man caught me and *planassed* me. I was about nineteen then.[54]

The band warfare continued on account of the music and rivalry to produce better sounding music, for better music attracted more girls. Most of the upper-class girls would not go to Laventille or John John to hang around men of a lower class, so they went to Woodbrook's Invaders panyard, as Mannette ponders. A rivalry related to music and women.

As previously stated, the Oval Boys often won the contests held around PoS, contests judged by music teachers from all over the islands. Contests were held at the Olympic Theatre, the Roxy Theatre, Skinner's Park, and other places. Winning these contests caused jealousy. Furthermore, Invaders' members lived in Woodbrook, in the vicinity of St. Clair, PoS's most affluent neighborhood. British, American, French, Canadian, and other Europeans lived in St. Clair. During Carnival, they dressed up in their rags, painted their faces, and jumped in Invaders band to its music that they loved, even though the next day they protested at the amount of noise the band made in its panyard.[55]

Another contributing factor to the clashes the Invaders had with other bands was the Beryl McBurnie's Dance Troupe, which was also from Woodbrook and Invaders played for her dance troupe. These associations with the affluent of St. Clair, McBurnie, and other socialites, all contributed to the jealousy, according to Mannette. When Invaders' members went into PoS and met members of bands from Laventille, John John, and Behind the Bridge, animosities surfaced and tempers along with them. The Invaders were called socialites and attacked, and Mannette as leader of the steel band fought back. His pride refused to allow him to take a beating from anyone without defending himself. He was no coward. In fact, they all fought back. They were men, and if they were with their women they dared not be shamed by having their masculinity threatened without retaliation. They refused to stand there after some one walked up behind them and *cuffed* them at the back of their head, in the presence of their girlfriends. They dared not be belittled. So, they carried their knives, machetes, and cutlasses and used them when they had to.

Additionally, Mannette as leader of the Invaders was their ready target. If he could be demoralized, then his entire steel band could be weakened and put out of all competitions. He and Invaders would be at the mercy of bullies who loved to prey on those perceived weak and vulnerable. The law of any jungle—colonial or otherwise—dictated survival. The spirit of any man demanded the right to dignity. The right of any human is to live in dignity. They all fought ferociously for this right.

Other area bands were also in rivalry: San Juan against Belmont, John John against Laventille, St. James against Belmont, San Juan against Laventille. At any given moment, any band could be in rivalry with another. And, when they clashed on Carnival day, the outcome was horrific. Because, when one thousand people were coming in one direction and another one thousand coming from another collided, all carrying their pans, they pushed and shoved each other to get by, with no one willing to yield to the other, regardless of age, color, or class. A cyclical Oedipus-Laius confrontational moment that makes us interrogate our own failure to learn from the mistakes of our ancient forebears.

Mannette's dismay today is at how a little pushing and shoving then escalated to violence. Sometimes, one band was going home and the other one was blocking the way of the players. Everyone was tired and tempers were short. It was hot; they were hungry; or, they just wanted to get it on with their selected woman for that Carnival Monday or Tuesday night. So many little factors could have contributed to the fights. Another factor that triggered the fighting was someone just accidentally dropping a bottle in a drunken stupor. The sound of the crash signaled a fight had broken out, that bottle-throwing at the enemy had begun. Feelings of revenge harbored all year round because someone had crossed someone else's path, or had cut a hand for spite, or had stolen a woman, and so on, got license for retaliation and the fighting began.

The older men wanted to stop the warring: Ossie Campbell, Barong, Oscar Pile, Guppee, to name a few. Once, they met in a yard lit by a circle of flambeaux and sat down under a tent to drink Carib beer and discuss how to end the warring. Mannette accounts that some youngsters did not want peace. When the meeting was in progress and they were negotiating the terms for peace, those who did not want peace remained on the outside grumbling and fretting about no need for peace. Suddenly, they started shelling bottles into the tent, not caring that they could hit some of their own older band members, men old enough to be their fathers. The meeting broke up as everyone scampered for cover and the younger men continued to shell the tent with bottles.

Though the meeting halted, attempts toward peace did not. The older men decided to find a safer place to meet and continue negotiations and chose the Quarry in John John, which was protected by a tall, perpendicular wall standing at a ninety-degree angle from the ground and many feet high. They thought the wall would be their protection. No one could enter the Quarry yard without being noticed and scaling the wall provided a feat for no coward. One Sunday evening, all the band leaders met there to talk with Pierre, Dennison, Goddard, and other leaders. Those youngsters, as Mannette refers to them, found a way to scale that wall and from the wall's flat top they showered down rocks onto the negotiators.

Mannette was himself particularly interested in peace. He had had too many close calls. One Carnival night, a big band was going up Charlotte Street, and a full-blown fight began directly in front of Hell Yard. He was still carrying his pan around his neck. Many times, those who were playing toward the back of the band did not know what was going on up front. He saw a man approaching him carrying a machete. As they neared each other, the man swung the machete at his face. Though Mannette tried to dodge him, the machete cut a vein over Mannette's right index finger. He dropped his pan and ran, leaving a trail of blood in his wake. The next day, the newspaper carried the news that Ellie Mannette's right hand was chopped off in PoS.[56]

Another night, a man fired some gun shots at him, and everybody thought he was surely killed. This happened on Wrightson Road and involved members from Funland, a Belmont band: Eddie Boome, Arthur Tramcar, and others. He had argued with them over something trivial and had left them at one club and gone to another called Stork. Eddie Boome with his gang followed him there. He was at the bar talking with another guy when he looked back and saw about ten of them (Boome and his Belmont gang) walking in. He next felt a thud on the back of his head that knocked him forward. This challenge led to a terrible fight between Eddie and him. Fortunately, Goldteeth, a Renegades member whom everyone respected, was there.

Since Mannette was alone, Goldteeth and his guys from Renegades came to his defense. Because of his esteem, when he called out, "No, all of yuh don't fight with Ellie, man. Let Ellie and Eddie fight it out," the rest of the gang retreated. He was saved from being jumped by the whole gang. He reminisces that night Goldteeth saved his life, even though Invaders and Renegades were strong rivals. He and Eddie Boome took the fight outside, which stopped when the police arrived. By then he was so angry, he rounded up a gang of Invaders guys and returned the following night to the Wrightson Road club looking for the Belmont gang to finish the fight.

Unknown to them, one of the guys from Eddie Boome's gang had a gun. Birdie, Francis Wickham, Ken Jones, and others were with Mannette, and they proceeded up Wrightson Road checking the various clubs looking for Eddie and his gang. By the time they got to the Diamond Horse Shoe Club, someone had already informed Eddie and his gang that Mannette was looking for them. When Mannette and his gang arrived, Eddie and his gang were standing on the pavement waiting for them. Mannette and his gang stayed in the road behind the line of cars parked along the curb and challenged Eddie to finish the fight that the police stopped the previous night. Then Mannette heard Birdie mutter, "Ellie, Ellie, watch it. A guy has something in his pocket." Thus alerted, nonetheless, he continued to challenge Eddie to come out in the road so they could finish their fight. Mannette had his hand in his shirt, ready to draw his knife from under his left armpit. Eddie had his hand in his shirt, ready to draw his knife, too. They were both strapped with knives, the nine-and twelve-inch ones popular in those days. Mannette's knife was about twelve inches. He and Eddie continued to taunt each other.

Suddenly, Mannette heard a loud, "Pow!" Immediately, he ducked behind a car and saw the fire of a bullet as it ricocheted along the roof of the car. Realizing that the man had a gun and that his knife was no match against a gun, he knew to get out of there instantly and ran up Tragarete Road. The man immediately followed after him and continued shooting, the sound of "Pow! Pow! Pow!" echoing almost simultaneously with the sounds of the bullets as they whizzed pass him. He fled pass Fatima College, continued down Gattica Street, up Baden Powell Street, and made it home safely. The next day he got a gun and went looking for Eddie Boome and his gang for revenge, again. This intense hatred for each other remained between the two for quite a while, with Eddie during another incident cutting a hole into Mannette's knee with an iron bolt.[57]

Continuing to identify all his trophy-scars of war, he recalls another fight that left a permanent scar over his left eye. This one happened at a dance in town over a girl named Elsie, and involved Ossie and a member of Desperadoes named Seth Banfield. Ossie was with Elsie, other guys were with their girls, and everyone was dancing and generally having a good time. Suddenly, a fight broke out and when Mannette rushed over to the fight in the corner of the hall, he saw his brother, Birdie,[58] on the ground being beaten up by a group of guys. He rushed into the crowd and tried to pull people off. Seth had a Vat 19 bottle. He states,

> When someone pulled my shirt and I turned around, Seth landed the bottle on my eye. The blow stunned me and knocked me backward. They had to take me to the hospital for stitches, eight or nine stitches for that gash. By the time I arrived at the hospital, the whole Invaders band was there. All the bad Invaders boys came to the Emergency Room with their machetes, knives, and iron bolts, so that once I was released we could go and find the culprits and have revenge. We left the hospital around 2:00 AM, blood all over me. This time I was wearing an all-white flannel suit for the dance, I led the way to John John Hill looking for these guys, about thirty of them. Because, from the time I got that cut they all gone and my boys came out.[59]

He recalls another incident that resulted in a cut on his left side, about three inches above his waist, during a fight that occurred at the Diamond Horseshoe Club. That gash required twenty-four stitches.

These reminiscences remind him of his general caution about all newspaper documentation of incidents because the Trinidad dailies almost never reported any of the stories accurately—what occurred, how and why, and so on. Those disdainful reporters never bothered to try to interview him or the men to get their perspectives. Their behavior simply made sensational news and fed into local propaganda that stigmatized the men as worthless *bad-johns*. Had anyone made the effort to perceive Mannette, in particular, as a man having dreams, goals, and a definite purpose; had anyone taken the trouble to deal with him not as a commodity but as a human being, that inquirer would have learnt that invariably these fracases were taking a toll on him. He dared not risk another slash on the eye that could blind him, or have a finger or hand chopped off, or have his knee broken that left him crippled for the remainder of his life, or any other physical assault. Instead, he and the men continued to be viewed as worthless bodies who could not be afforded such treatment that would have affirmed their human dignity. Equally valued, equally respected, and equally treated, their energies could have been channeled collaboratively and productively to the benefit of the entire nation.

Their life-threatening close shaves, the fatal ones that resulted in the senseless murders and resulting imprisonment and hanging, and all the other acts of reckless violence in which they embroiled, that stemmed from colonial oppression could have been mitigated, sometimes even averted. They were men, many of them frustrated to the point of pettiness that became cancerous. The hand turned against the eye. The body attacking itself because its nuclei had become unnaturally dysfunctional. Apathy or mere pococurantism fostered the east-west, ghetto-affluent neighborhood dichotomies. However, men were not cockroaches, nuisances to be squashed under a system's boots. They all deserved to live off the fruits of their labor, especially fruits that promised a harmonious environment. Hence, Mannette fully supported and participated in all peace-making efforts.

Later on, such efforts were promoted by influential people who were interested in seeing the Steelband industry go forward positively: Eric Williams, Lennox Pierre, Beryl McBurnie, Albert Gomes, and others who intervened in various ways. Seeing the potential for peace in corporate sponsorship and job opportunities, they pushed their agenda for peace among the bands, and worked with TTSA, later called NATTS, to this effect. While sponsorship was implemented by the panmen themselves and already underway, as Albert Jones's narrative accentuates, influential people began advancing the carrot of sponsorship as one mechanism toward peace. They determined that the financial support of five hundred to one thousand dollars came with the obligation for the men to respect the source of their financial support by not tarnishing the name and image of their sponsor, or risk losing sponsorship. They solicited the help of more private corporations to assume sponsorship, and with the vision of what their support promised for the entire nation, the peace process was underway.

Shell Oil was first to sponsor Invaders which became Shell Invaders. Others followed like Carib Lager (a beer company) who sponsored Tokyo and the band became Carib Tokyo. Solo (a sweet drink, or soda, company) sponsored Desperadoes; Pan Am sponsored North Stars; Esso sponsored Tripoli; and British Petroleum, Neal & Massey, Coco Cola, and other companies sponsored other bands. One cause for the warfare could be met head-on. The other cause was more elusive and intangible.

Mannette's heart and mind and soul were consumed with developing the steelpan. His family did not want him involved with Steelpan because of the reputation of panmen, and tolerated his involvement because it opened doors for them. Mannette's talents lessened the stinging reputation of the stigmatized panmen. Many of the élite who lived in the Woodbrook vicinity—the Hancocks, Woodens, Armstrongs, McNeeleys, Stollmeyers, and Pierres—loved to jump up in Invaders band at Carnival time. In fact, the only reason his parents got to know them was because of Pan. Doctors and lawyers who would not have anything otherwise to do with his parents came into the yard while they were practicing, followed the band on J'ouvert morning and jumped in *las' lap* with them. Obviously having a love-hate relationship with Pan and panmen, the high class loved steelband music but refused to validate the men who produced it. Mannette was aware that they respected, liked, and accepted him but to a limited extent. Such became evident while walking down Frederick Street. Upon approaching these same people who loved him at Carnival time, they averted their eyes from him. Not even a nod during the off-season to acknowledge his existence.

The painful memory of being snubbed in public is assuaged today by the knowledge of what he has accomplished both in Trinidad and the United States. In Trinidad, despite his reputation as a bad boy and because he was also involved with Beryl McBurnie's Little Carib Dance Theatre, Invaders became the band that accompanied Little Carib, as it is commonly called. There, he got to know the Espinets, Aubrey Adams, Albert Gomes, and all the people who patronized Little Carib. He proudly recalls having met Paul Robeson when he performed at Little Carib. Even more significant than meeting Robeson was his association with Eric Williams who also frequented there. All in all, Mannette was popular with the so-called socialites and developed the reputation of being one of the men who took the steel band out of the gutter and into the threshold of society. He dismisses the idea that he was the one responsible for taking the pan into high society and recognizes that music itself is to be so credited.

Fortuitously, TASPO arrived at an opportune moment. Without discounting the various publications and other versions, from Mannette's perspective TASPO became a reality under the industriousness of Lennox Pierre, a music teacher and lawyer, who saw that it would be a good thing for the stars of the various bands to travel abroad and display their talent. When the British festival approached, the panmen were informed that if they could form this band the government would send them to England to show off these new instruments. Mannette states that initially they did not take this talk seriously, even though Lennox Pierre got to work behind the scenes to make this idea become a reality. One day, Pierre called Mannette to inform him that he was one of the men mentioned and would be selected to go to England, if the men could get the band organized.

Despite Invaders not being a member of the steelband association,[60] he was one of the selected because his innovative contributions to the movement were well known. To become organized, the men needed to find an instructor to teach them music, even if a little, and to develop an understanding of musical terms and techniques. Eventually, the organizers of TASPO gathered the selected men in a community center in Cocorite and pointed out that if they were to go to England they had to come together as a team. They brought in all the leaders of the various bands whom Mannette recalls included: Andrew "Pan" de la Bastide, Winston "Spree" Simon, Theo Stephens, Patsy Haynes, Sterling Betancourt (now Sir Sterling Betancourt),[61] Tony Williams, Dudley Smith, Philmore "Boots" Davidson, Aubrey Bonaparte, Sonny Roach, and himself. Lieutenant Nathaniel Griffith, a police band director from [Barbados],[62] was then introduced as being brought in specifically to direct the band. TASPO met and rehearsed at the Cocorite Youth Centre and played in theatres—Globe, Olympic, and Roxy—and other places to raise money for the trip.

That moment when the panmen were dealing with the prospect of going to England, he was eager to put all the violence behind him. He eagerly anticipated learning much more from Lieutenant Griffith. He was impressed that when Griffith first arrived to hear them play and observed the different instruments and patterns and styles, one of the first things he did was point out that they were not playing on pitch. "You're not on pitch," he declared unceremoniously. The men had no tuning fork to tune their pans and used mouth-organs or whatever they could find to help them locate the sounds they were hearing in their heads. Griffith, on the other hand, used a violin. First, he played a note and the men copied it onto the pan as close as they could. Then, he played a note on the piano and the men did the same. Having set the standard for pitch, he then proceeded to set chromatic standards. None of them knew what he was talking about. At least speaking for himself, Mannette did not know what Griffith was talking about.

Griffith was generally a positive influence in Mannette's life and he remembers him fondly, despite the clash of two strong wills and personalities. He describes one deciding moment for himself and invariably the movement:

> We were gathered in the youth centre in Cocorite in a big, open concrete yard. He [Griffith] said to me, "Now, you're supposed to be the main boy in most of the work here. So, I want you to build me some steel bass drums, because we cannot go to England with one bass." At the time, we had just one caustic-soda bass drum with four notes. "So, you have to build the chromatic bass drum." "What is chromatic?" He then explained to me what he meant by

chromatic, and at the end of his explanation I said bluntly, "That's impossible. That just can't be built."

He replied, "I told you to build a steel drum, and I want you to build a steel drum," he said firmly. His manner brooked no argument. I was equally firm, "And, I telling you that can't be done. I don't care what you say. About chromatic,-somatic,-or whatever-matic. I know what I can do and I can't build what you talking about." I was shouting by this time. Who the hell this man think he was? Coming from wherever he come from to tell me what to do. We had some argument about this and slowly I felt myself yielding to the idea of what he was suggesting. Maybe, just maybe it was not impossible. Maybe, we can get something out of steel drums. I, for one, wanted to go to England looking and sounding good. This thing was too important to me. Finally, the desire to sound our best won and I decided to find some drums and try out his suggestion.

He was very pleased to see that I'd come around the day I told him I had some drums and ready to try his suggestion. That night, he came to the yard with even paper and pencil, ready to lay out his design of the notes. "Let's lay it out this way." He suggested how the notes could be arranged and grouped. Three drums with five notes each, with the lowest note being G. When I got started, I was no longer thinking impossible but how to make this thing a reality. I worked hard at this for weeks. When I was finally done, all he said by way of praise or compliment was, "You see? And you thought it couldn't be done. But look. You've made it happen. Now we can play music! We have a bass that can play the chromatic." This is how I learned how to make the bass drums and what chromatic really was.[63]

When they were finished with the bass, Griffith had another order for them to fill: "We have a single second and single guitar but we cannot use those. We have to have the double guitar and double cello." This was how the idea for those instruments came about, their reality being born by both Anthony Williams and Mannette. Without reservations, Mannette credits both himself and Williams for building the cello. They both started with two pans, which were called tune boom at the time, but ended up again meeting Griffith's expectation. So, for the England trip they had all chromatic sections.

He recalls that different men built the drums for TASPO. He and Spree Simon built their own lead pans, and Rudolph Stevens from San Fernando also built his own lead. Williams also built his lead and the cello for Bonaparte. Mannette also built a cello.[64] When the band sailed on July 5, 1951, aboard the SS San Mateo, it had six leads, two seconds, one bass, and two double cellos. However, they ended up with five lead players because Sonny Roach got so sick on their way to Barbados that when they arrived there he was placed on a ship bound for Trinidad and returned home.

He remembers vividly Griffith, a force to be reckoned with, commanded all the men's respect because he saw their capabilities and demanded that they rose not only to the occasions of becoming the first ambassadors of sorts for the country but also to their own potential. Reflecting upon the man himself, Mannette still marvels that he was so positively influential. He describes him as retired and in his early '50s,

> ... A short, heavy-set man of a brown complexion. A dynamic, hard-working man who pushed us hard. I worked well with him and had no problems with him. In fact, all the boys respected him a lot. He knew what he was about, what he wanted us to accomplish, and settled for nothing less. It was only after we were on that TASPO tour that the boys began misbehaving. Some wanted to stay [in England] and some wanted to go [home]. Griffith aggressively promoted the band while we were there. Got us gigs in France and Italy. His goal was to get us to travel all over Europe, introducing to the world something new, this phenomenon. He expected that people would respond well to us. They did in England and France.
>
> But the boys started rebelling, because some wanted to stay and some wanted to go home and caused an uprising against him. Well, they were already bad-behaved men who took their bad behavior with them all the way to England. The boys started their own uprising and rebelling against each other. It was not his fault, really. In fact, he did his best to have the boys work out their differences, but they had their bad behavior from home, which they brought with them. They were still bands warring against each other—Tripoli against John John, Tokyo against Casablanca against Invaders, and so on. Now, instead of an entire band it was the individual band member at war with another. They took sides. We divided into cliques. I, Aubrey Bonaparte, Stephen, Sterling Betancourt, and Andrew de la Bastide formed one clique. The other clique was the remaining men—five against five.[65]

The band remained in England for about seven to nine months and traveled and performed throughout the British Isles. From there, it proceeded to France, having been invited to play at a circus. It was there for three months when the men began misbehaving, most likely because some of them had become homesick and lonely; or simply as Mannette states, they had "brought their bad behavior with them and in Paris fought among themselves. One guy ended up in the hospital, so Lieutenant Griffith called for them to return home and aborted the tour," and, consequently, the band did not go on to Italy. Immediately after the fight among the men, Mannette himself decided he was ready to return home. For the most part, though, the trip inspired him tremendously. The introduction of the chromatic pan helped him to see the broader picture in developing the pan to play the classical music he was so deeply entrenched in. With this understanding of chromatics, he began to see how to develop pans for a full orchestra. In England, they had heard other bands play their music, too, and that affected him tremendously, to the extent that the music scholarship he had won held no appeal for him. He explains the reasons for refusing the scholarship.

While in England, Alfonso, the band's agent who managed the band's programs and performances, investigated the exact nature of the scholarship for Mannette. Upon contacting the Birmingham School of Music, Alfonso was informed that Mannette had to visit the school himself, so together they went. The School confirmed that it was an open scholarship, that Mannette's name was on record as the recipient of the scholarship, and what was required of him was to submit his Trinidad school transcript and his academic standing. Not knowing whether this information was available, he decided to turn it down, to forget about it. Mannette recounts that visit to the school:

> When I got there, they researched the information. "You're Elliott Mannette?" "Yes, I am." "You received an open scholarship from your government with no given time when to start. You may start today or next year. We'll give you a list of what you need to bring when you arrive, what financial obligations you're to meet, etc." I took the list and put it into my pocket. As we left, I turned to Alfonso and said, "I don't need this scholarship. I want to tune drums." He replied, "Well, at least you should go to school." That ended our conversation. After I returned to where we were staying at the King's Court Hotel on Hyde Park, I told them what transpired. "They want me to start school when I'm through with TASPO. But I'm not going. I don't want it."
>
> In my next letter home to my father, I wrote that I was not interested in the scholarship because I really wanted to tune drums. I wrote because I couldn't telephone. My father didn't have a phone in his house. I also wrote that we were going on to France for three months to perform after we were finished in England, and from France I planned to return home. The reason was that with thoughts of the chromatic, the close-up sight and sound of the big orchestras I heard at the Savoy, the symphonies I heard, made me wonder whether I could get these pans to sound like those orchestras. I got goose pimples just listening to these sounds and imagining the possibilities of the pan.
>
> Intuitively, I knew that I couldn't realize that dream in England. Besides which, by that time I'd completely forgotten all about the scholarship while my mind explored what I was envisioning. I couldn't wait to get back home and get to work. I had a picture and sound in my mind I wanted to develop and needed to be in the right environment to do this. I had a lot of ideas in my head about developing the instrument. Of bringing into practice and reality these ideas ... to [be able to] distinguish the voices within the orchestra. Voices that I wanted to be heard on the drum.[66]

Having already toyed with the idea of refusing the Birmingham scholarship because he could not fathom how it would serve his growing interest in building instruments that matched all the voices of the orchestra, the European tour helped him to crystallize the certainty that he needed to be in his natural environment to pursue his dreams of developing the pan. The scholarship would have transformed him into a colonial man, yes, but not an empowered, enabled one. He could not be like the two who "ran away and returned to England—Sterling Betancourt and Philmore Davidson—with the intention never to return to Trinidad." Not him. Not even a potential love-interest could dissuade him from returning.

While in England he met a White nurse, Nancy McIntyre, who was willing to support him financially had he decided to remain. But he refused her offer, returned the money (a large sum of pounds) she had given him, and returned home. He always felt, and still do, that returning to Trinidad was his best decision, despite what he faced, because his dream was to expand the concept of the steel band. Immediately upon returning from England, he got to work on the double second in 1952.

But returning was an unpleasant experience because of his refusal to make well his music scholarship. He painfully recalls those days:

> We got back home in January or February of '52 and I went straight to hunting for drums to build the double second. I listened for what I heard in England and knew what we did. I knew we were limited in our scope and I had to expand that scope. I also improved the bass from three [pans] to five.
>
> ... Percy Serrano and Bertie Marshall were the first ones to begin tuning with overtones and octaves. Percy's name is rarely mentioned because he left Trinidad for England and few people can remember him. But he did the first drum for Katzenjammers in '52. He was first to build notes that rang out. Bertie Marshall came after Percy. I struggled to get the ring of Percy and Bertie's drums, because my drums had a mellow sound and not that ring. But what I was going through didn't make anything easy.
>
> ... When I got home, I had to face all the ugly responses of the public regarding my decision. The newspapers called me names such as: worthless, having no ambition to study, didn't want to go to school, a vagabond, only wanted to come back home to play garbage cans and fight, and all that kind of nonsense. Even though the band had been formed and represented Trinidad, we still had the stigma of being bad boys. They still had bad attitudes toward us. We were all poor boys from Trinidad's lower class. My mother was a housewife and my father a poor man. All the TASPO members were poor men, too. They weren't working anywhere and came with no affluence. None of us was in middle or upper classes.

In fact, we were called boys from the gutter. These criticisms of me came from these middle and upper class people, not those in Pan. They felt so self-righteous in unleashing their scorn and contempt upon me. "I knew Ellie Mannette was no good and up to no good. Imagine that. He turned down a full government scholarship to beat pan. He has a fairly good high school education and refused the opportunity to improve himself with a college education." It was horrendous.

My parents were upset and threw me out. Sometimes, they relented and took me back in then threw me out again. My sisters helped me out a lot by taking me in during these times. I slept where I could and struggled a lot, grateful for those who would see me and tried to ignore those who held me in contempt. Before going to England, I could get drums a little freely because they were beginning to get around. Someone would occasionally sell or give me a drum. However, after all that name-calling, I couldn't even get a drum to buy. The oil company refused to sell me a drum. I would go to Shell Oil and request that they sell me that old, empty, unused barrel and they would refuse. My name was now associated with notoriety. They chased me away calling me the vagabond who refused a scholarship. That's when I turned to out-and-out stealing, and those stolen drums were cherished. It was hard when one got broken. It was a good thing I had the support of the other vagabonds.[67]

He further describes how he and the other vagabonds mastered their art of drum-stealing, which enabled them to build new pans during the years 1952 to 1957:

The naval base at Chaguaramas housed many abandoned drums which were piled high behind a very high fence, which yard was shaped like a horse-shoe, and protected by a guard and dog. From the Trinidad's people part of the island, we could see the drums. At the bottom of the fence there was a part of the yard that jutted out into the water. We timed the guard and dog as they made the rounds—a twenty-minute round—and posted two guys as lookouts to signal when the guard rounded the corner and was out of sight of the jutting land. The guys would signal with flashlights when they were coming back around—we had twenty minutes to steal a drum.

We swam out into the water and dog-paddled until the watchmen signaled to us that the guard had gone on the other side. Once we got the signal, we swam quickly into the compound, rushed into the yard, pulled some barrels down, threw them into the water and swam, pushing the drums ahead of us to the other side, where we would haul them on to the land and into the bushes. There, we'd cut them, then place them on our bicycles' handle and ride home. This theft went on for a few months because this was the best way we could get drums to develop.[68]

He catalogues and chronologizes his innovations and improvements made from stolen drums during the decade of the 1950s. The first instrument he made upon returning from England in '52 was the whole-tone double second, followed by the double guitar (first called the double cello) in '53 to '54, in '55 the five-bass, and the triple cello made in late '56. He marks '56 as special, the year of Sparrow's calypso, "Jean and Dinah," for which he created an accompaniment on the cello (made from galvanize drums) for this song. He recalls that Choy Amin and Bertram Inniss came to the Invaders panyard to listen to his rehearsal of this song.

Mindful that TASPO traveled with a bass section of three drums section, he informs it was later the two more drums were added to this section to make it a five-bass. Of the double second, he remarks that it was in low chromatic and played fairly well, and that the double guitars (also called double cello) were built by him and Tony Williams: he built it for Dudley Smith (from Belmont) and Williams built it for himself, as previously stated. He also rebuilt the double cello (or double guitar) by cutting the length, making it shorter, and called it the double guitar.

He relates that he dreamt of the cello—the diminished part, the placement of the notes, the exact notes. One morning, he awoke from sleep and drew out the design he saw in a dream on paper, and corrected his sketches on his way to work at Robinson Engineering. Then, that weekend he went looking for drums to build what he saw in a dream. So, the design and pattern of the cello that exists today came to him in a dream. He made the triple cello in '58 and the tenor bass in '59."[69] He offers some additional insight into what he sought to capture in each of his creations:

> When I decided to design the double second, somewhat after the single second whose notes included low G, low A, high G-sharp, high B-flat, low B, high C, and low C, I wanted the additional pan for range. I decided if I was scattering my notes on my original lead, then for this pan-section, I would design a right-hand second and a left-hand second. But I wanted both hands to play one note. So, I alternated the notes, left-right-left-right. I wasn't thinking in terms of where I was placing the notes. All I wanted to do was scatter the big notes. I didn't realize in so doing that I was forming the augmented pattern, [which] formed a geometric pattern. This happened quite accidentally.
>
> When I introduced the double guitar, I also at this time created my own pattern for the double guitar. Then the triple cello came out of my desire to get a full range of half tones, how to get the full range of overtones in half tones. This came in '58 to me in a dream. I got up in the middle of the night

and sketched out what I saw on paper. This, however, is not what it finally turned out to be. I had seen the small notes on the rim and the low notes in the middle. I had to change that because I found the little notes on the outer rim wasn't working. It wasn't until the early '70s that I finally changed it to what it is today. All those years, I'd been trying to improve what I did in '58. Some of these pans still exist, because I made these pans for some schools in New York—in Dundee and Jamestown, New York. Ron Miller, the professor there, wanted to change his drums for the ones today. I may take them back and include them in my archive. There's nothing else I can do with them. The high note on the rim is a strangled note that has no ring.

The tenor bass was innovated in '59 with four pans, each with six notes, starting with low E. Now, it starts with F. When we went to England, the lowest note was G. We just couldn't get it to go any lower. With the creation of the tenor bass, I had a little more practice at what I was doing. I tried the addition of the low E and found I could manage it.

When I first developed the second [pan], it was terrible with circular notes, not square notes like we have today. I placed less notes inside. Now, I have the B on one side and the A on the other side. On the left side, I put the B-flat and the A-flat. Now, these notes are on the inside. I had ten instead of eight notes around the rim.[70]

I also had a problem with sinking the drum to accommodate the number of notes I wanted to include. Without the proper tools and techniques, the surface kept breaking. Every time I tried to go down to five to six inches, the surface broke. I had to then settle for a shallower surface. That first set I built, Malcolm Weekes and Jerry Lopatten has a set of those drums.[71]

During this time, the bass was improved. He continues:

Still desiring to match the sounds I'd heard at the Savoy, I wanted pans with low notes. With experimentation, I went down from the G to the F then down to the E, after I'd changed from three notes to four notes. Then in 1955, I came out with the five-bass section. During '51 to '55, I learned how to manipulate the steel much better. I learned how to get the pitch to drop considerably. Eventually, I could get as low as C. The six-bass section with three notes each didn't come until the late '70s, '70 to '71. Jimmy Leyden was instrumental in this development. When I met Jimmy, I was working in New York City with my band. All the bands were still playing the five-barrel bass section. Each barrel had five notes. Now, the pans have three notes each. We came up with the cycle of fifths bass drums to go down to the B-flat. Jimmy and I started the low A, but I wasn't happy with it. Maybe, now I can get the A clearer.[72]

, this period, 1952 to 1955, was his most innovative, with some external influences, TASPO being the strongest and most positive. He dared to chart a course based on a drive, shaped by inspirational dreams that intimate that he may be a mystic, of sorts, and lived all the consequences of his choices. It mattered to him that his defiance of the colonial structure could have been his undoing. He was fully aware that many in Trinidad were more concerned with maintaining that structure even though they served the system as mere custodians of capitalism and colonialism (Fanon). He, on the other hand, could not be demoralized into living in a state of compromise merely to reaffirm anyone's school, regardless of the school's status. Rather, it mattered more to him that he remained true to himself, his vision for Pan, his right to define his goal and purpose in life, and all that defined his sense of self and being. While such clarity of mind and purpose is not unique to Mannette, one can not but wonder at the source of his inspiration. Indeed, who is this man whom some hail as a creative genius, a description to which he demurs?

Identifying himself as not a very spiritual person and no mystic, he states that he has not hesitated, however, to pray, to call on Jesus for help to understand how to create the pan he dreamed of. He does not perceive himself as having a muse, a particular source of inspiration for the pan, but notes that people have said to him he was here before. This is his second return to this life. He cites people who have said that his father was some old Egyptian or a Pharaoh who developed things, a Pharaoh's child. But he dismisses all such mythical and mystical ideas and instead claims that his source of inspiration was pragmatically classical music. He listened to all classics intently and desired to create instruments on which this music could be played, these voices be expressed. He wanted the voices of the orchestra to be expressed on pan. He perceives himself rather as very down-to-earth, grounded and close to the natural steel elements, that aspect of nature from which steel and things related emerge. The blacksmith. The silversmith.[73] Brathwaite in his poetry collections identifies this source of inspiration as Shango, and Albert Jones acknowledges both Shango and Rada who influenced the men of the various yards.[74]

Mannette recalls that even while he was creating these additions toward the creation of a complete steel symphonic orchestra, much internecine fighting and rivalry continued among the bands during these years. The men's travels abroad, of serving of ambassadors as sorts for Trinidad and Tobago, did little to nothing to change either the men's self-image or other people's image of the men, as previously stated. True, some had visited England, Europe, and various Caribbean islands. Yet, they were dogged with injurious insults born out of contempt for them as workers worthy of their hire, as the Invaders experienced when the band visited Aruba and Antigua. He recounts:

> … Invaders was hired by some lawyers to go to Aruba to play. We traveled to Aruba and when we got there we performed in a sports stadium. We played for two nights, and after playing we went the lawyers' office to collect our pay. They said they couldn't pay us because they didn't make enough money. We didn't believe them because we saw that a lot of people had attended the events of the two nights. The boys then started to make a lot of fuss, demanding some pay. This was two o'clock in the afternoon. We went calling at the office. One poked his head out of his upstairs window and yelled to us that we couldn't come up, to wait at the bottom of the steps. He withdrew his head.
>
> A few moments later, he looked out again and tossed out a small bundle to us. He'd wrapped a little money in tissue paper and tossed it out the window to us, standing at the bottom of the steps, like we were dogs. This happened in Aruba.
>
> … We also had some trouble in Antigua at a sports complex when they chased us around and wanted to beat us up. Other bands were there—Hell Gates and some others I can't recall right now. But because we were more advanced and played better than the other bands, we had to scamper for our lives to get away from those Antiguans.[75]

The Aruba incident still smarts today, just as much as the following one:

> A German producer got me and Rock Johnson, who is now deceased, to demonstrate to him in Invaders yard how to tune a pan. He came with his camera crew of three to four people, who documented the process of pan-building for world-wide use. We didn't even think of signing a contract with him. So, he took advantage of our naïveté. When we were finished, we both played solos, Rock on his pan and I on mine. This demonstration went on for a few days while he photographed and documented the entire process of pan-building (burning, tuning) and -playing.
>
> When he was finished, he told us to meet him at an office on Frederick Street at an appointed time to receive our payment. We'd charged him just a little for providing him this information. The charge wasn't much at all. When we arrived the next day, we were told that he'd already left his office to return to Germany. So, we called Customs to enquire about his departure. Customs confirmed that he had left and by that time was already in international waters. Because he was in international waters, they couldn't touch him. He was beyond the limits of Trinidad. The coast guard couldn't bring him back. The only thing that could be done was to contact his German firm and report him. I decided not to pursue it. But that betrayal hurt me.[76]

Hence, the men were dealing with frustration on multilevels: dehumanization; under-appreciation; being swindled repeatedly; and, in regard to the Trinidad public, being stereotyped and stigmatized as good-for-nothings, unambitious boys, not men, who were too myopic for their own good, despite their innovative accomplishments, recent travels, and experiences that exposed them to cultural sophistication, and thus were more accomplished than many of the Trinidad middle class. He concurs that the men's broadened scope of vision ought to have had a more compelling positive influence among them and affected their behavior. However, their penchant toward violence continued, the causes, he surmises, as being twofold: man's will to winning at any and all costs and to being bestowed all the favors and benefits of winning; and, man's desire for approval and the satisfaction that comes with societal approval and acceptance.

In particular, the men sought fair earnings and desirable women, with the competition for girls perceived as their "property" being the dominant catalyst. If a girlfriend was found speaking with a rival band member, a fight ensued—Casablanca, Renegades, Invaders, and Tokyo, among others—all embroiled in fights over a woman, his particular woman.[77] In Mannette's case, the midst of all, this he was also dealing with the responsibilities of being a father to a growing family.

Upon returning home with TASPO, he married Joyce Cumberbatch who had given birth to their first child, Kendall, during his absence. He then bore the responsibility of a husband and father, which coupled with the pursuit of his dream, was doubly challenging. Rebuffed by society, having difficulty finding a job, and stealing drums to build his instruments, he credits Joyce for being responsible for saving his life during this time. He states, "She paid the rent and helped me with clothes to wear and food to eat. Eventually, the rancor wore off and I got a job, and things began to improve for me. But those days were terrible for me, from '52 to '57."[78] He shares reservedly, for he is deeply respectfully of her memory and of how they first met:

> We used to practice in Invaders' yard in Woodbrook, but the neighbors complained and gave us a hard time. So, we went to practice in St. James in the backyard of the MacKenzie's home—Carl, Grace, and their brothers and sisters—a MacKenzie was a member of the band at the time. Joyce was a friend of the MacKenzies. And, though she lived in Belmont, she often visited the MacKenzie sisters. She loved the steel band and came to visit to hear the steel band. She would sit in the gallery/porch/verandah while the band was walking around the yard. While practicing, we marched around the yard while we played. That's where we met and became friends. She out-sat all the other girls

hanging around the yard, and then because by that time it was too late for her to go home by herself, I took her home.[79]

Grateful for her undying love and loyalty, he sees today more clearly what she meant to him and how her untimely death reshaped his view and treatment of women. His marriage to Joyce lasted ten years, ending when she died in late 1962. Their children include: Kendall, Karen, Earl, and Eric. She was a resolute wife who stood by him through all the negative news-reporting that portrayed him as a hooligan who wanted only to beat trash can, one who had no ambition to improve himself. Joyce offered him love, acceptance, and a home, unlike society who made him feel like its scourge and treated him like its whipping boy. She was his fortress against an entire country that seemed to be against him for refusing to accept the scholarship, including his parents. Upon marrying her in 1952, they lived in Belmont with her parents.

However, his parents and siblings were equally upset with his decision to get married, their ambivalence tempering their relationship. He thinks that they were secretly proud of him and his obvious exemplary inventive abilities. He speculates that they, however, possibly viewed his rejection of the scholarship then his untimely marriage to Joyce, a darker-skinned young woman who at the time was a nurse's aide, as hindrances to his ambition to make good for himself. It also pains him that no family member attended his wedding or gave him a wedding present. Not all his family members rejected him completely though, he remarks. He sometimes spent time with his sisters, Phyllis and Audrey, while waiting to get married. Nevertheless, during this time he felt he had no permanent home, which indeed was an unpleasant feeling.

The acrimony of public opinion lingered those ten years. However, the entire movement continued to face obstacles. One problem the men continued to encounter was having a place to build and tune the drums without harassment. He states, "Our reputation made our own progress and development difficult."[80] In Mannette's neighborhood in Woodbrook, the neighbors complained to the police about any noise, big or small, and so they were chased from Woodbrook to St. James. In St. James, in the area that is now the Jean Pierre Stadium, was once a big, open space that yawned into the Gulf of Paria, with mangrove trees at its waterfront. He began tuning and hammering his drums out there, away from people who may have complained about his disturbing the peace.

Panyards had also become the site for much fighting and quarreling, additional causes for the neighbors to complain. When they did, the police arrived and often seized the drums and destroyed them. All that labor for nothing, he observes. The irony of this was the same neighbors who complained and had the men running here and there to find a secure place to tune their drums were the first to jump in the bands on Carnival days, "Jumping higher than anyone else as they paraded down the streets ... on Carnival day...."[81] Despite these obstacles, the movement could not be stopped. Mannette could not be stopped.

Not only was his private family growing, the Invaders family was also, as well as his influence in getting others involved in the movement. He got started in 1951 the first all-women band, Girl Pat Steel Band,[82] under the directorship of Hazel Henley, and worked with other women interested in Pan, such as the Roberts sisters, Grace Baptiste, and others in the general vicinity of Picton Street. He also recalls that around this time Ray Holman began visiting the yard. He states:

> Ray was about eight years old when he started coming to the panyard. The older boys didn't want him in the yard at all and chased him away. But as head tuner and leader of the band, I encouraged them to leave him alone. Holman then stood right next to me to observe what I was doing. Even so, the older men still shouted at him, "Get out! We doh want you here! Your parents doh want you here! Go on! Go home!"[83]

Mannette, however, saw something in Ray and defended his right to be left alone, not to be interfered with. This began a lasting friendship between the two men, one that continues to today.

The presence of young Holman in their panyard and Mannette's insistence that he remain came from his innate desire not to keep what he was doing to himself. Even then, a part of his blossoming dream was the desire to leave a language, a system of building and tuning on which his students could build and improve the art form. Its geometry, engineering, science, musical templates for tuning, and codified language, all conveyed in ways his students could understand what he is trying to communicate to them began with Holman's presence in the panyard. Back then, he tried to communicate this when he visited QRC to conduct a mini workshop in 1964 to stimulate interest in Pan among the "college boys." Later, he built a set of drums for the monastery at Mount St. Benedict to perpetuate Pan. He remains proud of pioneering in these areas.

Back in the early '60s, he already knew intuitively that in order to accomplish the goal of leaving a lasting legacy, he needed to establish Pan in schools where he could work with students in order to communicate his thoughts to them in their language, being the bridge between the first generation of panmen and new one of pannists, conveying how to develop further and advance the art form. While the measure of his success, he maintains, is realized in his creation of seven of the ten sections that complete the steel orchestra—he credits Bertie Marshall, Anthony Williams, and Rudolph Charles with having developed the others—his eye was already on the future of where Pan can go.

Influential Relationships: Some Women and the U.S. Navy

Prior to his first marriage, one of the women he saw steadily was Norma Callender, already introduced. He reminisces on how she was almost destroyed because of her involvement with him:

> We met when I worked at Acme Engineering. The laundry at which she worked was right behind Acme. Both properties back each other and during lunch times when we sat in the back to eat we started talking. After meeting and talking through the wire-meshed fenced, finally we agreed to meet at a dance in St. James one Saturday night.... I saw her next on Monday and we continued to see each other regularly and intimately. Soon, the news spread that we were together. However, she had a boyfriend named Ellis, nicknamed Joebell. But once we started going together, she began to give him the cold shoulder. Apparently, his friends began to make a joke about it with him saying to him, "Ellie Mannette with your woman," telling him that his woman was pulling a fast one on him.
>
> One day, after she had left work and was riding home, he stopped her at the corner of George and Duke Streets. He was *liming* with his friends. He inquired about what was going on between us, that he'd heard rumors that she was seeing me. She replied, "I'm seeing Ellie because he's bright, and you need a flambeau on your head to be as bright as him." Her insult was added to the injury of making him look like a fool in front of his friends. No one made a fool of Joebell. As she turned away, he drew out his razor and sliced her down her back, from her neck to her lower spine. When she spun around in horror and surprise, he sliced her cheek, from the eye to the lip. "Take dat, yuh fuckin' whore." Excuse my language, but that's the way, and much worse than that, dem *bad-johns* used to talk. Myrna, I 'shame to tell you some of the things and ways we used to behave. Getting back to the story, he said, "Take yuh cut-up face and go to him, now," and walked away. "I hope yuh live to nevah walk again. Fuckin' whore." She fainted and came to in the hospital. [We] had been going together for six months. When I heard about the incident, I went immediately to the hospital and stayed the night at her bedside. Another woman almost destroyed over me. [*Shakes his head in dismay.*] After she recovered, we continued to see each other.
>
> As I said, I would give up one or even ten scholarships for the sake of Pan. But I would never be so callous and indifferent to the needs of women, if I had to live my life over again. I was young and flattered that so many girls—Chinese, Indian, Negro, Portuguese, all mixtures—were chasing after me. I was handsome, talented, and made a name for myself in the Steelband world.[84]

Though he then had a single-eyed but expansive vision and ambitious goal for Pan but tunnel-vision of women, he could not have known he was in the position eventually to be regarded as having stood on the cusp of Pan history.

In fact, as he and the other men state, none of them was aware of making history and so were inattentive to dates and to who was doing what, except for those who introduced something truly conspicuous, as his "baby bath pan." For instance, he had no intuition that he was on the verge of making history and linking irrevocably the United States and T&T. During those years of stealing drums from the Navy base, he was unaware that his name was becoming known and he was being marked for another man's ambition. He recounts most entertainingly how the realization of this came about:

> One day while working in my pan yard, a big white, Navy van pulled up outside. Seeing the Navy personnel dressed in their uniforms, I began running, certain they'd come for me to lock me up for stealing their drums. I reached the fence and was about to climb over when one of them shouted, "Mannette! Wait! Hey, Stop!" I paused at the bottom fence then climbed up. At the top, I turned around and asked, "What you want?" The naval officer replied, "I'm here to see Ellie Mannette." I asked, "What you want him for?" "Are you Ellie?" Refusing to identify myself, I asked again, "What you want him for?" He replied, "They want him down at the Navy base." Scared to death now, I was certain they would hold me down there for stealing their drums.
>
> I thought about my predicament for a moment before climbing down the fence. I walked toward the front of the yard and the parked van with its big, bold lettering, "U.S. Navy," and the men dressed in their U.S. Navy uniform. I asked one of them, "What you want me for at the base?" The officer replied, "Well, the admiral wants to see you. He wants to speak to you about building a Navy steel band." I replied, "Well, OK." I thought I may as well take the chance and get in. I was thinking that this may be a good way to get some drums without stealing them. So, I climbed into the van and went with them down to the Naval base.
>
> The admiral, Dan Gallery, was in Puerto Rico. The men at the Chaguaramas base telephoned him and I spoke with him. He introduced himself, "Mannette, I am Dan Gallery, the commander of the western hemisphere fleet. I understand that you've been stealing my drums. So, I want you now to build me some steel drums...." "How do I do that?" "I will fly you out to Puerto Rico and you will build them here." Of course, I agreed. What else could I do? I told him I didn't know how I'd get there because I had no passport. He said they'd take care of that. I would fly on a Navy plane, one of those Catalinas.... He further offered that I could stay as long as I wanted, which I did because I wasn't doing anything else of count.

> A few days later, the van returned and transported me to the Navy base from where I was placed on a Catalina [seaplane] and flown to Puerto Rico. I remained in Puerto Rico for three to four months. I lived on the barracks with the Naval people and got the Navy band started in 1957. When I returned, I wore a Navy uniform and lived like a member of the Navy, the only difference was I built drums while the sailors did their required Navy tasks. I remained there for almost a year, which earned me quite a bit of money. The U.S. dollar was much better than the Trinidad dollar. So when I returned home I could live a little better.[85]

The U.S. Navy afforded him travel for the first time to the United States in 1961. However, the racism he experienced firsthand destroyed his future incentive to visit, far less live, in the United States. He retells the incident with a tinge of rancor:

> ... They [whomever Admiral Gallery authorized] called and invited me to go to Charleston, South Carolina, because the Navy was leaving Puerto Rico for Charleston. So, I joined them again and went to Charleston. I stayed with them for a long time. Then in '61, I had to leave because of a racist incident.
> ... I was unaware of the exact nature of the U.S. political climate. We were in Charleston and had to go to Columbia to do a job. The band traveled on a big bus and from Columbia was going on St. Stevens, but I had to return to the Navy to continue working on a new drum. The commander advised me to take a bus from Columbia back to Charleston. The rest of the band was due to return at the end of the week.
> I boarded a bus in Columbia and took a seat in the front of the bus. All of a sudden, the bus driver turned and ordered me to the back of the bus, "You, there, get to the back!" I ignored him and continued to read my newspaper because I wasn't fully aware that the driver was actually addressing me. He repeated the order, "You, there, get back behind!" When I didn't move, the driver then suddenly pulled the bus over to the side of the road and came and stood over me and roared, "You! Get up! Get out!" I asked, "What is your problem?" Some colored guys at the back of the bus yelled, "—man, you come back here. You stupid, or something?" "What's the matter?" "You not supposed to sit up there."
> When I got to the back, I spoke to them explaining that I didn't know anything about this affair: "We living in Trinidad and Tobago don't know anything about riding at the back of the bus or about the fight for civil rights. Look, I want to go home. I want to go home right now." When I returned to the base, I told the commanding officer I wanted to go home right now. I persisted that I wanted to return home. Nothing they said could dissuade me. Reluctantly, they allowed me to return home.[86]

> I decided to return to Trinidad in '62, when the Navy finally allowed me to leave. Charlie Roeper was the first director of the steel band and Franz Grissom was the second. They invited me back several times but I refused. However, working for the Navy got me out of bad financial times. I was in real serious financial trouble. I was a young man without any serious job....[87]

Trinidad once more beckoned him and he had to return to the root of his inspiration, this time with the unnerving experience of racism reminding him that the world held little to no kindness toward or respect for the Black man. His will to rise up and be a man one more time was still located in his drive to build and tune pans. His satisfaction again still was found in pounding those drums, his preferred name for the instrument, hammering notes into sound that produced beautiful music in defiance of man's ugly behavior toward his fellow man. Many times, he went without sleep and food and was not bothered. His rest and sustenance resided in his passion to contribute something of surpassing beauty to society.

In 1963, he was awarded the Pegasus Award, which also has been awarded to Derek Walcott, Sybil Atteck, and Beryl McBurnie. He was indeed beginning to be acclaimed as a genius.

However, he modestly maintains that back then he could rely only on what he was looking for, knowing that what he was building did not previously exist anywhere. He was driven to continue going until he built what he could see and hear in his mind. As he went along, he states that success was realized when suddenly something clicked and he knew, "This is it! This is what I'm looking for!" His inspiration came from listening to classical music and all the various sounds he heard and wanted to create and capture on pan to match those sounds. All the voices of the orchestra matched with all the various pitches on pan. Not necessarily to sound like the violin or the cello but to create a distinct voice on pan that could capture the orchestral sounds. He continues to see an orchestra [as a multifaceted] sound of instrumental voices.

Back then, he listened attentively when he heard the playing of classical music on the radio to remember the voices. He listened attentively for a second playing to hear what he missed in his creation and was delighted when he heard and recognized what he had missed. Other builders then copied his work and simply changed the design to create a different sound, he surmises. For instance, Bertie Marshall and Tony Williams may have produced pans that sounded different from what he originally did by repositioning the notes, but he maintains his claim to being "the first," the original builder.

He points out that also during that time, despite the skills of the builder-tuner, he had no control over the physical composition of the steel. Thus, he had to work within those limitations as well. Some notes invariably produced particular color tones, depending on the composition of the steel, which in turn led him, and the rest of the men as well, to learn the behavior of steel while engaged in the building processes.

In 1964, while he was working at Shell Oil Company as a sales representative and found the job boring and tedious, he met Murray Narell.[88] Narell invited him to come to New York to build pans for community groups in Harlem, the Bronx, Bedford Stuyvesant, and Hybridge Gardens—the trouble spots of New York City. He informed him that he would not. He once had had a hard time in America and he did not wish to return to any of that unpleasantness. Narell tried to convince him that New York City was nothing like the south, but Mannette was undaunted and Narell left. The following years, about three years in a row, Narell returned to Trinidad and each time sought out Mannette in an effort to persuade him to come to New York City. He begged Mannette, "Please, come. Try out New York City. You'll have a good time there."[89]

Being advised by his father, who had allowed him to live back at home temporarily, at least to go and find out what it was all about—and because his curiosity got the better of him and also because his job at Shell Oil was not stimulating—he requested a nine-month leave of absence to visit New York City. His intention was to visit and see what Narell was doing, and most likely to stay because he was beginning to feel island-bound. He had exhausted his home's resources and was beginning to feel stifled. Attempts to take Pan into schools and beyond its stigmatized realm seemed stymied. In addition to his 1964 talk on Pan at QRC and drums tuned for Mount St. Benedict, with Tony Williams he had conducted a two-week workshop at the UWI, St. Augustine, which had been favorably but halfheartedly received. Stating he had his visa that classified him as H1,[90] a passport, and a ticket for nine days before he was due to travel on February 9, 1967, he arrived in the United States wearing a brown shirt-jack, and in one of the pockets he carried the now famous Oval Boys photograph. His arrival is another unforgettable moment. He states:

> I was classified as H1, for special skills. When I showed up at Immigration, the officer looked at my passport and asked, "Who are you? A sportsman?" I said, "No, you wouldn't understand who I am." He said, "Well, this is the second visa like this coming in this year. One from Japan, and now you. Classification H1. What skill do you have?" Again, I said, "You wouldn't understand. You wouldn't believe." Seeing he would not get an explanation from me, he finally

said, "Well, have a good stay in America." The classification meant I was doing something in this country that nobody else could do. Highly skilled. Which is why I had an H1 classification.[91] ... I came to work with the Labor Department [who] approved this classification.[92]

He credits his work with the U.S. Navy as being responsible for his immigration status, and for the many doors it opened to him in the United States.

The U. S. Navy Steel Band, which disestablished on October 1, 1999, began its forty-three year existence in 1957 and went through many transitions, including moving from San Juan, Puerto Rico, to New Orleans. Franz Grissom's narrative traces the band's formative years, 1957 to 1964, under the remarkable pioneer and war hero Admiral Dan V. Gallery. Grissom additionally recognizes the pivotal role Mannette played in launching the band, stating, "The Navy Steel Band would not be in existence today were it not for Ellie Mannette."[93] Yet, it was a mutually beneficial relationship for both Mannette and the Navy, and invariably the movement. Mannette points out:

> The Navy continued to have an interest in the development of the pan. They had tried sinking with a spoon machine, automation, hydraulics, laser to cut and place the notes. They continued to have an interest in developing the instrument, from which I benefited a lot. I made their drums and traveled with them throughout the United States and the world. From that, I received calls from many people who were referred by the Navy. The Navy was the only other band that had a complete outfit of chromed instruments similar to those here at Mannette Steel Drums.
>
> The Navy helped the entire Steelband movement a lot through me. They wanted to introduce me to high government and Navy officials last year, and they invited me a few times to a ceremony that would have honored my contributions to the Navy for forty years. But I refused because I did not care to be in the limelight. I preferred to develop the instruments. Make the instrument better. Teach the science of it so that the young people can make it better. The instrument still has too many flaws in the steel. We're getting steel that is only ninety percent good. I want to see us getting steel that is ninety-five percent good and then eventually one hundred percent good.
>
> Today's young people who have the desire and access to automation can do it. These young musicians can use the steel drum very effectively. They can tune, build, lecture, give performances and concerts. They can do whatever with it. This industry will be very profitable to them one day.
>
> ... My goal is to see the full quality orchestra. We are standing on the threshold of this excellent quality. We're working with metallurgists, physicists, engineers, and others to see this come about. I hope I live to see this.[94]

Mannette's unabashed enthusiasm for the movement's past, present, and future remains undiminished. After all, he denied conventional wisdom to pursue a dream. He violated societal law—and some would maintain moral law, too—to achieve an end. All the while, he refused to be side-tracked from his ultimate goal: to help produce a musical instrument that would be unrivaled among the entire world family of instruments.

The pattern in human history has revealed that when great men and women set out to accomplish an ambition, they will be tested, sometimes quite severely, to breaking points. Mannette is no exception. During the years of financial hardship, his involvement with the U.S. Navy rescued him from such hardship, and he remains grateful that he was better able to provide for his family while pursuing his dream. However, the sacrifice he paid was being away from home, missing see his children grow up, and the death of his first wife, Joyce. Maria "Vera" Pereira's vignette, appended to Mannette's, provides a glimpse of Joyce's illness and subsequent death.

The will to go on was made easier with the meeting of Jacqueline, whom everyone calls Jackie, who became his second wife. He speaks rather endearingly of her and how their relationship began:

> Jackie's family was middle class and lived in Cascade, a well-to-do family that didn't want Jackie to be involved with me at all because I was a panman, a *bad-john,* and vagabond in the eyes of the so-called socialites. Jackie was a musician.
>
> One time when I was working on a piece of music called "Dream of Aldwyn," we were trying to play it one night in the yard. She was there standing with a friend, a seamstress. I was standing there, too, listening to the band rehearse. We were standing close enough to each other for me to hear her say to her friend, "Oh, they're playing that piece of music wrong. It's not like that at all." I turned to her and arrogantly said, "What you talking about? What you know about the music?" She replied, "I'm telling you that I play that music and the way the band is playing is wrong. If you want me to show how it's wrong, you can come to my home tomorrow and I'll show you." "Where you live?"
>
> There was a friend of mine named Oswald Best. He, a couple of other friends, and I went to her house. When we got there, we were impressed with her house, which was located on a hill. The garage was dug out under the house and stairs led up to the main entrance. A four-to-five bedroom house, which in those days in Trinidad was huge and impressive. We parked on the street and went up the stairs and knocked on the front door. She came out and I said, "We're come to hear the music." She let us in and went over to the

piano and played the melody, first the way we were incorrectly doing it and then the way the music was written.

I was enthralled by her music literacy and her playing. I was speechless, too. When she was finished, all I could say was, "I see." She offered, "If you want me to help you, I can come down to help you guys because I know you're playing it wrong." That was the beginning of my friendship with Jackie. She began to drive down to the yard every day in her Austin Princess. Sometimes, their chauffeur drove her.[95]

In fact, she continued to offer suggestions on other songs the band was rehearsing, and most likely was in part responsible for the Invaders' growing reputation of being a band that played music excellently and had mastery of a classical repertoire. Their mutual interest in music and being perfectionists who held to the highest standards bonded them. They eventually got married in 1974 in New York. Still married to each other, she is an ordained reverend and continues to live in Manhattan, New York. He acknowledges fondly that she continues to be a most positive influence in his life. His children with Jackie are Nigel and Juliet, called Julie.

About women and his relationship in general with them, he observes that he did not treat them on the whole very well. Nor did they demand that he did. After all, prior to marriage and even during marriage, he had PoS's cream of the crop fawning over him and from which to choose. Not a good thing, he states pensively. While never physically abusive, he admits reflectively that he was rather cavalier about their emotions:

> I had a reckless behavior toward women, on the whole. I was young, bright, dressed well, and some said I was the one of the best dressed young men in PoS. I had a lot of attractive young women chasing after me. Sometimes, I came home from work at the Navy base to find six or seven girls sitting there waiting for me—Joyce, Norma, Sybil, Sheila, Grace, and sometimes Maria—one on the step, one inside with my father, one in the backyard, one sitting on the patio, one with the boys on the pan, one standing by the gate. I arrived home on my bicycle, walked pass all of them, went inside and changed my clothes. Then with a, "See y'all later," leave them all right there. I returned much later, when I knew they must have left by that time—eleven to twelve o'clock.[96]

One who out-sat them during this time was Maria "Vera" Pereira, of whom he speaks openly and describes as the prettiest woman he has ever known. Theirs was an off-and-on relationship beginning 1952, "with Maria being the persistent one and I being the stupid one," he claims. Her house on Jerry Street in St. James became the *liming* spot for the Invaders, where the men retreated to recuperate after violent confrontations with other bands. She was always his bulwark of support, the one to whom he turned whenever things were not going right in his marriage or with other women. They lost touch after she immigrated to the United States in 1962 and reunited in 1998.

The Later Years: The Hammer, the Music, and the Business (1967 to 2001)

Upon arrival in New York, Mannette lived with the Narells for approximately one year. Though Murray wanted him to remain living with them, he could not. He had to prepare a place for Jackie, for he knew he could not have his family living under another man's roof. Murray helped him find an apartment about two blocks away in Whitestone, Queens, and then assisted in getting Jackie to the United States. While living at the Narells, one incident marked history. On the day of his departure from Trinidad, Hamilton Jones gave him a photo of the Oval Boys, which he absented-mindedly put into his jacket pocket and promptly forgot about.

He was wearing the same jacket one day while romping in the snow with little Andy Narell (a Pan virtuoso and with whom he developed the quaduet, the last instrument made in 1996 to be attributed to him). The photo fell out of his pocket and Andy picked it up. By this time, it was fairly crumpled and not very impressive. He would have thrown it away but that Andy begged him to let him have it. Having no sentimental attachment to it, he agreed and thought no more of it. Years later, when someone said it was a shame no photos of the Oval Boys existed, lo and behold Andy produced it. That photo is now a trade photo and graces Mannette's office at Mannette Steel Drum Ltd (MSD), soon to be discussed, and the company's Internet Web site.

Murray helped to find a place at a friend of his, a guy named George—, who owned an apartment complex and also had a finished basement. He sublet to Mannette that basement, which allowed him to continue to work with the Narells. He lived in that basement for about five to six months until someone reported that they were illegally living there, probably because of the noise of the hammering and the music. In New York at that time, people were not supposed to be living in basements, even though it was a beautifully-finished basement, he recalls. Thus, according to the law, that place was not supposed to be rented out. Very apologetically, the landlord conveyed his regrets that though he liked them a lot they had to leave because someone would get him in trouble. Fortunately,

Jackie was working as a nurse's aide in an area hospital, and a friend of hers who was living in Jamaica, Queens, helped them to find an apartment there.

While living in Jamaica, in 1969 he formed a band called the Hummingbirds with some of the young people, and the landlord allowed them to practice in the basement. Comprised of fellow Trinidadians, the members included Bertram, Hollie, Errol (drummer), Herman, Baby Pierre, Lennox Ling, Elkie, Kente, and one more, whose named Mannette could not recall. He himself played the cello. Reportedly, the band did very well and performed at Carnegie Hall, Philharmonic Hall, Madison Square Garden, the Taft Hotel, the Sheraton Hotel, and the Hilton Hotel. He became a member of Local 802, the New York City musician union, in order to play at these big hotels. The band was also contracted by United Artists and Columbia Records, under Leroy—, who arranged for Nancy Wilson and others musicians of her caliber. It functioned through 1972 and disbanded because the guys did not want to rehearse, he states ruefully. They just wanted to show up for the gigs, play, get the money, and go their way. Many times they refused to set up and pull down the instruments and left all the work for Mannette, who soon tired of their attitude and behavior.

After the band dissolved, he began working with several poor community groups in and around the inner city: Harlem, Bronx, Bedford Stuyvesant, South Ozone Park, Hybridge Gardens, St. Nicholas, and others. He recalls that he worked for next to nothing building drums during those difficult years. Additionally, Murray introduced him to some of the neighborhoods that had never seen pan and were not interested in learning about it. His reception was cold in those particular neighborhoods.

He met James Leyden in the 1970s through George Gates who knew Murray Narell. Leyden is credited with taking Mannette to the next level in advancing the instrument's technology, introducing Mannette for the first time to the stroboscope and the tuning fork, or as Mannette puts it, "Jimmy introduced me to the language and technology of music."[97] The two first met when Leyden invited Mannette to the school at which he worked, Horace Greeley High School.

Leyden was also the one to invite him to Music Educators National Conference (MENC) and the Regional Music Educators National Conference (RMENC), where he was introduced to regional and national music educators. With them, he began to establish contacts with high schools and colleges whose music educators were interested in getting drums for their music programs. This is how he began building drums for programs in New York, Ohio, Arizona, and elsewhere. Once the drums were built and distributed, they had to be serviced, which led to his traveling to the various places to service them. With folks calling all the time requesting servicing, the demand for service became so intense he was hardly at home.[98]

On improving his technological skills, at the time he was tuning drums according to his ear and thought it was good. However, Leyden contradicted him that the drum was not good, that he needed to work with a machine, a stroboscope, which he explained and demonstrated to him and pointed out to him some techniques about harmonic overtones, relative tones, harmonic patterns, and the temperament of notes. They worked very closely for a few years, during which time he introduced the triple guitar[99] and brought out the six-bass section with three notes each. Prior to that time, all the bands were still playing the five-barrel bass section with each barrel having five notes. Today, the pans have three notes each. He and Leyden came up with the cycle of fifths bass drums to go down to the B-flat. They started with the low A, but he was not happy with it. Maybe now, he surmises, he can get the A clearer.[100] During this time, they both met Victor Brady who in his own way left a positive mark on Mannette.

Both Leyden and Mannette describe Brady as a flamboyant person, a great player of the double tenor who used four sticks to play, and even though he did not know how to read music, he was a fantastic player, a dynamic showman (the best showman with bells on his feet to keep his perfect rhythm, a one-man band of music and percussion). He played unimaginable melodies very impressively. Uncertain of exactly where Brady was born, either St. Croix or one of the Virgin Islands, Mannette cites him as one of the most demanding person he ever met who could tell whether a note was on perfect (absolute) pitch, despite being musically illiterate. He refused to accept a drum Mannette tuned unless it was perfect to his ear, which compelled Mannette to strive to an even higher standard and produce better work. Brady further demanded the best from all performing artists and consequently gave his best during every performance. His pans also had to look best, and he put a considerable amount of time into having them so highly polished they looked chromed.

Mannette additionally recalls his dealings with Rudolph Charles, who started to build six-and eight-and ten-barrel bass drums in the middle to late '70s and into the early '80s. During the '70s, he along with seven to ten panmen worked at the University Settlement, New York City. He described the environment

> as a large community center ... with several different rooms adjoining that we each occupied as work stations. There was Kim Loy Wong, Vincent Taylor, Ansell Joseph, Vincent Hernandez, Rudy King, and Rudolph Charles, just to name a few. No two of us could agree on patterns, tuning technique, ranges or anything. It was definitely an interesting period—to put it mildly—but I also

found it very frustrating. Everyone was more concerned about producing to make a fast dollar. There was not enough attention paid to quality.[101]

Of Charles, he states matter-of-factly that he really could not tune drums, not even for Desperadoes, when they lived in Trinidad. Corbeau Jack was the one who "went up to Laventille Hill to tune Despers' drums."[102] Nonetheless, Charles experimented with the large size bass sections, and called them names such as the rocket bass, and so on. However, Mannette with his eye trained on what is useful for the steel orchestra, dismisses such experimentation as

> just a gimmick. If you look at them, they only carry two notes. And they're not quality notes either. Let's face the facts. After the decibel begins to slow down and you go past low G, you can't really hear the sound. You can't hear it to recognize the pitch. What's the good having a sound you can't recognize? So, it's all a gimmick. He claims he went down to the low E. I said to him, "Don't fool yourself, Rudolph. You can't hear that." The strobe can't read it. The human ear can't hear. So what's the benefit, the value of having a sound you can't distinguish? You will hear a big old sound, like the rumble of thunder. This might satisfy some people. But overall, what's the value of that to the orchestra?[103]

The end of the 1960s into the '70s entailed his efforts to establish pans in schools, an idea started by Narell and Grissom, and then in colleges and universities. This he did through the many workshops he conducted on campuses, which included building and tuning pans for these various educational institutions. He lived the life of an itinerant artist traversing the U. S. interstates and highways on Greyhound buses and leaving his fingerprints on these campuses, literally. The price he paid for being more absent than present from his home and family—nine to ten months at a time—was separation from Jackie in 1982, with whom I spoke very briefly.

Without rancor, she shared that she had to allow him to pursue his dreams, for no one could stand in his way of making Pan into what he envisioned. They both would have been terribly unhappy had she attempted to impose upon him the standards of a traditional marriage and family, demanding that he was present for her and their children. She, likewise, did not have the spirit to live so unsettled a life, to be always on the road with children and not knowing how best to attend to their education, health, and so on.[104] They made their decision to live the way they have, and she is proud of all his accomplishments, awards, and distinguished recognitions. She is also happy about her own accomplishments.

Traveling alone changed for him, though. He met the Georges of Perry, Georgia, in 1980, shortly after the Georges had formed their family steel band, the Steel Bandits. This band accomplished some remarkable recognition worth mentioning. Before disbanding in 1994, during its fifteen-year history, President Ronald Reagan commended Inez (sixty-nine years old and originally from Marshalville, Georgia) and Joseph George (seventy-one years old and born in Barbuda) for their outstanding work as foster parents who offered their three biological children, plus twelve adopted and one foster for a total of sixteen children, not just a stable home but an enriched life through the opportunities afforded them as a very talented family steel band.

Equipped with the best of Mannette's drums, the band did benefit concerts for the National Adoption Conference in Chicago and the Cerebral Palsy of North Carolina, performed on the CBS *This Morning* show and at the Grammys, Los Angeles, and many five-star hotels and resorts. Daughter Kaethe, a former freelance journalist for the *Atlanta Journal-Constitution* and never a member of the band, in 1980 was at home visiting her biological parents when she and Mannette met for the first time. She had completed her Bachelor of Fine Arts degree the year before and begun to feel that her career was off to a fits-and-starts beginning. Fascinated by his work, they almost immediately formed a business relationship, one that lasts till today. Speaking quite candidly of her immediate attraction to him, she describes their first meeting:

> We met at the bus station. I had a preconceived notion of what a steelpan tuner looked like. When we (she and her mother) arrived, I noticed this man dressed immaculately in a three-piece suit. Immediately, I thought, "Oh! What a nice-looking man." He was all dapper and looked fine. I was looking for an old man in a straw hat. Ellie was hard to catch up with because of his schedule. So, my mother and I kept looking around for our prejudicial image of a steelbandsman/tuner. Meanwhile, my eyes would rest on him and I'd admire his handsomeness. My mother, a dramatic person, moaned, "I can't believe that he didn't come." But I couldn't believe he just didn't come.
>
> Finally, I decided to approach this man, who seemed to be waiting for someone and asked, "Are you Ellie Mannette?" And, he asked in turn, "Are you the Georges?" That was the beginning of our partnership. A little later, it developed into a romantic relationship. However, we soon learned that we work much better in a business relationship and make good working partners.[105]

Continuing to maintain a solid business relationship, George is called somewhat unflatteringly by some a "dragon lady." A diligent personal assistant and constant traveling companion, she zealously guards and monitors his daily schedule and dismisses all the negative monikers people have of her. She chooses to remain focused on what the two have accomplished professionally through the years. Mannette trusts her implicitly and credits her with having brought order to his somewhat chaotic life and respects her tremendously for absorbing the necessary transition he underwent from being easy-going and nonbusiness-like toward establish a professional, business-like image and operation.

One of the first things she did was to establish a fixed price for his drums, offer realistic delivery dates for orders, and coordinate his demanding daily and travel schedules. Still committed to servicing personally the educational institutions equipped with his instruments, he continues to travel to campuses but now in a customized van with a TV, sleeping accommodations, and water. George continues meticulously to plan, supervise, and document all the details of this rigorous life, schedule, and travels, including his historic homecoming trip to Trinidad in 2000, his first one home in thirty-three years. She is quite proud of what she has accomplished and refuses to allow anyone to diminish her or minimize her role in his professional life.

Contented with his many years of service at WVU, he does not regret having rejected residency offers from other colleges and universities. WVU's offer came at a time when he was ready to slow down from his constantly being on the road and was seriously considering a place where he could begin to build a permanent legacy. In accepting WVU's offer, he relinquished some income opportunities quite exceeding what the university offered. However, the trade-off was the autonomy to travel to other universities and colleges to continue retuning their drums, having already established his pans on approximately one hundred high schools, colleges, and university campuses. He desired to be in a position that allowed him to continue to fulfill his obligations to all the people for whom he had made pans. WVU offered him full latitude, and being the visionary that he is, he grasped the opportunity to be stationary at a place that allowed for stability while still being mobile and nurturing those roots already planted elsewhere.

His relationship with the institution began one day in 1991 while he was doing a five-day workshop at North Carolina University. At the time, he resided in Phoenix, Arizona. Upon its completion while he was packing up his tools to leave, he was approached by Phil Faini who had attended the workshop. Professors from other universities were present, and four bands performed, one of them being the U.S. Navy Steel Band. On that Saturday, Faini approached and complimented him for his precise work and his articulate and informative presentation. Then, he asked him if he would like to build drums for WVU. Not having yet introduced himself, Mannette asked bluntly, "Who are you and where are you from?" He introduced himself as the director of Percussions. Mannette said, "Well, it will take me some time to build the drums because I'm on tour right now. From here, I head to New York then Montana." They exchanged cards and promised to keep in touch.

After he returned home to Phoenix, about eight or nine months later, he received a phone call from Faini and agreed that was a good time for him to build the drums. When they were finished, since his travels were taking him pass WVU, he offered to drop them off. At the delivery, he inquired for some students to be gathered so he could instruct them on how to keep the drums in tune. Thus began his first informal instruction, which included showing them how to play the drums and maintain their care. Meanwhile, Drs. Faini and Wilson were observing his interaction with the students. When he was finished and departing with George, Faini stopped him to thank him for what he did with the students, who were obviously excited. "Looking at you and observing what you did, there was such energy. How about doing one semester with us?" He replied, "Once it can be arranged. Let's talk about it. But right now I have to go." George then asked, "If Ellie has to do a semester with you, how flexible will it be for him to travel around?" Faini replied, "I don't think that will be a problem." He and George agreed to think about it and left.

They proceeded to their next stop and on the road they called their answering service in Phoenix to check for messages. One was from Faini, which said that the position at WVU was open and he could start on January 15. He said, "We can't make it, Kaethe. I already have lined up several contracts around the country. Call and tell him that I can't come before the end of January." As it turned out, they did not arrive until the end of March, almost at the end of the semester, after WVU students came to Phoenix and took charge of the packing and moving of all his belongings.

Upon arrival, he was much surprised to receive a salary for the full semester, even though he did not arrive until the end, and was even more amazed that he was expected to accept the salary. He points out that was the beginning of the beautiful relationship he has maintained with the university. The following week he was offered a permanent position with agreements on his terms. He could not have asked for a more ideal relationship. A passionate teacher at heart, Mannette also seized the opportunity to settle down at WVU because he saw he could begin to develop a more systematic and focused approach to steeldrum teaching of the art form and the potential for manufacturing the instrument.

Many milestones were made in 1992 when he began to pave significantly the paths of his own leadership and organizational skills. First, it was the year he was established at WVU. Originally operating from the Creative Arts Center as artist-in-residence and head of the University Tuning Project (UTP), the program became underway with the drums originally owned by Steel Bandits. Mannette began shortly thereafter an apprenticeship program called Mannette Touch, which originally was an academic endeavor that flourished into a viable business based on the crafting and selling of his drums nationally and internationally. The year 1992 was also when he created the Ellie Mannette Award, bestowed biannually to those who have made significant contributions to the development of Pan. The first he awarded to Murray Narell; the '94 one to James Leyden; the '96 one to Ray Holman; and the '98 one to Robert "Robbie" Greenidge.

Both UTP and Mannette Touch shortly outgrew their location and relocated to its present location on Dents Way in Morgantown in November, 1998. Once more, the students packed and moved the operation but without official authorization of the university. All they knew was the program had outgrown its location and the time for trying on a new outfit had arrived. The new outfit fitted them appropriately, and on May 12, 2000, Mannette cofounded with George his own business, Mannette Steel Drums, Ltd., a merger of UTP and Mannette Touch. An impressive plant, it includes an engine room (a room for drums to be built and tuned), management offices, and workrooms for his key students.

Presently, the company's management staff includes a chief financial officer, a managing director of operations, a managing director of sales and marketing, and a managing director of tuning services. Other staff members comprise of the production team. The company produces two sets of instruments: the Signature Series and the Limited Edition.

He informs that he and his students communicate in a language that encodes pan-tuning techniques and a geometry for the pan templates that allows for the measurement of spaces and notes toward specifications for the future manufacturing of the instrument. These developments go to his commitment to advancing the art form, as he stated during his lecture at his annual 2001 workshop, "Meet Me in Morgantown" (MMIM).

Additionally in 1992, he and George launched MMIM. The first instructor at these workshops was Marc Svaline. He and Mannette first met in 1984, after Svaline decided that pan music was the type of music he wanted to include in his high school music curriculum at neighboring Washington High School. After extensive inquiry on purchasing instruments, he learned of Mannette who at the time lived in Perry, Georgia. He contacted him and ordered a lead, double second, a cello, and a bass, which were delivered that summer of 1984.

Svaline states, "That humble beginning has now grown to thirty-four sets of instruments and one of the largest steel bands in the United States."[106] Since 1984, I have come to recognize that I'm dealing with the greatest icon."[107] He recalls that the first workshop had about eighteen to twenty attendees, and the time was divided between building and playing. He can only see the industry continuing to grow and only a matter of time before it enters mainstream U.S. musical culture. The momentum cannot be slowed down: "With the number of writing and arranging for Pan, the music is becoming more readily available to the people. We are writing classics, music for Broadway, and so on. It can accompany soloists, Jazz, an infinitesimal array of diversity."[108]

During 1984 to 2000, Mannette with Jimmy Leyden ran a two-week workshop hosted by Portland State University, of which the Leyden's narrative provides more details.

The general atmosphere of the MMIM workshop is positive and infectious, and one can expect at any workshop a good dose of musical instructions being given by Ray Holman, Andy Narell, Jeff Narell, Tom Miller, and others who have distinguished themselves in the Caribbean and U.S. Pan world. Jeff Narell and Miller were quite excited about the 2001 MMIM workshop and had given up lucrative opportunities to offer their time to the workshop. Miller's first workshop was in 1995, though he first met Mannette in 1984 at a workshop he was conducting in Oregon with Jimmy Leyden and Andy Narell. He has since worked with Andy and Jeff Narell as well as David Rudder and is equally confident that it is just a matter of time before the music becomes mainstream. Miller has visited Trinidad and is much aware of the controversy swirling around some Trinidadians' concern that Mannette has given away their culture to men like Andy Narell, the chief beneficiary. He dismisses this charge and makes it analogous with "the prophet without honor in his own country" syndrome that stunts vision and inhibits progress. Continuing to describe Mannette's magnanimous contributions in scriptural language, he states:

> In Ellie's spreading the gospel of Pan, so to speak, the people of Trinidad should recognize that he has spread the culture of Trinidad and a worldwide appreciation of its culture. People who play pan and who go to Panorama know where the instrument came from and pay homage to Trinidad. People go to Trinidad not just for Carnival but to learn more of Trinidad's culture, not from a tourist's perspective but from a musician's standpoint. There's an

appreciation for Trinidad and it's hard to find such a small country as Trinidad, that commands this appreciation and interest.

For instance, pan-players and those involved in the Pan movement followed very closely the Abu Bakr uprising, avidly interested in seeing how the unrest panned out. They were very concerned about that whole incident. Should something like that happen elsewhere, say in Afghanistan, there would not be the same interest. Pan then has brought a level of empathy and sympathetic interest to Trinidadian affairs that would not exist otherwise. People were talking about it and wanted to see it resolved. People unknowledgeable about Pan and its origin had no awareness of what was going on. Yet, the uprising provided an opportunity to educate people about Pan and Trinidad. We got to talk to people about Trinidad, point it out on the map to those who'd never heard of Trinidad or knew where it was. It was great.[109]

Narell similarly dismisses the accusation that Mannette has betrayed his birthplace, as described in his narrative.

Two most gratifying moments in Mannette's saga are his 1999 trips to Washington, D.C. first to receive his NEA award when he met both President Bill Clinton and First Lady Hillary Rodham Clinton, and on a second trip to be honored by T&T's airline, BWIA. The airline now features Invaders steelband music played on pans manufactured by MSD and invited him to D.C. to mark the honorable moment. Being reunited with the Invaders for the first time in thirty-two years was indeed an emotional moment. He described how honored and exhilarated he felt after boarding the bus that transported the members of the Invaders and signing autographs on anything he was asked to write on. He really had no idea till that moment that he was indeed honored by Trinidadians as a great hero. The Invaders' reception made him feel like the cloud under which he left Trinidad had indeed begun to lift and he began to anticipate returning home, which occurred the following year.

In 2000, he was finally a prophet receiving honor in his own country when he visited home for the first time in thirty-three years, primarily to receive an honorary doctorate from the UWI, St. Augustine. He is notably the first pannist to be conferred such an honor. This acclamation process began a few years prior to Mannette's receipt of the National Heritage Fellowship from the National Endowment for the Arts. Brian Copeland points out that the Trinidad community was not influenced by the United States in its desire to honor him. While he frankly thinks that the award helped, "because the UWI decision body is very, very conservative," he regrets that he himself missed the deadline for the 1999 commencement ceremony. He states:

> We started quite late. The Department of which I am Head was only just recovering from some negative publicity,[110] so I was pretty much not open to much else. When the request for nominees came across my desk, I knew that I wanted to do something for the Pan world. My first instinct was to nominate Tony Williams and Ellie Mannette, as these, to my mind, were the last of the early pioneers. Later, when I spoke to Clém about the idea he suggested Bertie Marshall as well. We nominated all three with very sketchy details.
>
> By that time, my own work on the pan and the published literature had revealed the technical intricacies of the instrument. These tuners, particularly the early pioneers, are scientists in their own right, (like) Tony Williams, a humble man with a lot of knowledge. He did a lot of technical and artistic work. He is a self-taught genius. I checked the list of honorary awardees over the years and realized that none was ever awarded to tuners or pannists. I was painfully aware that many of the tuners worked under the worst of circumstances. They really deserve more recognition.[111]

Mannette's homecoming, as dubbed and coordinated by George, included much fanfare. Not only was he conferred the honorary doctorate but also received the Chaconia Silver Medal. The gold award is typically given to someone who has lived continuously in the country all his life. Nonetheless, he is contented that finally the nation is coming around to viewing pannists in a more positive light, even if not the most positive. For instance, some who traveled with Mannette were taken aback to sense that UWI, St. Augustine, was merely making a grand token gesture. His guest list to the dinner following the ceremony was a very short one of six, which forced him to exclude some thought appropriate to attending the dinner. The other honorary doctorate recipient's guest list was far longer than six, Mannette's party of academicians and students observed. Still, progress even in the form of baby steps is still progress.

Indeed, his return home was a subduing moment for many people, including many panmen who knew that once more *the west*, the middle class, was receiving more acclaim than *the east*. Ironically, Mannette's presence in Trinidad reiterated to panmen their place in society. Poet/prophet/artist LeRoy Clarke's view on Mannette's homecoming was particularly insightful. He candidly expressed how the unacclaimed panmen felt: pride that one of them made well for himself; the desire to close the distance created by self-imposed exile and fame and those who have not traveled or afforded the opportunity to become famous; the need to reconnect to one's source of invention and inspiration so as not to forget where one came from. Hence, the spoken question resonating among them was: will Mannette return and when? Will he make worthwhile and real his image not of a god on a pedestal but of a man like them walking among his people, reassuring them that fortune is happenstance but kindness and generosity are not? Apparently, the need for reassurance that he was not a Dickensian Pip who has forgotten his friends existed. Time will tell.

While maybe small steps are being made toward recognizing the greatness of panmen, back at his residentstate and the site of his workshops, Mannette towers. After returning from Trinidad, I wanted to witness firsthand whether, according to reports, Mannette was truly grandly received among Americans who loved Pan. I attended the 2001 workshop and was delighted. Not only was Mannette showered with adulation but I, as a fellow Trinidadian, was quite well received. Honey for a soul starved for acceptance as a human being, period.

Young pannists, high schoolers Cassie Kelly and Geoff Hohn, did not care that I was a college professor. They cared that I came from the land of Pan. They wanted to share willingly just how much Pan, Ellie, and the workshops meant to them. Cassie's first workshop was 1997 and she has attended every year since. Both members of the school band, Westwood Panhandlers, they dismiss the age differences of the attendees, some being their parents' and grandparents' ages, and in particular Mannette's. They find it totally cool how whenever he visits their school, he plays everyone's pan and gives individual instructions to all. They attend the workshop for that same spirit of encouragement and friendly yet professional support. Geoff who sported green hair throughout the week remarks that no one at the workshop found his hair color strange. Outside the workshop, people frowned upon his mark of individuality.

While both musically literate and advanced pan-players, they do not see that music illiteracy is any reason for anyone to stay away from the workshops. Cassie says, "You don't have to know music and even know the steelpan. Every year, I've seen people who have no music literacy or steelpan knowledge attend and have a great time. Some people think it's all so challenging because we learn so much stuff in such a short space of time." "Sure, it's a challenge," Geoff agrees, "but life is all about challenges."[112] Clearly, these inheritors of Mannette's legacy are already maximizing on it.

Mannette hopes to offer similar vital contributions to his homeland and welcomes the opportunity to work with Clément Imbert and Brian Copeland to accomplish this in an alliance with UWI, St. Augustine, when the time comes to make some larger steps. Nonetheless, he is quite impressed with the level to which Pan and its discussions have come in T&T, the United States, and other international countries. Exemplary in promoting scientific and engineering knowledge components to pan-building is the International Conference for Science and Technology of the Steelpan (ICSTS) held in Trinidad in 2000 (mentioned in Clifford Alexis's story), which drew attendees from as far away as Japan and Switzerland and closer to home from Guyana, Jamaica, and the United States. Pointing out that Trinidad is behind the rest of the world in focusing attention on the science of pan-building and -tuning, he draws attention to the work being done at the University of Texas El Paso by metallurgist Lawrence Muir and at NIU by physicist Thomas Rossing. Both, since 1996, have been conducting experiments on the properties of steel to remove the craft of pan-building from the realm of intuition, which is how Mannette has developed his techniques, into the realm of the objectivity of science. However, the work of these scientists and others is already being viewed as the co-optation of a folk art and culture into mainstream scientific endeavors. Clifford Alexis (see his narrative) argues that a conference such as the ICSTS is moving toward reifying imperial knowledge all over again.

Alexis indignantly refers to the process of accessing the panmen's knowledge of their art and then encoding the knowledge in recondite language as "exploitation in 3-D."[113] While the conference may be useful in debunking some of the myths and exposing some secrets of the trade, some participants of the conference found the esoteric scientific language overwhelming and exclusive of them.[114] Some uneducated first-generation tuners born in the 1920s and '30s did not advance beyond a seventh standard (sixth-grade) level, and those who did acquire a high school level of education still found it difficult to grasp or relate "the complexities of quadratic equations … to (tuning) the next instrument," a position taken by El Dorado Senior Comprehensive School steelband manager, Fazal "Moosh" Mohammed. Alexis argues that the time for the collaborative process between his school's music and physics teachers has arrived, for the benefit of students.[115] Unless such collaboration occurs, the next generation will express views similar to Pan pioneer Oscar Pile who claimed that much of the information flew over their heads (the first generation of pan-tuners) and the conference was not beneficial to them.[116]

Mannette, on the other hand, now an optimist about all things related to Pan, does not share these anxieties. Having worked with both Muir and Rossing and communicated effectively with them both, he is confident that those involved in Pan's R&D will find ways to communicate and advance the art form. He remains undaunted because he has witnessed and personally experienced how much the industry continues to evolve. He uses himself as a major example of how much concession is being made toward recognizing and giving panmen their overdue respect.

Conclusion: Sound Surpasses Fury

Humbled by the memory of some of the "idiotic and foolish things" he did in the past, he also regrets having disregarded the advice of the older people and just doing what he desired. He claims that nothing but human and divine intervention got him to where he is today. How else can he explain the way the stabbing of Ossie Campbell resulted?

About eight o'clock, Audrey returned with the good news that Ossie was not dead though still in a critical condition. "We'll let you know how he's recovering," she stated the obvious. She also brought him a change of clothes. The next day, a friend called "Low Eye" came by and Mannette had him throw away the clothes and the knife in a place called Slipway. With the news that Ossie was not dead, he decided to wait and see what happened next. He remained in that shack for three days with Audrey bringing him clothes and food. Finally, the news came that Ossie was recovering well.

With this news and the realization that he could not be charged for murder, he decided to surrender to the Criminal Investigation Department (CID), because the police was constantly in his father's yard and in the neighborhood investigating his whereabouts. Before going to the CID, he decided to visit Lennox Pierre for advice and to request that he accompany him to the CID. Pierre could not go with him at the time, so he took a taxi to the CID, walked into the station and up to the desk and said to the desk sergeant, "I understand that you are looking for Ellie Mannette in connection to an incident that took place a few days ago. Well, I'm here to turn myself in." He was taken into the back office and questioned. Afterward, he was put into a holding cell and later that evening someone posted bail for him and he was released. The case was set for September.

When the court date arrived, he went to court but Ossie, who was reported to have fully recovered, did not appear. He was somewhat relieved because he had no witnesses willing to come forward on his behalf and testify that he was attacked and merely defended himself. Not even John Sergeant, the tailor who helped to maintain his habit of dressing well in three-piece suits made from specially selected fabrics in colors of light green, blue, burgundy, and matching shoes: the outfits of the perfect *saga* boy. The case was postponed, but at the next appearance date again Ossie did not appear. Ossie's no-show occurred twice more. Finally, a warrant was issued for his arrest to appear and present his evidence against Mannette. Also, none of the other guys wounded that day ever showed up. None. He was simply amazed that Lady Luck was drumming out his good fortune once more.

Finally, Ossie was picked up and brought in. When the magistrate asked him to state his case, all he said was he wanted payment for his damaged shirt. Mannette was speechless. Just his shirt? No compensation for his injuries? Nothing? "The cost of your shirt?" the magistrate asked again for the record. "Fourteen dollars, sir." "And that's all the compensation you want?" "Yes, sir." Mannette continued to be astounded. Needless to say, Campbell's generosity and forgiveness was the beginning of a fast friendship and most likely set the tone for the end of the bands' rivalry.

He sometimes wonders today if his parents were stricter whether he could have been spared some headaches and heartaches. Without such strict parental discipline and guidance, he had to rely on instinct as well as intuition to cope with the violence and, consequently, developed being possessive to the point of domineering. He readily acknowledges that these traits make it difficult for anyone to put up with him and the world he shaped for himself, which except for his passion for Pan is otherwise quite loosely defined. However, he does not allow regret to inform his worldview, past or present. He did what was necessary, he states matter-of-factly. Any man tussling with steel and steel-willed men would understand and not condemn him. He adopted the persona of a vagabond—cussing, swearing, and fighting like one—without ever comprising his love for the art form. He wishes he were a little more caring of some of the people whom he came into contact with, though.

Indeed, Mannette's odyssey has brought him to a resting place, literally and figuratively. He says of where he currently is:

> I like the state (of West Virginia), its natural landscaping, the mountains. I loved it (when I first arrived) and decided to stay here. Since here, I've been offered opportunities at other universities, which I've turned down. I will remain loyal to WVU, which has been wonderful to me. I love the freedom I have in running these workshops every year, without the college officials looking over my shoulders or breathing down my back to scrutinize what I'm doing.[117]

He reflectively asks of his life: was and is it worth it? The sometimes three hours of sleep per night he gets. The noise from the tuning that leaves his ears ringing. The intense neck pain he occasionally suffers from the intense concentration he exerts while at work. The periodic breaks that allow his hearing to resume to normal and prevent permanent tone deafness because he refuses to use ear plugs, finding them undesirable to tuning. "Absolutely, yes!" he avers without a moment's hesitation.

Still a consummate perfectionist, he is occasionally dissatisfied with what he is doing because he believes that it could be done better. That someone will come along who can surpass what he has done does not bother him. In fact, his students know that he will be very disappointed if they do not produce a better drum than he ever has. His injunction to Carolyn Hendricks, Darren Dyke, Chanler Bailey, and the host of others with whom he works is to surpass him. They possess all his knowledge to take the lead pan, for example, and make it function as a solo drum, if they so desire. Whether the lead pan ever was intended to be a solo instrument or a member of an ensemble/orchestra depends on the dream. To build the almost perfect pan, the Stradivarius of steel that is recognizable by all and not just Phil Faini, continues to be his objective.

Recognizing that this dream may not be realized during his lifetime, he has transferred that burden to his current students and their struggle with steel to create the clear second octave that goes beyond G. He compares the fifty-year plus history of the pan with the five hundred-year history of the piano, for example, and knows that this newest percussion instrument has many miles to go before it can take its place along side the other more historical instruments.[118] In the early days of Pan, the men's efforts were grounded in the workings of the imagination that transformed an oil drum into a musical instrument. He is committed to leaving a legacy on which his students can build, a technology that can advance the art form. Should all be committed, not just his students, to its advancement, he has no doubt that in time Pan will take and hold its esteemed place in mainstream world music. Currently, many people still regard it as a folk instrument that ought to be limited to island music. How ridiculous, he reiterates in a sentiment shared by other pan-builders and -makers; however, it will take time for Pan to arrive at its zenith.

Yet, he worries that not enough is being done to advance the art form, to create what surpasses all existing accomplishments. He recognizes that some tuners in Trinidad, like "Guppy" Brown, are quite good but can do a better job of making both good high and low notes. This is his challenge to them. He additionally wishes that his influence extended beyond his immediate American students and apprentices to include some from Trinidad and the African American community, so that a more diverse representation of the next generation is receiving the knowledge of what he is passing on and not a single group, he says candidly and non-offensively. Hence, though the members of Sons of Steel, a group of six African American guys ranging in ages eleven to twenty-one years old and led by American thirty-one-year-old Tracy Thornton are not in his apprenticeship program, he is particularly proud of his role in bringing the band into existence and its current remarkable success.

During an informal conversation in 2000 at Mannette's then new site on 166 Dents Run Road, Thornton stated a carpe diem moment led to the group's formation the year before, following a summer camp program in Greensboro, North Carolina. He was enthused by the energy generated from the questions about steelpan coming from Arabian Lisbon, the youngest and a mere seven years old at the time; Adam Brady, then ten years; Jaren Doby, then twelve; and, Jai Doby, then fourteen. Recognizing that their avid interest, as well as remarkable talent, could be nurtured positively, Thornton suggested the formation of their own band, which led to Sons of Steel. He later added Nicholas "Nick" Hayes on drums, and he decided himself to play the tenor pan and percussion to complete the band's membership.

He is proud today, four years later in 2001, of what the boys have accomplished by remaining committed to their educational accomplishments in following a rigorous homeschooling program, despite their demanding tour schedule. They complete an average of fifteen tours annually, are on the road ten months, and have opened for Lauryn Hill and Jimmy Buffet. While addressing the 2001 MMIM audience, the boys avowed their ambitions to become a successful doctor, engineer, and computer analyst, with the band and its music being their vehicle. Playing for audiences as large as 30,000, they see that the band has enabled them to establish a pattern of success that boosts their confidence in their abilities to accomplish whatever they put their minds to. Thornton is happy to be a part in shaping their lives positively and attributes it back to Mannette's encouragement and support. He considers that Sons of Steel is a part of Mannette's legacy that extends beyond his direct program.

Mannette lives his belief posed in the rhetorical question: what does it profit a man to keep what he knows to himself? He answers:

> It does not profit you anything to keep what you know to yourself. If Ellie Mannette decided not to give these skills to the younger people, the art form will remain where it is and not improve. But I feel if I give it to intelligent, young people, they will advance it in the future. I don't care what you guys say, I will continue to give it to the young people. Even the Trinidad government is against me for this. They come here many a time and say I should go home and teach it to the young people down there at the university. I

shouldn't be teaching these people here, and a set of nonsense. But I'm not taking that on.

I'm very proud to see Darren, Carolyn, and Chanler and all these guys, what they've accomplished with something new in their lives. And you know what? They'll benefit considerably from this thing in the future. They'll live a big, happy, financially stable life from what they're doing here. Because I'll retire. Patrick Arnold is not tuning any more. Cliff Alexis will retire.... These young people are learning from a master and will surpass me. By the time I retire, there'll be thousands of steel bands across the country that need service. They must have service. These young people will clean up. The phones will be ringing off the hook. These guys have committed their lives to doing this: Robbie Davis, who has his master's degree, doesn't want to do anything else.... They will call the shots. No one can tell them anything because they have the clout.... Right now, I have hundreds of (school) programs to service. And, I enjoy doing this, not just for the money. It makes a lot of people happy. The young people enjoy playing. This is a real worthwhile program/ business.[119]

One needs only to tour his plant and be convinced that Ellie Mannette has little reason to regret following the sound of the drums that keep ringing from his heart and into the future. One of his dear friends, "Robbie" Greenidge who also calls him "Skip," sums up Mannette's story and its related issues well:

Progress happens and change takes place. There's nothing wrong with desiring national and international recognition; besides, eventually somebody would come along and take it (pan) out of Trinidad. He had become a great pan-tuner even before leaving Trinidad. If he wanted to become great internationally, he couldn't just stay in Trinidad. If you look at soccer and cricket and other sports that they play internationally, they didn't just stay at home playing. They went out into the world. Why then should Steelband be confined to Trinidad? No. It couldn't be. So, who better than someone who was there at almost the inception of Pan to spread its art form? Someone who has the status of a great piano tuner?

... As I said, he was already great in Trinidad but they didn't want to acknowledge his greatness. It's after he left they began to miss him and criticize him for leaving. He also had a great vision, a tremendous vision for Pan. So, the fella was merely trying to make a livelihood and living for himself doing what he does best. If it was me, I would have done the same. In fact, I left Trinidad in 1971 for the same reason.[120]

After all is said and done, Mannette still desires to awake every morning and do what he loves, knows, and does best: build and tune pans toward leaving the world the richest possible Pan legacy and a better place for his having been here.[121]

His story. His knowledge of Pan's history. His legacy. His voice in reverberation toward harmony.

Appendage

A Woman's Passion: *Maria Pereira's Vignette* [122]

Maria "Vera" Pereira *was born on December 7, 1932, in Barataria, Trinidad. She attended San Juan Government School, Osmond High School and Johnson Commercial School in San Juan, where she learned her secretarial skills. At age twenty, she moved to St. James.*

She immigrated to the United States in 1962 and has lived in Georgia since 1980. She retired in June 2003 as Sergeant Maria Pereira, *after seventeen and a half years of serving the Atlanta sheriff office. While filling her official duties,* Pereira *also served as Secretary of the Local 453 Union; Copresident of the Union; Chief Steward; Parliamentarian President and Secretary. During her tenure, in 1996 former President Bill Clinton recognized her commitment to the Sheriff's Office and the Union at a rally in Macon, Georgia. Incredibly youthful both physically and spiritually, she plans finally to learn to play the pan she should have learned years ago.*

Saturday night dances, with Cyril Ramdeo and his Union Orchestra performing at the Diamond Horseshoe Club located on Western Main Road, always promised the predictable and the unexpected. The pulsating rhythms of the lively calypso music compelled everyone to the dance floor. The last dance of the night always brought the expectation of something more to come, a climax. Loitering outside the club was merely a delay while waiting for any excuse to prolong the night, even if that excuse was a quarrel or a fight. Two panmen settling a score, or two girls attempting to stake their claim over one man. The police then arrived and restored order, and couples paired off and headed in various directions to complete what began on the dance floor or what got roiled up during the fight.

She had heard all about these dances and had moved to St. James to have fun.

Every one with a party-bone in his or her body went to the club. Each panman was a rooster around whom his flock of girls clucked for attention for a fun night, or more. At the moment, Ellie Mannette was the grand rooster, the craze. He with his devil-be-damned dismissal of what the newspapers or society said about him. He who had given up a Birmingham music scholarship and returned to Trinidad because Steelband and Calypso had a strange power over him. Young, bold, and the most handsome and gifted panman, he was taking Steelband to new realms all by himself, and people magnified him to unattainable heights. She had to see whom they were fussing over.

That first night, she was completely bowled over. She probably fell a little harder and faster than all the other women infatuated with him. For her, it was more than his handsome face. Something about him touched that part of her that said, "This is my man." And similarly to them, she was completely undaunted that each felt that she was his woman, including his wife Joyce whom she thought was a plain-Jane, if she ever saw one. Surely he could have done better.

Nothing happened that first night, nor did she expect anything to. The following Saturday night, she returned wearing a dress intended to cause more than a pause, a floral dress with spaghetti straps that hugged her petite frame. The dress worked. She could feel eyes upon her while she chatted with her girlfriends in one corner of the dance hall or when she was on the dance floor. Following one dance, she glanced in his direction and saw that he was looking. While she laughed and joked with her girlfriends, surreptitious glances in his direction confirmed that he was mesmerized.

He said he could not take his eyes off her. She was by far the prettiest young woman he'd laid eyes upon. One of the reasons he returned home was that English and European young women paled in comparison to Trini ones.

She was dizzy with the awareness of his attention. What to do next? He was married, so was she—but separated. Besides, in the club-scene everyone knew marriage didn't count. She thrilled every time their eyes made four across the dance floor.

Around midnight as the dance heated up, she decided to make the first move. He was talking with some of his friends at the bar when she beckoned him to come over. He didn't. Since Joyce wasn't in sight, she dared to approach him on the pretext of inquiring about playing Mas with Invaders. They chatted a while, danced a set or two, and she returned to her friends. They didn't dance again for the night, which made what happened upon her departure a surprise.

At the door, Joyce was waiting for her. She flashed-forward and saw the effects of the rage that was bound to match the fire in the woman's eyes and didn't have to wait long. She braced herself. Advancing toward her, Joyce planted herself squarely in her path and demanded, "I want *you* to tell *me* what *you* want with *my* husband." Every pronoun emphasized with a finger pointing at Maria then back at her own chest. Finished, Joyce waited with a tapping left foot, left hand on waist, and dangling right arm with clenched right fist, the fight stance that girls perfected during recess time on the school's playground.

Hands akimbo, saucily Maria replied, "If *you* have to ask then *you* shouldn't be with him in the first place."

"Stay away from meh husband, ah warning you, you little—."

"Or what? You big—yourself."

They were showering spit onto each other's faces as they attempted to out-scream and out-cuss each other. Then, the first shove was followed by a shove back, then the hair-pulling, nail-clawing at the face, and attempts to dig each other's eye out. Disfigurement the clear intent. By the time they were separated, her beautiful dress was ruined.

At home a little later, she decided that someone had to pay for her indignity and her dress. After all, all she did was talk to the man and he talked back. He didn't have to. They danced a little dance. That wasn't plenty. What right the woman had for coming at her, so? Eh, eh. Someone had to pay.

That next Sunday morning, with the torn dress in a brown paper bag, she presented herself at his house and demanded compensation for what his wife destroyed. They agreed to meet at Franco Beach House in Carenage, the rendezvous of lovers, later that afternoon. Their agreeing to meet at Franco's quickly established where their relationship was headed. She had no doubts about keeping their date but wondered about him. He did come.

They strolled along the beach for a while just talking about trivialities. Finally, they sat down on the dried limb of a fallen palm tree and she inquired about his travels. A comfortable topic for him, he delighted her through the remainder of the night and into the dawn with details on what TASPO did, where they went, whom they met, and how the men couldn't leave their bad behavior home. Exotic images that stirred in her a desire to see the world. Juicy details that wetted her appetite for travel and sample of life beyond a small island. He loved to talk and she enjoyed listening and dreaming. Just before sunrise, they parted and agreed to meet again.

The following months they met and just talked, sometimes at Franco's or her house. He had so much to get off his chest: his dreams for the steel band, frustrations about getting adequate drums for Pan, and, most of all, the longing for the violence between the bands to end. Far from being the tough *bad-john*, she saw what she intuitively felt drawn to that first night and would always love dearly: a gentle, sensitive man behind the tough bravado.

Eventually, he was not the only one hanging out at her house on Jerry Street but all the members of Invaders. In fact, after a fight with other band members, they all came to her house to patch their wounds or mend bruised egos.

On *Wajans* and *Wabines*

Trinidadian men were not expected to be true and faithful to one woman, not even their wives. Some "outside" women called *wajans* and *wabines* were so bold, they were known to confront wives on Frederick Street, or anywhere in public, and throw into the wives' faces, "*You* may have his ring, but *I* have his heart."

Wives learned to bear this humiliation with quiet dignity and not be reduced to further shame by fighting either verbally or physically with any *wajan* or *wabine*. A fight meant the wife never had a secure place in her husband's life to begin with, that she possibly trapped him into the marriage either with an unplanned pregnancy, her father's money, or obeah, as described in Mighty Sparrow's calypsos, "Mr. Walker" and "Melda." A fight meant the end of a forced marriage with the wife being left with nothing: no ring, no heart, and worst, no dignity.

Wives, consequently, mastered the scornful look they threw back at these *wajans* and *wabines* before striding away never once betraying their pain, despite its intensity. Queen Elizabeth II couldn't be more regal in stiff upper-lip composure.

Mistresses didn't instigate fights either; they didn't have to. They held the most secure position and didn't have to fight or confront a wife, *wajan*, or *wabine*. However, if a mistress' identity became known, she could be lowered if she were drawn successfully into a public fight, which the man was sure to hear of and then make peace by restoring one woman's position. Normally, he chose not to be bothered and left both wife and mistress to chase after a woman outside his reach or one who caused him little or no trouble, and returned later to women who were grateful for not having been deserted. These Trini men perfected the role of being a player before anyone else.

Who, however, could explain why some women propped up these men so? They sometimes made life a little too easy for men to make *sòts* of them. Those weren't the days for rationalizing behavior, though, neither the violent panmen's nor the women who fought for them.

That fight between Maria and Joyce was a foreboding one. If Maria were not careful she could lose Ellie even before anything began, before it was clearly established what role she played in his life, though it was clear the fight linked the three of them even before her role was established. Meanwhile, she steadily grew to love him deeply, to risk being made into a *sòt* while competing with others.

She also knew intuitively that no one and nothing held his affection as Pan did. Even if she tried, she could never have him all to herself. Never be first place in his heart. Such belonged to Pan only. For her to be first after Pan and second to no woman, she would have to sacrifice and allow him to develop his first love. She also knew from commonsense that he belonged to the world. He'd seen a little of it and could not disguise the longing to see more, a topic that tinged their conversation. Free-spirited. That was her man. She could only provide him the space to come and go as he pleased, trusting that in the end he would always find his way back to her.

It was a sacrifice she paid for over the years of always being out of his reach. Either someone else had asserted herself while she had hesitated, or Steelband's call had taken him to another land.

Color Stratification and Its Barriers

Something else caused her to hesitate. Her mother was Venezuelan and father Indian, which accounted for her heavily wavy hair and darker skin tone. She was what Trinidadians considered a *dougla*. Self-conscious about her skin tone, she feared rejection. He was light-skinned, having inherited his complexion from his mother, one of the most beautiful women Maria had ever seen, a light-skinned Spanish mixture with long, wavy hair. Ellie had told her none of his family attended his and Joyce's wedding, who had trapped him with an unplanned pregnancy. They complained he had "so many nice-looking women—meaning high-colored—desiring him and all he could end up with was that plain, Negro girl." Their rejection of his wife and ultimately his firstborn son was painful. Yet, he loved darker-skinned women: Norma, Joyce, now Maria. He wished society would mind its business and people would leave him alone to manage his private affairs. She herself got along well enough with his parents but maintained a respectful distance because of Joyce.

Maria longed to believe he really didn't care about skin color. That he secretly preferred the high-colored girls vying for his attention but was in rebellion of his family and society. She dared to believe when he said he didn't know why the hell people couldn't leave him alone and mind their own business. It was generally known that men of social mobility did not marry women who were darker than they. Since Pan promised no mobility, he had no one's expectations but his to meet.

His sisters also made it clear that their brothers' band with its reputation was beneath them and played Mas with Dixieland, the band that accommodated the socialites. They loved their brothers but didn't have to love his steel band or the people associated with it.

Consequently, she never bonded with his sisters and, instead, developed a close tie to "Birdie," a younger brother who drank a lot on Carnival day. So much so that he was always drunk even before the band reached the Savannah. His precious headpiece she alone had worked on all season would often be dragging on the ground before the band reached the judges. Every year it was the same, yet every year she hoped he would remain sober to keep his headpiece in place until after the judging. A hope on wings.

Costumepreparation was one reason she loved Carnival. No one cared for the drunkenness or self-destructive path upon which many girls ended. Nine months after Carnival the maternity ward at PoS General Hospital was always the busiest month of the year. For her, Carnival was a time for girlfriends to spend lots of hours helping to make costumes for the Mas band.

In the Invaders panyard, she was aware the girls were there not just to bead and bond but to get attention. But she could relax and enjoy the beading and bonding. She already had all the attention she desired. While playing Mas—she jumping up to music he played only for her, she felt—his eyes never wandered from her. He said he never let her out of his sight to make sure no one else was moving in on his Maria. She loved their secret glances as well as having a good jump-up time in the band. Hence, all the preparation was worth it, even if it meant beading throughout the night and sleeping at one's day job the following day.

She worked as a secretary for Martin Looby Contracting Company near to Marine Square. Around the country, bosses had reconciled with the fact that productivity slowed down during the Carnival season. Some knew better than to try to make demands on their workers, especially those who worked diligently during the off-season to play hard come Carnival Monday and Tuesday.

On Joyce's Death

After approximately six months, their friendship became intimate. They were fully aware the affair couldn't last and agreed to make the most of what they had. She was content just to enjoy their time together and not ask any questions, especially of the times he didn't come around. She believed when he said that she was his main one. She never asked among how many but guessed he saw four or five others during his absent spells. Eventually, after the uncertainty of not knowing when next she would see him and for how long became unbearable, she demanded a commitment. He agreed to move in with her and they enjoyed a year of stability from 1955 to '56.

Then, visibly his marriage began to crumble.

Though he always came home to her every night, sometimes quite late after steelband rehearsals, he always awoke her to reassure her that he was still hers.

However, some nights were disturbed by Joyce's visits. She stood outside and screamed expletives at him and Maria and demanded for him to come outside. She screamed herself hoarse before he went outside to calm her down and before the neighbors began complaining or called the police. They then argued furiously and always he ended up returning her home to her mother and their son, Kendall, then returning promptly to Maria.

Joyce's unseemly behavior made reconciling their marriage impossible. True, his own callous indifference to women's needs created a difficult marriage. He was to be blamed, he readily admitted. However, after moving in with Maria, Joyce was shattered and eventually became quite ill. Slowly, her health deteriorated, for she had simply given up the will to live. The doctors could find nothing physically wrong with her. She perked up every time he visited her at the hospital and slumped upon his departure. Her good health and spirit depended upon his presence, everyone but him could plainly see. Instead, he continued to behave as though he were footloose and fancy-free. Sometimes, not even Maria could pin him down.

Following Joyce's death in 1962, the doctors said she died literally from a broken heart—the only "illness" they could diagnose—he and Maria drifted apart. He could not get pass Joyce's final moments, including when her last breath expired for he happened to be there, having been compelled by a strong urge to visit her then. That image remained between him and other women for a while.

For Maria, their time together had been a bittersweet one, a chapter in her life that closed without any fanfare or ceremony. He just stopped coming around altogether, and when she left for New York later that year it was without so much as a good-bye to him.

Friends Forever

In 1981, she relocated to Atlanta, having wearied of big-city living. Shortly thereafter, they met again. At the time, she was free to pursue a lasting relationship. Since he did not inquire as to her status, she assumed that he was not free. The brief meeting brought back all the memories, though, and following it she inquired and learned that he was married. Oh, well, *c'est la vie*.

She began focusing on her career in the Atlanta sheriff office. After passing the examination for sheriff with impressively high scores, she began her ascent. She could finally make a comfortable living for herself and her daughter, Lynn, whom she had given birth to in Trinidad.

Quite a few years later, she was quite surprised to learn from Kim Loy, a former member of Highlanders then living in San Antonio, Texas, that he was being controlled by one Kaethe George. Kim described her as a very domineering young woman who blocked access to Ellie. Getting through her to Ellie was like breaking into Fort Knox. He was her prized gold whom no one would have. She didn't bother to get his number from Kim. She was too dismayed that the free-spirited man she once knew sounded like he was becoming *toutoulbé* in his old-age.

She could not but wonder: who the hell was this Kaethe George, anyway, this controlling young woman who probably forced her way into his life? How did she assume such power and control in his life and business? While she made up her mind she didn't want to have anything to do with him, she was intrigued. Thus, she kept abreast of his activities through mutual friends or articles published about him and his work.

A few years later, Lynn informed her that she heard he was living in Phoenix, Arizona. She urgently wanted to see him again and began inquiring on how to reach him. More than curiosity regarding Kaethe motivated her. This was the only man she had ever really loved and given herself freely to. He knew that. He'd said the same thing about her. Was love like that forever? She had to know.

In 1998, after obtaining his number from a mutual acquaintance, she phoned.
"This is Maria."
"Who Maria?"
"Maria." She refused to volunteer any more.
"Oh, my Maria." He laughed. He had not forgotten her. She laughed.

They spoke for about an hour, during which time she informed him that she was a deputy sheriff, a sergeant with the Fulton County sheriff department in Atlanta, Georgia. They agreed to meet.

What would he look like? A potbellied man turning seventy or so who had not kept up his health or appearance? What had she done? Would she pretend not to recognize him and walk away if from a distance he turned out to be a disappointment? How far would love go?

Though she knew she could never walk away, she was delighted to see he was still neat and trim. Her love and desire almost overwhelmed her, transporting her back to their passionate years.

He was equally happy to see she was even prettier than he remembered, and just as trim and petite. He, too, had thought of walking away if she had not kept up her appearance. Instead, his Maria's beautiful smile still wrapped itself warmly around his heart. Her eyes still laughed at the world she'd faced and conquered.

They agreed to a long distance affair, meeting once per month, or whenever they could.

He told her once in Atlanta, after showing her an article published about him and Pan, she should have been one of the pioneer female pan-builders and -tuners. How could she have? "Women couldn't even associate freely with panmen because of the stigma, much less consider getting involved in that," she reminisced. Continuing, "People really don't know how many sacrifices women back then made for Pan." She was referring to how women suffered dearly—some still do—for defying their families and society to become publicly involved with panmen or Pan.

Today, she continues to be thrilled to see so many women beating pan, back when she visited Trinidad in 1990, again in 2000, and very much present at MMIM.

Women, indeed, have arrived in Pan.

Glossary

Abbreviations
BG: British Guiana, now called Guyana
BOAC: British Overseas Airways Corporation
BWIA: British West Indies Airways
CASYM: Caribbean American Sports and Cultural Youth Movement (*Note*: The original name of the organization, which began in 1983, was Caribbean American Sports Youth Movement. "and Cultural" was added later with the addition of a steel orchestra.)
CID: Criminal Investigations Department
DCEU: *Dictionary of Caribbean English Usage*
DEWD: Development and Environment Works Division
NATTS: National Association of Trinidad and Tobago Steelbandsmen Association
NJAC: National Joint Action Committee
NIU: Northern Illinois University
NPR: National Public Radio
PoS: Port of Spain
PNM: People's National Movement
QRC: Queen's Royal College
RC: Roman Catholic
T&T: Trinidad and Tobago
T&TEC: Trinidad and Tobago Electric Company
TASPO: Trinidad All Steel Percussion Orchestra
TTSA: Trinidad and Tobago Steelband Association
UNC: United National Congress
USSBA: United States Steel Band Association
UWI: University of the West Indies
WIADCA: West Indian American Day Carnival Association
WSMF: World Steelband Music Festival
WVU: West Virginia University

Caribbean Creole

Note: some words have multiple meanings. For economy, definitions are provided for the reader's understanding of their contextual use in this work. Where indicated, *DCEU* provides their complete definition.

bad-john (bad john) • *n.* A violent man (*DCEU*); a lawless man who ironically enforced rules and discipline in Steelband.

bad-johnism • *n.* Violent and lawless conduct in the open (*DCEU*).

bad-talk • *n.* Malicious gossip or injurious half-truths (*DCEU*).

bad-talk • *v.* To speak maliciously (usu. in private conversation about a person, place, or thing) intending to cause discredit, disadvantage, or harm (*DCEU*).

bounce up with • *v phr.* To meet or run into someone by chance (*DCEU*).

cuff • *n.* A blow with the clenched fist; a blow with the fist, or with the open hand (*DCEU*).

cuff • *v.* To hit with the clenched fist; to punch (*DCEU*).

dougla(h) • *n.* A person of African and Indian ancestry (*DCEU*).

fore-day (fo'e-day) morning • *n phr.* Before dawn; the time between darkness and sunrise *DCEU*).

for true • *adv phr.* Really; truly; for a certainty (*DCEU*).

fraid • *adv often used as a vb.* (To be) frightened; (to be) afraid of (*DCEU*).

graff over • *v phr.* To experiment with (from the original verb "graft").

grind • *v.* To get into a state of inactive anger or fury (*DCEU*).

grundig • *n.* A pan invented by Neville Jules and named after a German radio that was marketed shortly after World War II. The grundig, which Jules abandoned, is the forerunner of the cello section of the steel band.

gym-boots (jim-boots) • *n.* Ankle-high, rubber-soled, canvas boots (sometimes with a rubber patch ankle-guard) (*DCEU*).

jokey • *adj.* Ridiculous, amusing, absurd (*DCEU*).

jook • *v.* **1** To stab or make a thrust at with a sharp-pointed instrument (*DCEU*). **2** To thrust one's hips back and forth sexually while dancing.

kyar • *v.* To can't; to cannot.

las' lap (last-lap) • *n.* The vigorous reveling and jumping-up in the streets in the final hours before midnight on Shrove Tuesday ending the Carnival celebrations (*DCEU*).

laywai' (laywait) • *v.* To waylay; to lie in wait for (*DCEU*).

liming • *n.* The habit or action of intentional idling in a public place or wasting time on a job (*DCEU*).

mash up • *v phr.* To destroy; to bring to an abrupt, noisy end; to break up by dealing smashing blows (*DCEU*). **2** To cease to exist.

nancy-story (anancy-story) • *n.* Nonsense; a lie (*DCEU*).
ole talk or old talk • *n.* Idle chatter; gossip; social chit-chat (*DCEU*).
ole talk or old talk • *v.* To indulge in idle chatter; to gossip; to talk irresponsibly for the sake of talking; to make empty promises (*DCEU*).
planass • *v.* To strike with the flat blade of a cutlass or machete (*DCEU*).
saga • *adj.* Very fashionable and showy; over-stylish; garish (*DCEU*).
sòt (sut) • *adj.* Stupid; silly; foolish (*DCEU*).
sòt (sut) • *n.* A fool (*DCEU*).
toutbagai • *n phr.* The whole lot; everything; everybody (*DCEU*).
tout moune (tout moon bagai) • *n phr.* Just about everybody; the world and his wife (*DCEU*).
toutoulbé • *adj.* Stupefied; dazed; madly in love (with the implication that this state has been brought about by witchcraft (*DCEU*).
wabine (wa(h)been) • *n.* A bad-woman; a prostitute (*DCEU*).
wajan (wajang, wajank) • *n.* **1** A bad-woman; **2** an expert at something (*DCEU*).
wine • *v.* (Esp of a woman) To dance erotically by swinging the hips vigorously while thrusting the buttocks back and forth (*DCEU*).
wining • *v.* Erotic or provocative dancing (*DCEU*).

Capitalization

Steelband, Steelpan, and/or Pan are all used interchangeably throughout the work. When referring to the art form, culture, or an academic degree program, the capital letter of the word(s) is used. When referring to the instrument, per se, the lower case letter is used.

Steel Band (as two words) is used when identifying the name of a specific steel band, for example, Tripoli Steel Band; or sometimes in reference to an unnamed steel band/steel bands.

Similarly to Steelband, the capital letter is used with Calypso, Carnival, and Soca when referring to the respective art forms. The lower case letter is used when referring to specific examples, as when the narrator implies calypso music without so stating: "He could sing calypso"; or, "You all are not doing calypso and you all don't look like calypso people." The lower case letter is also used when "steelband" is used as an adjective. This same rule is appled to Mas/mas.

Geographical Locations (not located on a T&T map)
Behind the Bridge: refers to all the areas beyond Piccadilly Street, located to the south-east of PoS: Calvary Hill, Clifton Hill, John John Hill, Reservoir Hill, and East Dry River, Laventille; also referred to collectively as the Laventille Hills or the Hill.
La Basse: located in the north-west of the island, a few miles south of PoS, along the Beetham Highway. It was located next to Shanty Town, where the poorest of the poor eked out a living. A large dung hill, it, along with Shanty Town, was demolished and made habitable during the early 1970s. Shanty Town was renamed Beetham Gardens and the La Basse was relocated to across the highway facing Beetham Gardens.

Conclusion

Many people have asked how I got these reticent pan-people to share their stories, in particular Ellie who had never before revealed some of these intimate details of his life. I think I reentered Pan at a critical time, as stated in the Introduction. The pan is now present on six of the seven continents, its indescribable sound continuing to fascinate people. How did this despised thing become a beloved instrument by so many people throughout the world? What quiet revolution has been underway, which began amongst some of the most despised people of the world? Who were these men whom the world needed to recognize as being responsible for giving us the only percussion instrument to have been invented during the twentieth century?

I began this work with a focus on Ellie, having accepted a visiting assistant professorship at WVU after Professor Patrick Conner informed me that he was there (my "steelqueen" e-mail address hinted at my interest in Steelband, which I still think is sheer brilliant of Professor Conner to have accurately guessed). I had pursued secretly my interest in Steelband as a child and adolescent in Trinidad, and recall the names Ellie Mannette, Neville Jules, and "Spree" Simon being at the forefront. One friend I had while living in Trinidad had made it his business to educate me about these men because I needed to know our history and culture, even though I was a girl. The information might be useful one day, he had said. The mystery of Ellie's departure from Trinidad was among the stories he shared. Therefore, when so many years later I learned I had the opportunity to meet him, I seized it.

One other person, however, really propelled me back into Steelband: my daughter, Miranda. She first heard pan music in utero (as did my son, Alex) while I was pregnant and a member of the second steel band in a church in Brooklyn, New York, named Glorious Freedom Steel Orchestra, a steel band I helped organize in 1976. I had immigrated to New York the year before with the knowledge that my high school alma mater, St. François Girls' College, was starting the first steel band for girls in the country, information that made enthusiastic approximately twenty fellow Caribbeans that it was acceptable for us to play pan in church. Then, the demands of motherhood superseded my commitment to the band, which was abandoned five years before the family relocated to Delaware in

1987. However, my husband and I often reminisced about our Steelband days, which peaked Miranda's curiosity.

Thus, when as a high school senior in 1995 she was required to complete a senior thesis, she decided to focus on Steelband. This entailed our reinvesting in a completely new set of instruments, which Terrance Cameron made, to complete the performance part of her thesis, hence the birth of Blaksilvah Steel Band. For the written part, I was appalled by the insufficient body of literature on the movement and wanted to change this. Steelband was too important to the next generation for there to be such a paucity of literature.

This desire to improve on Steelband's body of literature shaped my approach to Ellie. Our first conversation began with my saying, "Mr. Mannette," which he interrupted me by saying, "Call me, 'Ellie'; everybody does." I continued, "Thank you, Ellie, and for talking with me." "What is it you want?" I immediately launched into how there wasn't enough published material on Steelband. My daughter earned an A on the performance part of her senior thesis—having brought her training in classical piano to pan playing—but a B on the written part because we couldn't find enough material on Steelband. I wanted to change this and hoped he could help me. Young students and scholars deserved to know about Steelband, of which he was a big part, because people in Trinidad were still talking about him.

Very surprised, he interrupted, "They still talkin' 'bout me in Trinidad?" "They were, up until I left in 1975." "Well, I hope they talking 'bout how much I did for Steelband. People don't know about my work, my contributions." "Well, they deserve to: don't you agree?" With only the slightest hesitation, he agreed that maybe the time had come to get his story out. He had just been awarded the 1999 National Heritage Fellowship from the National Endowment for the Arts, which was bringing him and Steelband national and international attention. Also, UWI, St. Augustine, prior to the award, had discussed with him its conferral of an honorary doctorate degree. BBC Radio had recently interviewed him. With such honors and international attention being bestowed upon him, he felt the time had come for his story to be told.

As we talked, it became obvious to both of us that the story of Steelband was far bigger than he was, and that I would have to speak to other men in the movement. He willingly provided me with what contact information he had. Still, I sensed the story was bigger than the people who revolved around Ellie. Returning to Terrance, I shared with him my research interest and progress, and he willingly provided me names and contact information. Those contacts provided me additional ones, the result being this work.

Unheard Voices now stands as a part of a small but growing body of literature on the movement. Much work remains with many more stories to be documented. The call remains for scholars and researchers—not just a few such as Dr. Hollis Liverpool (Mighty Chalkdust), Selwyn Best, Gordon Rohlehr, and Donald Hill—to be diligent and aggressive in rising to the challenge and engage Steelband and Calypso as parts of western and world cultures. Now is the time to revolutionize curricula to include all voices. Only with these inclusions will our world community fully understand what George Lamming states in the Introduction of his classic novel *In the Castle of My Skin* (Schocken Books, 1983). In describing the Caribbean world, he writes that it

> ... is not simply poor. This world is black, and it has a long history at once vital and complex. It is vital because it constitutes the base of labor on which the entire Caribbean society has rested; and it is complex because Plantation Slave Society (the point at which the modern Caribbean began) conspired to smash its ancestral African culture, and to bring about a total alienation of man the source of labor from man the human person.
>
> The result was a fractured consciousness, a deep split in its sensibility which now raised difficult problems of language and values; the whole issue of cultural allegiance between the imposed norms of White Power, represented by a small numerical minority, and the fragmented memory of the African masses: between White instruction and the Black imagination. The totalitarian demands of White supremacy, in a British colony, the psychological injury inflicted by the sacred rule that all forms of social status would be determined by the degrees of skin complexion; the ambiguities among Blacks themselves about the credibility of their own spiritual history. (xi)

Later, Lamming argues that the journey toward a restored whole consciousness should be without fear that we may have to go beyond the boundaries of instruction and curricula that meet the approval of established academic learning (xix). *Unheard Voices* is such an attempt toward restoring the wholeness of human consciousness. Finally, *Unheard Voices* reiterates the lyrics of Singing Sandra's "Voices from de Ghetto," "We are not a forgotten people," and even more important, we, Caribbean and American pan-people, have not forgotten ourselves.

Notes

Introduction

1. The confluence continues through today, as reported in the following *New York Times* article: Ben Ratliff, "Sitar Meets Steel Pan, Naturally," *New York Times*, <http://query.nytimes.com/search/article-page.html?res=9C02E7D6133DF932A3575BC0A9669C8B63> (7 Oct 2002). Ratliff offers a positive review of Patasar and Harold Headley who combined to render the program's performance of music that combined Indian music, Calypso, and Jazz, called Indo-Calypso-Jazz.

2. Gordon Rohlehr in his essay "A Scuffling for Islands" points out that calypsonians were very much aware and were among the first West Indian artists to promote the idea of West Indian Federation and its call for Caribbean unity. Contemporaneously, the 1940s brought World War II, with its end in 1945 epochally marking the end of the reign of empire. The 1960s brought Independence to the four leading Caribbean countries: Jamaica (6 Aug 1962), Trinidad and Tobago (31 Aug 1962), Guyana (26 May 1966), and Barbados (30 Nov 1966).

3. Mas, the colloquial name for the masquerade of bands, is an activity of the Carnival season, whose activities include: the Crowning of the Calypso king and queen; the Crowning of the Carnival king and queen; J'ouvert, an early Monday-morning parade; Kiddies Carnival; the Road March winner, the calypso played by most bands on the road on Carnival days; Panorama, the official annual competition of steel bands; the Bomb winner, an off-stage steel band contest described in Neville Jules's story, and Las' Lap, the winding down of the festivities that begins on Tuesday night and continues into early Wednesday morning. Note that the pre-Carnival season begins immediately after Christmas and includes the preliminary competitions that climax during the last week and weekend prior to Carnival Monday and Tuesday. Carnival always precedes the Lenten season.

4. See Lloyd Best's "Not Pan in Schools but School in Pan: Reform of Panorama." *Trinidad Express*, 8 May 2001, <http://209.94.197.2/html1/prev/may01/may8/f6.htm>.

5. Jules's TASPO of 1946 was the brainchild of Prince Batson and Jules. They envisioned that one day the boys from Hell Yard (see Jules's narrative) would soar to great heights. According to Jules, even Dennis LeGendre, author of *Steelband in Perspective*, did not get the facts accurate. On page 31, LeGendre reports the name of the 1946 idea was TASPSO, Trinidad All Stars Philharmonic Steel Orchestra. Jules refutes that as misinformation and maintains he and Batson called the band TASPO, Trinidad All Stars Percussion Orchestra, and that the organizers of T&T TASPO simply appropriated his and Batson's idea, with merely one word changed.

6. Neville Jules's narrative suggests that he came up with the idea after 1948, which he describes in detail.

7. Both poems are published in *The Penguin Book of Caribbean Verse in English*, edited by Paula Burnett. London: Penguin Books Ltd., 1986.

8. Sandra des Vignes-Millington, "Voices from de Ghetto," *The Champions of Our Music*, CD, Ottic, Crosby's Music Centre, JW Productions. Composer, Christophe Grant. 1999.

9. Kim Johnson, "Pioneer on the Biscuit Drum: 'Patcheye' and Bar 20's Carlton 'Zigilee' Barrow," 13 Aug 2000, <http://www.pantrinbago.com/steelpan/briefhistory.htm> (19 Jul 2002). In this article, Johnson reports on his conversation with Henry "Patcheye" Pachot, the founder of Hill Sixty (named after the site for which the Germans and the British contested during World War I) was "one of the greatest biscuit drummers ever produced by the steelband movement." He lived on Clifton Hill, Laventille, and was influenced by the Shango tents that in 1938 attracted some of the best drummers. Later, he transferred leadership to Andrew "Pan" de la Bastide of Trinidad All Steel Percussion Orchestra (TASPO). Also in this article, Johnson writes that many men remained in the Hollywood, California area, and married American women to gain permanent residency and did not return to Trinidad upon the completion of the National Steelband's tour of the sixties. De la Bastide eventually made Los Angeles his permanent home where he died on November 19, 2002.

10. Ernest D. Brown, "Carnival, Calypso, and the Steelband in Trinidad." *The Black Perspective in Music.* 11. 1, 2 (1990): 83. In this article, Brown traces a lucid chronology of the country's emerging cultural history grounded in a hybrid African and European alternative lifestyle. Citing 1797 as the year Britain came into possession of Trinidad, he elucidates how Carnival emerged from concerted efforts by the British who for more than a century endeavoured "to Anglicize the culture" of its residual Spanish and French settlers' influences. Though somewhat scant on Steelband research but quite rich in Carnival and Calypso, his work provides excellent historical context for Pan's genesis in relation to Carnival and Calypso.

11. Kim Johnson, "The 'bad-john boys' from Belmont." *Sunday Express.* Sec. 2, 8 Mar 1998.

12. Terrance outfitted my family steelband in 1995 for my daughter Miranda to complete her senior high school thesis. See the Conclusion for further details.

13. The commercial aired on NBC and featured men in two ocean vessels, maybe Odysseus and his crew. The men in one vessel were struggling to keep going and were easily overtaken by the men in the other vessel who were energized by steelband music.

14. For further details on the crisis symphony orchestras face, see the following articles:
 Peter Daniels, "The Carnegie Hall-New York Philharmonic merger and the state of classical music." *World Socialist Web Site,* 10 Jul 2003, <http://www.wsws.org/articles/2003/jul2003/nyph-j10.shtml>.

 Joanne Laurier, "Detroit Symphony Orchestra faces $2 million deficit." *World Socialist Web Site,* 20 Dec 2003, <http://www.wsws.org/articles/2003/dec2003/tdso-d20.shtml>.

 Anne Midgette, "Decline in Listeners Worries Orchestras." *New York Times,* 25 Jun 2005, <http://www.nytimes.com/2005/06/25/arts/music/25ravi.html?incamp=article_popular_5>.

 Anthony Tommasini, "When the Bach Is Demonic, or No Sheep May Safely Graze." *New York Times,* 30 Jun 2005, <http://www.nytimes.com/2005/06/30/arts/music/30phil-extra.html?8dpc>.

15. Roberto Fernández Retamar, *Caliban and Other Essays*. Trans. Edward Baker. Minneapolis: U of Minnesota P, 1989.

16. Paulo Freire, *Pedagogy of Hope: Reliving Pedagogy of the Oppressed*. Trans. Robert R. Barr. New York: Continuum, 1994.

17. In the following listed works, Brathwaite discusses why Creole is the "nation language," a term he prefers over the colonial and racist one "dialect," of the Caribbean collective. Creole, he argues, shaped voice, song, and sound that became life-sustaining and death-defying during slavery, colonization, and colonialism:

    Edward Kamau Brathwaite, Address. Closing Conference Remarks. "North-South Counterpoints: Kamau Brathwaite and the Caribbean Word." Hostos Community College, Bronx, 24 Oct 1992.

    —. *Contradictory Omens: Cultural Diversity and Integration in the Caribbean*. 1974. Mona, Jamaica: Savacou Publications, 1985.

    —. *The Development of Creole Society in Jamaica, 1770–1820*. Oxford: The Clarendon Press, 1971.

18. Edouard Glissant, *Caribbean Discourse: Selected Essays*. Trans. J. Michael Dash. Charlottesville: UP of Virginia, 1992.

19. Voice here is being associated with nommo in contexts used by Kamau Brathwaite in *Roots*, where he defines nommo as the word or name that contains secrets and power (236); and by Ronald Jemal Stephens in "The Three Ways of Contemporary Rap Music" who defines nommo as the supernatural power of the spoken word, also present in the voice of the African drum (25–26).

20. For more information, see Simeon L Sandiford, ed, *Pan Sweet Pan: Steel Orchestras of the Caribbean* (Sanch Electronix Ltd, 2000), CD Booklet, 2–4. Also, Trinidadian journalist Terry Joseph and many others have already written that the name steelpan is not interchangeable with steel drum.

21. Robert "Robbie" Greenidge, during our 18 Jul 2001 conversation, thinks this is one of the jokes being played by Trickster god on everyone who feels he or she must know absolutely who that first man was. He says, "It could have been an old man living in the country (rural Trinidad) who quietly gave

his invention to a boy to go and jump up with in Carnival. Who really knows?" Indeed, who really knows who that first person was?

22. Nichole Christian, "Steel Bands Plan Boycott of Brooklyn's West Indian Parade," *New York Times*, 19 Jul 2001, <http://query.nytimes.com/search/restricted/article?res> (3 Jan 2003).

   Jon Pareles, "Sound of Steel in a Warm-Up for Carnival," *New York Times*, 7 Sep 1998, <://query.nytimes.com/search/article-page.html?res=9E04E1D6143EF934A3575AC0A96E958260>, (3 Jan 2003).

   Garry Pierre-Pierre, "A Crescendo in Steel," *New York Times*, 17 Dec 1998, <http://query.nytimes.com/search/article-page.html?res=9F0CE5DC133DF934A25751C1A96E958260>, (3 Jan 2003).

   Somini Sengupta and Garry Pierre-Pierre,"A Tradition Remade in Brooklyn; West Indians Prepare a Lavish, and Popular, Pageant," *New York Times*, 5 Sep 1998, <http://query.nytimes.com/search/article-page.html?pagewanted=all&res=9506E5DA173EF936A3575AC0A96E958260>, (3 Jan 2003).

Chapter 1

1. Telephone conversation, 22 Jul 2001. Follow-up calls continued throughout 2003.

2. Dawn Batson accounts of having received a similar treatment as a Bishop Ansty Girls' High School student during 1971–78, as narrated in her story.

Chapter 2

1. Personal conversation, 28 Sep 2002, at the home of his very dear friends, the Nelsons, who have co-organized the Trinidad All Stars Old Boys and Girls Association, an organization that is leading in a pioneer vision for the steelband movement. Follow up telephone conversations, 2002 into 2003.

2. In reference to Carlton Barrow, a.k.a. Carlton Constantine. For a brief narrative on his life, see Marcia Henville, "Memories of Old Man Zig," *Trinidad Express*, 4 Jan 1998, <http://209.94.197.2/jan/jan4/features.htm> (18 Oct 2002).

3. Bukka Rennie, "Pan Debate Must Open Up," *Trinidad Guardian*, 13 Nov 2000, <http://www.pantrinbago.com/steelpan/briefhistory.htm> (18 Oct 2002). Rennie in this article identifies this person as Cyril "Snatcher" Guy of Boom Town band from Tacarigua.

4. The closest I could get to Andrew "Pan" who died in 2002 was through a conversation by telephone with his niece on 27 Jun 2003, Shirlane Hendrickson Thomas, Calypso Queen, 1998 to 2001.

5. Ibid.

   Also, Beddoe is identified as a noted Orisha drummer, and the article alludes to the influence of Orisha in shaping the development of pan. According to Roberto Nodal in his essay "The Social Evolution of the Afro-Cuban Drum,"

   ... among the African Yoruba, the spirits of the deities of the Lucumí pantheon are called *orishas*, and include many gods well known to the African Yoruba: *Shangó*, the deity of the storm and lightning; *Obatalá*, god of war; *Ogún*, the god of iron and the mountains; *Eleggúa*, the guardian of the gateways and crossroads; *Ochún*, the river deity; *Yemayá*, the deity of the sea; *Babalú Ayé*, the healing god, and many others. Lucumí music thus is devoted mainly, though not exclusively, to the supplication and praise of these *orishas* or deities. (163–64)

6. Interview (radio). *Pan for the People*. 9 Mar 2002.

7. Felix I. R. Blake, *1995: The Trinidad and Tobago STEEL PAN: History and Evolution*. Published in Spain, Grafiques 85, S.L.—Molins de Rei.

8. Actually, Mannette claims to have created the double second in 1952 upon his return from England with TASPO.

9. Also called 'acoushi ants' in Guyana, bachac ants are large and voracious, reddish and sometimes black in color, and of many varieties (Allsop's *Dictionary of Caribbean Usage*, 57).

10. According to a 1998 article by Kim Johnson, "Killey and the Gonzales Rhythm Makers: The Scrap Iron Band of 1937: Wellington 'Killey' Yearwood" pan-bands were first formed in three locations: Big Yard on Woodford Street; Hell Yard on Charlotte Street; and Tantie Willie's Orisha

compound in Gonzales. Johnson continues that eighty-five year-old Yearwood as early as the 1920s was looking for a way to improve the sound of the bottle-and-spoon, which Jules discusses, and incorporated a brass shell-case his cousin had brought back from WW I. After the shell case was seized by Sergeant Caesar, the men generally lost their fascination for the "brass" instrument and returned to bamboo. However, in 1937, the band named First Eleven, of which he was a member, scrambled at the last minute to participate in that year's Carnival and hastily formed the first tin-pan band from scrap-iron. When the Belmont band heard them, its members discarded their bamboo into the river because the iron band drowned out their bamboo. By 1944, the Gonzales band had renamed itself Gonzales Rhythm Makers.

11. Road marches were appropriated to bands that marched while they were on the road rather than played Mas. The bands were judged very strictly and, therefore, were expected to adhere to the standards of a military band. Everyone in the band was expected to comply with the strict rules of military precision.

12. Jules is referring to Dr. Sidney Northcote, English adjudicator. For more details, see Steumple's *The Steelband Movement*, pp. 105–06.

Chapter 3

1. 1 Telephone conversation, 27 Aug 2002.

2. 2 I was delighted to hear Hugh Borde sharing his story on National Public Radio's *All Things Considered* with *The Kitchen Sisters* (Nikki Silva and Davia Nelson) on Tuesday, 4 Mar 2003. For more information, including photographs, visit <http://www.npr.org/programs/lnfsound/stories/current.html>.

3. 3 Desmond Bravo in our conversations on 23 and 25 Jun 2003 identifies Crick as the founder of Tripoli.

4. 4 For a brief biography on Hunte, see <http://www.mra.org.uk/fac/apr2000/profile2.html>.

Chapter 4

1. Personal conversations, 2002 into 2003, at his home in Brooklyn, New York, and via telephone.

2. Jones informed me that the origins of Kiddies Carnival began with a lady who had a private school on Henry Street and decided to bring out on Carnival Sunday a children's fair, to which the children came dressed in costumes. The fair lasted all day through five or six o'clock in the evening. Over the years, the fair came to be called Kiddies Carnival.

3. Kim Johnson, "The 'bad-john boys' from Belmont." *Sunday Express.* Section 2, 8 Mar 1998. Also, Jan Chatland, in "Descriptions of Various Loa of Voodoo," defines **Rada** as a loa who "represents the emotional stability and warmth of Africa, the hearth of the nation. Rada, derived almost directly from the Dahomean deity, is highly religious in nature," and "Rada drumming and dancing is on beat…., and stands for light and the normal affairs of humanity" <http://www.webster.edu/~corbetre/haiti/voodoo/biglist.htm>.

4. Pan-side refers to a regular steelband. Additionally, Ann Ward and Alison Taylor's "Iron & Steel: An Explique of a Typical Trinidad Pan Side" offers the following definitions for stage-side and road-side bands. The definitions are based on Maritime Life Hatters Steel Band of San Fernando, captained by Steve Achaiba, winner of 1975 Panorama. A stage-side band included: five high tenors, five low tenors, four double tenors, five double seconds, six double guitars, three triple guitars, three sets of cellos, and three sets of six-basses. A road-side band comprised of: ten high tenors, twenty low tenors, eight double tenors, ten double seconds, twelve double guitars, six triple guitars, eight sets of cellos, and six sets of six-basses. Both sides included an iron section or engine room of varying iron pieces.

5. In addition to the Rising Sun Steel Band photo featured in this book, Pan-around-the-neck is featured in Twentieth-Century Fox's *Island in the Sun* (1957), based on Alex Waugh's novel by the same title, featuring Dorothy Dandridge, Harry Belafonte, James Mason, Stephen Boyd, and others.

6. Deceased on Valentine's Day, 2003.

7. Kim Johnson, "Birth of Steelband Association: Pan Trinbago Honours Sydney Gollop's Contribution to Pan," *Sunday Express,* <http://www.nalis.gov.tt/steelbands/birthof_steelbandassociation.html#top> (18 Oct 2002).

8. Kim Johnson writes that Casablanca made a recording in 1947 and TASPO in 1951. See his article, "With Music in His Blood," *Trinidad*

Guardian, 21 Apr 2003, <http://www.guardian.co.tt/archives/2003-04-23/kim_johnson.html> (25 Aug 2003).

9. Note that Jones is not suggesting Antigua made the first steelband record, but that Antigua's record was being played on the radio. See also Kim Johnson's article that discusses how he unearthed the first steelband recording of Casablanca in 1947, which predates Antigua's of the 1950s: "With Music in His Blood: Oh Amadeus!" *Trinidad Guardian*, 21 Apr 2003, <http://www.guardian.co.tt/archives/2003-04-23/kim_johnson.html> (25 Aug 2003).

10. See Jules's story in which he offers an explanation for All Stars's nonparticipation in the festival from 1956 to 1966.

11. Stephen Steumple, *The Steelband Movement*, 105–16, corroborates the attempted colonial proscription on what the bands could and could not play.

12. See Cliff Alexis's narrative on how the name-change occurred.

13. Note that Jones is speaking of the 1950s to early '70s. Le Gendre notes in *Steelband in Perspective* that in 1973 at a conference that marked the "emancipation of the Panman," Williams instructed his Permanent Secretary to initiate courses in business management for panmen; however, music training, employment opportunities, standardization, a steelband factory, aid to unsponsored bands, and other economical boosts for panmen were still being explored (69–74).

14. According to Molineaux, this band of really little kids demonstrated the genius of young Trinidadians playing pan. He witnessed their arrival on the pan scene and was impressed.

15. Note that many readers will be quick to recognize that Reggae artists present deeply significant political and social commentaries in their lyrics, similarly to calypsonians, such as today's Spragga Benz, and Buju Banton. These younger artists do not overshadow Jimmy Cliff and Bob Marley who catapulted Reggae into the international limelight.

16. In 1881 and 1884, the British colonial authorities banned the use of the African camboulay drumming and Indian Hosay drumming, respectively. As the drums went underground, the African drummers adopted bamboo stools

as their "instrument" during Carnival and Emancipation celebrations, hence the name "tamboo-bamboo." All forms of drumming were again banned during WW II.

For more information on both bans, see Ernest D. Brown, "Carnival, Calypso, and the Steelband in Trinidad," *The Black Perspective in Music* 11.1, 2 (1990): 83. In this invaluable essay, Brown traces a lucid chronology of the country's history and emerging culture that was grounded in a hybrid African and European alternative lifestyle. Citing 1797 as the year Britain came into possession of Trinidad, he argues that Carnival emerged from more than one hundred years of concerted British efforts to anglicize the colony that had been influenced by Spanish and French settlers. Though somewhat scant on Steelband research but quite rich in Carnival and Calypso, his work provides excellent historical context that makes Pan's genesis in relation to Carnival and Calypso comprehensive and full-bodied. Brown's work helps to contextualize George Goddard's *Forty Years in the Steelbands: 1939–1979* (1991), a work seminal to the history of the Steelband movement. His work is an acute backdrop of what these stories merely intimate: a continuum of an instrument traced through colonial repression of the early twentieth century when all drums were banned, Emancipation and the celebration of freedom of the manumitted enslaved with drumming and dancing in the streets, and various West African musical and rhythmical expressions.

17. Honored in August 2003 at the 41st Independence Anniversary Ball in New York, along with Peter Minshall, Professor Courtney Bartholomew, (Professor) Emeritus of the University of the West Indies; Grace Blake, former executive director of the Apollo Theatre Foundation and motion picture producer for over 25 years; and David John, first vice president of Information Technology at Bayerische Landesbank, New York. See Sean Nero, "New York Honours Jit, Minshall," *Trinidad Guardian*, 13 Aug 2003, <http://www.guardian.co.tt/archives/2003-08-13/entertain4.html> (25 Aug 2003).

18. Since our conversation, Jones has been honored and awarded at the 2005 WSMF held at Madison Square Garden for his contributions to Pan both in Trinidad and the United States.

19. The two organizations reunited for the 2003 Brooklyn Panorama competition.

20. Terry Joseph, "Pannists Keep Vigil at Chaguaramas Pan Site," *Trinidad Express News*, 17 Nov 2002. The article reports that the battle for the site continues to the present.

21. In a follow-up conversation in August 2003, Jones informed me that talk is underway about the building of a cultural museum for Calypso, Carnival, and Steelband.

Chapter 5

1. Personal conversation, 16 Feb 2002, at his home in Brooklyn, New York.

2. Joyce Wadler, "His Incessant Racket Coaxes Steel Drums to Sing," *New York Times*, 1 Nov 2002, Metropolitan Desk, <http://query.nytimes.com/search/restricted/article?res> (23 Dec 2002).

3. For corroboration, see Norman Darway, "Story Behind the Steelpan," *Trinidad Express*, 20 Nov 2000, <http://www.pantrinbago.com/steelpan/briefhistory.htm> (23 Dec 2002).

4. Amy Alexander's *The Farrakhan Factor* (1998), pp. 26–28.

5. See Desmond Bravo's story for more details on Steelband in the United States in conjunction with the origin of Brooklyn's Labor Dad Parade.

6. Mikey Enoch died in 2003.

Chapter 6

1. Personal conversations, 23 and 25 Jun 2003, at his home in Philadelphia, Pennsylvania. Conversation concluded on June 25th with a meeting with members of his band, Pan Stars, now Pantastic.

Chapter 7

1. Personal conversation, 10 Jun 2003, at the home of Albert Jones.

2. Kim Johnson, "Pioneer on the Biscuit Drum: 'Patcheye' and Bar 20's Carlton 'Zigilee' Barrow,"13 August 2000, <http://www.pantrinbago.com/steelpan/briefhistory.htm> (19 Jul 2002). In this article, Johnson reports on his conversation with Henry "Patcheye" Pachot, the founder of Hill Sixty (named after the site for which the Germans and the British contested during World War I)

was "one of the greatest biscuit drummers ever produced by the steelband movement." He lived on Clifton Hill, Laventille, and was influenced by the Shango tents that in 1938 attracted some of the best drummers. Later, he transferred leadership to Andrew "Pan" de la Bastide of Trinidad All Steel Percussion Orchestra (TASPO). Also in this article, Johnson writes that many men remained in the Hollywood, California area, and married American women to gain permanent residency and did not return to Trinidad upon the tour's completion. This would explain why de la Bastide eventually made Los Angeles his permanent home where he died on November 19, 2002.

Chapter 8

1. Telephone conversation, 27 Jun 2003.

2. Sarah Van Gelder, "Freedom Sings: An Interview with Harry Belafonte," *Yes!* 21 (Spring 2002), <http://www.futurenet.org/21American/belafonte.htm>, <http://www.futurenet.org/21American/21toc_main.htm> (12 Apr 2003). In this article, Van Gelder informs that some calypsonians traveled to the United States during the 1930s and '40s and helped to lay the foundation for Belafonte's historical success with his long playing album *Calypso* (1956), a record that was the first in the history of U.S. music industry to sell more than one million copies.

3. Ernest D. Brown, "Carnival, Calypso, and the Steelband in Trinidad," *The Black Perspective in Music* 11.1, 2 (1990): 83–84.

4. Essiba Small, "Queen Title Stays in the Family: Shirlane Takes Sister's Crown," *Trinidad Express Features*, 11 Feb 1998, <http://209.94.197.2/feb/feb11/features.htm> (25 Jun 2003). The article discusses how Shirlane wins the victory from her sister, Lady Wonder. Also see, Josie-Ann Carrington, "Sheldon Reid is Young King: Shirlane's Second, Trini's Third," *Trinidad Express Features*, 13 Feb 1998, <http://209.94.197.2/feb/feb13/features.htm> (25 Jun 2003).

5. Refers to Raymond Quevedo, a.k.a. Atilla the Hun (1892–1962).

6. According to Peter Manuel, et al, "Rum and Coca Cola" is a Lord Invader's original. See *Caribbean Currents: Caribbean Music from Rumba to Reggae* (Philadelphia: Temple UP, 1995), p. 189.

7. Ibid, p. 193.

Chapter 9

1. Personal conversation, 28 Sep 2002, at his Brooklyn, New York home.

Chapter 10

1. Personal conversation, 19 Jul 2001, at MMIM workshop.

2. The Keith Smith Column, "Troubling Times for Narell." *Trinidad Express*, 3 Feb 2000, <http://209.94.197.2/feb00/feb23/opinion.htm> (18 Oct 2002).

3. Andy did respond to my e-mail request for an interview. His demanding schedule did not allow him to engage a full interview at the time. The Steelband world eagerly anticipates his story.

4. See <http://www.npr.org/programs/btaylor/pastprograms/anarell.html>.

5. Michelle Loubon, "Honouring the Man with the Pan," *Sunday Guardian*, 2 Feb 2003, 52 People.

6. "Crazy's Tribute to 'Ellie Man'," *The Bomb*, 31 Jan 2003, Showtime.

7. Announcement, "TT National Junior Panorama Competition 23 Feb 2003," *Saturday Express*, 22 Feb 2003, Section 2.

Chapter 11

1. Telephone conversations, 24 Aug 2001 and 28 Jun 2003. His narrative includes his article found on the internet at the Panyard's website and used with his permission.

Chapter 12

1. Telephone conversation, 17 Aug 2001 and 29 Jun 2003.

Chapter 13

1. Telephone conversations, 11, 12, and 13 Aug 2002.

2. Moral Rearmament (MRA): An evangelical movement founded by a U.S. evangelist and former Lutheran pastor, Frank Buchman, in the 1920s. It initially received the most support at Oxford University and was called the Oxford Group until 1938. It sought the regeneration of individuals and

nations through conversion, God's personal guidance, and living in purity, unselfishness, honesty, and love. The Macmillan Encyclopedia 2001,© Market House Books Ltd 2000: http://www.xrefer.com/entry/510477. Today, the organization is called Initiatives of Change: http://www.sobertimes.com/AA-Pages.htm. Note: see also <http://www.schillerinstitute.org/calendars/lar_show.html>, <http://www.uk.initiativesofchange.org/discovering/update.html>.

3. Hailed as the "Paganini of the Pan," Liam Teague has distinguished himself as the recipient of many awards in his homeland of T&T. In the fall of 1992, he was the co-winner of the National Steelband Festival solo championship of T&T and has also won championships for his skill on the violin and recorder. Along with performing for heads of state and dignitaries of his country, Teague has also performed for Prince Edward of Great Britain, and Carlos Andres Perez, former President of Venezuela. Liam Teague has appeared as soloist for the MC Hammer tour of Trinidad. Teague's international performances include appearances in the United States, Italy, France, Germany, the Czech Republic, Taiwan, Korea, Canada, Panama, Barbados, and Jamaica. Under the baton of Dr. Paul Freeman, Teague with the Chicago Sinfonietta gave the world premier of Jan Bach's "Concerto for Steelpan and Orchestra" in 1995 at Symphony Hall. He has since played the piece with the Czech National Symphony in Prague, the Sinfonia Da Camera, the Rockford Symphony, the Peoria Symphony, the Northwest Indiana Symphony and the Dartmouth Wind Ensemble.

4. Refers to the Harry U. Lawrence Law, <http://www.leg.state.vt.us/docs/2002/journal/hj010126.doc>.

Chapter 14

1. Telephone conversation, 8 Oct 2002.

2. See Teague's interview in the Trinidad Express Features, 3 Jan 2002 that offers a different timeline on the chronology. I draw attention to the conflict in accounts to accentuate what all the men state unequivocally: that they were not paying attention to specific dates. The significance of the event itself is what became fixed in memory. Teague's interview can be found at: <http://www.trinidadexpress.com/features.asp?mylink=2003-01-03%2Ffeatures%2FI%20want%20to%20give%20back.htm&mydate=2003-01-03&mypage=features>.

3. Telephone conversation, 8 Oct 2002.

4. Amadinda-Ugandan log xylophone. Also known as embairé. The standard instrument includes fifteen keys: <http://www.worldmusicportal.com/Instruments/instruments.htm>.

Chapter 15

1. Telephone and personal conversations, 31 Jan 2002, 7 Feb 2002, 10 Mar 2002, and 26 Sep 2002. Personal conversations were conducted at his plant in Pittsburgh, Pennsylvania.

2. Kim Loy Wong currently resides in the United States Anthony "Tony" Williams and Bertie Marshall reside in Trinidad.

3. Kamau Brathwaite says in his poetry collection, *Barabajan Poems*, that the winds of invention of the music transported the sound over the waves and those attuned picked up on these sound waves. The sound of the steelband was carried on the waves of the Caribbean Sea and delivered onto the shores of the various islands.

4. Tom Reynolds is from St. Croix U.S. Virgin Islands. For more information on Reynolds, see <http://www.tropicalhammer.com/florida/shop/>.

5. See Albert Jones's narrative for an account of the early days of steelband organization in Trinidad.

6. Forbes Burnham was the first president of Guyana and served from 1964 to 1987.

7. Cliff Alexis is on the faculty of NIU School of Music. See his story for more details.

8. One of the best known U.S.-born pannists, his father Murray Narell is reputed as being the first one to launch steelband programs in New York City schools for students-at-risk. See Jeff Narell's narrative for more details.

9. See Vincent Hernandez's story for when the bore pan was introduced into the movement.

10. At the time of this conversation, Solomon was unaware that Mannette had established his steel drum company, called Mannette Steel Drums Ltd., in 2000.

11. Here is one example of how Solomon, who is unfamiliar with Brathwaite's poetry, speaks similarly in poetic language of the Caribbean experience.

12. Solomon is referring to some Caribbean foods such as flying fish and coucou (Barbados, Trinidad and Tobago, Guyana, St. Vincent), roti (Trinidad, Guyana, Jamaica), pelau (Trinidad, Bahamas), callaloo (Trinidad), accra (Grenada) or fish cake (Barbados), ackee (Jamaica). These foods are not unique to the islands I have listed because as island migration occurred, the foods and dishes traveled with the people who established them wherever they made their abode. Some foods, however, remain typically associated with a particular island.

13. The *Dictionary of Caribbean English Usage*, edited by Richard Allsop, states the word "was borrowed as an appropriate indigenous label for the National Day celebrations of the newly designated Co-operative Republic of Guyana in 1970" (374).

Chapter 16

1. Telephone conversation, 24 Jun 2003.

2. Ann Ward and Alison Taylor, "Iron & Steel: An Explique of a Typical Trinidad Pan Side." The following definition is based on Maritime Life Hatters Steel Band of San Fernando, captained by Steve Achaiba, winner of 1975 Panorama. A stage-side band included: five high tenors, five low tenors, four double tenors, five double seconds, six double guitars, three triple guitars, three sets of cellos; three sets of six-basses. A road-side band comprised of: ten high tenors, twenty low tenors, eight double tenors, ten double seconds, twelve double guitars, six triple guitars, eight sets of cellos; six sets of six-basses. Both sides included an iron section or engine room of varying iron pieces.

3. Actually, the first known company to make steelband accessories is Solomon Steelpan Company, owned by Guyanese Philbert "Phil" Solomon of Pittsburgh, Pennsylvania. He began his company in 1990. Panyard Inc. of

Akron, Ohio began its operation a few years later. See Solomon's story for more details.

4. Molineaux is referring to the Price-Whitmyre hydroforming process that many men have spoken about and I have addressed in the Introduction.

5. The brainchild of Teddy Osei, a Ghanaian sax player, composer, and drummer who came to London to study music, Osibisa was one of the first African bands to win worldwide popularity. Their mix of African (especially highlife) and Caribbean forms made them a sensation in the mid '70s and their popularity continues today, even though recording dates have fallen off. ~ J. Poet, All Music Guide *Written by J. Poet,* <http://music.yahoo.com/ar-260304-bio—Osibisa>.

6. When I first contacted Othello to make an appointment, we began a conversation about the violence in Steelband because I mentioned that one former police I interviewed (referring to Randolph "Rannie" Babb) maintains that the followers of steelbands caused the violence. Othello maintained there was no distinction between the followers and the players. As long as he was associated with a steelband, the entire band had the reputation. This is the conversation to which he is referring.

I wish here to acknowledge what Chan LeePow has also said during our 18 Jun 2003 conversation on Mas, having played Mas with Harold Saldena. As a boy during the '50s, he witnessed the bottle-and stone-pelting, pans being used as weapons, the *mashing up* of pans during riots. One vivid riot was between Sunland and Desperadoes one Carnival Tuesday when Sunland refused to allow an ambulance through with a wounded Despers's player. Word quickly spread and Despers descended on Park Street between Frederick and Henry Streets, where one of the bloodiest riots unfolded before his eyes. He was petrified as he stood beneath a tree and saw blood flow freely from ghastly wounds. He further recalled that people left slippers and shoes behind as they scampered for their lives, and the next day lined up at a police station to claim their footwears, whatever was left of them. The leaving of personal belongings behind was also common to the riots.

Chapter 17

1. Telephone conversation, 21 Jun 2003.

2. See Othello Molineaux's narrative, En. 2.

Chapter 18

1. Personal conversation, 9 Aug 2002, at an Elkton, Maryland public park.

Chapter 19

1. Personal conversation, 10 Feb 2002, at their home in Philadelphia, Pennsylvania.

Chapter 20

1. Telephone conversation, 13 Aug 2002.

Chapter 21

1. Telephone conversation, 31 Aug 2002. He boasts of having been married for nineteen years in December and has four beautiful children with his wonderful wife, Merry. They met in grad school, and he regards her like all good things in life as a gift from God. Their children's ages range from nine to fourteen years: Montoya M. (fourteen years), Aminta J. (twelve years), Jasmine (eleven), and Elijah (nine).

2. Derek Walcott, *Dream on Monkey Mountain: And Other Plays*. New York: The Noonday Press, Farrar, Straus and Giroux, 1992.

3. Moses is referring to my sharing what the other men have said about the name of the instrument, and my favoring Sandiford's definition of the instrument. He was unfamiliar with Sandiford's work, which I encouraged him to examine because it sounded to me that he was more so agreeing than disagreeing with Sandiford. We indeed had a heated discussion over this issue.

Chapter 22

1. Our personal conversations began informally in 1999 at the University Tuning Project, Morgantown, West Virginia. They continued formally at his home in 2000 and continued through 2002. Additionally, much thanks to Kaethe George for making available the cassette taped interviews of Ellie with Chris Tanner in 1998.

2. Mannette is one of nine persons born outside the United States to receive this award. In a personal conversation (22 Sep 1999), he reiterated that the award was more in recognition for Pan than of himself and his contributions to the development of the instrument. By remaining focused on the fact that his life's work has been all about developing and promoting the instrument, he humbly received the award in honor of all the panmen who deserve to be recognized both in Trinidad and abroad, he stated emphatically.

3. Current official sponsor of the Invaders since 1998, <http://209.94.197.2/nov/nov22/general.htm>.

4. Personal conversation, 20 Aug 2001.

5. A type of piranha fish whose species infests the Gulf of Paria.

6. According to Bravo, Mannette was also called Barracuda because of his own bad reputation. He thinks the nickname was later appropriated to the pan Mannette made.

7. Dennis Le Gendre, *Steelband in Perspectives*. On page 61, Le Gendre notes that under Andrew de la Bastide's tutelage, Callender became the first female to master the ping-pong.

8. Some controversy revolves around the first appearance of the big pan. Both Neville Jules's story and Bukka Rennie's article published in the *Trinidad Guardian*, "Pan Debate Must Open Up," assert that Mannette was not the first to introduce the big pan to the public. While Jules, during our conversation, could not readily recall the name of the player to introduce the big pan, Rennie's article states unequivocally that Cyril "Snatcher" Guy of Tacarigua was the first one to introduce the big pan to the public.
See the entire article published on 13 Nov 2000 at <http://www.pantrinbago.com/steelpan/briefhistory.htm>.

9. David Brewster, "Meet Me Down by the Croisée," published in *Trinidad Express Online*, 6 Jul 2002, <http://209.94.197.2/html1/prev/aug01/aug3/f7.htm>. Mastifé, born Eugene de la Rosa, died at age seventy-nine of prostate cancer on 10 Dec 2002: see, David Brewster, "Bad-john 'Mastifé' Dies at 79," *Trinidad Express News*, 11 Dec 2002, <http://www.trinidadexpress.com/News.asp?mylink>.

10. According to Molineaux, "Patsy" Haynes died in New York City in 1998.

11. Marcia Henville, "Pan Pioneers: Memories of Old Man Zig," *Trinidad Express Online* (4 Jan 1998). This article describes how notes were introduced to the pan in the late thirties.

12. For a wonderful short story about this art form, see Willi Chen's "The Stickfighter," published in *Caribbean New Wave: Contemporary Short Stories* (published by Heinemann, 1990; edited by Stewart Brown).

13. Personal conversation, 22 Jul 2001.

14. Lecture, 15 Jul 2001, MMIM workshop.

15. Queen's Park Oval is commonly called "The Oval."

16. See Kim Johnson's article published in the *Trinidad Express Online* "Bye bye, Blackbird" (21 Nov 1999) for Vernon "Birdie" Mannette's role in starting Oval Boys.

17. Ibid.

18. This is one aspect of the controversy around whether this incident occurred, or it became folklore and eventually fact. In addition to Rudy King's challenge to this as actual fact, see also "Story behind the steelpan" by Norman Darway published at <http://www.pantrinbago.com/steelpan/briefhistory.htm>. Originally published on 20 Nov 2000.

19. Mannette's interview with Chris Tanner, 4 Oct 1998.

20. Lecture, 15 Jul 2001, MMIM workshop; Personal conversations, 22 Jul 2001, 6 Aug 2001, and 20 Aug 2001.

21. Lecture, 15 Jul 2001, MMIM workshop.

22. Sweet oil was a type of cooking oil (like Canola and other vegetable oil) manufactured and sold by a company located on the road from Laventille to San Juan. The barracuda was then not made from an abandoned garbage can but from one of these drums.

23. See the Jules's narrative for the history of All Stars, which was never called Red Army. Prior to being All Stars, the band was called Second Fiddle and Cross of Lorraine. Also, as Jules's narrative delineates, "Fisheye" was never a member of All Stars. He was a member of Second Fiddle; then when Second Fiddle split up due to a controversy he caused, he left and joined Invaders. Second Fiddle was afterward renamed All Stars.

24. Personal conversation, 22 Jul 2001.

25. Jules's narrative also describes that All Stars maintained a strict code of discipline and was never involved in band violence, not as a band. Individual members who infracted the rules were without ceremony dismissed from All Stars.

26. Personal conversation, 22 Jul 2001.

27. Guy Claxton, "What's the Big Idea?" *The Observer*. 22 Sep 2002, <http://www.observer.co.uk/magazine/story/0,11913,796509,00.html>.

28. 28 Lecture, 15 Jul 2001, MMIM workshop.

29. Ibid.
Also, see Neville Jules's conversation for another version of this innovation.

30. Jules's narrative renders a different version regarding the creation of the guitar pan, which credits Philmore "Boots" Davidson, while maintaining that Boots duplicated a pan he had made a few weeks earlier in 1948 or '49, called the quatro. According to Molineaux, Davidson died in New York City in 2002.

31. Personal conversation, 22 Jul 2001.

32. Daryl Cumber Dance, *New World Adams: Conversations with Contemporary West Indian Writers*, Yorkshire, England: Peepal Tree Books, 1992. P.152.

33. See <http://www.geocities.com/timothybathory/TheWorldatWarErwinRommel.htm> for a brief account of this historical incursion.

34. Mannette's interview with Chris Tanner, 4 Oct 1998.

35. Albert Jones credits Neville Jules for creating the tune boom.

36. See the Neville Jules's narrative for the more accurate history.

37. Ibid.

38. Personal conversation, 22 Jul 2001.

39. Lecture, 15 Jul 2001, MMIM workshop.

40. Auntie Kay, the host of the only children's program aired on radio, emphasized proper (colonial) stage decorum and schooled children, on air, on proper introduction of themselves and their rendition. It was well known that it was an honor to be featured on the Auntie Kay children's program.

41. Mannette's interview with Chris Tanner, 4 Oct 1998.

42. Lloyd Best, "Not Pan in Schools but School in Pan: Reform of Panorama," *Trinidad Express*, 8 May 2001, <http://209.94.197.2/html1/prev/may01/may8/f6.htm>.

43. Workshop session, WVU, Morgantown, 20 Jul 2001.

44. Ibid.

45. Ibid.

46. Jules's conversation offers that he is the creator of the *grundig*, which Albert Jones's story corroborates. Jones credits Jules for creating both the *grundig* and tune boom.

47. Ibid.

48. Mannette's interview with Chris Tanner, 4 Oct 1998.

49. Ibid.

50. Mannette's interview with Chris Tanner, 28 Nov 1998.

51. Kim Johnson, "The Great Bonaparte." *Trinidad Internet Express*, 22 Oct 2000.

52. Beryl McBurnie (1913–2000) is recognizably one of the most distinguished Trinidadians in promoting Arts and Culture in Trinidad and Tobago. Internationally renowned, her brief biographies and pertinent information on her life and death can be found at the following Web sites: <http://209.94.197.2/apr00/apr1/general.htm>, <http://209.94.197.2/apr00/apr2/opinion.htm>, <http://209.94.197.2/nov/nov22/general.htm>, <http://www.nalis.gov.tt/Biography/bio_BERYLMCBURNIE_pleofcentury.htm>, <http://www.geocities.com/ronemrit/profiles/mcburnie.html>, <http://www.pantrinbago.com/BerylMcBernie2.htm>.

53. For more details and others' perspectives on the Trinidad All Steel Percussion Orchestra, see *Trinidad Express Online*, 27 Apr 2000, 27 Jul 2001, and 22 Oct 2000. <http://www.seetobago.com/trinidad/pan/sr/sr00024.htm>.

54. Personal conversation, 22 Jul 2001.

55. Mannette's interview with Chris Tanner, 4 Oct 1998; personal conversation, 22 Jul 2001.

56. Personal conversation, 22 Jul 2001.

57. Ibid.

58. Bravo states that eventually from all this violence, "Birdie," also nicknamed Pablo and reputed to be Invaders "cutter-man" for his readiness with the blade, spent approximately six months in prison.

59. Ibid.; Personal conversation, 22 Jul 2001.

60. Personal conversation, 28 Oct 1999. Invaders did not become a member of the association until June 29, 1959. He attributes his hesitation to joining to his being cautionary about the association's commitment to assisting the panmen. When he was convinced that their efforts were genuine and the association's officials were not wasting anyone's time, Invaders joined.

61. Betancourt is the first panman (and only one to date) to receive an MBE from Queen Elizabeth II in June 2002 for his work in Pan <http://209.94.197.2/html1/prev/apr02/apr2/o1.htm>.

62. Mannette, as well as all newspaper articles I have examined, reports conflicting information on Griffith's origins. Mannette thinks he came from Antigua, while some articles report him as coming from Barbados and St. Lucia.

63. Lecture, 15 Jul 2001, MMIM workshop.

64. Ibid.

65. Personal conversation, 22 Jul 2001.

66. Lecture, 15 Jul 2001.

67. Mannette's interview with Chris Tanner, 28 Nov 1998.

68. Ibid.

69. Lecture, 16 Jul 2001.

70. Personal conversation, 20 Aug 2001; interview with Chris Tanner, 4 Oct 1998.

71. Mannette's interview with Chris Tanner, 28 Nov 1998.

72. Ibid.

73. Personal conversation, 6 Aug 2001.

74. See Albert Jones's story.

75. Personal conversation, 6 Aug 2001.

76. Ibid.

77. Lecture, 15 Jul 2001.

78. Personal conversation, 6 Aug 2001.

79. Ibid.

80. Lecture, 16 Jul 2001.

81. Ibid.

82. According to Molineaux, Girl Pat Steelband was formed for class reasons. See his narrative for what he states as having witnessed firsthand.

83. Lecture, 15 Jul 2001.

84. Personal conversation, 6 Aug 2001.

85. Mannette's interview with Chris Tanner, 28 Nov 1998.

86. Lecture, 16 Jul 2001.

87. Ibid.

88. See Vincent Hernandez's story that contradicts this date.

89. Ibid.

90. **H1B** classification applies to persons in a specialty occupation which requires the theoretical and practical application of a body of highly specialized knowledge requiring completion of a specific course of higher education. This classification requires a labor attestation issued by the Secretary of Labor (65,000). This classification also applies to government-to-government research and development, or co-production projects administered by the Department of Defense (100). **H-2A** classification applies to temporary or seasonal agricultural workers; **H-2B** classification applies to temporary or seasonal non-agricultural workers. This classification requires a temporary labor certification issued by the Secretary of Labor (66,000), <http://www.us-immigration.org/visa_emptemp.htm>.

91. Lecture, 16 Jul 2001.

92. Mannette's interview with Chris Tanner, 28 Nov 1998.

93. Ibid.

94. Personal conversations, 28 and 29 Jul 2001.

95. Ibid.

96. Ibid.

97. Mannette's interview with Chris Tanner, 28 Nov 1998.

98. Personal conversation, 6 Aug 2001.

99. Ibid.

100. Mannette's interview with Chris Tanner, 28 Nov 1998.

101. Ibid.

102. Interview with Kaethe George, published in *Percussive Notes*, October 1994.

103. Personal conversation, 6 Aug 2001.

104. Mannette's interview with Chris Tanner, 28 Nov 1998.

105. Personal conversation, 24 Aug 2001.

106. Personal conversation, 19 Jul 2001.

107. This perspective may be somewhat inaccurate. Some U.S. steelbands include sixty to eighty sets of instruments and almost one hundred players on pans and percussions, as can be seen at the annual Brooklyn Panorama competitions. Svaline probably means high school steelbands.

108. Personal conversation, 19 Jul 2001.

109. Personal conversation, 17 Jul 2001.

110. Personal conversation, 20 Jul 2001.

111. E-mail interview, 19 Aug 2001. Also note that Copeland did not specify and did I press the matter.

112. Personal conversation, 21 Jul 2001.

113. Conversation on 7 Oct 2002.

114. Ibid.

115. Terry Joseph, "Hiding Pan Facts under Canopies." *Trinidad Internet Express*, 31 Oct 2000.

116. Terry Joseph, "Unite for the Common Pan." *Trinidad Internet Express*, 3 Nov 2000.

117. Personal conversation, 22 Jul 2002.

118. Ibid.

119. Ibid.

120. Personal conversation, 18 Jul 2001.

121. Ibid.

122. Maria Pereira's narrative grew out of our initial conversation on 22 Jul 2001 at Mannette's home in West Virginia. Many telephone conversations followed that clarified her ongoing role in Mannette's life, and why she is formally introduced at the WVU's workshops.

Other Interviewees

Bishop, Rondell "Pompey," 25 Jun 2003

Brady, Adam, 17 Jul 2001

Bravo, Desmond, 23 and 25 Jun 2003

Clarke, LeRoy, 30 Oct 2000

Copeland, Brian, 20 Jul 2001

Doby, Jai, 17 Jul 2001

Doby, Jaran, 17 Jul 2001

Dodds, Neil "Fat man," 25 Jun 2003

Feldman, Howie, 18 Jul 2001

Greenidge, Robert "Robbie," 18 Jul 2001

Hayes, Nicholas, 17 Jul 2001

Headley, Harold, 16 Jul 2001

Hohn, Geoff, 16 Jul 2001

Imbert, Clément, 20 Jul 2001

Kelly, Cassie, 16 Jul 2001

Lee-jah, 25 Jun 2003

LeePow, Carmen and Chan, 16 Jun 2003

Lisbon, Arabian, 17 Jul 2001

McIntosh, Dwight, 10 Aug 2002

Miller, Tom, 17 Jul 2001

Mundy, Clarence "Dinks," 25 Jun 2003

Raymond, Brian, 25 Jun 2003

Solomon, Fauna, 10 Mar 2002

Solomon, Janera, 10 Mar 2002

Solomon, Jonnet, 10 Mar 2002

Solomon, Leigh, 10 Mar 2002

Svaline, Marc, 19 Jul 2001

Thornton, Tracy, 17 Jul 2001

978-0-595-40153-6
0-595-40153-8

Printed in the United States
71737LV00003B/11